From the photo album

An early picture shows a giant boojum tree guarding the San Borja runway

Author measuring Benjamin Hill last August - sure didn't need a sweater

From the photo album

An early picture shows a giant boojum tree guarding the San Borja runway

Author measuring Benjamin Hill last August - sure didn't need a sweater

Airports of Mexico and Central America

16th Edition

by Arnold D Senterfitt

with words, pictures, and
runway measurements gathered
during a few hundred
pleasant flights

The information in this book has been compiled from many sources, primarily personal on-scene visits by the author. Although every effort has been made to assure accuracy, no warrant is made and no responsibility is assumed to any person oz persons in connection with the use of this information contained herein or later made a part of this book adding to, or deleting, or otherwise affecting these contents.

This book is copyrighted under the Universal Copyright Convention per the notice affixed below. The book may not be photocopied, nor reproduced electronically nor mechanically, it may not be translated, nor reduced to any machine readable form nor in any other form whether in whole or in part without specific advance permission in writing from the copyright holder.

NOTICE

Intentional or willful violations of the copyright law may result in: **Civil damages** of up to $50,000 in addition to: **Actual damages** in addition to: **Criminal penalties** of up to one year imprisonment in addition to: **Fines** of up and including $10,000 per page copied.

ISBN 0-937260-01-0

Copyright © 1982 Arnold D Senterfitt

All Rights Reserved This book is protected throughout the world under provisions of the International Copyright Convention

Previous editions Copyright ©1964, 1965, 1966, 1967, 1968, 1969, 1970, 1971, 1972, 1973, 1974, 1975, 1976, 1978, 1979, 1980 by Arnold D Senterfitt

International Standard Book Number 0-937260-00-3

Printed and bound in the United States of America

Cartography and photographs not bylined are by the author

Cover by Robert Bausch

Pasteup by Hallie Wyckoff

Send all orders and correspondence to:

The Pathfinders
Post Office Box 11950
Reno, Nevada 89510

Author's Preface

Comfortable chair, but then I'm not being sacrificed

Author with Lic. Miguel Aleman of Mexico's Tourism Council

El Arco Center/Approach/Tower/Ground Control during an early Baja 1000 road race-photo by Don Downie

In the Beginning. . .

Since the early sixties the purpose of this book has been to offer general aviation families the tools needed to see, to explore, and to enjoy interesting cities or towns which are almost next door and where the cost to visit is quite low.

In your airplane you are a few hours from hundreds of wonderful places the airlines don't reach, whereas airline passengers are limited to imitations of Miami or Las Vegas. They will only read about the places you go so easily.

For Example

If you and I are bound for Club Med at Playa Blanca on the Coconut Coast we merely buzz the red roofed hotel at 500' agl to alert a cab, then land near the lighthouse at Punta Farallon 2 miles SE. Airline passengers can only get there after four dusty hours in a bus from Puerto Vallarta or Manzanillo.

Time Runs Backward

Acapulco airline passengers only see a smeary version of the earth forty thousand feet below through two layers of plexiglass. They miss the intimate view of miles and miles of white sandy beaches, and of coconut plantations going by your window. They couldn't even imagine our liesurely view of towns sitting up in the mountain peaks.

And if the whim strikes you, any route to anywhere has dozens of small town airports where one can casually stop for a can of fruit juice obtainable at the inevitable store, called 'tienda'. At these stops you will see village life as it has been for a very long time. Woodcutters sell their product from house to house, everyone works at the slow but steady pace in the tropics as they harvest mangoes, papaya, coconuts. That era exists now; it is waiting for you.

What'll It Be?

Whether you decide to pitch a tent and stay for days or to saunter around for a few hours then continue on your way is your choice. You might get acquainted with a duster pilot who could help you find and see the intimate side of that area. If you are a hunter there is always a chance of hunting anything from birds to mountain lion.

No Imagination

What you read in these pages is what I found when there. I made a normal landing to measure and evaluate the runway. I did not land at the risk of Grace's or my life or to the airplane I was flying. Each time I pushed my wheel from one runway end to the other, bought gasoline if they said it was available. If towers are listed I've talked to them in English. If they preferred my agonizingly slow Spanish, or gave me a clue they don't handle English well, the airport page itself will say so.

Follow A Coward

Actually, I prefer the flying part to be smooth, weather clear, and a choice of fuel stops conveniently near one another. I prefer to confine the vibrantly exciting part to the sightseeing. I like to see mountains jump up ten or more thousand feet out of the tropical bench, volcanos we can circle and marvel at. And I like flying down a beach looking at manta rays with twenty foot wingspans playing on the edge of the surf line. If someone wants to say I'm a chicken pilot I'll accept that as a compliment.

First Book

In nineteen years this book has grown from five hand-drawn instant printed sheets. As I learned to draw better and mispell less often these books went through fourteen editions of the original *Airports of Baja California* then thirteen editions of a separate book, *Airports of Mexico and Belice* later called *.. and Central America*. The two books were merged in 1980 into the 560 page fifteenth composite edition. This 16th edition is a total revision of the 15th, a hundred-some pages thicker.

First Airplane

You may see an occasional photo in here of my first airplane, the round engined Cessna 195, name of N1537D. That big old pussycat taught me much about flying as we went together throughout Mexico and a few trips to Belice. After thirteen years of enjoying the luxury of an aisle between the front seats and a quiet 1800 RPM cruise a friend named Martin Litton, who had coveted 37D since I bought it finally got his way as I moved up to a lighter and quicker Cessna 180 called N180EE.

Wow! Visibility!

Soon as I got over being able to see outside, 180EE and I really had fun. We often went solo through Central America to Panama and Colombia either on survey flights or leading Baja Bush Pilots expeditions. We made that 55 hour round trip enough times that I assume EE could have done it without me.

Flying Station Wagon

Recently we found 92R, a Cessna 185, and at last a comfortable allowable cabin load. Without seats five and six, two couples of us can carry enough to camp in luxury if we want to do so. Grace and I've enjoyed camping a lot but with the limited Useful Loads of the past we couldn't take anyone else.

It's All Your Fault

All of the important improvements in this book are here because you said please and kept insisting. Border crossing details in the 1965 edition, an aerial photograph of each airport in 1968, more countries in the 70s, IFR plates for information in 1980, Reader Reports in 1982.

Through sheets called PREPs we will update the material in this book, such as the latest version of TCAs in Latin America (TCA doesn't mean there what it does here).

Reader Reports Help Everyone

Notice in this edition there are Reader Reports; there will be more in the next edition. Just drop me a note at the address on page 4, tell me what you've found where and we'll tell everyone else. A postcard is fine, or a letter, whatever. Just write.

One Man Band

Since I am a combination pilot/writer/photographer/typist/gopher/mapmaker and janitor, please be patient. When you write in I try to answer in the same calendar year but don't always succeed. But maybe you'll see your name in the next book or get a telephone call from someone saying "...hey, Arnold just told me you know all about..." Your picture could be in the next edition, particularly if you were on a Baja Bush Pilots trip.

Doing this book is a lot of fun. I hope you get that feeling in reading through it and using it. And as you get to the various places you can extend your pleasure to others with Reader Reports.

Using This Book

The materials in this book help you get ready, out the door, across any border. Next, the Area and Airport pages tell you the specifics for each place based on what Grace and I find to see/do there. Basically if you start from right here and proceed page-by-page, you will cover what you need to know and in the correct order.

Getting Ready: This **Introduction** Section

Here in this section **Reminiscing** on 9 and 10 is a pleasant way to get a feel for the country of Mexico and the pleasant things that have happened on my trips. That flows nicely into **For Women Only**(ask her permission first!).

The volatile money situation, drinking water, the fly-together group called Baja Bush Pilots, insurance needs, subject of gasoline, are covered painlessly. Basically, the Introduction Section introduces you and sets the stage for the specific details to follow.

Border Crossing

This book is your Open Sesame to crossing into and out of ten sovereign nations, each jealously unique in what they want for prior reporting, flight plans, personal documentation. Thats why this section needs 61 pages. Starting with pages 42/43 **All Border Data** first you get a summary, then details. 42/43 is a summary of what you need to cross into and out of all ten countries. (This section gets specific here only on the US/Mexico crossings. Central America will come later in its own section.) The rest of **Border Crossing** section takes you through the precise details of getting back and forth without fuss.

Actual Forms

The forms shown in this book are often on the sloppy and pocket smudged because they are actual. Those pieces of paper often rode around with me for a few weeks, then I was given permission to bring them home to use them in this book as an example. And Marvin Patchen and Robert Young are not my aliases. At one time or another during preparation for this edition I've been between airplanes so have ridden with them. You may notice a Flight Plan or other forms used from those flights. Bob has a 210, Marvin a Skylane. Forms from me will show either my former Cessna 180 or present Cessna 185.

Be **Very** Sure of. . .

You will get tired of plowing through the US Customs and Agriculture rules for what kind of jewelry you can bring back from which countries but don't skip anything on the US Customs reprint of "**Customs Guide for Private Flyers**(sic). That part will keep you out of trouble by telling you to be sure and call FSS before crossing the US border. It is vital that, on return to US airspace that you notify FSS the right amount of time *before crossing into US Airspace*. Not before you taxi up to Customs or before landing at the US airport. Customs people have a $500 fine habit if we forget and violate this.

105: Sample Airport Then the Good Stuff

Airport data in this book starts with an outline of how airport information is arranged on each of the hundreds of airport pages. Some readers like to put a little magic tape tab on page 105 so they can flip back to it easily.

The Good Stuff

Each of the six geographic areas of this book begins with a double page **Area Chart** followed by an **Area Index**, a **Briefing** for that area, then the airport pages with lots of extra pages included to talk about interesting places to see and things to do.

Central America Section

This section is unique in that it deals with eight countries' border crossing needs plus the airports therein. I've reprinted the **All Border Data** on pages 542/543 then proceeded to discuss each countries' own application. There are many new airports in this section which Grace and I enjoyed finding then discovering new friends. You'll learn how easy it is when you start flying with this book.

The Appendix is an Appendix

Anything that doesn't fit anywhere else seems to end up in the Appendix. This one has Climate Charts, how to avoid $50 telephone calls, **Aircraft Spanish** which is actually a misnomer, it is more correctly **Pilot Spanish**. You can use it not just to order Avgas, file flight plans, but also to buy dinner, groceries at a market, etc.

Still With Me?

That's an overview of what you will find from here on page 7 through to whatever the last page number turns out to be as we go through the final days of putting this book together. I'm having a good time going to all these place to gather information so you can pick what you'd like to do and where. As you go to the places in this book we could meet and say hello. I'll be the one with the measuring wheel.

Table of Contents

Introduction 9

background about Mexico and Central America written from the left seat of N4492R and its predecessors

Border Crossing 40

step-by-step border proceedures; not only how, but why

Baja California Area 104

Sample Airport 104,105
Area Charts 106,107
Baja Cfa. Index 108
Baja Cfa. Briefing 109
Airports begin page 112

Northwest Mexico 258

Area Chart 262,263
NW Area Index 264
NW Area Briefing 265
First airport 266

Northeast Mexico 338

NE Area Chart 338,339
NE Index 340
NE Briefing 341
First airport 342

Coconut Coast 418

Area Charts 418,419
Area Index 420
Area Briefing 421
First airport 422

Yucatan Area 484

Yucatan Area 484,485
Yucatan Index 486
Yucatan Briefing 487
First airport 488

Central America 534

CA Area Charts 534,535
CA Index 536
CA Briefing 537
CA Border Crossing 538-547
CA First airport 548

Appendix 619

Where we put the extra information which will make your trip more enjoyable

Introduction   Reminiscing 9

To me, flying in Mexico and Centro America is...

The Mexico City cab driver, anxious to improve his English, drove slowly all the way from the airport to prolong his mobile learning session then carefully deducted twenty percent from the meter for the lesson... Back when my Spanish was even worse than it is now, the tower at Ciudad Victoria one day responded to my too rapid call in English with their own much much slower English: "please talk more slowly." My reply in very slow, tortured Spanish brought their instant Spanish response: "Oh, in that case talk faster."...

At the airport restaurant in San Luis Potosi back in the eight cent peso days the lady served served a ham sandwich and coffee for $1.50 pesos then hovered around to be sure it was worth the full twelve cents...

Although overwhelmed with curiosity about my airport measuring wheel the very courteous people at Tecolutla were much too polite to quiz me directly. Instead they asked my wife all the questions, having first asked for my help as interpreter...the gas man at los Mochis, long after quitting time and his tanks were at normal empty anyway. He rassled those big tanks to drain the last drops out so I could get on home for Christmas...

El Paso airport can be interesting when it gets busy. One day I was told to follow a T-34, which should have been a military two place Bonanza. Turned out to be a Lockheed Jetstar bizjet. But he had his problems too: the biplane he was following was doing aerobatics on final...

One of the San Carlos Bay hotels has long supplied only salt water in their toilets and lavatories. Each room has a carefully typed notice about the salt water both in Spanish and in English. The English version says it's 'temporary' but in the Spanish one that one word is missing...

Under the bandstand in downtown Oaxaca (wah-HAH-cah) the city has built stalls and rents them to various purveyors of goods. A lady named Marie Elena has two of them side by side for well diversified activities. The left one uses its three foot frontage for the manufacture and sale of candies, the right one is the jewelry factory specializing in intricate gold earrings and such, at only a percent or two more than bullion prices...for reasons I've yet to discover, cemeteries and airports seem to occur together in about a third to half the Latin cities you visit. At places as diverse as Mision Santa Catarina in Baja California, la Pesca in Sinaloa, and dozens more, you touch down within a few feet of a fully operational graveyard. If there is a message involved, I for one am not listening...

Those poor guys who are given the job of reporting arrivals and departures of aircraft at remote airports in various parts of Mexico. With their very tidy forms they note each pilot name, license, aircraft type and registration in exactly measured data blocks. We tourist pilots slop up the work trying to stuff our nine digit pilot license numbers into space for the Mexican pilot's four digits or less...

Considerate airport and airways people everywhere, typified by the lady maned Chepina, for many years queen of 126.9 in Central Mexico. One day I was VFR ontop from Tampico to Veracruz over a solid layer and my ADF was acting up. Although Veracruz Vor was scheduled for shutdown to get routine maintainance that would have left me with dead recking only. Chepina had them delay an hour until I was well past...the big Yucatecan mystery about the huge meathooks on hotel walls finally solved one day when a desk clerk asked whether we would prefer beds or hammocks (HAH-mah-kahs)... a hotel manager tossed a party for some of us one day to express his appreciation for having six rooms occupied simultaneously. All the drinks and so forth were put on our tab, but as he was patient to explain, we were certainly not charged for his labor in doing the ordering for us...

Local taildragger pilots throughout Latin America are carefully aware of the landings of each tourist taildragger. Anything less than a squeaker causes funny grins amongst local pilots. By common consent a round of soft drinks buys their eternal silence. If you are having an off day use a technique I discovered: landings made during the 1 pm to 3 pm siestas are exempt. That has saved me a bundle...

The boys at Roatan's Coxen Hole airport selling you on the idea of a guard for your treasured airplane. (It certainly isn't necessary.) For three or five dollars a day they promise to stay within arm's reach both day and night. But after you make the deal they will be off the airport before you are...

Sophisticated pedestrians at Costa Rica's Puntarenas intown airport walk in and around aircraft landing or taking off or taxing just like pedestrians weave through car traffic in Manhattan. Regulars yell !Clear! before starting to crank and all that but taxi as though no one was around. Sure is worrisome the first couple times...

Baja California's paved highway has brought resounding changes to the peninsula. Places which before had had no more than a car a week now get hundreds. Any U.S. three day weekend causes an invasion of campers. Oldtimer Mexicans who have spent their lives teetering on starvation now have trouble knowing what to do with all the money they are making...

Leo Lopez, the Cessna dealer in Chihuahua, taught himself to fly before 1920 by rebuilding a wreck he found in the mountains. He rebuilt it once to start flying, then several other times as he learned survivable lessons... at Isla Porvenir in Panama San Blas indian ladies sell reverse applique panels called 'molas' to tourist ladies. Airtaxis bring them to the 1480' runway in Britten Norman Islanders, the British STOL airplane. You notice from the worn grass those airplanes consistantly turnoff at the 900' mark. When the Islanders need help they add a stock Aztec. Better than four landings out of five that airplane turns off the cement onto the grass at least two hundred feet shorter...

Notice sometime the Cessna 206 based at Barra Navidad: the owner has solved the problem of wheelbarrowing onto very rough runways by using a few links of chain to keep the oleo from extendinging. Neat installation..... Although you are certainly close to pyramids on final at Tikal, many are skeptical; they haven't been there but still they doubt the fact. Still haven't decided whether to mention on the airport page that you must be careful to avoid the pyramids on short final...

Lady Customs inspector at Tapachula, when told we were returning from Colombia, all but took the airplane apart. She even made Ralph Powers dismantle his Colombian rocking chair. First Mexico Customs inspection I've even seen in well over a hundred trips there over the past in three four years. Later, Customs people told me privately that the responsible word is 'Colombia'...

Leaving Minatitlan one morning I was worried about possible heavy turbulence from wind coming north through the Isthmus of Tehuantepec. After asking around, one of the local airtaxi pilots took a couple minutes to suggest going via the west side of Lago Catemaco. He said there'd be some pretty healthy jiggling over at the NW corner of that range. Sure enough it was a good ride, almost entirely smooth except for that one place he'd told me to expect a couple minutes of real healthy bouncing. Found out later several other norhtbound tourist aircraft had turned back because of turbulence they got in the first minute. Usually not a bad idea, rough as it was in that spot. But asking with a Spanish/English dictionary in hand could have saved them a day's delay...

Out in Yucatan the airtaxi pilots are the ones in the Cessna 180s with the XA-registration. In the rest of Mexico airtaxis will usually be a Cessna T206 or bigger. Look for the XA-(three letters) registration, that always means airtaxi or airline.

Proud Hospitality

The United States' neighbor to the south has the oldest culture in this hemisphere. Mexico had universities more than four hundred years ago; it had printing presses a full century before we did. In fact, young ladies dressed in silks and satins from the Orient wore perfumes from Persia and rode in fancy carriages on wide paved boulevards while our own ancestors had yet to explore the other side of the Hudson River.

Great numbers of foreign visitors have long been coming from all over the world. The earliest confirmed tourists arrived just a thousand years ago. Mexicans still welcome you as an individual. They are glad you came and want you to enjoy what they can offer you. This marvelous pride makes Mexico a special place to visit: you are a guest not just another tourist.

National Town Monuments

Mexico is a very beautiful, wondrously different country. Even the small villages cast a romantic spell regardless of how rustic and modest in material things. There is always a plaza of some sort with a church alongside, often a bandstand in a town square.

In a country with hundreds of beautiful villages there are some so perfect the government of Mexico has set them aside so that future generations will have a first hand look at their heritage.

Alamos, in the Northwest section, is a very nice example. You see the colonial architecture everywhere you look, from hotels to churches. About the only intrusion is a foosball table tucked away in a corner of the central market where it won't intrude.

Guanajuato's airport is isolated and hard to get a taxi, but the city itself is well worth some trouble. Noteworthy not only for the sweeping examples of colonial architecture, that city is the cradle of liberty for the Republic.

Here Father Hidalgo gave his famous 'grito', or cry for independence, the end of France's attempted colonization took place here when the 'Emperor' Maximillian was executed by Juarez' army. You find the important features of Mexico's march to independence in many obscure parts of this beautiful city. The colonial treasure laws will assure that for many more years Mexicans and even tourists yet unborn will appreciate that cultural heritage.

The Happy Maya

In Yucatan you will meet a pure race of brilliant people who have been there for thousands of years. They are tiny, cheerful, smiling people who find life in this century a bit rough but maybe their day will come again. You sure hope so after meeting them.

When you see Chichen-Itza, in the Yucatan Area, you will understand. Then after meeting your first ever-helpful Mayan you won't believe all that stuff about their human sacrifices. It must have been the work of those mean Toltecs who then blamed it on the gentle Maya.

The Women

Mexico and Centro America may be our own neighbors but their faces are toward Europe. We've had little influence on its people except for material things. Our movies influence their dress and their ideas about us but that's about all.

Even a hairdresser in a little shop with no hot water has been to Paris for a few weeks to learn good hair styling. It never crossed her mind to go to New York or Miami to learn those skills.

Quaint Hotels

Many of us prefer quaint sidestreet hotels with some comforts. Cheer up, there are lots of them but they are not well publicized. In this book they are usually the ones shown with the lower prices on airport page hotel listings.

It is best to go look for yourself to see if the report meets your own expectations and if they have room for you. The more desirable ones too often have no telephones or interest in answering the mail. They are too busy making delicious meals and keeping the place spotless.

Cab Driver Reservations

Asking a cab driver to pick a hotel for you can be risky. He will want to see you in the flossiest place the city has to offer either because he thinks all tourists are 'ricos' or because those places pay him the best commissions.

If you must rely on the driver, don't hesitate to ask him to take you to other

For Women Only

places if you don't like the first ones. Go in yourself to see if space is available.

Conventional Motel Choices

There is no shortage of good to deluxe hotels in Mexico, as a glance in this book or at the AAA Tour book will show. Rates are only a rough guide to the kind of service you'll receive, but they are at least a place to start.

In hotels that have both American Plan (with meals) and European Plan (no meals), you must ask if the rates quoted cover meals and if so how many. Disregard any signs: overhead or in tour books, including this one.

Under some circumstances, you may even ask that they write down for you the room rate in pesos, "con (o sin) alimentos," with (or without) meals.

Clothing to Take Along

Synthetic blend permanent press clothes are marvelous for travelers in the temperate areas of Mexico and Centro America. They are comfortable, can be quickly washed even in a hotel basin and are ready to wear the next morning.

In the tropics nothing, but nothing is as comfortable as cotton. It does get wrinkled and takes much too long to dry for hotel basin laundry. A favorite solution is to go with cotton in the tropics and send them to the hotel laundries. City hotels usually have printed lists in the room with prices and when you can expect clothing back.

Day after tomorrow service is standard. Getting the laundry back tomorrow afternoon costs fifty to a hundred percent more. Do remember that everything is washed as though it was a rugged cotton and very soiled. Your husband, if he notices, may be surprised that all laundered clothing is meticulously hand ironed, including his socks.

High Country Clothing

The Central Plains of Mexico and many cities in Centro America are high enough to make a light wool dress comfortable at any time of year. Guatemala City, San Salvador, San Jose in Costa Rica can be cool through the evening and until late morning.

If you will be in the plains of Mexico during the winter do plan to have more wools and other warm clothing. During those months it will be cold at in Mexico City's mile and a half altitude. The rest of the year a warm sweater or sweater jacket will take care of unexpected cool days.

Scarfs, Hats, etc.

Scarfs are handy but a soft straw or washable cotton hat with a narrow brim will endear itself to you on a trip that may take you from the beach to the big city in one day with no time for hairdos. The narrow brim is easy to wear in an airplane and protects your hair and skin.

The acceptance of hairpieces is a boon to travelers and those who just don't like hats. Falls and stretch wigs are perfect for instant recovery from a wet windy beach. They don't need a special box and most wash like a hankie.

Hotel Warmth

Few hotels in the Latin countries have really warm bed clothes. Winter travel calls for either a wool blanket per person, or better yet a SPACE blanket each. This is a sheet of plastic the size of a double bed with a special silvery coating on one side which returns about eighty percent of your body heat.

SPACE blankets work very well, weigh only 5 ounces, fold to a package the size of a pair of mens socks. It is quite handy in the airplane as well. Wrapped around your feet one will fill in for an aircraft cabin heater which skimps on properly heating some parts of the passenger compartment.

Clothing and Dress

In larger cities well dressed women wear things from Europe or in European styles. Since you are able to travel it seems reasonable to the average Mexican that you should be able to dress adequately well. That doesn't mean a gold lame gown in the evening or a full sable coat.

People in Latin America are truly offended by women of any age wearing shorts anywhere. Tennis courts would be the only exception. If someone in your party is dressed in an unusual way the feelings of people in your host society will be reflected in the type of service you receive.

For Women Only

Be Sure To Take

Carry a good supply of facial tissues, whatever cosmetics you are using, and a few basic medicines. Include aspirin, kaopectate, Gelusil, vaseline, mild laxatives, and bandaids. You'll want to have both sunscreen and suntan lotion. These basic supplies are also available at any town or city farmacia (farr-mah-SEE-yah).

Every So Often..

Only in the largest cities and resorts do you encounter the tourist-hardened Mexican. Perhaps you have met his counterpart in New York, Chicago, Los Angeles, or Paris. He usually has a dull but hard and poorly paying job or he's working for his father-in-law, or both. Maybe he's been mistreated by the Ugly Tourist and takes it out on everyone.

Ask How Much

To avoid being affected by this type be cautious about assuming exactly what you understand on first presentation. Make every effort to be sure that other person understands what it is that you expect of him. Since money gets involved, be sure you know what quantity and which kind. 'Dollars' sometimes can mean pesos, sometimes U.S. dollars.

Be gentle but persistent. If you don't understand the answer repeat your request or question until you do. You may discover the prices or rates as first quoted or that you noticed will actually include less than you would expect.

This is always true in restaurants where you might think the low prices are very very low if you didn't know that diners in Latin America order a la carte. Example.

Order Food Thoroughly

Certainly off the tourist route and even sometimes on it, restaurant menus are a la carte. Everything, but everything, must be ordered individually. Bread does not come with an entree unless specifically ordered. Nor does butter automatically come with bread unless it is specifically ordered. Vegetables do not come with meat unless specifically ordered.

There are some very few complete meals such as the universal favorite: braised ribbons of beef with avocado, salad, a chocolate sauce, and potato. This is ordered as 'Carne Asada Tampiqueno' (CARR-nay ah-SAH-dah tomm-pee-CANEyo); i.e. in the style of Tampico. In most places you order it by just asking for 'Tampiqueno'.

Step by step by step by step...

For other meal choices, plan to order step by step by step by step: any items you forget won't appear at the table. Coffee with cream? order cream (CRAY-mah); sugar too? (ah-soo-CARR). Napkin? (sair-vee-YETT-ah). Order each and everything you want. Remember step by step by step by step...

After the adventure of getting along without what you've always thought were necessities a time or two you'll catch on. In the process you will learn some new foods which could become new favorites. Most of us who travel southward much find it does expand our tastes considerably.

A useful tip: in your uncertainty you will be frowning at the menu a lot those first few times. To reassure the waiter or waitress that you aren't upset at them, say a pleasant please a lot: (pore fah-VORR).

Latin Men

One word of advice girls. If you are sixteen or ninety and think a Latin male from eight to eighty is flirting with you, he isn't. He is serious. How you handle the first few seconds of this new relationship makes a lot of difference in the outcome.

If you flush or dimple up, you're on! Coming to your senses a few seconds later won't help; he'll only think you are being coy. Best to not notice any advance, however subtle. Large dark sunglasses are one way to maintain useful ignorance.

Officials

Latin government officials are most often men; let your husband handle all customs and immigration procedures. If you try to help in a situation that has become bogged down your intrusion may be resented, regardless of your obvious beauty and shrewd insight. Particulary the latter. Latin officials have their own systems; relations are smoother when we are gracious guests.

14 For Women Only

Should you find yourself dealing directly with officials, be patient and listen. Patience is infectious: if you are, he will be. Don't start hauling money or getting upset or nervous because he doesn't understand you or you him. Once you understand what is needed, do just that. If you then thank him for all his help you will part friends.

Town Saint's Days

Plan to do a lot of looking at town fiestas. They are local celebrations; you will seldom be asked to dance by anyone within a mile of being sober, any more than your husband would be expected to dance with a local lady. However if things are getting dull, that latter is bound to start a riot.

To Sum Up

The more you travel in other lands the more you will realize all peoples are pretty much alike. You are worried about taxes, ways of the younger generation, the funny things being done in our nation's capital. So is everyone living in each and every country you visit. With that for starters, you'll find it easy to get along well with people you meet.

The Golden Rule is never truer than when traveling.

VFR Altitudes

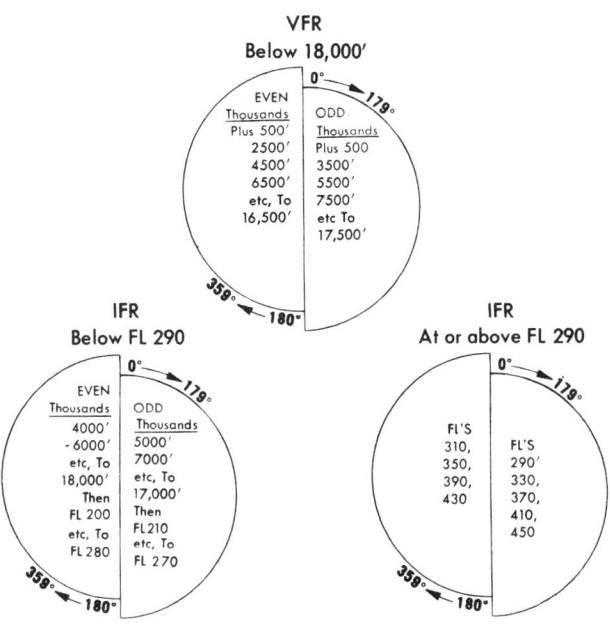

EXCEPTIONS:
1. VFR flights are not authorized above 18,000'

they called them 'dollars' before we did   **Mexico's Money**   15

Throughout Mexico and Central America the basic unit of currency is called 'peso'. Whatever country you're in, the national name is attached, i.e. Mexican peso, Colombian peso, etc. The Honduras lempira is called a 'peso' so long as you remember to say 'Honduran peso.'

Mexican pesos at this writing have have just been devalued to less than one cent U.S. Yesterday's rate was 124 pesos per US dollar. Before leaving on a trip check your bank for the current exchange rate. In Mexico the banks and change houses normally stay within two or three percent of that. Best exchange rate will be at a Mexican bank, worst at a US bank.

Cab drivers and airport fuel sellers can be very convincing about "a new exchange rate of an hour ago." Happened to me yesterday, see page 25.

When buying with dollars and getting pesos in change, or vice versa, you are frankly vulnerable to creative change making. Once the other person learns you are slow at figuring rates or aren't sure of the values of bills and coins, you are about to get a lesson. When you are new at this, best to keep the amounts involved small and inexpensive.

The first and really absolute don't ever forget piece of wisdom is: stay in one currency. When the deal is dollars pay and get change in dollars. If pesos, stay in that kind of pesos entirely: don't mix currencies.

Get started by changing about a hundred or two dollars at a U.S. bank, then change more locally once you learn the ropes. Whatever U.S. dollars you have along should emphasize tens and twenties, plus about ten, one dollar bills for each day of your trip. Use these for small expenditures, cabs and tips.

In Baja California you won't need to change to pesos at all; the dollar is so widely used it is sometimes hard to get pesos there when you want them.

General Carranza was president of Mexico in the middle 1910s. This sort of purplish hundred peso note is worth about seventy five US cents. In September 1982 it'd buy more than a gallon of 100/130 at a controlled airport or nearly two gallons of 80/87 or a quart of oil.

Mexico's greatest independence hero, the beloved Benito Juarez, graces the fifty peso note.   This will buy a third of the cab from Vallarta's airport to town or a beer when you get there.

Allende is pictured on the red colored twenty.

Father Hidalgo, the Samuel Adams of Mexico. He triggered the country's independence and lived to direct it only for a short time. This ten peso note will buy part of a bottle of mineral water some places, it will need help at others.

A heroine of the revolution, this lady's five peso note is now replaced mostly by a five peso coin. This bank note is still used in smaller towns though.

Health

Water IS Necessary

You must drink water, in the tropics you need to drink quite a lot of water to feel good.

One Glass Each Hour

In the tropics my hundred ninety pound body needs eight to ten ounces of liquid per daylight hour. Less than that causes one to feel out-of-sorts, and vaguely unwell. In the more temperate High Country or along the coasts as little as one glass every two to four hours feels right.

Do It Yourself

Although it isn't, if you act as though much of the tap or unbottled water you will encounter is a problem you will get along best. We have a great temptation to heed sincere assurances that "the water here is purified". The water certainly has been through a thing which removed large impurities but not bacteria or virus. Since it hasn't any leaves or twigs, in the waiter's eyes it is purer than what he drinks hence it is purified. But it can cause you serious problems.

Those with travel experience carefully purify any water which does not come from a sealed bottle opened in their presence. This guards against the possibility of a waiter pouring local tap-water into a mineral water bottle when he is very anxious to provide you with what they've just run out of.

In Mexico the mineral water is called by the name 'Tehuacan' (tay-wah-KONN) after the spa city in Puebla from which most of it comes. It is widely available, not expensive, and can be supplemented by your trusty iodine purification system described in the next part.

Water, Not Beer

We're talking about the equivalent of two six packs a day per person. It would not be possible for me to function if much of that was beer or flavored soft drinks. It needs to be either water from my iodine purifying jug (next pages) or normally available mineral water. Either is healthy, purified, safe, and readily available.

Doctors and Medicines

If it should come to that, there are pharmacies -farmacias- (farr-mah-SEE-yuss) in towns and cities of all sizes. You are able to purchase everything for an upset stomach there. This includes the staples such as aspirin (oss-pur-EE-nah), kaopectate (kaopectate), lomatil (low-mah-TEEL), etc. Tetracycline (tetra-see-CLEEN-ah) can get one in trouble if taken without a doctor's instructions. Mostly that one gets reserved for fever associated problems.

English Speaking Doctors

Your best source for a local physician is the hotel desk or the city's Turismo office. Another is the worldwide listing from Iamat. To be listed in that directory the licensed physician must agree to a specified reasonable fee scale and to provide forwarding of calls to an English speaking colleague when he is not himself available. Very handy to have, that book is available by sending $9.55 to Iamat, 350 Fifth Avenue Suite 5620, New York, NY 10001 USA. Allow three weeks.

Caution

There is a medicine very popular in Latin America, which was recommended in many of the older guidebooks. Called Entero Vioformo or sometimes just Vioformo. Brown tablets in a glass tube, many travelers were advised to take one or more tablets per day to prevent digestive upsets.

You should be aware that that it was withdrawn from the U.S. market because of indications that it was responsible for retina damage. Careful: many sources still recommend it.

Gamma Globulin

Several of the problems you hear about can be avoided by a combination of moderation in physical activities and by being reasonably careful about what and where you eat. To be doubly sure many of us routinely have gamma globulin shots not less than every six months. It discourages any hepatitis virus looking for a new host.

Next..

The iodine water treatment system is important to having maximum fun on frequent trips to Latin America. It sure has opened new worlds to the author and to many others who now 'wouldn't leave home without it.'

continued on page 637

Baja Adventures
a fascinating book written by two great people   **17**

BY MARVIN & ALETHA PATCHEN

"Enjoyable...informative...nostalgic...This book brings Baja right into your living room...Highly recommended for old-timers and novices alike."
— Tom Miller, co-author, *Baja Book II*

"Marv Patchen is that rare bird who is both good at flying and telling stories. His aerial exploration has giving him a view of Baja that most long to see."
— Arnold Senterfitt, author, *Airports of Mexico and Central America*

"The Patchens have cruised the Sea of Cortez in the luxury of seagoing yachts. They have also splashed through those waters with just a pair of canoes lashed together so that they could camp on otherwise inaccessible beaches. They are true, latter-day explorers who have many tales to tell, and the skills to tell them well."
— Dix Brow, author, *Boating in Mexico*

Adventure comes in many forms in Baja California. One's imagination is the only limitation. Marvin and Aletha Patchen have looked for adventure in Baja in more ways than perhaps anyone else. Jeeps, dune buggies, motorcycles, campers, three-wheelers, go-carts, yachts, canoes, kayaks, skiffs, helicopters, airplanes of all sizes and a lot of hiking and skin diving have all been their modes of exploration. If you're a first-timer to Baja or a veteran traveler, you'll enjoy BAJA ADVENTURES. It's fun reading and you'll learn from it, too. It's bound to be an inspiration whether you travel by land, air or sea.

Today people are discovering that the word "Baja" is synonomous with adventure and that it need not cost an arm and a leg to be a participant. BAJA ADVENTURES is a testimony to the fact that adventures lie around every corner on the peninsula. It is not a guide book, nor a scientific journal, yet one can learn much from it. The information on trip planning, outfitting and selection of vehicles, boats and aircraft is solid and easy to assimilate as it is woven into a collection of adventures dating back over 30 years. Everyone will enjoy this 192-page book with over 120 photographs.

BAJA ADVENTURES BY LAND, AIR, AND SEA may be ordered from B. K. Palmer Co., 225 Hope, Ramona, CA 92065, by sending $9.95 plus $1.30 for tax and shipping.

Baja Bush Pilots
Where Grace and I go have fun with friends

We just arrived at Isla Porvenir, on the Caribbean Coast of Panama.

Puerto Vallarta, Acapulco, Oaxaca, are names to most pilots but frequent and familiar sights to members of a flying family group called 'Baja Bush Pilots.

Six to ten times a year we strap on our airplanes a go explore together.

In all honesty we don't spend a lot of time at the touristy places which are so over-written about, rather we emphasize the comfortable and always interesting less publicized spots. Acapulco, a city of half a million, is there if we need it, but we have other choices.

First publicly announced in 1970 when the author was giving a seminar Flying in Mexico, the Bush Pilots have now been on about eighty trips together with the author leading in his airplane. Usually fifteen airplanes make up a Bush Pilots group trip, all but three times the author led the group either from his airplane or riding with someone else.

We have been into or through Mexico on more than ninety percent of the trips. So far we've racked up almost four hundred stays at various Mexico destinations. Many of the people pictures in this book were taken of members, with permission of course, on those trips.

All C.A. Countries

We have stopped or stayed in all Central American countries at one time or another, never when there was any hint of problems. We're very careful not to go where we are not thoroughly welcome. The author checks ahead of time with an onscene pre-run to verify our level of welcomeness.

Favorite Islands

We have developed some special feeling about the islands in this book. We've

Baja Bush Pilots enjoying an early Loreto Date Festival in Baja California's original capital.

discovered Islas Roatan, Porvenir, and Contadora are fun places but we certainly don't overlook Ambergris, Cozumel, or the camping possibilities at Caye Chapel where the hotel is infrequently open.

No Super Pilots

Members of the Baja Bush Pilots are a standard cross-section of active pilots. Most of us have instrument ratings, nearly all but not all, own the airplanes they are flying. Those planes range from fixed pitch four place to and beyond retractables. Under ten percent are twins. If we had an average airplane it would be a Cessna Skylane or Cherokee 235 or Arrow. In the first five years of the Baja Bush Pilots our most populous single airplane was the Cessna 172 but the above

Jack makes that vital first cup of coffee; Fort Yukon, Alaska during a Bush Pilots trip.

Baja Bush Pilots

more Bush Pilots information on pages 427, 502.

During a membership skills demo Jerry is off well before the Endmark.

two models have now edged it out.

As pilots we in the Bush Pilots we think of ourselves as still learning about flying, none of us has all the answers. We are certainly not superpilots. Our members are mature people who are also pilots. Age is not a factor, just maturity. On our two and three week Panama trips we go into and out of many countries, deal with dozens of inspectors. We find border crossings go best if we are low pressure people and are able to roll with it.

We Go There As Friends

Of course the biggest factor in the Bush Pilots is that when we visit somewhere we have been there or nearby before, we are known, and people enjoy seeing the Bush Pilots again. Altho you may not have been on that first Bush Pilots trip to the East Cape to help Jacob Malin catch his first marlin on our East Cape expedition in 1971, you do get caught up in the recollection when Carlos and others of us begin reminiscing.

New Places Too

When we go to places we haven't been recently, we are are still remembered from last time even if last time was quite awhile back. On a 1972 trip across Yucatan all fifteen of us stopped for fuel at a place not normally a fuel stop but one I'd arranged for ahead of time, conditionally. Last summer I was there again. The fuel men got great pleasure out of remembering with me that nearly nine years ago visit of all the pretty airplanes and courteous people.

Planning Ahead

In the Bush Pilots we let everyone along the way know well ahead of time that we are coming, who will be with us, their airplane type and registration, and all details. At in-country airports virtually none of this is required but we have learned that officials, fuel sellers, and everyone else appreciates knowing what to plan on from us.

No Loopholes

These early and comprehensive notifications mean we signup well ahead with everyones pilots license numbers, passport numbers. etc. And we are carefull to be nice. Some pilots, not in our group, try to avoid departure tax for their passenger wife by getting her a student pilot license. But the exception for crew is for licensed crew only. We smooth this out ahead of time with our

We've shown off our insignia on trips ranging from Point Barrow, Alaska to Cape Horne, Argentina.

members to speed the process in each country whose border we cross.

The Best $19 . . .

You may join the Bush Pilots easily-details are on page 21 where you will also learn about an insurance policy to further speed Mexico trip planning and going. Our members who use that policy routinely say that by itself that policy saves them several times the nineteen dollars a year.

It's Getting Late

Don't delay signing up for the Baja Bush Pilots, you've already missed one Alaska trip to Point Barrow, a flight to Cape Horne at the tippy tip of South America, seven or eight to Panama, and at least fifty more to other places we're rather not tell you about because it'll just make you sad.

To make it easy, we are going to Alaska in the Summer of 1983 and Panama comes often, as do many others. Cape Horne is a biggy we will do about every four years; our experience from last time will make the next one shorter by fifteen to twenty tach hours.

"... California pilots are lucky to have an experienced veteran in aviation insurance ..."

Bill Gilchrist, President of Franklin Insurance Service Corporation offers a rare blend of:

- 27 Years of flying experience in California and Mexico.
- 35 Years of thoughtful insurance coverage and service in Southern California.
- Creator of the Baja Bush Pilots Mexican Policy.
- Always current on Flying regulations and insurance needs.

For all your California and Mexico Insurance needs:

FRANKLIN INSURANCE SERVICE CORPORATION

5252 Balboa Avenue   Suite 800
San Diego, CA 92117   278-2000

Public Liability Insurance

Whatever we carry in the way of aircraft insurance here in the U.S., when we cross the border into the Republic of Mexico we must have a valid Mexican public liability insurance policy.

At the time we check in with Civil Aviation at our airport of entry the man will ask for proof of insurance written on a Mexican company. The reason is simple: over the years Mexicans who were injured by tourist cars or airplanes haven't gotten what they thought were fair settlements from non-Mexican companies.

Sometimes in the past a driver or pilot involved in an accident would show a policy which in fact was not a good one. With those problems local officials began insisting on cash bonds of several thousands of dollars when an accident occurred. If the driver couldn't post the bond he had to stay until the money was posted. Often his hometown newspaper decided that was 'ransom.'

Insurance is Better

It is a relief that the aviation authorities have cleared up the confusion. Now that everyone has a policy we know there won't be any more misunderstandings on that score. We can confine ourselves to picking the best way of getting needed coverage.

Annual or Flight

You have a choice of two principle ways to get the required liability coverage: an annual policy or trip by trip coverage. Each has its own points to consider.

$1.50 per Day

Members of Bush Pilots Internacional have the option of an annual thirty day coverage policy for $35, covers the minimums as specified in the rules. There are no reports to make before or after trips to start or stop coverage. You do need to keep a record of how many days you were in Mexico during your policy year.

Any days beyond prepaid thirty days incountry will be charged at $1.10 per day but that will comeup only at the time of annual renewal.

Advantages: 1) lowest cost, 2) no pretrip or postrip reporting requirements, 3) honor system bookkeeping, 4) the actual policy in your hands.

Disadvantages: 1) Must be a member of Bush Pilots Internacional ($19 a year), 2) $35 annual minimum premium.

$5-$6 a Day

A credit card system is the other main choice. You apply for and receive a plastic card. When you want to start your coverage in the aircraft listed on your application you telephone or write to the office telling them what date you will be leaving. Coverage starts that day and will continue either until you told them to stop it or until you phone or write to say you've returned.

The plastic card itself carries your name and account number, plus a request on the back in Spanish that anyone needing to inquire may send a collect wire asking whether your insurance policy is actually in force.

Advantages: no mimimum, credit card sized 'policy'.

Disadvantages: 1) application fee, policy fees, plus insurance premium itself will take costs into the $5-$6 per day range. 2) If you forget to call before leaving you have no coverage, 3) Should a local official want to get sticky, the plastic card is not itself proof of insurance. Only after he has sent a wire then received a confirming one will he have proof that you are in fact insured.

Do It

Whatever method you use to get coverage be doggoned sure you have a policy of some kind running before you leave home on your trip south. Not only is it required by law, the risks involved are simply not worth it for a buck a day.

For Application

Annual policy: Bush Pilots Internacional, Postal Drawer 27310, Escondido, California 92027

Card: MacAfee and Edwards, 3105 Wilshire Blvd, Los Angeles, CA 90010

Dirt Field Techniques

During the multi-hundreds of dirt field landings needed to find, measure, and evaluate the airports in the various editions of this book the author has evolved some dirt runway evaluating techniques. Using these methods, you can fly safely in and out of dirt airports throughout the world in virtually any normal production airplane. Using these you can decide, while still in the air, whether you want to land under the conditions that day, and how you will go about doing it safely.

The following three step system will open to you hundreds of interesting small towns you would otherwise never get to see and enjoy.

HIGH-LOW-CLOSE Looks

Begin with the HIGH Look which is just a few left 360s at 1,000', made so you can get acquainted with the area. Among other things look for nearby settlements which might produce pesky pedestrians, gullies pointing anywhere near the runway, or anything unusual. When you are satisfied that you have a good overall picture move down for the 300' to 500' AGL LOW Look.

Low Look

While making passes with the runway on your left check carefully for approach obstructions, ditches affecting the runway, cattle or burros. The first pass is to look for holes and soft spots. On the second I like to pick out both a touchdown spot and 'Go Around If Not Down By' spot.

It is better for the airplane if you can touchdown where the airplane will coast to a parking area with almost no blasts of power. The power needed to make turns on the runway will raise tons of avoidable dust. With these details arranged in your mind, go get intimate with this runway.

50' Closeup Look

At pattern altitude I like to get the airplane ready as though for a landing so I can concentrate on looking carefully. Down at this altitude with the runway on the left it is easy to spot holes, animal or vehicle tracks, to help decide if this is going to be a landing. A cow pushes down about 200 psi on the runway, a truck or airplane thirty to forty. If a vehicle left deep tracks then it is certainly too soft for us; but if a cow did, that is something else.

When you like what you see the IF we land works up to PROBABLY. Go back to pattern altitude, get the airplane ready and make the approach. If all goes really well and you feel good, land.

But for me if the approach is even a teeny tiny bit off or doesn't feel just exactly right, that pass becomes another Closeup Look and we go back for another. On each Closeup Look you get that much smarter about the runway.

After you do land be careful on rollout. Carb heat needs to come off and the flaps come up (flaps, not gear). Dust is not a friend to either.

Easy Does It

While taxiing it is vital to use brakes little if at all and to apply just enough power to keep the airplane moving. The final spotting the airplane into an actual tying down place should be done by hand with the towbar. Shut the engine off and do this last part carefully to save props and engines, just in case we plan to use them again.

Tying Down

Nearly all the airports in this book have tiedown areas, but almost none have ropes and anchors which would securely hold your airplane in even a moderate blow. For adequate protection you will need to carry your own tiedowns. In Bush Pilots Internacional we made up a kit with six pieces of thirty inch rods (building contractors know

Dirt Field

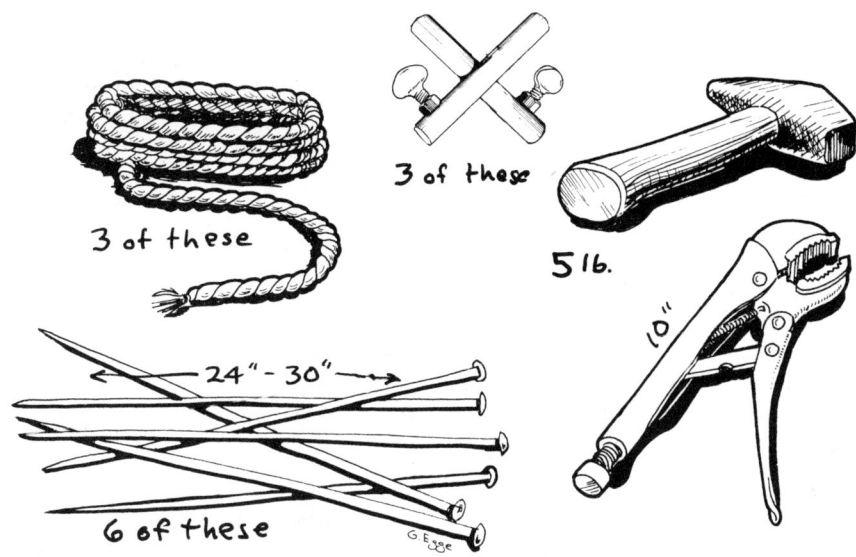

about REE-bar), a five pound short handled sledge to pound them in, 10" visegrips to get them out later, and three each fifteen to twenty foot pieces of half to five eighths rope. The rods we use are aluminum in T3 or T6 hardness; this material is harder to find than rebar but much easier to use.

Stakes are slant-driven into the ground with their tops leaning out from the tiedown ring so they are about forty five degrees the ground's surface. The kit I use was madeup by Paul Baxter of Siletz, Oregon and has welded bracket guides to hold two stakes in a cross. With them in the ground fully, there is about two tons of earth holding me at each tiedown. Hard to beat that for security. Forget piles of rocks, screw-in stakes, or sacks of sand; their benefit is purely cosmetic.

Departure

Before cranking up it is a good idea to first layout in your mind the shortest easiest route from this tiedown spot to the start of your takeoff roll. It is even better for the airplane if you've first hand pushed push it around to point in the taxiing direction.

On startup by keeping the idle under 1000 rpm you will minimize dusting of yourself and others. You may need 2000 rpm but only for those few seconds needed to get rolling. Then power can be reduced to just enough to keep moving.

Blasting Idiot

On dirt we never ever do a conventional paved airport runup or magcheck, unless of course our propellors are too long and we want them shorter. That would also sandblast every airplane around. Most of us either forego magchecks while on dirt or, if we really must do one we borrow the seaplane technique.

Accelerate to magcheck rpm as a part of the takeoff run, quickly switch back and forth. If all is well, go to full throttle and continue takeoff. But if something just isn't quite right we've only used three hundred feet so we stop easily and think it over.

Your Turn

These ideas have been in use for several years both by the author and by members of Bush Pilots Internacional. Pleased members have been able to fly everything from Bonanzas and Cherokees to Mooneys and Vikings off dirt runways from Point Barrow, Alaska to the tip of South America.

But these ideas are just that: ideas you can use to build your own methods. They are not intended to be the last word on the subject. When you come up with ways of doing this let me know, I'd be delighted to have you improve on my ideas.

MacKenzie Aviation
Sharpen your skills for the trip

The clear air at Ramona, California has been an excellent training site since the Navy established the airport during World War 2. The 4,000+ foot lighted, paved runway is still a favorite for training exercises.

Ron MacKenzie's fixed base operation offers a choice of a full Bush Flying Course, a Mountain Flying curriculum, or a **Get Re-Acquainted With Your Airplane** session for those who've gotten busy and want to polish their skills.

Cessnas-Pipers-King Airs-Boeings

Ron's instructor staff is widely qualified. Type ratings range from 707s, Citations, Lears, KingAirs, to popular General Aviation singles and light twins. Each instructor flies regularly in the aircraft in which he is qualified.

Full weekend sessions may be arranged for anyone who would like to make a concentrated effort. Not only are there **five IFR airports** within twenty miles, but Ramona itself has an approach as well.

Ron's **Pinch Hitter** course which can be given the spouse either in a MacKenzie airplane or in the family one. An advantage of using Ron's is that both husband and wife can save time by taking dual at the same time.

The **Lunchbreak course** is a concentrated training sequence set in one midday session. It consists of three to four hours of ground and flight instruction starting daily in the late morning for a thorough, combined IFR and VFR skill review. Just the thing to brush up before a safe, fun Mexico trip.

If Mountain flying interests you there are two good instructors on the staff with thousands of hours in the Ecuadorian mountains. Maybe Bush Flying? Some of these instructors flew Cessna 180s in and out of rice paddies in Chiapas, oil fields in Venezuela, and hauled missionaries around Guatemala's jungles and sierras.

Whatever instructor skill you need, talk to Ron and you'll be flying much quicker and with confidence.

MacKenzie Aviation

A Full Service FBO

Flight Instruction—A&P, AI Shop— *Instant* Fuel Service

In quiet, clear Ramona, California

Telephone 714-789-6384

Gasoline 25

Smoothing the Way

No matter where you stop for fuel in Latin America there have been hundreds or thousands of us there ahead of you. The gas sellers have learned that English 'Gasoline' sounds reasonably close to Spanish 'Gasolina' (goss-oh-LEE- nah). They've had fun with 'oil'. Aceite (ah-SAY-tay), but if you forget just opening the cowl will put the point across.

At Baja California's Rancho Santa Ynez, gasoline is thoroughly filtered and carefully measured

The facilities for putting gasoline into your aircraft vary widely, as the photographs here show, ranging from the most modern high pressure millimicron filtered facilities, to modest systems elsewhere on the scale.

Don't let appearances deceive. Many Baja California ranches have been vital aviation gasoline outlets for twenty to thirty years. Often cowboy looking cowboys have for years been parking their horses, correctly identifying and properly fueling 80/87 vs 100/130 octane Bonanzas, Cessnas, etc. before getting on with cow chasing.

Chamois?

In my experience anyone who sells gasoline to airplanes already has funnels, filters or chamoises(?), and can make change. At one time or another I've bought gasoline that was filtered through regular chamoises, often through synthetic ones, and once through Rene Villavicencio's felt hat. And after filling each time there was enough dirt and water in the bottom after fueling to say filtering was a good idea but not so much as to worry. And each time the airplane ran just fine.

I have never found it necessary to put even one gallon of gas in any airplane without filtering.

Black Blob = Gas

In this book airports where gasoline is routinely available are clearly marked twice. First, on each airport page itself the page number for gaoline- selling airports are printed in white numbers on black backgrounds rather than the usual black numbers on white paper. Second, the same thought is used on the Area Charts at the beginning of each section.

Gasoline's Everyplace

The black boxes with white numbers are where you can buy gasoline. Again, both on the Area Charts and airport page, white page numbers on a black blob sell aviation grade gasoline.This way you can pick them out quickly.

You Speak, I'll Listen

If you find anything in this book different from your experience anywhere, please let me know. Drop me a note to the address on page 4. The PREPS will carry changes. I may not answer your letter in the same century it was written but you will probably see your in the next edition as the source or as a Reader Report. That is my way of saying thank you.

Meantime, at present prices for aviation gasoline in Mexico you can't afford to stay home. Get going!

Filling 180EE's tip tanks at La Paz on a typical nice day there

26 Gasoline *what the paperwork looks like*

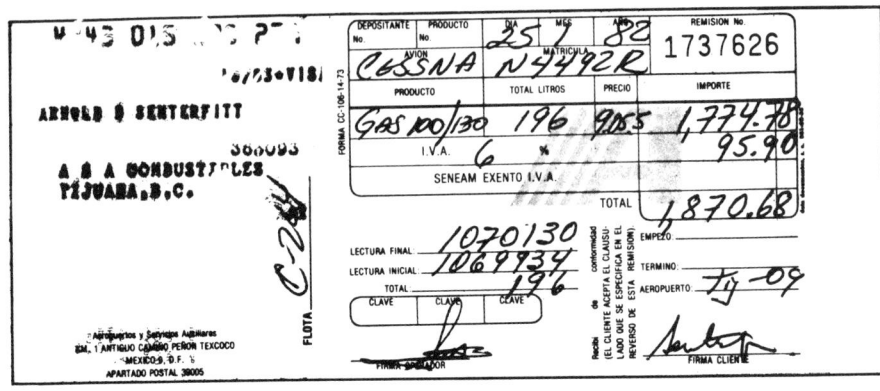

Both when I made the purchase of "GAS 100/130" January 25, 1982 for Cessna 92R (delivery slip above) and when I bought 80/87 for Marvin's Skylane yesterday, (delivery slip below) I paid for the transactions with my VISA card. The system is that on credit card sales to slips are prepared: Fuel Delivery Slip, and a separate VISA/MC Charge Slip.

Gasoline 27

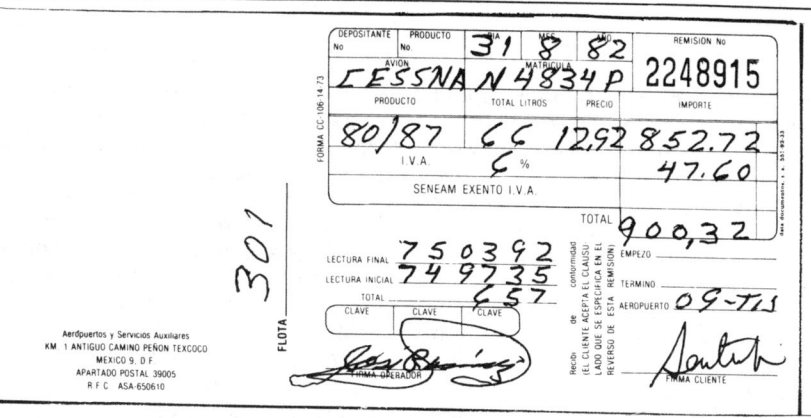

Yesterday I wanted to check a new system being used so Marvin and I flew into Tijuana, fueled 92 liters worth the aforesaid VISA, then we flew around for awhile and came back to Tijuana, topped off with 66 more liters paid for in US dollars at whatever rate the fuel seller said, and went home. In those two fueling sessions we learned some things.

January Was 100/130

The fuel purchase in January was exchanged at the old rate for the peso and cost me about eighty-five cents a gallon for prime 100/130 aviation fuel. What with the peso jumping around a lot I wondered what to expect on the last day of August, 1982.

Half The Price

First, the 92 liters of 80/87 it took to fillup on our first Tijuana stop, charged on my VISA, will end up costing me about eighty US cents per US gallon. That's because the price I pay will be the peso rate on the day that voucher arrives in Mexico City, not an off-the-wall gasboy's rate.

Fifty Over

The second lesson was, paying in US dollars and trusting the fuel seller to give us something like the official bank rate was optimistic. Near as I can figure, 66 liters for $15 US dollars was $1.16 a gallon, once and a half the credit card cost.

These gas men see dozens of US aircraft a day come and go, from watching how others were handled that day it is my opinion that this was a typical example of what would happen had you taxied in for fuel behind or ahead of us that day, on the very latest possible day before this book went to press.

Need a Quart?

The very popular U.S. oil, Aersohell W is only seen in Mexico as some local pilot's private stock. Excepting Mexico, every place in this book with gas in this book carries Shell routinely. In Mexico you do see Texaco both in compounded (detergent) and uncompounded (mineral oil) at the usual airports with fuel. Esso oil is also available uncompounded in heaviest weights.

50=100

Oil grades in Latin America are known by the Saybolt numbers, not by our usual Society of Automotive Engineers ones. You and I think of it as Shell (SAE) 50, in most other countries it is called (Saybolt) Grade 100. In Spanish,(cien, see-ENN). If you want 40 weight, be sure to tell the man 'ochenta' (oh-CHENN-tah) so he'll put in Grade 80. For a really big number, Esso's SAE 60 goes to a hundred twenty (see-ENN-toe BAIN-tay) there.

Check It Yourself

Mostly the gas pumps in Latin America deal with local airplanes whose pilots prefer to keep their own accounting of the oil status. Almost never have I been asked anything about oil, even years ago when flying the 195 which had a 5 gallon oil tank and regularly used two quarts for every hour that tached by. On that rascal if you didn't carry oil in gallon cans you'd wear yourself out going up and down the ladder.

Fussy? Carry Your Own

If you will be using much of a non-available oil, either take a good supply with you or switch. Some pilots, heading for fifty hours in Mexico only, change to Texaco before the trip, use only Texaco in Mexico, then change back on return home.

28 Mechanical Help

THE Problem

Most pilots worry too much about those stories which start "It is a crime to have airplane trouble..." The answer: baloney. Scare stories come in all sizes. Where there are airplanes there are going to be occasional service difficulties or even accidents. It is important to know the right steps should a problem surface around you. No one expects superhuman solutions, just legal ones.

Bad stories may get started when someone tries to quietly slip the wings off his bent airplane and smuggle it home without telling anyone he'd had a problem. The usual official result is a fine for working on an airplane without being a licensed mechanic.

Typical of Latin countries, the Republic of Mexico has laws which are very similar to the U.S. regarding airplane mechanical problems and who can legally work on them. The rules are that you can do some very minor things yourself such as changing a tire. Bigger problems need the attention of a federally licensed, in their country Mexican licensed, aircraft mechanic.

Airplane problems divide into the two phases first of getting the airplane on the ground if the problem occurs in the air, then second going through the administrative or repair steps. If the landing itself is a problem we'll get into those details further down in the paragraph 'Bent Airplane'.

Perfect Example

Couple years ago an incident occurred which was a textbook example of how to handle both parts of the problem the right way all the way through.

Bush Pilots Internacional had been at Loreto on our annual Ladies' Funny Fishing Tournament. When the problem began Jack Ross was heading home a day early. The rest of us were flying up for our usual shelling on the beach at Punta Chivato which we've been doing for the past ten years when visiting Loreto.

Jack called me to say his engine was beginning to run rough, power seemed to be off as evidenced by five mph less airpeed. Rule One: Alert another pilot then keep him posted on what is happening and what you intend to do.

Pick an Easy Airport

Next, he decided a landing was necessary but not instantly so picked forty mile distant Serendidad at Mulege as the nearest fully suitable airport. It is an active airport which already has overnight guards if his stay should stretch; the runway is plenty long. Hotel Serenidad itself is on the opposite side of the runway from the parking area.

Although closer, Santa Rosalia's runway is badly positioned: afternoon west winds make that a leeside runway. He already had enough problems.

Altitude is Money

Third, he proceeded to Serenidad at six five; with that altitude, he'd always be within easy gliding distance of at least one of three less suitable but existing interim airports. For this sort of problem Santa Rosalia, Rancho San Lucas, and Punta Chivato aren't all that great but if the situation deteriorated he'd have a known place to go where others of us could come help.

Count the Cylinders

On the ground do whatever your own skills are. After his uneventful landing Jack looked over the engine, couldn't find the problem, so I took him and his passengers back to Loreto. Later that day one of the other members who is an A&P went by and discovered a hairline width crack between the spark plug holes on number three cylinder. The suitable repair was a replacement cylinder.

Local Licensed Mechanic

In Loreto Jack talked to Oscar Flores, the licensed Mexican airline A&P who also has a J3 Cub. Oscar agreed another cylinder was needed, told Jack he'd be available the next Thursday. By telephone Jack arranged with his mechanic at home for a cylinder then called a friend who'd fly him and the cylinder back to Serenidad.

Report the Problem: Twice

Both Mexico's Civil Aviation department and the U.S. FAA will want to know something happened. Civil Aviation is the FAA of Mexico; you report to the commander of the controlled airport of entry as you leave the country. They want at least a handwritten narrative of

Mechanical Help

what happened, what you have done, what you plan do and when. If you don't have a licensed Mexican mechanic by now the commander will be able to suggest someone. More often than not this office has already heard about the accident. Your being willing to report the incident both confirms it and speaks of your honesty.

General Declaration: Keep It

Understand that the General Declaration you receive on entering the country is a permission for that airplane to be in the Republic: surrender it only when the airplane itself departs the country, not when you do.

Import the Parts Legally

Mexican import duty on aircraft parts is low, two to five percent. The quickest way to take them into Mexico is to call a Customs Broker from home to do your forms and handling. Saves a couple three hours or more. Jack did that and was able to sail through the clearance process at Tijuana.

Your Own Mechanic Too?

Most mechanics in Mexico work for the airlines; they don't always have the small airplane parts, tools, and manuals. Although they welcome someone who is well equipped, a tourist U.S. mechanic actually doing work is flatly illegal and it is enforced. He can watch, that's all.

Expect Shop Rates

Although work might be done out in the open somewhere, expect to pay something near your normal shop rates for the mechanic and his helper. As a bargaining point, the helper is usually considered part of the mechanic, so you pay for one, not two. In casual situations such as this the mechanic may ask what you think the job was worth then settle for that amount or something near it.

Runup and Test Fly

Jack imported the cylinder, his home-base mechanic was delighted to accept a couple days paid vacation in Mulege where Oscar met them. After the cylinder was installed and the airplane test flown okay, Jack threw a party for Oscar, his helper, and the ones who'd come with him from Van Nuys. Next morning everyone went home.

U.S. Customs Formality

Repairs made just so you could continue a flight are not dutiable to U.S. Customs. Unless you had your airplane painted or upholstered or otherwise increased in value while outside the U.S., you owe no Customs duty on returning home. It would be a good idea to tell the inspector you had work done on the airplane just so everyone is working with the same information, but the five percent duty on paint or labor or fabrics will not apply to you.

The key words are 'necessary to flight'; if the repairs were, no duty. Otherwise, pay the man $5 per hundred dollars of what you laid out.

Now the FAA

The Friendlies require any serious work on an airplane be done by or under the supervision of a U.S. licensed Aircraft and/or Powerplant mechanic (A&P). The FAA does not presently recognize Mexican A&P mechanics' licensure for certified work or logbook entries on U.S. registry aircraft. The work done by Oscar had to be signed off by a licensed U.S. A&P.

In this case it was duly entered by Jack's mechanic who watched Oscar doing the work. In order to conform with Mexican law about no gainful employment, he did get get in one full day of great fishing while the work was being done instead of being paid as an A&P, but he was content.

No A&P Along?

But what if you or I have a problem, get it fixed locally then go on our way without having a handy U.S. licensed A&P to watch? We still need to get some U.S. A&P to signoff the work when we return home if the job would normally require a licensed mechanic when that same job is done in the U.S. In most cases that means talking to whomever keeps up with your airplane. Not a bad idea for you to take lots of closeup pictures of the work being done just in case he's curious.

Their Law=Our Law, Almost

Remember that Latin American countries have laws about who is licensed to work on airplanes, same as the FAA does. Generally if you comply, there,

MUSTANG

Aviation Enterprises

1424 CONTINENTAL STREET-BROWN FIELD-SAN DIEGO, CALIFORNIA 92173-714-690-2669

HELP IS AVAILABLE!!

We now have a unique service available for those with a mechanical problem in Baja California or in mainland Mexico and need parts to get going.

Here at Mustang we can help with the largest part of that problem by being sure that you won't lack for airplane parts. We can make up a kit of whatever parts and tools you need to get going, then will ship the package to you wherever you are. We will even see to it that the box contains safety wire, solvent, even rags. In short everything you need to get back in the air and headed home.

What gets us started is you telling us with a HELP MESSAGE where you are, what kind of problem you are having. Send that via any northbound airplane; ask the pilot to pass it to us. We are right next door to U.S. Customs at Brown Field in California, page 115 in this book.

To be the most usefulness, that HELP Message should include your airframe make, model, and serial, the problem you are having and what parts you need. If you know part numbers send those also. For billing purposes include with your HELP message a major credit card.

We will get new parts, include the tools you will need, box everything properly, legally import them to Mexico, and either take them to Tijuana to await a southbound airplane, or contact San Diego FSS for a southbound airplane. If you have another preference for shipping include it in your HELP Message.

You will be charged only the current catalog list prices for the parts we ship to you. When you stop in and return the tools we've sent and sign the invoice we will return your credit card to you.

For lightning fast service we can even charter fly the parts directly to you. Also, if you are stranded in a remote area and can't find the necessary Mexican mechanic we know several and can either fly one to you with your parts or include a note in the box telling you the local mechanic's name and how to locate him.

We all hope there are never any problems but if one should come up we'll make doggoned sure you get going again quickly.

Question? Call us,

Charley Farrar, Chief Pilot
Al

Mechanical Help

Bent Airplane

If your problem is bent metal, that will mean an insurance claim. U.S. insurors have always preferred, at least from what I have observed, to send their own claims men to the scene for care or retrieval of the airplane. You need only post a guard on the airplane, pay him $10 a day for the first week, report, then give the General Declaration to the insurance company. The report of this more serious accident should be made in person to the commander's office of the nearest controlled airport.

Injuries

In the event of an accident serious enough to cause injuries to occupants of the aircraft or to those outside, the general rule is take care of the injured people first then do administrative details. This means that although the accident investigator wants parts of the airplane left where they stopped falling, care of the injured comes first.

Your Liability

You carry insurance to take care of people who may be hurt or lose property. Problem is that just having a piece of paper is no guarantee that you actually do have currently inforce, valid insurance coverage which will pay real money. Where injuries or damage involve local residents or their property a local law enforcement man is going to be concerned that you, as the highly probable responsible party, will pay whatever the costs will be.

Be Damned Helpful

In an accident situation in which you are the pilot, a law enforcement officer will be called upon to make some difficult decisions about you with very little to go on. He must decide whether the liability insurance policy you show is a good one and whether you should be allowed to return home without posting a cash bond. All he will have to help him decide will be what he has seen or is told about your behavior.

If in the process of whatever happened a family's milk cow gets wiped out or a brick maker's freight burro is injured, it would be to your definite best interests to immediately replace them or it without waiting for adjustors or a court.

A family with a small child needs milk twice a day every day. Someone who has a burro to carry loads he'd carry on his own back otherwise, will need to carry freight before he next buys food. Don't waste any time.

Forget the Bad Word

Nobody wants the pilot in jail just because he had an accident. That only becomes a factor when the policeman has reason to worry that the pilot does not have a good policy, or any. Or the policeman could decide, based on the pilot's actions, that locally damaged property might not be recompensed properly once the pilot is not there. Over the past years that latter has happened enough for any local law enforcement officer to take that possibility into consideration.

Problem: Emotion

The hard part is to go on functioning when someone is hurt, several people are hysterical, the lady whose cow got hurt has newborn infant needing milk for her next feeding in an hour. With this walk-through preparation you know what to expect should this problem ever present itself anywhere around you.

Say Again

It is worth repeating: if you have a mechanical problem in Latin American country and follow the rules the FAA has for that level of repair you will be okay. If you blow a tire, fix it or call on your local Llanteria (yonntair-REE-yah), tire repair yard.

But if there is something more than the FAA would let you do yourself, or if you want to play it extra safe get a locally licensed mechanic for absolutely anything the airplane needs. You may need to feed him parts, maybe tools, and manuals, do that too as necessary. That's the way to stay on the good side of the Civil Aviation departments once a mechanical problem develops.

Regulations

CIRCULAR of December 15, 1979

I. This circular is applicable to private aircraft of foreign nationality and foreign registration of any type, whose maximum capacity is 16 passenger seats and for which there is no transportation charge. On these aircraft, they can only transport people who have been invited and under no circumstances any cargo, merchandise, or articles of any kind that are not for the personal use of the crew or their guests.

When the capacity of the aircraft is greater than 16 seatsd, in order to be able to operate in Mexican territory, application for approval must be applied for at least five working days before the date of the scheduled trip and written permission must be obtained from Directorate of Civil Aeronautics.

II. In order to enter Mexican territory, all privately owned foreign civil aircraft destined exclusively for private purposes, recreation, or transiting Mexico, must comply with the following requirements:

A. Jet or turbine aircraft can and should use for their entry or departure from Mexico any of the airports listed below:

Acapulco, Gro.	Mexico, DF
Cancun, Q.Roo	Merida, Yucatan
Cd Acuna, Coahuila	Monterrey, Nuevo Leon
Cd Juarez, Chih.	Nogales, Sonora
Cozumel, Q Roo	Nuevo Laredo, Tamps.
Chetumal, Q Roo	Piedras Negras, Coah.
Chihuahua, Chih.	Puerto Vallarta, Jal.
Guadalajara, Jalisco	San Jose del Cabo, BCS
Guaymas, Sonora	Tampico, Tamaulipas
Hermosillo, Sonora	Tapachula, Chiapas
la Paz, BCS	Tijuana, BCN
Manzanillo, Colima	Torreon, Coah.
Matamoros, Tamps.	Veracruz, Ver.
Mazatlan, Sinaloa	Zihuatanejo, Gro.
Mexicali, BCN	

II-B. Piston engine aircraft of one and two engine will use for their entry/departure from Mexico the following border internacional airports:

Northern Zone	
Ciudad Acuna, Coah.	Mexicali, B.Cfa.Norte
Ciudad Juarez, Chih.	Nogales, Sonora(part time)
Hermosillo, Sonora	Nuevo Laredo, Tamps.
➤La Paz, Baja Cfa.Sur	Piedras Negras, Coah.
➤Loreto, B.Cfa.Sur	Reynosa, Tamps.
Matamoros, Tamps.	➤San Jose del Cabo, BCS
	Tijuana, B.Cfa.Norte

South and Southeastern Zones

For flights from or to the south and southeastern borders of Mexico, use of these following airports of entry or departure are authorized:

Cancun, Q.Roo	Cozumel, Q.Roo
Chetumal, Q.Roo	Tapachula. Chis.

II-C. At each airport of entry/departure the crew and passengers comply with the formalities of Customs, Immigration, and Health. as they enter or depart the Mexican Republic.

II-D. The crew comply with security standards established by the general communications systems law and its regulations, as well as the provisions of their own country's regulations regarding registration, operating weight, first aid and instruments. Foreign aircraft entering the Mexican Republic must carry certificates of registry and airworthiness, licenses for flight personnel, and other pertinent documents.

II-E Aircraft must follow the air routes established by the Secretariat of Communications and Transports and will be subject to the regulatory procedures contained in the official Mexican aeronautics information publication.

II-F The pilot of an aircraft proceeding to land at a border airport of entry or departure must communicate with that airport by radio or by other means, of their intention to land. Notification via FSS followed by a call 10 to 30 miles out will suffice. Jet and turbine aircraft overflying the border will announce their entry into Mexican airspace by calling the nearest ATC facility.

II-G In compliance with the provisions of articles 351 and 352 of the General Communications System Law, the operator of the aircraft must have insurance to guarantee the payment of damages caused to third parties on the ground due to operations within the Republic of Mexico. Public Liability minima there established are:

Aircraft whose gross takeoff weight is 5000 kgs (10,200 lbs) or less:$ 60,000.00
Aircraft of 20,000 kg (44,000 lbs):$ 150,000.00
Aircraft to 40,000 kg (88,000 lbs):$ 600,000.00
This insurance must be arranged with a Mexican insurance company.

III. Crews of aircraft entering Mexico shall, at the airport of entry, fill out and/or sign the form GHC-001 shown on page XX — which is then taken each to the Mexican Customs and Mexican Immigration desks. Either the Airport Commandant or his representative will then approve the document and deliver the original document to the pilot. That document must then be kept aboard the aircraft until that aircraft itself departs the Republic of Mexico. It must be available for inspection by competent authorities within the Republic.

Once these procedures have been met at the airport of entry the foreign aircraft may then operate freely within the Republic of Mexico, subject only to the aeronautical regulations set forth in the Law of General Communications.

IV. In instances where a rented aircraft is used without the services of a charter pilot, it will be permitted to enter the nation if it has either one or two engines and a maximum of eight seats. If the aircraft either has three or more engines or will seat more than eight persons total, flights into the Republic of Mexico by that aircraft must be approved in advance by the Civil Aviation office, Department of Internacional Air Transport, Universidad y Xola, Mexico.

V. Departing the Republic of México:

VI. The aircraft must enter and depart the Republic carrying the same crew and passengers. In case a different crew is to be used, permission for such change must be obtained in advance from the Commandant of the first airport of entry. If presented with a substantial reason he may, providing there is no infringement of the Law of General Communications, approve and make note of such approval on the form GHC- 001. Author note: Be absolutely sure the notation is written on the GHC-001 if you request and receive such permission.

VII. The provisions of this circular are subject to the principle of reciprocity and therefore will not be in effect for aircraft registered in countries which do not grant these same privileges to Mexican aircraft in private service.

This circular revokes all previous ones regarding the processes of entry into the Republic of Mexico for foreign aircraft; it becomes effective this date.

Parties interested in this circular may contact the Department of Civil Aviation, Department of Internacional Air Transport, Avenida Universidad y Xola, Mexico 12, D.F. or by telephone 905-519-8183 or 905-591-7625.

Signed: Ing. Jorge Ceniejas
Director General

Author's Note: where comments or clarifications have been added within the text, they have been enclosed by the kind of brackets used to surround this sentence.

How they work   Mexican Regulations at work   TCA

One of the confusing parts of international travel is that we sometimes discover other people use 'our' terms to mean something else. Take TCA. Here in the US we use it to mean a **Terminal** Control Area, a big area where everyone is under positive control. But everyone else in the world uses the term to mean a **Traffic** Control Area, a not very tall, small area a place where there is a tower.

Compounding the problem is that the very popular US WACs carry the designation TCA without distinguishing between a hundred mile diameter, 20,000' high Terminal Control Area which has Approach Control and the much smaller, say ten or twenty mile diameter two to four thousand foot high traffic control area which has no Approach Control, only a tower, often part- time at that. Taking a deep breath I decided, in this book, to tell you on each and every affected page which is in effect list the size every time so we can all remember.

Much as I dislike inventing language, two at least slightly different terms seemed called for.

Throughout this book I have used the term TCA in big letters to mean a big Terminal Control Area and tca in little letters to mean the much smaller in size traffic control area. Thus, on the airport pages every TCA is shown as 50 mile radius, 100 mile diameter, twenty thousand feet high. But tca in little letters defines areas that are all smaller, but different sizes and heights. Each page with a tca I've spelled out the diameter and top for that particular place.

Big = TCA   little = tca

34 Camping

Staying at a pleasant hotel with interesting sights just outside the door, a native market day down the street or marvelous discos going until dawn is lots of fun. But camping on a quiet beach or in a jungle town can be an experience you will long treasure.

Camping has given us the key to dozens of unique places in Mexico and Centro America, places we just couldn't have enjoyed any other way.

We've camped on an island in the western Caribbean, in the ruins of Yucatan, at airports in countless small towns. A never to be forgotten thrill is your first midnight stroll in an now abandoned Mayan city where a thousand years ago a quarter million lived.

It is a real treat to fix morning coffee on the tail of your airplane while seals watch you safe in the ocean forty fifty feet away.

The Auburns

All of this became possible because one day in the sixties Bob Auburn convinced me to take camping seriously. Marion and Bob made those popular Flyers Night films of flying interesting places. While I was searching out runways to measure they were searching out places to film. We met a lot.

Bush Pilots members camped at Punta Final's spare runway

They encouraged us to do more than just unroll a sleeping bag on the ground when the weather prevented our going on. We did and camping has now become a vital part of our trip planning.

The first camping was on the 1969 series of updating flights which led to the second edition of 'Airports of Mexico and British Honduras". Worked great: it was possible to stay in some interesting towns which had no hotels of any kind, not even the modest dollar-a-nighters we'd used now and again.

For the first time we could go any doggoned place we wanted. There'd be a hot meal at night, a dry place to stay, and a good breakfast in the morning. We discovered we particularly liked uninhabited islands.

On the first of those trips we slept in our tent nine nights. If you want to count, that tent, stove, and utensils we bought especially for camping cost us ninety-three dollars. Add about twenty more for food, and those overnight stays at some of the most interesting places we've ever visited cost us eleven twelve dollars a night for two. Now we're down to food cost alone.

Poptent

The one piece of camping equipment which made this possible is called a Pop Tent. Nine feet in diameter and six feet high when set up, it's only ten inches in diameter and twenty four inches long as baggage. It weighs an easy eighteen pounds, has front and back insect screens, zipper closing front door and back window. Surprisingly, the thing will go back into the cloth bag it comes in.

In the years since, we've bought and/or tried others but the nine foot diameter Poptent is our hands down favorite. We started with the too small seven. Although I'm only six one I had to sleep scrunched up.

We find the nine comfortable for two in either a zipped together single large or two separate sleeping bags, with room on the sides for our clothes. The center fixture will take either clothes hangers or your garment bag. We couldn't be happier with our "casa compana".

Breakfast Box

Next in importance is our Breakfast Box. At first I used an old fiberboard camera case about twelve inches high by ten deep and maybe twenty-two inches long. That was too heavy so now an ordinary carton with lid carries our aluminum cookset, six stainless Sierra cups with wire handles, bottles of coffee, tea, sweetener if you use it. Quaker instant oatmeal comes in envelopes, each

Camping 35

having a different thing added, like raisins, dates, etc. There's also a plastic stirring spoon in there.

Place settings can be either your stainless from home or a set of camper's bolt-together knife, fork, and spoon for each person.

Estufa

You have a choice on stoves: backpackers' single burner or an easier to get along with 2 burner Coleman. After using each on trips through Latin America, Alaska, and even the U.S. my opinion is that the extra ten or so pounds for two burners has a lot going for it. They cost almost the same. You can cook two things at once, sure. But also

Our seven footer popped at Emiliano Zapata in the Yucatan section.

the two burner stove is stable, doesn't tip or otherwise get skittish. We use gasoline out of the tanks whether we're running 80 or 100, and have for years without a problem.

Water Works

Iodine purified water is in one or two of those readily available squishy collapsible two and a half gallon plastic jugs. A quart canteen to drink from is handy.

Food Box(es)

Our pantry is a cardboard box in the airplane. It includes paper plates in both the large and saucer sizes. Cans of stew, desserts, pork and beans of course, whatever one expects of a pantry.

Establish Camp First

When we pick an overnight spot we first setup camp, then explore until almost dark, coming back in time to have dinner with sunset.

On arrival I just stop the airplane and look around for an overnight parking place. If possible pushing the airplane there by hand is good if there is help. Parking with the tail pointing into the wind it keeps gasoline fumes away from the tail where the stove is setup on the horizontal stabilizer. For some reason the tent seems to always be on the right side; I don't know why.

Takes about fifteen minutes to get things out of the airplane, tent popped and stocked with our sleeping things and luggage. The stove is carried empty of fuel, it now gets filled with gasoline from the wing tanks and will be ready when we come back from exploring.

One night it was on a little island or key off Belice called Caye Chapel; another night we set up housekeeping at a town called Emiliano Zapata where we shooed a few hundred head of curious Brahma cattle away just before going to sleep.

At Caye Chapel we explored the beach and swam in the Caribbean. We watched fish jump and saw beautiful birds soaring in a peaceful evening sky. Emiliano Zapata is a small but bustling town on the Usumacinta (oo-soo-mah-SEENtah) River which then flows south a little further to become the border between Mexico and Guatemala.

You see a variety of tents on Bush Pilots' camping expeditions but consistantly pleasant people.

VARI-PROBE™

Flashlight for Pilots

ADJUSTABLE from brilliant white to a soft red flood: Ideal for inspection or cockpit

EXPLOSION-PROOF: Meets Military Standard 810

RUGGED anodized aluminum construction

LIFETIME WARRANTY

WATERPROOF

Available in 2-7 cells

A Code Four Product

Police Equipment Division
L.A. Screw Products Inc
8401 Loch Lomond Drive
Pico Rivera, CA 90660

DEALER INQUIRIES INVITED

With the 185 we enjoy camping even more now

I was between airplanes in the Summer of 1981 but needed to gather more of the updating material for this 16th edition; Marvin Patchen volunteered. He and I lived in his Robertson Skylane for the next three weeks. We camped all but two of the nights we were away, cooked for ourselves each camping morning and night and, as a test, had nearly all our non-fresh food with us on departure from San Diego.

It was July, we saved weight by not needing warm clothes. Stopping to measure airports at about a hundred different places meant we would never be in one place, cold or warm, for very long. Altitude of our stops ranged from a cool seven thousand feet to several sea level tropics stops. We just carried windbreakers and decided to tough it out.

21 Days Without M ☆ A ☆ S ☆ H

We watched a midnight lightning show at Navajoa, were entertained by muffler- less trucks alllllll through the night at Puerto Lazaro Cardenas. The floor show at Villahermosa was 727s going and coming til past midnight. The navy men in the two big hangars at Isla Mujeres graciously went about their evening and night quietly. At Barra Cazones, Marvin found a fellow baseball fan as I updated the 15th edition page 334 by pushing the wheel from river to yon fence over paving which the tropics climate has reduced to gravel with the last few asphalt drops fading from it.

As usual the menu did not include freeze dried foods. Because water is needed to make them usable we find it easier to just carry canned foods. Main dishes such as pork and beans, vienna sausages with various vehicles, chile con carne, or a can of roast beef require no special skills or equipment to prepare. We discovered that for two hungry men almost any combination was delicious. It may not sound like it sitting there comfortably in your chair, but a can of chile con carne and a can of baked beans stirred together and heated in the same pan are delicious after a day of ten landings and ten wheelpushings.

We bought fresh fruits in settlements as the opportunity presented. This is the way you get papaya, cocos, mangoes, etc. But produce found in big city supermarkets isn't quite the same quality.

Big Poptent

We had along Grace and my twenty pound, nine foot poptent. Where bugs were not a problem Marvin slept outside. I generally slept inside mainly to compare this tent with our square ones. At fifteen pounds less weight and considerably fewer parts to assemble the poptent was a winner for traveling. Our eight by ten foot Sears tent is twenty five percent bigger in floor area so it will be used for our longer camping stays.

Marvin and I had a good time on that trip but I did miss not having Grace along, just as he missed Aletha's company. He and I are fortunate that our wives are good company wherever we decide to go look.

Family Style

It is a real pleasure to go camping with Grace. She is a good sport about choppy air or rocky camping sites or unprotected Facilities. Long as we have a beach campsite now and then she is content. Son Johnny, altho most of us need a ladder to get up to where we can say hello to him, is even more inquisitive than I am. He can spot passing satellites by the dozens in the night sky and loves new places.

Family camping to us involves bringing along but seldom using a tent. Away from US cities the star cover is bright and clearly visible, satellites go by, it is surprising how many shooting stars there are. Nobody wants to miss the continual starshow.

For a short 3 day updating trip last month our menu was simplicity itself. Grace made a flock of baloney sandwiches which she served for breakfast, lunch, and dinner. Supplemented by fruits and various vegetables, no one was hungry. It must have been nutritionally adequate, for the first time in years I didn't go on my usual salad eating jag after we returned.

Now with an airplane which has a thousand pound allowable cabin load after the 80 gallon tanks are full, we can at last carry four adults, all our camping gear, and still have a hundred or two pounds leftover for souvenirs. You will certainly be hearing more from us on this subject.

Flying Samaritans
weekend fly-in medical clinics help remote areas

A toylift to Baja California's El Rosario in 1961 turned out to be successful beyond anyone's wildest dreams, and in the most unexpected, story-book way. It was so successful in fact that it resulted in healthier children and parents in Northwest Mexico, school teachers with rambunctious children ready and eager to learn more. And indians on reservations in two countries have begun getting medical care they never had before. All because Dale Hoyt is easily embarrassed.

Starting With One
A San Diego physician and pilot, Dale Hoyt was asked to fly his Bonanza and haul some toys and hander outers and did. But while the toy party went on Dale noticed that many El Rosario people were in obvious need of medical attention. With the nearest physician ten to twelve hours away by car (a hundred miles) sick people either got well or didn't.

Avoiding the limelight, Dale quietly asked whether anyone would like to see a doctor and was inundated with patients. When he ran out of supplies in an hour the door was closed and sick people came in the windows. What could he do.

He promised to return on his next day off in two weeks and did, many times.

Then Another
The second physician to start helping was Dr Diane Trembly, then the floodgates opened. Nurses, lab techs, dentists, pilots, everyone wanted to help. Aileen Saunders Mellotte had put together the original toylift, now she stepped in to help Dr. Hoyt organize what had come out of it. Since it was a group of samaritans who flew, the club name Flying Samaritans was adopted.

Like Downtown
Soon El Rosario had regular every two weeks clinics put together usually at the last minute. Typically a team would arrive early Saturday afternoon from San Diego, work until everyone (often a hundred or more) was seen by a doctor, sleep a little, then do followups Sunday before a mid afternoon departure for home.

As a club it went through some growing pains. Aileen had to go back to her job so this author reluctantly 'temporarily' accepted what became a two year term as the Flying Samaritans' second president. It meant a trip per week for two years, untold hours in rented airplanes, then later in my Cessna 195 going back and forth to set up clinics, surgical weekends.

Organize and Expand
For starters we faced a new low. When I asked to see everyone's licenses to do what they had been doing in the Samaritans we lost our two busiest 'pilots' and one 'dentist'.

The next two years were busy as we incorporated, got the IRS to agree we were nonprofit and charitable therefore deductible. Membership went from eleven to a tad under three hundred. We opened regular clinics at San Ignacio, Bahia Asuncion, Colnett, on the Reservation at Mision Santa Catalina. And we were still getting to El Rosario every two weeks as before.

Typical Team
We made up modules of a pilot, a doctor, an interpreter, and a nurse or lab technologist. If we could find a multi-skilled person we could make up for it by sending along either extra medicines or another skill mentioned on the Want List i.e. dentist or orthopedist.

The author would, at first, just fly the airplane and work on-scene with medical charts, or chase medicines. Later, after some training, I took and developed X-rays. As my Spanish got almost passable I'd translate in the treatment room if they were really desperate.

Many Chapters

Now past twenty years old, the Flying Samaritans long since outgrew being just a San Diego organization. With chapters throughout California, each of which supports a given clinic site, the Samaritans today have grown beyond just helping in Mexico. It is an overlooked point that many reservation indians in the U.S. get no medical care. Some Flying Samaritans chapters support that need.

Individuals often become interested in helping a particular problem or area not already getting needed assistance and a new effort is begun. One man's interest in helping eye patients results in traveling eye surgery clinics every few months in previously planned places to the benefit of both eye patients and Mexican physicians who are invited to come work, often with the some of the finest surgeons in their field.

Its Something Special

Whether our help is in collecting medicines or sorting them or comforting a sick lady we can't understand through mere language, there is a niche for any skill or ability. Mostly we learn we are more capable than we ever suspected.

Call Bob or Dick

If you do decide to do something in the Samaritans I can, through experience, make you two absolute, rock-ribbed promises. It will be one of the more rewarding times in your life, and certainly one of the most frustrating. What will at first appear to you as doing things backward will,by your third or sixth trip, turn out to be the best way as you learn the rest of the reasons for it. The trick is in not suggesting anything until that magic six comes and goes.

Some of the Flying Samaritans clinics in Baja California.

It is hard, but worth it.

If you'd like to know more about the Flying Samaritans let me introduce you to Bob Morris 415-494-2033 near San Francisco or Dick Leubben at 213-377-8147.

Bob uses his 172 to help with the indians in Northern California. Dick's interest is in the clinics in Mexico, much closer to the LA area and quick to reach in his Cherokee 235. Either will put you in touch or just answer your questions. Call them.

42 All Border data

PERSONAL PAPERS

COUNTRY	Neighbors	Visa requirement	Tourist Permit	Get it where
Belice	Mexico Guatemala	No	Yes	At Airport of Entry
Colombia	Panama South America	No	Yes	Any Colombian Consular Office
Costa Rica	Nicaragua Panama	No	Yes	At Airport of Entry
El Salvador	Guatemala Honduras	Visa or Tourist Permit	Either, not both	At Airport of Entry
Guatemala	Mexico Belice Honduras El Salvador	Visa or Tourist Permit	Either, not both	At Airport of Entry
Honduras	Guatemala El Salvador Nicaragua	Visa or Tourist Permit	Either, not both	At Airport of Entry
Mexico	U.S.A. Belice Guatemala Texas	Only if on business	Yes, for tourists	Tourist Permit at Airport of Entry
Nicaragua	Honduras Costa Rica	Visa or Tourist Permit	Either, not both	A Consulate or Embassy
Panama	Costa Rica Colombia	Yes, or pay $10 fine		Any Panamanian Consular Office

All Border data

FOR AIRCRAFT ENTRY

Need written permission?	If not, what is needed	Address for letters	Telex/TWX Telegraph Address	COUNTRY
No	Flight Plan	Chief Aviation Officer Box 367 Belice, Belice, C.A.	CIVILAR BELICE	**Belice**
No	Flight Plan 2 hours ahead		AEROCIVIL BOGOTA	**Colombia**
No	24 hr. notice and Flight Plan	DGAC* Box 5026 San Jose, C.R. C.A.	AEROCIVIL SAN JOSE	**Costa Rica**
Yes	At least 48 hr. notice	DGAC* Apto Ilopango San Salvador, El Salvador, C.A.	AEROCIVIL EL SALVADOR	**El Salvador**
24 hr. Notice: will reply if refused	Letter or wire	DGAC* Aeropuerto La Aurora Guatemala City, Guatemala, C.A.	AEROCIVIL GUATEMALA	**Guatemala**
Notice	Letter or wire	DGAC* Apartado Postal 250 Tegucigalpa, Honduras, C.A.	DIRGA TEGUCIGALPA	**Honduras**
Not if 15 or less seats; 8 if rented	Flight Plan	DGAC* Dpto Transport Int'l Universidad y Xola Mexico 12, D.F.	CIVILAIR MEXICO	**Mexico**
24 hr. Notice Confirm by Radio @ Frontier	Letter or wire	Ministerio de la Defensa Apartado 87 Managua, Nicaragua, C.A.	DIDAC MANAGUA or Telex 1369 AEROCIVIL NIC	**Nicaragua**
24 hr. notice	Flight Plan	DGAC* Apartado 7501 o 7615 Panama 5, R.P.	AEROCIVIL PANAMA or Telex 2057/0143/2618	**Panama**

*DGAC means Director General de Aviacion Civil

44 Checklist: Depart U.S.—Arrive México *plan ahead*

Four to six weeks before departure

1. If you haven't used Mexican liability insurance before, check the Insurance details on page 21 and get started right now to arrange it.
2. Make hotel reservations: if you're going on a U.S. 3 day weekend these should be made even further ahead, like five to seven weeks
3. The name under which the airplane is registered on the U.S. Registry of Civil Aircraft: is it your own name? If so, fine, but if it is anyone else's name, get notarized permission from him to take the aircraft to México. If a corporation, even your own, get permission from an officer of that corporation.
4. Apply at your County Clerk or Passport Office for passports for everyone who will be aboard. Although not required, these are the best form of citizenship proof you can possibly have. Takes about 2-3 weeks.

One week before departure

1. If the kind of Mexican liability policy you chose requires some notification ahead of time, do it today.
2. Verify that everyone who will be aboard has passports; anyone without should be sure to have a notarized statement that they are U.S. citizens to show the Migración inspector to get a Tourist Permit.
3. If there will be any minor children aboard *without both parents*, get a notarized permission from the parent not along, for the other to take the child(ren) away from their home and into the Republic of México.
4. Get an hour or two in your airplane this week, preferably with all seats occupied and tanks full.

Day of departure

1. File a Flight Plan with your own FSS, taking you to the airport of entry in Mexico. They'll also have weather into Mexico available, tell them to ask Kansas City.
2. When you are within range of a border FSS you may, if you wish, change your Flight Plan into a Round Robin, giving you Search and Rescue protection within México.

At Mexican Airport of Entry

1. Use normal tower-controlled airport procedures.
2. On rollout after landing give point of departure, destination, number of passengers on board; park in area indicated by tower.
3. Before starting clearance processing, tell fueling man what you-want and leave your credit card with him.
4. At Civil Aviation Desk fill out Blue Form—page 47— then add information for Flight Plan—page 48 —and sign both. When General Declaration is filled out for you sign
→ 5. You will pay 150 pesos ($6.00) for VFR flight plan or 400 pesos for IFR flight plan fee and receive a receipt at this time.
6. Over at Migración office get/have signed Tourist Permits for all onboard; the inspector will add his signature and stamp to your General Declaration.
7. Whether or not Customs inspects your aircraft they'll add their part to your Declaration for the last step of your clearance into México.
8. Go back to the plane, pay the fuel tab, and be on your way to a world of fun places to see and enjoy.

Copyright © 1976 Arnold Senterfitt

getting started right   **Arrival in México 45**

Departing US: Flight Plan Only

Unique among countries represented in this book, the U.S. does not have a requirement that we make a special stop when leaving for another country. Aside from filing a flight plan you just yell clear, crankup and leave. This assumes you are not flying a World War 2 fighter or a Viet Nam era gunship, each of which are subject to understandable arms control.

You may either file that flight plan approaching the border or, if your last leg into Mexico is a few hundred miles, file the border crossing part whenever it is convenient for you.

Mexican Airport of Entry AOE

A year or more ago the US Drug Enforcement Agency influenced Mexico to stop allowing single engine aircraft to use interior to Mexico Airports of Entry. That is now fading but the lions share of arrival/departure single engine recip traffic uses a border Mexican AOE.

You will find the controllers' English is excellent, they use standard phrases the same as any other tower. If it weren't for their asides to Spanish-speaking traffic you could still be at an airport near home.

As at any other controlled airport, call ten miles out for traffic sequencing unless there is a US tower or TCA to prevent doing so. With almost no exceptions, the Tower and Ground frequencies are the same so there is no switching on rollout.

Where From - Where To - How Many

On turning off the active runway tell the controller where you are coming from, **your destination that day**, and how many people are on board, and if you will be needing fuel. He will direct you to park in the appropriate area. Generally that means you've parked at the fuelling facility. Order fuel, leave your credit card with the man and head for the brief clearance proceedings listed opposite.

Civil Aviation is First

At this office you start with the Blue Form, page 47, then you spectate while the man fills out your General Declaration, page 54, then your Flight Plan, page 49. You are sometimes asked to either fill these in yourself or to add parts of them so it helps to have this book open and following the process.

The General Declaration is your permission to be in Mexico as the pilot of the listed airplane carrying the people specified, for a time not to exceed the Expiration Time shown in the form's top right corner.

Migracion and Aduana or Customs

Tourist permits, described in detail on pages 52 and 53, are required for each person over fifteen (15) years old who is on board. Younger children may be included on either parent's Permit but that is sometimes a sticky item if for any reason the child makes part of the trip with the other parent or whatever. Best to have a Permit for each person over the age of, say, five.

Aduana (ah-DWON-ah), Customs, inspectors seldom really go look at an airplane, they mostly just sign their blank on the General Declaration and wish you a good trip. If someone gotup on the wrong side or whatever, they will conduct a courteous and tentative inspection. They are great students of human nature and can quickly distinguish between someone who is nervous about crossing into a foreign country and someone else who is trying to pull off an illegal trick of some kind.

Civil Aviation Again

At some airports of entry you finish the clearance process by stopping back by the Civil Aviation desk on your way to the airplane. Usually to drop off the other General Declaration forms. Often they will pass along your flight plan at this time.

On Your Way

Now you have now been through all the hoops and are legally in a foreign country! Stop at the fuel facility to sign your tab and be on your way. Next time, knowing how easy it will be will make it that much faster too. Now go have yourself lots of fun. . . . . .

Copyright © 1976 Arnold Senterfitt

46 Notarized Permission

Special Renter Pilots Rule

Pilots who are flying rented aircraft into Mexico are required to show they have written permission from the registered owner of the aircraft to take it into the Republic of Mexico. This is to prevent Mexico from being at all involved in the stolen airplane process.

Even Your Own

This rule applies even if the airplane is owned by your own corporation. You still must have a properly attested _notarized_ permission to fly that airplane in Mexico. The signatory should be an officer of the corporation signing by title, and it helps if the notarized instrument is on corporate stationery.

Belice Too

Boys at the Civil Aviation office at Belice International tell me they intercept about ten to twenty airplanes a year by doing this. They think it is worth the trouble.

Here is an outline of what you could use; doesn't need to be exactly this way, so long as it contains the elements.

PERMISSION
(USE CORPORATE LETTERHEAD)

This is to certify that _____ has permission
                                   NAME OF PILOT

of this corporation to fly _____
                                   AIRCRAFT REGISTRATION

a _____ into and through
           MAKE AND MODEL

the Republic of Mexico and Centro America during the months of

_____ year 19_____.

Sign _____
                    NAME

_____
           TITLE

Notarize   here

NOTE
copyright holder's permission granted to photocopy this page for personal, use, not for commercial purposes.

your report of Arrival/Departure is called the **Blue Form** 47

On every arrival or departure at a controlled airport in Mexico this blue paper form is The Source. You list the various facts which the dispatcher then uses to prepare whatever documents you will need next.

Incountry/Internacional Arrivals

If you are either enroute or just starting out for somewhere, part of the Blue Form's information goes into the Flight Plan shown on page 48. If this leg brought you into Mexico, the Blue Form will contribute to your next flight plan plus the General Declaration you need to fly around inside the country.

Should you be leaving here for a destination outside the Republic of Mexico you will be asked to turn in the General Declaration you received on arrival in the country. The dispatcher will then file an internacional flight plan for your signature, and will ask you to check out with Migracion. This is nearly always just adding your single entry permit to the growing stack on the dispatcher's desk. About one time out of fifteen he will ask you to check with Customs, aduana (ah-DWONN-ah).

2/3 Size

① Airport—La Paz
② Aircraft—Cessna   ③ Type—180   ④ Registration—N180EE
⑤ Pilot—A. Senterfitt   ⑥ His lic.-1350059   Copilot—not required
⑧ Class of flight—Private   ⑨ From—San Diego
⑩ No. passengers—0   Remarks: ⑪
     ⑫ A/C Serial—31546
⑯ to: Palmas de Cortés (from here)   ⑬ Owner-same as pilot ⑭ Phone
     ⑮ Pilot address—

⑰ (Arrival) at 2215 Greenwich time, March 24, 1976

⑱ Pilot's signature   ⑲ Dispatcher's signature

Copyright © 1976 Arnold Senterfitt

48 Mexico Flight Plan — translated

In Mexico you are required to file and close flight plans wherever there are facilities to do so. 'Facilities' may mean a tower, or just a man with pads of forms. The practice again: file and close where there are facilities. No facilities, you can't open one, no facilities, you can't close one.

```
                              — 2/3 SIZE —
                                                    PLAN DE VUELO.
   seneam              VFR  [✓]       LUGAR: Hmo.
   SCT                 IFR  [ ]       FECHA: 26/IV/82
                                                              F-I-74
A) IDENTIFICACION Y/O  B) TIPO DE AERONAVE  C) MATRICULA  D) NIVELES DE CRUCERO Y RUTA
   PART                   C-185            XA-492R          65'
E) TIEMPO ESTIMADO ENTRE ESCALAS:                          HORA DE SALIDA
   Hmo.  00+40   BHK                                 F) PROPUESTA  G) EFECTIVA
H) VELOCIDAD VERDADERA  I) AEROPUERTO ALTERNO(S)  J) RADIO FRECUENCIAS A BORDO  K) COMBUSTIBLE A BORDO
                                           TRANS       RECEPC      HORAS   MINUTOS
                                                                    05      00
L) NOMBRE DEL COMANDANTE  M) NUMERO LICENCIA  N) DOMICILIO  O) COLOR DE LA AERONAVE  P) DESTINO FINAL
   ARNOLD SENTERFITT      1350059             U.S.A.         BCO / AMA.             BHK.
OBSERVACIONES:                                           Q) CIERRE PLAN DE VUELO CON:

   PAX. 3
                                                         R) CLOSE FLT PLAN WITH:

COMANDANTE DE LA AERONAVE            DESPACHADOR
SECCION SUPERIOR: PARA IFR LLENE TODOS LOS DATOS, PARA VFR TODOS, EXCEPTO LOS SOMBREADOS.   T.G.N.
ORIGINAL: PARA EL PILOTO, COPIA: DESPACHADOR, COPIA: COMANDANCIA, COPIA: ASA.
```

SENEAM is the aviation branch of:
SCT the Secretary of Communications and Transport
LUGAR 3 letter ident of where we are now *HMO = Hermosillo*
FECHA date, written Day/month in Roman Numerals/Year *April 26, 1982*
A Identification Y/O Identification, as airline flight number and/or *PART is short for Particular, the word for private aircraft*
B Tipo de Aeronave (or) type of aircraft *C185 = Cessna 185*
C MATRICULA Aircraft Registration or side number
D NIVELES DE CRUCERO Y RUTA Crossing altitudes and route *he just put 65' for 6500'*
E TIEMPO ESTIMADO ENTRE ESCALAS Time estimated between stops *from here HMO, no hours plus forty minutes to BHK, Bahia Kino*
HORA DE SALIDA Departure Time: **F PROPUESTA** Proposed
   G EFECTIVA Actual
*SHADED AREA IS FOR IFR
* **H VELOCIDAD VERDADERA** True airspeed
* **I AEROPUERTO ALTERNO(S)** Alternate Airport(s)

* **J RADIO FRECUENCIAS A BORDO** Radio frequencies aboard *they want to know either "VHF" or "HF" or both*
K COMBUSTIBLE A BORDO Fuel on board in hours/minutes
L NOMBRE DEL COMANDANTE Pilot's name
M NUMERO LICENCIA His pilots license number
N DOMICILIO His country of residence
O COLOR DE LA AERONAVE Aircraft Color *BCO/AMA = Blanco/Amarillo = White/Yellow*
P DESTINO FINAL Final destination *Bahia Kino*
OBSERVACIONES Remarks *list here number of passengers*
Q CIERE PLAN DE VUELO CON: Close flight plan with: *the soldiers manning the building at Kino aren't yet part of this system*
R CLOSE FLIGHT PLAN WITH same, but in English
COMANDANTE DE LA AERONAVE Pilot's Signature *Readable or not*
DESPACHADOR Signature: *in practice this is a personal logo, for identification, not intended to be read as a word*

Fine print at the bottom says:
1st line "Top part, for IFR fill in everything. For VFR all but shaded area"
2nd line "Original to the pilot, copy: Despatcher, copy: Airport Commander. copy: ASA"

PLAN DE VUELO

sct

REC. 36151

LUGAR: MXL
FECHA: 08/09/81

VFR [x]
IFR [ ]

A) IDENTIFICACION Y/O	B) TIPO DE AERONAVE	C) MATRICULA	D) NIVELES DE CRUCERO Y RUTA.
08M	C 210	N9408M	VFR

E) TIEMPO ESTIMADO ENTRE ESCALAS: MXL/CXL 0:10

H) VELOCIDAD VERDADERA	I) AEROPUERTO ALTERNO(S)	M) NUMERO LICENCIA	J) RADIO FRECUENCIAS A BORDO		O) COLOR DE LA AERONAVE	HORA DE SALIDA	
			TRANS	RECEPC		F) PROPUESTA	G) EFECTIVA

						K) COMBUSTIBLE A BORDO	
		195727			B/N	HORAS 05	MINUTOS 00

L) NOMBRE DEL COMANDANTE	N) DOMICILIO					P) DESTINO FINAL
R. D. YOUNG	USA					CXL

Q) CIERRE PLAN DE VUELO CON: ALA 12:31

OBSERVACIONES: 3 PAX:

R) CLOSE FLT PLAN WITH.

_____
COMANDANTE DE LA AERONAVE

_____
DESPACHADOR

SECCION SUPERIOR: PARA VFR LLENE TODOS LOS DATOS. PARA VFR TODOS EXCEPTO LOS SOMBREADOS.
ORIGINAL: PARA EL PILOTO, COPIA: DESPACHADOR, COPIA: COMANDANCIA, COPIA: ASA.

Flight Plan Fee — *dollar and a quarter in September, 1982*

RECIBO DE DESPACHO

SERVICIOS A LA NAVEGACION EN EL ESPACIO AEREO MEXICANO

BOULEVARD PUERTO AEREO 485
DELEGACION VENUSTIANO CARRANZA
15500 MEXICO, D.F.

NUMERO: 20093-82

DIA	MES	AÑO
25	01	82

RECIBIMOS EN REPRESENTACION DE LA TESORERIA DE LA FEDERACION

DE: A. SENTERFITT

CANTIDAD CON LETRA: CIENTO CINCUENTA PESOS 00/100

IMPORTE: $ 150.00

POR CONCEPTO DE SERVICIOS DE DESPACHO E INFORMACION DE VUELO

EN: TIJ/SAN

A LA AERONAVE: CESSNA 185 N 4492 R

PLAN DE VUELO: IFR ☐ VFR ☒

SOLICITADO POR

USUARIO

A. SENTERFITT
ANTONIO Arreola A.
NOMBRE Y FIRMA DEL DESPACHADOR

420-6

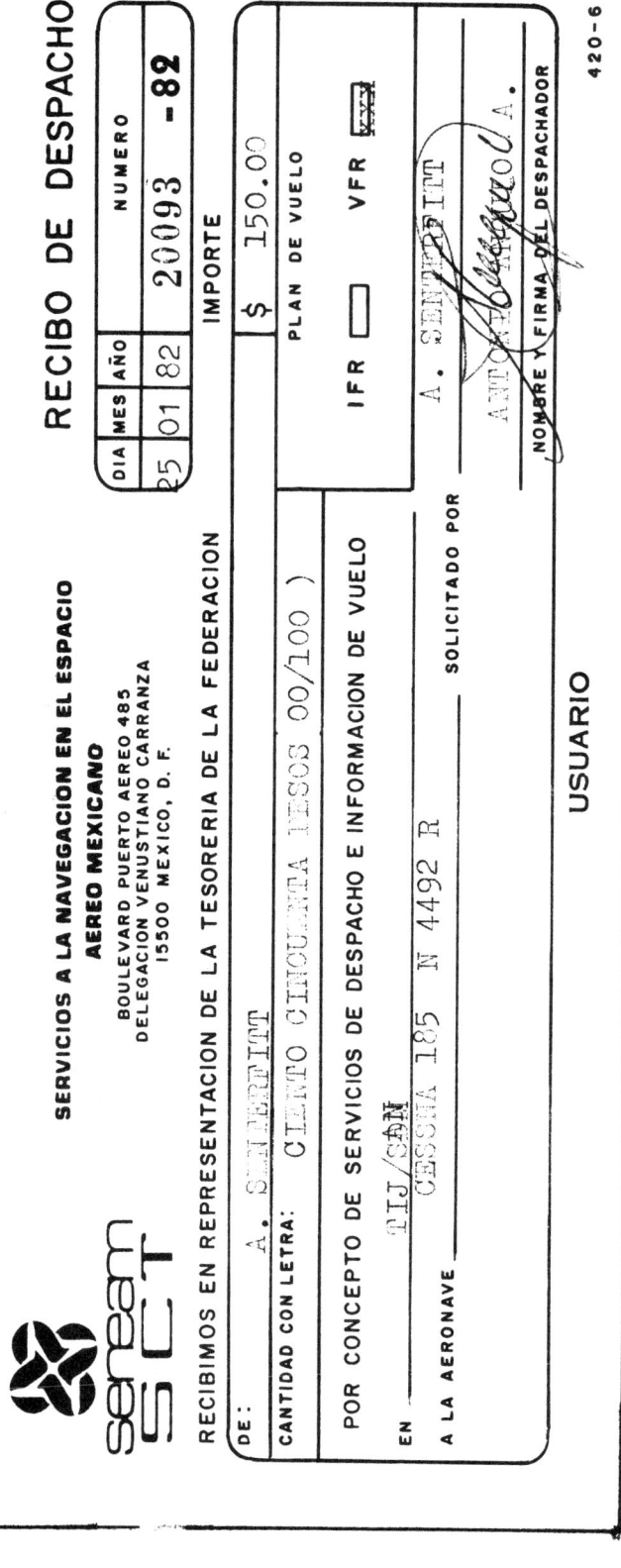

To help pay for the inter-station communications equipment and the people to run them, Mexican Civil Aviation has instituted a Flight Plan fee: $150 pesos VFR($1.25 US at this writing) or $400 pesos IFR(now about $3.25 US). This receipt from a flight in January-notice date 25-01-82 at upper right- says the National Treasury of the Federation has received of A. Senterfitt $150, amount in letters one hundred fifty pesos for the concept dispatch and flight information of a flight to TIJ(Tijuana) from SAN(San Diego) in the aircraft Cessna 185 N4492R. This is the User's Copy, note 'Usario' and is actual size.

NOTARIZED STATEMENT

I, the undersigned, hereby swear and affirm that I am a citizen of the United States of America by virtue of _____ birth _____ naturalization, which took place in the city of _____ and within the state of _____ on date _____ .

Dated _____

    Signed _____
    Name Printed _____
    Address _____
    City _____ State _____ Zip _____

NOTARY

State of _____
County of _____

On this _____ day of _____, 19 _____ before me _____ a Notary Public in and for said County and State, duly commissioned and sworn, personally appeared _____ known to me to be the person _____ whose name _____ subscribed to the within instrument, and acknowledged that _____ he _____ executed same.

IN WITNESS THEREOF, I have hereto set my hand and affixed my official seal the year and date in this certificate first above written.

(Seal)

                                    _____
                                    Notary Public in and for said County and State

Furnished by Arnold D Senterfitt

52   Tourist Permit — single entry

These Single Entry Tourist Permits are the way to go: airport Migracion inspectors have a stacks of them ready for your arrival. You merely show your passport or other proof of citizenship, you are generally handed one of these and you fill out the top two thirds yourself.; see the notarized form page 51.

Then you turn it over, and here's the tricky part. You need to sign both the pink and the blue copies but LIFT THE CARBON OUT OF THE WAY BEFORE YOU SIGN EACH ONE.

The inspector then fills in the bottom, stamps both copies and gives you one to take along. Don't forget that whatever proof of citizenship you offered to get this Permit must accompany you on the trip where you use this document.

(With the permission of an immigration inspector I brought this home from a trip in 1976 to put in the tenth edition of 'Airports of Baja California' and the eighth edition of 'Airports of Mexico'. It is still a current form.)

Copyright © 1976 Arnold Senterfitt

if you go back and forth a lot this one is handy **Tourist Permits 53**

Passports are Best Proof

No longer is there any reason not to use passports as once there was; you'll find these are welcomed by Migración inspectors. If you are not able to have a passport for each person on board, get Notarized Statements; birht certificates are alone as proof are okay for men and un-married women. Married women need to have the birth certificate backed up by a notarized statemnet.

Remember, if you .....

....have any minor children aboard but not *both* parents, be sure the parent along has a notarized permission from the other parent giving an okay to take that child away from the family home and into México. You may not always need to have this, but when you need it *you need it*.

Multiple Entry Permits

This is the sort of permit I use mostly; this last time I was out of pictures and used a half dozen or so Single Entry ones while trying to get that done. Note that under proof of citizenship -shownhere as 'actual citizenship' it shows my passport number and place of issue: Los Angeles. This one is good for any number of entry/departure round trips within a six month (seis meses) period. Each entry and departure is stamped on the back and the number of entries much match

1/2 Size

Copyright © 1976 Arnold Senterfitt

M8-B10

54 General Declaration — front

Each foreign nation your enter requires, among other things, that you file and have onboard during your time there a document called, in ICAO —International Civil Aviation Organisation—terms, a General Declaration. This document lists pertinent aircraft/crew/passneger data and must be either aboard or in possession of the pilot at all times while in the host country. Typically it is surrendered on departure from that nation.

México has just recently changed their old 'Form 40' declaration to this streamilined version which can be made out in a flash. On the Blue Form—page 47—you've listed everything they need to make this out for you.

Notice on this one that three of uswent into México on January 3, and the expiration of this document would have been June 3. All of the data is typed in, but only on a single side.

After I signed it, the Civil Aviation office stamp and signature is in the SCT box, then we checked with Migración, they stamped and signed in the right-most box, Customs did their thing in the left-most box, and the document was handed to me. Note the word 'piloto' on the right margin: that is my copy.

Once this was in my hands it was my permission to be in México with the aircraft described, for a period ending June 3. If I wanted to stay any longer I'd simply go to the nearest Internacional Airport and get a new declaration, or 'Aircraft Entrance' as it says on the form.

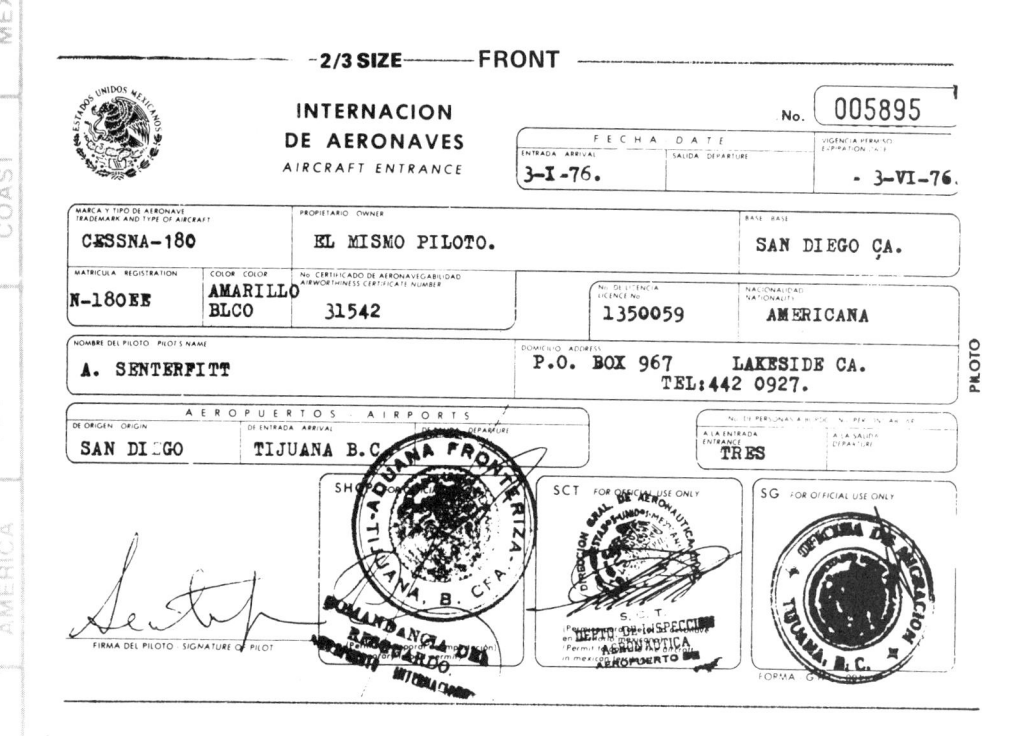

— 2/3 SIZE ——— FRONT —

INTERNACION DE AERONAVES — AIRCRAFT ENTRANCE

No. 005895

FECHA DATE — ENTRADA ARRIVAL: 3-I-76. — SALIDA DEPARTURE — VIGENCIA PERMISO EXPIRATION: - 3-VI-76.

MARCA Y TIPO DE AERONAVE / TRADEMARK AND TYPE OF AIRCRAFT	PROPIETARIO OWNER	BASE BASE
CESSNA-180	EL MISMO PILOTO.	SAN DIEGO CA.

MATRICULA REGISTRATION	COLOR COLOR	No. CERTIFICADO DE AERONAVEGABILIDAD / AIRWORTHINESS CERTIFICATE NUMBER	No. DE LICENCIA / LICENCE No.	NACIONALIDAD / NATIONALITY
N-180EE	AMARILLO BLCO	31542	1350059	AMERICANA

NOMBRE DEL PILOTO / PILOT'S NAME: A. SENTERFITT
DOMICILIO ADDRESS: P.O. BOX 967 LAKESIDE CA. TEL: 442 0927.

AEROPUERTOS · AIRPORTS
DE ORIGEN ORIGIN: SAN DIEGO
DE ENTRADA ARRIVAL: TIJUANA B.C.
DE SALIDA DEPARTURE:
No. DE PERSONAS A BORDO — A LA ENTRADA ENTRANCE: TRES — A LA SALIDA DEPARTURE:

SH... / SCT FOR OFFICIAL USE ONLY / SG FOR OFFICIAL USE ONLY

FIRMA DEL PILOTO · SIGNATURE OF PILOT

M8-B10

Copyright © 1976 Arnold Senterfitt

General Declaration — back

The back of the General Declaration form is seldom used any more but here is what it looks like just in case you need to know. If you are asked to sign this side as well as the front be sure to **first lift the carbon out of the way before signing.**

Back

The English words under each of the three blocks of information are these:

Sanitary Declaration

The pilot declares under oath a) that the aircraft referred to in this declaration has not been during the last 40 days in infected zones from which quarantinable requirements are demanded. b) that in the State where outgoing aircraft is located does not exist any contagious infectious disease.

Inspection (Animal and Vegetable)

For faster inspection , don't bring to México: plants, fruits, seeds, soil, etc. in case of pets request information from: Secretaria de Turismo, Av. Juárez No. 92, México 1, D.F., or any office of tourism in the locality.

Declaration Related to the Classification of Private Service Aircraft

The pilot also declares under oath: a) that this aircraft has not taken nor will take any cargo or merchandise. b) that the aircraft refered to in this declaration is considered in the classification of private service aircraft and that it is not used for (profit).c) that the flight plan has been presented asking at the same time that the message be transmitted through the appropriate channel of the country of departure and RAMSA in México with enough anticipation so that the message (be reached) before the arrival of the aircraft. d) that the dat (data) furnished in the present document are true and exact.

Copyright © 1976 Arnold Senterfitt

M8-B10

56 Departing México/Arrival U.S.—Checklist *a quick summary*

30 Minutes south of the U.S. Border
1. **File Flight Plan** with FSS: either a border crosser or trigger the return half of your previously filed roundrobin
2. Gather up: **General Declaration, all Tourist Permits**
3. Have someone make a list of all foreign purchases; US Customs will want this when you get to the US side.

At the Mexican Airport of Departure
1. Put in **fuel order, leave credit card with gas man** before leaving the aircraft for clearance process
2. At Civil Aviation desk **hand in General Declaration,** have Tourist Permits to show number of passengers on departure from México
3. You will pay 150 pesos ~~($6.00)~~ for VFR flight plan or 400 pesos for IFR flight plan fee and receive a receipt at this time.
4. Hand in **Tourist Permits to Migración**.
5. Should Customs want to inspect your airplane they will let you know.
6. **Sign fuel invoice** and retrieve your credit card, paying cash can be expensive unless you have exact change.
7. Tip $1.00 to $2.00 to each office as you are leaving it.

After Liftoff, before arrival at US Airport of Entry
1. Be sure on your initial call to the U.S. facility that they understand you are coming from Mexico. The controller may even remind you of the rule requiring you to call to FSS ~~at least fifteen minutes~~ before entering US airspace. Don't be upset: he's trying to save you a $500 fine which gets assessed to often already. Again NOTIFY FSS ~~15 MINUTES~~ BEFORE YOU ENTER U.S. AIRSPACE. Not REPEAT not, ~~fifteen minutes~~ before you taxi up to Customs.

Time for advance notification varies by place—see pages 84 to 90

At U.S. Airport of Entry
1. Ask Ground Control to direct you to the **International Clearance Area**.
2. You will fill out a little form, both sides; **lift carbon when writing on the back**.
3. The inspector will transfer information to a full sized form, plus he will **ask to see your pilot's license**.
4. **List of Foreign Purchases** will come in handy: he will ask what you bought and for how much: he already knows how much so be nice.
5. Although aircraft **inspection is usually perfunctory** if the computer finds a bad guy with a similar license number or aircraft registration they could get really into the aircraft, asking about secret compartments, thumping wing panels, etc.

Departing México

You Cannot Export:

The government of México exercises controls preventing the export of certain materials/articles either under their constitution or via regulations from various governmental agencies. **You may not legally export** gold, those articles of antiquity which are a part of the cultural history of the nation such as mission artifacts, ancient stone carvings—fakes are okay—nor marine animals such as shrimp, abalone, lobster, or clams. These latter may be exported only if you are in possession of a receipt showing they were purchased from a person or agency having the concession to take them from the sea and sell: this generally means the local fishing cooperativo.

If you seek to export stone carvings or other reproductions, be prepared to prove they are *not* real ones you've stolen from an archeological site, or maybe bought from someone who robbed a site.

Why Border Airports of Entry?

There have been so many drug-related problems along the border that now both the US and Mexico are requiring that all clearances be made near the frontier. Mexico originally was to use Nogales for Arizonians but lack of an IFR procedure shot it down so Hermosillo is still in the picture. On the U.S. side Customs isn't too happy at anything further from the border than Tucson.

There is a hidden benefit: gasoline prices. At this writing you save about a dollar per gallon on fuel purchased in Mexico. By stopping at the border on your way out you tip-topoff at bargain rates for the same quality avgas.

The Departure Procedure

It is always best, since you are in an airplane, to think of the **Civil Aviation** office first. That's where you drop off your general declaration, show the man how many passengers were aboard so he can fill in the "person aboard at departure" blank on the declaration, file a flight plan to the U.S. Although there are no longer fees to pay, sometimes you may be told "that will be $1". It's another way of asking for a tip. I generally tip $1.00 to $2.00 to each office on entry to the country: Civil Aviation, Migración, and Customs

You turn in your tourist permit at **Migración** if you were using a onetime, or single entry, or have the multiple entry permits signed off. The first lady inspector I've seen at an airport was at Migración one day at Ciudad Juárez; the men seemed to be moving very carefully around her.

Customs, or **Aduana** *(ah-DWAH-nah)* seldom wants to look at your airplane on departure from the Republic unless you have been reported ahead as carrying artifacts or other no-no things. The Ramp Agent is, for departure from the nation, just as important as he was during your entry process. As with any other office on earth, there are not enough so one may be helping several airplanes at once.

Should Customs decide they do want to see inside your airplane the Ramp Agent will usually be the one to let you know, often by holding up a hand gesturing with the thumb and index finger close together: the universal signal for 'just a little' time.

IFR Departures: Follow Your Clearance

The reason so few single engine IFR departure clearances are issued is that too many U.S. pilots do not provide proper reports: usually they immediately start talking to the U.S. facility. You'll get a handoff at the right time anyway, but follow please? It is important for all of us who want a departure after you.

Copyright © 1976 Arnold Senterfitt   M8-B10

FRONTERA MEXICANA:

**Informacion de
Cuarantena Agricola
de los Estados Unidos**

AVISO A TODO VIAJERO. Declare todos los artículos agrícolas que triaga de México. Al lo hacerlo, le puede resultar en demoras y confiscación de los artículos que de otra manera fueran permitidos. Ciertas frutas, verduras, carnes, y aves llevadas de los Estados Unidos a México no se permite regresar. Infórmese con anticipación con los inspectores del Departamento de Agricultura.

ARTICULOS PROHIBIDOS

Artículos agrícolas que pueden llevar plagas de plantas o enfermedades de animales están prohibidos.

FRUITAS Y VERDURAS. Toda la fruta que no está en la siguiente lista está prohibida. Papas y camotes están prohibidos. (*Excepciones:* Papas y camotes cocidos están permitidos. Aguacate sin semilla está permitido, excepto en el estado de California.)

PLANTAS Y SEMILLAS. Se require permiso especial. Algunas plantas están prohibidas. Infórmese con anticipación con los inspectores de agricultura. (*Excepción:* Partes de planta seca, para uso medicinal por ejemplo, están permitidos.)

CARNES. *Carne de puerco,* cruda o cocida, incluyendo salchichas, carnes frias, carnitas, o tacos de carne de puerco están prohibidos. (*Excepciones:* Carne de puerco enlatada que no require refrigeración, y chicharrones secos están permitidos.) *Aves de granja*—carne cruda de gallina o pavo o de aves silvestres está prohibido. (*Excepción:* Carne de ave cocida.) *Aves y animales de caza*—infórmese con anticipación con los inspectores de agricultura. *Otras carnes*—se limita la cantidad de carne a 50 libras por persona.

HUEVOS. Prohibidos. (*Excepción:* Huevos cocidos.)

AVES VIVAS. Aves caseras de granja y silvestres están prohibidas. Para la importación de aves proprios, infórmese con anticipación con los inspectores de agricultura.

PAJA. En general, prohibida.

ARTICULOS PERMITIDOS

Además de los artículos mencionados como excepciones, muchos artículos están permitidos si pasan la inspección, es decir que no tengan plagas, arena, o tierra.

FRUTAS Y VERDURAS. La siguiente fruta está permitida: Dátil, fresa, limón, litchi, melón, mora, papaya, piña, plátano, tuna, uva, y zarzarora. Toda la verdura está permitida con la excepción dada anteriormente. Quimbombó (okra) se requiere permiso especial.

ADEMAS. Se permite lo siguiente: Almendras, bellotas, cacahuates, granos de cacao, castañas, cocos (sin cascara o sin leche), nueces, piñones, tamarindos, y "waternuts."

U.S. DEPARTMENT OF AGRICULTURE
Animal and Plant Health Inspection Service

☆ U.S. Government Printing Office: 1980—311-725/2895

Furnished by Arnold D Senterfitt

MEXICAN BORDER:

U.S. Agricultural Quarantine Information

NOTICE TO TRAVELERS. Declare all agricultural items you bring from Mexico. Failure to do so may result in delay of your trip and confiscation of items that otherwise would be permitted entry. Fruits, vegetables, meats, and birds taken from the United States to Mexico may not be allowed to reenter. Consult in advance with inspectors of the U.S. Department of Agriculture.

PROHIBITED ITEMS

Agricultural items are prohibited if they can carry plant pests or animal diseases.

FRUITS AND VEGETABLES. All fruit not on the permitted list, below, is prohibited. Potatoes are prohibited, including Irish potatoes, sweet potatoes, and yams. (*Exceptions:* Cooked potatoes are permitted. Avocadoes without seeds are permitted, except in California.)

PLANTS AND SEEDS. Special permits are required. Some plants are prohibited. Check in advance with agricultural inspectors. (*Exception:* Dried plant parts, such as for medicinal purposes, are permitted.)

MEAT AND GAME. Pork—raw and cooked, including sausages, cold cuts, skins, and pork tacos are prohibited. (*Exceptions:* Shelf-stable, canned pork and hardcooked pork skins (cracklings) are permitted.) Poultry—raw meat from both domesticated and game fowl is prohibited. (*Exception:* Thoroughly cooked poultry.) Game—check with agricultural inspectors in advance. Other meat—imports limited to 50 pounds per person.

EGGS. Prohibited. (*Exception:* Boiled and cooked eggs.)

LIVE BIRDS. Wild and domesticated birds, including poultry, are prohibited. To import personally owned pet birds, contact agricultural inspectors in advance.

STRAW. Generally prohibited.

PERMITTED ITEMS

In addition to the excepted items listed above, many agricultural items are permitted if they pass inspection to be sure they are free of pests, soil, sand, and earth.

FRUITS AND VEGETABLES. Permitted fruits are: Bananas, blackberries, cactus fruits, dates, dewberries, grapes, lemons, limes (sour), lychees, melons, papayas, pineapples, and strawberries. All vegetables are permitted, except for those on the prohibited list, above. Okra, however, is subject to certain restrictions.

NUTS. Permitted items are: Acorns, almonds, cocoa beans, chestnuts, coconuts (without husks, or without milk), peanuts, pecans, pinons (pinenuts), tamarind beans, walnuts, and waternuts.

U.S. DEPARTMENT OF AGRICULTURE
Animal and Plant Health Inspection Service

Program Aid 941
Revised October 1978
Slightly revised October 1980

Furnished by Arnold D Senterfitt

60 Travel Tips

TRAVELERS' TIPS
ON BRINGING FOOD, PLANT, AND ANIMAL PRODUCTS INTO THE UNITED STATES

AGRICULTURAL INSPECTION

Foods and plant and animal products from foreign countries are inspected at U.S. ports of entry by the U.S. Department of Agriculture (USDA).

Travelers often think that quarantine restrictions are aimed only at commercial importers. This is not true. Restrictions apply to anyone who brings or mails agricultural items to this country. Personal luggage and "carry-on" baggage are major channels for the international spread of agricultural pests and diseases.

Inspectors of USDA's Animal and Plant Health Inspection Service (APHIS) determine if agricultural items are free from pests and diseases or pose a pest risk to this country. Small quantities of admissible agricultural items are usually released without expense or undue delay to the traveler.

Materials requiring extensive inspection, testing, or treatment often are held until they can be certified free of pests. Some items may be refused entry.

If there is evidence or a high likelihood that agricultural items carry pests or diseases, the items are not permitted entry. APHIS inspectors take them for destruction without reimbursement.

EVEN ONE CAN HURT

Some travelers with one or two fruits or sausages in the luggage, or a pet bird in a cage, are amazed that "just one" can be a problem. In fact, even one can hurt.

One piece of fruit, one piece of sausage, or one pet bird could be the means of accidentally introducing destructive pests or diseases into this Nation. In 1971, an imported, diseased parrot was responsible for an outbreak of exotic Newcastle disease in U.S. poultry. Nearly 12 million exposed chickens were destroyed to control the deadly virus. Commercial poultrymen received over $26 million in indemnities.

Plant and animal pests and diseases cost Americans over $12 billion annually. Many of our most destructive pests are foreigners that cause greater damage in the United States than in their native environment, where natural enemies may hold them in check.

A Special Message for Travelers

A few minutes to become familiar with restrictions on bringing back agricultural items can save you time and money It is illegal to bring many types of meats, fruits, vegetables, plants, animals, and plant and animal products into the United States without approval from the U.S. Department of Agriculture.

These restrictions are intended to protect the plant and animal life of this country. Agricultural items can harbor foreign insects and diseases that could cause severe damage to U.S. crops, forests, gardens, and livestock.

We ask your cooperation in bringing into the United States only those agricultural items that are approved for entry.

CLEARING U.S. CUSTOMS

You must declare, on a U.S. customs declaration form, all food, plant, and animal products you acquired abroad, before your arrival in the United States. Undeclared items subject you to a fine.

Furnished by Arnold D Senterfitt

Travel Tips 61

Declaration forms are given to travelers on airplanes, ships, and trains. When you pass through customs inspection, the agent may call in an APHIS agricultural inspector to check if your agricultural items can be brought in safely.

SMUGGLING

Smuggling of food, plant, and animal products into the United States is a Federal offense. Persons found guilty of such smuggling are subject to a fine and/or imprisonment.

IF YOU VISIT A FARM OVERSEAS

The U.S. customs declaration form also asks you to declare if you visited a farm or ranch in a foreign country. Unknowingly, you may have picked up a livestock disease on your shoes or clothes.

Highly contagious livestock diseases, such as African swine fever and foot-and-mouth disease, are prevalent in many foreign countries. These diseases do not affect humans but will debilitate or kill animals.

When you pass through inspection, an agricultural inspector will determine how to minimize any disease risk. These precautions help keep foreign livestock diseases from infecting animals here.

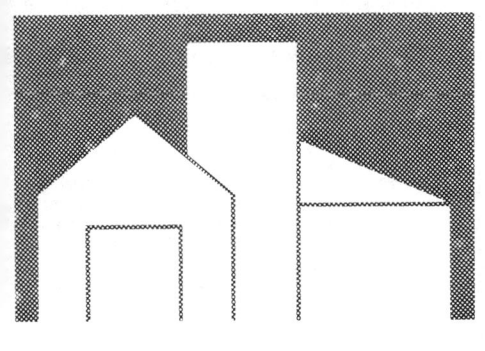

OBTAINING PERMITS

A written permit is required before restricted items may be brought into the United States. Look in the separate sections below for instructions for importing animals and birds, plants, and plant materials. Only residents of the United States may apply for permits, but they may do so on behalf of foreign visitors who intend to bring in restricted items.

LIVE ANIMALS AND BIRDS

The U.S. Department of Agriculture restricts the entry of pet birds and many other live animals, poultry, and other birds (and hatching eggs).

Some animals are prohibited; others must be held in USDA animal import centers or by the owner for 30 to 60 days after entry. For all animal-related information and permits, write: Veterinary Services, USDA-APHIS, Federal Building, Hyattsville, MD 20782.

Travelers can arrange to bring in one or two pet birds (but no more), provided the birds were in the owner's possession for 90 days before entry. In the future, more stringent requirements for pet birds are likely—such as a 30-day quarantine in an import station at the owner's expense. This is similar to the procedures now followed for commercial bird imports. So, it is best not to buy pet birds overseas or take any out of the country for later return to the United States.

Animals and birds must be inspected by APHIS veterinarians before they may enter the country. Make advance arrangements because this inspection service is available only at certain ports. In addition, the U.S. Public Health Service restricts imports of dogs, cats, monkeys, and birds.

MEAT, HUNTING TROPHIES, AND OTHER ANIMAL PRODUCTS

USDA also restricts imports of meat, game animal carcasses and hunting trophies, hides, dairy products, and other animal products. Fresh meat is generally prohibited from many countries.

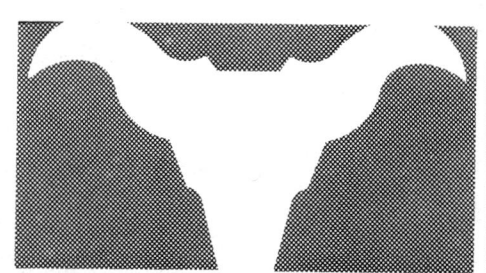

Canned meat is permitted if the inspector can determine that it is commercially canned, hermetically sealed, and storable without refrigeration.

Other canned, cured, and dried meat is severely restricted from most countries. For details, contact an APHIS field office (see list on page 58.

PLANT MATERIALS

A USDA permit is required before certain plant materials can be brought into the United States. These include fruits, vegetables, and plants or plant parts intended for growing. The entry status of various plants is specified in the lists on pages 58 to 59.

To obtain a permit, write: Permit Unit, USDA-APHIS-PPQ, Federal Building, Hyattsville, MD 20782.

MAILING PLANTS HOME

All plant materials you carry with you from overseas are examined at customs inspection on your return to the United States. You may, however, mail restricted materials directly to one of the plant inspection stations listed below. Ask the Permit Unit, address above, for mailing labels when you apply for a permit.

In mailing: (1) Be sure to write your name and home address on a sheet of paper put inside the package. After clearance, your package will be forwarded to you without additional cost. (2) Mark the outside of the package to show its contents. (3) Send the package to: U.S. Department of Agriculture, APHIS, PPQ, using one of the following addresses:

Border Inspection Sta.
Rm. 202
Nogales, AZ 85621

9650 S. La Cienega Blvd.
Bldg. D. North
Inglewood, CA 90301

Agriculture Building,
Rm. 101
Embarcadero at
Mission Street
San Francisco, CA 94105

P.O. Box 43-L
San Ysidro, CA 92070

Miami Inspection Sta.
P.O. Box 592136
Miami, FL 33159

P.O. Box 29757
Honolulu, HI 96820

P.O. Box 20037
Airport Mailing Facility
New Orleans, LA 70140

Plant Importations Office
209 River St.
Hoboken, NJ 07030

John F. Kennedy
International Airport
Plant Inspection Sta.
Cargo Building 80
Jamaica, NY 11430

P.O. Box 3386
Old San Juan, PR 00904

P.O. Box 306
Brownsville, TX 78520

Cordova Bridge Sta.
Rm. 172-A
3600 East Paisano
El Paso, TX 79905

P.O. Box 277
Laredo, TX 78040

Federal Office Building
Rm. 9014
Seattle, WA 98104

Furnished by Arnold D Senterfitt

WHAT YOU CAN BRING HOME

The entry status of agricultural products differs by type of item, intended use, and destination. The lists on the following pages will give you some idea of the entry status of agricultural items commonly brought in by travelers. Many common foods, plants, animals, and plant and animal products available in foreign countries are admitted without restriction other than inspection. Some are prohibited. And a few items are admitted only conditionally under permit.

Any item, however, may be refused entry if the inspector has reason to believe it poses a pest risk under current conditions. Restrictions apply to agricultural items, whether they are carried as baggage or are mailed to the United States from a foreign country.

ENTRY STATUS LISTS

Exceptions — The following list of the entry status of products from most overseas areas does *not* apply to products from Canada, Mexico, Hawaii, Puerto Rico, and the U.S. Virgin Islands. For this information, see page 54.

Products from Most Overseas Areas

Animal hair, wool or bristles.
Must be scoured, dyed, or thoroughly washed.

Animals.
Includes live cattle, swine, deer, horses, sheep, mules, burros, goats, dogs used around livestock and zoo animals. Also see: "Live Animals and Birds," p. 3.

Bakery goods.
Includes breads, cakes, cookies, and similar items.

Bamboo.
Dried poles only.
All other parts.

Beads and curios.
Made of seeds.
Made of jequirity beans.

Berries (fresh).
See: "Plant Materials."

Birds.
See: "Live Animals and Birds."

Bonsai trees.
See: "Plants."

Candies.

Cheeses (fully cured).

Chestnuts.

Christmas greens and foliage.
Fresh or dried.
Pine branches.

Citrus peels (fresh or dried).
From most countries.

Travel Tips

	PROHIBITED	GENERALLY PROHIBITED	RESTRICTED	PERMIT REQUIRED	TREATMENT REQUIRED	ADMITTED
Coconuts. Without husks. With husks — into Hawaii and Florida only						●
Coffee beans. Roasted. Unroasted and dried. Into most states. Into Hawaii and Puerto Rico.	●		●			●
Coffee berries.	●					
Cones of trees.						●
Corn, and related plants, such as broomcorn, sorghum, and Job's tears. See: "Plant Materials," p. 4.		●				
Corn husks.		●				
Cotton. Medicinal (swabs, bandages). Bolls, other plant parts. See: "Plant Materials," p. 4.		●				●
Dairy products, fresh items from most countries. See also: "Cheeses," p. 6.	●					
Disease organisms and vectors. For exceptions for scientific and educational purposes, write: Quarantines, USDA-APHIS-PPQ, Federal Building, Hyattsville, MD 20782.	●					
Dried foods (polished rice, beans, coffee, tea, shelled nuts).						●
Eggs (from poultry and other birds). See: "Live Animals and Birds," p. 3.	●					
Fish. Canned. Other than canned. See: "Meat, Hunting Trophies, and Other Animal Products," p. 4.			●			●
Flower bulbs. Most types. Anemone bulbs from Germany. Gladiolus bulbs from Africa.	● ●		●			
Flowers. Fresh cut or dried. Fresh camellias and gardenias. Coming into California. Coming into Florida.	● ●			●		●
Foliage, for decoration. Fresh cut leaves and branches. Pine, rice, sugarcane, citrus, and wheat foliage.	●					●
Fruits. Canned or processed. Some fresh fruits. Other fresh fruits. See: "Plant Materials," p. 4.	●		●			●
Game (animals or birds). See: "Meat, Hunting Trophies, and Other Animal Products," p. 4.		●				
Hay, straw or grass (from most countries).	●					
Herbarium materials. Most species. Witchweed (*Striga* spp.). Illegal drugs (materials under Controlled Substances Act).	●					●
Herbs (for medicine or food).						●
Hides and skins (fully tanned). See: "Meat, Hunting Trophies, and Other Animal Products," p. 4.						●
Insects. Dried and preserved. Live, in any stage of development. For exceptions for scientific and educational purposes, write: Quarantines, USDA-APHIS-PPQ, Federal Building, Hyattsville, MD 20782.	●					●
Jams and jellies (canned or processed).						●
Leather products, including suede.						●
Lichens.			●			
Meat. See: "Meat, Hunting Trophies, and Other Animal Products," p. 4.						
Mexican jumping beans.						●
Mushrooms.						●
Nuts (outer husk must be removed). Most kinds. Chestnuts. Acorns.			●			● ●
Packing materials. Peat moss, sphagnum moss, wood shavings, sawdust, paper, and excelsior. Most other plant and animal materials.			●			●
Pets (dogs, cats, monkeys, birds). See: "Live Animals and Birds," p. 3.						
Plants. Most dried plants, flowers, and leaves for herbarium or decoration. Live plants (shrubs, trees, fresh cuttings intended for growing). Some live plants are prohibited; others require special post-entry growing authorization; contact a USDA office, see pp. 15 and 16. Citrus leaves, rice straw or hulls, sugarcane, and witchweed. All plants in soil.	● ●			●		●
Rice straw and hulls.	●					
Rocks and minerals (cleaned).						●
Sauces (canned or processed).						●
Scientific materials. For permits to import serums, animal or plant disease organisms, vectors, and specimens of animals or their parts, write: Quarantines, USDA-APHIS-PPQ, Federal Building, Hyattsville, MD 20782.			●	●		

Furnished by Arnold D Senterfitt

64 Travel Tips

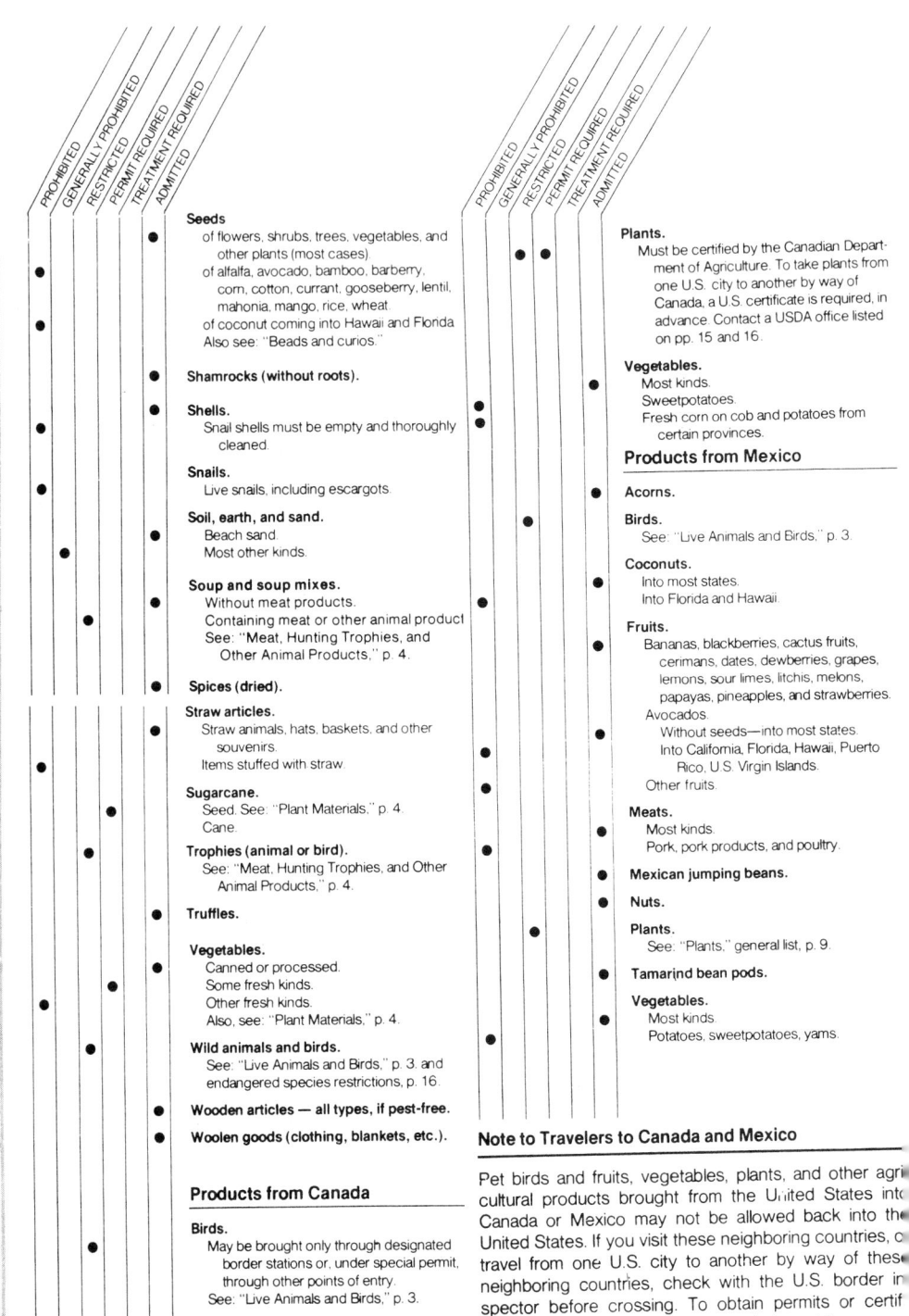

	PROHIBITED	GENERALLY PROHIBITED	RESTRICTED	PERMIT REQUIRED	TREATMENT REQUIRED	ADMITTED
Seeds						●
of flowers, shrubs, trees, vegetables, and other plants (most cases).						
of alfalfa, avocado, bamboo, barberry, corn, cotton, currant, gooseberry, lentil, mahonia, mango, rice, wheat.	●					
of coconut coming into Hawaii and Florida	●					
Also see: "Beads and curios."						
Shamrocks (without roots).						●
Shells.						●
Snail shells must be empty and thoroughly cleaned.						
Snails.	●					
Live snails, including escargots.						
Soil, earth, and sand.						
Beach sand.						●
Most other kinds.				●		
Soup and soup mixes.						
Without meat products.						●
Containing meat or other animal product						
See: "Meat, Hunting Trophies, and Other Animal Products," p. 4.						
Spices (dried).						●
Straw articles.						
Straw animals, hats, baskets, and other souvenirs.						●
Items stuffed with straw.		●				
Sugarcane.						
Seed. See: "Plant Materials," p. 4.						
Cane.			●			
Trophies (animal or bird).						
See: "Meat, Hunting Trophies, and Other Animal Products," p. 4.						
Truffles.						●
Vegetables.						
Canned or processed.						●
Some fresh kinds.					●	
Other fresh kinds.	●					
Also, see: "Plant Materials," p. 4.						
Wild animals and birds.			●			
See: "Live Animals and Birds," p. 3. and endangered species restrictions, p. 16.						
Wooden articles — all types, if pest-free.						●
Woolen goods (clothing, blankets, etc.).						●

Products from Canada

Birds.
May be brought only through designated border stations or, under special permit, through other points of entry.
See: "Live Animals and Birds," p. 3.

Fruits.
Most kinds.
Black currants.

Meats and dressed poultry (most kinds).

	PROHIBITED	GENERALLY PROHIBITED	RESTRICTED	PERMIT REQUIRED	TREATMENT REQUIRED	ADMITTED
Plants.	●	●				
Must be certified by the Canadian Department of Agriculture. To take plants from one U.S. city to another by way of Canada, a U.S. certificate is required, in advance. Contact a USDA office listed on pp. 15 and 16.						
Vegetables.						●
Most kinds.						
Sweetpotatoes.						
Fresh corn on cob and potatoes from certain provinces.						

Products from Mexico

Acorns.					●	
Birds.						
See: "Live Animals and Birds," p. 3						
Coconuts.						
Into most states.						●
Into Florida and Hawaii.						
Fruits.						●
Bananas, blackberries, cactus fruits, cerimans, dates, dewberries, grapes, lemons, sour limes, litchis, melons, papayas, pineapples, and strawberries.						
Avocados.						
Without seeds—into most states.						
Into California, Florida, Hawaii, Puerto Rico, U.S. Virgin Islands.						
Other fruits.						
Meats.						
Most kinds.						
Pork, pork products, and poultry.						
Mexican jumping beans.						●
Nuts.					●	
Plants.						
See: "Plants," general list, p. 9.						
Tamarind bean pods.						●
Vegetables.						
Most kinds.						
Potatoes, sweetpotatoes, yams.						

Note to Travelers to Canada and Mexico

Pet birds and fruits, vegetables, plants, and other agricultural products brought from the United States into Canada or Mexico may not be allowed back into the United States. If you visit these neighboring countries, or travel from one U.S. city to another by way of these neighboring countries, check with the U.S. border inspector before crossing. To obtain permits or certificates in advance, write to one of the addresses on page **65**.

Furnished by Arnold D Senterfitt

Travel Tips 65

WHAT ABOUT YOUR CAR?

Cars that were used abroad and still have foreign soil clinging to them must be cleaned at the owner's expense before release at the port of arrival. This restriction does not apply to passenger cars coming from Canada or Mexico.

COMMERCIAL SHIPMENTS

This booklet pertains only to food, plant, and animal products brought into the United States by travelers. For information about commercial shipments of foreign agricultural materials, contact one of the offices listed below, or write: Quarantines, USDA-APHIS-PPQ, Federal Building, Hyattsville, MD 20782.

FOR MORE INFORMATION

Specific information is available for travelers visiting Mexico and those wishing to bring back foreign plants. Write USDA-APHIS, Washington, DC 20250 for: *Visiting Mexico* or *Shipping Foreign Plants Home*. For more detailed information, write: Quarantines, USDA-APHIS-PPQ, Federal Building, Hyattsville, MD 20782, or contact the nearest inspection station. Look in the telephone directory under U.S. Department of Agriculture, Animal and Plant Health Inspection Service, in the following locations:

Alabama: Mobile
Alaska: Anchorage
Arizona: Nogales, Phoenix, San Luis, Tucson (airport)
Bahamas: Nassau
Bermuda: Hamilton
California: Alameda, Calexico, Fairfield (Travis AFB), Los Angeles (airport), Oakland, San Diego (airport), San Francisco, San Pedro, San Ysidro
Colorado: Denver
Connecticut: Wallingford
Delaware: Dover, Wilmington
Florida: Ft. Lauderdale, Jacksonville, Key West, Miami, Pensacola, Port Canaveral, Riviera Beach, Tampa
Georgia: Atlanta, Savannah
Hawaii: Hilo, Honolulu
Illinois: Chicago
Louisiana: Baton Rouge, New Orleans
Maine: Bangor, Portland
Maryland: Baltimore
Massachusetts: Boston
Michigan: Detroit
Minnesota: Duluth, St. Paul
Mississippi: Gulfport
Missouri: Kansas City, St. Louis
New Jersey: Hoboken, Moorestown, Wrightstown
New York: Buffalo, Jamaica (JFK International Airport), New York, Ogdensburg, Rouses Point
North Carolina: Morehead City, Wilmington
Ohio: Cleveland
Oregon: Astoria, Coos Bay, Portland
Pennsylvania: Philadelphia
Puerto Rico: San Juan
Rhode Island: Warwick
South Carolina: Charleston
Tennessee: Memphis
Texas: Brownsville, Corpus Christi, Dallas, Del Rio, Eagle Pass, El Paso, Galveston, Hidalgo, Houston, Laredo, Port Arthur, Presidio, Progreso, Roma, San Antonio
U.S. Virgin Islands: St. Thomas Island (Charlotte Amalie); St. Croix Island (Christiansted)
Virginia: Chantilly (Dulles International Airport), Newport News, Norfolk
Washington: Blaine, Seattle, Tacoma
Washington, D.C.
Wisconsin: Milwaukee

Columns: PROHIBITED / GENERALLY PROHIBITED / RESTRICTED / PERMIT REQUIRED / TREATMENT REQUIRED / ADMITTED

- Garlic.
- Ginger roots.
- Gourds.
- Herbs.

Insects.
Dried and preserved.
Live (in any stage of development). For exceptions for scientific and educational purposes, write: Quarantines, USDA-APHIS-PPQ, Federal Building, Hyattsville, MD 20782.

- Medicinal plants (dried).

Plants.
Plants without soil, and cuttings. Must be certified pest-free. For arrangements, call Puerto Rico Department of Agriculture at 724-0422 or Virgin Islands Department of Agriculture at 772-0990.
Cactus plants and cuttings.
Plants in soil.

Seeds.
Most dried seeds.
Cottonseed.

Shells.
For restrictions, see "Shells," general list, p. 9.

Snails.

Soil, earth, and sand.
Beach sand.
Most other kinds.

- Sugarcane.
- Tamarind bean pods.

Vegetables.
Beans (fresh shelled), calabazas, chayotes, eggplants, leeks, onions, peas, pumpkins, most root crops, squash.
Sweetpotatoes and most other vegetables.

urnished by Arnold D Senterfitt

Pilots Reservation Service
⇨ at 714-291-3491 ⇦
is a source of reservations
at many of these hotels

Travel Tips

OTHER FEDERAL REQUIREMENTS

Several Government agencies, in addition to USDA, have requirements affecting overseas travelers. Below is a listing of these additional requirements and ways to get more information about them.

U.S. CUSTOMS SERVICE

Collects import duties (tax) on items acquired abroad and coordinates all inspection of passenger baggage. For information, read: "Customs Hints for Returning U.S. Residents—Know Before You Go." Contact: U.S. Customs Service, P.O. Box 7118, Washington, DC 20044.

U.S. DEPARTMENT OF STATE

Assures that travelers have proper travel documents. For information, read: "Your Trip Abroad." Contact: Passport agencies located in Boston, Chicago, Honolulu, Los Angeles, Miami, New Orleans, New York, Philadelphia, San Francisco, Seattle, and Washington, D.C. Prospective visitors to the United States should contact the nearest U.S. consulate.

U.S. PUBLIC HEALTH SERVICE

Restricts imports of dogs, cats, monkeys, and pet birds that may affect human health. For information, read: "How to Import Pets But Not Disease." Also advises travelers on how to safeguard their health and well-being while overseas and avoid bringing human diseases to the United States. For information, read, "Health Information for International Travel." Contact: Center for Disease Control, Atlanta, GA 30333.

Furnished by Arnold D Senterfitt

U.S. DEPARTMENT OF JUSTICE

Regulates imports of narcotics and other substances under the Controlled Substances Act of 1970. Contact: Drug Enforcement Administration, 1405 Eye St., N.W., Washington, DC 20537.

U.S. FISH AND WILDLIFE SERVICE

Restricts or prohibits imports of many species of animals and plants, including those considered endangered and threatened. Regulations cover wildlife and game birds plus trophies, hair, leather, eggs, and other parts and products of regulated animals. For information, read: "Facts About Federal Wildlife Laws."

For imported endangered plants only, USDA has responsibility to examine the plants and the accompanying documents to assure compliance with the Convention on International Trade in Endangered Species. USDA, however, has no authority to issue documents to allow endangered plant species to enter the country.

Documents must be obtained prior to shipment. For information on where to obtain them, contact: Federal Wildlife Permit Office, U.S. Fish and Wildlife Service, Washington, DC 20240.

FLYING TO MEXICO?
CALL US FOR HOTEL RESERVATIONS
714-942-3111

CARDIFF BY THE SEA TRAVEL
119 ABERDEEN DRIVE, CARDIFF BY THE SEA, CA 92007

WE HAVE MEXICO TOURIST CARDS, FISHING LICENSES AND BOAT PERMITS. NO SERVICE CHARGES — WE ARE WORLD-WIDE HOTEL, AIRLINE, STEAMSHIP, TOUR, U-DRIVE & CHARTER AGENTS. **AL WAGNER**

This is a reprint of the 1982 Edition of the Customs' Guide. In order to save space, northern border airports have been omitted as listed on page 81 under "Coverage." — *Arnold*

U.S. CUSTOMS GUIDE For

PRIVATE FLYERS
(General Aviation Pilots)

1982 Edition

ask for information

If in doubt as to proper procedure to follow, DON'T GUESS. ASK YOUR LOCAL CUSTOMS OFFICERS. Also, inquire as to changes in the list of airports, hours of service, etc. that may have occurred after publication of this pamphlet.

Published by the Department of the Treasury, U.S. Customs Service
Washington, D.C. 20229
Telephone 202-566-2366

March 1982

Furnished by Arnold D Senterfitt

Contents

introduction, 69

scope and definitions, 69

outward flights, 70

inward flights, 70

    Providing Notification to Customs, 70
    Special Reporting Requirements—Southern Border, 71
    Exemption from Special Landing Requirements, 72
    To Customs Designated "International Airports," 72
    To "Landing Rights" Airports, 74
    To Other Airports, 74
    What to Report, 74
    Short Flights, 74
    Changing Destination En Route, 74
    Documentation and Examination on Arrival, 75
    Personal Exemptions, 75
    Plant and Animal Quarantines, 75
    Repairs to Private Aircraft, 76
    In Case of Emergency, 76
    Returning Without Landing, 76
    Hours of Service, 76
    Overtime Charges, 76
    Customs Bonds, 78
    Penalties for Violations, 78
    Customs Districts, 79
    Customs Regions, 80

list of airports/customs services, 81

For sale by the Superintendent of Documents, U.S. Government
Printing Office, Washington, D.C. 20402

Introduction

Customs Guide for Private Flyers is for you—the private and corporate pilot—on business or pleasure flights to and from foreign countries. It sets forth the basic Customs requirements, provides a list of airports at which Customs clearance may be obtained and explains overtime charges.

You can facilitate your air travel if you know Customs regulations and follow them. Additional valuable information on regulations concerning international flights is available in the International Flight Information Manual published by the Federal Aviation Administration (FAA) and sold by the Superintendent of Documents, U.S. Government Printing Office, Washington, D.C. 20402.

If you are in doubt, don't guess. Ask your local Customs officers or the Customs officers at the airport of your intended return to the United States.

Happy landing!

Scope and Definitions

1. The information in this pamphlet applies to private aircraft of both United States and foreign registry.

2. Customs requirements vary according to whether an aircraft is operating as a commercial or private flight. It is the nature of each particular flight that determines whether an aircraft is operating in a private or commercial capacity. The owners, aircraft type, or predominant usage of the aircraft has little bearing on this determination. In fact, **many corporate and business aircraft typically operate as "private aircraft" for Customs purposes.**

   Aircraft not qualifying as private aircraft must comply with the applicable entry and clearance requirements for commercial aircraft as specified in Part 6, Customs Regulations (19 CFR Part 6). For additional information on these requirements, please contact the nearest U.S. Customs office.

3. For Customs purposes, a "private" aircraft is any civilian aircraft not being used to transport persons or property for compensation or hire. A "commercial" aircraft is any civilian aircraft being used in the transportation of persons or property for compensation or hire.

   The term "person transported for compensation or hire" means a person who would not be transported unless there was some payment or other consideration, including monetary or services rendered, by or for the person and who is not connected with the operation of the aircraft or its navigation, ownership or business.

   The major criterion for determining whether an aircraft is private or commercial will be the use of the aircraft on a particular flight, and this determination would be the same if the owner or lessee is a corporation, partnership, sole proprietorship or an individual.

   An aircraft will be presumed not to be carrying persons or merchandise for hire, and thus will be a private aircraft for Customs purposes, when the aircraft is transporting only the aircraft owner's employees, invited guests, or the aircraft owner's own property. This presumption may be overcome by evidence that the employees, "guests", or property are being transported for compensation or other consideration. If an aircraft is used by a group of individuals, one of whom is the pilot making the flight for his own convenience, and all persons aboard the aircraft including the pilot contribute equally toward payment of the expense of operating the aircraft owned or rented by them, the aircraft would be considered private.

Furnished by Arnold D Sentertitt

Usually those aircraft arriving in the United States which have raised the question as to whether they are private or commercial are operated by the owner or lessee. For purposes of determining if an aircraft is private or commercial, the lessee of an aircraft will be considered as its owner if the pilot is a regular employee of the lessee and the lessee has complete control of the aircraft and its itinerary. Accordingly, aircraft operated by the owner or by a lessee as described in the preceding sentence will be classified as private or commercial depending on the use of the aircraft on a particular flight, that is, whether the aircraft is being used in the transportation of persons or property for compensation or hire. On the other hand, a leased aircraft will be considered commercial for Customs purposes if the pilot and/or crew are part of the leasing arrangement of the aircraft.

4. The term "international airport" means any airport designated by the Secretary of the Treasury or the Commissioner of Customs as a port of entry for civil aircraft arriving in the United States from any place outside thereof and for cargo carried on such aircraft. This pamphlet lists all such airports that have been officially designated to date. (**Note: Frequently the word "international" is included in the name of an airport for other than Customs purposes, in which case it has no special Customs meaning.**)

5. The term "landing rights airport" means an airport at which permission to land may be granted by the appropriate Customs officer with acknowledgement of the Immigration and Naturalization Service, the Public Health Service, and the Animal and Plant Health Inspection Service of the Department of Agriculture. Such landing rights are required before an aircraft may land at an airport which has not been designated for Customs purposes as an international airport.

6. The term "United States" for Customs purposes includes the States, the District of Columbia, and Puerto Rico. This does not include U.S. possessions. For information regarding those areas, refer to the FAA International Flight Information Manual.

Outward Flights

advance notice of arrival in Canada and Mexico

Many countries, including Canada and Mexico, require advance notice of the intent of pilots to arrive in those countries.

Under agreements between the United States, Canada, and Mexico, operators of private planes may, in most cases, include this advance notice in a flight plan to be filed prior to departure from the United States with the nearest FAA Flight Service Station. That station will then cause the message to be transmitted to the proper authorities in the country of destination without further responsibility on the part of the pilot or operator. Contact the nearest FAA Flight Service Station regarding this procedure.

Aircraft carrying passengers or cargo for hire or compensation are not considered to be "private aircraft" for Customs purposes and must comply with the clearance requirements specified for commercial aircraft as set forth in Part 6, Customs Regulations.

Inward Flights

providing notification to customs

In order to have an officer present to provide Customs service for you and your aircraft, Customs must be notified of your intention to land and time of arrival or penetration.

This notification may be provided through FAA; however, this entails the relaying of information and is not as timely or reliable as direct communication. It is recommended that, if possible, pilots attempt to communicate directly with Customs by telephone or other means to insure that an officer will be available at the time requested. It is the ultimate responsibility of the pilot to insure Customs is properly notified, and the failure to do so may subject the pilot to penalty action (see "Penalties for Violations"). The last section of this guide lists telephone numbers to facilitate this notification process.

special reporting requirements—southern border

All pilots of private aircraft arriving from a foreign place in the western hemisphere south of 33 degrees north latitude which cross into the U.S. over a point on the U.S. border between 95 and 120 degrees west longitude, are required to communicate to Customs by telephone, radio or other means either directly or through the FAA Flight Service Station, their intention of landing and the intended point and time of border crossing not less than 15 minutes prior to crossing the border.

Due to unreliable communications relay from Mexico, a flight plan filed in Mexico may not be transmitted in time to meet this reporting requirement even though the flight plan included "ADCUS" or "Advise Customs." Pilots are advised to rely solely upon telephone or radio communication to notify Customs of intended arrival on a timely basis.

The report to Customs must include the following:
- Type of aircraft and registration number
- Name of aircraft commander
- Number of United States citizen passengers
- Number of alien passengers
- Place of last foreign departure
- Other countries visited
- Estimated time and location of crossing United States border
- Name of nearest intended United States airport of first landing (one of the designated airports listed below unless an exemption has been granted)
- Estimated time of arrival

All private aircraft, unless exempted, are required to land at one of the specially designated airports listed below. The letter code following airport name indicates location on map, see page 5.

Location	Name
Arizona	
Douglas	Bisbee-Douglas International Airport (a)
Nogales	Nogales International Airport (b)
Tucson	Tucson International Airport (c)
Yuma	Yuma International Airport (d)
California	
Calexico	Calexico International Airport (e)
San Diego	Brown Field (f)
San Diego	San Diego International Airport (g) (Lindbergh Field)
Texas	
Brownsville	Brownsville International Airport (h)
Del Rio	Del Rio International Airport (i)
Eagle Pass	Eagle Pass Airport (j)
El Paso	El Paso International Airport (k)
Laredo	Laredo International Airport (l)
McAllen/Hidalgo	Miller International Airport (m)
Presidio	Presidio-Lely International Airport (n)

Furnished by Arnold D Senterfitt

Except for Tucson and Yuma, 24-hour free inspection service will be available on weekdays, Monday through Saturday, at the airports designated above when staffed by Customs officers as opposed to inspecting officers from other agencies. Customs overtime charges up to a maximum of $25 will be assessed for inspectional services provided on Sundays and holidays before 8:00 A.M. and after 5:00 P.M.

Flyers intending to clear Customs at Tucson International and Yuma International Airports Monday through Saturday can check with Customs (at the telephone numbers listed in this guide) concerning possible overtime charges. Outside of scheduled tour of duty Customs officers clearing private aircraft do so on a reimbursable overtime basis only.

exemption from special landing requirements

Private aircraft owners may request an exemption from the requirement of landing at a designated airport. The request shall be submitted to the Customs officer in charge of the airport of first landing at which Customs processing is desired (this will usually be the base airport or airport nearest to requestor's residence or home office). If the request is for an exemption covering a number of flights over a period of one year, it must be submitted to the Customs officer at least 30 days prior to the anticipated first arrival. If the request is for an exemption covering a single flight, it must be submitted to the Customs officer at least 15 days prior to the anticipated arrival.

Private aircraft owners applying for an exemption must furnish the following information:

Aircraft registration number
Identity of aircraft (make and model number)
Names and addresses of owners of the aircraft
Names and addresses of all crewmembers
Names of usual or potential passengers to the extent possible
Name of anticipated airport of first landing in the United States
Place or places from which the flight(s) will originate

The private aircraft owner will be notified by the district director, in writing, of the action taken on his request.

The exemption, once granted, will permit the aircraft to proceed to any airport in the U.S. which is staffed by Customs. Aircraft exempted from landing at the airports designated above must comply with the advance notice and landing rights request requirements described under "International Airports" and "Landing Rights Airports."

to customs designated "international airports"

It is unnecessary for aircraft arriving at these airports to request permission to land or "landing rights" from Customs. However, an advance notice of the estimated time of arrival (in local time) is required to be transmitted to U.S. Customs for each flight. In general, 1-hour advance notice is sufficient, although you will note in the "Special Arrangements or Restrictions" column that a longer time is required at certain airports. Aircraft operators must bear in mind that this advance notice is predicated on the time that the Customs officer receives the notification, and not on the time that the flight plan or message is filed.

Except in the case of "Short Flights" (see below), requests to transmit such notices may be included in flight plans to be filed at certain airports in Canada and Mexico under agreements with those countries. Information concerning the availability of this service at United States airports has been included in the column "FAA Flight Plan Notification Available." If "Advise Customs" or "ADCUS" is not included on the flight plan, FAA will not advise Customs of intended arrival. The pilot is ultimately responsible for insuring that Customs is properly notified.

At those airports where the flight plan notification service is not available, notices of arrival must be transmitted directly to U.S. Customs.

For private aircraft arriving in the United States from certain foreign areas south of the United States, refer to "Special Reporting Requirements" under Inward Flights.

Furnished by Arnold D Senterfitt

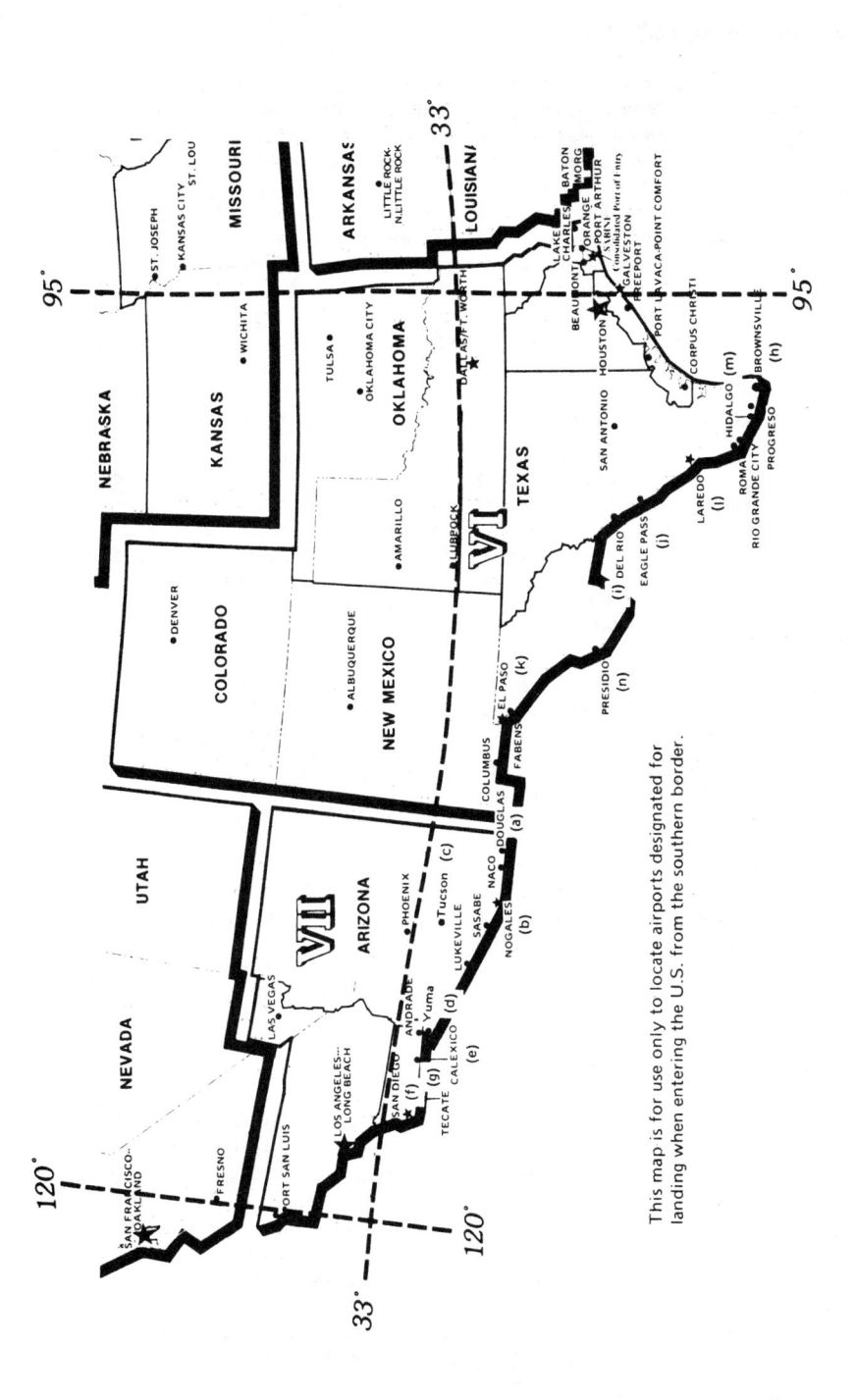

This map is for use only to locate airports designated for landing when entering the U.S. from the southern border.

to "landing rights" airports

In addition to advance notice of arrival as described under "International Airports," specific permission to land at "Landing Rights" airports must be obtained in advance of contemplated use. Except in the case of "Short Flights" advance notice of arrival may be transmitted to Customs in flight plans where flight notification service is rendered. Such notices will be treated as applications for permission to land although the pilot is still ultimately responsible for insuring that Customs is properly notified, and pilots should be aware that "landing rights" can be denied if inspection service cannot be provided. If the notification service is not available, pilots must submit applications for landing rights and provide arrival notices directly to U.S. Customs.

Customs officers may at their discretion grant blanket "Landing Rights" to persons to land at certain airports for a specified period of time, in which event advance notices of arrival will be the only requirement.

to other airports

Permission to land at airports other than "international" and "landing rights" airports may be obtained in some limited cases; however, advance arrangements (preferably in writing) must be made with the Customs office nearest the airport of intended arrival. Advance notice of arrival is required as usual. Pilots should be aware that mileage and per diem costs may be accrued in addition to any overtime charges if applicable.

what to report

Except at airports where the flight plan notification service is rendered, applications for landing rights and arrival notices shall specify:

> Type of aircraft
> Registration marks
> Name of commander
> Place of last departure
> Other countries visited
> Airport of arrival and code designation
> Number of alien passengers
> Number of citizen passengers
> Estimated time of arrival

The above requirements do not apply to private aircraft arriving in the United States from certain foreign areas south of the United States. (See "Special Reporting Requirements" under Inward Flights.)

short flights

If flying time from the foreign airport to the U.S. airport is less than 1 hour, the pilot should request his application for landing rights, when required, and transmit his arrival notice directly to the U.S. Customs office before departure from the foreign airport (unless prior arrangements were made). This is necessary to allow inspectional personnel to be assigned and at the airport prior to arrival of the aircraft. FAA cannot guarantee delivery of a message (under the flight plan notification arrangement) in sufficient time on such short notice. It is still the pilot's responsibility to give timely notice even though a flight plan has been filed.

For private aircraft arriving in the United States from certain foreign areas south of the United States, refer to "Special Reporting Requirements" under Inward Flights.

changing destination en route

Pilots may find it necessary or convenient to change the intended airport of destination en route; however, definite confirmation **from Customs** permitting a change must be received. Failure to obtain permission in advance to alter the airport of destination may result in Customs initiated penalty action.

To avoid the possibility of incurring overtime charges at two airports, it is important that pilots immediately cancel their request for overtime service at airport of original destination when diversion to a different airport occurs. If the request to cancel overtime services arrives too late to prevent the officer from leaving for the original airport, it is possible that the aircraft operator may incur overtime charges at both airports.

documentation and examination on arrival

Private aircraft are required to report directly to Customs for inspection immediately upon arrival. Normally a Customs officer (or an officer from the Immigration and Naturalization Service or Department of Agriculture) will be present if a pilot has given proper advance notice of arrival. Should no inspecting officer be present, the pilot should report his arrival to Customs by telephone or most convenient means. He should keep the aircraft, passengers, crewmembers, baggage, food and cargo intact in a segregated place until the officer arrives or until he has received special instructions from a Customs officer.

The pilot should provide the necessary information to assist the inspecting officer in the preparation of the required documentation unless the pilot has prepared the necessary documents in advance (obtainable from Customs). The forms required for private aircraft arrivals are:

    I-92 A—Report of Private Aircraft Arrival
    CF 178—Private Aircraft Inspection Report

The pilot may also be requested to produce for inspection a valid airman's certificate, medical certificate (14 CFR 61.3) and the aircraft registration certificate.

Crew and passenger baggage will be examined in the same manner as that of other international travelers. A verbal declaration of articles acquired abroad will suffice, except that a written declaration, Customs Form 6059-B (or appropriate substitute), shall be presented when duty is to be collected or when the inspecting officer deems a written declaration necessary. Noncommercial cargo and unaccompanied baggage carried on board private aircraft shall be accounted for on a baggage declaration (CF 6059-B) prepared by the pilot in command, and appropriate entry for same shall be required. Customs officers will furnish the necessary forms. In addition, the inspecting officer may require that all personal items, baggage and cargo be removed from the aircraft for inspection, and he may physically inspect the aircraft. It is the responsibility of the pilot to assist in opening baggage and compartments.

personal exemptions

Persons engaged in the operation of a private aircraft are not considered crewmembers for tariff purposes, and they are to be treated as returning residents for exemption purposes (19 CFR 148.61). For additional information about exemptions and the importation of typical tourist items, refer to the Customs pamphlets *Know Before You Go*, and *Customs Hints for Visitors (Nonresidents)*.

plant and animal quarantines

The importation of plants, plant products, all birds, certain animals, meats, and meat and animal products is regulated by the U.S. Department of Agriculture (USDA) to prevent the introduction of plant and animal pests and diseases. Agricultural items should not be brought to the United States in lunches or otherwise unless you are informed in advance by Agriculture inspectors of the Animal and Plant Health Inspection Service (APHIS) or Customs officers that such items are admissible. Prohibited items on board will be confiscated. Any such products on board the aircraft must be called to the attention of the inspecting officer by oral declaration. An APHIS inspector must be present when you return from an area where there has been an outbreak of destructive pests or diseases. Customs will advise APHIS of flights arriving from, or stopping in, such an area.

Furnished by Arnold D Senterfitt

For further information on this subject, refer to the FAA International Flight Information Manual or contact USDA.

Endangered species of plant and animal wildlife and products thereof may be prohibited or require permits or certification by the U.S. Fish and Wildlife Service.

repairs to private aircraft

Aircraft belonging to a resident of the U.S. and taken abroad for noncommercial purposes and returned by the resident shall be admitted free of duty upon being satisfactorily identified. Repairs made abroad to such aircraft, if incidental to use abroad, must be reported to Customs but are not subject to duty. Repairs not incidental to use abroad and alterations and additions made abroad shall be assessed with duty up to their value at the rate at which the aircraft itself would be dutiable if imported. Accessories acquired abroad are dutiable as if separately imported.

In the event that foreign-made parts, such as spare engines, must be replaced abroad, these parts may be dutiable upon reentry to the United States. The reimportation of U.S.-made parts may require entry. It is advisable that the nearest U.S. Customs office be contacted for clarification of this matter in each particular instance.

in case of emergency

If an emergency landing is made in the United States, the pilot should report as promptly as possible by telephone or most convenient means to the nearest Customs office. He should keep all merchandise or baggage in a segregated place and should not permit any passenger or crewmember to depart the place of arrival or commingle with the public without official permission, unless it is necessary for preservation of life, health, or property.

returning without landing

Aircraft returning to the United States or Puerto Rico without having landed outside the United States are not required to give advance notice of arrival or report to Customs.

hours of service

Generally speaking, free service is provided at airports during regular business hours (usually 8 AM to 5 PM), Monday through Saturday, and from 8 AM to 5 PM on Sundays and national holidays. However, tours of duty at airports are based on the need for services and are altered at some ports to coincide with schedule changes and peak workloads. The normal hours of service are listed in this booklet; however, to be absolutely positive that overtime charges will not accrue, private aircraft operators may contact, prior to departure, the Customs officer in charge at the U.S. airport of intended arrival in order to ascertain those hours during which free service can normally be expected. Phone numbers which may be used for this purpose are listed herein.

overtime charges

Federal laws[1] require that Customs officers be paid extra compensation for services performed outside of regular hours of duty on weekdays, and on Sundays and holidays. The same laws require that, except for specific functions and between the hours of 8 AM and 5 PM on Sundays and holidays, the Government be reimbursed for the cost of these services by the parties requesting them. When no overtime bond is on file at the port of entry to cover overtime reimbursement, cash deposit (payable in U.S. currency or checks drawn on U.S. banks) must be made to the inspecting officer for services rendered.

---

[1] 19 U.S.C. 261, 267, and 1451

BORDER CROSSING

DEPARTMENT OF THE TREASURY
UNITED STATES CUSTOMS SERVICE

PRIVATE AIRCRAFT INSPECTION REPORT
6.2, 6.14, C.R.

PARTIAL LIST OF COUNTRY CODES

AC	ANTIGUA	DR	DOMINICAN REPUBLIC	MX	MEXICO	ST	ST. LUCIA
BB	BARBADOS	EL	EL SALVADOR	NA	NETHER-LANDS	TD	TRINIDAD & TOBAGO
BD	BERMUDA	GJ	GRENADA		ANTILLES	TK	TURKS & CAICOS IS
BF	BAHAMAS	GP	GUADELOUPE	NU	NICARAGUA	VC	ST. VINCENT
BH	BRITISH HONDURAS	GT	GUATEMALA	PN	PANAMA	VE	VENEZUELA
CA	CANADA	GY	GUYANA	PQ	CANAL ZONE	VI	BRITISH V.I.
CJ	CAYMAN IS	HA	HAITI	SC	ST. CHRISTO-PHER-NEVIS-	VQ	V I (U.S.)
CK	COCOS IS	HO	HONDURAS		ANGUILLA		
CO	COLOMBIA	JM	JAMAICA	SQ	SWAN IS		
CS	COSTA RICA	MB	MARTINIQUE				

1. AIRCRAFT NUMBER `31:`
2. SYSDINO `20:A`
3. PILOT NAME `38:` Last Name / First Name / M.I.
4. FOREIGN DEPARTURE Last Foreign City / Country Code
5. ARRIVAL IN U.S. U.S. Airport Code / Time of Arrival / Arrival Date (MMDDYY)
6. AIRCRAFT `61:` Make / Model / Color(s)
7. PILOT DATA `66:` Pilot's name as in Item no. 3 above / Date of Birth (MMDDYY) / License No. / Nationality

8. PILOT ADDRESS
9. OWNER NAME AND ADDRESS
10. FOREIGN ITINERARY
11. DATE/TIME OF DEPARTURE FOR U.S.
12. U.S.-BASED AIRCRAFT ONLY ▶ a. U.S. Airport of Departure b. Date/Time of U.S. Departure

13. PASSENGERS

a. Last Name	b. First Name	M.I.	d. Nationality	Date of Birth

INSPECTOR SIGNATURE & BADGE NO.

Agriculture Data
- ☐ Fruits ☐ Plants
- ☐ Meats ☐ Veget.
Country of Origin

PAIRS Entry
- Sta. Code:
- Date:
- Time:

Inspection Data
- Travel Time:
- Waiting Time:
- Inspection Time:

☐ INS ☐ USDA ☐ OTHER: _____

(PAIRS ENTRY—New Record: Items 1, 3, 4, 5, 6, & 7. Modify: Items 1, 2, 3, 4, 5, & 7 if new.)

GPO 946-690

Customs Form 178 (10-30-81)

Furnished by Arnold D Senterfitt

Operators of private aircraft will be processed free of overtime charges during regular hours of duty (usually 8 AM to 5 PM) on weekdays, and from 8 AM to 5 PM on Sundays and holidays. Overtime charges will accrue after regular hours of duty on weekdays, and before 8 AM and after 5 PM on Sundays and holidays. However, at the specially designated airports along the southwest border (see page 3), Customs overtime charges will accrue only before 8 AM and after 5 PM on Sundays and holidays. If an officer from an inspecting agency other than Customs is providing the service, overtime charges after regular working hours during weekdays may be incurred.

A maximum of $25 has been established on a private aircraft pilot's liability for the cost of all overtime services performed by Federal inspection service employees in connection with each arrival or departure.[1] Overtime charges are prorated if services are performed for more than one operator or owner by the same inspector during an overtime assignment. Depending on the overtime charge and the number of inspections performed, the cost can be less than the $25 maximum. However, private aircraft operators should expect to pay $25 for overtime services. Refunds, if applicable, will usually be made at a later date by Customs' central accounting office.

For information about requirements of other Federal inspectional agencies and the manner in which overtime services are performed by them, operators should contact the respective services listed below:

APHIS Port Operations Staff
U.S. Department of Agriculture
Federal Building
Hyattsville, Md. 20782

Chief, Quarantine Branch
Epidemiology Program
Center for Disease Control
Atlanta, Georgia 30333

Associate Commissioner, Management
U.S. Immigration and Naturalization Service
425 Eye Street, N.W.
Washington, D.C. 20536

customs bonds

Customs term bonds are available which would largely preclude the need for cash deposits for payment of overtime services, penalty assessments, etc. Customs Form 7569, "Vessel, Vehicle, or Aircraft Bond (Term)," and Customs Form 7599, "Bond for Use in Connection with Requests for Overtime Services Made by or on Behalf of Parties in Interest (Term)" could be of particular advantage to aircraft owners and operators who frequently travel abroad. It is recommended that a copy of the bond be carried aboard the aircraft to simplify verification. The application for a bond should be accompanied by a Customs Form 53, "Bond Transcript," which permits the automating of bond data nationwide. For further information, contact the nearest Customs office.

penalties for violations

Since the law provides for substantial penalties for violations of the Customs regulations, aircraft operators and pilots should make every effort to comply with them. Examples of the more common violations and resulting penalties include:
- Failure to report arrival [19 CFR 6.2(a)]—$500
- Failure to obtain landing rights [19 CFR 6.2(a)]—$500
- Failure to provide advance notice of arrival [19 CFR 6.2(b)]—$500
- Failure to provide penetration report on southwest border [19 CFR 6.14(a)]—$500.

---

[1] 49 U.S.C. 1741

Furnished by Arnold D Senterfitt

- Departing without permission or discharging passengers or cargo without permission [19 CFR 6.2(c)]—$500
- Importation of contraband, including agriculture materials, or undeclared merchandise—can result in penalty action and seizure of aircraft which varies according to the nature of the violation and pertinent provision of law.

If a penalty is incurred, application may be made to the Customs officer in charge for a reduction in amount or cancellation, giving the grounds upon which relief is believed to be justified. If the operator or pilot desires to further petition for relief of the penalty, he may appeal to the appropriate District Director of Customs. If still further review of the penalty is desired, written appeal may be made to the proper Regional Commissioner of Customs and, in some cases, to Customs Headquarters.

customs districts

Address all correspondence to the District Director of Customs at the following locations (Roman numerals preceding addresses indicate the region in which the district is located):

VIII	Anchorage, Alaska 99501 / 620 E. Tenth Ave.
III	Baltimore, Maryland 21202 / 103 S. Gay St.
I	Boston, Massachusetts 02109 / 2 India St.
I	Bridgeport, Connecticut 06609 / 120 Middle St.
I	Buffalo, New York 14202 / 111 West Huron St.
IV	Charleston, South Carolina 29402 / P.O. Box 876
IX	Chicago, Illinois 60607 / 610 S. Canal St.
IX	Cleveland, Ohio 44114 / 55 Erieview Plaza
VI	Dallas / Ft. Worth, Texas / 75261 / P.O. Box 61050
IX	Detroit, Michigan 48226 / 477 Michigan Ave.
IX	Duluth, Minnesota 55802 / 515 W. First St.
VI	El Paso, Texas 79985 / Bldg. B, Room 134 Bridge of the Americas (P.O. Box 9516)
VIII	Great Falls, Montana 59401 / 215 1st Ave. N.
VIII	Honolulu, Hawaii 96806 / 335 Merchant St.
VI	Houston / Galveston, Texas 77052 / 701 San Jacinto St.
VI	Laredo, Texas 78040 / Mann Road & Santa Maria
VII	Los Angeles / Long Beach / 300 S. Ferry St. San Pedro, California 90731
IV	Miami, Florida 33131 / 77 S.E. 5th St.
IX	Milwaukee, Wisconsin 53202 / 628 E. Michigan St.
IX	Minneapolis, Minnesota 55401 / 110 S. Fourth St.
V	Mobile, Alabama 36602 / 250 N. Water St.
V	New Orleans, Louisiana 70130 / 423 Canal St.
II	New York, New York New York Seaport Area, New York, New York 10048 Customhouse, 6 World Trade Center Kennedy Airport Area, Jamaica, New York 11430 Seaboard World Building 178 Newark Area, Newark, New Jersey 07114 Airport International Plaza
VII	Nogales, Arizona 85621 / International & Terrace Sts.
III	Norfolk, Virginia 23510 / 101 E. Main St.
I	Ogdensburg, New York 13669 / 127 N. Water St.
IX	Pembina, North Dakota 58271 / Post Office Bldg.
III	Philadelphia, Pennsylvania 19106 / 2nd & Chestnut Sts.
VI	Port Arthur, Texas 77640 / 5th & Austin Ave.
I	Portland, Maine 04111 / 312 Fore St.
VIII	Portland, Oregon 97209 / N.W. Broadway & Glisan Sts.

Furnished by Arnold D Senterfitt

I	Providence, Rhode Island 02903 / 24 Weybosset St.
I	St. Albans, Vermont 05478 / Main & Stebbins Sts.
IX	St. Louis, Missouri 63105 / 120 S. Central Ave.
IV	St. Thomas, Virgin Islands 00801 / P.O. Box 510
VII	San Diego, California 92188 / 880 Front St.
VIII	San Francisco, California 94126 / 555 Battery St.
IV	San Juan, Puerto Rico 00903 / P.O. Box 2112
IV	Savannah, Georgia 31401 / 1 East Bay St.
VIII	Seattle, Washington 98174 / 909 First Ave.
IV	Tampa, Florida 33602 / 301 S. Ashley Dr.
III	Washington, D.C. 20041 / Dulles Int'l Airport Gateway Bldg. No. 1
IV	Wilmington, North Carolina 28401 / 2094 Polk St.

(Note: New York has Area Directors instead of District Directors)

customs regions

Address all correspondence to the Regional Commissioner of Customs at the following locations:

I	Boston, Massachusetts 02110 / 100 Summer St.
II	New York, New York 10048 / 6 World Trade Center
III	Baltimore, Maryland 21202 / 40 S. Gay St.
IV	Miami, Florida 33131 / 99 S.E. 5th St.
V	New Orleans, Louisiana 70112 / 423 Canal St.
VI	Houston, Texas 77002 / 500 Dallas St.
VII	Los Angeles, California 90053 / 300 N. Los Angeles St. / P.O. Box 2071
VIII	San Francisco, California 94105 / 211 Main St.
IX	Chicago, Illinois 60603 / 55 E. Monroe St.

customs headquarters

Washington, D.C. 20229 / 1301 Constitution Avenue, N.W.
Attn: Office of Border Operations

Airports at Which Customs Service Is Normally Available

Information in this section is provided in the following order:
1st line:
Location / Name of Airport / Code / FAA Flight Plan Notification/Customs (USCS) Phone Number (2nd line used if more than one phone number).
Remaining lines:
Special Arrangements or Restrictions.

- • indicates for Customs purposes "international airport;" all others are "landing rights" airports. See pages 2 and 4 for explanation of these terms.

† indicates USCS 24-hour numbers; F.S. indicates FAA Flight Service number.

The term "advance arrangements must be made" means that inspection services cannot be provided on a timely basis if only advance notice of arrival is given. Arrangements in writing or by telephone must be made prior to the flight by the pilot.

The term "regular business hours" means 0800 to 1700 hours, Monday through Saturday, except where otherwise indicated and these are the hours that the Customs office is normally staffed to make arrangements for service.

The notation "MP/F: 10," or other number, indicates maximum number of passengers which may be cleared per flight.

As noted below, this reprint includes only airports in the states you might use coming home from Mexico or Centro America. — Arnold

INDEX

Page					
82	Alabama		~~Kentucky~~		~~North Dakota~~
	~~Alaska~~	85	Louisiana		~~Ohio~~
82	Arizona		~~Maine~~	87	Oklahoma
82	Arkansas		~~Maryland~~		~~Oregon~~
83	California		~~Massachusetts~~		~~Pennsylvania~~
	~~Colorado~~		~~Michigan~~	87	Puerto Rico
	~~Connecticut~~		~~Minnesota~~		~~Rhode Island~~
	~~Delaware~~	85	Mississippi	87	South Carolina
	~~District of Columbia~~		~~Missouri~~		~~Tennessee~~
84	Florida		~~Montana~~	88	Texas
	~~Georgia~~		~~Nebraska~~		~~Utah~~
	~~Hawaii~~	86	Nevada		~~Vermont~~
	~~Idaho~~		~~New Hampshire~~	89	Virgin Islands
	~~Illinois~~		~~New Jersey~~		~~Virginia~~
	~~Indiana~~	86	New Mexico		~~Washington~~
	~~Iowa~~		~~New York~~	90	West Virginia
	~~Kansas~~	86	North Carolina		~~Wisconsin~~
					~~Wyoming~~

Furnished by Arnold D Senterfitt

ALABAMA

Birmingham / Birmingham Municipal / BHM / FAA: Yes / USCS 205-254-1464.
   On-call basis. 2 hours advance notice required. MP/F: 20

Huntsville / Huntsville Madison County Jetplex / HSV / FAA: Yes / USCS 205-772-3404.
   On-call basis. 2 hours advance notice required.

Mobile / Bates Field / FAA: Yes / USCS 205-690-2111.
   On-call basis. 2 hours advance notice required during regular business hours, 0800-1700, Monday through Saturday. 3 hours advance notice after regular business hours.

Montgomery / Dannelly / MGM / FAA: Yes / USCS 205-254-1464 (Birmingham).
   Not staffed by Customs. Advance arrangements must be made for inspection by Customs through Birmingham.

ALASKA *(not included)*

ARIZONA

Douglas / • Bisbee Douglas Int'l / DUG / FAA: Yes / USCS †602-364-8486.
   F.S. 602-364-8487
   Communicate direct via radio or telephone to Customs or FAA intention to land and advise intended point and time of border penetration not later than 15 minutes prior to entering U.S. airspace.

Nogales / • Nogales Int'l / OLS / FAA: Yes / USCS †602-287-2562.
   F.S. 602-287-4092.
   Communicate direct via radio or telephone to Customs or FAA intention to land and advise intended point and time of border penetration not later than 15 minutes prior to entering U.S. airspace.

Phoenix / Sky Harbor Int'l / PHX / FAA: Yes; if radio contact with tower /
   USCS 602-261-3514. F.S. †602-275-4121.
   1 hour advance notice required during regular business hours, 0800-1700, Monday through Friday. 2 hours otherwise. MP/F: 25.
   Private aircraft entering U.S. from south of the border not designated to land at Sky Harbor Int'l.

Tucson / • Tucson Int'l / TUS / FAA: Yes / USCS †602-287-2562.
   F.S. 602-889-9689.
   Communicate direct via radio or telephone to Customs or FAA intention to land and advise intended point and time of border penetration not later than 15 minutes prior to entering U.S. airspace. Free Customs service varies. During one 2-week period, service is free 0800-1700 hours, Monday through Sunday. The following 2-week period, service is free 0800-2000 hours, Monday through Saturday and 0800-1700 hours on Sundays and holidays. All other times on an overtime basis.

Yuma / • Yuma Int'l / YUM / FAA: Yes / USCS †602-627-8326, 602-627-8821
   (San Luis). F.S. 602-726-2550, 1000 to 1800 hours only.
   Communicate direct via radio or telephone to Customs or FAA intention to land and advise intended point and time of border penetration not later than 15 minutes prior to entering U.S. airspace. Free Customs service provided 0900-1700 hours, Monday through Sunday; overtime basis all other times.

ARKANSAS

Little Rock / Adams Field / LIT / FAA: Yes / USCS 501-378-5289.
   On-call basis. 2 hours advance notice required.

Furnished by Arnold D Senterfitt

CALIFORNIA

Calexico / • Calexico Int'l / CXL / FAA: Yes / USCS 714-357-1195, †714-357-4841.
F.S. 714-352-8740.
Communicate direct via radio or telephone to Customs or FAA intention to land and advise intended point and time of border penetration not later than 15 minutes prior to entering U.S. airspace.

Eureka / Eureka / EKA / FAA: Yes / USCS 707-442-4822.
On-call basis. 2 hours advance notice required.

Fresno / Fresno Municipal / FAT / FAA: Yes / USCS 209-487-5460.
On-call basis. 1 hour advance notice required during regular business hours, 0800-1700, Monday through Friday. Advance notice by 1630 Friday on all flights requesting service on Saturdays and Sundays. MP/F: 10.

Los Angeles / Los Angeles Int'l / LAX / FAA: Yes / USCS 213-642-5926, 213-646-2937, 213-646-2938, †213-642-5116.
1 hour advance notice required. Regular business hours. 0800-1700, Monday through Friday. Advance arrangements must be made during other times. Int'l Arrivals Bldg. usually not available for private aircraft. MP/F: 10.

Oakland / Metropolitan Oakland Int'l / OAK / FAA: Yes / USCS 415-876-2812 (San Francisco).
On-call basis. 2 hours advance notice required. Regular business hours, 0800-1700, Monday through Friday. Advance arrangements must be made for service during other times, in writing or by telephone, prior to flight by pilot.

Sacramento / Sacramento Metropolitan / SMF / FAA: Yes / USCS 415-876-2812 (San Francisco).
On-call basis. 4 hours advance notice required during regular business hours, 0800-1700 Monday through Friday. Pilot must make advance arrangements in writing or by telephone prior to flight.

San Diego / • San Diego Int'l (Lindbergh) / SAN / FAA: Yes / USCS †714-428-7207
F.S. 714-291-6381.
Communicate direct via radio or telephone to Customs or FAA intention to land and advise intended point and time of border penetration not later than 15 minutes prior to entering U.S. airspace.

San Diego / Brown Field / SDM / FAA: Yes / USCS †714-428-7207.
F.S. 714-291-6381.
Communicate direct via radio or telephone to Customs or FAA intention to land and advise intended point and time of border penetration not later than 15 minutes prior to entering U.S. airspace.

San Francisco / San Francisco Int'l / SFO / FAA: Yes / USCS 415-876-2812.
1 hour advance notice required during regular business hours, 0800-1700, Monday through Saturday; 2 hours advance notice required during regular business hours, 1700-2400 hours, Monday through Saturday. Advance arrangements must be made during other times, in writing or by telephone, prior to flight by pilot.

San Jose / San Jose Municipal / SJC / FAA: Yes / USCS 415-876-2812 (San Francisco)
Advance permission required. MP/F: 6

COLORADO *(not included)*

CONNECTICUT *(not included)*

DELAWARE *(not included)*

DISTRICT OF COLUMBIA *(not included)*

FLORIDA
Fort Lauderdale / • Fort Lauderdale-Hollywood Int'l / FLL / FAA: Yes / USCS 305-522-3218.
   Regular business hours, 0800-2000, Monday through Saturday.

Fort Lauderdale / Executive / FXE / FAA: Yes / USCS 305-771-8095.
   Regular business hours, 1100-1900, Monday through Saturday. Tower will direct flyers to Customs ramp. MP/F: 20.

Fort Pierce / St. Lucie County / FPR / FAA: Yes / USCS 305-461-1200.
   1 hour advance notice required.

Jacksonville / Jacksonville Int'l / JAX / FAA: Yes / USCS 904-791-2775.
   Not staffed by Customs. Advance arrangements must be made for Customs inspection by party of interest prior to departure. Regular business hours, 0800-1700, Monday through Friday. Saturday and Sunday requests for service must be made prior to 1700 hours Friday.

Key West / • Key West Int'l / EYW / FAA: Yes / USCS 305-294-1044, 305-296-5411.

Marathon / Marathon / MTH / FAA: Yes at Key West / USCS 305-743-3575, 305-743-6054.
   2 hours advance notice required at all times. MP/F: 20.

Melbourne / Melbourne Regional / MLB / FAA: Yes. Direct radio contact. / USCS 305-783-2066.
   On-call basis. 2 hours advance notice required.

Miami / • Chalk's Seaplane Base / X44 / FAA: No / USCS 305-350-5261.
   After regular business hours, call 305-526-2875.

Miami / • Miami Int'l / MIA / FAA: Yes / USCS 305-526-2875.

Miami / Opa-Locka / OPF / FAA: Yes / USCS 305-688-0832.
   Regular business hours, 1100-1900, Monday through Saturday. 1 hour advance notice required.

Orlando / Orlando Int'l / MCO / FAA: Yes / USCS 305-420-6308
   Regular business hours, 0800-1700, Monday through Saturday. Tower will direct to Customs ramp. One hour advance notice required.

Panama City / Panama City-Bay County (Fannin Field) / PFN / FAA: Yes / USCS 904-785-4688.
   Advance arrangements must be made during regular business hours, 0800-1700, Monday through Friday. MP/F: 20.

Pensacola / Pensacola Municipal / PNS / FAA: Yes / USCS 904-432-6811.
   On-call basis. 3 hours advance notice required. MP/F: 20.

St. Petersburg/Clearwater / St. Petersburg-Clearwater / PIE / FAA: Yes / USCS 813-536-7311.
   1 hour advance notice required.

Furnished by Arnold D Senterfitt

Tampa / • Tampa Int'l / TPA / FAA: Yes / USCS 813-228-2395.
Nights: 813-228-2385
1 hour advance notice required.

West Palm Beach / • Palm Beach Int'l / PBL / FAA: Yes / USCS 305-683-1806.
Regular business hours, 0800-1700, Monday through Sunday.

GEORGIA *(not included)*

HAWAII *(not included)*

IDAHO *(not included)*

ILLINOIS *(not included)*

INDIANA *(not included)*

IOWA *(not included)*

KANSAS *(not included)*

KENTUCKY *(not included)*

LOUISIANA
Baton Rouge / Ryan / BTR / FAA: Yes / USCS 504-355-1932.
On-call basis. 2 hours advance notice required.

Lake Charles / Lake Charles Municipal / LCH / FAA: Yes / USCS 318-439-5512.
2 hour advance notice required.

New Orleans / New Orleans Int'l (Moisant Field) / MSY / FAA. Yes / USCS 504-467-4319.
Nights: 504-589-6804.
2 hours advance notice required. Regular business hours, 0800-1700, Monday through Saturday.

New Orleans / New Orleans Lakefront Airport / NEW / FAA: Yes / USCS 504-467-4319.
Nights: 504-589-6804.
On-call basis. 2 hours advance notice required. Regular business hours, 0800-1700, Monday through Saturday. MP/F: 20.

MAINE *(not included)*

MARYLAND *(not included)*

MASSACHUSETTS *(not included)*

MICHIGAN *(not included)*

MINNESOTA *(not included)*

MISSISSIPPI
Gulfport / Gulfport Biloxi Regional / GPT / FAA: Yes / USCS 601-864-6794.
On-call basis. 2 hours advance notice required during regular business hours, 0800-1700, Monday through Friday. MP/F: 10.

Furnished by Arnold D Senterfitt

Pascagoula / Jackson County / PGL / FAA: No / USCS 601-762-7311.
On-call basis. 2 hours advance notice required during regular business hours, 0800-1700, Monday through Friday.

MISSOURI *(not included)*

MONTANA *(not included)*

NEBRASKA *(not included)*

NEVADA
Las Vegas / McCarran Int'l / LAS / FAA: Yes / USCS †702-385-6480.
On-call basis. 1 hour advance notice required during regular business hours, 0800-1700, Monday through Friday; 2 hours otherwise. MP/F: 25.

Reno / Reno Int'l / RNO / FAA: Yes / USCS 702-784-5585.
On-call basis. 2 hours advance notice required. Arrangements should be made during regular business hours, 0800-1700, Monday through Friday, for all flights. MP/F: 25.

NEW HAMPSHIRE *(not included)*

NEW JERSEY *(not included)*

NEW MEXICO
Albuquerque / Albuquerque Int'l / ABQ / FAA: Yes / USCS 505-766-2621.
2 hours advance notice required during regular business hours, 0800-1700, Monday through Friday. At least 3 hours otherwise.

NEW YORK *(not included)*

NORTH CAROLINA
Charlotte / Douglas Municipal / CLT / FAA: Yes / USCS 704-392-9328.
On-call basis. 1 hour advance notice required during regular business hours, 0830-1700, Monday through Friday. 3 hours notice required after 1700 hours and on Saturdays, Sundays, and holidays.

Greensboro / Greensboro/Highpoint/Winston-Salem Regional / GSO / FAA: Yes / USCS 919-761-3001 (Winston-Salem).
On-call basis. 2 hours advance notice required during regular business hours, 0830-1700, Monday through Friday. 3 hours notice required after 1700 hours and on Saturdays, Sundays and holidays. Charge is made for mileage.

Raleigh-Durham / Raleigh-Durham / RDU / FAA: Yes, but not satisfactory due to prior assignment of Customs personnel. / USCS 919-541-5211.
Advance arrangements must be made for Customs inspection by party of interest prior to departure. Regular business hours, 0800-1700, Monday through Friday. Saturday and Sunday requests for service must be made prior to 1700 hours Firday. Requests for holiday service must be made prior to 1700 hours on the preceding work day. Charge is made for mileage.

Wilmington / New Hanover County / ILM / FAA: Yes / USCS 919-343-4616.
On-call basis. 2 hours advance notice required during regular business hours. 3 hours notice required after 1700 hours and on Sundays and holidays.

Winston-Salem / Smith Reynolds / INT / FAA: Yes / USCS 919-761-3001.
   On-call basis. 1 hour advance notice required during regular business hours, 0830-1700, Monday through Friday. 3 hours notice required after 1700 hours and on Saturdays, Sundays, and holidays.

NORTH DAKOTA *(not included)*

OHIO *(not included)*

OKLAHOMA
Oklahoma City / Will Rogers World / OKC / FAA: Yes / USCS 405-231-4347.
   Advance arrangements must be made. Regular business hours, 0830-1700, Monday through Friday. Saturday and Sunday requests for service must be made prior to 1700 hours on Friday. MP/F: 8 (including crew).

Tulsa / Tulsa Int'l / TUL / FAA: Yes / USCS 918-835-7631.
   Advance arrangements must be made. Regular business hours, 0830-1700, Monday through Friday. Saturday and Sunday requests for service must be made prior to 1700 hours on Friday. MP/F: 8 (including crew).

OREGON *(not included)*

PENNSYLVANIA *(not included)*

PUERTO RICO
Culebra / Culebra / CPX / FAA: No / USCS 809-742-3531.
   1 hour advance notice required during regular business hours. Arrivals from U.S. Virgin Islands only.

Isla de Vieques / Vieques / VQS / FAA: No / USCS 809-741-3991.
   1 hour advance notice required during regular business hours. Arrivals from U.S. Virgin Islands only.

Mayaguez / Mayaguez Airfield / MAZ / FAA: No / USCS 809-832-0042, 809-832-8308.
   On-call basis. 1 hour advance notice required.

Ponce / Mercedita / PSE / FAA: No / USCS 809-842-3195, 809-842-1030.
   On-call basis. 1 hour advance notice required.

San Juan / Puerto Rico Int'l / SJU / FAA: Yes / USCS 809-791-5245, 809-791-0220.
   Regular business hours, 0800-2400, Monday through Saturday.

San Juan / San Juan/Isla Grande / SIG / FAA: Yes / USCS 809-725-6911.
   Regular business hours, 0800-1900, Monday through Saturday.

RHODE ISLAND *(not included)*

SOUTH CAROLINA
Charleston / Charleston Municipal / CHS / FAA: Yes / USCS 803-744-0712, †803-723-1272.
   1 hour advance notice required.

Greer / Greenville-Spartanburg / GSP / FAA: Yes / USCS 803-877-8006.
   1 hour advance notice required during regular business hours.

Furnished by Arnold D Senterfitt

TENNESSEE *(not included)*

TEXAS

Amarillo / Amarillo Int'l / AMA / FAA: Yes / USCS 806-376-2347.
  Advance arrangements must be made. Regular business hours, 0830-1700, Monday through Friday. Saturday and Sunday requests for service must be made prior to 1700 hours on Friday. MP/F: 8 (including crew).

Austin / Robert Mueller Municipal / AUS / FAA: Yes / USCS 512-397-5309.
  Advance arrangements must be made. Regular business hours, 0830-1700, Monday through Friday. Saturday and Sunday requests for service must be made prior to 1700 hours on Friday. MP/F: 10 (including crew).

Beaumont / Jefferson County / BPT / FAA: Yes / USCS 713-982-2832 (Port Arthur).
  On-call basis. 2 hours advance notice required. Regular business hours, 0800-1700, Monday through Friday.

Brownsville / • Brownsville Int'l / BRO / FAA: No / USCS 512-542-4232.
  Communicate direct via radio or telephone to Customs or FAA intention to land and advise intended point and time of border penetration not later than 15 minutes prior to entering U.S. airspace.

Corpus Christi / Corpus Christi Int'l / CRP / FAA: Yes / USCS 512-888-3352.
  On-call basis. 2 hours advance notice required. Regular business hours, 0800-1700, Monday through Friday.

Dallas / DFW Regional / DFW / FAA: Yes / USCS 214-574-2131, 0830-1700 hours.
  F.S. 214-350-7340 after 1700 hours.
  1 hour advance notice required prior to 1700 hours. 2 hours notice after 1700 hours.

Dallas / Dallas Love Field / DAL / FAA: Yes / USCS 214-574-2131.
  2 hours advance notice required. After 1700 hours call FAA 214-350-7340.

Del Rio / • Del Rio Int'l / DRT / FAA: Yes / USCS 512-775-8502.
  Communicate direct via radio or telephone to Customs or FAA intention to land and advise intended point and time of border penetration not later than 15 minutes prior to entering U.S. airspace.

Eagle Pass / • Eagle Pass Municipal / EGP / FAA: No / USCS 512-733-9468.
  Communicate direct via radio or telephone to Customs or FAA intention to land and advise intended point and time of border penetration not later than 15 minutes prior to entering U.S. airspace.

El Paso / • El Paso Int'l / ELP / FAA: Yes / USCS 915-543-7430.
  Communicate direct via radio to FAA or telephone to Customs intention to land and advise intended point and time of border penetration not later than 15 minutes prior to entering U.S. airspace.

Ft. Worth / Meachem Field / FTW / FAA: Yes / USCS 214-574-2131.
  On-call basis. 2 hours advance notice required. No service after 1700 hours unless arrangements made prior to 1700 hours.

Furnished by Arnold D Senterfitt

Galveston / Scholes Field / GLS / FAA: Yes / USCS 713-763-1211 ext. 623.
   Saturdays: 713-763-2214.
   Landing rights granted in case of emergency with concurrence of the other interested agencies.

Houston / Houston Intercontinental / IAH / FAA: Yes / USCS 713-443-4356.
   1 hour advance notice required during regular business hours, 0800-1700, Monday through Saturday. 2 hours otherwise.

Houston / William P. Hobby / HOU / FAA: Yes / USCS 713-921-4107.
   1 hour advance notice required during regular business hours; 2 hours otherwise. MP/F: 20 (including crew) with concurrence of other interested agencies.

Laredo / • Laredo Int'l / LOI / FAA: Yes / USCS 512-722-1113.
   Communicate direct via radio or telephone to Customs or FAA intention to land and advise intended point and time of border penetration not later than 15 minutes prior to entering U.S. airspace.

Lubbock / Lubbock Int'l / LBB / FAA: Yes / USCS 806-762-7458.
   Advance arrangements must be made. Regular business hours, 0800-1630, Monday through Friday. Saturday and Sunday requests for service must be made prior to 1630 hours on Friday. MP/F: 8 (including crew).

McAllen / • Miller Int'l / MFE / FAA: Yes / USCS 512-843-2231.
   Communicate direct via radio or telephone to Customs or FAA intention to land and advise intended point and time of border penetration not later than 15 minutes prior to entering U.S. airspace.

Presidio / • Presidio-Lely Int'l / TX07 / FAA: Yes / USCS 915-229-3349.
   On-call basis. 1 hour advance notice required during regular business hours, 0830-1700, Monday through Friday. 2 hours advance notice required after 1700 hours Monday through Friday or anytime on Saturday, Sunday, and holidays.

San Antonio / San Antonio Int'l / SAT / FAA: Yes / USCS 512-822-0471, 512-229-5137.
   1 hour advance notice required during regular business hours. 2 hours otherwise.

UTAH (not included)

VERMONT (not included)

VIRGIN ISLANDS
St. Thomas / Harry S. Truman / STT / FAA: Yes / USCS 809-774-1719 (Charlotte Amalie).
   1 hour advance notice required during regular business hours, Sundays, and holidays.

St. Croix / Alexander Hamilton / STX / FAA: Yes / USCS 809-778-0216 (Christiansted).
   1 hour advance notice required during regular business hours. 2 hours advance notice required at other times and on Sundays or holidays.

VIRGINIA (not included)

WASHINGTON (not included)

Furnished by Arnold D Senterfitt

WEST VIRGINIA

Charleston / Kanawha / CRW / FAA: Yes / USCS 304-343-6181 ext. 423 or 424.
   1 hour advance notice required. Regular business hours, 0800-1700, Monday through Friday. Prior arrangements must be made for Saturday and Sunday arrivals.

Huntington / Tri-State / HTS / FAA: Yes / USCS 304-343-6181 ext. 423 or 424.
   On-call basis. Advance arrangements must be made.

WISCONSIN *(not included)*

WYOMING *(not included)*

PRECLEARANCE FROM THE VIRGIN ISLANDS

Private aircraft departing the U.S. Virgin Islands destined for the mainland or Puerto Rico may request preclearance service at St. Croix and St. Thomas. This service will be provided 0800 to 1700 hours, Monday through Sunday. Preclearance outside of these hours may be authorized at the discretion of the District Director on a case-by-case basis. All private aircraft pilots desiring preclearance to the U.S. are required to make advance arrangements for clearance directly with Customs or through the Federal Aviation Administration by radio or other means. FAA will notify Customs of all preclearance requests.

At time of preclearance, you will complete a General Declaration (CF-7507) which will be authenticated by the inspecting officer as evidence of your having been precleared.

If for any reason you find that you cannot come directly to the U.S. (must stop for refueling or any other reason), your preclearance becomes invalid and you must report to Customs on your arrival in the U.S. or Puerto Rico.

Use of the General Declaration, although not required for general aviation aircraft unless carrying persons or cargo for hire, will serve as evidence of your having been precleared if challenged upon your arrival in the Customs territory. However, this does not preclude reinspection by Customs, although such reinspection would be rare.

Customs Publication No. 513

KNOW BEFORE YOU GO

customs hints for returning u.s. residents

This booklet is to inform U.S. residents going abroad of key United States Customs regulations and procedures. Your use of this information will enable our inspectors to complete your baggage examination without difficulty on your return.

In an effort to facilitate your Customs clearance new legislation now in effect increases your personal exemption and provides a flat rate of duty which will enable you to determine in advance how much duty will be paid if you acquire up to $600 worth of dutiable articles in excess of your personal exemption. And there are special provisions made if you visit our insular possessions—the U.S. Virgin Islands, American Samoa, or Guam—as they depend largely on tourist trade.

Facilitation is our key word. Our efforts include developing new procedures and patterns for inspection, putting into effect long-sought legislative changes mentioned above, negotiating with airport managers for adequate space, and processing your immigration/customs clearance with a friendly smile and a "Welcome Home."

We also make an intensive effort to acquaint you with our procedures and the requirements and restrictions which must be enforced in order to maintain the vital health and economy of our Nation. So take a few minutes and become familiar with our *Customs Hints* . . . before you go.

If you have any questions, or suggestions, let us hear from you. Our district customs offices as well as our overseas locations are listed on page 30. If you wish to write, address your letter or post card to Customs, P.O. Box 7118, Washington, D.C., 20044

Have a good trip!

Furnished by Arnold D Senterfitt

Know Before You Go

CONTENTS

Your Declaration 93
    Oral, written, family

Warning—Penalties 94
    Undervaluation, failure to declare

Your Exemption 94
    $300, $600, $25
    Cigars, cigarettes, alcoholic beverages
    Time limitations

Gifts 95
    Mailed to friends and relatives
    Accompanying you

Articles: Free of Duty or Dutiable 95
    Personal belongings mailed home
    Duty-free products from developing countries
    Foreign-made articles taken abroad
    Vehicles, airplanes, boats taken abroad
    Household effects
    Flat rates of duty
    Payment of duty
    Various rates of duty

Prohibited and Restricted Articles 98
    Prohibited items
    Automobiles
    Biological materials, books
    Cultural property (pre-Columbian)
    Firearms, ammunition
    Food products, fruits, vegetables, plants
    Meats, livestock, poultry
    Medicine containing narcotics
    Merchandise from Rhodesia, North Korea, Vietnam, Cambodia, Cuba
    Trademarked articles
    Wildlife and fish

Customs Pointers 101
    Traveling back and forth across the border
    "Duty-free" shops, sales slips
    Packing your baggage, photographic film
    Shipping Hints: mail, express, freight
    Unaccompanied tourist purchases
    Storage charges

Locations of Customs Offices 103

your declaration

ALL articles acquired abroad and in your possession at the time of your return must be declared. This includes:

Furnished by Arnold D Senterfitt

- Gifts presented to you while abroad, such as wedding or birthday presents.
- Repairs or alterations made to any articles taken abroad and returned, whether or not repairs or alterations were free of charge.
- Items you have been requested to bring home for another person.
- Any articles you intend to sell or use in your business.

In addition, articles acquired in the U.S. Virgin Islands, American Samoa, or Guam and not accompanying you must be declared at the time of your return.

The price actually paid for each article must be stated on your declaration in U.S. currency or its equivalent in country of acquisition. If the article was not purchased, obtain its fair retail value in the country in which it was acquired.

Note: The wearing or use of any article acquired abroad does not exempt it from duty. It must be declared at the price you paid for it. The customs officer will make an appropriate reduction in its value for wear and use.

Oral Declaration

Customs declaration forms are distributed on vessels and planes and should be prepared in advance of arrival for presentation to the immigration and customs inspectors. Fill out the *identification* portion of the declaration form. You may declare orally to the customs inspector the articles you acquired abroad, if the articles are accompanying you and you have not exceeded the duty-free exemption allowed. A customs officer may, however, ask you to prepare a written list if it is necessary.

Written Declaration

A written declaration will be necessary when:
- The total fair retail value of articles acquired abroad exceeds your personal exemption.
- More than one quart of alcoholic beverages, 200 cigarettes (one carton), or 100 cigars are included.
- Some of the items are not intended for your personal or household use, such as commercial samples, items for sale or use in your business, or articles you are bringing home for another person.
- Articles acquired in the U.S. Virgin Islands, American Samoa, or Guam are being sent to the U.S.
- A customs duty or internal revenue tax is collectible on any article in your possession.

Family Declaration

The head of a family may make a joint declaration for all members residing in the same household and returning *together to the United States.* Example: A family of four may bring in articles free of duty valued up to $1,200 retail value on one declaration, even if the articles acquired by one member of the family exceeds the personal exemption allowed.

Know Before You Go

Infants and children returning to the United States are entitled to the same exemption as adults (except for alcoholic beverages). Children born abroad, who have never resided in the United States, are entitled to the customs exemptions granted nonresidents.

Visitors to the United States should obtain the leaflet *Customs Hints for Visitors (Nonresidents)*.

Military and civilian personnel of the U.S. Government should obtain the leaflet *Customs Highlights for Government Personnel* for information about their customs exemptions when returning from an extended duty assignment abroad.

warning!

If you understate the value of an article you declare, or if you otherwise misrepresent an article in your declaration, you may have to pay a penalty in addition to payment of duty. Under certain circumstances, the article could be seized and forfeited if the penalty is not paid.

If you fail to declare an article acquired abroad, not only is the article subject to seizure and forfeiture, but you will be liable for a personal penalty in an amount equal to the value of the article in the United States. In addition, you may also be liable to criminal prosecution.

Don't rely on advice given by persons outside the Customs Service. It may be bad advice which could lead you to violate the customs laws and incur costly penalties.

If in doubt about whether an article should be declared, always declare it first and then direct your question to the customs inspector. If in doubt about the value of an article, declare the article and then ask the customs inspector for assistance in valuing it.

Customs inspectors handle tourist items day after day and become acquainted with the normal, current foreign values. Moreover, current commercial prices of foreign items are available at all times and on-the-spot comparisons of these values can be made.

It is well known that some merchants abroad offer travelers invoices or bills of sale showing false or understated values. This practice not only delays your customs examination, but can prove very costly.

Play it safe—avoid customs penalties

Furnished by Arnold D Senterfitt

your exemptions

In clearing U.S. Customs, a traveler is considered either a "returning resident of the United States" or a "nonresident."

Generally speaking, if you leave the United States for purposes of traveling, working or studying abroad and return to resume residency in the United States, you are considered a returning resident by Customs.

Residents of American Samoa, Guam, or the U.S. Virgin Island, who are American citizens, are also considered as returning U.S. residents.

Articles acquired abroad and brought into the United States are subject to applicable duty and internal revenue tax, but as a returning resident you are allowed certain exemptions from paying duty on items obtained while abroad.

$300 Exemption

Articles totaling $300 (based on the *fair retail value* of each item in the country where acquired) may be entered free of duty, subject to the limitations on liquors, cigarettes, and cigars, *if:*

• Articles were acquired as an incident of your trip for your personal or household use.

• You bring the articles with you at the time of your return to the United States and they are properly declared to Customs. Articles purchased and left for alterations or other reasons cannot be applied to your $300 exemption when shipped to follow at a later date.

• You are returning from a stay abroad of at least 48 hours. Example: A resident who leaves United States territory at 1:30 p.m. on June 1st would complete the required 48-hour period at 1:30 p.m. on June 3rd. This time limitation does not apply if you are returning from Mexico or the Virgin Islands of the U.S.

• You have not used this $300 exemption, or any part of it, within the preceding 30-day period. Also, your exemption is not cumulative. If you use a portion of your exemption on entering the United States, then you must wait for 30 days before you are entitled to another exemption other than a $25 exemption, see page 9.

• Articles are not prohibited or restricted. See page 19.

Cigars and Cigarettes: Not more than 100 cigars and 200 cigarettes (one carton) may be included in your exemption. Products of Cuban tobacco may be included if purchased in Cuba, see page 22. This exemption is available to each person regardless of age. Your cigarettes, however, may be subject to a tax imposed by state and local authorities.

Liquor: One quart (32 fluid ounces) of alcoholic beverages may be included in this exemption if:

• you are 21 years of age or older,

• it is for your own use or for use as a gift, and

• it is not in violation of the laws of the state in which you arrive.

Information about state restrictions and taxes should be obtained from the state government as laws vary from state to state.

Alcoholic beverages in excess of the one quart limitation are subject to duty and internal revenue tax.

Shipping of alcoholic beverages by mail is prohibited by United States postal laws.

Metric conversion will not be applied to customs exemptions until mandatory on January 1, 1980.

$600 Exemption

If you return directly or indirectly from the Virgin Islands of the United States, American Samoa, or Guam, you may receive a customs exemption of $600 (based on the fair retail value of the articles in the country where acquired). Not more than $300 of this exemption may be applied to merchandise obtained elsewhere than in these islands.

Residents, 21 years of age or older, may enter one U.S. gallon of alcoholic beverages (128 fluid ounces) free of duty and tax, *provided* not more than one quart of this amount is acquired elsewhere than in these islands.

Articles acquired in and sent from these islands to the United States may be claimed under your duty-free personal exemption if properly declared, see page 29.

Other provisions under the $300 exemption apply.

$25 Exemption

If you cannot claim the $300 or $600 exemption because of the 30-day or 48-hour minimum limitations, you may bring in free of duty and tax articles acquired abroad for your personal or household use if the total fair retail value does not exceed $25. This is an individual exemption and may not be grouped with other members of a family on one customs declaration.

You may include any of the following: 50 cigarettes, 10 cigars, 4 ounces of alcoholic beverages, or 4 ounces of alcoholic perfume.

If any article brought with you is subject to duty or tax, or if the total value of all dutiable articles exceeds $25, no article may be exempted from duty or tax.

gifts

Bona fide gifts of not more than $25 in fair retail value where shipped, can be received by friends and relations in the United States free of duty and tax, if the same person does not receive more than $25 in gift shipments in one day. The "day" in reference is the day in which the parcel(s) are received for customs processing. This amount is increased to $40 if shipped from the U.S. Virgin Islands, American Samoa, or Guam. These gifts are not declared by you upon your return to the States.

Perfume containing alcohol valued at more than $5 retail, tobacco products, and alcoholic beverages are excluded from the gift provision.

Gifts intended for more than one person may be consolidated in the same package provided they are individually wrapped and labeled with the name of the recipient.

Be sure that the outer wrapping of the package is marked 1) unsolicited gift, 2) nature of the gift, and 3) its fair retail value. In addition, a consolidated gift parcel should be marked as such on the outside with the names of the recipients listed and the value of each gift. This will facilitate customs clearance of your package.

If any article imported in the gift parcel is subject to duty and tax, or if the total value of all articles exceeds the bona fide gift allowance, no article may be exempt from duty or tax.

If a parcel is subject to duty, the United States Postal Service will collect the duty plus a handling charge in the form of "Postage Due" stamps. Duty cannot be prepaid.

You, as a traveler, cannot send a "gift" parcel to yourself nor can persons traveling together send "gifts" to each other. Gifts ordered by mail from the U.S. do not qualify under this duty-free gift provision and are subject to duty.

Gifts accompanying you are considered to be for your personal use and may be included within your exemption. This includes gifts given to you by others while abroad and those you intend to give to others after you return. Gifts intended for business or promotional purposes may not be included.

other articles: free of duty or dutiable

Some products from certain developing countries may enter the United States free of duty under the Generalized System of Preferences (GSP). For further details, obtain the leaflet *GSP and The Traveler* from your nearest Customs office.

Personal belongings of United States origin are entitled to entry free of duty. Personal belongings taken abroad, such as worn clothing, etc., may be sent home by mail before your return and receive free entry provided they have not been altered or repaired while abroad. These packages should be marked *"American Goods Returned."* When a claim of United States origin is made, marking on the article to so indicate facilitates customs processing.

Foreign-made personal articles taken abroad are dutiable each time they are brought into our country unless you have acceptable proof of prior possession.

Furnished by Arnold D Senterfitt

96 Know Before You Go

Documents which fully describe the article, such as a bill of sale, insurance policy, jeweler's appraisal, or receipt for purchase, may be considered reasonable proof of prior possession.

Items, such as watches, cameras, tape recorders, or other articles which may be readily identified by serial number or permanently affixed markings, may be taken to the Customs office nearest you and registered before your departure. The Certificate of Registration provided will expedite free entry of these items when you return. Keep the certificate as it is valid for any future trips.

Registration cannot be accomplished by telephone nor can blank registration forms be given or mailed to you to be filled out at a later time.

Automobiles, boats, planes, etc., or other vehicles taken abroad for noncommercial use may be returned duty free by proving to the customs officer that they were taken out of the United States. This proof may be the state registration card for an automobile, the Federal Aviation Administration certificate for an aircraft, a yacht license or motorboat identification certificate for a pleasure boat, or a customs certificate of registration obtained before departure.

Dutiable repairs or accessories acquired abroad for articles taken out of the United States must be declared on your return.

Warning: Catalytic equipped vehicles (1976 or later model years) driven outside the United States, Canada, or Mexico will not, in most cases, meet EPA standards when brought back to the U.S. As unleaded fuel generally is not available in other countries, the catalytic converter will become inoperative and must be replaced. Contact Environmental Protection Agency, Public Information Center (PM-215), Washington, D.C. 20460, for details and exceptions.

Your local Customs office has the following leaflets which will be of interest—*Importing a Car, Pleasure Boats,* and *Customs Guide for Private Flyers.*

Household effects and tools of trade or occupation which you take out of the United States are duty free at the time you return if properly declared and entered.

All furniture, carpets, paintings, tableware, linens, and similar household furnishings acquired abroad may be imported free of duty, *if*:
* They are not imported for another person or for sale.
* They have been used abroad by you for not less than one year or were available for use in a household in which you were a resident member for one year. This privilege does not include articles placed in storage outside the home. The year of use need not be continuous nor does it need to be the year immediately preceding the date of importation. Shipping time may not be included in the computation of the one year in use. For information on freight shipments, see page 28.

Items such as wearing apparel, jewelry, photographic equipment, tape recorders, stereo components, and vehicles are considered as personal articles and cannot be passed free of duty as household effects.

Furnished by Arnold D Senterfitt

Articles imported in excess of your customs exemption will be subject to duty unless the items are entitled to free entry or prohibited.

The inspector will place the items having the highest rate of duty under your exemption and duty will be assessed upon the lower rated items.

After deducting your exemption and the value of any articles duty free, a flat rate of duty will be applied to the next $600 worth (fair retail value) of merchandise. Any dollar amount of an article or articles over $600 will be dutiable at various rates of duty based, in most cases, on wholesale value.

Articles to which the flat rate of duty is applied must be for your personal use or for use as gifts and you cannot receive this flat rate provision more than once every 30 days, excluding the day of your last arrival.

The flat rate of duty is 10% based on fair retail value in the country of acquisition including Communist block countries, and *articles must accompany you.*

The flat rate of duty is 5% for articles purchased in the U.S. Virgin Islands, American Samoa, or Guam, whether the articles accompany you or are shipped.

Example: You acquire goods valued at $1500 from:

	U.S. insular possessions	Other countries or locations
Personal exemption (free of duty)	Up to $600	Up to $300
Flat duty rate	Next $600 at 5%	Next $600 at 10%
Various rates of duty	Remaining $300	Remaining $600
Total	$1,500	$1,500

The flat rate of duty will apply to any articles which are dutiable and cannot be included in your personal exemption, even if you have not exceeded the dollar amount of your exemption. Example: you are returning from Europe with $200 worth of articles which includes 2 quarts of liquor. One quart will be free of duty under your exemption, the other dutiable at 10%, plus any internal revenue tax.

Members of a family residing in one household traveling together on their return to the U.S. will group articles for application of the flat duty rate without regard as to which member of the family may be the owner of the articles.

Payment of duty, required at the time of your arrival on articles accompanying you, may be made by any of the following ways:
* U.S. currency (foreign currency is not acceptable)
* Personal check in the exact amount of duty, drawn on a national or state bank or trust company of the United States, made payable to the "U.S. Customs Service."
* Government check, money orders or traveler's checks are acceptable if they do not exceed the amount of the duty by more than $50. [Second endorsements are not acceptable. Identification must be presented; e.g. traveler's passport or social security card.]

Know Before You Go

Rates of Duty

Various rates of duty for some of the more popular items imported by tourists are provided for use as an advisory guide only. If you have dutiable articles not subject to a flat rate of duty, the customs officer examining your baggage will determine the rates of duty.

Rates of duty on imported goods are provided for in the Tariff Schedules of the United States. These are two duty rates for each item, known as "column 1" and "column 2." Column 1 rates are those afforded most favored nations, while column 2 rates are much higher, sometimes as high as 90%, and apply to products from the following Communist countries, with the exception of Romania, Yugoslavia, Poland, and Hungary.

Albania, Bulgaria, China (any part of which may be under Communist domination or control), Czechoslovakia, Estonia, Germany (the Soviet zone and the Soviet sector of Berlin), Indochina (any part of Cambodia*, Laos, or Vietnam* which may be under Communist domination or control), Korea* (any part of which may be under Communist domination or control), Kurile Islands, Latvia, Lithuania, Outer Mongolia, Southern Sakhalin, Tanna Tuva, Tibet, Union of Soviet Socialist Republics and the area in East Prussia under the provisional administration of the Union of Soviet Socialist Republics.

Products of the above countries are dutiable at the column 2 rates of duty shown in parenthesis in the listing that follows, even if purchased in or sent from another country. Example: A table cloth or cloisonne vase made in the Peoples Republic of China and purchased in Hong Kong would be dutiable at the column 2 rate. If the article accompanies you, however, it may be entered under your duty-free personal exemption or the flat rate of duty allowance.

*Goods from, or products of, these countries are subject to foreign assets controls, see page 22.

ALCOHOLIC BEVERAGES

	Int. Rev. Tax (per gal.*)	Customs Duty (per gal.*)	
Beer	$9 bbl (31 gal.)	6¢	(50¢)
Brandy	$10.50	50¢ to $5	($5.00)
Gin	$10.50	50¢	($5.00)
Liqueurs	$10.50	50¢	($5.00)
Rum	$10.50	$1.75	($5.00)
Vodka	$10.50	$1.25	($5.00)
Whisky*			
Scotch	$10.50	51¢	($5.00)
Irish	$10.50	51¢	($5.00)
Other	$10.50	62¢	($5.00)
Wine			
Sparkling	$2.40-$3.40	$1.17	($6.00)
Still	17¢-$2.25	31½¢-$1	($1.25)

*Per U.S. gallon (128 fluid ounces) if under 100 proof. Duty and tax are based on proof gallon if 100 proof or over.

Furnished by Arnold D Senterfitt

ANTIQUES produced prior to 100 years before the date of entry—Free (Free)
(Have proof of antiquity obtained from seller.)
AUTOMOBILES, passenger—3% (10%)

BAGS, hand, leather—8½ to 10% (35%)
BAMBOO, manufacturers of—12% (45%)
BEADS: Imitation precious and semi-precious stones—
   7 to 13% (40 to 75%)
   Ivory—10% (45%)
BINOCULARS, prism—20% (60%)
   Opera and field glasses—8½% (45%)
BOOKS, foreign author or foreign language—Free (Free)

CAMERAS:
   Motion picture, over $50 each—6% (20%)
   Still, over $10 each—7½% (20%)
   Cases, leather—8½ to 10% (35%)
   Lenses—12½% (45%)
CANDY:
   Sweetened chocolate bars—5% (40%)
   Other—7% (40%)
CHESS SETS—10% (50%)
CHINA:
   Bone—17½% (10¢ per dozen pcs. + 70%)
   Nonbone, other than tableware—22½% (70%)
CHINA TABLEWARE, nonbone, available in 77-piece sets.
   Valued not over $10 per set—10¢ doz. + 48% (10¢ doz. + 70%)
   Valued over $10 but not over $24 per set—10¢ doz. + 55% (10¢ doz. + 70%)
   Valued over $24 but not over $56 per set—10¢ doz. + 36% (10¢ doz. + 70%)
   Valued over $56 per set—5¢ doz. + 18% (10¢ doz. + 70%)
CIGARETTE LIGHTERS:
   Pocket, valued at over 42¢ each—22½% (110%)
   Table—12% (60%)
CLOCKS:
   Valued over $5 but not over $10 each—75¢ + 16% + 6¼¢ for each jewel ($3 each + 65% + 25¢ for each jewel)
   Valued over $10 each—$1.12 each + 16% + 6¼¢ for each jewel ($4.50 each + 65% + 25¢ for each jewel)
CORK, manufactures of—18% (45%)

DOLLS AND PARTS—17½% (70%)
DRAWINGS (works of art), done entirely by hand—Free (Free)

EARTHENWARE TABLEWARE, available in 77-piece sets
   Valued not over $3.30 per set—5¢ doz. + 14% (10¢ doz. + 50%)
   Valued over $3.30 but not over $12 per set—10¢ doz. + 21% (10¢ doz. + 50%)
   Valued over $12 per set—5¢ doz. + 10½% (10¢ doz. + 50%)

FIGURINES, china—12½ to 22½% (70%)
FILM, imported, not qualifying for free entry is dutiable as follows:
   Exposed motion-picture film in any form on which pictures or sound and pictures have been recorded, developed or not developed, is dutiable at 48/100ths of a cent per linear foot. (3¢ per linear foot)
   Other exposed or exposed and developed film would be classifiable as photographs, dutiable at 4% of their value. (25%)

Know Before You Go

FLOWERS, artificial, plastic—21% (60%)
FRUIT, prepared—35% or under (40% or under)
FUR:
 Wearing apparel—8½ to 18½% (35 to 50%)
 Other manufactures of—8½ to 18½% (50%)
FURNITURE:
 Wood, chairs—8½% (40%)
 Wood, other than chairs—5% (40%)

GLASS TABLEWARE valued not over $1 each—20 to 50% (60%)
GLOVES:
 Not lace or net, plain vegetable fibers, woven—25% (25%)
 Wool, over $4 per dozen—37½¢ lb. + 18½% (50¢ lb. + 50%)
 Fur—10% (50%)
 Horsehide or cowhide—15% (25%)
GOLF BALLS—6% (30%)

HANDKERCHIEFS:
 Cotton, ornamented—4¢ each + 40% (4¢ each + 40%)
 Cotton, plain—25% to 5¢ lb. + 35% (37% to 10¢ lb. + 67%)
 Linen, machine hemmed—9% (50%)

IRON, travel type, electric—5½% (35%)
IVORY, manufactures of—6% (35%)

JADE:
 Cut, but not set and suitable for use in the manufacture of jewelry—2½% (10%)
 Other articles of jade—21% (50%)
JEWELRY, precious metal or stone:
 Silver chief value, valued not over $18 per dozen—27½% (110%)
 Other—12% (80%)

LEATHER:
 Pocketbooks, bags—8½ to 10% (35%)
 Other manufactures of—4 to 14% (35%)

MAH-JONGG SETS—10% (50%)
MOTORCYCLES—5% (10%)
MUSHROOMS, dried—3.2¢ lb. + 10% (10¢ lb. + 45%)
MUSICAL INSTRUMENTS:
 Music boxes, wood—8% (40%)
 Woodwind, except bagpipes—7½% (40%)
 Bagpipes—Free (40%)

PAINTINGS done entirely by hand—Free (Free)
PAPER, manufactures of—8½% (35%)
PEARLS:
 Loose or temporarily strung and without clasp:
  Genuine—Free (10%)
  Cultured—2½% (10%)
  Imitation—20% (60%)
 Temporarily or permanently strung (with clasp attached or separate)—12 to 27½% (45 to 110%)
PERFUME—8¢ lb. + 7½% (40¢ lb. + 75%)
POSTAGE STAMPS—Free (Free)
PRINTED MATTER—2 to 7½% (25 to 45%)

RADIOS:
 Transistor—10.4% (35%)
 Other—6% (35%)
RATTAN:
 Furniture—16% (60%)
 Other manufactures of—12½% (45%)
RECORDS, phonograph—5% (30%)
RUBBER, natural, manufactures of—6% (35%)

Furnished by Arnold D Senterfitt

SHAVER, electric—6½% (35%)
SHELL, manufactures of—8½% (35%)
SHOES, leather—2½ to 20% (10 to 30%)
SKIS and SKI EQUIPMENT—8 to 9% (33.3 to 45%)
 Ski boots—Free to 20% (Free to 35%)
STEREO EQUIPMENT
 depending on components—5 to 10.4% (35%)
STONES, CUT BUT NOT SET:
 Diamonds not over one-half carat—4% (10%)
 Diamonds over one-half carat—5% (10%)
 Other—Free to 5% (10 to 20%)
SWEATERS, of wool, over $5 per lb.—37½¢ lb. + 20% (50¢ lb. + 50%)

TABLEWARE AND FLATWARE:
 Knives, forks, flatware
  Silver—4¢ each + 8½% (16¢ each + 45%)
  Stainless steel—½ to 2¢ + 6 to 17½% (2 to 8¢ + 45%)
 Spoons, tableware
  Silver—12½% (65%)
  Stainless steel—17% (40%)
TAPE RECORDERS—5½ to 7½% (35%)
TOILET PREPARATIONS:
 Not containing alcohol—7½% (75%)
 Containing alcohol—8¢ lb. + 7½% (40¢ lb. + 75%)
TOYS—17½% (70%)
TRUFFLES—Free (Free)

VEGETABLES, prepared—17% (35%)

WATCHES, on $100 watch, duty varies from $6 to $13 ($24 to $52)
WEARING APPAREL:
 Embroidered or ornamented—21 to 42½% (45 to 90%)
 Not embroidered, not ornamented
  cotton, not knit—8 to 21% (37½ to 45%)
  cotton, knit—21% (45%)
  linen, not knit—7½% (35%)
  manmade fiber, knit—25¢ lb. + 32½% (45¢ lb. + 65%)
  manmade fiber, not knit—25¢ lb. + 27½% (45¢ lb. + 65%)
  silk, knit—10% (60%)
  silk, not knit—16% (65%)
  wool, knit—37½¢ lb. + 15½ to 32% (50¢ lb. + 50%)
  wool, not knit—25 to 37½¢ lb. + 21% (33 to 50¢ lb. + 45 to 50%)
WOOD:
 Carvings—8% (33.3%)
 Manufactures of—8% (33.3%)

prohibited and restricted articles

Because customs inspectors are stationed at ports of entry and along our land and sea borders, they are often called upon to enforce laws and requirements of other Government agencies. For example, the Department of Agriculture is responsible for preventing the entry of injurious pest, plant, and animal diseases into the United States. The customs officer

Know Before You Go 99

cannot ignore the Agriculture requirements—the risk of costly damage to our crops, poultry and livestock industry is too great.

Certain articles considered injurious or detrimental to the general welfare of the United States are prohibited entry by law. Among these are *absinthe, liquor-filled candy, lottery tickets, narcotics and dangerous drugs, obscene articles and publications, seditious and treasonable materials, hazardous articles (e.g., fireworks, dangerous toys, toxic or poisonous substances), products made by convicts or forced labor, and switchblade knives.*

Other items must meet special requirements before they can be released. You will be given a receipt for any articles retained by Customs.

Automobiles

Imported motor vehicles are subject to safety standards under the Motor Vehicle Safety Act of 1965 and air pollution control standards under the Clean Air Act of 1968.

A prospective purchaser should know that most vehicles manufactured abroad in conformity with U.S. standards are exported for sale in the U.S. It is highly unlikely that a vehicle obtained abroad meets U.S. emission and safety standards. Claims by a dealer or other seller that a vehicle meets such standards—or can be readily brought into compliance—can be accepted only at a great risk. Noncomplying vehicles must be brought into compliance, exported, or destroyed.

It is strongly recommended that before you purchase a vehicle abroad, you contact the Environmental Protection Agency, Washington, D.C. 20406, and the Department of Transportation, Washington, D.C. 20590, to determine admissibility of the vehicle. Also obtain a copy of our leaflet *Importing a Car.*

Biological Materials

Biological materials of public health or veterinary importance (disease organisms and vectors for research and educational purposes) require import permits. Write to the Foreign Quarantine Program, U.S. Public Health Service, Center for Disease Control, Atlanta, Ga. 30333.

Books

"Piratical" copies of copyrighted books—those produced without the authorization of the copyright owner—are prohibited, such as unauthorized photo-offset copies of American bestsellers and expensive textbooks produced and sold in the Far East for a fraction of what their cost would be if produced in the U.S.

Cultural Property

An export certificate may be required by certain Latin American countries in order to import pre-Columbian monumental and architectural sculpture or murals, whether they are shipped directly or indirectly from the country of origin into the U.S.

Firearms and Ammunition

Firearms and ammunition are subject to restrictions and import permits approved by the Bureau of Alcohol, Tobacco and Firearms (ATF). Applications to import may be made only by or through a licensed importer, dealer, or manufacturer. Weapons, ammunition, or other devices prohibited by the National Firearms Act will not be admitted into the United States unless by specific authorization of ATF.

No import permit is required when it is proven that the firearms or ammunition were previously taken out of the United States by the person who is returning with such firearms or ammunition. To facilitate *reentry*, persons may have them registered before departing from the U.S. at any Customs office or ATF field office. However, not more than three nonautomatic firearms and 1,000 cartridges therefor, will be registered for any one person. Quantities in excess of those indicated are subject to the export licensing requirements of the Office of Munitions Control, Department of State, Washington, D.C. 20520.

For further information, contact the Bureau of Alcohol, Tobacco and Firearms, Department of the Treasury, Washington, D.C. 20226.

Residents of the U.S. carrying firearms or ammunition with them to other countries should consult in advance the customs officials or the respective embassies of those countries as to their regulations.

Food Products

Bakery items and all cured cheeses are admissible. The USDA Animal and Plant Health Inspection Service leaflet, *Travelers' Tips,* provides detailed information on bringing food, plant, and animal products into the U.S.

Fruits, Vegetables, Plants

Fruits, vegetables, plants, cuttings, seeds, unprocessed plant products, and certain endangered plant species, are either prohibited from entering the country or require an import permit. Every single plant, plant product, fruit or vegetable must be declared to the customs officer and must be presented for inspection, no matter how free of pests it appears to be. Canned or processed items are admissible.

Applications for import permits or requests for information should be addressed to Quarantines, USDA-APHIS-PPQ, Federal Bldg., Hyattsville, Md. 20782.

Gold

Gold coins, medals, and bullion, formerly prohibited, may be brought into the U.S.; however, copies of gold coins are prohibited if not properly marked.

Meats, Livestock, Poultry

Meats, livestock, poultry, and their by-products (such as sausage, paté), are either prohibited or restricted from entering the United States, depending on the animal disease condition in country of origin. Fresh meat is generally prohibited from most countries. Canned meat is permitted if the inspector can determine that it is commercially canned, cooked in the container, hermetically sealed, and can be kept without refrigeration. Other canned, cured, or dried meat is severely restricted from most countries.

Furnished by Arnold D Senterfitt

All prohibited importations will be seized and destroyed unless the importer returns them immediately to their country of origin.

You should contact Quarantines, USDA-APHIS-PPQ, Federal Building, Hyattsville, Maryland 20782, for detailed requirements.

Merchandise

Merchandise originating in Rhodesia, North Korea, Vietnam, Cambodia, and Cuba (and all goods containing Cuban components) are prohibited from being imported without a Treasury license under regulations of the Office of Foreign Assets Control (FAC).

Under a general license issued by FAC, travelers visiting North Korea, Vietnam, Cambodia, or Cuba may purchase and bring into the United States $100 worth of articles (based on retail value). These articles must be for personal use, not for resale, and must accompany the traveler. The allowance may only be used once every 6 months.

Journalists, news and documentary film makers, and others who visit these countries for professional purposes, may acquire, without limit, films, magazines, books, and similar publications which are directly related to their professional activities and for their own use, not for resale. These items need not be accompanied and may be shipped to the U.S.

Articles from Rhodesia and articles which are products of these countries arriving from any other country are prohibited unless a license is obtained from FAC. Example: Cigars made of Cuban tobacco if imported from another country are prohibited without a license. These licenses are strictly controlled and for all practicable purposes may be considered unavailable to tourists.

Copies of FAC regulations, Cuban Assets Control Regulations, and Rhodesian Sanction Regulations may be obtained from the Office of Foreign Assets Control, Department of the Treasury, Washington, D.C. 20220.

Medicine/Narcotics

Narcotics and dangerous drugs are prohibited entry and there are severe penalties if imported. A traveler requiring medicines containing habit-forming drugs or narcotics (e.g., cough medicines, diuretics, heart drugs, tranquilizers, sleeping pills, depressants, stimulants, etc.) should:
- have all drugs, medicinals, and similar products properly identified;
- carry only such quantity as might normally be carried by an individual having some sort of health problem;
- have either a prescription or written statement from your personal physician that the medicinals are being used under a doctor's direction and are necessary for your physical well-being while traveling.

Money

Although there is no limitation in terms of total amount, if you transport or cause to be transported (including by mail or other means), more than $5,000 in monetary instruments on any occasion into or out of the United States, or if you receive more than that amount, you must file a report (Customs form 4790)

Furnished by Arnold D Senterfitt

with U.S. Customs. Ask a customs officer for the form at the time you arrive or depart with such amounts, or obtain the form from any Customs office. Monetary instruments include U.S. or foreign coin, currency, traveler's checks, money orders, and negotiable instruments or investment securities in bearer form.

Pets

There are controls, restrictions, and prohibitions on entry of animals, birds, turtles, wildlife, and endangered species. Cats and dogs must be free of evidence of diseases communicable to man. As a general rule, vaccination against rabies is not required for cats, but a vaccination is required for dogs. Two personally owned pet birds may be entered provided they were in the owner's possession for 90 days prior to entry. Animals and birds must be inspected by APHIS veterinarians, located only at certain ports, before they may enter the country. Monkeys or any non-human primates may not be imported. If you plan to take your pet abroad or import one on your return, obtain a copy of our leaflet *Pets, Wildlife, U.S. Customs*.

You should check with state, county and municipal authorities about any restrictions and prohibitions they may have before importing a pet.

Trademarked Articles

Foreign-made trademarked articles may be limited as to the quantity which may be brought into the United States if the registered trademark has been recorded by an American trademark owner with U.S. Customs.

The types of articles usually of interest to tourists are 1) lenses, cameras, binoculars, optical goods; 2) tape recorders, musical instruments; 3) jewelry, precious metalware; 4) perfumery; 5) watches, clocks.

Persons arriving in the U.S. with a trademarked article are allowed an exemption, usually one article of a type bearing a protected trademark. An exempted trademark article must accompany you and you can claim this exemption for the same type of article only once each 30 days. The article must be for your personal use and not for sale. If an exempted article is sold within 1 year following importation, the article or its value is subject to forfeiture.

If the trademark owner allows a quantity in excess of the aforementioned exemption for its particular trademarked article, the total of those trademarked articles authorized may be entered.

Consents for popular tourist articles are contained in our leaflet *Trademark Information for Travelers*.

Wildlife and Fish

Wildlife and fish are subject to certain import and export restrictions, prohibitions, permits or certificates, and quarantine requirements. This includes:
- wild birds, mammals including marine mammals, reptiles, crustaceans, fish, and mollusks;
- any part or product, such as skins, feathers, eggs; and
- products and articles manufactured from wildlife and fish.

If you contemplate purchasing articles made from wildlife, such as tortoise shell jewelry, leather goods,

Know Before You Go

articles made from whalebone, ivory, skins, or fur, please contact—before you go—the U.S. Fish and Wildlife Service, Department of the Interior, Washington, D.C. 20240. That agency also prescribes the limits on migratory game birds, prior to each hunting season.

If you plan to import fish or wildlife, or any product, article or part, check with Customs or Fish and Wildlife first, as only certain ports are designated to handle these entries. Additional information is contained in our leaflet *Pets, Wildlife, U.S. Customs.*

Federal regulations do not authorize the importation of any wildlife or fish into any state of the United States if the state's laws or regulations are more restrictive than any applicable Federal treatment. Wild mammals or birds, taken, killed, sold, possessed, or exported to the United States in violation of any foreign laws are not allowed entry into the United States.

customs pointers

Traveling Back and Forth Across Border

After you have crossed the United States boundary at one point and you swing back into the United States to travel to another point in the foreign country, you run the risk of losing your customs exemption unless you meet certain requirements. If you make a "swing back," don't risk your exemptions—ask the nearest customs officer about these requirements.

"Duty-Free" Shops

Articles bought in "duty-free" shops in foreign countries are subject to U.S. Customs exemptions and restrictions.

Articles purchased in U.S. "duty-free" shops are subject to U.S. Customs duty if reentered into the U.S. Example: Liquor bought in a "duty-free" shop before entering Canada and brought back into the United States will be subject to duty and internal revenue tax.

Keep Your Sales Slips

You will find your sales slips, invoices, or other evidence of purchase not only helpful when making out your declaration but necessary if you have unaccompanied articles being sent from the U.S Virgin Islands, American Samoa, or Guam.

Packing Your Baggage

Pack your baggage in a manner that will make inspection easy. Do your best to pack separately the articles you have acquired abroad. When the customs

Furnished by Arnold D Senterfitt

officer asks you to open your luggage or the trunk of your car, please do so without hesitation.

Photographic Film

All imported photographic films, which accompany a traveler, if not for commercial purpose, may be released without examination by Customs unless there is reason to believe they contain objectionable matter.

Films prohibited from entry are those that contain obscene matter, advocate treason or insurrection against the United States, advocate forcible resistance to any law of the United States, or those that threaten the life of or infliction of bodily harm upon any person in the United States.

Developed or undeveloped U.S. film exposed abroad (except motion-picture film to be used for commercial purposes) may enter free of duty and need not be included in your customs exemption.

Foreign film purchased abroad and prints made abroad are dutiable but may be included in your customs exemption.

Film manufactured in the United States and exposed abroad may be mailed home. Use the mailing device or prepaid mailer provided by the manufacturer or processing laboratory for this purpose. Mark the outside wrapper *"Undeveloped photographic film of U.S. manufacture—Examine with care."*

Delivery can be expedited if the package is addressed to your dealer or a processing laboratory for finishing. If the package is a prepaid processing mailer, no customs arrangements need be made. If not, arrange before you leave for the laboratory or dealer to accept and enter the film. If delivery is refused, the film must be sent to a warehouse and becomes subject to a storage fee.

Delivery can be expedited if the package is addressed to the manufacturer of the film. All customs requirements will be taken care of by the manufacturer who is well informed on customs procedures.

If none of the above suggestions can be used, address the package to yourself.

Shipping Hints

Merchandise acquired abroad may be sent home by you or by the store where purchased. As these items do not accompany you on your return, they cannot be included in your customs exemption, and are subject to duty when received in the U.S. Duty cannot be prepaid. There are, however, special procedures to follow for merchandise acquired in and sent from the U.S. Virgin Islands, American Samoa, or Guam. See page 29.

All incoming shipments must be cleared through U.S. Customs. Customs employees cannot, by law, perform entry tasks for the importing public, but they will advise and give information to importers about customs requirements.

Customs collects no fee except the customs duty (if any) as provided for in the tariff schedules. Any other charges paid on import shipments are for handling by freight forwarders, commercial brokers, or for other delivery services.

102 Know Before You Go

Note: Customhouse brokers are not U.S. Customs employees. Fees charged by the brokers are based on the amount of work done, not on the value of the personal effects or of the tourist purchase you shipped. The fee may seem excessive to you in relation to the value of the shipment. The National Customs Brokers & Forwarders Association is well aware of the difficulties and excessive expense incurred by tourists shipping items home. Their advice is "Ship the easy way—take it with you in your baggage or send it by parcel post prepaid."

Mail shipments (including parcel post) have proven to be more convenient and less costly for travelers. Parcels must meet the mail requirements of the exporting country as to weight, size, or measurement.

The U.S. Postal Service sends all incoming foreign mail shipments to Customs for examination. Packages free of customs duty are returned to the Postal Service for delivery to you by your home post office without additional postage, handling costs, or other fees.

For packages containing dutiable articles, the customs officer will attach a mail entry showing the amount of duty to be paid and return the parcel to the Postal Service. The duty and a postal handling fee will be collected when the package is delivered.

If you pay the duty on a package but feel that the duty was not correct, you may file a protest. This protest can be acted on only by the Customs office which issued the mail entry receipt—Customs form 3419—attached to your package. Send a copy of this form with your letter to the Customs office at the location and address shown on the left side of the form. That office will review the duty assessment based on the information furnished in your letter and, if appropriate, authorize a refund. If duty is refunded, the postal handling fee will also be refunded. If an adjustment is made with a partial refund of duty, the postal handling fee will not be refunded.

Another procedure would be not to accept the parcel. You would then have to provide, within 30 days, a written statement of your objections to the Postmaster where the parcel is being held. Your letter will be forwarded to the issuing Customs office. The shipment will be detained at the post office until a reply is received.

Express shipments may be sent to the United States from Canada and Mexico and by air freight from other countries. The express company or its representative, when properly licensed, usually acts as the customhouse broker for you and clears the merchandise through Customs. A fee is charged for this service.

Freight shipments, whether or not they are free of duty at the time of importation, must clear Customs at the first port of arrival into the United States, or, if you choose, the merchandise may be forwarded in customs custody (in bond) from the port of arrival to another customs port of entry for customs clearance.

All arrangements for customs clearance and forwarding in bond must be made by you or someone you designate to act for you. Frequently, a freight forwarder in a foreign country will handle all the necessary arrangements, including the clearance through Customs in the United States by a customhouse broker. A fee is charged for this service. This fee is not a Customs charge. If a foreign seller consigns a shipment to a broker or agent in the United States, the freight charge is usually paid only to the first port of arrival in the United States. This means there will be additional inland transportation or freight forwarding charges, brokers' fees, insurance, and other items.

An individual may also effect the customs clearance of a single noncommercial shipment for you if it is not possible for you to personally secure the release of the goods. You must authorize and empower the individual in writing to execute the customs declaration and the entry for you as your unpaid agent. The written authority provided to the individual should be addressed to the "Officer in Charge of Customs" at the port of entry.

Unaccompanied tourist purchases, acquired in, and sent directly from the U.S. Virgin Islands, American Samoa, or Guam, may be entered, if properly declared and processed, as follows:

- Up to $600 free of duty under your personal exemption. Remember, that if up to $300 of this amount was acquired elsewhere than in these islands, those articles must accompany you at the time of your return for duty-free entry under your personal exemption.
- An additional $600 worth of articles, dutiable at a flat 5% rate of duty.
- Any amount over the above, dutiable at various rates of duty.

The procedure outlined below must be followed:

Step 1. You will: a) list all articles acquired abroad on your baggage declaration (Customs form 6059B) except those sent under the $40 bona fide gift provision to friends and relatives in the U.S.; b) indicate which articles are unaccompanied; c) fill out a Declaration of Unaccompanied Articles (Customs form 255) for each package or container to be sent. This form may be obtained when you clear Customs if it was not available where you made your purchase.

Step 2. Customs at the time of your return will: a) collect duty and tax if owed on goods accompanying you; b) verify your unaccompanied articles against sales slips, invoices, etc.; c) validate form 255 as to whether goods are free of duty under your personal exemption or subject to a flat rate of duty. Two copies of the 3-part form will be returned to you.

Step 3. You will return the yellow copy of the form to the shopkeeper (or vendor) holding your purchase and keep the other copy for your records. You are responsible for advising the shopkeeper at the time you make your purchase that your package is not to be sent until this form is received.

Step 4. The shopkeeper will place the form in an envelope and attach the envelope securely to the outside of the package or container, which must be clearly marked *"Unaccompanied Tourist Purchase."* This is the most important step to be followed in order for you to receive the benefits allowed under this procedure.

Furnished by Arnold D Senterfitt

Know Before You Go   103

Step 5. The Postal Service will deliver the package, if sent by mail, to you after Customs clearance. Any duty owed will be collected by the Postal Service plus a postal handling fee; or

You will be notified by the carrier as to the arrival of your shipment at which time you will go to the Customs office processing your shipment and make entry. Any duty or tax owed will be paid at that time. You may employ a customhouse broker to do this for you. A fee will be charged by the broker.

Storage charges. Freight and express packages delivered before you return (without prior arrangements for acceptance) will be placed in storage by Customs after 5 days, at the expense and risk of the owner. If not claimed within one year, the items will be sold.

Mail parcels not claimed within 30 days will be returned to the sender unless a duty assessment is being protested.

Every effort has been made to indicate essential requirements; however, all regulations of Customs and other agencies cannot be covered in full.

Customs offices will be glad to advise you of any changes in regulations which may have occurred since publication of this leaflet.

District Directors of Customs are located in the following cities:

Anchorage, Alaska 99501	907/279-2543
Baltimore, Md. 21202	301/962-2666
Boston, Mass. 02109	617/223-6598
Bridgeport, Conn. 06609	203/366-7851
Buffalo, N.Y. 14202	716/842-5901
Charleston, S.C. 29402	803/724-4312
Chicago, Ill. 60607	312/353-6100
Cleveland, Ohio 44114	216/522-4284
Detroit, Mich. 48226	313/226-3177
Duluth, Minn. 55802	218/727-6692
El Paso, Tex. 79985	915/533-7454
Galveston, Tex. 77550	713/763-1211
Great Falls, Mont. 59401	406/453-7631
Honolulu, Hawaii 96806	808/546-3115
Houston, Tex. 77052	713/226-4316
Laredo, Tex. 78040	512/723-2956
Los Angeles, Calif. (see San Pedro)	
Miami, Fla. 33131	305/350-4806
Milwaukee, Wis. 53202	414/224-3924
Minneapolis, Minn. 55401	612/725-2317
Mobile, Ala. 36602	205/690-2106
New Orleans, La. 70130	504/589-6353
*New York, N.Y. 10048	212/466-5550
Nogales, Ariz. 85621	602/287-4955
Norfolk, Va. 23510	804/441-6546
Ogdensburg, N.Y. 13669	315/393-0660
Pembina, N.D. 58271	701/825-6201
Philadelphia, Pa. 19106	215/597-4605
Port Arthur, Tex. 77640	713/982-2831
Portland, Maine 04111	207/775-3131
Portland, Oreg. 97209	503/221-2865
Providence, R.I. 02903	401/528-4383
St. Albans, Vt. 05478	802/524-6527
St. Louis, Mo. 63105	314/425-3134
St. Thomas, V.I. 00801	809/774-2530
San Diego, Calif. 92188	714/293-5360
San Francisco, Calif. 94126	415/556-4340
San Juan, P.R. 00903	809/723-2091
San Pedro, Calif. 90731	213/548-2461
Savannah, Ga. 31401	912/232-4321
Seattle, Wash. 98174	206/442-5491
Tampa, Fla. 33602	813/228-2381
Washington, D.C. 20018	202/566-8511
Wilmington, N.C. 28401	919/763-9971

*Write to Regional Commissioner of Customs.

Should you need Customs assistance while abroad, you can visit or telephone our representatives located at the American Embassy or consultate in . . .
  London / 499-1212
  Paris / 265-7400, ext. 8241 or 48
  Rome / 4674, ext. 475 or 533
  Bonn / 8955, ext. 3207 or 331-435
  Tokyo / 583-7141, ext. 7205
  Hong Kong / 239-011, ext. 243-4
  Mexico City / 553-3333, ext. 687
  Montreal / 514-281-1456
or our preclearance operations in . . .
  Montreal / 514-636-3875
  Toronto / 416-676-2606
  Winnipeg / 204-774-5391
  Calgary / 403-276-0693
  Vancouver / 604-278-1825
  Bermuda / 809-293-0353
  Nassau / 809-327-7126
  Freeport / 809-352-7256

Frequently, we are asked questions which are not Customs matters. If you want to know about . . .

Passports. Contact the Passport Field Agency nearest you. Field agencies are located in Boston, 02203; Chicago, 60604; Detroit, 48226; Honolulu, 96850; Los Angeles, 90261; Miami, 33130; New Orleans, 70130; New York, 10021; Philadelphia, 19106; San Francisco, 94102; Seattle, 98174; and Washington, D.C. 20524. Some Clerks of Court and Postal Clerks also issue passports.

Visas (if required). Get in touch with the appropriate Embassy in Washington, D.C., or nearest consular office.

Inoculations. Contact your local or state health department.

Baggage allowance. Ask the airline or steamship line you are traveling on about this.

Currency of other nations. Your local bank can be of assistance.

Foreign countries. For information about the country you will visit or about what articles may be taken into that country, contact the appropriate Embassy, consular office or tourist information office.

One last word, should you have any complaints, write the Special Assistant to the Commissioner for Public Affairs, U.S. Customs, Washington, D.C. 20229, or call 202-566-2475.

DEPARTMENT OF THE TREASURY
U.S. CUSTOMS SERVICE
Washington, D.C. 20229
1978
Customs Information Series T:78-1

☆ U. S. GOVERNMENT PRINTING OFFICE : 1979 O - 282-785

Furnished by Arnold D Senterfitt

Dictionary

$ or $E hotel rate of $30-$35 US dollars per couple per night, room only.
$A $30-$35 hotel rate per couple per night including meals, i.e. American Plan. $$ = $60-$70, $$$ = $90-$110, etc.
Adjacent immediately adjoining
Apch or Approach normally operating approach control services.
Elev or Elevation height of surface above mean sea level
B'cast Commercial broadcast station operating at least during daylight hours.
BYO this item or service not normally available, it is therefore suggested that you Bring Your Own.
Cards type of credit cards accepted for goods or service mentioned.
Cash-Yes will accept both US dollars and the local currency.
Central in the middle or principle part of the town or city.
City Ident three or four letter identification for that place. If none is already assigned the author will assign one and denote it with a following minus sign: ABC is country-assigned, ABC- was assigned by the author pending an official designation.
Dash - this item not normally available.
Dme computed distance not to exceed 100 from a normally operational Distance Measuring Equipment facility. For distances over 100 see n.mi.
Fuel aviation grade fuel normally available, either 80(80/87), 100(100/130), or JP(Jet Fuel).
GMT Greenwich Mean Time, also called Universal Time, Zulu time, etc. World-wide reference time of day at zero degrees longitude.
ICAO International Civil Aircraft Organisation, the world standard maintaining group.
Internacional Latin American Airport of Entry (AOE) and departure. One of these must be must be site of your first and last landing in that country.
International US Airport of Entry. Must be site of your first landing in US; no requirement for a stop on departure from the U.S. except for ex-military aircraft subject to embargoes, etc.
JN US Air Force Jet Navigation chart, scale approximately 28 nautical miles per inch.
Major (credit card) large US oil company credit cards accepted.
Major (repairs) comprehensive aircraft repair includes capability for wing or fuselage rebuild.
MC Mastercard will be accepted for goods or services listed.
Minor (repairs) maintainance limited to tire changing and correction of obvious missing screws, etc.
Ndb Non directionally radiating radio beacon suitable for use with an ADF.
Repairs as listed will vary between 'minor' for tire changing, etc, to 'major' for airframe rebuild. 'Yes' indicates somewhere between.
Sectional chart whose scale is about 7 nautical miles per inch.
tca tower controlled area as whose horizontal dimensions and vertical height are as listed. Radio call on passing nominally required for aircraft inside the tca limits.
TCA Approach control facility which covers a 50 mile radius by 20,000' high Control Area. Radio call on passing nominally required during hours of operation for aircraft within the TCA.
US Time either EST or CST or MST or PST. Note West Coast PDT = MST, used from late April to late October.
Visa credit card accepted for good or services listed.
Vor VHF Omnirange station.
VorDme Vor with normally operating Distance Measuring Equipment.
WAC World Aeronautical Chart, scale about 14 nautical miles per inch.
Yes (repairs) Available at some level between tirechanging and major overhaul; I haven't yet found out exactly what level applies.

Sample Airport 105

JET CHART	WAC	SECTIONAL	LATITUDE	LONGITUDE	US TIME	FOR GMT ADD	ICAO IDENT	TOWN IDENT
JN-46	CH-22 No. ✱ ADS-15	TPC H-22B	30°44'	112°10'	MST	7	-	CAB

OTHER COMM Traffic 122.75   *see page 93
CITY 1 mile E   POPULATION 31,000
FROM Hermosillo   FREQ 112.8 TRACK 318°,115 n.mi.
FROM Nogales   FREQ 108.2 TRACK 227°,81Dme
FROM Punta Peñaso FREQ 112.8 TRACK 105°,79Dme
FUEL sometimes   CARDS -   CASH? Pesos
REPAIRS Minor   TIEDOWN BYO

HOTEL	RATE	WHERE	TEL
Motel el Camino	$	Central	2-04-66

This town airport gets a slight amount of use from dusters, fumigators in Spanish, who do not have their own airports. It is nearest to the city so you tend to come here first, but the Manjarés Airport has more dependable fuel and no cars on the runway.

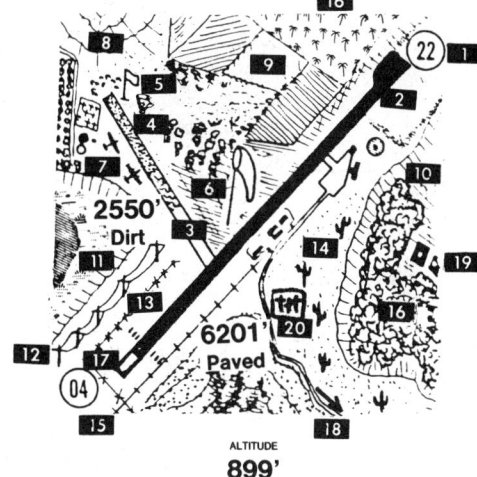

2550' Dirt
6201' Paved
ALTITUDE 899'

1. Runway designator: magnetic heading to the nearest ten degrees; i.e. 04 indicates runway heading between 035 and 044 degrees magnetic.
2. Paved surface
3. Dirt or sod
4. Gravel surface
5. Wind indicator, not windsock
6. Windsock
7. Parking area noted either by airplane symbols, or by the words 'Park' or 'Parking'
8. Contours of a hill
9. Tilled land
10. Dropoff, may also be noted in feet of elevation difference
11. Marsh or mushy area, chancy even for walking
12. telephone, power, or telegraph line on poles
13. Barbed wire fence
14. Cardon cactus, similar to Arizona's sahuaro
15. Single set of railroad tracks
16. Trees or jungle
17. Runway ends; on the photograph arrows are often added if the runway is at all obscure.
18. Skinny arrow points to the settlement if either not obvious or where there is a choice.
19. Buildings
20. Campo santo, or cemetary (see note on page titled Latin America Is..)

Name* = Not yet complete, see PREPS
MROC   ICAO (International) identifier

BLX   'Official national identifier

HOT-   minus sign indicates author's assigned an identifier for his file purposes where no others were known

✱ One of some 300 airports to be shown on the upcoming 15th Edition of Arnold Senterfitt's WAC scale "Complete Chart of Baja California and Northwest Mexico"

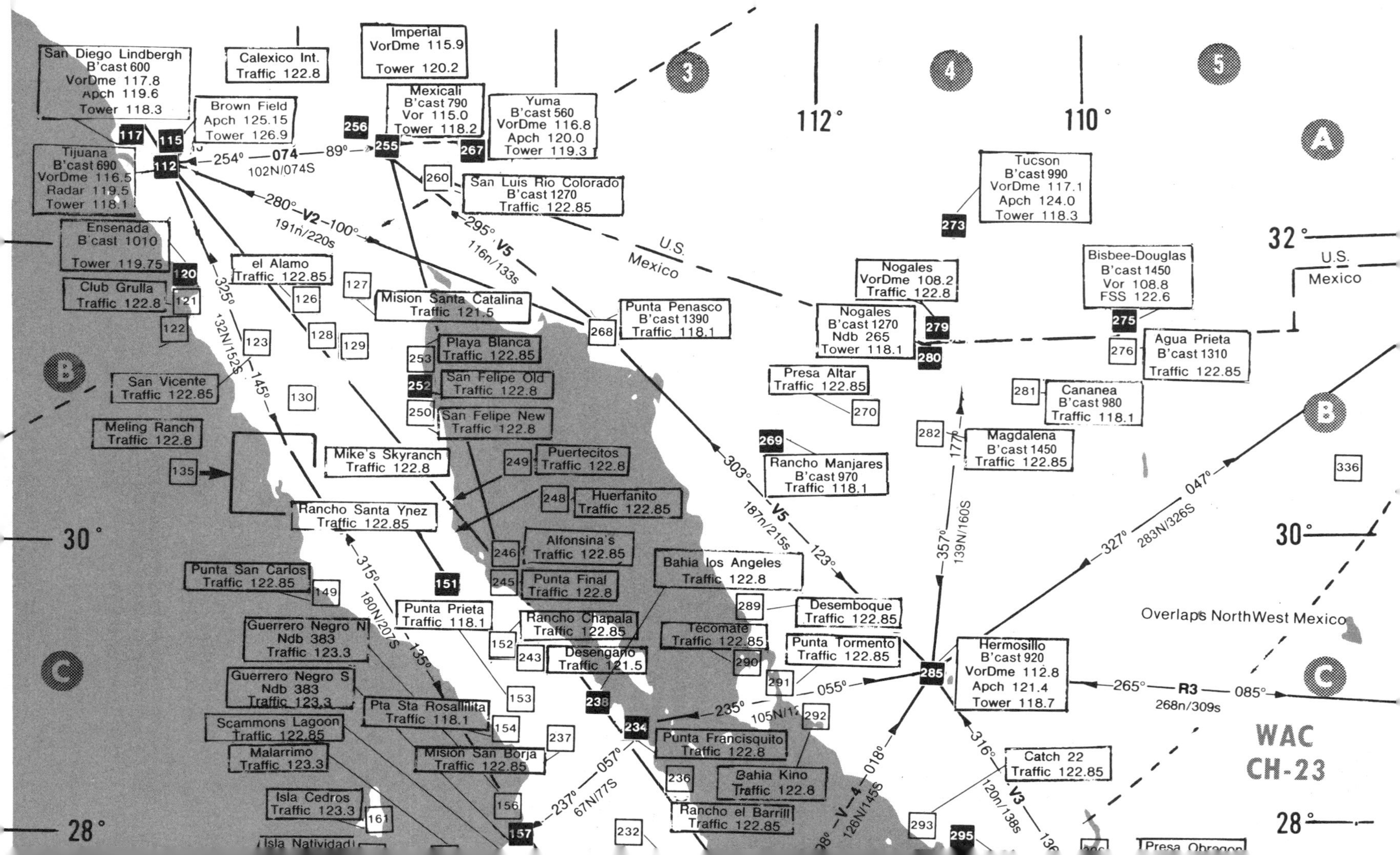

San Diego Lindbergh B'cast 600 VorDme 117.8 Apch 119.6 Tower 118.3
Calexico Int. Traffic 122.8
Imperial VorDme 115.9 Tower 120.2
Brown Field Apch 125.15 Tower 126.9
Mexicali B'cast 790 Vor 115.0 Tower 118.2
Yuma B'cast 560 VorDme 116.8 Apch 120.0 Tower 119.3
Tijuana B'cast 690 VorDme 116.5 Radar 119.5 Tower 118.1
San Luis Rio Colorado B'cast 1270 Traffic 122.85
Tucson B'cast 990 VorDme 117.1 Apch 124.0 Tower 118.3
Ensenada B'cast 1010 Tower 119.75
el Alamo Traffic 122.85
Club Grulla Traffic 122.8
Mision Santa Catalina Traffic 121.5
Punta Penasco B'cast 1390 Traffic 118.1
Nogales VorDme 108.2 Traffic 122.8
Nogales B'cast 1270 Ndb 265 Tower 118.1
Bisbee-Douglas B'cast 1450 Vor 108.8 FSS 122.6
Agua Prieta B'cast 1310 Traffic 122.85
San Vicente Traffic 122.85
Playa Blanca Traffic 122.85
San Felipe Old Traffic 122.8
San Felipe New Traffic 122.8
Presa Altar Traffic 122.85
Cananea B'cast 980 Traffic 118.1
Meling Ranch Traffic 122.8
Magdalena B'cast 1450 Traffic 122.85
Mike's Skyranch Traffic 122.8
Puertecitos Traffic 122.8
Rancho Manjares B'cast 970 Traffic 118.1
Huerfanito Traffic 122.85
Rancho Santa Ynez Traffic 122.85
Alfonsina's Traffic 122.85
Bahia los Angeles Traffic 122.8
Punta San Carlos Traffic 122.85
Punta Final Traffic 122.8
Desemboque Traffic 122.85
Punta Prieta Traffic 118.1
Rancho Chapala Traffic 122.85
Tecomate Traffic 122.85
Punta Tormento Traffic 122.85
Guerrero Negro N Ndb 383 Traffic 123.3
Desengaño Traffic 121.5
Hermosillo B'cast 920 VorDme 112.8 Apch 121.4 Tower 118.7
Guerrero Negro S Ndb 383 Traffic 123.3
Pta Sta Rosalllita Traffic 118.1
Scammons Lagoon Traffic 122.85
Punta Francisquito Traffic 122.8
Malarrimo Traffic 123.3
Mision San Borja Traffic 122.85
Bahia Kino Traffic 122.8
Catch 22 Traffic 122.85
Isla Cedros Traffic 123.3
Rancho el Barrill Traffic 122.85
Isla Natividad
Presa Obregon
Overlaps NorthWest Mexico
WAC CH-23
U.S. Mexico
U.S. Mexico
112°
110°
32°
30°
30°
28°
28°
3
4
5
A
B
B
C
C
254° —074— 89°
102N/074S
280°—V2—100°
191n/220s
295° V5
116n/133s
325°
132N/152S
145°
315°
180N/207S
135°
303°
V5
187n/215s
123°
177°
357°
139N/160S
047°
327°
283N/326S
265° R3 085°
268n/309s
055°
235°
105N/1
018°
V 4
126N/145S
057°
237°
67N/77S
316°
V3
120n/138s
136
117 115 112 256 255 267 260 273 120 121 122 123 126 127 128 129 130 135 268 279 280 275 276 253 252 250 270 281 282 269 336 249 248 246 245 151 149 289 152 243 290 291 285 153 238 234 292 154 237 236 156 157 161 232 293 295

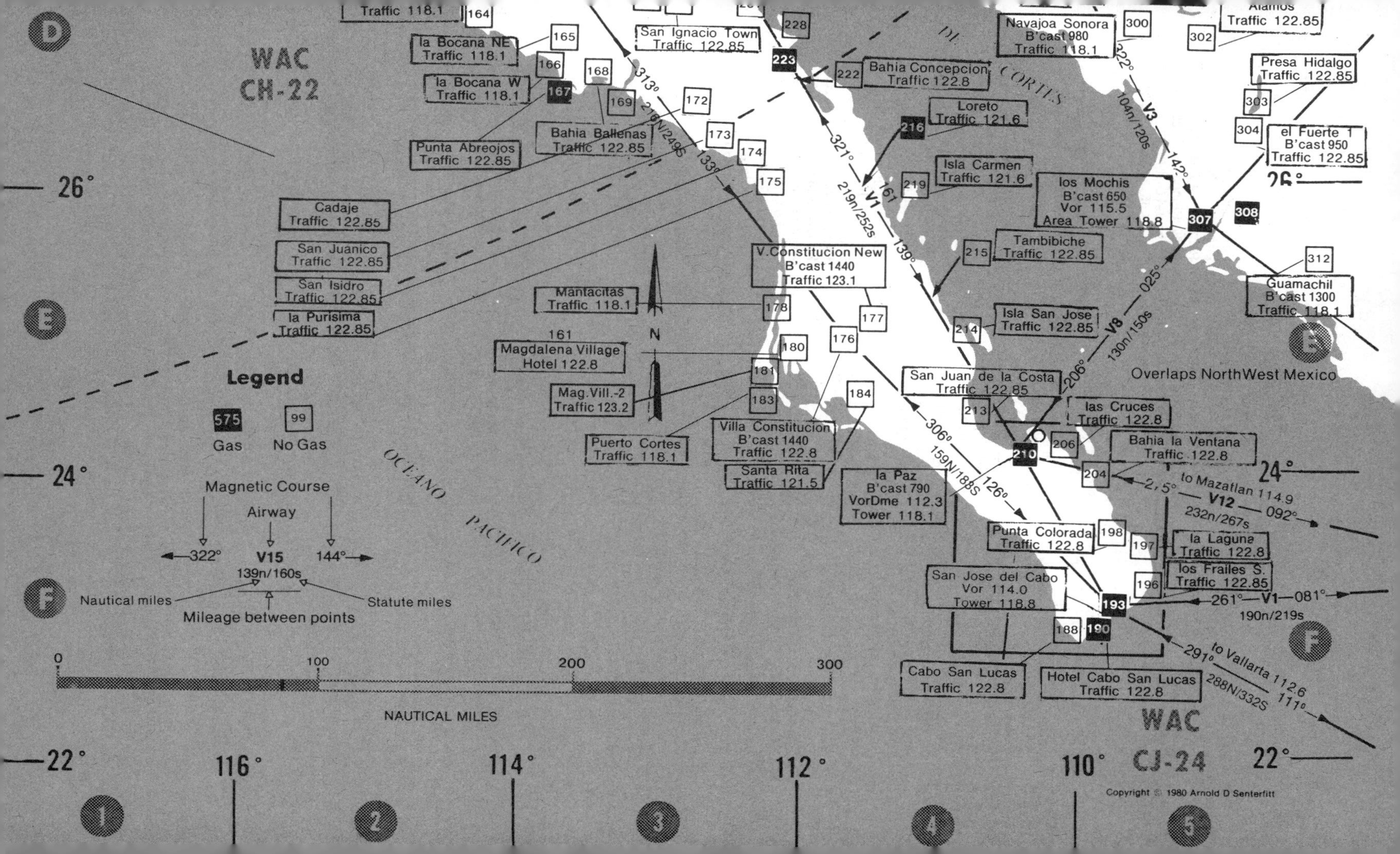

WAC CH-22
WAC CJ-24
Traffic 118.1
164
San Ignacio Town Traffic 122.85
228
223
Navajoa Sonora B'cast 980 Traffic 118.1
300
Alamos Traffic 122.85
302
la Bocana NE Traffic 118.1
165
166
la Bocana W Traffic 118.1
167
168
169
Punta Abreojos Traffic 122.85
Bahia Ballenas Traffic 122.85
172
173
174
175
313°
218N/249S
133°
Bahia Concepcion Traffic 122.8
222
CORTES
Presa Hidalgo Traffic 122.85
303
304
el Fuerte 1 B'cast 950 Traffic 122.85
322°
V3
104n/120s
142°
Loreto Traffic 121.6
216
321°
161
V1
219n/252s
139°
Isla Carmen Traffic 121.6
219
los Mochis B'cast 650 Vor 115.5 Area Tower 118.8
307
308
Cadaje Traffic 122.85
San Juanico Traffic 122.85
San Isidro Traffic 122.85
la Purisima Traffic 122.85
V.Constitucion New B'cast 1440 Traffic 123.1
Tambibiche Traffic 122.85
215
312
Guamachil B'cast 1300 Traffic 118.1
Mantacitas Traffic 118.1
178
177
176
Isla San Jose Traffic 122.85
214
025°
V8
130n/150s
206°
N
161
Magdalena Village Hotel 122.8
180
181
183
184
Mag.Vill.-2 Traffic 123.2
San Juan de la Costa Traffic 122.85
213
Overlaps NorthWest Mexico
Legend
575 Gas
99 No Gas
Puerto Cortes Traffic 118.1
Villa Constitucion B'cast 1440 Traffic 122.8
Santa Rita Traffic 121.5
306°
159N/188S
126°
las Cruces Traffic 122.8
206
210
Bahia la Ventana Traffic 122.8
204
OCEANO PACIFICO
la Paz B'cast 790 VorDme 112.3 Tower 118.1
2,5°
to Mazatlan 114.9
V12
092°
232n/267s
Magnetic Course
Airway
322°
V15
144°
139n/160s
Nautical miles
Statute miles
Mileage between points
Punta Colorada Traffic 122.8
198
197
la Laguna Traffic 122.8
los Frailes S. Traffic 122.85
196
San Jose del Cabo Vor 114.0 Tower 118.8
193
261°
V1
081°
190n/219s
188
190
Cabo San Lucas Traffic 122.8
Hotel Cabo San Lucas Traffic 122.8
291°
to Vallarta 112.6
111°
288N/332S
0
100
200
300
NAUTICAL MILES
D
E
F
26°
24°
22°
116°
114°
112°
110°
1
2
3
4
5
Copyright © 1980 Arnold D Senterfitt

108 Baja California Index

Sequence: Place, Ident, Page

Abreojos,Punta,PAB,167
Alfonsina's,ALF-,246
Asuncion,Bahia,BSU,164

B los Angeles-Munoz,BLX4-,239
BLX-Diaz,BLX2-,240
Bad Picture,261
Bahia Asuncion,BSU,164
Bahia Ballenas,BBS-,168
Bahia Ballenas Map,BBS-,169
Bahia Chileno,HCB-,190
Bahia Concepcion,MLG5-,222
Bahia Magdalena,MAG-,182
Bahia Tortugas,BTO,163
Bahia la Ventana,VNT-,204
Bahia los Angeles New,BLX1-,242
Bahia los Angeles-SE,BLX3-,238
Bahia's Hotels,241
Baja Calif Index,108
Baja Calif. Area,106
Baja Calif. Briefing,109
Baja Cfa Shipwrecks,179
Baja Mar,HGL-,119
Baptist Mission,BPT-,136
Black Warrior Map,GNO,155
Briefing-Malarrimo,MMO-,160
Brown Field Int'l,SDM,113
Brown IFR,SDM,112

Cabo San Lucas,CSL,188
Cabo San Lucas detail,CBO-,187
Cadaje,CJE-,172
Cadena,DNA-,249B
Calentura,HOT-,125
Calexico International,CXL,256
Calmalli,CAI,233
Castel Resort Hotel,SFE,251
Cielito Lindo,MTA-,142
Club Grulla,GRU-,121
Colnett West,CNT-,133
Colnett-East,CNT-,132
Coloradito,DTO-,249A
Concepcion,Bahia,MLG5-,222

Desengano,DNO-,243
Dictionary,104

El Alamo,LAM-,126
El Arco,LRC-,232
El Huerfanito,HFO-,248
El Marmol,MRM-,150
El Rosario East,ERO,146
El Rosario West,ERO,147
El Tule,HCB-,190
Ensenada,ENS,120

Francisquito,FQT-,234
Fulano's Restaurant,FOOD,209

Guadalupe New,TCT,118
Guadalupe Old,LIF,117
Guerrero Negro Map,155
Guerrero Negro So.,GNO,157
Guerrero Negro-N,GNO,156

Hamilton Ranch,HAM-,134
Hortaliza,HRT-,131

Hotel Baja Mar,BJM-,189
Hotel Borrego de Oro,PCH,228
Hotel Cabo San Lucas,HCB-,190
Hotel Castel,251
Hotel De Anza,257
Hotel Francisquito,FQT-,235
Hotel Palmilla,PMA-,191
Hotel Punta Pescadero,PES-,203
Hotel Serenidad,SRD-,223
Hotel las Arenas,205

Imperial IFR,IPL,258
Imperial VFR,IPL,259
Isla Carmen,ICM,219
Isla Cedros,ICD,161
Isla Natividad,TVD-,162
Isla San Jose,ISJ,214

La Bocana,BCN1-,165
La Bocana,BCN2-,166
La Paz IFR,LAP,210
La Paz Int'l,LAP,211
La Paz Military,LAP,212
La Purisima,PUR,175
La Ventana,ABU-,197
Laguna San Ignacio,LSG-,169
Lands End,CBO-,187
Las Cruces,RAC,206
Las Palmas,BHP,201
Lindbergh IFR,LIF,114
Lindbergh Int'l,LIF,115
Llano Colorado,LLN-,124
Loreto IFR,LTO,216
Loreto Int'l,LTO,217
Loreto Map,LTO,218
Los Frailes South,FRY-,196

Magdalena Village 1,MVG1-,180
Magdalena Village 2,MVG2-,181
Malarrimo,MAL-,159
Malarrimo Briefing,160
Map-Black Warrior,GNO,155
Map: Bahia Ballenas,BBS-,169
Map: Loreto Area,LTO,218
Map: Mulege,MLG,225
Map:Laguna San Ignacio,LSG-,169
Matancitas,MTB,178
Meling Ranch,MEL-,130
Mexicali IFR,MXL,254
Mexicali Int'l,MXL,255
Mike's Skyranch New,MSK-,129
Mina Volcanes,VOL-,141
Miraflores,MFL-,194
Mision San Borja,BRJ-,237
Mision Santa Catalina,CAT-,127
Mulege Map,225
Mulege Municipal,MLG,227
Mulege View,MLG,224
Mulege West,MLGW-,226

Natividad,Isla,TVD-,162

Ojo de Liebre,SCM-,158
Old Mill,MOL-,139

P.San Carlos Brief.,PSC-,148
Palmas de Cortes,BHP,201
Papa Fernandez',PPF-,247

Pedregal,EGA-,140
Pescadero,Pta.,PES,202
Pichilingue,PCH-,207
Playa Blanca,BCA-,253
Playa del Oro,PLO-,143
Pto.Adolfo Mateos,Jr,MTB,178
Puertecitos,PTO-,249
Puerto Cortes,PTC,183
Puerto Refugio,244
Puerto Santo Tomas,STO-,122
Punta Abreojos,PAB,167
Punta Chivato,PCH,228
Punta Colorada,PCL,198
Punta Final,PFL-,245
Punta Francisquito,FQT-,234
Punta Pescadero,PES,202
Punta Prieta,PRT-,153
Punta Pulpito,PUL-,221
Punta SanCarlos,PSC-,149
Punta Sta Rosallilita,RLL-,154

Rancho Buena Vista,BSA,200
Rancho Chapala,CHP-,152
Rancho Robertson,ROB-,144
Rancho Rosarito,RCO-,220
Rancho San Lucas,RSL-,229
Rancho Santa Ynez,YNZ-,151
Rancho Valladolid,VDO-,138
Rancho el Barril,BRL-,236
Rancho el Cipres,CIP,208
Rancho el Leonero,LEO-,199
Rancho el Socorro,SOC-,145

Sample Airport,104
San Felipe New,SFE,250
San Felipe Old,SFE,252
San Ignacio Downtown,SIB2-,171
San Ignacio West,SIB,170
San Ignacio,Laguna,LSG-,169
San Isidro,YSD-,174
San Jose IFR,SJD,192
San Jose del Cabo,SJD,193
San Juan de la Costa,JDC-,213
San Juanico,SCO,173
San Luis Rio Colorado,RIO-,260
San Pedrito,PED-,186
San Quintin Map,SQN,135
San Quintin Military,SQN,137
San Vicente,SVC-,123
Santa Rita,SRT-,184
Santa Rosalia,SRL,231
Santa Rosalia IFR,SRL,230
Santiago,STG,195
Scammons Lagoon,SCM-,158
Serenidad,Hotel,SRD-,223

Tambibiche,TBB-,215
Tecate,TCT,116
Tijuana IFR,TIJ,110
Tijuana Int'l,TIJ,111
Todos Santos,TST,185
Turtle Bay,BTO,163

V Constitucion New,VCT2-,177
V.Constitucion,VCT,176
Valle de Trinidad,VTR-,128

Baja California Briefing

Area includes: From the northwestern corner of Mexico. Southeastward 700 n.mi. to Cabo San Lucas

Best Known For: Sea of Cortes fishing, posh Cabo hotels.

But it Also Has: Snorkling at Loreto, shopping in Tijuana, giant gray whales at Scammons Lagoon, weekend gold panning at Meling.

Cities: Tijuana, Mexicali, San Felipe, Mulege, Loreto, La Paz, Cabo San Lucas.

Altitude: sealevel to Sierra San Pedro Martir's 10,156'.

Climate: North half similar to Southern California, bottom half ten degrees warmer

Weather of Note: High humidity hurricane season annually from August 1 to October 15

Special Feature: Baja California's south end is one full time zone east of its north end. If you are flying south the whole length in one day remember sunset will be an hour earlier at your destination.

Shopping Tips: Tijuana's million plus population seems to support lots and lots of storekeepers. Widest market place you can imagine, some of the items are made in the back or down the street. San Diegans buy wrought iron in fancy shapes, often redesigned on the spot, same per pound price whether intricate or just bars.

Primitive pottery shares a store with Hummel figurines while shoes made in Leon range in price and value about the same. For best imported buys hurry- Baja California's designation as a free trade zone is about to expire. When it does, there will be no more duty free stores in NW Mexico.

Liquors: if you like gin try the Oso Negro 80, naturally it is called 80 octane. If Beefeaters is your favorite Oso Negro ginebra 100 tastes exactly the same. Rum, called 'ron' in Spanish is in good supply thanks to the big sugar crops of Southern Mexico.

Familiar brand liquors such as scotches are available either plainly labelled as licensed to be produced in Mexico, or imported. There have been no recent reports of counterfeit or otherwise confusing labels. If you see Cutty Sark it is the real Cutty.

Remarks: It is easy to have fun in Baja California since there is so much variety. Wives whose husbands can't live without fishing have learned to go along, first being sure to specify Cabo San Lucas for the delightful hotels and imaginative boutiques. They find the sun shines through a liquid-feeling air that is impossible to imagine until you've tried it and returned a few times, not able to believe the first times.

For mid-peninsula fun try snorkling the undersea grottos off Isla Carmen's WNW side or a ride up to Mission San Javier. Sportsmen in the know are about the only ones who use Todos Santos' airport. They are heading up the sierra for some rare hunting. A few others go there in early summer for the panocha, or sugar, cooking.

If you have occasion to stop there, Navy people at Puerto Cortes are certainly hard workers with excellent morale. A brief courtesy call on the Commanding Officer is in order.

Ace-in-the-hole: In the event weather goes against you somewhere on the peninsula don't push it. There is at least daily bus service along the paved highway to the nearest airline-served city. If an appointment at home is really so important try leaving the driving to them.

TIJUANA, B.C.N.
VOR/DME PISTA 27

RADIO	TWR	118.1	ELEV. *499'*
131.2 y	APP	119.5 y 126.3	VAR.MAG 14° E
130.0	EMER	121.5	TIJ ·· ·· ·——

ENERO-30-1981/154

110

Caution — For Information Only — Not for Aerial Navigation

PRECAUCION: DESDE LA BASE "REAM" DE LOS EUA DESPEGAN AVIONES EN VUELO POR INSTRUMENTOS, AL SUR DE ELLA HAY UNA ZONA DONDE SE REALIZAN PRACTICAS DE TIRO AEREO CONTRA BLANCOS REMOLCADOS.

RESTRICCION
VELOCIDAD MAXIMA DE APROXIMACION (IAS) 160 KTS O MINIMA DE MANIOBRA DESDE D-15

DME TIJ 116.5

NAAS REAM
NAAS BROWN

250° / 045° / 100° / 280° / 7000' / 1100' (601') / 5000' / 3700' / 2900'

5200'
3400'

PRECAUCION: AL ESTABLECER CONTACTO VISUAL CON LA PISTA NO ABANDONE RADIAL DE APROXIMACION FINAL HASTA D-5

VOR/DME
ELEV. *499'*

FALLIDA: ASCIENDA EN **RADIAL 250°** CON VIRAJE DE GOTA A LA **IZQUIERDA** DENTRO DE 10 M.N. Y PROSIGA HACIA EL **VOR/DME-TIJ** HASTA LA ALTITUD MINIMA DE ESPERA.

CATEGORIA	DIRECTO PISTA 27 MDA *1100'* (601')	CATEGORIA	CIRCULANDO MDA
A	1 (1600 M)	A	*1200'* (701') – 1 (1600 M)
B		B	
C	1 ¾ (2800 M)	C	*1200'* (701') – 2 (3200 M)
D	2 (3200 M)	D	*1200'* (701') – 2 ¼ (3600 M)

CAMBIOS: AJUSTE DE MINIMOS e IDENTIFICACION VOR

SCT-DGAC-SENEAM
TIJ-VD-1

SUNRISE & SUNSET – GMT   **SALIDA y PUESTA del SOL – GMT**

15th of	JAN	FEB	MAR	APR	MAY	JUN	JUL	AUG	SEPT	OCT	NOV	DEC	
SUNRISE	1449	1430	1358	1318	1249	1240	1251	1311	1331	1351	1417	1442	SALIDA
SUNSET	0104	0133	0155	0217	0239	0256	0256	0233	0154	0115	2447	2443	PUESTA
15° de	ENE	FEB	MAR	ABR	MAY	JUN	JUL	AGO	SEP	OCT	NOV	DIC	

To get local time just subtract 'GMT ADD'
PARA OBTENER TIEMPO LOCAL SUSTRIAGA 'GMT ADD'

Tijuana Internacional Baja Calif. Norte   *tee-WHAH-na*   111

JET CHART	WAC	SECTIONAL	LATITUDE	LONGITUDE	US TIME	FOR GMT ADD	ICAO IDENT	TOWN IDENT
JN-46	CG-18	ADS-15 Los Angeles	32°31'	116°59'	DST	8	MMTJ	TIJ

TCA TO: 20,000'   RADIUS 50 n.mi.   HOURS 1400-0400Z
APPROACH 119.5   TOWER 118.1   GROUND 118.1
OTHER COMM SAN FSS 122.4, Brown 126.9
CITY Adjacent   POPULATION 700,000+
LOCAL VorDme   FREQ 116.5   WHERE Here   HOURS 24
B'CAST FREQ 690   WHERE 4 mi W   HOURS 24
FROM San Quintín   FREQ 113.3   TRACK 325°, 138n.mi.
FROM Mexicali   FREQ 115.0   TRACK 253°, 45n.mi.
FUEL 80, 100, JP   CARDS Visa, MC   CASH? Yes
REPAIRS Minor   TIEDOWN BYO

HOTEL	RATE	WHERE	TEL
Conquistador	$$$	Central	903-386-4801
Palacio Azteca	$$	Central	903-386-5301

AOE 24 hrs

Concrete
Normal traffic

Asphalt
Overflow Traffic

ELEVATION
499'

Easy clearances, fast gas service, on the ball controllers, and low traffic density are the reasons many of us prefer this as an internacional airport. Although the city approaches one million people, having two runways keeps things orderly.

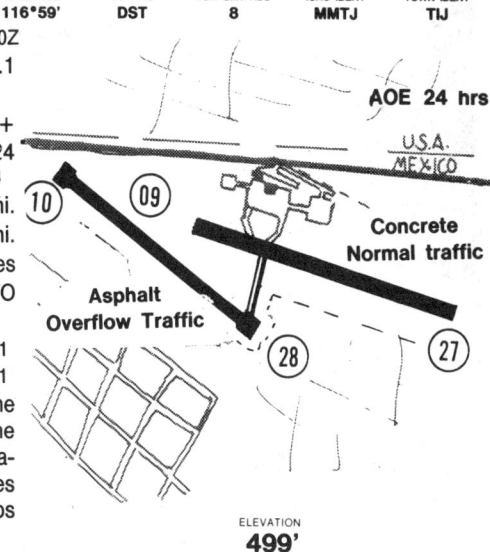

Amdt 2
VOR-A

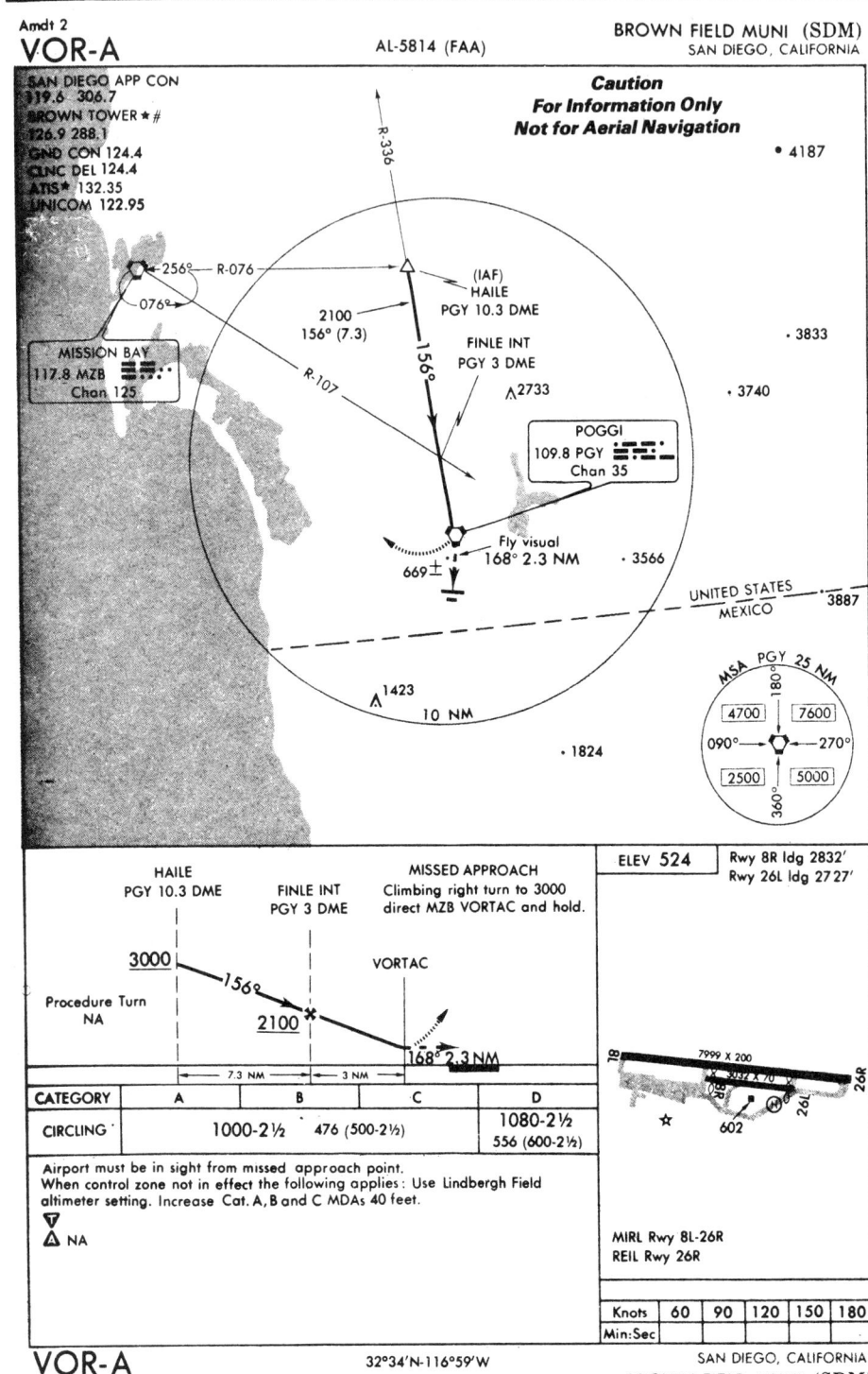

AL-5814 (FAA)

BROWN FIELD MUNI (SDM)
SAN DIEGO, CALIFORNIA

SAN DIEGO APP CON
119.6 306.7
BROWN TOWER ★ #
126.9 288.1
GND CON 124.4
CLNC DEL 124.4
ATIS ★ 132.35
UNICOM 122.95

Caution
For Information Only
Not for Aerial Navigation

MISSION BAY
117.8 MZB
Chan 125

R-336
256° ← R-076
076°
2100
156° (7.3)
R-107
156°
(IAF) HAILE
PGY 10.3 DME
FINLE INT
PGY 3 DME
△ 2733
POGGI
109.8 PGY
Chan 35
Fly visual
168° 2.3 NM
669±
• 3566
• 4187
• 3833
• 3740

UNITED STATES / MEXICO
• 3887

△ 1423
10 NM
• 1824

MSA PGY 25 NM
4700 | 7600
090° —◇— 270°
2500 | 5000

	HAILE PGY 10.3 DME	FINLE INT PGY 3 DME	MISSED APPROACH Climbing right turn to 3000 direct MZB VORTAC and hold.

3000
156°
Procedure Turn NA
2100
VORTAC
168° 2.3 NM
7.3 NM   3 NM

ELEV 524
Rwy 8R ldg 2832'
Rwy 26L ldg 2727'

7999 X 200
602

CATEGORY	A	B	C	D
CIRCLING	1000-2½	476 (500-2½)		1080-2½ 556 (600-2½)

Airport must be in sight from missed approach point.
When control zone not in effect the following applies: Use Lindbergh Field altimeter setting. Increase Cat. A, B and C MDAs 40 feet.
▽
△ NA

MIRL Rwy 8L-26R
REIL Rwy 26R

Knots	60	90	120	150	180
Min:Sec					

VOR-A

32°34'N-116°59'W

SAN DIEGO, CALIFORNIA
BROWN FIELD MUNI (SDM)

California **Brown Field** 113

JET CHART	WAC	SECTIONAL	LATITUDE	LONGITUDE	US TIME	FOR GMT ADD	ICAO IDENT	TOWN IDENT
JN-46	CG-18 ADS-15	Los Angeles	32°34'	116°59'PST	8	-	SDM	

APPROACH - TOWER 126.9 GROUND 121.6 AOE 24 hrs
OTHER COMM ATIS 119.35, FSS 122.4, Fuel 123.5
CITY 5 miles NW POPULATION 750,000+
FROM Tijuana FREQ 116.5 TRACK NE,2Dme
FROM Mexicali FREQ 115.0 TRACK 254°,90n.mi
FROM La Paz FREQ 112.3 TRACK -,-
FUEL 80, 100, JP CARDS Major CASH? Yes
REPAIRS Major TIEDOWN Yes

Although an easy little-traffic airport, too many reports come in here about the attitude of the inspecting officers. Often pilots choose to use Lindbergh Field for later crossings. Personally I have had no problems nor experienced any unusual delays here after several years.

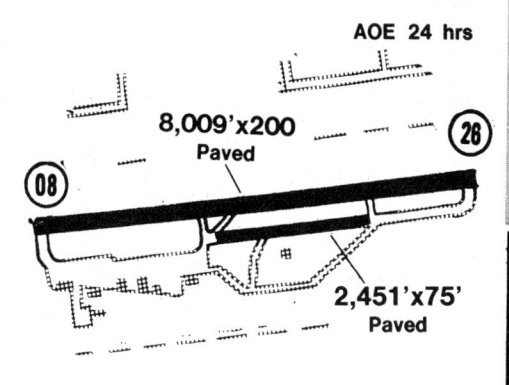

8,009'x200 Paved
2,451'x75' Paved

ELEVATION
501'

ILS RWY 9 — SAN DIEGO INTL-LINDBERGH FIELD (SAN)

Amdt 10
AL-373 (FAA)
SAN DIEGO, CALIFORNIA

SAN DIEGO APP CON 127.3 323.0
LINDBERGH TOWER 118.3 270.9
GND CON 123.9
CLNC DEL 125.9
ATIS 134.8

OCEANSIDE 115.3 OCN Chan 100
JULIAN 114.0 JLI Chan 87
MISSION BAY 117.8 MZB Chan 125
LOCALIZER 110.9 I-SAN Chan 46

SARGS (IAF) I-SAN 10.1 DME
GATTO INT I-SAN 5.6 DME
2000 NoPT 092° (4.5)
2500 to Sargs Int/DME
MZB 10 DME Arc
LMM BOING 245 AN

MSA AN 25 NM: 4700 / 2100 / 5200 (140°, 230°, 340°)

Missed Approach
Climb to 1000, climbing left turn to 3000 direct MZB VORTAC then via MZB R-326 to Carif Int.

Remain within 10 NM
GS 3.22° TCH 84* *Displ Thld
4.7 NM

ELEV 15
TDZE 14
Rwy 9 ldg 8697'
Rwy 13 ldg 3888'
Rwy 27 ldg 7590'
Rwy 31 ldg 4038'
092° 5.4 NM from Gatto Int I-SAN 5.6 DME
TDZ/CL Rwy 9-27
MIRL Rwy 13-31
HIRL Rwy 9-27

CATEGORY	A	B	C	D
S-ILS 9		350/50	336 (400-1)	
S-LOC 9	540/50	526 (600-1)	540-1½ 526 (600-1½)	540-1¾ 526 (600-1¾)
CIRCLING	780-1 765 (800-1)	800-1¼ 785 (800-1¼)	800-2¼ 785 (800-2¼)	820-2½ 805 (900-2½)

Inoperative table does not apply.
ILS unusable from MM inbound.
Air carrier will not reduce landing visibility due to local conditions.

FAF to MAP 4.7 NM

Knots	60	90	120	150	180
Min:Sec	4:42	3:08	2:21	1:53	1:34

ILS RWY 9   32°44'N–117°11'W   SAN DIEGO, CALIFORNIA
SAN DIEGO INTL-LINDBERGH FIELD (SAN)

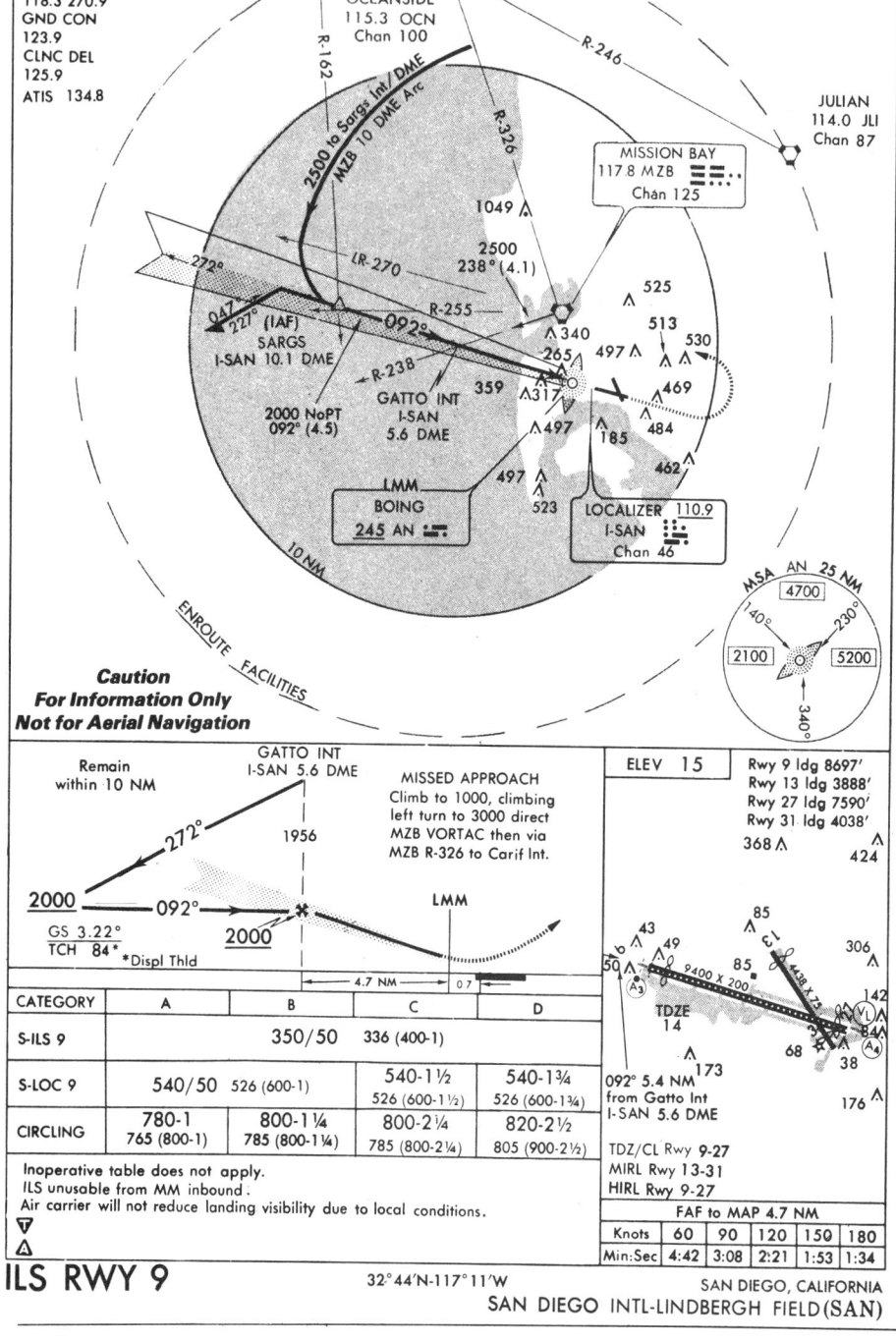

SUNRISE & SUNSET – GMT   SALIDA y PUESTA del SOL – GMT

15th of	JAN	FEB	MAR	APR	MAY	JUN	JUL	AUG	SEPT	OCT	NOV	DEC
SUNRISE	1451	1431	1359	1319	1249	1240	1251	1312	1332	1352	1418	1443
SUNSET	0105	0133	0156	0218	0240	0258	0257	0234	0155	0116	2447	2444
15° de	ENE	FEB	MAR	ABR	MAY	JUN	JUL	AGO	SEP	OCT	NOV	DIC

To get local time just subtract 'GMT ADD'
PARA OBTENER TIEMPO LOCAL SUSTRIAGA 'GMT ADD'

Lindbergh Field Int'l California

JET CHART	WAC	SECTIONAL	LATITUDE	LONGITUDE	US TIME	FOR GMT ADD	ICAO IDENT	TOWN IDENT
JN-46	CG-18 So. ADS-15	Los Angeles	32°44'	117°11'	PST/PDT	8/7	-	LIF

115

APPROACH 119.6   TOWER 118.3   GROUND 121.7
OTHER COMM ATIS 133.35, FSS 122.4, ILS 110.9
CITY All sides   POPULATION 700,000
LOCAL VorDme FREQ 117.8 WHERE 4 miles NW HOURS 24
B'CAST FREQ 600   WHERE 4 mi E   HOURS Daylight
FROM Tijuana   FREQ 116.5   TRACK 308°, 17Dme
FROM Ensenada FREQ Airport TRACK 317°, 64n.mi.
FUEL All grades   CARDS All major   CASH? Yes
REPAIRS Major   TIEDOWN Yes

HOTEL	RATE	WHERE	TEL
Royal Inn	$$$	1 mile S	-
Motel Six	$$	2 miles No.	-
Hilton	*$$$	1 mile W	-

dozens of others
Site of the famous Flight 182 ramming a Cessna 172 from behind

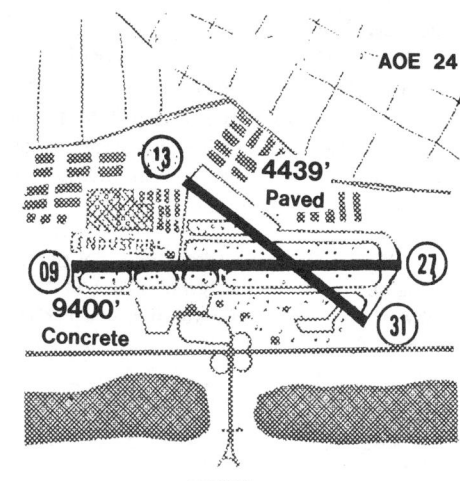

AOE 24

4439' Paved

9400' Concrete

ELEVATION
18'

116 Tecate   Baja Calif. Norte   *teh-COTT-ay*

JET CHART	WAC	SECTIONAL	LATITUDE	LONGITUDE	US TIME	FOR GMT ADD	ICAO IDENT	TOWN IDENT
JN-46	CG-18 So. ADS-15	Los Angeles	32°32'	116°38'	PST	8		TCT

OTHER COMM Traffic 122.85
CITY 3 miles N   POPULATION 27,000
B'CAST FREQ 1380   WHERE 2 mi NE   HOURS Daylight
FROM Tijuana   FREQ 116.5   TRACK 074°, 17Dme
FROM Mexicali   FREQ 115.0   TRACK 253°, 72n.mi.
FROM Julian   FREQ 114.0   TRACK 168°, 37Dme
FUEL -   CARDS -   CASH? -
REPAIRS -   TIEDOWN BYO

Often used as a dragstrip, the parallel ridge very near on the upwind side can cause downwind problems during the usual windy afternoons.

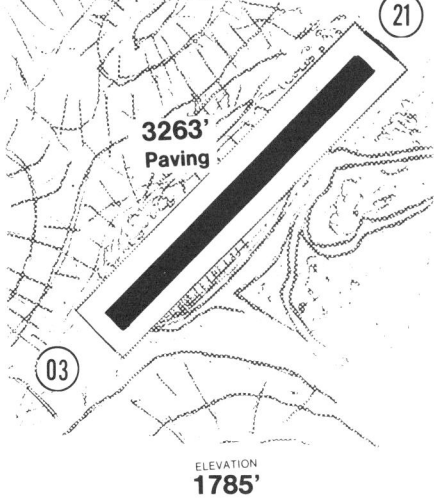

3263' Paving

ELEVATION
1785'

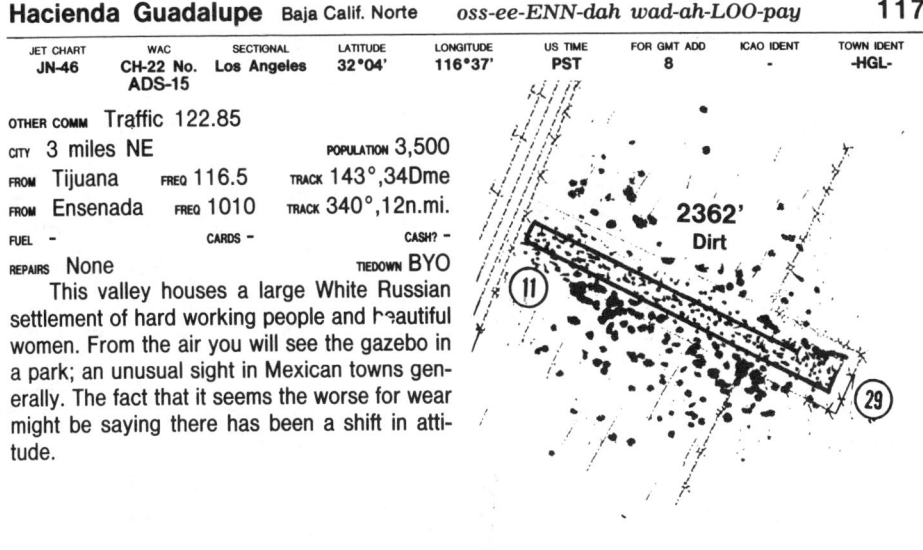

Hacienda Guadalupe   Baja Calif. Norte   *oss-ee-ENN-dah wad-ah-LOO-pay*   117

JET CHART	WAC	SECTIONAL	LATITUDE	LONGITUDE	US TIME	FOR GMT ADD	ICAO IDENT	TOWN IDENT
JN-46	CH-22 No. ADS-15	Los Angeles	32°04'	116°37'	PST	8	-	-HGL-

OTHER COMM Traffic 122.85
CITY 3 miles NE   POPULATION 3,500
FROM Tijuana   FREQ 116.5   TRACK 143°,34Dme
FROM Ensenada   FREQ 1010   TRACK 340°,12n.mi.
FUEL -   CARDS -   CASH? -
REPAIRS None   TIEDOWN BYO

    This valley houses a large White Russian settlement of hard working people and beautiful women. From the air you will see the gazebo in a park; an unusual sight in Mexican towns generally. The fact that it seems the worse for wear might be saying there has been a shift in attitude.

2362'
Dirt

ELEVATION
1065'

118 Guadalupe New   Baja Calif. Norte   *wah-dah-LOO-pay*

JET CHART	WAC	LATITUDE	LONGITUDE	US TIME	FOR GMT ADD	ICAO IDENT	TOWN IDENT
JN-46	CH-22	32°08'	116°31'	PST/PDT	8/7		

OTHER COMM Traffic 124.7
TOWN 3/4 mi West   POPULATION est 2000
FROM Tijuana   FREQ 116.5   TRACK 123°, 32.6Dme
FROM Mexicali   FREQ 115.2   TRACK 231°, 71.4Dme
FROM Julian   FREQ 114.0   TRACK 186°, 68.9Dme
AVGAS-   CREDIT CARDS-   CASH TYPE-
REPAIRS AVAILABLE -   TIEDOWNS? BYO

This airport and several others serve brandy distilleries in the Republic of Mexico, all owned by the same conglomerate.

This airport is used a lot by Capt. Miguel Marquez in the company's Cessna 402. Mike is one of the few pilots with 20,000+ hours of just bush flying. For a time he worked for one company so anzious for fares that they regularly made road and beach landings in a DC-3 to pick up or drop passengers. That's getting experience the hard way.

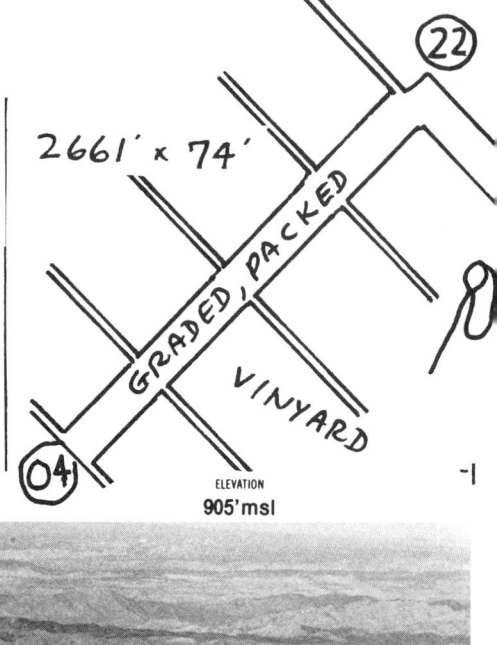

2661' x 74'
GRADED, PACKED
VINYARD
ELEVATION
905' msl

BAH-hah MARR Baja Calif. Norte **Baja Mar Resort** 119

JET CHART	WAC	LATITUDE	LONGITUDE	US TIME	FOR GMT ADD	ICAO IDENT	TOWN IDENT
JN-46	CG-18	32°03'	116°52'	PST/PDT	8/7		BJM-

OTHER COMM Traffic 124.5
SETTLEMENT 0.5mile SW   POPULATION Increasing
FROM Tijuana   FREQ 116.5   TRACK 157°, 29.3Dme
FROM Mexicali FREQ 115.0   TRACK 233°, 90.7Dme
FROM Julian   FREQ 114.0   TRACK 197°, 76.1Dme
AVGAS-   CRED CARDS-   CASH TYPE
REPAIRS AVAILABLE -   TIEDOWNS? BYO

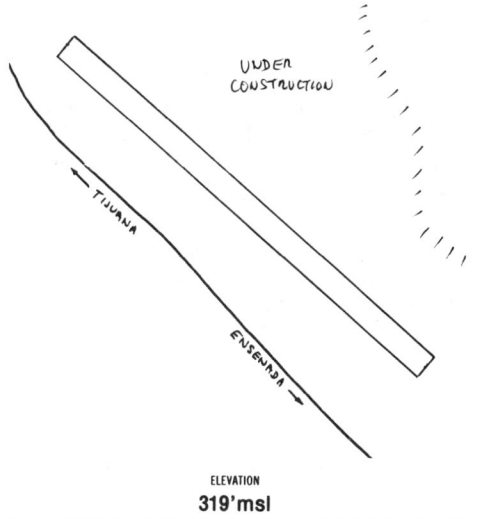

Newest of the new developments on the West Coast a very few miles from Tijuana, this piece of coastline takes in two spectacular views; a magnificent sweep of coastal beauty seen from the highway, central part and along the low bluffs sealions 'tiptoe' in for a bashful peak at people.

The developers are serious: choices of condos, lots, apartments, are now somewhere between plans and ready for occupancy.

ELEVATION
319'msl

120 Ensenada Baja Calif. Norte   *enn-senn-AH-dah*

JET CHART	WAC	SECTIONAL	LATITUDE	LONGITUDE	US TIME	FOR GMT ADD	ICAO IDENT	TOWN IDENT
JN-46	CH-22 No. ADS-15	TPC H-22A	31°48'	116°36'	PST	8	-	ENS

APPROACH - TOWER 119.75? GROUND 119.75?
CITY 5 miles No. POPULATION 71,000
B'CAST FREQ 1010 WHERE 5 mi No. HOURS Daylight
FROM Tijuana FREQ 116.5 TRACK 147°, 49Dme (10)
FROM Mexicali FREQ 115.0 TRACK 220°, 86n.mi.
FROM San Quintin FREQ 113.3 TRACK 324°, 84n.mi.
FUEL 100 CARDS - CASH? Pesos
REPAIRS Minor TIEDOWN BYO

HOTEL	RATE	WHERE	TEL
San Nicolas	$$$	Central	903-399-1901
Travelodge	$$	Central	800-255-3050
Bahia	$$	Central	-

And many many others.

Joint civil-military airport to serve a city popular with the yachting set who crowd in here annually for the Newport to Ensenada Race, and many smaller races as well.

4715' Paved (28)

ELEVATION
25' to 37'

Club Grulla Baja Calif. Norte   *cloob* GROO-*yah*   **121**

JET CHART	WAC	SECTIONAL	LATITUDE	LONGITUDE	US TIME	FOR GMT ADD	ICAO IDENT	TOWN IDENT
JN-46	CH-22 No. ADS-15	TPC H-22A	31°42'	116°38'	PST	8	-	GRU-

OTHER COMM Traffic 122.85
SETTLEMENT Club SW corner   POPULATION -
FROM Tijuana   FREQ 116.5   TRACK 148°,53Dme
FROM Ensenada   FREQ Airport TRACK 178°,6n.mi.
FROM Mexicali   FREQ 115.0   TRACK 220°,90n.mi.
FUEL -   CARDS -   CASH? -
REPAIRS -   TIEDOWN BYO

Private hunting and fishing club, you can legally land here but the cold shoulder you get would freeze the whatevers off an anything.

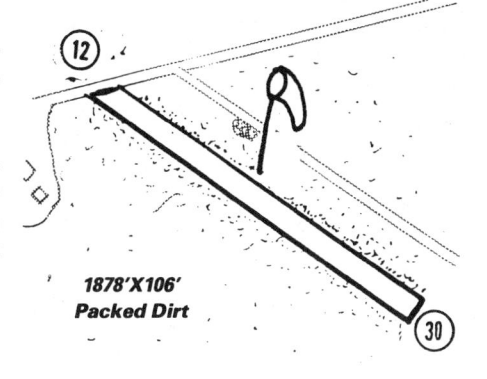

1878'X106'
Packed Dirt

ELEVATION
13'

122 Puerto Santo Tomás — Baja Calif. Norte

PWAIR-toe SAHN-toe toe-MOSS

JET CHART	WAC	SECTIONAL	LATITUDE	LONGITUDE	US TIME	FOR GMT ADD	ICAO IDENT	TOWN IDENT
JN-46	CH-22 No. ADS-15	TPC H-22A	31°31'	116°39'	PST	8	-	-STO-

OTHER COMM Traffic 122.85
SETTLEMENT Plant 3/4 mile SE   **POPULATION** 25
FROM Tijuana   **FREQ** 116.5   **TRACK** 152°, 64Dme
FROM Ensenada **FREQ** Airport **TRACK** 175°, 16n.mi.
FROM San Quintin **FREQ** 113.3 **TRACK** 314°, 71n.mi.
FUEL -   **CARDS** -   **CASH?** -
REPAIRS -   **TIEDOWN** BYO

2317' Packed

ELEVATION
71' to 84'

Although a bit close to the city for camping, you will be in good company. A mile or so North is a famous cabaña.

It was built by an LA Times writer named Jack Smith using his landlord as a contractor. The very long series of articles was later compiled into a book called "God and Mr Gómez"; an excellent place to reach a decent understanding of how things go.

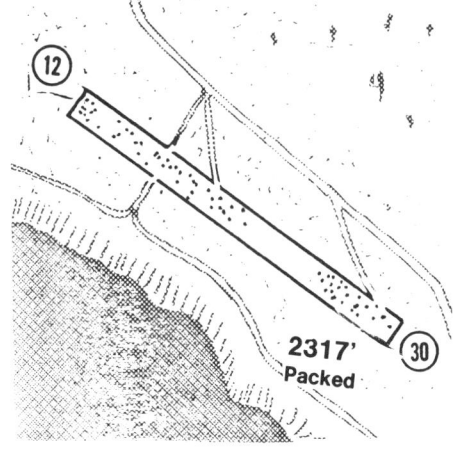

San Vicente   Baja Calif. Norte   *sahn bee-SENN-tay*   123

JET CHART	WAC	SECTIONAL	LATITUDE	LONGITUDE	US TIME	FOR GMT ADD	ICAO IDENT	TOWN IDENT
JN-46	CH-22 No. ADS-15	TPC H-22A	31°20'	116°15'	PST/PDT	8/7	-	-SVC-

OTHER COMM Traffic 122.85
SETTLEMENT 1/4 mile W   POPULATION 2,000
FROM Tijuana   FREQ 116.5   TRACK 137°,82Dme
FROM San Quintin   FREQ 113.3   TRACK 326°,51n.mi.
FROM Meling Ranch FREQ airport   TRACK 294°,35n.mi.
FUEL -   CARDS -   CASH? -
REPAIRS Minor   TIEDOWN BYO
    HOTEL   RATE   WHERE   TEL

Important because this little valley usually heats up much earlier than the often foggy coast. Many a time I've been able to stop here for an hour or two waiting for Colnett or Hamilton to go VFR. Henrietta (Ketta) MacFarland will put you up at her house just North of runway heading on the East side of the paved highway.

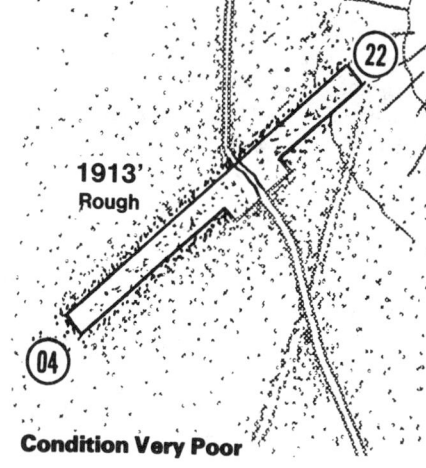

1913'
Rough

Condition Very Poor

ELEVATION
337'

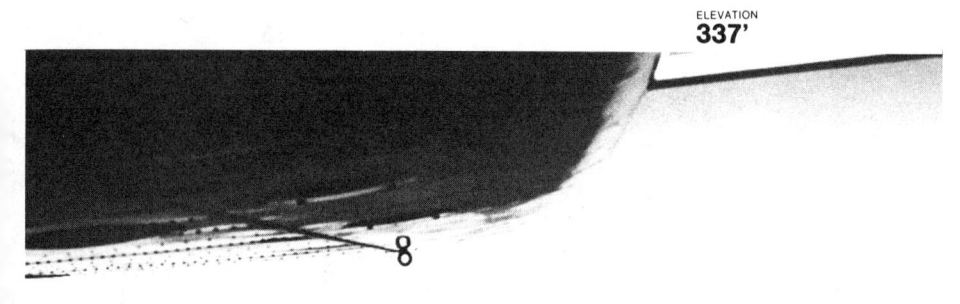

124 Llano Colorado   Baja Calif. Norte   YAH-no coe-loe-RAH-doe

JET CHART	WAC	SECTIONAL	LATITUDE	LONGITUDE	US TIME	FOR GMT ADD	ICAO IDENT	TOWN IDENT
JN-46	CH-22 ADS-15	TPC H-22A	31°15	116°08	PST	8	-	-

OTHER COMM Traffic 122.85
SETTLEMENT E end   POPULATION Ranch
FROM Tijuana   FREQ 116.5   TRACK 137°,88Dme,
FROM Mexicali   FREQ 115.0   TRACK 195°,95Dme,
FROM San Quintín   FREQ 113.0   TRACK 335°,46n.mi.,
FUEL -   CARDS -   CASH? -
REPAIRS -   TIEDOWN BYO

2440' Packed

Part of México's attempted agricultural transition to larger, more efficient farming operations. There are several crops in this farming complex which is almost doing pure research toward production of more food for a burgeoning population. Presently most of the south end of this San Vicente valley is involved in this farm, as is Valle de Trinidad east of here, and Calentura just up the draw.

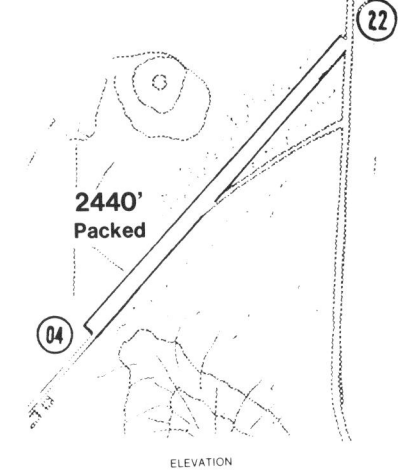

ELEVATION
681'

la Calentura   Baja Calif. Norte   *lah call-enn-TOO-rah*   **125**

JET CHART	WAC	SECTIONAL	LATITUDE	LONGITUDE	US TIME	FOR GMT ADD	ICAO IDENT	TOWN IDENT
JN-46	CH-22 No. ADS-15	TPC H-22A	31°16	116°01'	PST	8	-	-

OTHER COMM   Traffic 122.85
SETTLEMENT   In valley   POPULATION   Ranch
FROM   Tijuana   FREQ 116.5   TRACK 133°, 90Dme,
FROM   Mexicali   FREQ 115.0   TRACK 192°, 92Dme,
FROM   San Quintín   FREQ 113.3   TRACK 342°, 46n.mi.,
FUEL   -   CARDS   -   CASH?   -
REPAIRS   -   TIEDOWN   BYO

So seldom used by 'outside' aircraft that no has ever complained about the forest of tent stakes at the upper end. They are just waiting for an unwary pilot to shred a tire. With the distinct slope of this runway few pilots will see those stakes up close. PS: park sideways.

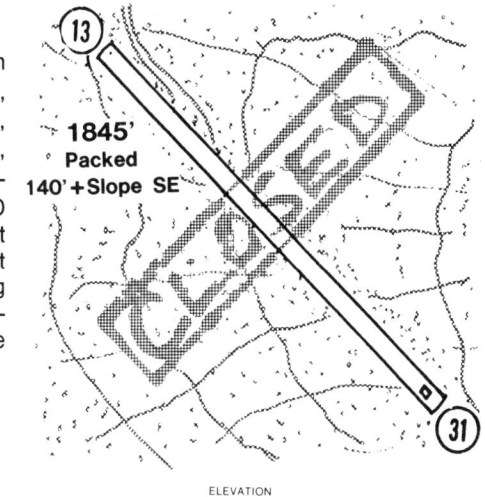

1845'
Packed
140' + Slope SE

ELEVATION

126 el Alamo Baja Calif. Norte   *ell AHH-lah-moe*

JET CHART	WAC	SECTIONAL	LATITUDE	LONGITUDE	US TIME	FOR GMT ADD	ICAO IDENT	TOWN IDENT
JN-46	CH-22 No. ADS-15	Los Angeles	31°36'	116°02'	PST	8	-	-LAM-

OTHER COMM Traffic 122.85
SETTLEMENT West end   POPULATION 37
FROM Tijuana   FREQ 116.5   TRACK 130°,72Dme
FROM Ensenada   FREQ 1010   TRACK 105°,32n.mi.
FROM San Quintin FREQ 113.3   TRACK 344°,66n.mi.
FUEL -   CARDS -   CASH? -
REPAIRS -   TIEDOWN BYO

At least a dozen old gold mines do this area, including four to six within half a mile of your airplane. A botanical curiosity exists here: gardners tell several plants grow here which are only known grow where gold ore is found.

With the departure of the Mesa family for Tijuana we no longer have a guide to the various workings but exploring on your own is fun too.

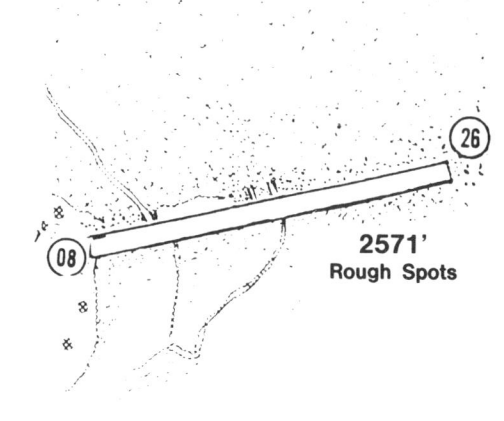

2571'
Rough Spots

ELEVATION
3730'

Misión Santa Catalina Baja Calif. Norte   *meese-ee-OWN*   **127**

JET CHART	WAC	SECTIONAL	LATITUDE	LONGITUDE	US TIME	FOR GMT ADD	ICAO IDENT	TOWN IDENT
JN-46	CH-22 No. ADS-15	TPC H-22A	31°40'	115°49'	PST	8	-	-CAT-

OTHER COMM Traffic 122.85
SETTLEMENT 3/4 mile So.   POPULATION 145
FROM Tijuana   FREQ 116.5   TRACK 117°,79Dme
FROM Mexicali   FREQ 115.0   TRACK 192°,64n.mi.
FROM San Quintín FREQ 113.3   TRACK 351°,69n.mi.
FUEL -   CARDS -   CASH? -
REPAIRS -   TIEDOWN BYO

Reservation for the Pai Pai Indians of the Yuma nation, and an original stop for the Flying Samaritans' medical teams, the combination of poor runway condition and density altitudes over 8,000' in summer has caused the group to use el Alamo nearby instead. Interesting very isolated people here, not helped by a deteriorating runway. Unless changes are made pretty soon look for this one not to be in the next edition.

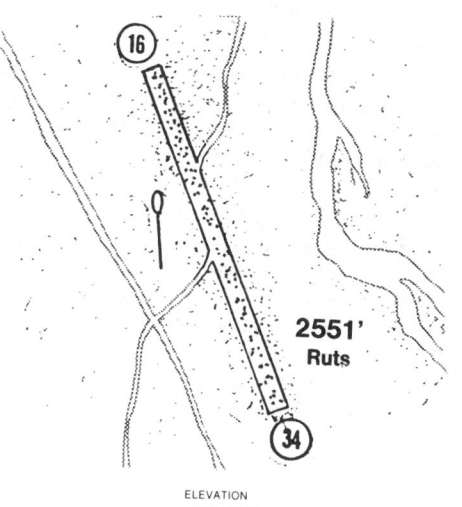

2551'
Ruts

ELEVATION
3919'

128 Valle de Trinidad Baja Calif. Norte *BAH-yay deh-treen-ee-DOD*

JET CHART	WAC	SECTIONAL	LATITUDE	LONGITUDE	US TIME	FOR GMT ADD	ICAO IDENT	TOWN IDENT
JN-46	CH-22 No. ADS-15	TPC H-22A	31°24'	115°43'	PST	8	-	-VTR-

OTHER COMM Traffic 122.85
SETTLEMENT 1/4 mile N   POPULATION 975
FROM Tijuana   FREQ 116.5   TRACK 123°,95Dme
FROM Mexicali   FREQ 115.0   TRACK 184°,78n.mi.
FROM San Quintin FREQ 113.3   TRACK 358°,54n.mi.
FUEL -   CARDS -   CASH? -
REPAIRS -   TIEDOWN BYO

Plenty of precipitation in the mountains. No and So provides a good ground water table in this small valley. One large and several small farms are creating an agricultural boom. Store for camping supplies, car gas, refreshments.

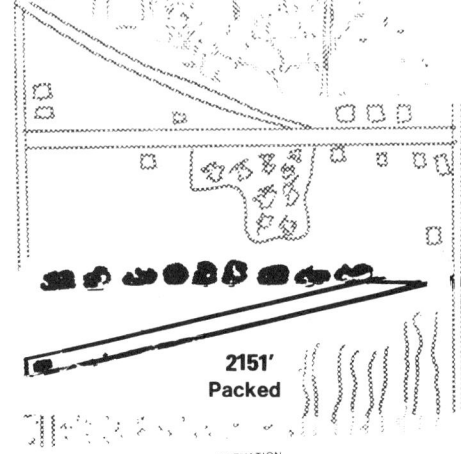

2151'
Packed

ELEVATION
2015'

Mike's New* Baja Calif. Norte   129

JET CHART	WAC	SECTIONAL	LATITUDE	LONGITUDE	US TIME	FOR GMT ADD	ICAO IDENT	TOWN IDENT
JN-46	CH-22 ADS-15	TPC H22A	31 11'	115 40'	PST	8		SKY-

OTHER COMM Hotel 122.8

CITY			POPULATION
LOCAL	FREQ	WHERE	HOURS
FROM Tijuana	FREQ 116.5	TRACK 126°, 104 n.mi.	
FROM Mexicali	FREQ 115.0	TRACK 180°, 90Dme	
FROM San Quintin	FREQ 113.3	TRACK 006°, 43.5 n.mi.	
FUEL —		CARDS —	CASH? —
REPAIRS —			TIEDOWN
HOTEL	RATE	WHERE	TEL
Skyranch	$$	2 SE	

Remarks: On the latest possible visit before printing this new runway had some small but sturdy trees ready to catch a wing at those marked locations alongside the runway. When they are chopped down so I can land and measure you will read length and condition in the PREPS.

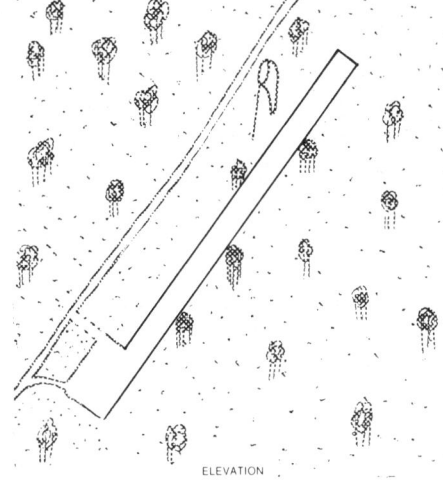

ELEVATION

130 Meling Ranch Baja Calif. Norte

MELL-ing ranch

JET CHART	WAC	SECTIONAL	LATITUDE	LONGITUDE	US TIME	FOR GMT ADD	ICAO IDENT	TOWN IDENT
JN-46	CH-22 No. ADS-15	TPC H-22A	30°58'	115°44'	PST/PDT	8/7	-	-MEL-

OTHER COMM Ranch 122.8 prior request
SETTLEMENT Ranch 3/4 mile SW   **POPULATION** 25
FROM Tijuana   **FREQ** 116.5   **TRACK** 132°, 114 n.mi.
FROM Mexicali   **FREQ** 115.0   **TRACK** 181°, 101 n.mi.
FROM San Quintin   **FREQ** 113.3   **TRACK** 008°, 30 n.mi.
FUEL 100 prior req.   **CARDS** -   **CASH?** Dlls
REPAIRS Minor   **TIEDOWN** BYO

HOTEL	RATE	WHERE	TEL
Guest Ranch	$$A	here	714-466-6872

The legendary Rancho San José dates from late in the eighteenth century when Grandfather Johnson's health needed a change from South Texas. He was fascinated by these mountains where he founded a placer gold mine, raised cattle and four children.

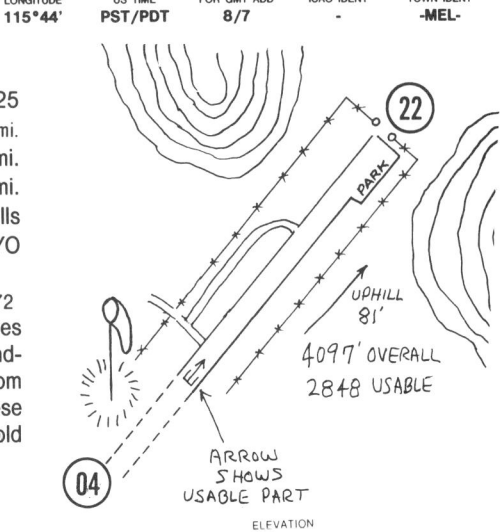

UPHILL 81'
4097' OVERALL
2848 USABLE
ARROW SHOWS USABLE PART

ELEVATION 2285' to 2370'

Hortaliza Baja Calif. Norte *or-tah-LEE-sah* **131**

JET CHART	WAC	SECTIONAL	LATITUDE	LONGITUDE	US TIME	FOR GMT ADD	ICAO IDENT	TOWN IDENT
JN-46	CH-22 No. ADS-15	TPC H-22A	30°57'	115°58'	PST	8	-	-HRT-

OTHER COMM Traffic 122.85
SETTLEMENT 1/10 mile N   POPULATION Ranch
FROM Tijuana   FREQ 116.5   TRACK 138°, 107 n.mi.
FROM San Quintín FREQ 113.3 TRACK 344°, 27 n.mi.
FUEL -   CARDS -   CASH? -
REPAIRS -   TIEDOWN BYO

One of the Flying Samaritans stops (see index) to bring medical care to the remote areas. This Samaritans group is from the LA area; they make this clinic site every four weeks. When they are not here the runway is even harder to spot.

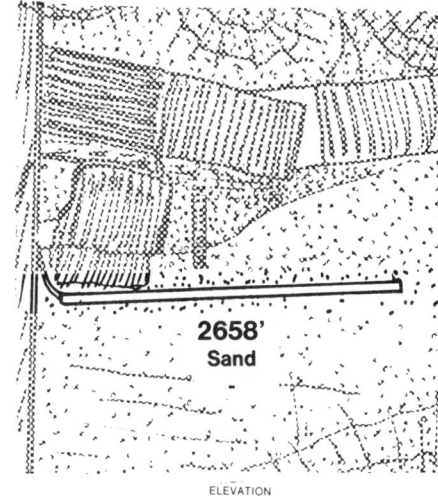

2658'
Sand

ELEVATION
322'

132 Colnett East — Baja Calif. Norte — coe-loe-NETT

JET CHART	WAC	SECTIONAL	LATITUDE	LONGITUDE	US TIME	FOR GMT ADD	ICAO IDENT	TOWN IDENT
JN-46	CH-22 No. ADS-15	TPC H-22A	31°05'	116°13'	PST/PDT	8/7	-	-CNT-

OTHER COMM Traffic 122.85
SETTLEMENT 3/4 mile E   POPULATION 750
FROM Tijuana   FREQ 116.5   TRACK 156°, 96Dme
FROM San Quintin FREQ 113.3 TRACK 323°, 38n.mi.
FUEL -   CARDS -   CASH? -
REPAIRS -   TIEDOWN BYO

HOTEL	RATE	WHERE	TEL
Rancho Grande	–$	Here	-

One of the early Flying Samaritans' Clinic sites, we were bringing medical help to this town via this runway back in the early nineteen sixties. The closer to the clinic of Colnett's two runways, this one does get lots of ruts from campers who chew it up by driving on the runway during or after a rain. Suggest you look it over carefully before deciding to land.

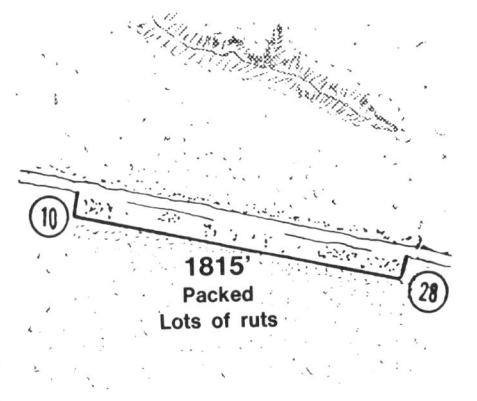

⑩ 1815' Packed Lots of ruts ㉘

ELEVATION **255'**

Colnett West
Baja Calif. Norte coe-loe-NETT **133**

JET CHART	WAC	SECTIONAL	LATITUDE	LONGITUDE	US TIME	FOR GMT ADD	ICAO IDENT	TOWN IDENT
JN-46	CH-22 No. ADS-15	TPC H-22A	31°05'	116°15'	PST/PDT	8/7	-	-CNT-

OTHER COMM Traffic 122.85
SETTLEMENT 4 miles East   POPULATION 750
FROM Tijuana   FREQ 116.5   TRACK 157°,96Dme
FROM San Quintin FREQ 113.3   TRACK 322°,38n.mi.
FUEL -   CARDS -   CASH? -
REPAIRS -   TIEDOWN BYO

HOTEL	RATE	WHERE	TEL
Rancho Grande	–$	4 miles E	-

Colnett's original runway which enabled the medical teams of the Flying Samaritans to bring medical care to Colnett residents unable to travel long distances to see a physician.

Starting in late sixty three we were continually having tire problems after landing here. Finally we discovered the subminiature cacti.

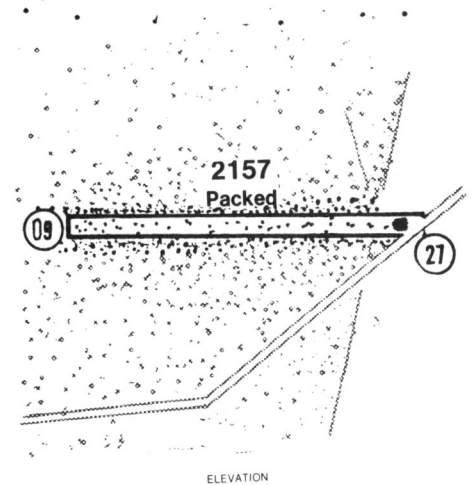

2157
Packed
09   27

ELEVATION
295'

134 Hamilton Ranch   Baja Calif. Norte

JET CHART	WAC	SECTIONAL	LATITUDE	LONGITUDE	US TIME	FOR GMT ADD	ICAO IDENT	TOWN IDENT
JN-46	CH-22 No. ADS-15	TPC H-22A	30°45'	115°58'	PST/PDT	8/7	-	-HAM-

OTHER COMM	Traffic 122.85		
SETTLEMENT	Ranch N side		POPULATION 1
FROM Tijuana	FREQ 116.5	TRACK 140°,120 n.mi.	
FROM Mexicali	FREQ 115.0	TRACK 184°,119n.mi.	
FROM San Quintin	FREQ 113.3	TRACK 341°,14n.mi.	

HOTEL	RATE	WHERE	TEL
Hamilton Ranch	-	-	-

A popular movie stars' orgy site during the 1930s when Stinson Reliants and big Wacos brought high rollers here for quiet weekends far from prying eyes.

More recently this was an ordinary guest ranch run by Margo Ceseña until her death almost two years ago. Closed now, the future of the ranch is in doubt as her US nephew and heir tries to figure out whether he will run it or just what.

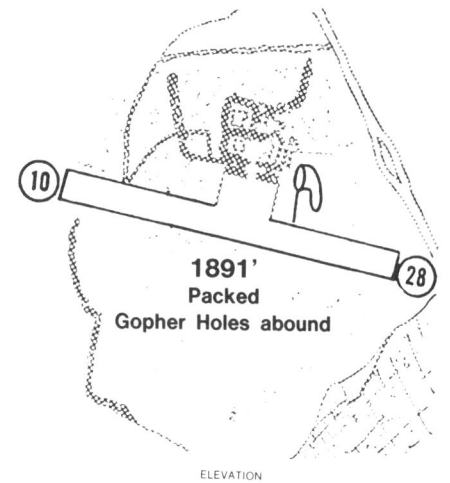

1891'
Packed
Gopher Holes abound

ELEVATION
181' to 197'

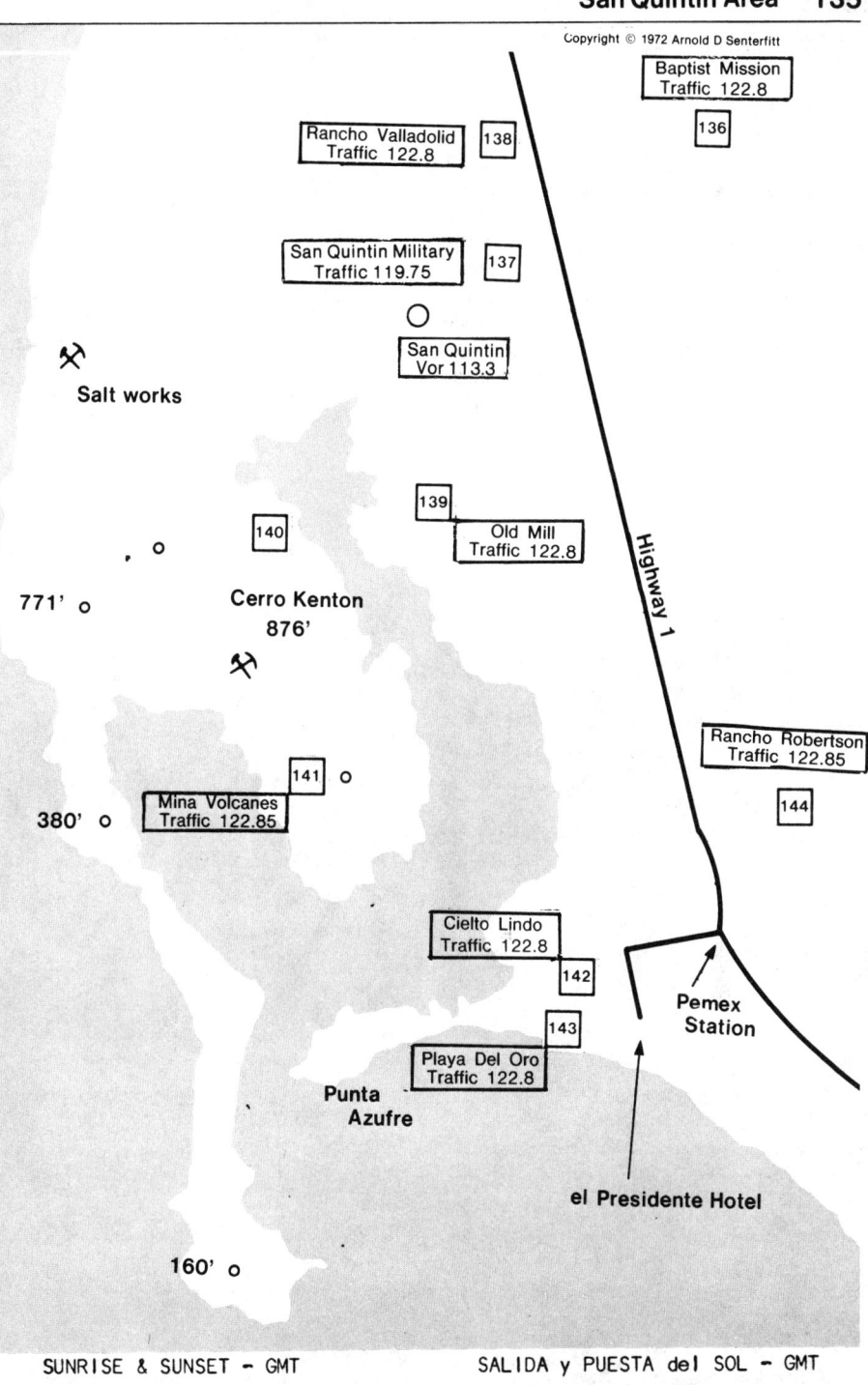

San Quintin Area 135

Baptist Mission
Traffic 122.8

136

Rancho Valladolid
Traffic 122.8

138

San Quintin Military
Traffic 119.75

137

San Quintin
Vor 113.3

Salt works

140

139

Old Mill
Traffic 122.8

Highway 1

771'

Cerro Kenton
876'

Rancho Robertson
Traffic 122.85

144

141

Mina Volcanes
Traffic 122.85

380'

Cielto Lindo
Traffic 122.8

142

Pemex
Station

143

Playa Del Oro
Traffic 122.8

Punta
Azufre

el Presidente Hotel

160'

SUNRISE & SUNSET - GMT							SALIDA y PUESTA del SOL - GMT					
15th of	JAN	FEB	MAR	APR	MAY	JUN	JUL	AUG	SEPT	OCT	NOV	DEC
SUNRISE	1441	1424	1353	1316	1249	1240	1251	1310	1328	1346	1409	1433 SALIDA
SUNSET	0104	0131	0151	0211	0230	0247	0247	0226	0149	0112	2446	2444 PUESTA
15° de	ENE	FEB	MAR	ABR	MAY	JUN	JUL	AGO	SEP	OCT	NOV	DIC

INTRODUCTION

BORDER CROSSING

BAJA CALIFORNIA

NORTHWEST MEXICO

NORTHEAST MEXICO

COCONUT COAST

YUCATAN

CENTRO AMERICA

APPENDIX

Copyright © 1972 Arnold D Senterfitt

136 Baptist Mission Baja Calif. Norte

JET CHART	WAC	SECTIONAL	LATITUDE	LONGITUDE	US TIME	FOR GMT ADD	ICAO IDENT	TOWN IDENT
JN-46	CH-22 No. ADS-15	TPC H-22A	30°35'	115°56'	PST/PDT	8/7	-	-BPT-

OTHER COMM Traffic 122.8
SETTLEMENT NE Side   POPULATION 75
LOCAL Vor   FREQ 113.3   WHERE 4 miles W   HOURS 24
FROM Tijuana   FREQ 116.5   TRACK 143°, 133 n.mi.
FROM Mexicali FREQ 115.0   TRACK 182°, 130 n.mi.
FUEL 80 Emergency   CARDS -   CASH? Pesos
REPAIRS Minor   TIEDOWN BYO

Loren Long's small full service hospital is an asset to the San Quintín valley: they treat health problems first, then discuss religion. Local efforts are reinforced by physicians of all specialties available from their US practices less than two hours away.

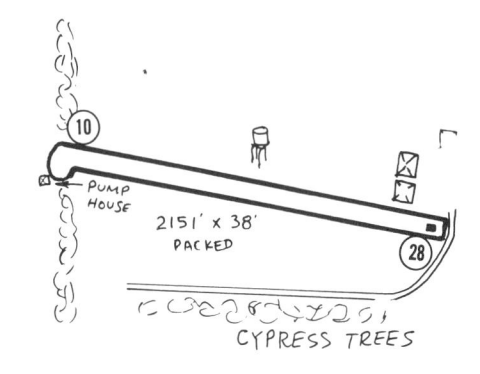

ELEVATION
215'

San Quintín Military   Baja Calif. Norte   *sohn keen-TEEN*   137

JET CHART	WAC	SECTIONAL	LATITUDE	LONGITUDE	US TIME	FOR GMT ADD	ICAO IDENT	TOWN IDENT
46	CH-22 No. ADS-15	TPC H-22A	30°33'	115°58'	PST	8	-	-SQM-

OTHER COMM   Traffic 118.1-
SETTLEMENT   SE End   POPULATION   Army base
FROM   Tijuana   FREQ 116.5   TRACK 142°, 129.2 n.mi.
FROM   Mexicali   FREQ 115.0   TRACK 183°, 130.7 n.mi.
FROM   la Paz   FREQ 112.3   TRACK 312°, 489.1 n.mi.
FUEL -   CARDS -   CASH? -
REPAIRS -   TIEDOWN BYO

HOTEL	RATE	WHERE	TEL
el Presidente	$$$	8 mi So.	
Old Mill	$$	4 mi SW	-
Ernesto's	$$	4 mi SW	-

At this writing, the only paved airport in the San Quintín area, the soldiers have been good about permitting landings by twins unsuitable for the dirt airports around here. Otherwise, the hotel airports are more convenient in this taxi-less farming community.

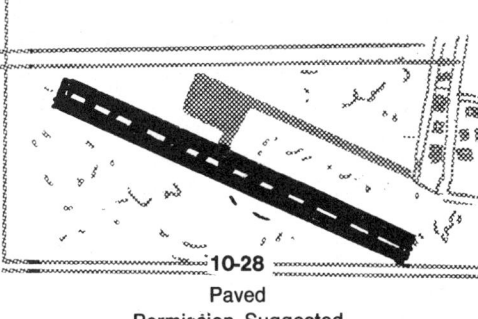

10-28
Paved
Permission Suggested

ELEVATION
213'

138 Rancho Valladolid   Baja Calif. Norte   *bye-ah-doe-LEED*

JET CHART	WAC	SECTIONAL	LATITUDE	LONGITUDE	US TIME	FOR GMT ADD	ICAO IDENT	TOWN IDENT
JN-46	CH-22 No. ADS-15	TPC H-22A	30°34'	115°57'	PST/PDT	8/7	-	-VDO-

OTHER COMM   Traffic 122.8-
SETTLEMENT   1/2 mile S   POPULATION   900
LOCAL   Vor   FREQ 113.3   WHERE 3 miles NW   HOURS 24
FROM   Tijuana   FREQ 116.5   TRACK 143°, 130 n.mi.
FROM   Mexicali   FREQ 115.0   TRACK 184°, 129n.mi.
FUEL   Private stock 80   CARDS -   CASH? Yes
REPAIRS   Minor   TIEDOWN BYO

HOTEL	RATE	WHERE	TEL
Old Mill	$$	4 miles W	-
Ernesto's	$$	4 miles W	-

A busy agricultural strip in the lush San Quintín valley where much of Southern California's table vegetables are grown. At various times you may see any kind of aircraft from pressurized twins to modest dusters parked here.

2227'
Hard Dirt

ELEVATION
65'

Old Mill Baja Calif. Norte   *Molino Viejo* **139**

JET CHART	WAC	SECTIONAL	LATITUDE	LONGITUDE	US TIME	FOR GMT ADD	ICAO IDENT	TOWN IDENT
JN-46	CH-22 No. ADS-15	TPC H-22A	30°30'	115°58'	PST	8	-	-MOL-

OTHER COMM Traffic 122.8
SETTLEMENT 1/2 mile SW   POPULATION 75
LOCAL Vor FREQ 113.3 WHERE 2 miles N. HOURS 24
FROM Tijuana FREQ 116.5 TRACK 143°, 136 n.mi.
FROM Rancho Sta Ynez FREQ airport TRACK 292°, 73n.mi.
FUEL Seldom 100/130   CARDS –   CASH? Yes
REPAIRS –   TIEDOWN BYO

HOTEL	RATE	WHERE	TEL
Al Vela's Old Mill	$$	1/2 mi.SW	-
Ernesto's	$$	1/2 mi SW	-

Rough runway taking you to nice people. Al and Dorothy Vela have been running the Old Mill several years. Although architecturally a 30s Motor Court, their personal charm makes it special.

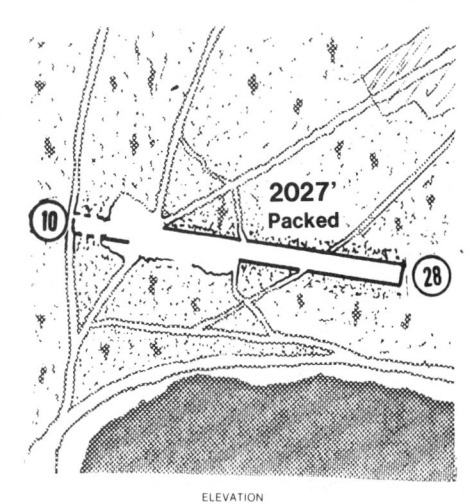

ELEVATION
71'

140 Pedregal, BCN Baja Calif. Norte *pedd-ray-GAL*

JN CHART	WAC	SECTIONAL	LATITUDE	LONGITUDE	US TIME	FOR GMT	ICAO	TOWN ID
JN-46	CH-22 ADS-15	TPC H22A	30°28'	115°57'	PST	+8	-	PDD –

OTHER COMM Traffic 124.5
SETTLEMENT Adjacent   POPULATION 3 to 40
LOCAL Vor   FREQ 113.3   WHERE 3 miles NE
FROM Tijuana   FREQ 116.5   TRACK 142°, 134.8 n.mi.
FROM Mexicali   FREQ 115.0   TRACK 182°, 135.2 n.mi.
FROM Ensenada   FREQ Adf1010   TRACK 143°, 86.7 n.miles
AVIATION GAS ·   CARDS ·   CASH TYPE ·
REPAIRS AVAILABLE ·   TIEDOWNS BYO

2299'x46' Packed Dirt

6' Mound

Uphill 17'

1570' TO TOP

ELEVATION
11' to 28 msl'

The fishermen of San Quintin now have their own fly-in homesites for lease, here across from the Old Mill area. Well on their way to their second dozen homes built, everyone is very handy to the runway. This area is about to bust wide open with development; if anyone were thinking about moving in that direction, they shouldn't wait too long. 16-140

Mina Volcanes   Baja Calif. Norte   *MEE-nah vole-CAH-ness*   **141**

JET CHART	WAC	SECTIONAL	LATITUDE	LONGITUDE	US TIME	FOR GMT ADD	ICAO IDENT	TOWN IDENT
JN-46	CH-22 No. ADS-15	TPC H-22A	30°26'	115°59'	PST/PDT	8/7	-	-VOL-

OTHER COMM Traffic 122.85
SETTLEMENT Isolated   POPULATION -
LOCAL Vor   FREQ 113.3   WHERE 4 miles N   HOURS 24
FROM Tijuana   FREQ 116.5   TRACK 145°, 136 n.mi.
FROM Mexicali   FREQ 115.0   TRACK 184°, 137 n.mi.
FUEL -   CARDS -   CASH? -
REPAIRS -   TIEDOWN BYO

The mining activity was removing lava gravel from San Quintín's four volcanic hills for use as concrete aggregate. That stopped twenty years ago, leaving this gently rolling surface to the occasional campers who treasure total isolation.

With this mini-peninsula teetering on the verge of explosive development, any day you can expect to see city level constructions replace this total isolation. It was fun.

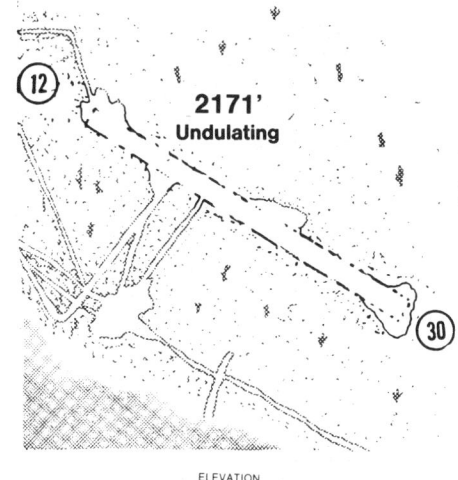

2171'
Undulating

ELEVATION
25' to 35'

142 Cielito Lindo Baja Calif. Norte *see-ay-LEE-toe LEEN-doe*

JET CHART	WAC	SECTIONAL	LATITUDE	LONGITUDE	US TIME	FOR GMT ADD	ICAO IDENT	TOWN IDENT
JN-46	CH-22 No. ADS-15	TPC H-22A	30°34'	115°55'	PST	8	-	-MTA-

OTHER COMM Traffic 122.8
SETTLEMENT Motel Adjacent SW   POPULATION 15-35
LOCAL Vor   FREQ 113.3   WHERE 335°   HOURS 6n.mi.
FROM Tijuana   FREQ 116.5   TRACK 156°, 139 n.mi.
FROM Mexicali   FREQ 115.0   TRACK 181°, 138n.mi.
FUEL Expensive 100/130   CARDS -   CASH? -
REPAIRS -   TIEDOWN BYO

HOTEL	RATE	WHERE	TEL
Cielito Lindo	$$	here	-
el Presidente	$$	1 mile SE	-

An airport for Cielito Lindo and el Presidente hotels. If you stay at el Presidente make it the West rooms, the East ones are too near a huge generator plant. Cielito Lindo is quiet; you get to bed with the chickens.

A tip: park only on the West side of the parking area to limit the very fine silt dust getting into your airplane's every nook and cranny.

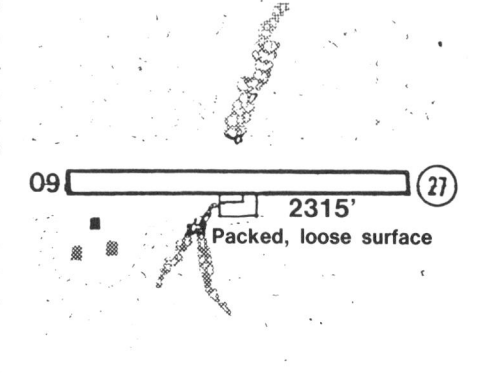

09 ⟶ 2315' ⟵ 27
Packed, loose surface

ELEVATION
19'

Playa de Oro   Baja Calif. Norte   *PLY-ah dell OH-roe*   **143**

JET CHART	WAC	SECTIONAL	LATITUDE	LONGITUDE	US TIME	FOR GMT ADD	ICAO IDENT	TOWN IDENT
JN-46	CH-22 No. ADS-15	TPC H-22A	30°03'	115°56'	PST/PDT	8/7	-	-PDO-

OTHER COMM Traffic 122.8
SETTLEMENT Ranch NE corner   POPULATION about 5
LOCAL Vor   FREQ 113.3   WHERE 5 mi. NW   HOURS 24
FROM Tijuana   FREQ 116.5   TRACK 156°,140 n.mi.
FROM Mexicali FREQ 115.0   TRACK 181°,139n.mi.
FUEL -   CARDS -   CASH? -
REPAIRS -   TIEDOWN BYO

HOTEL	RATE	WHERE	TEL
el Presidente	$$	0.5 mile E	-

This runway has definite rough spots but there is an unlimited supply of three- to four-inch-diameter sand dollars ready to be picked up over in the beach dunes. All us kids like to take them home.

To land any closer to the beach than this you'd need to be rolling on the sand, a no no of course because of the marvelous corrosion it generates.

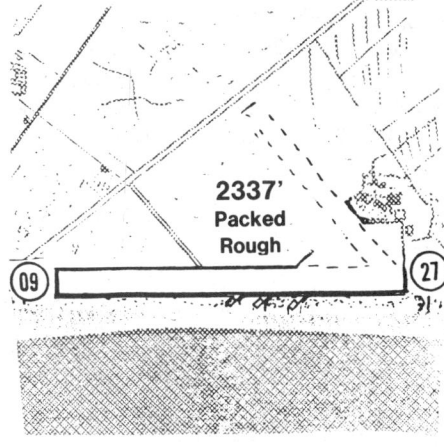

2337'
Packed Rough

09   27

ELEVATION
13'

144 Rancho Robertson Baja Calif. Norte

JET CHART	WAC	SECTIONAL	LATITUDE	LONGITUDE	US TIME	FOR GMT ADD	ICAO IDENT	TOWN IDENT
JN-46	CH-22 No. ADS-15	TPC H-22A	30°26'	115°52'	PST	8	-	-

OTHER COMM Traffic 122.8
SETTLEMENT West side POPULATION Ranch
FROM San Quintín FREQ 113.3 TRACK 120°, 6n.mi.,
FROM NA FREQ 116.5 TRACK 141°, 138 n.mi.
FROM Rcho Sta Ynez FREQ airport TRACK 290°, 69n.mi.,
FUEL - CARDS - CASH? -
REPAIRS - TIEDOWN BYO

Very interesting lady, Mrs Robertson is of a pioneer family in this area, wonderful lady.

No longer used much, this was a pioneer ranch in the San Quintin valley and a famous one. Now off the beaten track things are kind of coasting waiting for the next move. With full-scale development of the area about to bust out things could get busy at the drop of a pin. First thing to disappear will be this airport.

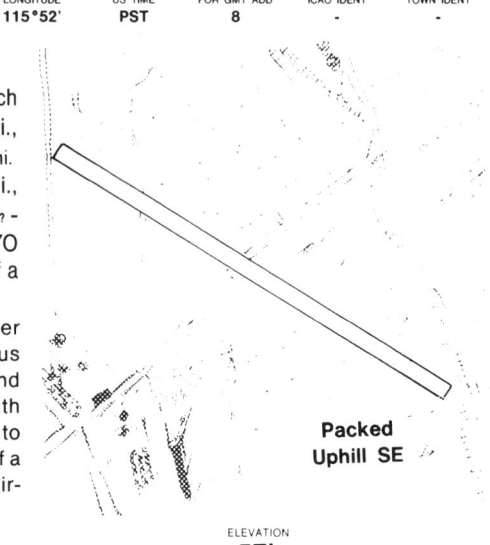

Packed
Uphill SE

ELEVATION
57'

Rancho el Socorro Baja Calif. Norte *ell so-CORE-oh* **145**

JET CHART	WAC	SECTIONAL	LATITUDE	LONGITUDE	US TIME	FOR GMT ADD	ICAO IDENT	TOWN IDENT
JN-46	CH-22 No. ADS-15	TPC H-22A	30°19'	115°49'	PST	8	-	-SOC-

OTHER COMM Traffic 122.85
SETTLEMENT Both sides   **POPULATION** 29
FROM San Quintín **FREQ** 113.3 **TRACK** 141°,14n.mi.
FROM Tijuana **FREQ** 116.5 **TRACK** 140°,146 n.mi.
FROM Rancho Sta Ynez **FREQ** airport **TRACK** 297°,64n.mi.
FUEL -   **CARDS** -   **CASH?** -
REPAIRS -   **TIEDOWN** BYO

Pleasant beachside lots available here for either trailers or cabins. Must be ten or twelve at last count. Be sure to ask permission for camping.

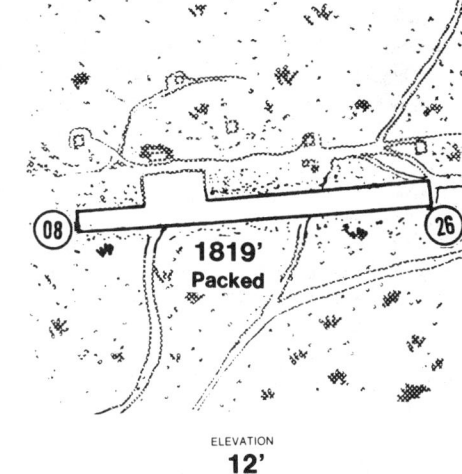

1819' Packed

ELEVATION
12'

146 el Rosario East   Baja Calif. Norte   *ell roce-ARR-ee-yoh*

JET CHART	WAC	SECTIONAL	LATITUDE	LONGITUDE	US TIME	FOR GMT ADD	ICAO IDENT	TOWN IDENT
JN-46	CH-22 No. ADS-15	TPC H-22A	30°05'	115°45'	PST	8	-	-ROS-

OTHER COMM   Traffic 118.1
SETTLEMENT   2.5 miles So.   POPULATION 900
FROM   San Quintín   FREQ 113.3   TRACK 146°, 27n.mi.
FROM   Tijuana   FREQ 116.5   TRACK 142°, 161 n.mi.
FROM   Rancho Sta Ynez FREQ airport TRACK 276°, 54n.mi.
FUEL   Some 80/87   CARDS -   CASH? Yes
REPAIRS   Minor   TIEDOWN BYO

HOTEL	RATE	WHERE	TEL
Casa Espinosa	-$	In town	-

3115' Packed Some holes

The Flying Samaritans' founding clinic was here in Anita Espinosa's living/dining room. Over nearly twenty years of that flying doctor's effort we've had many delightful experiences here and at other places where later clinics were established. Check the Index for details.

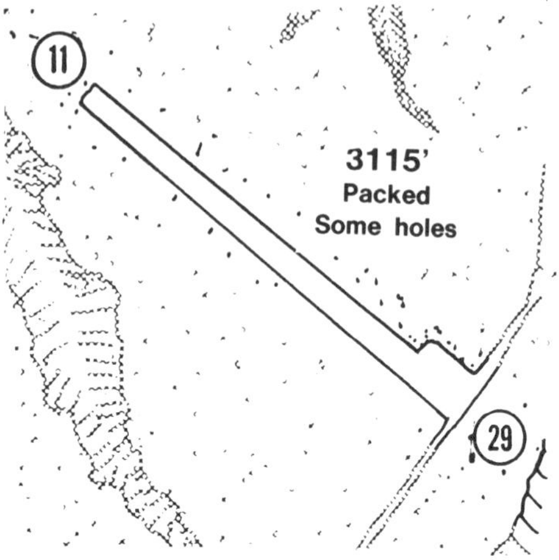

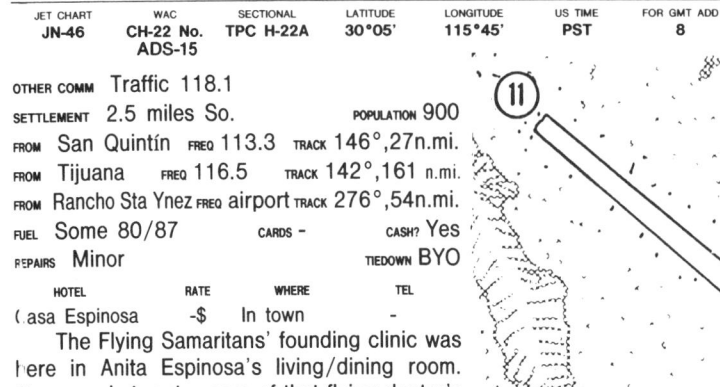

ELEVATION **855'**

el Rosario West Mesa Baja Calif. Norte   *ell roce-ARR-ee-oh*   **147**

JET CHART	WAC	SECTIONAL	LATITUDE	LONGITUDE	US TIME	FOR GMT ADD	ICAO IDENT	TOWN IDENT
JN-46	CH-22 No. ADS-15	TPC H-22A	30°04'	115°45'	PST	8	-	-ROS-

OTHER COMM Traffic 118.1
SETTLEMENT 3 miles So.   POPULATION 900
FROM San Quintín FREQ 113.3 TRACK 147°, 28n.mi.
FROM Tijuana FREQ 116.5 TRACK 142°, 162 n.mi.
FROM Rancho Sta Ynez FREQ airport TRACK 275°, 55n.mi.
FUEL Some 80/87   CARDS -   CASH? Yes
REPAIRS Minor   TIEDOWN BYO

HOTEL	RATE	WHERE	TEL
Casa Espinosa	-$	Central	-

Built in WW2 for the coastal patrol aircraft, this was the Flying Samaritans' first airport when we started bringing medical care to remote parts of the peninsula. Still my favorite of the two runways on this mesa.

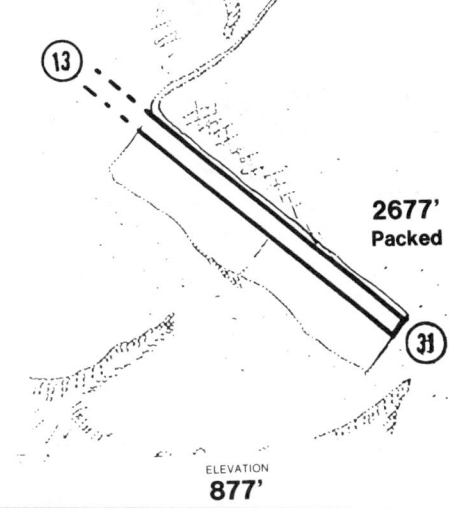

2677'
Packed

ELEVATION
877'

Punta San Carlos Briefing

Anne Curl with several dinners for she and Jerry

Baja Bush Pilots' Shore Survival practice

A favorite August camping spot for the Baja Bush Pilots and for a pooped airport measurer looking for a quiet place to stop for lunch or to spend the night. The Pacific both lulls you to sleep and gently awakens you the next morning.

The Cocker Spaniels of the sea are the California Sealions which very quietly lift their heads up out of the water to watch us pitching tents, cooking on the tail of the airplane, and in general behaving like people. When we are a little too obviously watching, they will silently submerge, move fifty or sixty feet then just as silently reappear. Watching them is just the level of activity one needs to start awakening to a new day.

Keep in mind here that the shorter runway is the better surface. But do also remember that as you taxi over to cliffside parking to be careful of the Baja Bush Pilots' barbeque pit in the middle of our usual covered wagon circle of airplanes. It is a soft area because we re-dig that hole each time and reuse the large stones for our pit barbeque.

The pit barbeque system is that we all bring firewood, build a good intense two hour fire to thoroughly heat these stones, clean out the fire and put in our pre-seasoned cloth covered meats and bury it under a few feet of dirt. Next afternoon we reopen the pit and start eating fantastic foods oS It is easiest to spot the soft plan ah witu first shut down and walk around before taxiing.

Cliffside bother you? We routinely park ten or more of our airplanes within thirty to forty feet of the cliff's edge.

Beachcombing is excellent, the lobster fishermen are more often here during months which contain an 'R', careful of those August tropical showers. And don't forget to either take all your trash with you or bury it more than two feet below the surface. Either action makes you a paidup member of the Punta San Carlos Chamber of Commerce.

Author measuring the shorter runway

Punta San Carlos   Baja Calif. Norte   *POON-tah sahn-CARR-loce*   **149**

JET CHART	WAC	SECTIONAL	LATITUDE	LONGITUDE	US TIME	FOR GMT ADD	ICAO IDENT	TOWN IDENT
JN-46	CH-22 No. ADS-15	TPC H-22A	29°38'	115°32'	PST	8	-	-PSC-

OTHER COMM Traffic 122.85
SETTLEMENT 1 mile E   POPULATION 0 to 50
FROM Tijuana   FREQ 116.5   TRACK 142°,191 n.mi.
FROM San Quintin   FREQ 113.3   TRACK 142°,58n.mi.
FROM Rancho Sta Ynez FREQ Airport TRACK 252°,41n.mi.
FUEL -   CARDS -   CASH? -
REPAIRS -   TIEDOWN BYO

1515'
Fine Gravel
Nice

44' MSL

ELEVATION
55'

Excellent camping with lobster for eating only. Fishing laws reserve all shellfish for commercial Mexican fishermen so they catch; you buy, cook, and eat. Not a bad arrangement.

As is the case with camping at Rancho X, if you camp here on the bluff next to the sea, the seals will so quietly stick their heads up out of the water and watch everything you are doing.

I prefer the shorter strip because it is usually smoother, once you find its south end.

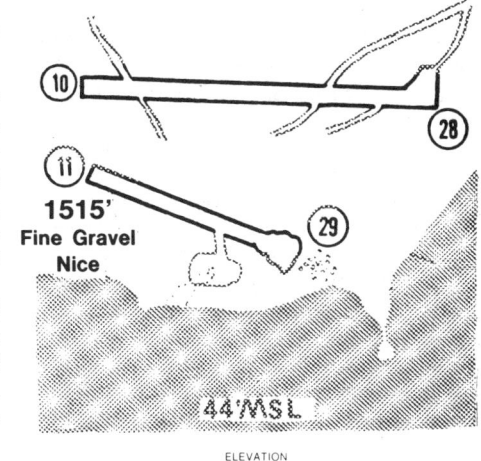

150 el Marmol   Baja Calif. Norte   *ell MAR-mole*

JET CHART	WAC	SECTIONAL	LATITUDE	LONGITUDE	US TIME	FOR GMT ADD	ICAO IDENT	TOWN IDENT
JN-46	CH-22 No. ADS-15	TPC H-22A	29°58'	114°54'	PST	8	-	-MRM-

OTHER COMM Traffic 122.85
SETTLEMENT 1 mile East   POPULATION Zero
FROM San Quintin FREQ 113.3 TRACK 107°, 67 n.mi.
FROM Pta Peñasco FREQ 112.1 TRACK 205°, 106 n.mi.
FUEL -   CARDS -   CASH? -
REPAIRS -   TIEDOWN BYO

Would you believe an onyx schoolhouse set in a few more acres of loose, ready to be picked up, onyx? No? Then pass right on by, the shock could do you in.

Of the few remaining buildings from an onyx ghost town, the two foot thick walled school is the most intact. But by wandering around you will find plenty to gather for home. Don't get too much, as others did and dropped it on the walk back to the plane as you noticed while walking in.

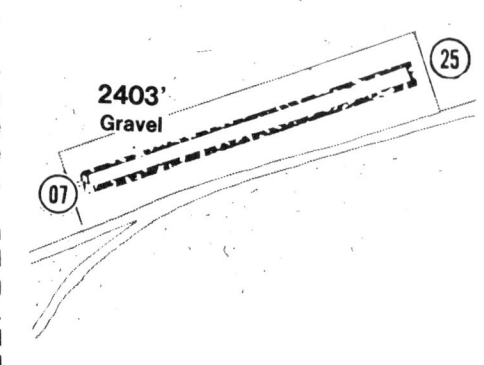

2403'
Gravel

ELEVATION
1843'

Rancho Santa Ynez   Baja Calif. Norte   *RON-cho SON-tah ee-NESS*   **151**

JET CHART	WAC	SECTIONAL	LATITUDE	LONGITUDE	US TIME	FOR GMT ADD	ICAO IDENT	TOWN IDENT
JN-46	CH-22 No. ADS-15	TPC H-22A	29°48'	114°46'	PST	8	-	SNZ

OTHER COMM Traffic 122.85
SETTLEMENT Ranch adjacent N   POPULATION 7
FROM Mexicali   FREQ 115.0   TRACK 152°, 172n.mi.
FROM Tijuana   FREQ 116.5   TRACK 131°, 200 n.mi.
FROM San Quintin FREQ 113.3   TRACK 112°, 76n.mi.
FUEL 80, 100, JP   CARDS -   CASH? Yes
REPAIRS Minor   TIEDOWN BYO

HOTEL	RATE	WHERE	TEL
Casa Josefina	-$	Here	-
el Presidente	$$	1 KM No.	-

A dependable fuel stop for many years made more so now with the 24,000 gallon capacity tanks. Owner Dona Josefina has a lunchstand, a few bunks in clean but spartan rooms, and two acre lots available on long-term lease. Excellent mid-peninsula stop.

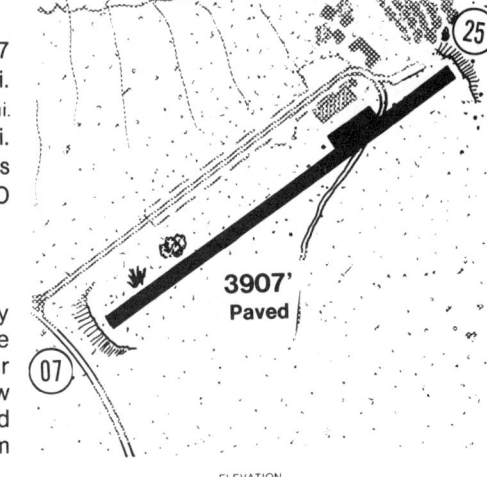

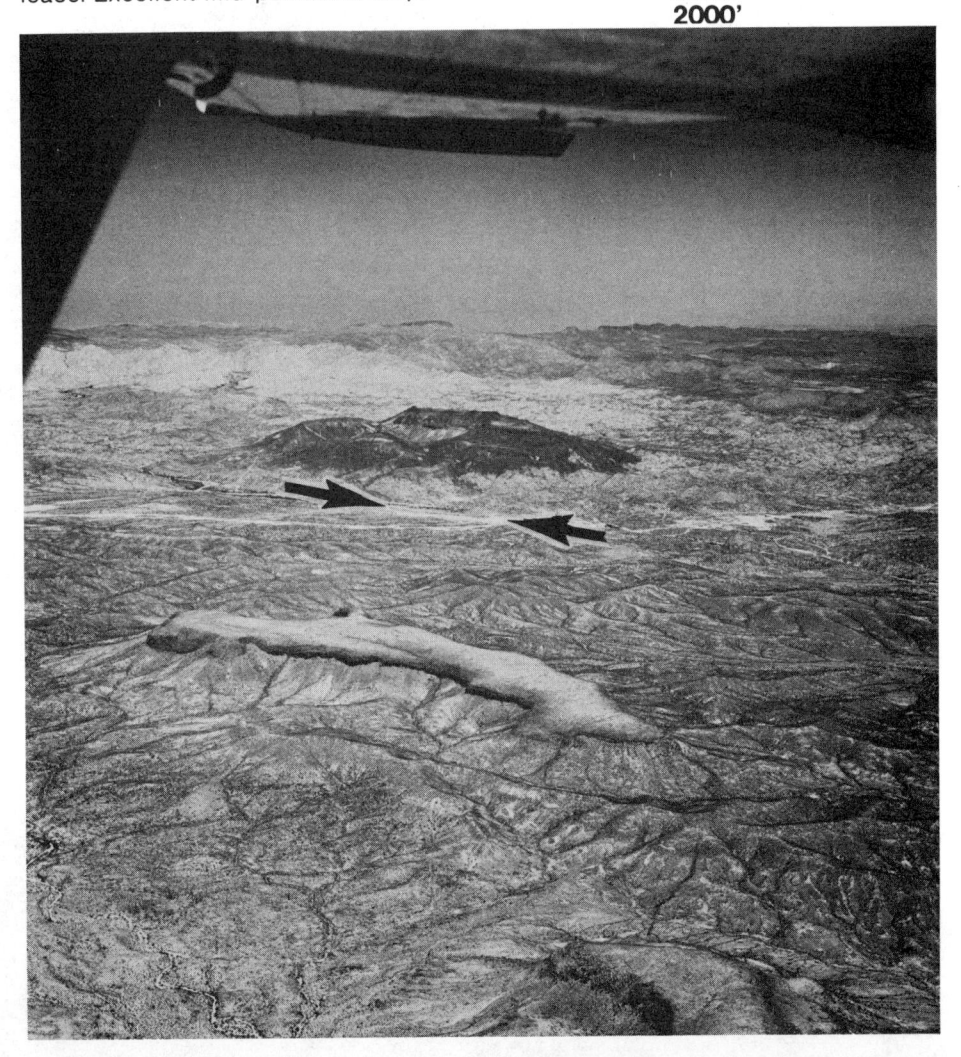

3907'
Paved

ELEVATION
2000'

152 Rancho Chapala Baja Calif. Norte *RON-cho chop-AH-lah*

JET CHART	WAC	SECTIONAL	LATITUDE	LONGITUDE	US TIME	FOR GMT ADD	ICAO IDENT	TOWN IDENT
JN-46	CH-22 No. ADS-15	TPC H-22B	29°26'	114°22'	PST	8	-	-CHP-

OTHER COMM Traffic 122.85
SETTLEMENT 1 mile SE POPULATION 5 to 20
FROM San Quintín FREQ 113.3 TRACK 117°,106n.mi.
FROM Punta Peñasco FREQ 112.1 TRACK 189°,129 n.mi.
FROM Rancho Sta Ynez FREQ airport TRACK 125°,33n.mi.
FUEL -   CARDS -   CASH? -
REPAIRS -   TIEDOWN BYO

The dry lakes immediately south were, for years and years, the only hard flat place on the highway for hundreds of miles. After days of five sometimes wowee! twelve mph, drivers could live it up by turning sixty for a mile or two. Then it was back to a subsonic speed.

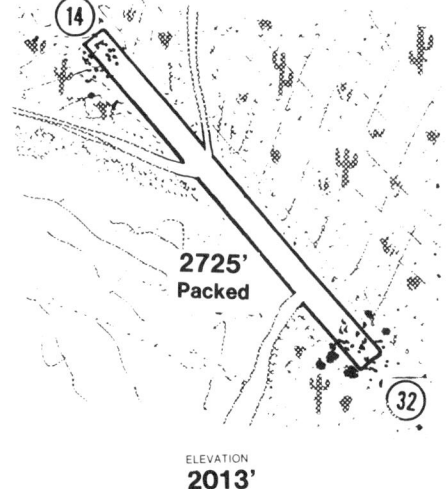

2725' Packed

ELEVATION
2013'

Punta Prieta   Baja Calif. Norte   *POON-ta pree-ETT-ah*   153

JET CHART	WAC	SECTIONAL	LATITUDE	LONGITUDE	US TIME	FOR GMT ADD	ICAO IDENT	TOWN IDENT
JN-46	CH-22 No. ADS-15	TPC H-22B	28°57'	114°10'	PST	8	-	-PRT-

OTHER COMM Traffic 118.1
SETTLEMENT 1/8 mile NW   POPULATION 59
FROM Guerrero Negro FREQ 382 TRACK 345°, 60n.mi.
FROM San Quintín FREQ 113.3 TRACK 122°, 133n.mi.
FROM Rancho Sta Ynez FREQ airport TRACK 138°, 63n.mi.
FUEL -   CARDS -   CASH? -
REPAIRS -   TIEDOWN BYO

Highway department built this runway when Highway One was getting done. Soldiers will meet your landing but they are nice guys and are more curious than anything else. Restaurant up the street. You and your children will get a kick out of those giant cardón (cactus) on two sides. Look like sahuaro but they're quite different up close.

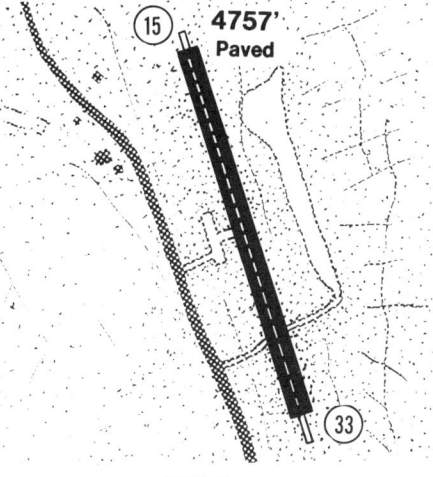

4757'
Paved

ELEVATION
859'

154 Pta Santa Rosallilita Baja Calif. Norte *sahn-ta rose-ah-lee-lEET-ah*

JET CHART	WAC	SECTIONAL	LATITUDE	LONGITUDE	US TIME	FOR GMT ADD	ICAO IDENT	TOWN IDENT
JN-46	CH-22 No. ADS-15	TPC H-22B	28°42'	114°13'	PST	8	-	-RLL-

OTHER COMM Traffic 118.1
SETTLEMENT 1/2 mile S POPULATION about 50
FROM San Quintín FREQ 113.3 TRACK 126°, 143n.mi.
FROM Guerrero Negro FREQ 382 TRACK 339°, 44n.mi.
FUEL - CARDS - CASH? -
REPAIRS - TIEDOWN BYO

If you don't mind the walk, there are some fine camping beaches around here. The little island just up the beach is almost covered with birds and seals a lot of the time. They appreciate quiet neighbors.

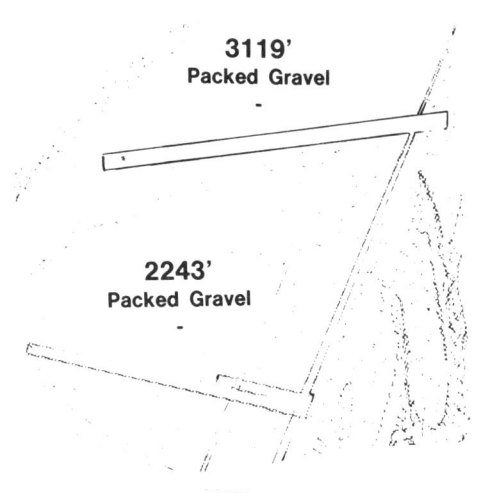

3119'
Packed Gravel
-

2243'
Packed Gravel
-

ELEVATION
113'

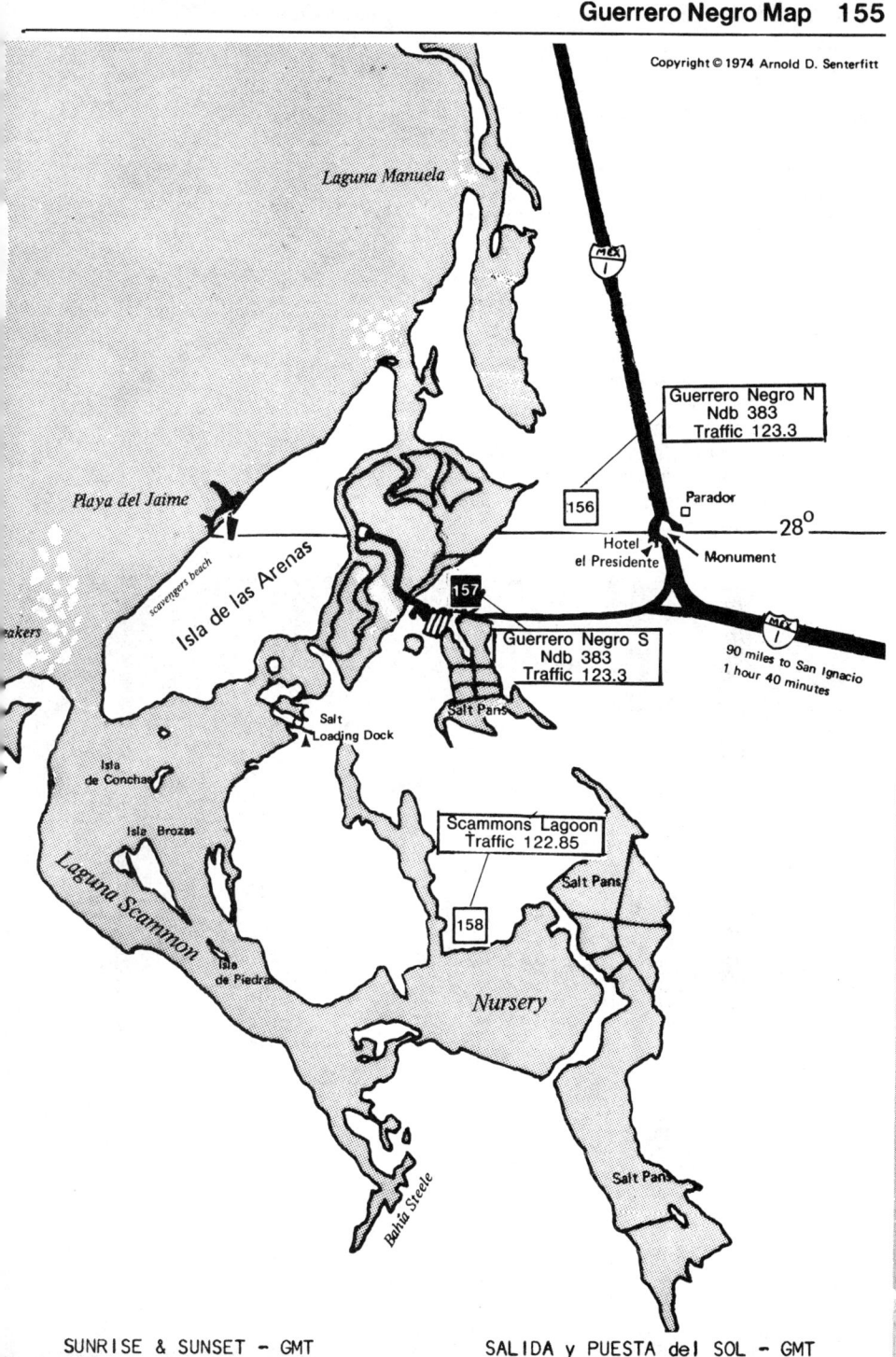

Guerrero Negro Map 155

Copyright © 1974 Arnold D. Senterfitt

Laguna Manuela

Guerrero Negro N
Ndb 383
Traffic 123.3

156

Parador

Playa del Jaime

28°

Hotel el Presidente — Monument

scavengers beach

Isla de las Arenas

157

Guerrero Negro S
Ndb 383
Traffic 123.3

90 miles to San Ignacio
1 hour 40 minutes

Salt Loading Dock

Salt Pans

Isla de Conchas

Isla Brozas

Scammons Lagoon
Traffic 122.85

158

Salt Pans

Laguna Scammon

Isle de Piedra

Nursery

Salt Pans

Bahía Steele

SUNRISE & SUNSET - GMT   SALIDA y PUESTA del SOL - GMT

15th of	JAN	FEB	MAR	APR	MAY	JUN	JUL	AUG	SEPT	OCT	NOV	DEC	
SUNRISE	1428	1413	1345	1311	1246	1239	1249	1306	1321	1336	1357	1420	SALIDA
SUNSET	0102	0126	0144	0201	0218	0233	0234	0214	0141	0107	2443	2442	PUESTA
15° de	ENE	FEB	MAR	ABR	MAY	JUN	JUL	AGO	SEP	OCT	NOV	DIC	

To get local time just subtract 'GMT ADD'
PARA OBTENER TIEMPO LOCAL SUSTRIAGA 'GMT ADD'

INTRODUCTION | BORDER CROSSING | BAJA CALIFORNIA | NORTHWEST MEXICO | NORTHEAST MEXICO | COCONUT COAST | YUCATAN | CENTRO AMERICA | APPENDIX

156 Guerrero Negro Baja Calif. Norte   goo-RARE-oh NEGG-roe

JET CHART	WAC	SECTIONAL	LATITUDE	LONGITUDE	US TIME	FOR GMT ADD	ICAO IDENT	TOWN IDENT
JN-46	CH-22 No. ADS-15	TPC H-22B	28°01'	114°05'	MST	7	-	GRN

OTHER COMM Exportadora 123.3; Salt Company
CITY 4 miles S   POPULATION 3,500
LOCAL Ndb FREQ 383 WHERE 4 mi. SSW HOURS on request
FROM San Quintin FREQ 113.3 TRACK 137°,179n.mi.
FROM Santa Rosalia FREQ 112.6 TRACK 282°,103n.mi.
FROM S.J. del Cabo FREQ 114.0 TRACK 310°,380n.mi.
REPAIRS -   TIEDOWN BYO

HOTEL	RATE	WHERE	TEL
el Presidente	$$	1.5 miles SE	-
Motel la Duna	$	East of town	-

No fuel at this airport: see other one
Built so the President of México could stop here and dedicate the transpeninsular highway. Too far from town for the infrequent air taxis, and with no Baja California air line service these past years, not much happens here. See the downtown airport.

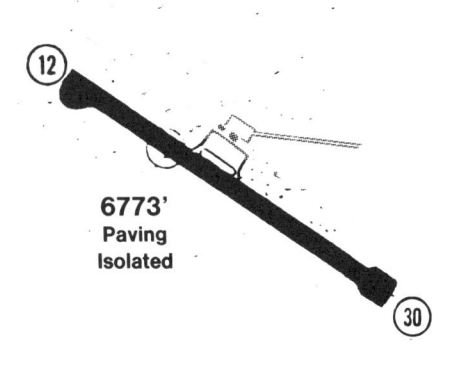

6773'
Paving
Isolated

ELEVATION
15' to 25'

Guerrero Negro-S Baja Calif. Sur   *goo-RARE-oh NEGG-roe*   **157**

JET CHART	WAC	SECTIONAL	LATITUDE	LONGITUDE	US TIME	FOR GMT ADD	ICAO IDENT	TOWN IDENT
JN-46	CH-22 ADS-15	TPC H-22C	27°58'	114°02	MST	7	-	GNO

OTHER COMM Traffic 123.3
CITY Adjacent SW   POPULATION 3,500
LOCAL GN   FREQ 383   WHERE Adj SW   HOURS Varies
FROM Santa Rosalia FREQ 112.6 TRACK 281°, 101 n.mi.,
FROM San Quintín FREQ 113.3 TRACK 133°, 182 n.mi.,
FROM Hermosillo FREQ 112.8 TRACK 235°, 171 n.mi.
FUEL Some 100   CARDS -   CASH? Yes
REPAIRS Minor   TIEDOWN BYO

HOTEL	RATE	WHERE	TEL
el Presidente	$$	1 mi NE	Tvl Agt
la Duna	$	3/4 mi E	-
Baja Sur	$	3/4 mi E	-

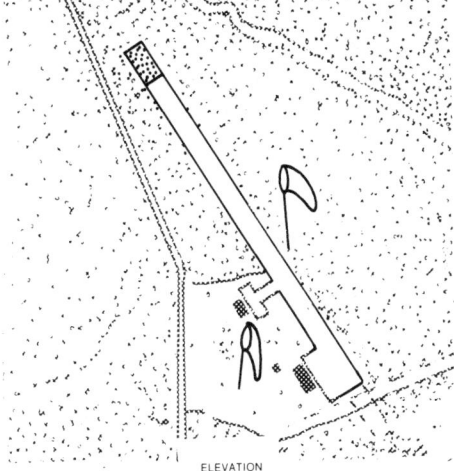

ELEVATION

158 Scammons Lagoon — Baja Calif. Sur

JET CHART	WAC	SECTIONAL	LATITUDE	LONGITUDE	US TIME	FOR GMT ADD	ICAO IDENT	TOWN IDENT
JN-46	CH-22 No. ADS-15	TPC H-22B	27°46'	114°04'	MST	7	-	-SCM-

OTHER COMM Traffic 122.85
CITY 14 miles NNW POPULATION 5,100
FROM Guerrero Negro FREQ 382 TRACK 155°, 14n.mi.
FROM San Quintín FREQ 113.3 TRACK 136°, 192n.mi.
FROM Santa Rosalia FREQ 112.6 TRACK 275°, 100n.mi.
FUEL - CARDS - CASH? -
REPAIRS - TIEDOWN BYO

Closest you can get to the Nursery of this whales lagoon but the airport is closed when the whales are here. Just as well, you see nothing from the beach. Best to fly at 1,000' and look down; the view is excellent.

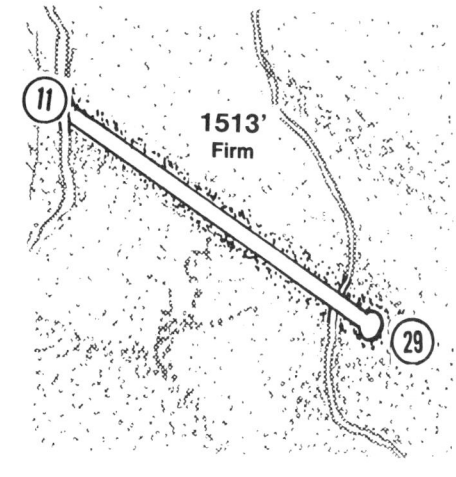

1513' Firm

ELEVATION
55'

Playa Malarrimo　Baja Calif. Sur　　*PLY-ah mal-ah-REE-ma*　**159**

JET CHART	WAC	SECTIONAL	LATITUDE	LONGITUDE	US TIME	FOR GMT ADD	ICAO IDENT	TOWN IDENT
JN-46	CH-22 No. ADS-15	TPC H-22C	27°48'	114°43'	MST	7	-	-MAL-

OTHER COMM　Traffic 123.3
SETTLEMENT　Adjacent NE　　POPULATION 0 to 65
FROM　Guerrero Negro FREQ 382 TRACK 240°,34n.mi.
FROM　San Quintín FREQ 113.3 TRACK 146°,176n.mi.
FROM　Santa Rosalia FREQ 112.6 TRACK 271°,135n.mi.
FUEL　-　　CARDS -　　CASH? -
REPAIRS　-　　TIEDOWN BYO

If anyone ever tells you they were camped here and the whales kept them awake, believe it. From about December until March the California grays are in the Scammons Lagoon area from Alaska. Females in the lagoons, males outside. All night long hundreds of males patrol this coast each one spouting every few minutes. Sounds like a convention of freight trains after the wind dies down about 3 a.m. Good luck on sleeping.

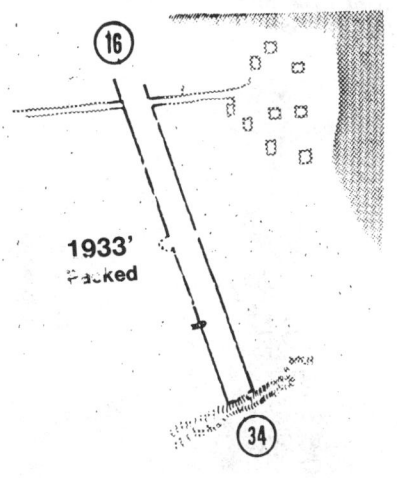

1933'
Packed

ELEVATION
16' to 30'

160 Malarimmo Briefing

mal-ah-REE-moe

Local fishermen with smaller versions of lobster and fish you can buy here.

On dirt runways we do all final positioning of aircraft by hand.

A favorite whale-visiting place during the annual December to March California gray whale visits to the nearby lagoons where they birth this year's children and make whooppee for the two years from now generation. When the Baja Bush Pilots are in town we camp, eat lobster, and listen to passing male whales trumpet all thru the night. Sounds a bit like steam locomotives running slowly.

The first 26 Baja Bush Pilots planes outnumber the number of houses in town.

Isla Cedros Baja Calif. Sur

EES-lah SEDD-roce **161**

JET CHART	WAC	SECTIONAL	LATITUDE	LONGITUDE	US TIME	FOR GMT ADD	ICAO IDENT	TOWN IDENT
JN-46	CH-22 No. ADS-15	TPC H-22A	28°02'	115°11'	MST	7	-	ICD

OTHER COMM Company radio 123.3; same for traffic
CITY 3 miles N   POPULATION 5,500
FROM Guerrero Negro FREQ 382 TRACK 262°, 57n.mi.
FROM San Quintin FREQ 113.3 TRACK 163°, 154n.mi.
FUEL Emergency: flown in from G. Negro CARDS - CASH? -
REPAIRS -   TIEDOWN BYO

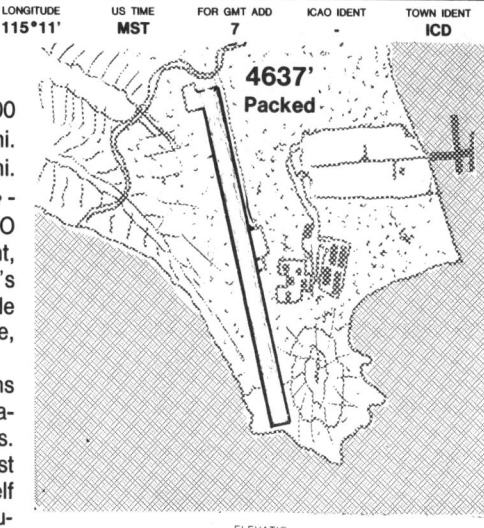

4637' Packed

ELEVATION
62' to 77'

If ever anything was hidden in plain sight, Cedros is. Heading north or south along Baja's West coast it is almost a fixed spot on your side window for an hour or more; go look sometime, it is interesting.

At this south end salt by the millions of tons arrives by barge from Guerrero Negro's lagoons for shipment to the world markets. Northwest a few miles the island's West Coast is a scavenger's beach deluxe. The town itself is up that road North. No cabs but you can usually negotiate something. Give it a try.

162 Isla Natividad   Baja Calif. Sur   *EES-lah naw-tee-vee-DOD*

JET CHART	WAC	SECTIONAL	LATITUDE	LONGITUDE	US TIME	FOR GMT ADD	ICAO IDENT	TOWN IDENT
JN-46	CH-22 No. ADS-15	-	27°41'	115°10'	MST	7	-	-TVD-

OTHER COMM Traffic 123.3
SETTLEMENT Adjacent SW   **POPULATION** 400
FROM Guerrero Negro **FREQ** 382 **TRACK** 272°, 56n.mi.
FROM San Quintin **FREQ** 113.3 **TRACK** 154°, 167n.mi.

Site of an early engineering test model solar seawater distillation system which did work and well. This population was perfect for the test. They have plenty of sun, barge water in from Cedros for drinking and watering flowers. Brainchild of a modest La Jollan named Horace McCracken, these units are now used in many other places.

READER REPORT Satelite television has come to Natividad. Each of the fishermens houses have 40 channels of color TV. People here use lobsters to repay favors like a plane ride to Cedros, etc. —J Sprague, California.

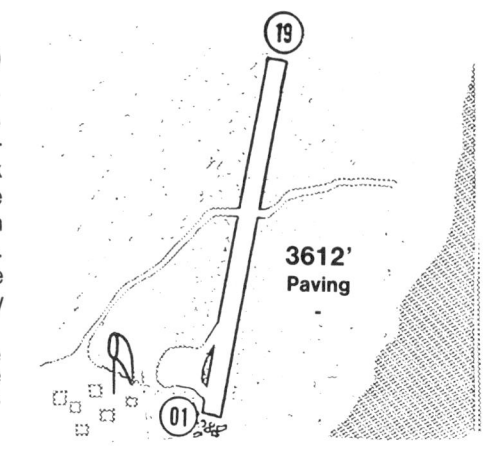

3612' Paving

ELEVATION
40' to 60'

Bahía Tortugas Baja Calif. Sur   *bah-EE-yah tore-TOO-guss*   163

JET CHART	WAC	SECTIONAL	LATITUDE	LONGITUDE	US TIME	FOR GMT ADD	ICAO IDENT	TOWN IDENT
JN-46	CH-22 No. ADS-15	TPC H-22C	27°42'	114°55'	MST	7	-	BTO

OTHER COMM Traffic 118.1
SETTLEMENT 1 mile West   **POPULATION** 4,100
FROM Guerrero Negro **FREQ** 382 **TRACK** 238°, 46n.mi.
FROM San Quintín **FREQ** 113.3 **TRACK** 149°, 179n.mi.
FROM Santa Rosalia **FREQ** 112.6 **TRACK** 270°, 141n.mi.
FUEL 80/87 by truck?   **CARDS** -   **CASH?** Pesos
REPAIRS Minor   **TIEDOWN** BYO

Almost totally enclosed bay near Baja California's middle is a favorite stop for boats beating northward from Cabo San Lucas. Those few tourists arriving by air may be accommodated at a rustic motel in town, not that far from the infamous Casa Azul.

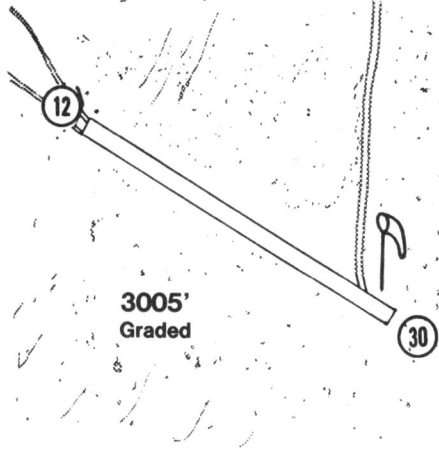

3005'
Graded

ELEVATION
105'

164 Bahía Asunción Baja Calif. Sur bah-EE-yah oss-oon-see-OWN

JET CHART	WAC	SECTIONAL	LATITUDE	LONGITUDE	US TIME	FOR GMT ADD	ICAO IDENT	TOWN IDENT
JN-46	CH-22 So. ADS-15	TPC H-22C	27°11'	114°16'	MST	7	-	BSU

OTHER COMM Traffic 118.1
SETTLEMENT 4 miles SW   POPULATION 3,500
FROM San Quintin FREQ 113.3 TRACK 142°, 217n.mi.
FROM Guerrero Negro FREQ 382 TRACK 174°, 46n.mi.
FROM Santa Rosalia FREQ 112.6 TRACK 255°, 100n.mi.
FUEL Some 100   CARDS -   CASH? Pesos
REPAIRS -   TIEDOWN BYO

HOTEL	RATE	WHERE	TEL
Local hotel	-$	Central	-

One of two islands along this coast is located at the tippy end of that point near town. It is seal-encrusted a lot of the year when the seals, properly California Sea Lions, use the island's isolation for breeding and birthing. Buzz town at 500' AGL for a cab.

2914'
Packed
Some ruts

3977'
Hard

ELEVATION
199'

la Bocana-1 Baja Calif. Sur

lah boe-CAH-nah **165**

JET CHART	WAC	SECTIONAL	LATITUDE	LONGITUDE	US TIME	FOR GMT ADD	ICAO IDENT	TOWN IDENT
JN-46	CH-22 So. ADS-15	TPC H-22C	26°38'	113°41'	MST	7	-	-BCN1-

OTHER COMM Traffic 118.1
SETTLEMENT 2 miles WSW   POPULATION 1.100
FROM Guerrero Negro FREQ 382 TRACK 156°,70n.mi.
FROM Santa Rosalia FREQ 112.6 TRACK 237°,83n.mi.
FUEL 100 Sometimes   CARDS -   CASH? Pesos
REPAIRS -   TIEDOWN BYO

Not much to look at, however this runway is dry, hard, has good approaches and even sometimes a windsock might be seen. What more could you ask.

Typical of this coast, expect morning stratus with a 600' ceiling and burnoff VFR about nine to eleven a.m. If you camp here, there is not one even tiny stick of wood to be found: bring everything.

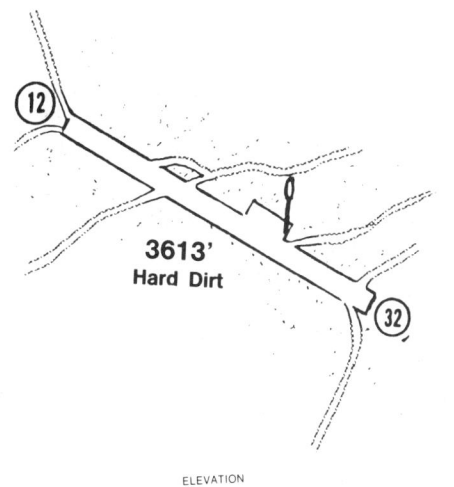

3613'
Hard Dirt

ELEVATION
147'

166 la Bocana   Baja Calif. Sur   *lah boe-CAH-nah*

JET CHART	WAC	SECTIONAL	LATITUDE	LONGITUDE	US TIME	FOR GMT ADD	ICAO IDENT	TOWN IDENT
JN-46	CH-22 No. ADS-15	TPC H-22C	26°50'	113°41'	MST	7	-	-BN-

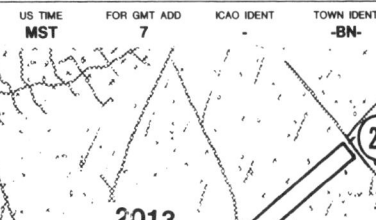

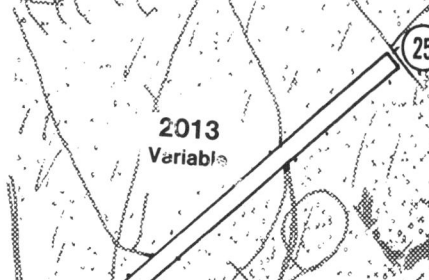

OTHER COMM   Traffic 118.1
SETTLEMENT   Adjacent NW   POPULATION 1,100
FROM   Guerrero Negro   FREQ 382   TRACK 155°, 70n.mi.
FROM   Santa Rosalia   FREQ 112.6   TRACK 238°, 82n.mi.
FUEL   100 sometimes   CARDS -   CASH? Pesos
REPAIRS   -   TIEDOWN BYO

Fishermens village along the 'nose' of Baja California, this runway can be squishy if you combine high gross with small tires.

Quickest test is to look at your tire pressure: 30 or below is usually okay. Over 30 psi of air pressure in your tires means you could duplicate Ed Murnane's experience of all but burying a Coast Guard SA-16 on this runway. His tire pressure that day was 105 psi.

ELEVATION
Sea level

Punta Abreojos Baja Calif. Sur   *POON-tah obb-ray-OH-HOSE*   167

JET CHART	WAC	SECTIONAL	LATITUDE	LONGITUDE	US TIME	FOR GMT ADD	ICAO IDENT	TOWN IDENT
JN-46	CH-22 So. ADS-15	TPC H-22C	26°45'	113°34'	MST	7	-	PAB

OTHER COMM Traffic 122.95
CITY 1 mile W   POPULATION 3,000
FROM Guerrero Negro FREQ 382 TRACK 148°,77n.mi.
FROM Santa Rosalia FREQ 112.6 TRACK 231°,77n.mi.
FROM Mulegé FREQ Serenidad TRACK 251°,86n.mi.
FUEL 100   CARDS -   CASH? Any
REPAIRS Minor   TIEDOWN BYO

  Casa Villavicencio: bring sleeping bags
  Fishing village with a button factory: a Japanese concern hires local girls to punch disks out of shells from abalone, clam, and other shellfish. No cottage industry, they have their own building.
  René Villavicencio still runs the store and a 'camping in' place to stay. But nowadays his camp at Bahia Ballenas is preferred.

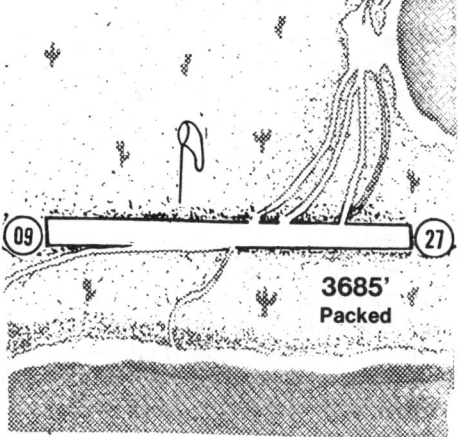

3685'
Packed

ELEVATION
3

168 Bahia de las Ballenas — Baja Calif. Sur — bah-EE-yah day loss bah-YAY-nuss

JET CHART	WAC	SECTIONAL	LATITUDE	LONGITUDE	US TIME	FOR GMT ADD	ICAO IDENT	TOWN IDENT
JN-46	CH-22 So. ADS-15	TPC H-22C	26°49'	113°28'	MST	7	-	-BBS-

OTHER COMM Traffic 122.85
SETTLEMENT NE side   **POPULATION** 10
FROM Guerrero Negro **FREQ** 382 **TRACK** 144°, 75n.mi.
FROM Santa Rosalia **FREQ** 112.6 **TRACK** 235°, 70n.mi.
FROM Loreto **FREQ** Airport **TRACK** 293°, 124n.mi.
FUEL 100 prior Req.   **CARDS** -   **CASH?** Yes
REPAIRS -   **TIEDOWN** BYO

HOTEL	RATE	WHERE	TEL
Casa René	-$	here	-

3654' Packed Sand Hard
06 / 24

ELEVATION
10'

Here on the side of the bay of ballenas, (bah-YAY-nuss) whales, you have a ringside seat at the annual arrival from the Arctic of several hundred thirty- to fifty-ton mammals. They make this four-month trip for calving and to whoop it up for the next crop of two-ton babies.

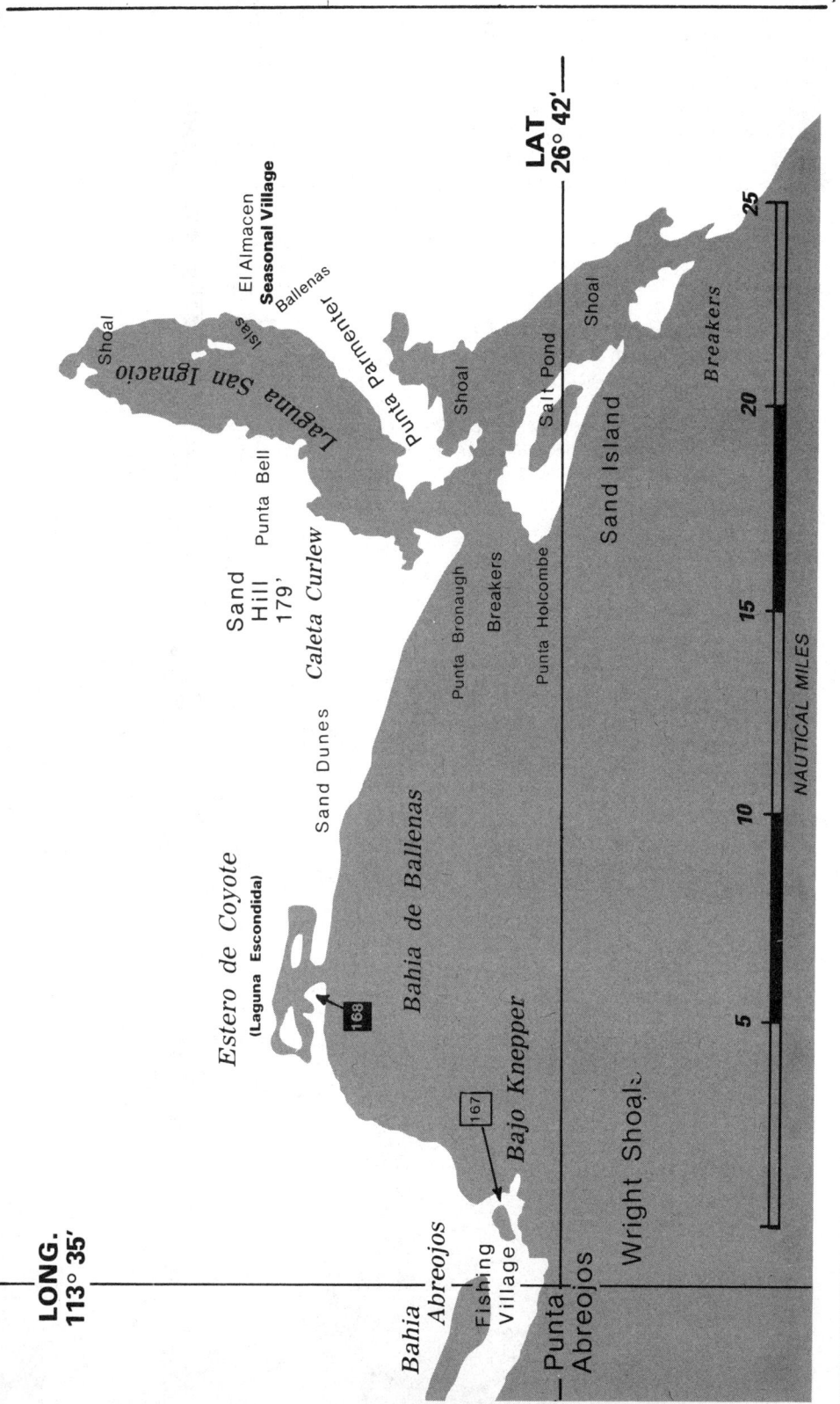

Bahia de las Ballenas 169

LONG. 113° 35'

LAT 26° 42'

- Bahia Abreojos
- Fishing Village
- Punta Abreojos
- Wright Shoals
- Bajo Knepper
- Estero de Coyote (Laguna Escondida)
- Bahia de Ballenas
- Sand Dunes
- Sand Hill 179'
- Caleta Curlew
- Punta Bell
- Laguna San Ignacio
- Shoal
- Isias
- Ballenas
- El Almacen — **Seasonal Village**
- Punta Parmenter
- Shoal
- Punta Bronaugh
- Breakers
- Punta Holcombe
- Salt Pond
- Shoal
- Sand Island
- Breakers

167
168

NAUTICAL MILES
5 10 15 20 25

San Ignacio-West Baja Calif. Sur   *sahn igg-NAH-see-oh*

JET CHART	WAC	SECTIONAL	LATITUDE	LONGITUDE	US TIME	FOR GMT ADD	ICAO IDENT	TOWN IDENT
JN-46	CH-22 So. ADS-15	TPC H-22C	27°18'	112°56'	MST	7	-	SIB

OTHER COMM Traffic 122.85
CITY 3 miles E   POPULATION 4,000
FROM Guerrero Negro FREQ 382 TRACK 111°, 71n.mi.
FROM Santa Rosalia FREQ 112.6 TRACK 258°, 35n.mi.
FROM Loreto FREQ Airport TRACK 303°, 114n.mi.
FUEL -   CARDS -   CASH? -
REPAIRS Minor   TIEDOWN BYO

HOTEL	RATE	WHERE	TEL
el Presidente	$$	Central	-
la Posada	$	Central	-

36 / 18
4947' Paved Crosswind
ELEVATION 889'

The combination of a prevailing 90° crosswind, instant access from the highway, and isolation from the city make this an uncomfortable place to park. Mostly pilots send their passengers to town by cab, then take their airplanes to the Downtown airport which has far better security although it is not generally a great runway.

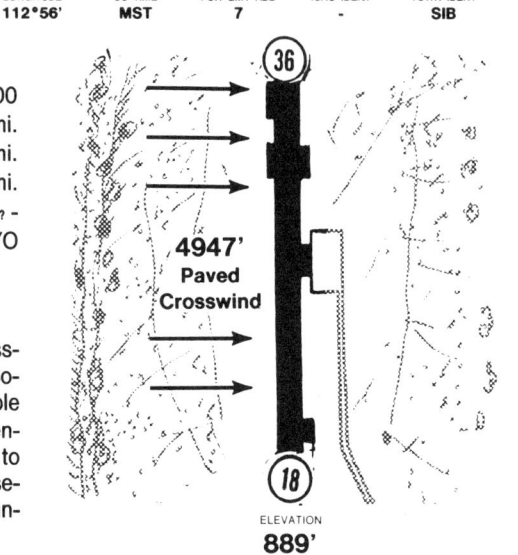

San Ignacio Downtown			Baja Calif. Sur			*sahn igg-NAH-see-oh*			**171**
JET CHART	WAC	SECTIONAL	LATITUDE	LONGITUDE	US TIME	FOR GMT ADD	ICAO IDENT	TOWN IDENT
JN-46	CH-22 So. ADS-15	TPC H-22C	27°17'	112°53'	MST	-	-	SIB

OTHER COMM Traffic 122.85
CITY 3/8 mile SW POPULATION 4,000
FROM Guerrero Negro FREQ 382 TRACK 110°,74n.mi.
FROM Santa Rosalia FREQ 112.6 TRACK 257°,32n.mi.
FROM Mulegé Serenidad FREQ airport TRACK 285°,53n.mi.

FUEL -   CARDS -   CASH? -
REPAIRS -   TIEDOWN BYO

HOTEL	RATE	WHERE	TEL
el Presidente	$$	Central	-
la Posada	$	Central	-

Already an ancient city when the Spaniards came to Baja California in the 1500s, San Ignacio's artesian river and natural agriculture makes it a true oasis. The mission is of hand hewn pink stone blocks hauled by men to the central plaza.

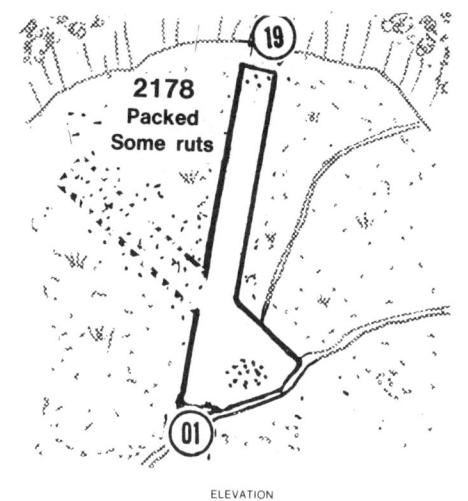

2178
Packed
Some ruts

ELEVATION
497'

172 Cadajé   Baja Calif. Sur   *ah-dah-HAY*

JET CHART	WAC	SECTIONAL	LATITUDE	LONGITUDE	US TIME	FOR GMT ADD	ICAO IDENT	TOWN IDENT
JN-46	CH-22 So. ADS-15	TPC H-22C	26°25'	112°29'	MST	7	-	-CJE-

OTHER COMM Traffic 122.85-
SETTLEMENT 0.2 miles NE   POPULATION 100
FROM Santa Rosalia FREQ 112.6 TRACK 180°, 54n.mi.
FROM Guerrero Negro FREQ 382 TRACK 128°, 125n.mi.
FROM La Paz   FREQ 112.3   TRACK 310°, 182 n.mi.
FUEL -   CARDS -   CASH? -
REPAIRS -   TIEDOWN BYO

A true Baja California oasis: people found a little water and have built a settlement around it. Clean, tidy place with a small general store where you can find a soft drink, some crackers, and very basic canned things. Flying Samaritans clinic site.

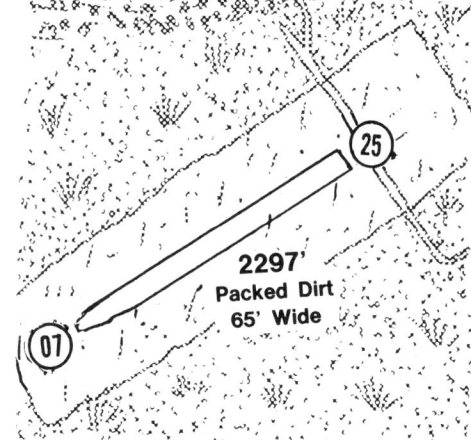

2297' Packed Dirt 65' Wide

ELEVATION
210'

San Juanico Baja Calif. Sur   *sawn waun-EE-coe*   173

JET CHART	WAC	SECTIONAL	LATITUDE	LONGITUDE	US TIME	FOR GMT ADD	ICAO IDENT	TOWN IDENT
JN-46	CH-22 So. ADS-15	TPC H-22C	26°17'	112°29'	MST	7	-	SCO

OTHER COMM Traffic 122.85
SETTLEMENT 1/4 mile SE   POPULATION 400
FROM Santa Rosalia FREQ 112.6 TRACK 178°, 67n.mi.
FROM La Paz   FREQ 112.3   TRACK 309°, 176 n.mi.
FROM Loreto   FREQ Airport   TRACK 276°, 64n.mi.
FUEL -   CARDS -   CASH? -
REPAIRS -   TIEDOWN BYO

Fishing village and a Flying Samaritans monthly stop, the lack of parking indicates they can't handle two airplanes at once.

At least one US pilot of a light twin likes to land here on the sand; don't be surprised to see an airplane parked inches above high tide.

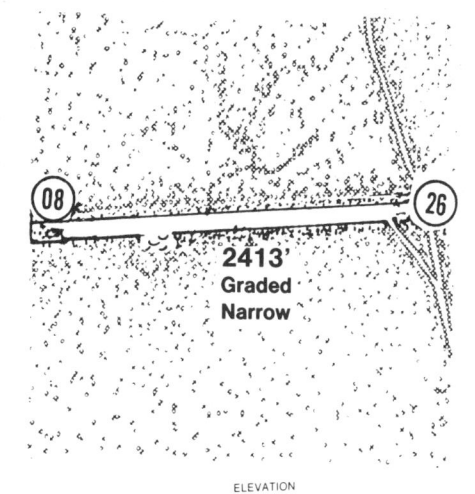

2413'
Graded
Narrow

ELEVATION
85'

174 San Isidro Baja Calif. Sur *sohn ee-SEED-roe*

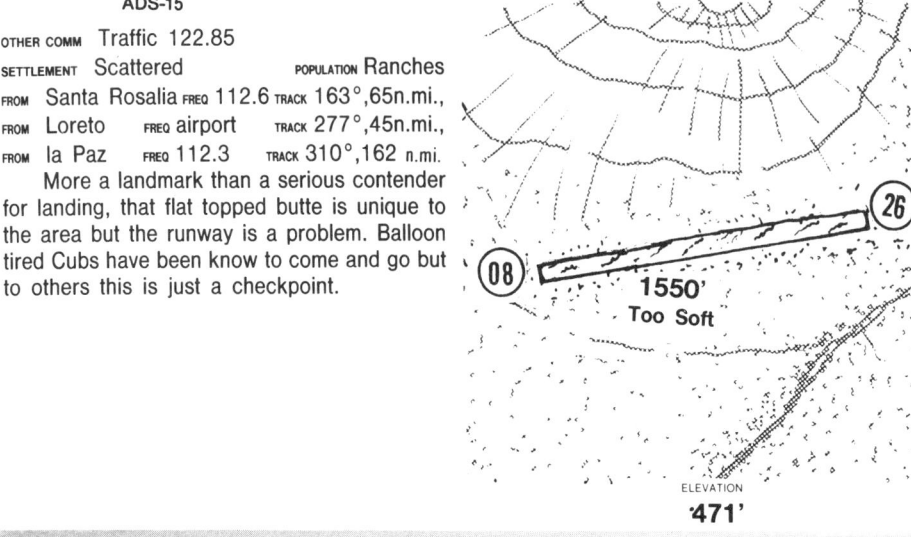

JET CHART	WAC	SECTIONAL	LATITUDE	LONGITUDE	US TIME	FOR GMT ADD	ICAO IDENT	TOWN IDENT
JN-46	CH-22 So. ADS-15	TPC H-22C	26°13'	112°11'	MST	7	-	-

OTHER COMM Traffic 122.85
SETTLEMENT Scattered   POPULATION Ranches
FROM Santa Rosalia FREQ 112.6 TRACK 163°, 65n.mi.,
FROM Loreto   FREQ airport   TRACK 277°, 45n.mi.,
FROM la Paz   FREQ 112.3   TRACK 310°, 162 n.mi.

More a landmark than a serious contender for landing, that flat topped butte is unique to the area but the runway is a problem. Balloon tired Cubs have been know to come and go but to others this is just a checkpoint.

1550'
Too Soft

ELEVATION
'471'

la Purísima Baja Calif. Sur *lah poo-REE-see-mah* 175

JET CHART	WAC	SECTIONAL	LATITUDE	LONGITUDE	US TIME	FOR GMT ADD	ICAO IDENT	TOWN IDENT
JN-46	CH-22 So. ADS-15	TPC H-22C	26°09'	112°08'	MST	7	-	PUR

OTHER COMM Traffic 122.85
CITY 3 miles NE   POPULATION 800
FROM Santa Rosalia FREQ 112.6 TRACK 162°, 72 n.mi.
FROM La Paz   FREQ 112.3 TRACK 311°, 157 n.mi.
FROM Loreto   FREQ Airport TRACK 272°, 44 n.mi.
FUEL -   CARDS -   CASH? -
REPAIRS -   TIEDOWN BYO

3527'
Firm Dirt
E end rough

ELEVATION
697'

This lonely airport far from even a tiny town has a good reason for being here: it intersects the famous Jesuit Trail. Predecessor to all the highways of today, it was a five-foot-wide thoroughfare connecting the missions and ranches of all three Californias. Kept carefully maintained and smooth for the weekly postal riders who had absolute right of way this four-hundred-year-old highway remains as a reminder today.

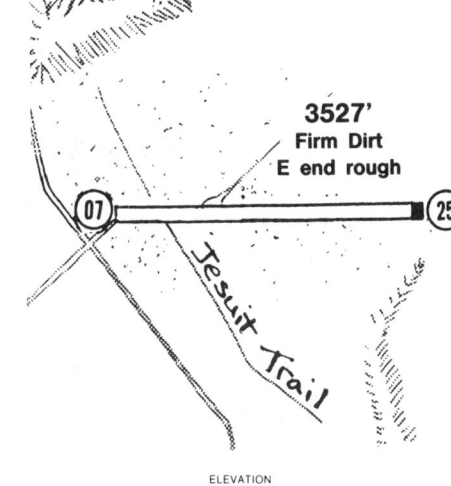

176 Villa Constitución Baja Calif. Sur *VEE-yah con-stee-too-cee-OWN*

JET CHART	WAC	SECTIONAL	LATITUDE	LONGITUDE	US TIME	FOR GMT ADD	ICAO IDENT	TOWN IDENT
JN-46	CH-22 So. ADS-15	TPC H-22C	25°05'	111°41'	MST	7	-	VCT

OTHER COMM Traffic 118.1
CITY 1/2 miles SE
POPULATION 31,000
B'CAST FREQ 1440   WHERE -   HOURS Daylight
FROM Santa Rosalia FREQ 112.6 TRACK 155°,138n.mi.
FROM La Paz   FREQ 112.3   TRACK 299°,95Dme
FROM Loreto   FREQ Airport   TRACK 188°,57n.mi.
FUEL 80 ocasionally   CARDS -   CASH? Pesos
REPAIRS Minor   TIEDOWN BYO

HOTEL	RATE	WHERE	TEL
Hotel Maribel	$	Central	2-01-55
Hotel Casino	-$	Central	2-00-04

Mostly a duster (fumigator) strip to serve the rapidly growing agriculture belt of Southern Baja California. Every few years an airline pops up briefly: VCT gets Air Service for awhile, then back to normal. Bustling city with easy telephone service to all points.

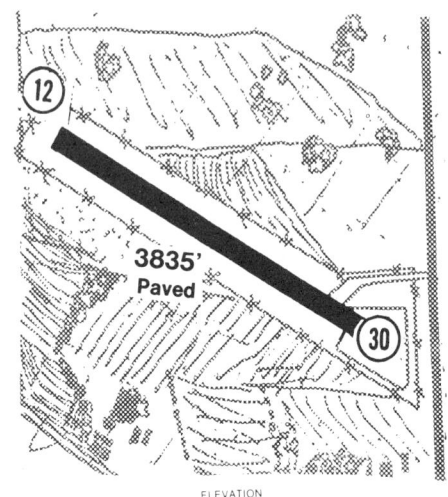

3835' Paved

ELEVATION **137'**

Villa Constitucion New — Baja Calif. Sur — *VEE-yah cone-stee-too-see-OWN* — 177

JN CHART	WAC	SECTIONAL	LATITUDE	LONGITUDE	US TIME	FOR GMT	ICAO	TOWN ID
JN-61	CH-22 ADS-15	TPC H22C	25°07'	111°27'	MST	+7	-	VCT

OTHER COMM Traffic 124.1
CITY 4 miles SW
B'Cast 1440 WHERE 4 mi SW
FROM La Paz FREQ 112.3
FROM Santa Rosalia FREQ 112.6
FROM Loreto FREQ 113.4

POPULATION 21,000
HOURS Daylight
TRACK 302°, 86.1 Dme
TRACK 148°, 139 n.mi.
TRACK 172°, 52.1 Dme

AVIATION FUEL ·   CREDIT CARDS ·   CASH TYPE ·
REPAIRS AVAILABLE ·   TIEDOWNS ·

Data Incomplete

FARM
DOWNHILL 9'
FARM

178 Matancitas Baja Calif. Sur *ma-tawn-SEE-tuss*

JET CHART	WAC	SECTIONAL	LATITUDE	LONGITUDE	US TIME	FOR GMT ADD	ICAO IDENT	TOWN IDENT
JN-46	CH-22 So. ADS-15	TPC H-22C	25°11'	112°07'	MST	7	-	-MTC-

OTHER COMM Traffic 118.1
CITY Cannery town Adjacent POPULATION 3,500
FROM Santa Rosalia FREQ 112.6 TRACK 165°, 128n.mi.
FROM La Paz FREQ 112.3 TRACK 294°, 118 n.mi.
FROM V.Constitución FREQ 1440 TRACK 274°, 24n.mi.
FUEL Some 80 CARDS - CASH? Pesos
REPAIRS Minor TIEDOWN BYO

Busy packing plant with a Cessna 172 fish spotter airplane. Resulting town is a chance to get basic supplies if you're camping in the area. I have purchased 80/87 here but three hours is lightning fast, plan four.

Avoid landing or taxiing on the dark part: they dry their black nets on the light tan runway.

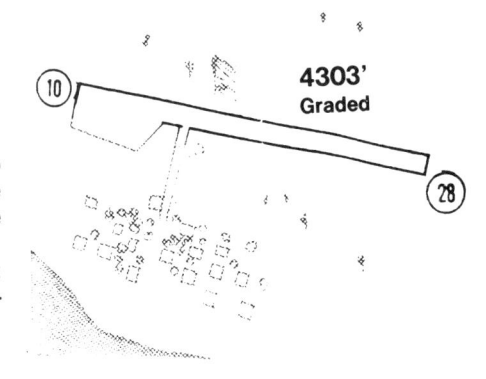

4303'
Graded

ELEVATION
27'

they're sort of fading away   **Baja California's Shipwrecks**   **179**

For its length and purported maritime hazardousness, Baja California hasn't had all that many shipwrecks in the twenty-some years I've been looking out the window of an airplane. These three, plus a Navy vessel north of Ensenada and a ferry which blew up in La Paz are all I've seen which involve ocean-going vessels.

It is interesting to see these and speculate how much better you and I would've handled each situation.

Fish Story

There is a story about the trawler which I first saw in the early sixties. The story came to me later and may or may not be strict truth. Seems it was not a Mexican vessel but was fishing in Mexican waters by undercover techniques. They'd come in at night, set their fish traps, marking them with underwater sonic buoys and go back out to international waters. Next night they'd ADF in to the traps, harvest them, then wait out the day safely in international waters. With only simple farmers and cowboys as adversaries they were doing well.

But, the story goes, the simple cowboys found out. One day they roped a buoy and drug it half a mile up this very canyon. That night when the trawler came tracking inbound on that buoy they needed wheels and didn't have them.

Personally, I am skeptical about the truthfulness of that story but I do like how it comes out. And until it faded away a few years ago we did have a shipwreck to prove it.

Within a mile of the light at Cabo San Lazaro, this ship is a mid- to late- seventies wreck.

This wreck is well off the beaten track, about halfway between Cabo San Lazaro and Matancitas. Apparently being dismantled by one man working alone, I've watched him at it for eight or ten years now.

East of San Jose del Cabo, this fishing trawler of an un-named Oriental country was reportedly lured ashore by clever cowboys. Wreckage has now mostly broken up.

180   Baja Calif. Sur   **Magdalena Village**

JET CHART	WAC	SECTIONAL	LATITUDE	LONGITUDE	US TIME	FOR GMT ADD	ICAO IDENT	TOWN IDENT
JN-46	CH-22 ADS-15	TPC H22C	24°51'	112°04'	MST	7		MVG-

OTHER COMM Hotel 122.8
CITY 1 mile West   POPULATION 3,000

LOCAL	FREQ	WHERE	HOURS
FROM Sta Rosalia	EQ 112.6	TRACK 163°	148 n.mi.
FROM La Paz	FREQ 112.3	TRACK 283°	106 n.mi.
FROM V.Const.	FREQ 1440	TRACK 225°	25.2 n.mi.

FUEL –   CARDS –   CASH? –
REPAIRS –   TIEDOWN BYO

HOTEL	RATE	WHERE	TEL
M Village	$$$	2 SE	–

4271' Packed
ELEVATION 34'

Remarks: New runway to Baja California's airports, this one replaces the old Puerto San Carlos just west. That has been overbuilt and disappeared. This is the site of Ed Tabor's new fishing place, supplementing not replacing the original Flying Sportsmens Lodge in Loreto.

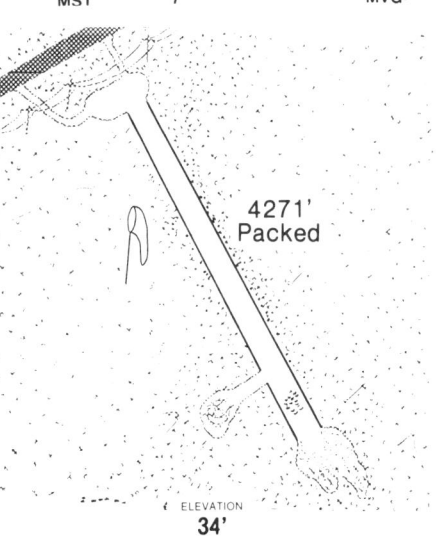

Magdalena Village SW   Baja Calif. Sur   *mog-dah-LAY-nah*   181

JN CHART	WAC	SECTIONAL	LATITUDE	LONGITUDE	US TIME	FOR GMT	ICAO	TOWN ID
JN-46	CH-22 ADS-15	TPC H22C	24°47'	112°07'	MST	+7	-	MVG2 –

OTHER COMM Traffic 124.2
SETTLEMENT Adjacent
B'cast 1440   WHERE 8 miles NE
FROM La Paz   FREQ 112.3
FROM Santa Rosalia   FREQ 112.6
FROM Loreto   FREQ 113.4
   Hotel
   Magdalena Village

POPULATION 10-50
HOURS Daylight
TRACK 294°, 107 n.mi.
TRACK 164°, 151 n.mi.
TRACK 196°, 81.8 Dme
Where   Rattel
Here   Tvl Agt

**1537'x56'
Packed Dirt**

A short, wide strip alongside the windy Bahia de la Magdalena. In late winter and early Spring the California Gray whales are here to birth and to make whoop-pee, causing the next crop of whales. This fishing village is intended for the 'fishing is everything' sort of angler. Women are usually more comfortable elsewhere.

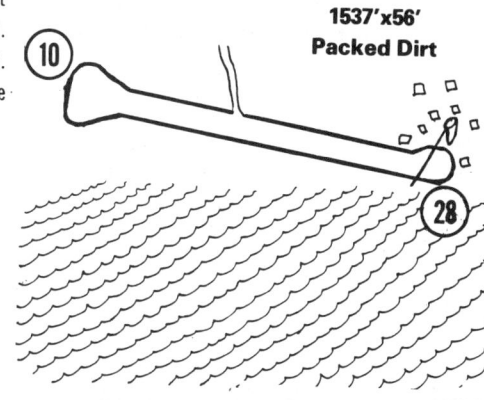

182 Bahía Magdalena Baja Calif. Sur ba-EE-yah mog-da-LAY-na

JET CHART	WAC	SECTIONAL	LATITUDE	LONGITUDE	US TIME	FOR GMT ADD	ICAO IDENT	TOWN IDENT
JN-46	CH-22 So. ADS-15	TPC H-22C	24°39'	112°09'	MST	7	-	-MAG-

OTHER COMM Traffic 121.5
SETTLEMENT Camp 1/4 miles SE POPULATION 0 to 200
FROM Santa Rosalia FREQ 112.6 TRACK 176°, 159 n.mi.
FROM La Paz FREQ 112.6 TRACK 279°, 106 n.mi.
FROM V. Constitución FREQ 1440 TRACK 213°, 37 n.mi.
FUEL - CARDS - CASH? -
REPAIRS - TIEDOWN BYO

Very poor airport, suitable only for helicopters and STOL aircraft you didn't want to keep. A Supercub pilot tells me he uses this; he is welcome to it.

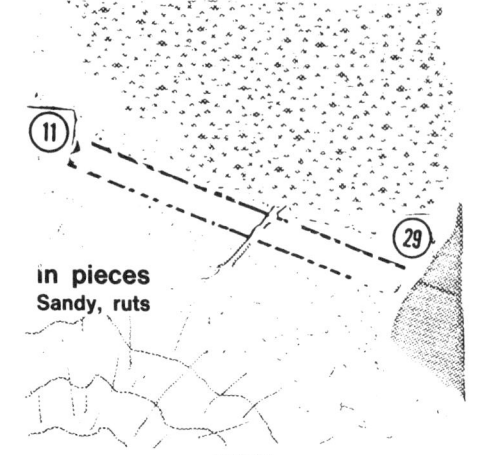

in pieces
Sandy, ruts

ELEVATION
13' to 30'

Puerto Cortés Baja Calif. Sur *PWAIR-toe core-TESS* 183

JET CHART	WAC	SECTIONAL	LATITUDE	LONGITUDE	US TIME	FOR GMT ADD	ICAO IDENT	TOWN IDENT
JN-46	CH-22 So. ADS-15	TPC H-22C	24°29'	111°51'	MST	7	-	PTC

OTHER COMM Traffic 118.1
SETTLEMENT Navy base East side POPULATION 900
FROM Santa Rosalia FREQ 112.6 TRACK 162°, 170n.mi.
FROM La Paz FREQ 112.3 TRACK 276°, 86Dme
FROM V. Constitución FREQ 1440 TRACK 182°, 38n.mi.
FUEL 80 sometimes CARDS - CASH? Pesos
REPAIRS Very minor TIEDOWN BYO

An isolated Navy base with a good crew of sharp, hardworking people. Former military will understand the courtesy of calling on the CO. The rest of us can merely ask to be introduced and exchange pleasantries, same thing. Pleasant way to get acquainted.

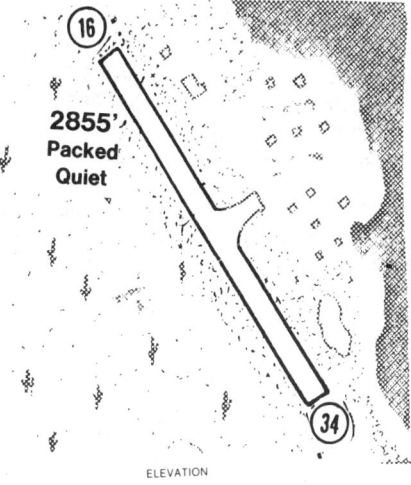

2855'
Packed
Quiet

ELEVATION
11'

184 Santa Rita Baja Calif. Sur SAHN-tah REE-tah

JET CHART	WAC	SECTIONAL	LATITUDE	LONGITUDE	US TIME	FOR GMT ADD	ICAO IDENT	TOWN IDENT
JN-46	CH-22 So. ADS-15	TPC H-22C	24°36'	111°39'	MST	7	-	-SRT-

OTHER COMM Traffic 122.85
SETTLEMENT 1/4 mile E   POPULATION 21
FROM V. Constitución FREQ 1440 TRACK 146°, 31n.mi.
FROM La Paz   FREQ 112.3   TRACK 285°, 70Dme

Store and gas station, a SE curve here breaks the longest straightaway of Highway One.

After watching the condition of this runway over the years, if I had a problem and needed to land quickly it would be on the highway.

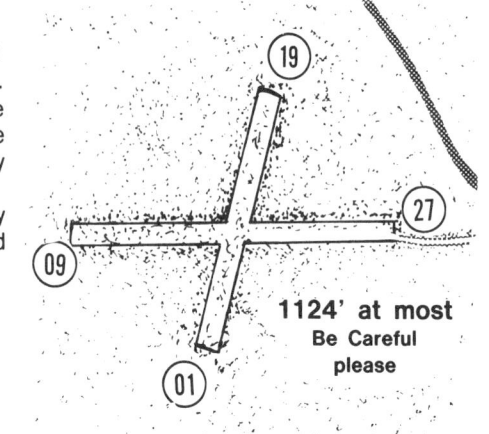

1124' at most
Be Careful please

ELEVATION
115'

Todos Santos Baja Calif. Sur   *TOE-doce SAHN-toce*   185

JET CHART	WAC	SECTIONAL	LATITUDE	LONGITUDE	US TIME	FOR GMT ADD	ICAO IDENT	TOWN IDENT
JN-46	CJ-24 No. ADS-15	TPC J-24A	22°30'	110°12'	MST	7	-	TST

OTHER COMM Traffic 122.85
CITY 1 mile SW   POPULATION 5,500
FROM La Paz   FREQ 112.3   TRACK 155°,36Dme
FROM S.J. del Cabo FREQ 114.0 TRACK 296°,35n.mi.
FUEL -   CARDS -   CASH? -
REPAIRS -   TIEDOWN BYO

Sitting straddle the Tropic of Cancer, these sugarcane fields announce the annual 'panocha', the almost black cake of sugar formed by cooking down the juice from crushed cane.

The restored mission and many other sights are here to be enjoyed. Most of us flash through and miss nearly everything. Try it slow.

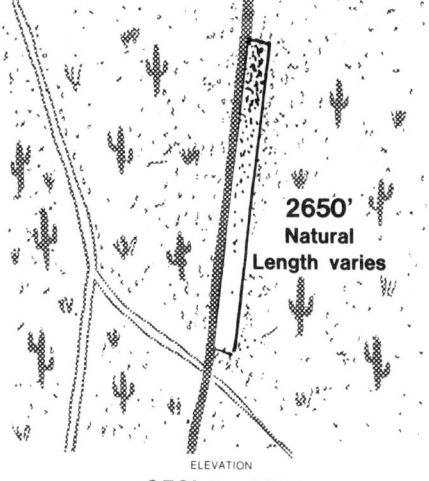

2650' Natural
Length varies

ELEVATION
350' to 383'

186   San Pedrito   Baja Calif. Sur   *sahn pay-DREE-toe*

JET CHART	WAC	SECTIONAL	LATITUDE	LONGITUDE	US TIME	FOR GMT ADD	ICAO IDENT	TOWN IDENT
JN-46	CJ-24 No. ADS-15	TPC J-24A	23°35'	110°13'	MST	7	-	-PED-

OTHER COMM   Traffic 122.85
SETTLEMENT   Ranch S side   POPULATION 7 to 20
FROM   La Paz   FREQ 112.3   TRACK 158°, 41Dme
FROM   S.J. del Cabo   FREQ 114.0   TRACK 285°, 33n.mi.
FUEL -   CARDS -   CASH? -
REPAIRS -   TIEDOWN BYO

Interesting place to land since the runway slopes to the right and to the left, each at some point of your touchdown and rollout. Nice place to stop for a cool dip, lunch, and to be on your way. Overnight stays are not all that welcome.

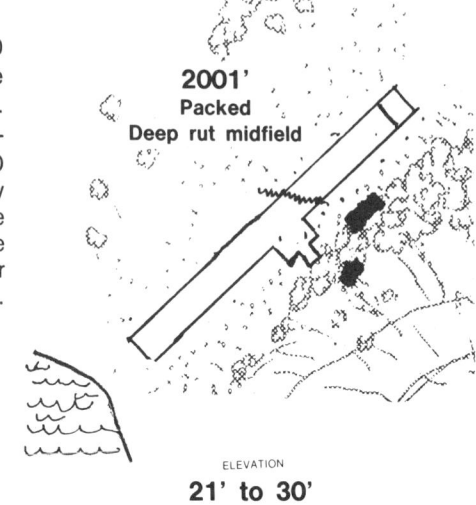

2001'
Packed
Deep rut midfield

ELEVATION
21' to 30'

GALEON
RESTAURANT

Gourmet Food
Served In A
Spanish Colonial
Setting

the finest restaurant
on the Baja peninsula

OPEN NOON TO 11 PM - ALL YEAR ROUND TEL: 3-0443

In front of the marina   Cabo San Lucas BCS

an intimate full resort hotel

HOTEL Solmar

Instant Telephone Reservations

706-843-0022

by mail:
P.O. Box 8
Cabo San Lucas
Baja California del Sur, Mexico

Cabo San Lucas map

Isla Espiritu Santo

Ferry to Los Mochis

Pichilingue 207
Bahia de La Paz

Isla Cerralvo

208 206 Club las Cruces

212 La Paz Military

210
La Paz
Tower 118.1
VorDme 112.3

Punta Arena de la Ventana

204

Ferry to Mazatlan

Principle La Paz Hotels:
 Econohotel Palmira, 2 mi North
 El Presidente Sur, 3 mi NE
 Gran Hotel Baja, Back bay
 Hotel Calafia, So side of city
 Motel la Perla, Waterfront
 Hotel la Posada, Back bay
 Hotel la Purisima, Commercial
 Hotel los Arcos, Central

202 Punta Pescadero

Bahia de las Palmas

Palmas de Cortes
201
  Rancho Buena Vista
200
  Punta Colorada
  198

197 Spectacular Reef

Todos Santos 185

186
San Pedrito

195

196
Los Frailes South

San Jose del Cabo **175**
VorDme 114.0
Tower 118.9

Shipwreck

191 Hotel Palmilla

190 Hotel Cabo San Lucas

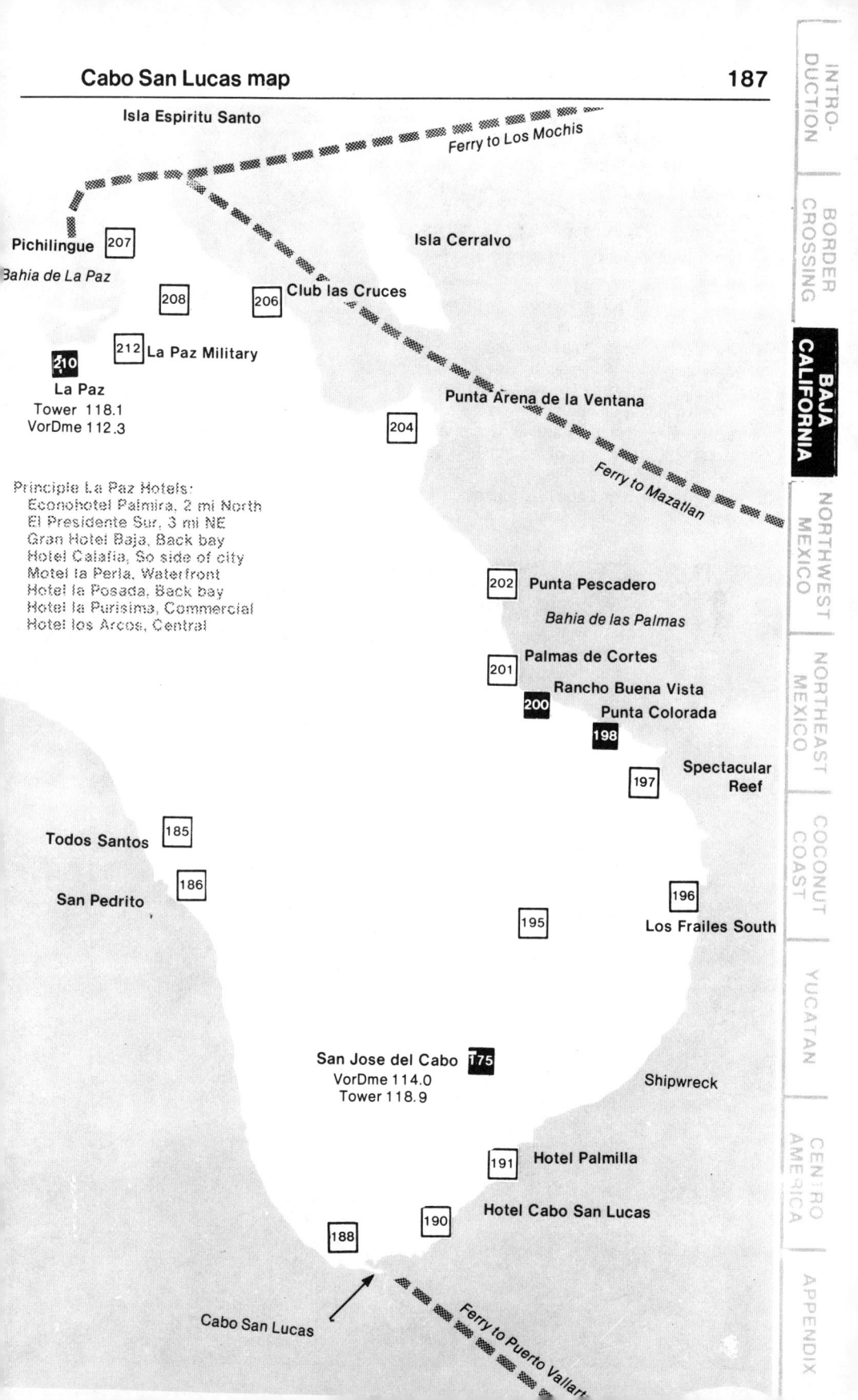

188

Cabo San Lucas

Ferry to Puerto Vallarta

INTRODUCTION | BORDER CROSSING | **BAJA CALIFORNIA** | NORTHWEST MEXICO | NORTHEAST MEXICO | COCONUT COAST | YUCATAN | CENTRO AMERICA | APPENDIX

188 Cabo San Lucas   Baja Calif. Sur   *CAH-boe sahn LOO-cuss*

JET CHART	WAC	SECTIONAL	LATITUDE	LONGITUDE	US TIME	FOR GMT ADD	ICAO IDENT	TOWN IDENT
JN-46	CJ-24 No. ADS-15	TPC J-24A	22°56'	109°56'	MST	7	-	CSL

OTHER COMM Traffic 122.8
CITY 4 miles S   POPULATION 4,500
FROM S.J. del Cabo FREQ 114.0 TRACK 213°,19n.mi.
FROM La Paz   FREQ 112.3   TRACK 150°,72Dme
FUEL 100 prior request   CARDS -   CASH? Pesos
REPAIRS -   TIEDOWN BYO

HOTEL	RATE	WHERE	TEL
Cabo S. Lucas	$$$$	On bay	-
Finisterra	$$$$	Abv bch	-
Hotel Solmar	$$$E	Ocean bch	-
Mar de Cortés	$E	In town	Cabo 3-00-32

Known locally as 'the airport on the hill', be sure on landing that there are no piles of dirt on the runway and that one of the hotels is sending a cab.

This is the real Cabo San Lucas: a local confusion in hotel names might have led you astray.

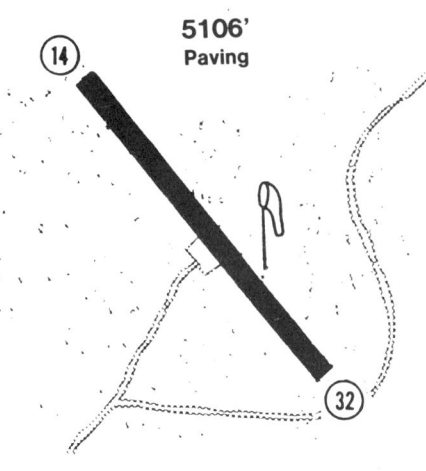

(14) 5106' Paving (32)

ELEVATION
457'

FOR THE FUN OF A LIFETIME!

Escape to romantic, sun-filled Cabo San Lucas where the days are as lazy or as exciting as you want them to be. The fun-filled Hotel Cabo Baja offers it all. Glistening white sand beaches. Three swimming pools. Whirlpool spa with an unsurpassed view of the arch at lands-end where the Pacific meets the Sea of Cortez.

Want excitement? We've got it all. World-class marlin, swordfish and sailfish. Sailing. Scuba diving. Snorkling. Lighted tennis courts. Beach volleyball. And there's disco dancing every night under the stars.

There's more. Romantic moonlight. Tropical flowers. Balmy ocean breezes. Room service. Valet service. Exotic food and drink. Air conditioned rooms with a view of the sea and beautiful courtyards. For the fun of a lifetime . . . HOTEL CABO BAJA HAS IT ALL.

HOTEL CABO BAJA
"The friendliest hotel in Cabo"

FOR RESERVATIONS, HAVE YOUR TRAVEL AGENT CALL:

San Diego	California	Nationwide
(714) 459-0251	(800) 542-6028	(800) 854-2026

190 Hotel Cabo San Lucas Baja Calif. Sur

JET CHART	WAC	SECTIONAL	LATITUDE	LONGITUDE	US TIME	FOR GMT ADD	ICAO IDENT	TOWN IDENT
JN-46	CJ-24 No. ADS-15	-	22°57'	109°49'	MST	7	-	-HCB-

OTHER COMM Hotel Cabo 122.8
SETTLEMENT Across Hiway   POPULATION Resort
FROM la Paz   FREQ 112.3   TRACK 145°, 73Dme
FROM S.J. del Cabo FREQ 114.0 TRACK 195°, 16n.mi.
FUEL Some 100   CARDS -   CASH? Dlls.
REPAIRS -   TIEDOWN BYO

HOTEL	RATE	WHERE	TEL
Hotel Cabo	$$$$	here	-
H. Finisterra	$$$$	7 mi W	Tvl agt
H. Solmar	$$$	8 mi W	Tvl agt

Sometimes called 'el Chileno', or 'el Tule', sometimes just 'Cabo San Lucas', this posh hotel has an appealing bay of its own. Built about twenty years ago as the second complete resort hotel in the Cabo San Lucas area, and still a leader today.

2905'
Graded
Steep slope

ELEVATION
160'-195'

Las Cruces Palmilla Baja Calif. Sur *pall-MEE-yah* 191

JET CHART	WAC	SECTIONAL	LATITUDE	LONGITUDE	US TIME	FOR GMT ADD	ICAO IDENT	TOWN IDENT
JN-46	CJ-24 No. ADS-15	TPC J-24A	23°01'	109°43'	MST	7	-	-PMA-

OTHER COMM Unicom 122.8
SETTLEMENT Resort across highway   POPULATION 200
FROM S.J. del Cabo FREQ 114.0 TRACK 176°,10n.mi.
FROM La Paz   FREQ 112.3   TRACK 139°,73Dme
FUEL 100 prior request   CARDS -   CASH? Yes
REPAIRS -   TIEDOWN BYO

HOTEL	RATE	WHERE	TEL
H. Palmilla	$$$$	here	-

4201'
Graded Dirt

ELEVATION
80' TO 105'

This quietly attractive complete resort hotel helped make the name Cabo San Lucas special. The suites and condominia are tastefully furnished, the pavillions are set off nicely by a selection of statuary in the Colonial style. The wide veranda take in the full sweep of this meeting place of the Sea of Cortés and the Pacific Ocean.

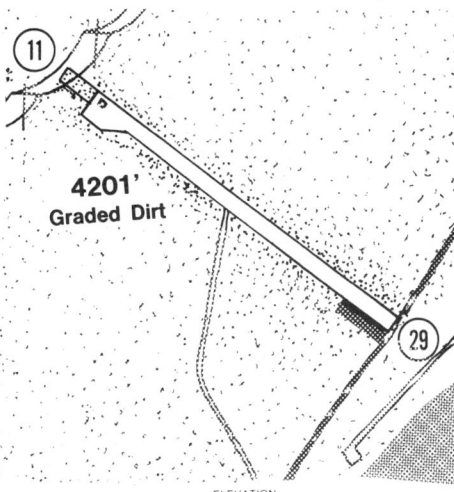

SAN JOSE DEL CABO, B.C.S.
VOR/DME PISTA 16

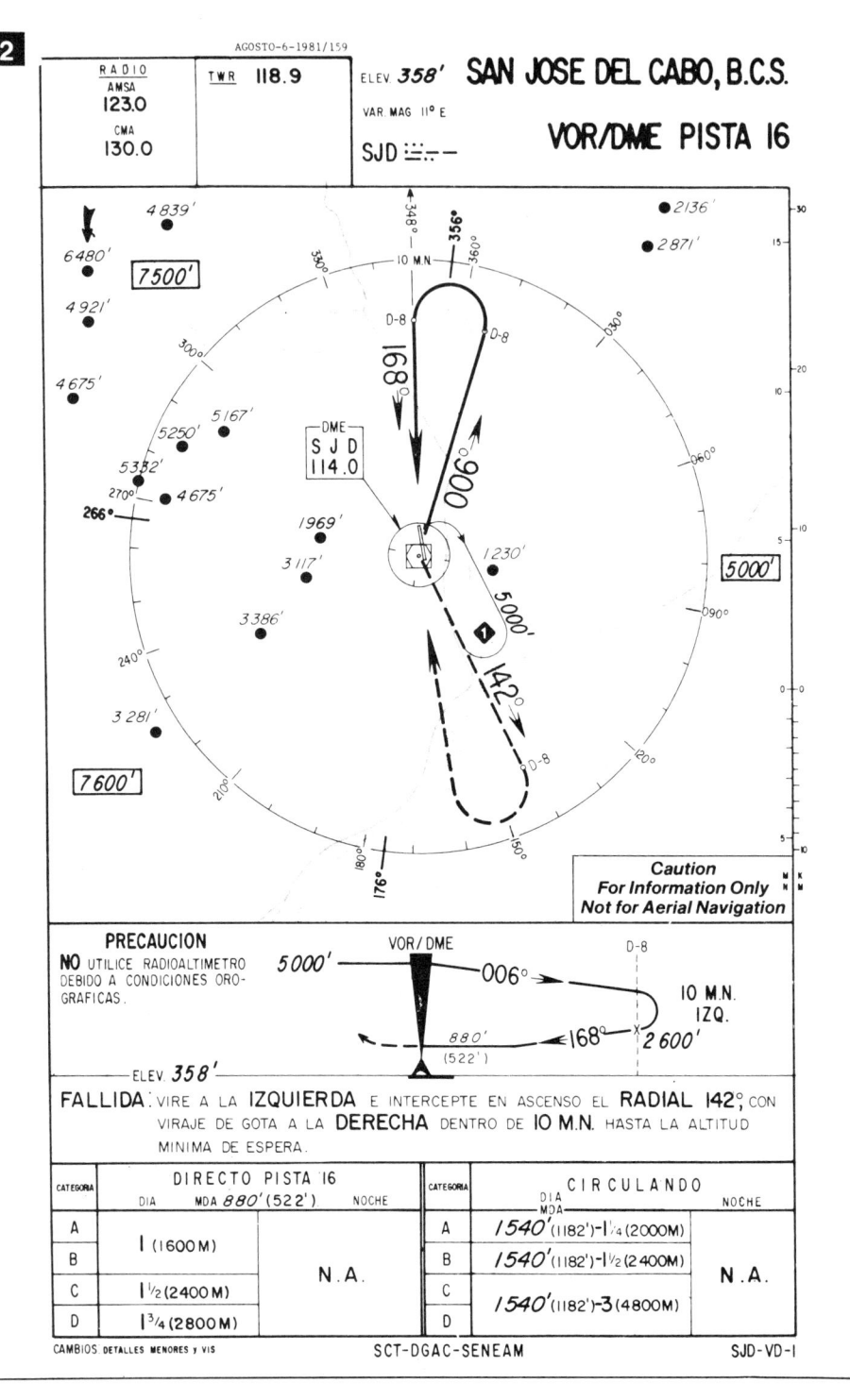

RADIO AMSA 123.0 — CMA 130.0
TWR 118.9
ELEV 358'
VAR. MAG 11° E
SJD ·--- ·-·· —··

AGOSTO-6-1981/159

Caution — For Information Only — Not for Aerial Navigation

PRECAUCION: NO UTILICE RADIOALTIMETRO DEBIDO A CONDICIONES OROGRAFICAS.

VOR/DME — 5000' — 006° — D-8 — 10 M.N. IZQ. — 168° — 2600' — 880' (522') — ELEV 358'

FALLIDA: VIRE A LA **IZQUIERDA** E INTERCEPTE EN ASCENSO EL **RADIAL 142°**, CON VIRAJE DE GOTA A LA **DERECHA** DENTRO DE **10 M.N.** HASTA LA ALTITUD MINIMA DE ESPERA.

CATEGORIA	DIRECTO PISTA 16 DIA MDA 880' (522')	NOCHE	CATEGORIA	CIRCULANDO DIA MDA	NOCHE
A	1 (1600M)	N.A.	A	1540' (1182') - 1¼ (2000M)	N.A.
B	1 (1600M)	N.A.	B	1540' (1182') - 1½ (2400M)	N.A.
C	1½ (2400M)	N.A.	C	1540' (1182') - 3 (4800M)	N.A.
D	1¾ (2800M)	N.A.	D	1540' (1182') - 3 (4800M)	N.A.

CAMBIOS: DETALLES MENORES y VIS — SCT-DGAC-SENEAM — SJD-VD-1

SUNRISE & SUNSET – GMT   SALIDA y PUESTA del SOL – GMT

15th of	JAN	FEB	MAR	APR	MAY	JUN	JUL	AUG	SEPT	OCT	NOV	DEC	
SUNRISE	1402	1351	1327	1258	1237	1232	1241	1255	1305	1315	1332	1352	SALIDA
SUNSET	2454	0114	0127	0139	0152	0205	0207	0151	0122	2453	2434	2435	PUESTA
15° de	ENE	FEB	MAR	ABR	MAY	JUN	JUL	AGO	SEP	OCT	NOV	DIC	

To get local time just subtract 'GMT ADD'
PARA OBTENER TIEMPO LOCAL SUSTRIAGA 'GMT ADD'

San Jose del Cabo Internacional
Baja Calif. Sur *sohn hoe-SAY dell CAH-bow* **193**

JET CHART	WAC	SECTIONAL	LATITUDE	LONGITUDE	US TIME	FOR GMT ADD	ICAO IDENT	TOWN IDENT
JN-46	CJ-24 No. ADS-15'	TPC J-24A	23°10'	109°42'	MST	7	-	SJD

AOE 9am-1pm, 3-5pm MST

- tca to: 5,000'msl   CENTER AT VorDme   RADIUS 10 mi.
- APPROACH -   TOWER 118.9   GROUND 118.9
- CITY 6 miles S   POPULATION 3,900
- LOCAL Vor   FREQ 114.0   WHERE here   HOURS 24
- FROM La Paz   FREQ 112.3   TRACK 132°, 66Dme
- FROM Mazatlán   FREQ 114.9   TRACK 260°, 192 n.mi.
- FUEL 80,100,JP   CARDS Visa,MC   CASH? Yes
- REPAIRS Minor-BYO   TIEDOWN

HOTEL	RATE	WHERE	TEL
las Cruces Palmilla	$$$$	8 mi SW	-
Cabo San Lucas	$$$$	14 mi SW	-
Hyatt San Lucas	$$$$	19 mi WSW	-

This readily expandable airport serves Cabo San Lucas, the posh tip of Baja California. In a boom limited only by hotel space, new tourists are just now discovering what others have been enjoying for nearly a thousand years.

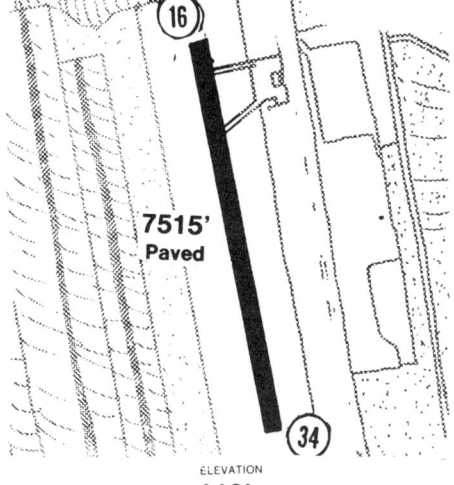

16 / 7515' Paved / 34

ELEVATION **110'**

194 Miraflores   Baja Calif. Sur   Baja Calif. Sur   *meer-ah-FLO-ress*

JET CHART	WAC	SECTIONAL	LATITUDE	LONGITUDE	US TIME	FOR GMT ADD	ICAO IDENT	TOWN IDENT
JN-46	CJ-24 ADS-15	TPC J-24A	23°22	109°47	MST	7	-	-

OTHER COMM Listen 118.9
SETTLEMENT 0.5 mile North   POPULATION 1200
FROM San José   FREQ 114.0   TRACK 327°,13Dme,
FROM la Paz   FREQ 112.3   TRACK 137°,54Dme,
FROM Santiago FREQ airport TRACK 199°,9n.mi.,
FUEL -   CARDS -   CASH? -
REPAIRS -   TIEDOWN BYO

CAUTION this airport has had little care for several years, approach it very carefully.

This city was was once a busy leather center for the area, but heavy demands have long since outstripped the supplies both of of leather and of craftsmen to work it. Today selling articles made elsewhere takes the place of locally crafted ones. In factory mass production quality is higher but that certain charm is missing.

2715'
Natural
Careful!

ELEVATION
781'

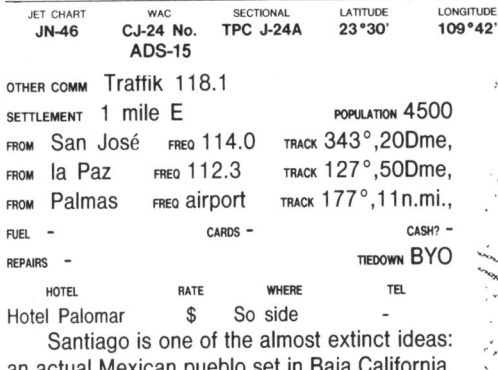

Santiago   Baja Calif. Sur   *sonn-tee-OGG-oh*   195

JET CHART	WAC	SECTIONAL	LATITUDE	LONGITUDE	US TIME	FOR GMT ADD	ICAO IDENT	TOWN IDENT
JN-46	CJ-24 No. ADS-15	TPC J-24A	23°30'	109°42'	MST	7	-	STG

OTHER COMM Traffik 118.1
SETTLEMENT 1 mile E   POPULATION 4500
FROM San José   FREQ 114.0   TRACK 343°,20Dme,
FROM la Paz   FREQ 112.3   TRACK 127°,50Dme,
FROM Palmas   FREQ airport TRACK 177°,11n.mi.,
FUEL -   CARDS -   CASH? -
REPAIRS -   TIEDOWN BYO
   HOTEL   RATE   WHERE   TEL
Hotel Palomar $ So side   -

Santiago is one of the almost extinct ideas: an actual Mexican pueblo set in Baja California. There is colonial architecture, a sugarcane raising area, it also is the administrative center for the valley. The pace, while liesurely, is certainly not slow. Stores, one service station, the valley's post office, all need to be seen.

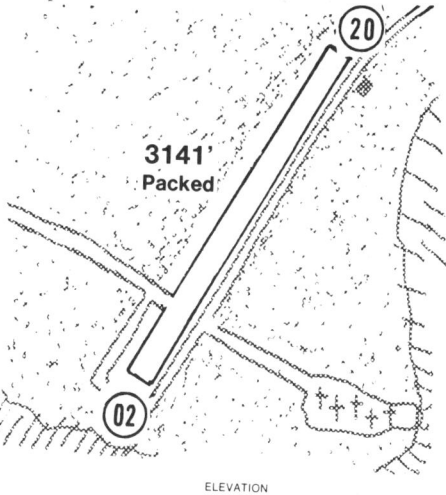

3141' Packed

ELEVATION
437'

196 los Frailes

loe fry-EE-less

JET CHART	WAC	SECTIONAL	LATITUDE	LONGITUDE	US TIME	FOR GMT ADD	ICAO IDENT	TOWN IDENT
JN-46	CJ-24 No. ADS-15	TPC J-24A	23°21'	109°26'	MST	7	-	-FRY-

OTHER COMM Traffic 122.85
SETTLEMENT Ranch 1/4 mile E   POPULATION 3
FROM La Paz   FREQ 112.3   TRACK 118°, 67Dme
FROM S.J. del Cabo FREQ 114.0 TRACK 039°, 20n.mi.

Wear polaroid glasses to notice how close the very blue water comes to the beach. That says there is a very steep bottom gradient. Bet you could catch marlin from the beach if you could get a good cast. Excellent camping spot.

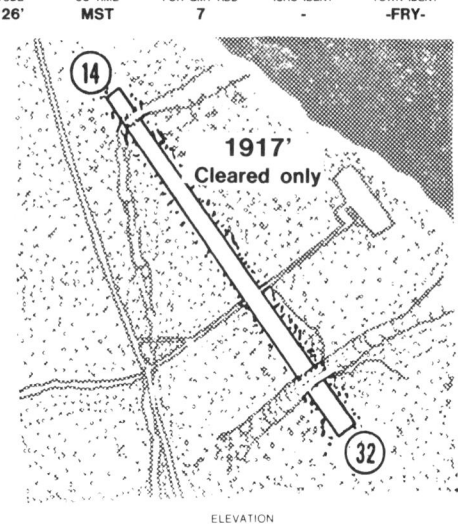

1917'
Cleared only

ELEVATION
17' to 33'

la Laguna Baja Calif. Sur *lah lah-GOO-nah* 197

JET CHART	WAC	SECTIONAL	LATITUDE	LONGITUDE	US TIME	FOR GMT ADD	ICAO IDENT	TOWN IDENT
JN-46	CJ-24 No. ADS-15	TPC J-24A	23°31'	109°27'	MST	7	-	-ABU-

OTHER COMM Traffic 122.8
SETTLEMENT Resort 0.7 miles NE   POPULATION 20
FROM La Paz   FREQ 112.3   TRACK 59Dme,
FROM S.J. del Cabo FREQ 114.0   TRACK 021°,26n.mi.
FUEL 100 prior request   CARDS -   CASH?
REPAIRS -   TIEDOWN BYO

HOTEL	RATE	WHERE	TEL
Laguna Guesthouse	$$$$?	here	Trvl agt?

A smallish resort overlooking its own corner in the Sea of Cortés, a six couple party has the entire hotel to itself. Situated just south of the lighthouse at Punta Arena, sandy point, the Guesthouse is that rare really quiet place if you all want it so, or it can all but jump off its foundations if you all prefer. A dream come true.

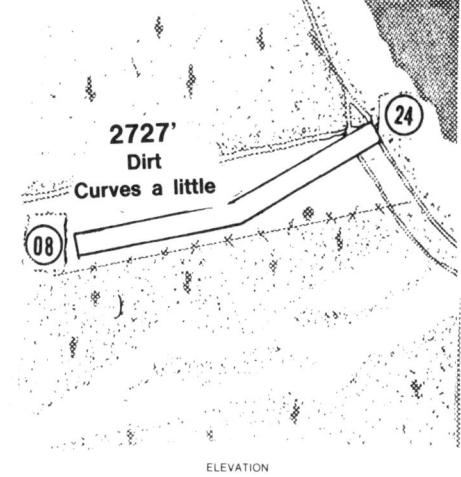

2727'
Dirt
Curves a little

ELEVATION
28' to 42'

198 Punta Colorada   Baja Calif. Sur   *POON-tah coe-loe-RODD-oh*

JET CHART	WAC	SECTIONAL	LATITUDE	LONGITUDE	US TIME	FOR GMT ADD	ICAO IDENT	TOWN IDENT
JN-46	CJ-24 No. ADS-15	TPC J-24A	23°35'	109°30'	MST	7	-	-CDA-

OTHER COMM   Hotel unicom 122.8
SETTLEMENT   Resort 3/4 mile NE   POPULATION 50
FROM   La Paz   FREQ 112.3   TRACK 111°,55Dme
FROM   S.J. del CCabo FREQ 114.0 TRACK 013°,29n.mi.
FUEL   100 prior request   CARDS -   CASH? Yes
REPAIRS   Minor   TIEDOWN BYO

HOTEL	RATE	WHERE	TEL
Punta Colorada	$$$A	here	-

Bobby and Chacha von Wormer are both hotel owners and leaders of a big fan club. Nearly every guest you meet here has come here before. They enjoy Chacha's food, Bob's overseeing the boats and the hotel in general. A few people are even talking condominium so they will be more a part of things.

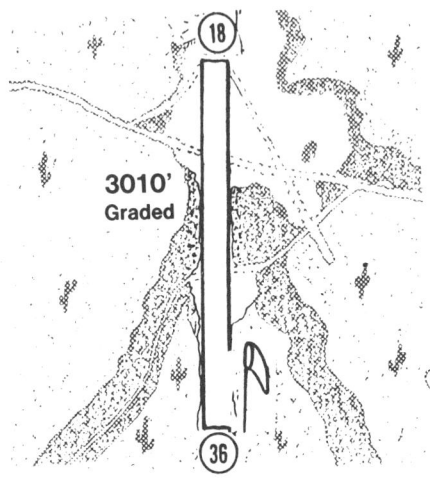

3010'
Graded

ELEVATION
11' to 38'

Rancho el Leonero Baja Calif. Sur   ... *ell lee-oh-NARE-oh*   **199**

JET CHART	WAC	SECTIONAL	LATITUDE	LONGITUDE	US TIME	FOR GMT ADD	ICAO IDENT	TOWN IDENT
JN-46	CJ-24 No. ADS-15	TPC J-24A	23°38'	109°39'	MST	7	-	-ERO-

OTHER COMM Traffic 122.8
SETTLEMENT NE side   POPULATION 3
FROM San José/Cabo FREQ 114.0 TRACK 355°, 28Dme,
FROM la Paz   FREQ 112.3 TRACK 118°, 47Dme,
FROM Mazatlán   FREQ 114.9 TRACK 269°, 189 n.mi.
FUEL -   CARDS -   CASH? -
REPAIRS -   TIEDOWN BYO

Once owned by a man who was a legend of sorts in Baja California, this hot property is now in the midst of a painful change in ownership. It would be at least impolite to use the words 'land grab' around here. Visitors are a problem: they haven't yet figured out a way to tell you to leave.

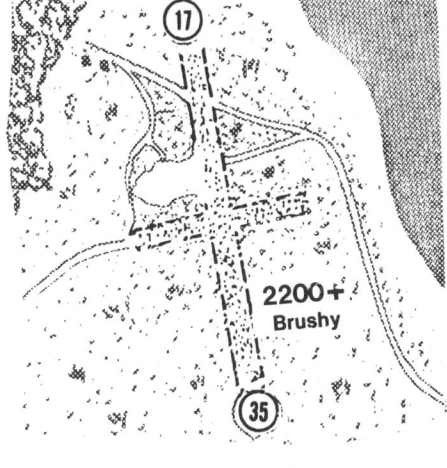

ELEVATION
31'

200 Rancho Buena Vista   Baja Calif. Sur   *RONN-cho BWANE-ah VEES-tah*

JET CHART	WAC	SECTIONAL	LATITUDE	LONGITUDE	US TIME	FOR GMT ADD	ICAO IDENT	TOWN IDENT
JN-46	CJ-24 No. ADS-15	TPC J-24A	23°39'	109°42'	MST	7	-	-BUV-

OTHER COMM   Hotel Unicom 122.8
SETTLEMENT   Resort adjacent   POPULATION 100
FROM   la Paz   FREQ 112.3   TRACK 112°,44Dme
FROM   San José   FREQ 114.0   TRACK 350°,29n.mi.
FUEL   100 prior request   CARDS -   CASH? Yes
REPAIRS   Minor   TIEDOWN BYO

HOTEL	RATE	WHERE	TEL
Rnch. Buena Vista	$$$	here	-
Spa Buena Vista	$$	1/2 mile S	-

The standard for comparison among fishing resorts, Colonel Gene's ideas continue with Chuck Walters and Ted Bonney. To the completely dedicated fisherman, This Is It.

Whether it is boats, gear, fishing wardens, information about what to catch where, good food, well stocked bar, quick service, the answer is Buena Vista; you'll prove it every time

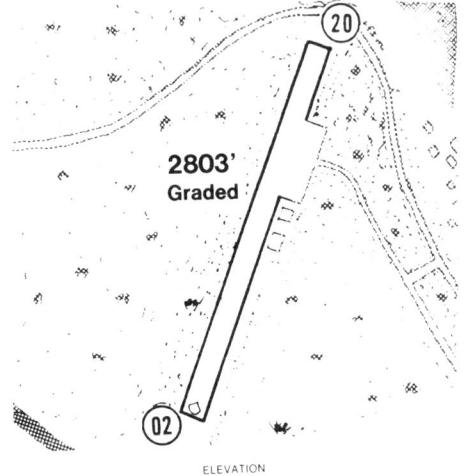

2803' Graded

ELEVATION
15' to 41'

Palmas de Cortés
Baja Calif. Sur *PALL-muss day core-TESS* **201**

JET CHART	WAC	SECTIONAL	LATITUDE	LONGITUDE	US TIME	FOR GMT ADD	ICAO IDENT	TOWN IDENT
JN-46	CJ-24 No. ADS-15	TPC J-24A	23°41'	109°42'	MST	7	-	-BHP-

OTHER COMM Traffic 122.8
SETTLEMENT Resort adjacent   POPULATION 39
FROM La Paz   FREQ 112.3   TRACK 111°,42Dme
FROM S.J. del Cabo   FREQ 114.0   TRACK 350°,31n.mi.
FUEL 100   CARDS -   CASH? Yes
REPAIRS Minor   TIEDOWN BYO

HOTEL	RATE	WHERE	TEL
Palmas de Cortés	$$$E	here	-
Playa Hermosa	$$E	Adjacent N	same

Favorite of many pilots because any room is less than a minute's walk from the airplane. While the beaches are beautiful, food excellent, air balmy, it adds a lot that you can easily slip away for a minitrip around Cabo San Lucas.

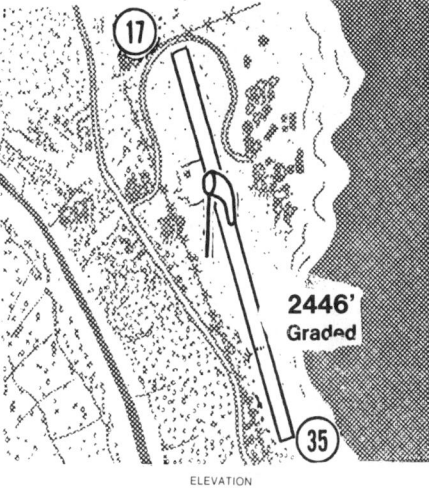

2446' Graded

ELEVATION **17'**

202 Punta Pescadero Baja Calif. Sur *POON-tah pess-cah-DARE-oh*

JET CHART	WAC	SECTIONAL	LATITUDE	LONGITUDE	US TIME	FOR GMT ADD	ICAO IDENT	TOWN IDENT
JN-46	CJ-24 No. ADS-15	TPC J-24A	23°48'	109°42'	MST	7	-	-PES-

OTHER COMM Hotel Unicom 122.8
CITY Resort 3/4 mile SE   POPULATION 100
FROM La Paz   FREQ 112.3   TRACK 104°,38Dme
FROM S.J. del Cabo FREQ 114.0 TRACK 349°,38n.mi.
FUEL 100 prior request   CARDS -   CASH? Yes
REPAIRS -   TIEDOWN BYO

HOTEL	RATE	WHERE	TEL
Pta Pescadero	$$$$	here	415-948-5505

These twenty rooms overlooking fishermen's point make for an ideal guest list. You will quickly be on a first name basis with the other guests who are also enjoying an exquisitely small, almost personal-sized resort.

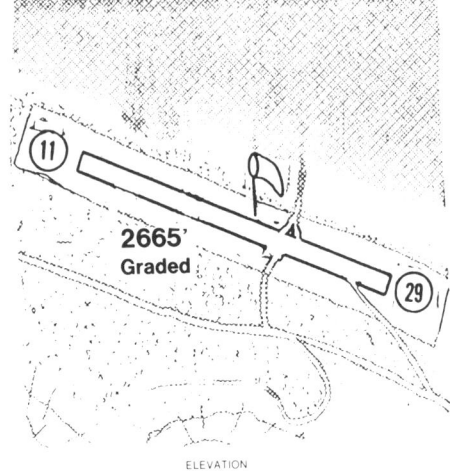

2665' Graded

ELEVATION
44' to 67'

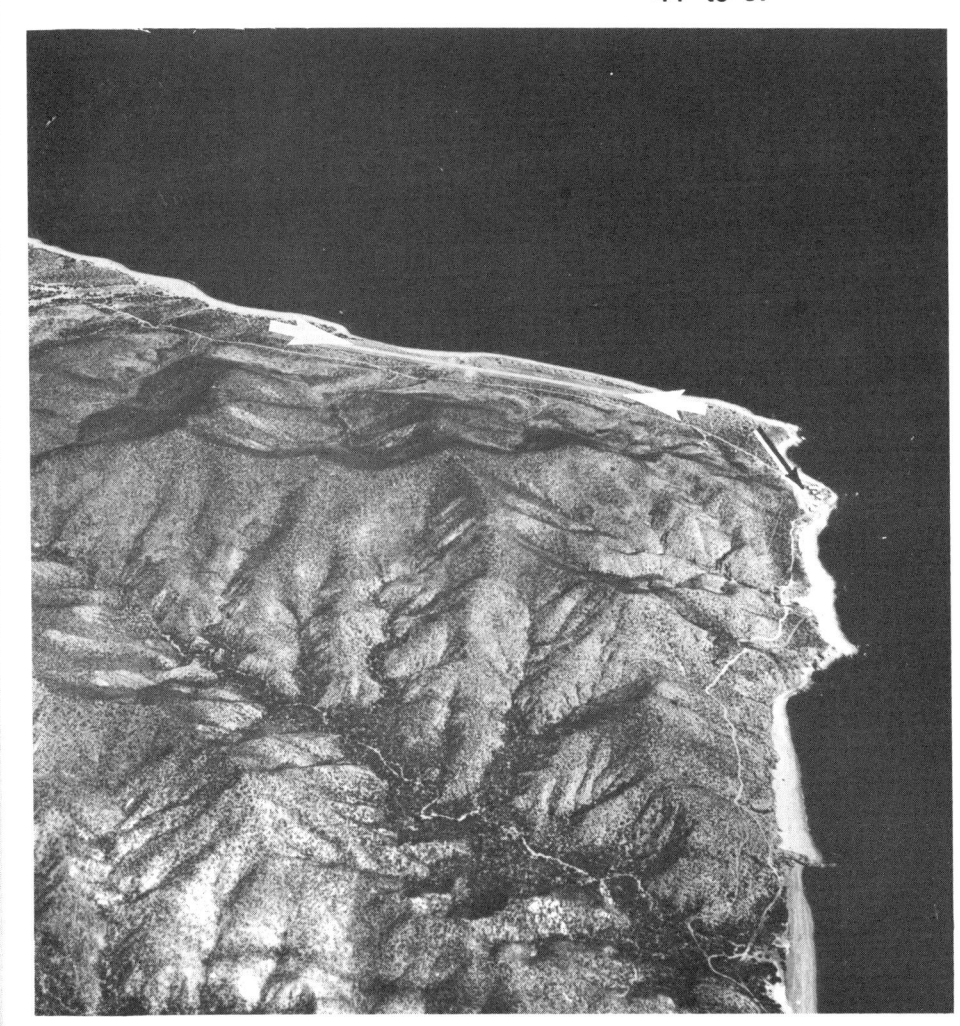

Hotel Punta Pescadero — *The premier East Cape resort*

One of the world's great sport fishing grounds where Marlin, Broadbill, Rooster, Sail, Yellowtail, etc. Swim, Snorkel, Scuba in comfortable waters alive with spectacular underwater life just a few feet from your comfortable room.

Enjoy warm hospitality of 20 sea-view rooms then dine under the stars a few steps from a delightful fresh water pool. The *complete* retreat—air for scuba, boats for fishing, miles of unspoiled beaches for sunning, shelling, exploring.

for Reservations call 415-948-5505
or write
Post Office Box 1044
Los Altos, California 94022

204 Bahía de la Ventana Baja Calif. Sur *bah-EE-yah day lah venn-TAH-nah*

JET CHART	WAC	SECTIONAL	LATITUDE	LONGITUDE	US TIME	FOR GMT ADD	ICAO IDENT	TOWN IDENT
JN-46	CJ-24 No. ADS-15	TPC J-24A	24°20'	109°51'	MST	7	-	-VNT-

OTHER COMM Traffic 122.85
CITY Resort 1 mile NNE POPULATION 20
FROM La Paz FREQ 112.3 TRACK 088°,27Dme
FROM S.J. del Caboor FREQ 114.0 TRACK 340°,51n.mi.
FUEL - CARDS - CASH? -
REPAIRS - TIEDOWN BYO

HOTEL	RATE	WHERE	TEL
Under construction	-	-	-

Newest East Cape resort, lucky guests here will have either side of the prominent Punta la Ventana available for fishing with miles and miles of quiet clean white sandy beaches.

VNT

442' Soft
3780' Graded

ELEVATION
73'

HOTEL LAS ARENAS
AT Bahia de la Ventana, near La Paz, Mexico

Look – Out Bar

Virgin Beaches

Big Game Fishing

For Reservations & Information Call NOW:

FREE (California) 800 - 352-4334 — Nationwide except CA 800-423-4785

Los Angeles Area - (213) 949-0201

206 (las Cruces) Palmilla Baja Calif. Sur *loss CROO-sess pal-MEE-yah*

JET CHART	WAC	SECTIONAL	LATITUDE	LONGITUDE	US TIME	FOR GMT ADD	ICAO IDENT	TOWN IDENT
JN-46	CH-22 So.	TPC H-22C	24°12'	110°05'	MST	7	-	LCS
		ADS-15						

OTHER COMM Unicom 122.8
SETTLEMENT 1/4 mile E   POPULATION 100
FROM La Paz   FREQ 112.3   TRACK 053°, 18Dme
FROM Santa Rosalia FREQ 112.6 TRACK 133°, 221n.mi.
FROM S.J. del Cabo FREQ 114.0 TRACK 333°, 66n.mi.
FUEL guest' 100 prior req.   CARDS -   CASH? Yes
REPAIRS -   TIEDOWN BYO

HOTEL	RATE	WHERE	TEL
Club las Cruces	$$$$	here	-

A marvelously relaxing resort on the Sea of Cortés. The architecture, furnishings, and staff combine to make this private club an unforgettable experience. There are boats, all manner of sports equipment, badminton courts, tennis, etc.

When you see this remote setting and its quietly expressed taste you'll never forget it.

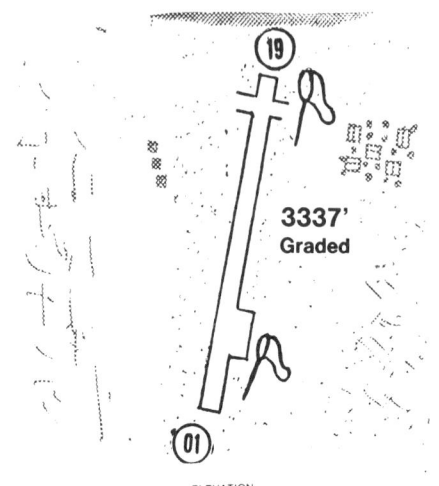

3337'
Graded

ELEVATION
10' to 28'

Pichilingue   Baja Calif. Sur   *peah-ee-LEEN-gay*   **207**

JET CHART	WAC	SECTIONAL	LATITUDE	LONGITUDE	US TIME	FOR GMT ADD	ICAO IDENT	TOWN IDENT
JN-46	CH-22 So. ADS-15	TPC H-22C	24°16'	110°18'	MST	7	-	-PCH-

OTHER COMM La Paz 118.1 for Traffic
SETTLEMENT 1/16 mile SE   POPULATION 5
FROM La Paz   FREQ 112.3   TRACK 356°,10Dme
FUEL -   CARDS -   CASH? -
REPAIRS -   TIEDOWN BYO

⑯
1734
Rough Gravel
Numerous holes
㉞
ELEVATION
53'

Aside from isolation, about the only feature here is the small salt works at the South end. Read up on salt evaporation ahead of time so you can better appreciate it. Doggoned process is very complicated.

Pretty place but unless you have a whole bunch of prop clearance, these lava rocks could mess up things considerably.

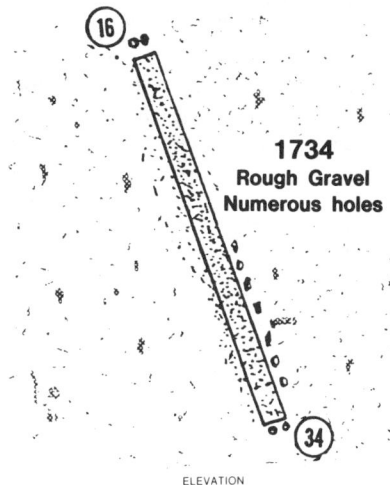

208 Rancho el Ciprés   Baja Calif. Sur   ... ell see-PRESS

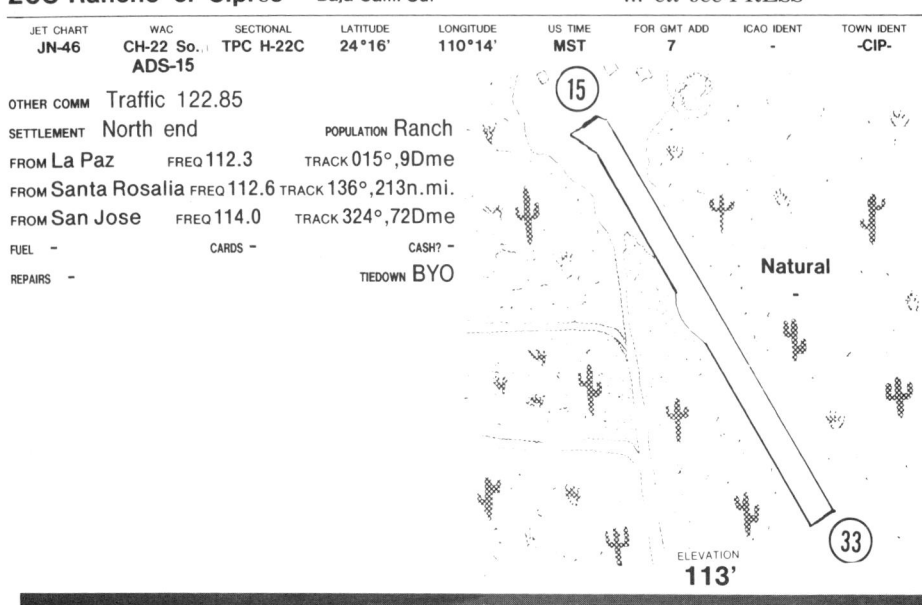

JET CHART	WAC	SECTIONAL	LATITUDE	LONGITUDE	US TIME	FOR GMT ADD	ICAO IDENT	TOWN IDENT
JN-46	CH-22 So. ADS-15	TPC H-22C	24°16'	110°14'	MST	7	-	-CIP-

OTHER COMM Traffic 122.85
SETTLEMENT North end   POPULATION Ranch
FROM La Paz   FREQ 112.3   TRACK 015°, 9Dme
FROM Santa Rosalia FREQ 112.6 TRACK 136°, 213n.mi.
FROM San Jose   FREQ 114.0   TRACK 324°, 72Dme
FUEL -   CARDS -   CASH? -
REPAIRS -   TIEDOWN BYO

Natural
-

ELEVATION
113'

you hear it on 122.9 a lot: "See you at Fulano's"

FULANO'S

RESTAURANT — BAR

Freshest lobster in La Paz

Centrally located at the waters' edge

Open daily from noon til midnight

AT AVENIDA OBREGON NUMBER 340 ALTOS
TEL 2-23-22

LA PAZ, B.C.S.
VOR/DME PISTA 18

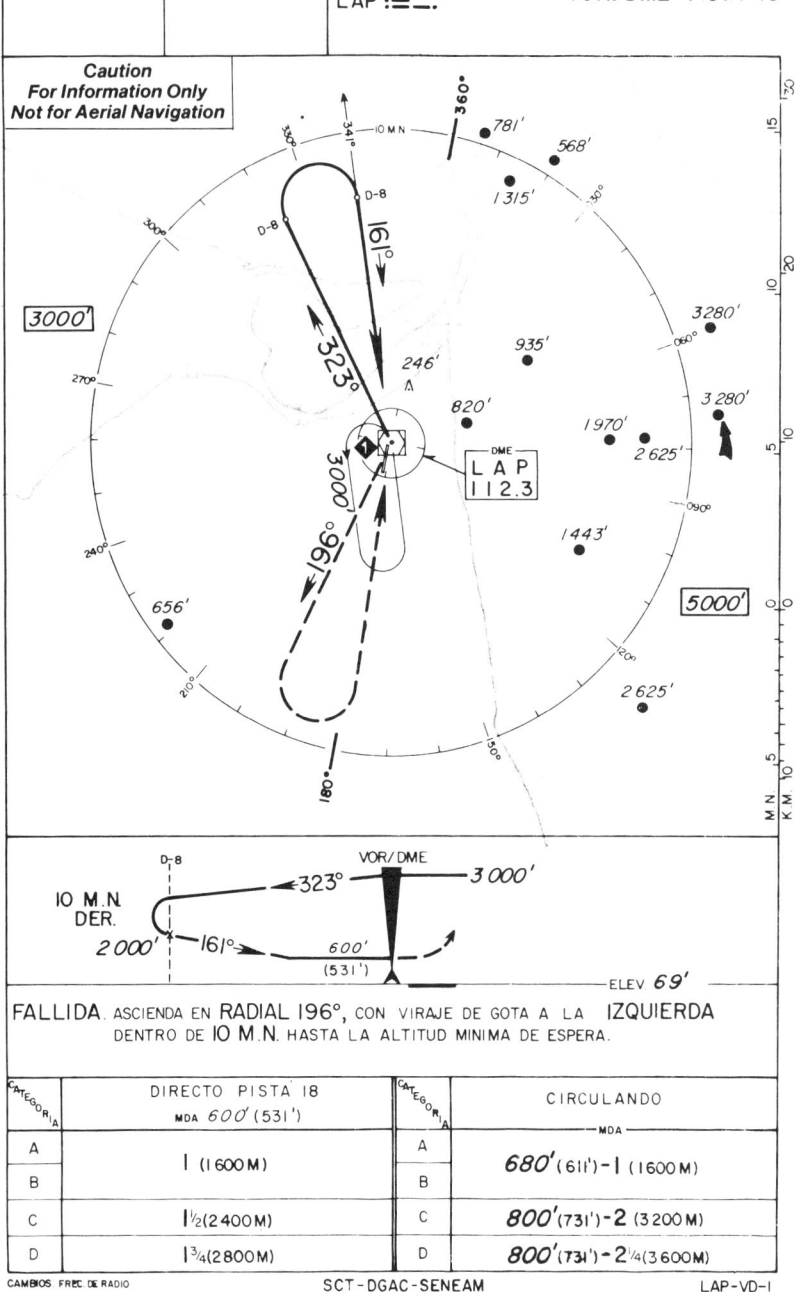

RADIO		TWR	ELEV **69'**
AMSA	CMA	118.1	VAR. MAG. 11° E
131.0 y 130.0			LAP :=:..

AGOSTO-6-1981/159

Caution
For Information Only
Not for Aerial Navigation

DME LAP 112.3

FALLIDA. ASCIENDA EN **RADIAL 196°**, CON VIRAJE DE GOTA A LA **IZQUIERDA** DENTRO DE **10 M.N.** HASTA LA ALTITUD MINIMA DE ESPERA.

CATEGORIA	DIRECTO PISTA 18 MDA 600' (531')	CATEGORIA	CIRCULANDO — MDA —
A	1 (1600 M)	A	680' (611') - 1 (1600 M)
B		B	
C	1½ (2400 M)	C	800' (731') - 2 (3200 M)
D	1¾ (2800 M)	D	800' (731') - 2¼ (3600 M)

CAMBIOS FREC. DE RADIO   SCT-DGAC-SENEAM   LAP-VD-1

SUNRISE & SUNSET — GMT   SALIDA y PUESTA del SOL — GMT

```
15th of   JAN   FEB   MAR   APR   MAY   JUN   JUL   AUG   SEPT  OCT   NOV   DEC
SUNRISE   1406  1354  1330  1259  1238  1233  1242  1256  1307  1318  1336  1356   SALIDA
SUNSET    2455  0116  0130  0142  0156  0210  0211  0155  0125  2455  2435  2436   PUESTA
15° de    ENE   FEB   MAR   ABR   MAY   JUN   JUL   AGO   SEP   OCT   NOV   DIC
```

To get local time just subtract 'GMT ADD'
PARA OBTENER TIEMPO LOCAL SUSTRIAGA 'GMT ADD'

La Paz Internacional   Baja Calif. Sur   *lah PAH-ss*   **211**

JET CHART	WAC	SECTIONAL	LATITUDE	LONGITUDE	US TIME	FOR GMT ADD	ICAO IDENT	TOWN IDENT
JN-46	CJ-24	ADS-15 / TPC J-24A	24°04'	110°21'	MST	7	MMLP	LAP

- TCA TO: 20,000'   RADIUS 50 n.mi.   HOURS 1400-0400Z
APPROACH 120.6   TOWER 118.1   GROUND 118.1
CITY 6 miles NNE   POPULATION 80,000
LOCAL VorDme   FREQ 112.3   WHERE here   HOURS 24
B'CAST FREQ 790'   WHERE 6 mi NNE   HOURS Daylight
FROM Santa Rosalia FREQ 112.6 TRACK 136°, 213 n.mi.
FROM S.J. del Cabo FREQ 114.0 TRACK 324°, 72 n.mi.
FROM los Mochis FREQ 115.5 TRACK 205, 131 n.mi.
FUEL 80,100,JP   CARDS Visa,MC,etc   CASH? Yes
REPAIRS Yes   TIEDOWN BYO ropes
HOTEL   RATE   WHERE   TEL
el Presidente $$E   Back bay   -
Econohotel La Paz $$E   N side   -

AOE 9am-1pm, 3-5pm MST

8282' Concrete Uphill 8° N

ELEVATION 48' to 51'

City of peace, La Paz sits on the edge of the well named Vermillion Sea. You will discover how true some afternoon as the sun gets low. The reflection across La Paz bay is a brilliant orangey red which will stick in your memory.

READER REPORT Found a great cab driver, Jose Whitney, Taxi Nr 10, Hotel El Presidente tel 2-40-70. Speaks excellent English, and very helpful.—T. Lieb, California

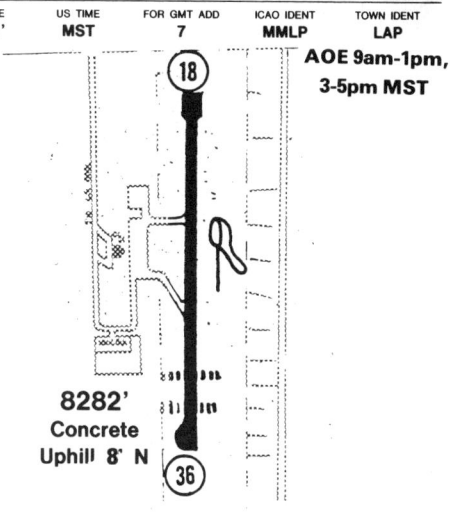

212 la Paz Military Baja Calif. Sur *lah PAH-ss*

JET CHART	WAC	SECTIONAL	LATITUDE	LONGITUDE	US TIME	FOR GMT ADD	ICAO IDENT	TOWN IDENT
JN-46	CJ-24 No. ADS-15	TPC J-24A	24°07'	110°17'	MST	7	-	-LAP2-

OTHER COMM La Paz tower 118.1
CITY 4 miles N   POPULATION 80,000
FROM La Paz   FREQ 112.3   TRACK 050°,4Dme
FUEL -   CARDS -   CASH? -
REPAIRS None   TIEDOWN BYO

Gradually being phased out as the squeeze for city land intensifies, Air Force will move to Internacional one day. Meantime this is an alternate; use La Paz tower.

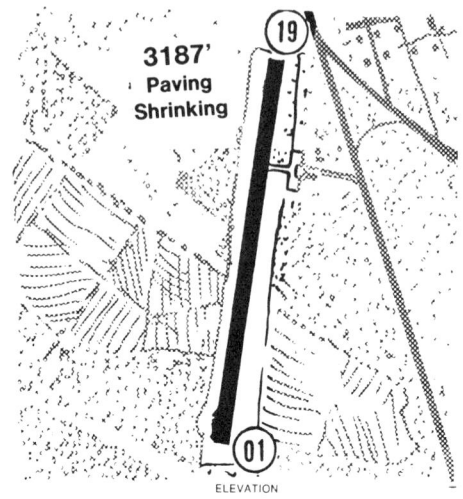

3187'
Paving Shrinking

ELEVATION
87'

San Juan de la Costa Baja Calif. Sur   *sawn whonn day lah COCE-tah*   213

JET CHART	WAC	SECTIONAL	LATITUDE	LONGITUDE	US TIME	FOR GMT ADD	ICAO IDENT	TOWN IDENT
JN-46	CH-22 So. ADS-15	TPC H-22C	24°23'	110°42'	MST	7	-	-JDC-

OTHER COMM Traffic 122.85
SETTLEMENT West side 1/4 mile POPULATION 500, inc.
FROM La Paz   FREQ 112.3   TRACK 310°,34Dme
FROM Loreto   FREQ Airport   TRACK 149°,102n.mi.
FROM V. Constitución FREQ 1440 TRACK 117°,69n.mi.
FUEL -   CARDS -   CASH? -
REPAIRS -   TIEDOWN BYO

New phosphorous find in the mountains started the activity. A resort will follow, probably bus service in a year or two. Right now you can still see the old ranch house and talk to the people who lived here in total isolation for generations. Hope they made a bundle.

This Bay of La Paz can be unpleasant: when area ceilings are below a thousand feet don't be surprised to find zero, zero conditions over the water.

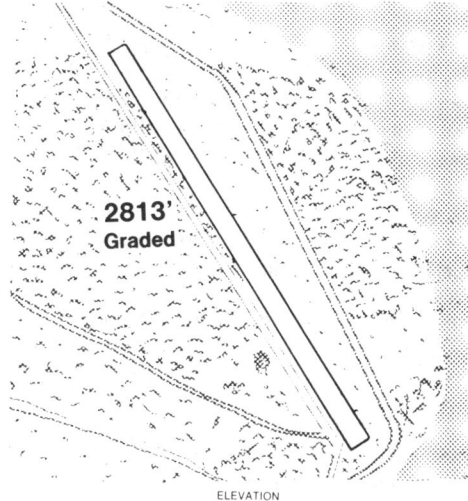

2813'
Graded

ELEVATION
25'

214 isla San José   Baja Calif. Sur   *EES-lah sahn hoe-SAY*

JET CHART	WAC	SECTIONAL	LATITUDE	LONGITUDE	US TIME	FOR GMT ADD	ICAO IDENT	TOWN IDENT
JN-46	CH-22 So. ADS-15	TPC H-22C	24°56'	110°38'	MST	7	-	ISJ

OTHER COMM Traffic 122.85
SETTLEMENT 0.2 miles W   POPULATION 0 to 2
FROM La Paz   FREQ 112.3   TRACK 324°,53Dme
FROM Santa Rosalia FREQ 112.6 TRACK 136°,169n.mi.
FROM Los Mochis FREQ 115.5   TRACK 227°,106n.mi.
FUEL -   CARDS -   CASH? -
REPAIRS -   TIEDOWN BYO

The lack of easily found water limits the possibilities of settlement for now. But the waters abound with fish, seawater conversion is on the horizon. Meantime, camp here by yourself. About the only disturbance you'll find is a nut occasionally stopping to measure the runway again. It'll cost you a cup of coffee to tell me these runway numbers are not reciprocals and for me to say neither are the two ends of this curving runway.

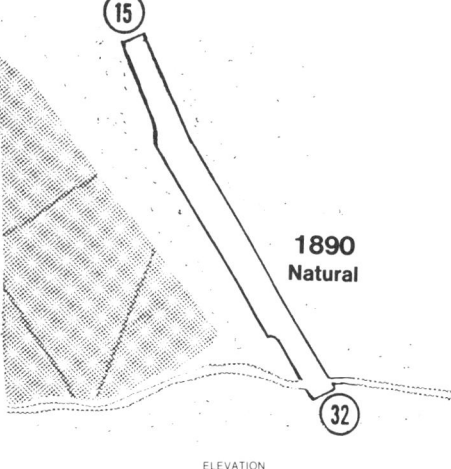

1890 Natural

ELEVATION
12' to 28'

Tambibiche   Baja Calif. Sur   *tomm-bee-BEE-chay*   **215**

JET CHART	WAC	SECTIONAL	LATITUDE	LONGITUDE	US TIME	FOR GMT ADD	ICAO IDENT	TOWN IDENT
JN-46	CH-22 So. ADS-15	TPC H-22C	25°15'	110°58'	MST	7	-	-TBB-

OTHER COMM Traffic 122.85-
SETTLEMENT Ranches NE side   POPULATION 55
FROM Loreto   FREQ Airport   TRACK 143°,49n.mi.
FROM La Paz   FREQ 112.3   TRACK 324°,79Dme
FROM Los Mochis   FREQ 115.5   TRACK 241°,112n.mi.
FROM V. Constitución FREQ 1440   TRACK 059°,40n.mi.
FUEL -   CARDS -   CASH? -
REPAIRS -   TIEDOWN BYO

Lots of activity here every other October as we Bush Pilots use 1200' of this runway for demonstrations.

You can rent a ponga for fishing, a mule for riding if you are really brave, or walk up to that interesting bay north. You need to figure out how to pay for something with a gallon of gas. The two remaining smokers here desperately need fuel for their Zippos but are bashful.

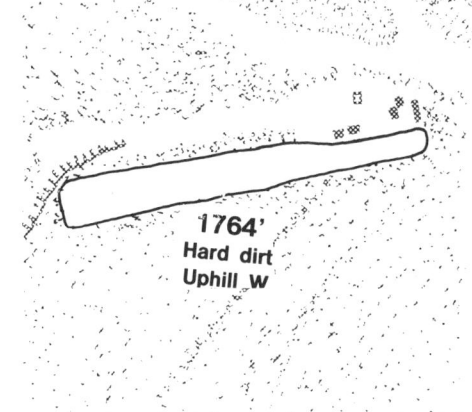

1764'
Hard dirt
Uphill W

ELEVATION
45' to 64'

*IFR procedure
not available
at press time.*

Loreto Internacional — Baja Calif. Sur — low-RETT-toe — 217

JET CHART	WAC	SECTIONAL	LATITUDE	LONGITUDE	US TIME	FOR GMT ADD	ICAO IDENT	TOWN IDENT
JN-46	CH-22 So. ADS-15	TPC H-22C	25°59'	111°24'	MST	7	-	LTO

APPROACH - TOWER 118.4 GROUND 118.4
LOCAL NAVAID VorDme FREQ 113.2 WHERE Here HOURS 24
CITY 1 mile E POPULATION 3,500
FROM Tijuana FREQ 116.5 TRACK 128°, 485 n.mi.
FROM Mexicali FREQ 115.0 TRACK 138°, 465 n.mi.
FROM La Paz FREQ vorDme TRACK 112.3, 142° 126Dme
FUEL 80, 130/130 CARDS Visa, MC CASH? Any
REPAIRS Minor TIEDOWN BYO

HOTEL	RATE	WHERE	TEL
Hotel Oasis	$$	Central	Yes
el Presidente	$$$	N side	-
Hotel Misión	$$	Central	-

AOE 9am-1pm, 3-5pm MST

7610' x 197'

ELEVATION 15' to 26'

A favorite Bush Pilots Internacional destination, we have our annual Ladies' Fishing Tournament here in October. That's the one where ladies have a slight extra handicap of whatever it takes for them to win all the prizes.
READER REPORT Don't miss eating at Don Luis' restaurant: fantastic.— P Shoemaker, Arizona

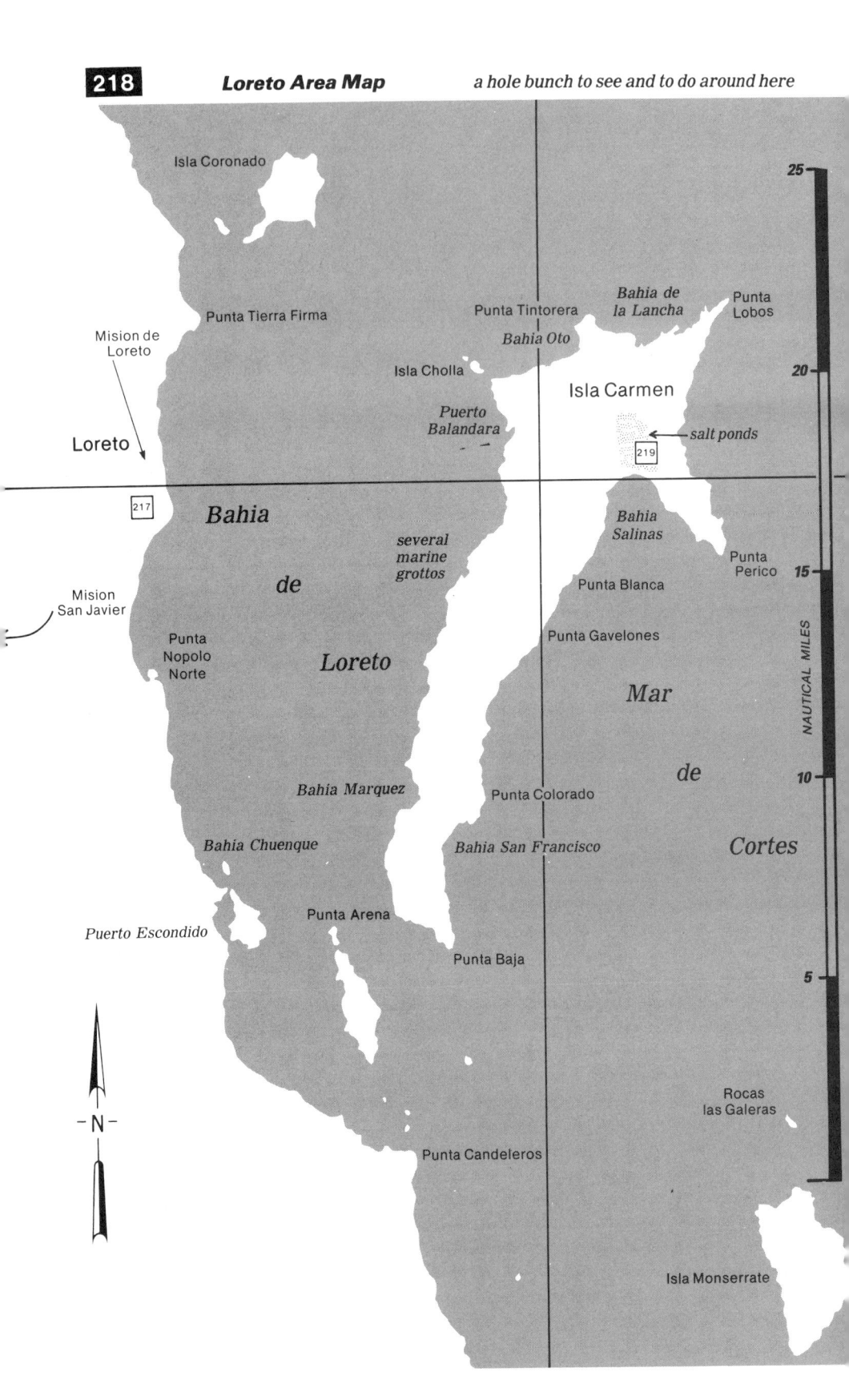

218   **Loreto Area Map**   *a hole bunch to see and to do around here*

Isla Carmen   Baja Calif. Sur   *EES-lah CARR-mun*   **219**

JET CHART	WAC	SECTIONAL	LATITUDE	LONGITUDE	US TIME	FOR GMT ADD	ICAO IDENT	TOWN IDENT
JN-46	CH-22 So. ADS-15	TPC H-22C	25°59'	111°07'	MST	7	-	-CAR-

OTHER COMM Traffic 121.6
SETTLEMENT 0.3 miles SW   POPULATION 5 to 20
FROM Loreto   FREQ Airport   TRACK 076°, 13 n.mi.
FROM Santa Rosalia FREQ 112.6 TRACK 128°, 101 n.mi.
FROM Cd. Obregón FREQ 115.1 TRACK 310°, 109 n.mi.
FUEL -   CARDS -   CASH? -
REPAIRS -   TIEDOWN BYO

Source of salt since the earliest explorers came to Baja California. Variously reported as 98 to 99 percent pure, the salt consists of both ancient salt from the time when this was a newly opened volcano, until recently when it has been an evaporative salt producer.

Also an excellent place to fly in and walk over to the beaches. Bring lunch, a snorkel and fins for an unforgettable day. Choose either the East side or the NW beaches near the grotto.

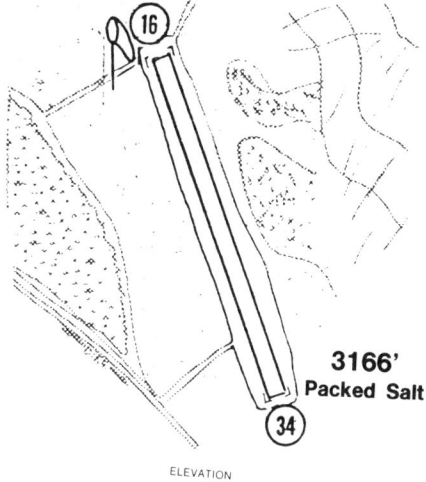

3166' Packed Salt

ELEVATION
26'

220 Rancho Rosarito Baja Calif. Sur

RON-cho rose-ah-REE-toe

JET CHART	WAC	SECTIONAL	LATITUDE	LONGITUDE	US TIME	FOR GMT ADD	ICAO IDENT	TOWN IDENT
JN-46	CH-22 So. ADS-15	TPC H-22C	26°34'	111°39'	MST	7	-	-RCO-

OTHER COMM Traffic 122.95
SETTLEMENT Restaurant across highway POPULATION 17
FROM Santa Rosalia FREQ 112.6 TRACK 132°56n.mi.,
FROM Mulegé FREQ Serenidad TRACK 126°,27n.mi.
FROM Loreto FREQ airport TRACK 324°,39n.mi.
FUEL -   CARDS -   CASH? -
REPAIRS -   TIEDOWN BYO

Built for the highway crews to come and go, easy to keep an eye on road work, you would certainly have all the hunting to yourself here. From one runway measuring stop to the next I almost never see wheel tracks of another airplanes.

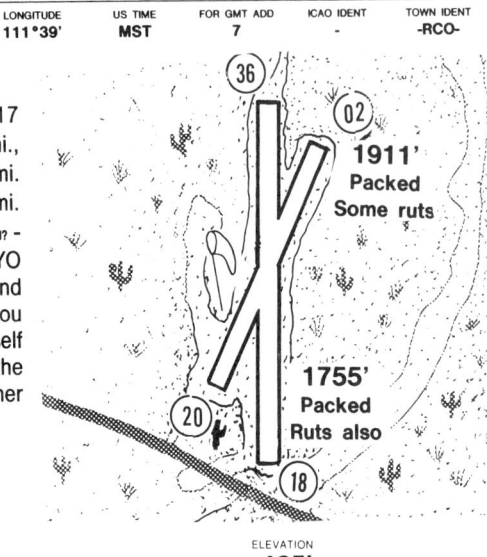

36 / 02
1911'
Packed
Some ruts

1755'
Packed
Ruts also

20 / 18

ELEVATION
465'

Punta Pulpito Baja Calif. Sur   *POON-tah pool-PEE-toe* 221

JET CHART	WAC	SECTIONAL	LATITUDE	LONGITUDE	US TIME	FOR GMT ADD	ICAO IDENT	TOWN IDENT
JN-46	CH-22 So. ADS-15	TPC H-22C	26°38'	111°36'	MST	7	-	-PUL-

OTHER COMM Traffic 122.95
SETTLEMENT Ranch 1/4 mile E   POPULATION 11
FROM Santa Rosalia FREQ 112.6 TRACK 127°, 54n.mi.
FROM Mulegé FREQ Serenidad TRACK 125°, 26n.mi.
FROM Loreto FREQ Airport TRACK 328°, 42n.mi.
FUEL -   CARDS -   CASH? -
REPAIRS -   TIEDOWN BYO

Cattle buyers land here to deal for range stock raised by the ranch. Those guys are something else: they don't seem to mind the brush or smaller ruts.

Then every once in awhile you see a tourist airplane here as someone has discovered a way to have a beach of their very own.

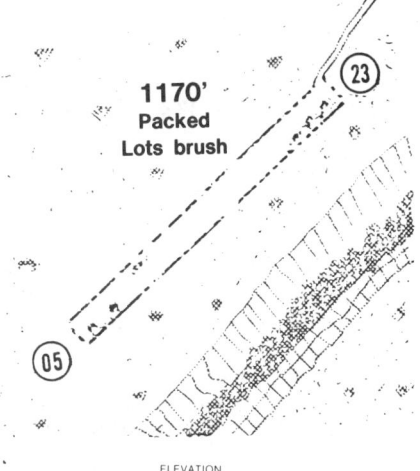

1170'
Packed
Lots brush

ELEVATION
179' to 190'

222   Baja Calif. Sur   **Bahía Concepción**

JET CHART	WAC	SECTIONAL	LATITUDE	LONGITUDE	US TIME	FOR GMT ADD	ICAO IDENT	TOWN IDENT
	CH-22 DS-15	TPC H22B	26 46'	111 55'	MST	7		MLG5-

OTHER COMM Traffic 122.8
Settlement 1/4 mi East   **POPULATION** Varies

LOCAL	FREQ	WHERE	HOURS
FROM Sta Rosalia	FREQ 112.6	TRACK 136°,39Dme	
FROM Loreto	FREQ 113.2	TRACK 316°,56Dme	
FROM Cd. Obregon	FREQ 115.1	TRACK 240°,119n.mi.	
FUEL	CARDS -		CASH? -
REPAIRS			TIEDOWN

Strictly a one-way airport for the pretty Bay of Conception area; there is plenty of runway if one is careful and prepared. Realize you can only approach over the south end, there is no go-around. And the approach end may be squishy if the tide is in. We stuck a Cessna 402B here first time I measured this, so do be careful with heavy airplanes which have high tire pressures.

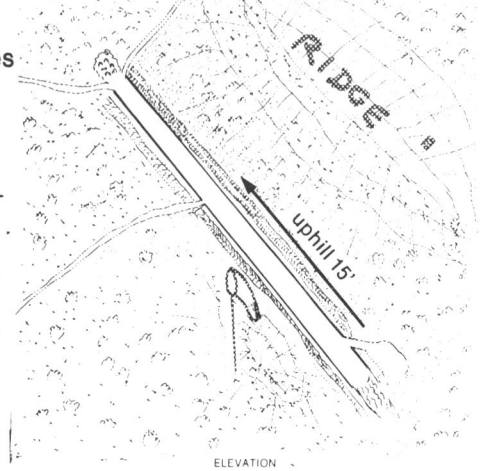

ELEVATION
7' to 22'

Hotel Serenidad   Baja Calif. Sur   *sair-enn-ee-DODD*   **223**

JET CHART	WAC	SECTIONAL	LATITUDE	LONGITUDE	US TIME	FOR GMT ADD	ICAO IDENT	TOWN IDENT
JN-46	CH-22 So. ADS-15	TPC H-22C	26°54'	111°59'	MST	7	-	SRD-

OTHER COMM Traffic 122.8
CITY 0.7 miles W   POPULATION 3,450
FROM Santa Rosalia FREQ 112.6 TRACK 135°, 29 n.mi.
FROM La Paz   FREQ 112.3 TRACK 318°, 189 n.mi.
FROM d. Obregón   FREQ 115.1 TRACK 241°, 122 n.mi.
FUEL 80, 100   CARDS -   CASH? Yes
REPAIRS In Loreto   TIEDOWN BYO

HOTEL	RATE	WHERE	TEL
Hotel Serenidad	$$	here	-
las Casitas	$	Central	-
Old Hacienda	$	Central	-

Handy place to stay if you want to airplane sightsee. Your parked airplane is literally less than a minute's walk from your room. Good dependable avgs supply adds to the possibilities of visiting the West Coast for a day. You can be over there and back with a load of clams or lobster by lunch time if you're in a hurry.

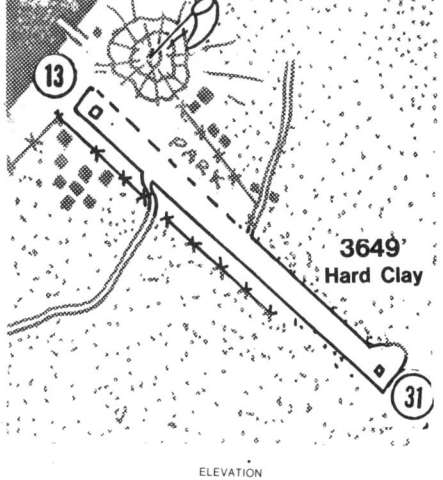

3649'
Hard Clay

ELEVATION
10' to 22'

Enroute to La Paz or Cabo from the north, you see this view of Mulege from the left seat on your way by. Town is on your left, just on the north side of the river, the mission is south across the river to your right. In town are both the modest Hotel Old Hacienda presided over by owner/host Al Cuesta, and the tiny hotel called George's Las Casitas.

Hotel Serenidad and Hotel Mulege are near the Sea of Cortes, each has a runway nearby. Serenidad's is immediately on the premises, the other a quarter mile distant. Plenty of taxis make all of Mulege readily accessible to the other parts.

Known Best for the territorial honor prison which housed inmates with work-in-town privileges, the mission, and a relaxed way of life. The honor prison idea is fading away, but the mission is being reborn in the government's restoration program. Not even the occasional long distance telephone service has changed the easy going pace.

But also has: clamming trips by cab to Bahia Concepcion, visits to ancient painted caves, good to excellent fishing on the Sea of Cortes. At last count there was one-count 'em one-swimming pool in town, at Hotel Mulege.

Shopping tips: Nancy at Nancy's Gift Shop in town has good taste and a pleasant manner, both of which are reflected in her stock. This is also the one place in town with color film in various kinds and sizes. A supermarket on the square has small store items plus a liquor department.

Although a new city by Mexican standards, the mission dates from just 1705, Mulege is an interesting oasis to visit, to explore, and to add to your list of places you will revisit.

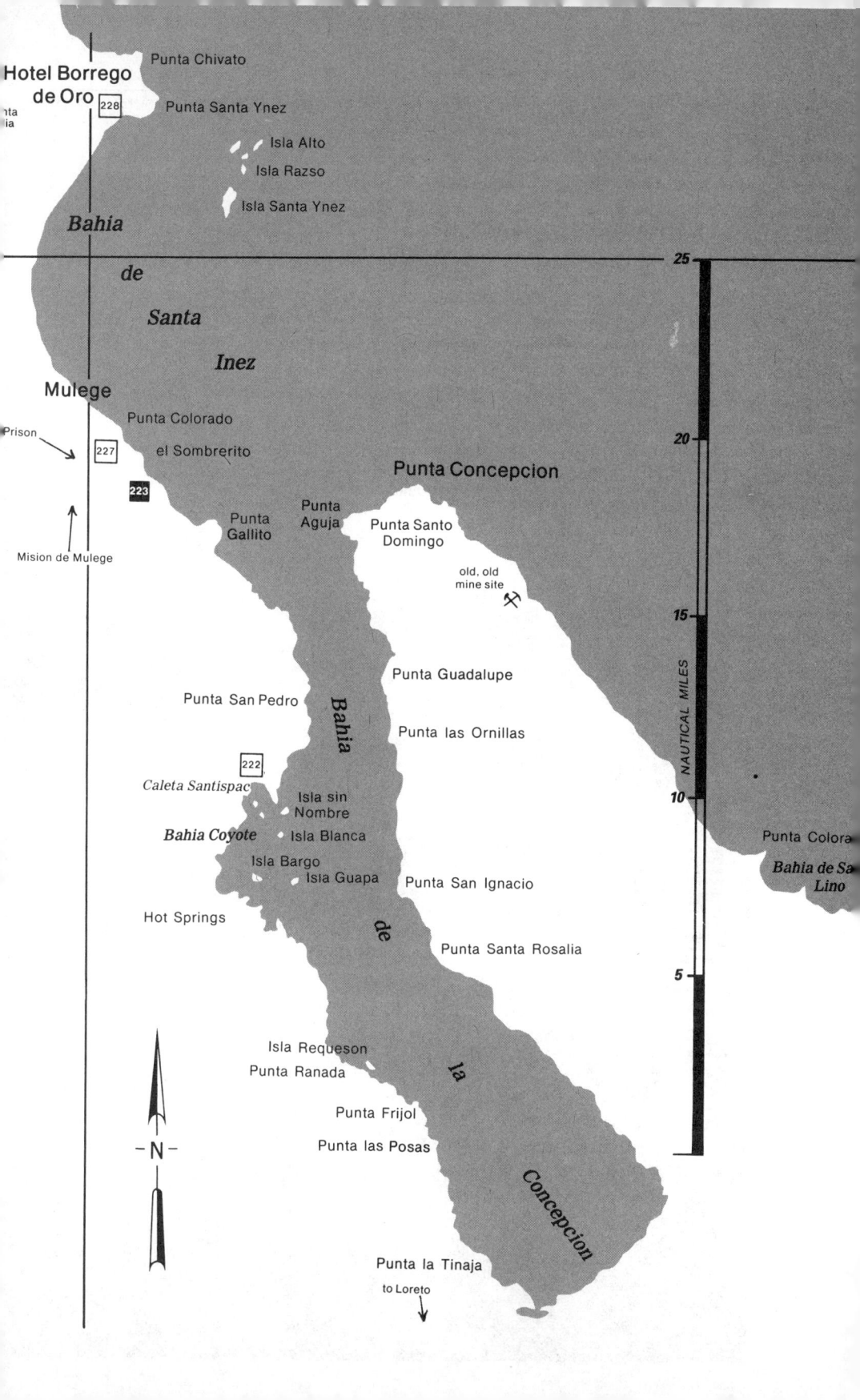

Map of Bahía Concepción area

- Hotel Borrego de Oro
- Punta Chivato
- 228
- Punta Santa Ynez
- Isla Alto
- Isla Razso
- Isla Santa Ynez

Bahia de Santa Inez

- Mulege
- Prison
- Punta Colorado
- el Sombrerito
- 227
- 223
- Punta Concepcion
- Punta Gallito
- Punta Aguja
- Punta Santo Domingo
- old, old mine site
- Mision de Mulege
- Punta Guadalupe
- Punta San Pedro
- Punta las Ornillas
- 222
- *Caleta Santispac*
- Isla sin Nombre
- *Bahia Coyote*
- Isla Blanca
- Isla Bargo
- Isla Guapa
- Punta San Ignacio
- Punta Colora
- *Bahia de Sa Lino*
- Hot Springs
- Punta Santa Rosalia
- *Bahia de la Concepcion*
- Isla Requeson
- Punta Ranada
- Punta Frijol
- Punta las Posas
- Punta la Tinaja
- to Loreto

— N —

NAUTICAL MILES: 5, 10, 15, 20, 25

226　Mulegé-West　Baja Calif. Sur　　　　moo-la-HAY

JET CHART	WAC	SECTIONAL	LATITUDE	LONGITUDE	US TIME	FOR GMT ADD	ICAO IDENT	TOWN IDENT
JN-46	CH-22 So. ADS-15	TPC H-22C	26°53'	112°04'	MST	7	-	-

OTHER COMM Traffic 122.8
CITY 5 miles East　　　　POPULATION 3,100
FROM Santa Rosalia FREQ 112.6 TRACK 142°, 28n.mi.
FROM Cd. Obregón FREQ 115.1 TRACK 241°, 128 n.mi.
FUEL 80 or 100 by truck　　CARDS -　　CASH? Yes
REPAIRS In Loreto　　　　TIEDOWN BYO

HOTEL	RATE	WHERE	TEL
Old Hacienda	$	Town	-
las Casitas	$	Central	-
Hotel Serenidad	$$	Gulfside	-
Hotel Mulegé	$$	E side	-

Best of the Mulegé airports, may be difficult to get a cab out here from town. Try calling Serenidad on 122.8 and ask them to send one.

Remember, although this is a hard packed surface it is still dirt and those disciplines could help.

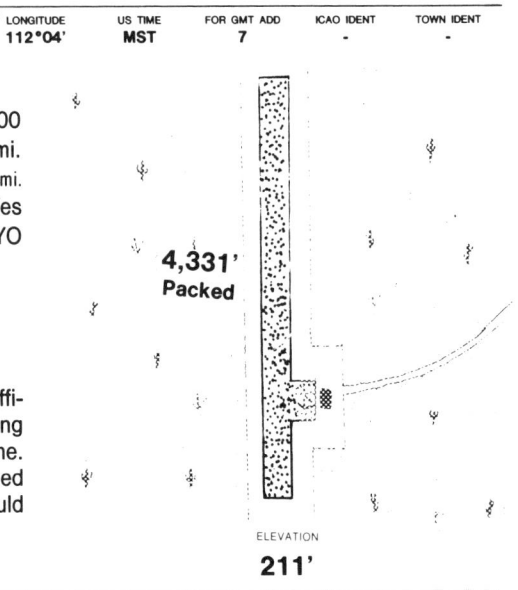

4,331'
Packed

ELEVATION
211'

Mulegé Municipal Baja Calif. Sur *moo-la-HAY* 227

JET CHART	WAC	SECTIONAL	LATITUDE	LONGITUDE	US TIME	FOR GMT ADD	ICAO IDENT	TOWN IDENT
JN-46	CH-22 So. ADS-15	TPC H-22C	26°55'	111°59'	MST	7	-	-HML-

OTHER COMM Traffic 122.8
CITY 3/4 miles West   POPULATION 3,100
FROM Santa Rosalia FREQ 112.6 TRACK 134°, 29 n.mi.
FROM La Paz   FREQ 112.3   TRACK 319°, 189 n.mi.
FROM Bahia Ballenas FREQ airport TRACK 073°, 81 n.mi.
FUEL 80,100 by truck   CARDS -   CASH? Yes
REPAIRS in Loreto   TIEDOWN BYO

HOTEL	RATE	WHERE	TEL
Hotel Mulegé	$$	1/16 mi E.	-
Hotel Serenidad	$$	Gulfside	-
las Casitas	$	Central	-
Old Hacienda	$	Central	-

Not many pilots are accustomed to landing on a runway more than a wingspan higher at one end than the other. My way is to make a flat, very low short final and wait for the runway to come get me.

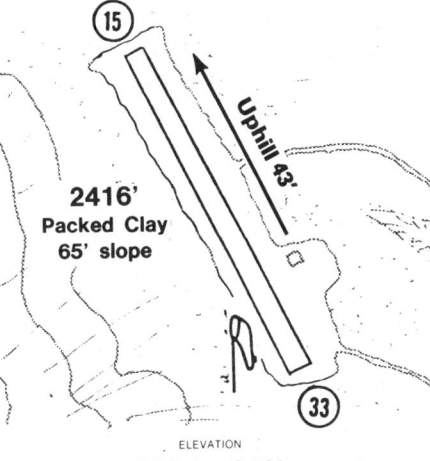

2416'
Packed Clay
65' slope

Uphill 43'

ELEVATION
180 to 213'

228 Punta Chivato — Baja Calif. Sur

POON-tah chee-VOTT-oh

JET CHART	WAC	SECTIONAL	LATITUDE	LONGITUDE	US TIME	FOR GMT ADD	ICAO IDENT	TOWN IDENT
JN-46	CH-22 So. ADS-15	TPC H-22C	27°04'	111°59'	MST	7	-	-CHV-

OTHER COMM Traffic 122.85
SETTLEMENT Abandoned resort   POPULATION 9
FROM Santa Rosalia FREQ 112.6 TRACK 119°, 21 n.mi.
FROM Mulegé Serenidad FREQ airport TRACK 352°, 12 n.mi.
FROM La Paz FREQ 112.3 TRACK 325°, 201 n.mi.
FUEL -   CARDS -   CASH? -
REPAIRS -   TIEDOWN BYO

In early 1982 the hotel was still a long way from re-opening but some lot leases are being offered. Hear much enthusiasm from those customers who've put their money down but the office people seem reluctant to talk for publication.

Meantime the shelling is excellent on the beach west of where the runways almost join. So many that if you don't see the shells you like just dig down an inch to open an entirely new selection.

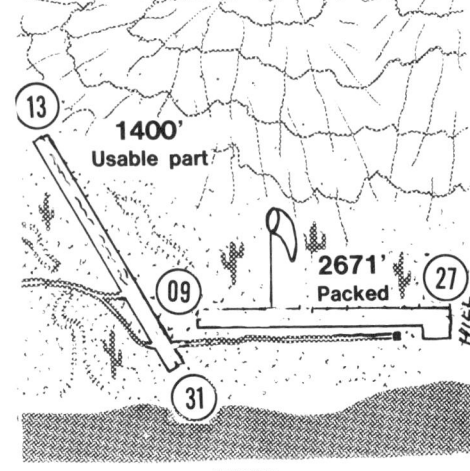

ELEVATION
31' to 65'

Rancho San Lucas   Baja Calif. Sur   *RONN-cho SAWN LOO-cuss*   229

JET CHART	WAC	SECTIONAL	LATITUDE	LONGITUDE	US TIME	FOR GMT ADD	ICAO IDENT	TOWN IDENT
JN-46	CH-22 So. ADS-15	TPC H-22C	27°13′	112°15′	MST	7	-	-RSL-

OTHER COMM   Traffic 122.85
SETTLEMENT   Army platoon adjacent   POPULATION 150
FROM   Santa Rosalia   FREQ 112.6   TRACK 148°, 6 n.mi.
FROM   Ciudad Obregon FREQ 115.1 TRACK 252°, 131 n.mi.
FUEL -   CARDS -   CASH? -
REPAIRS -   TIEDOWN BYO

'Down the hill' from Santa Rosalia, this is an often mentioned replacement for the occasionally hazardous airport there. Use with caution, the gravel is large and not many planes come here per year.

This shallow bay would be an interesting place to explore with your brought along folding boat, to check that sunken boat, or to see how many clams live on the mangroves.

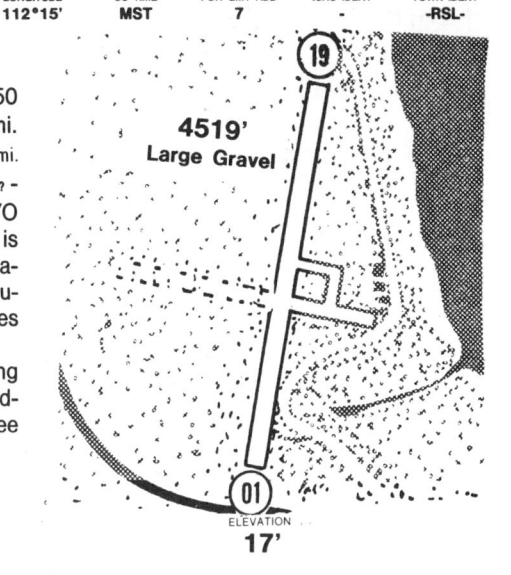

4519'
Large Gravel

ELEVATION 17'

STA ROSALIA, B.C.

AERODROMO
VOR—A
112.6 MHZ
SRL

RADIO:	TORRE DE CONTROL	ELEV. 341'
DIA: 123.0		VAR. MAG. 12° E
NOCHE: 123.0	C. APROXIMACION	C. TERRESTRE

MAYO 15-1975/113

Caution
For Information Only
Not for Aerial Navigation

FALLIDA: VIRE A LA **IZQUIERDA** E INTERCEPTE EN ASCENSO EL **RADIAL 010°** Y PROSIGA EN TRAYECTORIA DE APROXIMACION HASTA LA ALTITUD MINIMA DE ESPERA.

ELEV. 341'

CATEGORIA	DIRECTO PISTA	CATEGORIA	CIRCULANDO DIA	NOCHE
A		A	1660' (1319')-2	
B	N.A.	B	—	N.A.
C		C		
D		D		

CAMBIOS: DETALLES MENORES   S.C.T.-D.G.A.C.   T, C   SRL-V-1

SUNRISE & SUNSET - GMT   SALIDA y PUESTA del SOL - GMT

15th of	JAN	FEB	MAR	APR	MAY	JUN	JUL	AUG	SEPT	OCT	NOV	DEC	
SUNRISE	1420	1406	1338	1304	1240	1233	1243	1300	1314	1329	1349	1411	SALIDA
SUNSET	2456	0120	0137	0153	0210	0225	0226	0207	0134	0100	2437	2436	PUESTA
15° de	ENE	FEB	MAR	ABR	MAY	JUN	JUL	AGO	SEP	OCT	NOV	DIC	

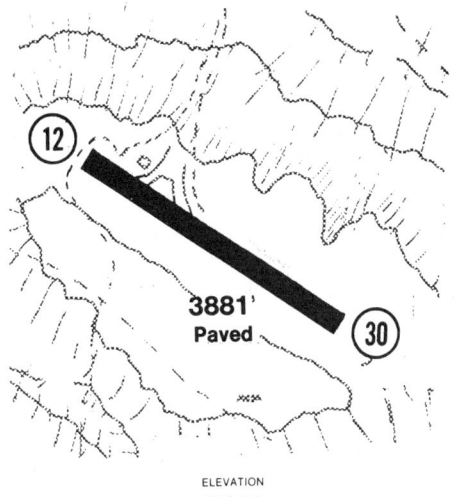

Santa Rosalia Baja Calif. Sur *SAHN-tah rose-ah-LEE-yah* 231

JET CHART	WAC	SECTIONAL	LATITUDE	LONGITUDE	US TIME	FOR GMT ADD	ICAO IDENT	TOWN IDENT
JN-46	CH-22 So. ADS-15	TPC H-22C	27°18'	112°17'	MST	7	-	SRL

OTHER COMM Traffic 118.1
CITY 3/4 mile N   POPULATION 21,000
LOCAL Vor Dme FREQ 112.6 WHERE Adjacent hill HOURS 24
FROM G. Negro   FREQ 382   TRACK 102°, 102 n.mi.
FROM Bahia los Angeles FREQ airport TRACK 135°, 120 n.mi.
FROM La Paz   FREQ 112.3   TRACK 321°, 219 n.mi.
FUEL Private stock   CARDS -   CASH? -
REPAIRS Minor   TIEDOWN BYO

HOTEL	RATE	WHERE	TEL
Hotel el Morro	$$	So of town	2-01-75
Hotel Central	$	Central	-

Caution: Be very careful here when West winds blow: they spill over the ridge adjacent to the runway and can cause severe downdrafts just as you approach flareout.

3881' Paved

ELEVATION **331'**

232 el Arco Baja Calif. Sur *ell ARR-coe*

JET CHART	WAC	SECTIONAL	LATITUDE	LONGITUDE	US TIME	FOR GMT ADD	ICAO IDENT	TOWN IDENT
JN-46	CH-22 No. ADS-15	TPC H-22C	27°59'	113°25'	MST	7	-	-LRC-

SETTLEMENT 1.5 miles N   POPULATION 1,100
OTHER COMM Traffic 118.1
FROM Santa Rosalia FREQ 112.6 TRACK 292°, 71
FROM Guerrero Negro FREQ 382 TRACK 079°, 36n.mi.
FROM Hermosillo FREQ 112.8 TRACK 239°, 143 n.mi.
FUEL -   CARDS -   CASH? -
REPAIRS Minor   TIEDOWN BYO

HOTEL	RATE	WHERE	TEL
el Arco Hilton	Free	Ground	-

Spurred on by the steadily increasing market for copper, el Arco's vast deposits are at last being developed. Copper is easily seen by wiping one of the whitewashed runway markers to discover it is blue-green copper ore: the big-time aint far away. Good place to see curious cirio trees up close, and to show children that 'jumping cactus' really do jump. Well, sort of.

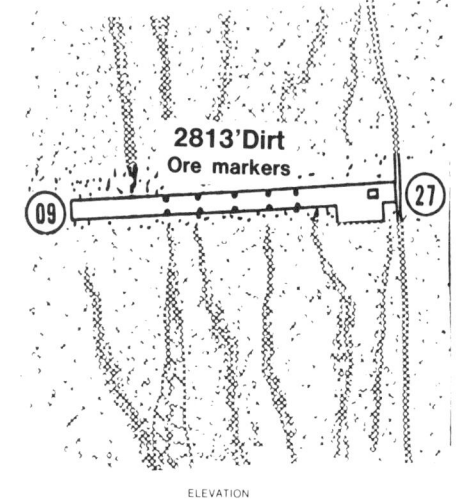

2813' Dirt
Ore markers
09 27

ELEVATION
720'

Calmallí Baja Calif. Norte *call-mah-YEE* 233

JET CHART	WAC	SECTIONAL	LATITUDE	LONGITUDE	US TIME	FOR GMT ADD	ICAO IDENT	TOWN iDENT
JN-46	CH-22 No. ADS-15	TPC H-22B	28°06'	113°26'	MST	7	-	-CMI-

OTHER COMM Traffic 122.85
SETTLEMENT Ranch 1 mile W   POPULATION 12
FROM Santa Rosalia FREQ 112.6 TRACK 296°, 78n.mi.
FROM Guerrero Negro FREQ 382 TRACK 068°, 34n.mi.
FROM Bahia los Angeles FREQ airport TRACK 161°, 52n.mi.
FUEL -   CARDS -   CASH? -
REPAIRS -   TIEDOWN BYO

Site of a gold mine busy in the 1930s, there is still some equipment to see and to admire. We've camped here and it is a chance to enjoy the exploring. The newly discovered copper deposits in the area promise great things will be happening again.

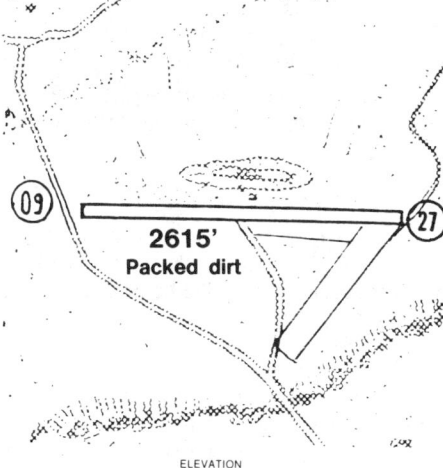

2615'
Packed dirt

ELEVATION
1065'

234 Francisquito Baja Calif. Norte *fronn-sis-KEE-toe*

JET CHART	WAC	SECTIONAL	LATITUDE	LONGITUDE	US TIME	FOR GMT ADD	ICAO IDENT	TOWN IDENT
JN-46	CH-22 No. ADS-15	TPC H-22B	28°24'	112°53'	MST	7	-	-FQT-

OTHER COMM Unicom 122.8 in the bar
SETTLEMENT Resort East end **POPULATION** 30
FROM Santa Rosalia **FREQ** 112.6 **TRACK** 315°, 69n.mi.
FROM Bahia los Angeles **FREQ** airport **TRACK** 121°, 49n.mi.
FROM Rancho Sta Ynez **FREQ** airport **TRACK** 116°, 84n.mi.
FUEL 100 **CARDS** - **CASH?** Yes
REPAIRS - **TIEDOWN** BYO

HOTEL	RATE	WHERE	TEL
Hotel Francisquito	$E	Here	714-870-7551

Runway 31 is being changed to parking and standby use leaving the better approached 34. Fulltime Unicom 122.8.

New operators are taking Francisquito out of its doldrums with new boats, scuba equipment, volley ball, sidetrips to the painted caves, and lots of enthusiasm. Looks like now Francisquito will at last be off and running.

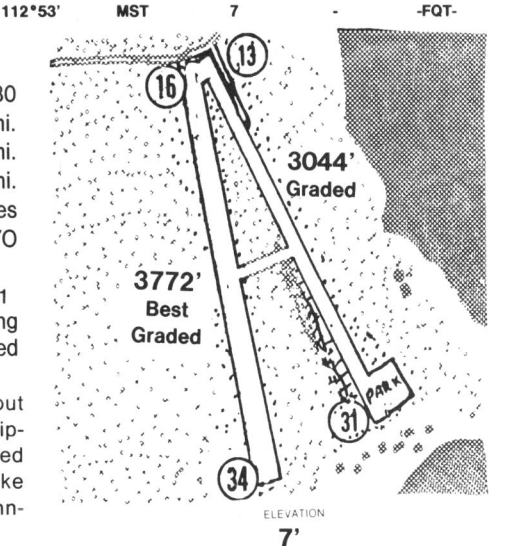

3044' Graded
3772' Best Graded

ELEVATION 7'

PUNTA SAN FRANCISQUITO TOTAL ESCAPE

Air Miles

SAN DIEGO 390 mi.	PHOENIX 300 mi.	EL PASO 450 mi.
SAN FRANCISCO 800 mi.	LOS ANGELES 550 mi.	ORANGE 490 mi.

APPROX. STATUTE MILES

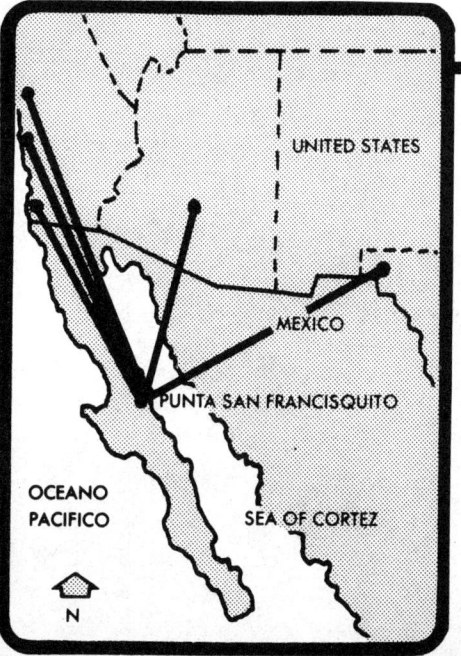

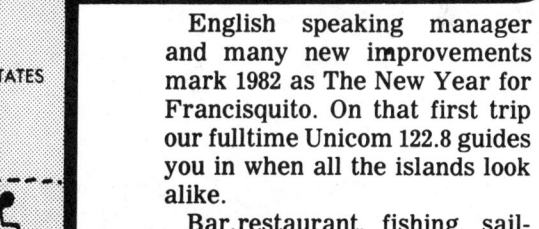

English speaking manager and many new improvements mark 1982 as The New Year for Francisquito. On that first trip our fulltime Unicom 122.8 guides you in when all the islands look alike.

Bar, restaurant, fishing, sailing, scuba diving, boating, and all the fun stuff to make an unforgettable vacation: your best taste of the tropics in Baja California!

$38 per person per day with three great meals

**Reservations
714-870-7551**

236 Rancho el Barrill Baja Calif. Norte *ell bah-REEL*

JET CHART	WAC	SECTIONAL	LATITUDE	LONGITUDE	US TIME	FOR GMT ADD	ICAO IDENT	TOWN IDENT
JN-46	CH-22 No. ADS-15	TPC H-22B	28°18'	112°54'	MST	7	-	-BRL-

OTHER COMM Traffic 122.85
SETTLEMENT Ranch adjacent East POPULATION big family
FROM Mexicali FREQ 115.0 TRACK 140°, 290n.mi.
FROM Santa Rosalia FREQ 112.6 TRACK 320°, 70n.mi.
FROM Bahia los Angeles FREQ airport TRACK 126°, 53n.mi.
FUEL 100 sometimes CARDS - CASH? Yes
REPAIRS - TIEDOWN BYO

Couple centuries ago the Villavicencios (vee-yah-vee-SENN-see-ohs) settled at wells from here across to the Pacific. The cowboy side of the family, typified by José Rosas and his son 'Poley' will tell you about painted caves in the area and will, for a few dollars each, truck you around to see those ancient graffiti.

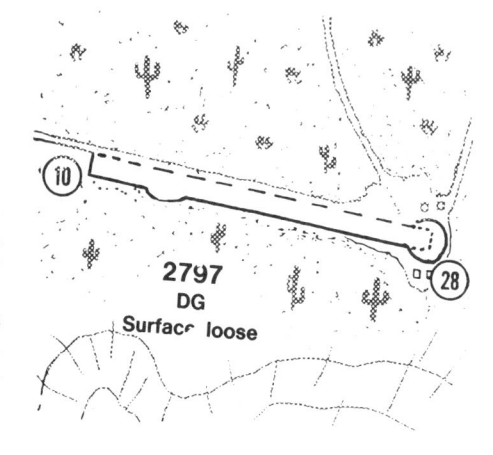

2797 DG
Surface loose

ELEVATION
70'

Misión San Borja Baja Calif. Norte *meese-ee-OAN sohn BORE-hah* **237**

JET CHART	WAC	SECTIONAL	LATITUDE	LONGITUDE	US TIME	FOR GMT ADD	ICAO IDENT	TOWN IDENT
JN-46	CH-22 No. ADS-15	TPC H-22B	28°46'	113°54	MST	7	-	-

OTHER COMM Traffic 122.85
SETTLEMENT 1 mile No. POPULATION 80
FROM San Quintín FREQ 113.3 TRACK 120°,149n.mi.,
FROM Bahia los Ang. FREQ airport TRACK 227°,22n.mi.,
FROM Santa Rosalia FREQ 112.6 TRACK 304°,123n.mi.,
FUEL - CARDS - CASH? -
REPAIRS - TIEDOWN BYO

Just a few minutes flying time from Bahia de los Angeles, this famous mission is being refurbished by a Mexican government program. Interesting for its stone circular stairway and arched ceilings plated with tile, and the never completed roof, this was one of the Jesuits' last missions in the Californias.

Today's residents have a soft drink stand and grocery, do some farming.

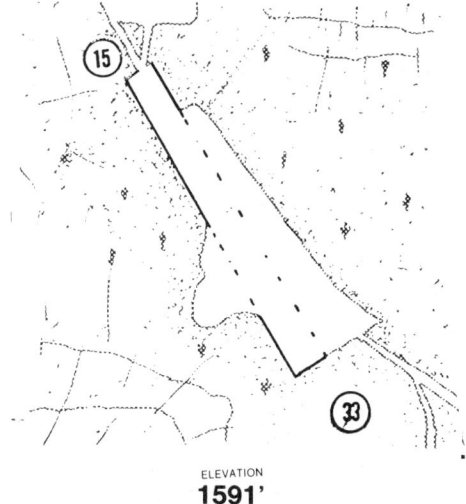

ELEVATION
1591'

237A Midriff Islands   *Las Islas de la Cintura*

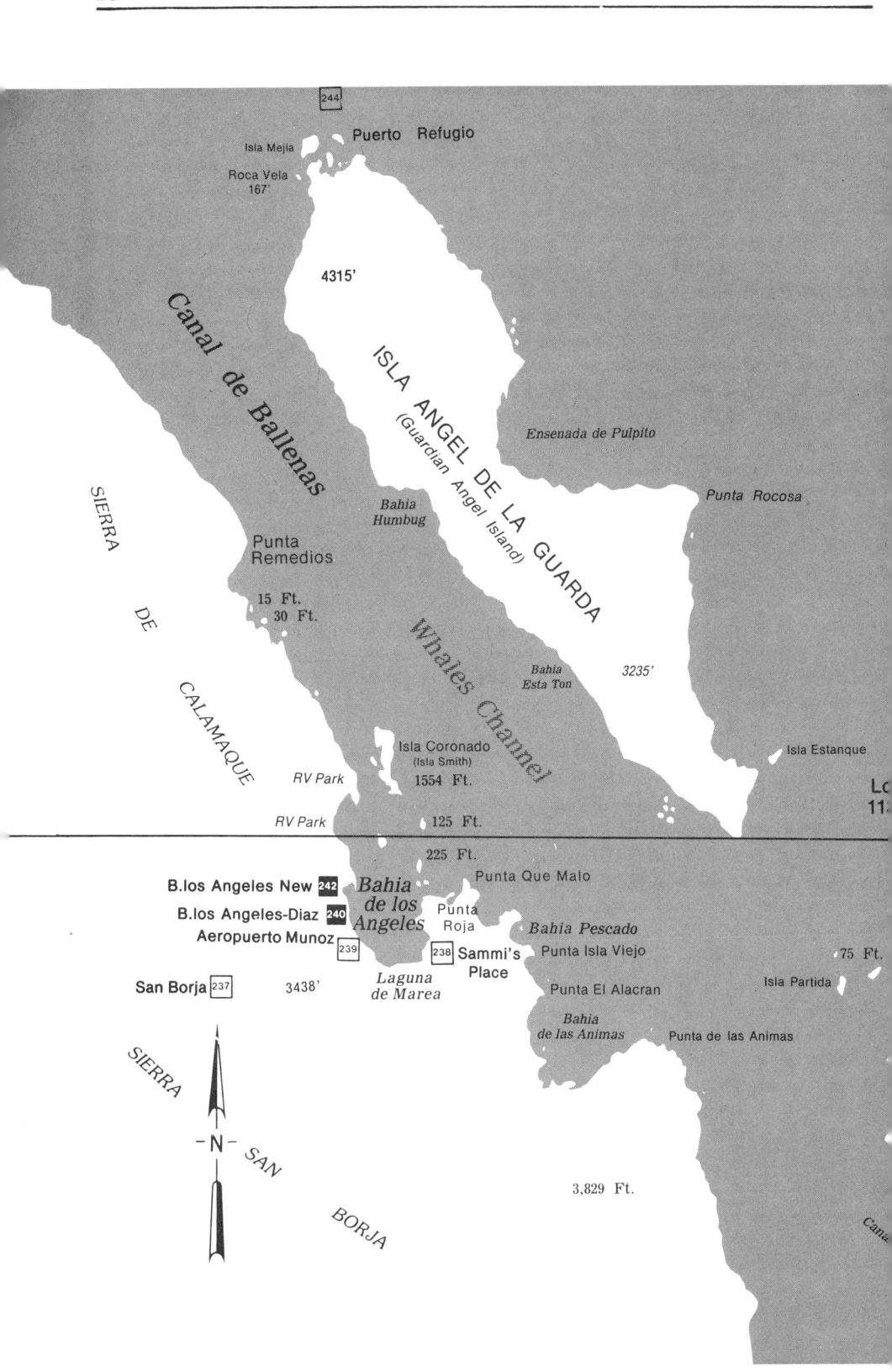

Puerto Refugio
Isla Mejia
Roca Vela 167'
244

4315'

ISLA ANGEL DE LA GUARDA
(Guardian Angel Island)

Canal de Ballenas

Ensenada de Pulpito

Punta Rocosa

SIERRA DE CALAMAQUE

Bahia Humbug

Punta Remedios

15 Ft.
30 Ft.

Whales Channel

Bahia Esta Ton

3235'

Isla Coronado
(Isla Smith)
1554 Ft.

Isla Estanque

RV Park

RV Park   125 Ft.

225 Ft.

Punta Que Malo

B.los Angeles New 242   *Bahia*
B.los Angeles-Diaz 240   *de los*   Punta   *Bahia Pescado*
Aeropuerto Munoz 239   *Angeles*   Roja
                              238 Sammi's   Punta Isla Viejo   75 Ft.
San Borja 237   3438'   Place
                 Laguna   Punta El Alacran   Isla Partida
                 de Marea
                              Bahia
                              de las Animas   Punta de las Animas

SIERRA
-N- SAN
BORJA

3,829 Ft.

237 B

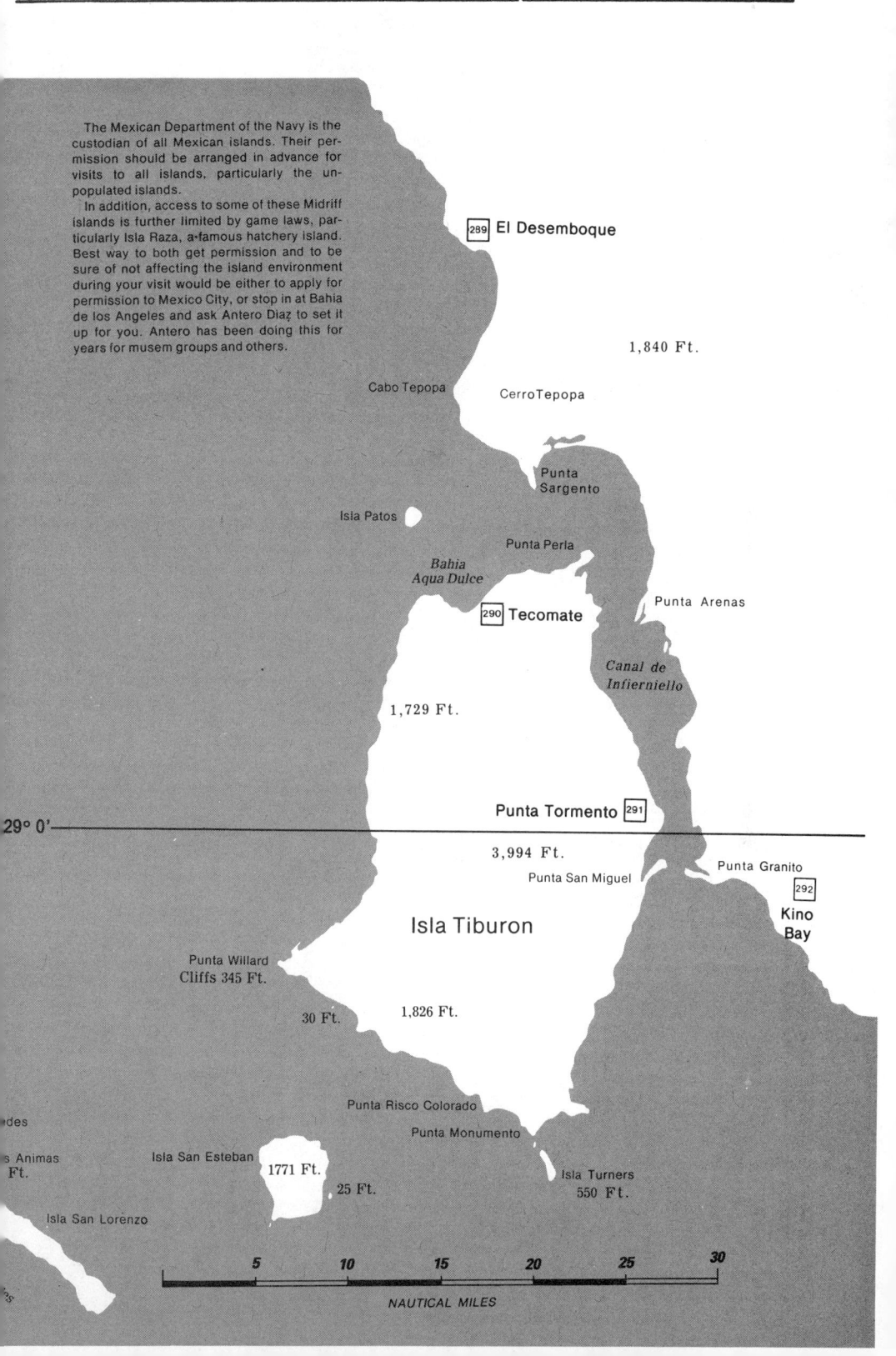

The Mexican Department of the Navy is the custodian of all Mexican islands. Their permission should be arranged in advance for visits to all islands, particularly the unpopulated islands.

In addition, access to some of these Midriff islands is further limited by game laws, particularly Isla Raza, a famous hatchery island. Best way to both get permission and to be sure of not affecting the island environment during your visit would be either to apply for permission to Mexico City, or stop in at Bahia de los Angeles and ask Antero Diaz to set it up for you. Antero has been doing this for years for musem groups and others.

[289] El Desemboque

1,840 Ft.

Cabo Tepopa   CerroTepopa

Punta Sargento

Isla Patos

Punta Perla

Bahia Aqua Dulce

[290] Tecomate

Punta Arenas

Canal de Infierniello

1,729 Ft.

Punta Tormento [291]

29° 0'

3,994 Ft.
Punta San Miguel   Punta Granito

[292] Kino Bay

Isla Tiburon

Punta Willard
Cliffs 345 Ft.

30 Ft.   1,826 Ft.

Punta Risco Colorado
Punta Monumento

Animas
Ft.

Isla San Esteban   1771 Ft.
                    25 Ft.   Isla Turners
                                   550 Ft.

Isla San Lorenzo

0 5 10 15 20 25 30
NAUTICAL MILES

238 Sammi's Place Baja Calif. Norte

JET CHART	WAC ★	SECTIONAL	LATITUDE	LONGITUDE	US TIME	FOR GMT ADD	ICAO IDENT	TOWN IDENT
JN-46	CH-22 No.	TPC H-22C	28°54'	113°27	PST	8	-	-SAM-

OTHER COMM Traffic 122.8
CITY 5 miles NW   POPULATION 326
FROM San Quintin FREQ 113.3 TRACK 116°,161n.mi.
FUEL Trucked 80,100   CARDS -   CASH? Yes
REPAIRS -   TIEDOWN BYO
FROM Mexicali   FREQ 115.0 TRACK 142°,233 n.mi.
FROM San Quintin FREQ 113.3 TRACK 112°,162 n.mi.
FROM Sta Rosalia FREQ 112.6 TRACK 315°,114n.mi.

A trailer/RV facility by Antero (Papa) Diaz, there are several lots leased here now, a few weekend cabins have been finished, others still in construction. Lot rental is low, there are men around who can be persuaded to promise they'll work on your project. Seems to go best if they help you work on your project.

The spectacular backbay fishing has so far been kept under wraps.

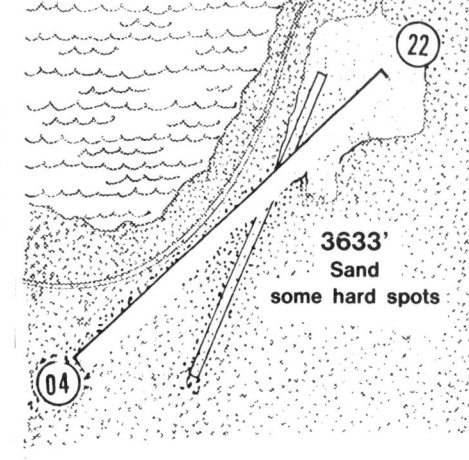

3633'
Sand
some hard spots

ELEVATION
7'

BLX-Muñoz Baja Calif. Norte   moon-YOCE   239

JET CHART	WAC	SECTIONAL	LATITUDE	LONGITUDE	US TIME	FOR GMT ADD	ICAO IDENT	TOWN IDENT
JN-46	CH-22 No. ADS-15	TPC H-22B	28°52'	113°31'	PST	8	-	-BLXM-

OTHER COMM Traffic 122.8
SETTLEMENT 3 miles NW   POPULATION 611
FROM San Quintín FREQ 113.3 TRACK 117°, 160 n.mi.
FROM Punta Peñasco FREQ 112.1 TRACK 170°, 152 n.mi.
FROM Hermosillo FREQ 112.8 TRACK 075°, 131 n.mi.
FUEL 80, 100, by truck   CARDS -   CASH? Yes
REPAIRS Minor   TIEDOWN BYO

HOTEL	RATE	WHERE	TEL
Casa Diaz	$	3 miles N	-
Hotel Vitta	$$	3 miles N	-

Fine camping and swimming on an isolated beach with occasional campers heading SE to Sammi's place. One day this runway will be paved and everything will get busy. For now, enjoy the quiet.

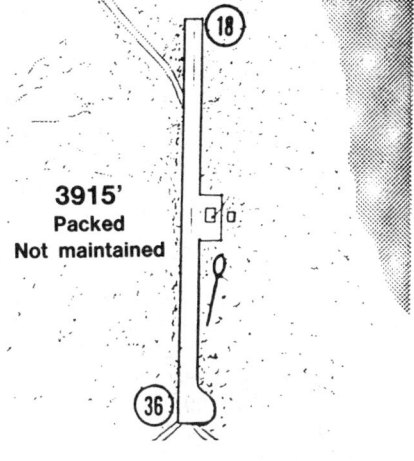

3915'
Packed
Not maintained

ELEVATION
11' to 17'

BLX-1

Isla Angel de la Guarda

240 Bahía de los Angeles Baja Calif. Norte *bah-EE-yah day loce-ONN-hell-ess*

JET CHART	WAC	SECTIONAL	LATITUDE	LONGITUDE	US TIME	FOR GMT ADD	ICAO IDENT	TOWN IDENT
JN-46	CH-22 No. ADS-15	TPC H-22B	28°57'	113°33'	MST	7	-	BLX

OTHER COMM Traffic 122.8
SETTLEMENT West side   POPULATION 650
FROM Punta Final FREQ Airport TRACK 129°62n.mi.,
FROM Santa Rosalia FREQ 112.6 TRACK 314°,120n.mi.
FROM Hermosillo FREQ   TRACK 112.8,074°132 n.mi.
FUEL 80, 100   CARDS -   CASH? Yes
REPAIRS Very minor   TIEDOWN BYO

HOTEL	RATE	WHERE	TEL
Casa Diaz	$A	3/4mi So	-
Hotel Vitta	$$$A	3/4mi So.	714-298-4958

Begun in the '30s by a pioneering couple Antero, and his wife Cruz, Diaz as an alternative to the kitchens at the then mine a mile south, today 'Bahia' is expanding.

The Diaz' rooms and boat rentals, gas for boat, car, and plane kept the presence of the bay alive. Now the Hotel Vitta, the RV Park 3 mi NE, say development is about to deluge us.

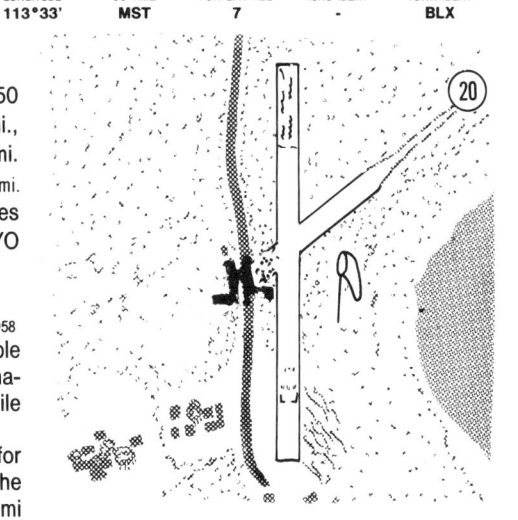

ELEVATION
5' to 12'

2 hotels now and more coming — Bahia's Hotels

This spectacular bay dotted with interesting islands has a backdrop of the mile-high Sierra San Borja mountain range on the left. For years 'the Bay' was kept alive by the Diaz (pronounced DEE-uss) family. Papa and Mama are the hardest working pair you'll find. With their modest hotel called Casa Diaz, in spite of some unbelievable difficulties over the years they been keeping 'the bay' going as a dependable fuel and meal stop since the 1930s.

When the early dirt highways were washed out repeatedly Papa still managed to get aviation gasoline here for us. Often the cost to them was a set of new truck tires each way from Ensenada. When even that ran low they'd ration out what they did have, selling you enough to make your next stop of Mexicali or Mulege. Nobody had to do completely without.

Now the highway brings drive-in visitors by the hundreds, bulk gas trucks are willing to come here on schedule at a delivery cost of a penny or two a gallon.

And more hotels. So far one new hotel is in-place, others have been promised. Through it all, Papa and Mama Diaz continue to provide simple rooms, set a good table, and keep prices under control. There's turtle steak in season, veal at other times. A playful Papa Diaz will, with an almost straight face, try to convince you the meat is really burro.

Rare photo: Papa and Mama Diaz not working

It is a mark of Mama Diaz' excellent kitchen that so many of us get hungry, wherever we are, at just the mention of 'Bahia'.

No advance reservations at family style Casa Diaz; there's always room for another plane load. Plenty of self service beer and soft drinks. For harder stuff bring your own. Whether you are staying a few days or just making a fuel stop, doing it with Papa and Mama Diaz makes you a part of Baja's history.

Villa Vitta
HOTEL RESORT SPA
Bahia de los Angeles, B.C.
México

$44.05
PER DAY + TAX
PER PERSON
(DOUBLE OCC.)
LODGING
AND MEALS
INCLUDED

RESTAURANT (TILL 2200)   COCKTAIL BAR
AIR CONDITIONED — POOL — JACUZZI
FISHING — AVGAS AVAILABLE
AIR TRANSPORTATION ARRANGED
— BRAND NEW BOATS AVAILABLE —

IMMEDIATE RESERVATIONS
(714) 298-4958
(PRICES SUBJECT TO CHANGE WITHOUT NOTICE)

242 Bahia de los Angeles New Baja Calif. Norte *bah-EE-yah day loce ONN-hell-uss*

JET CHART	WAC	LATITUDE	LONGITUDE	US TIME	FOR GMT ADD	ICAO IDENT	TOWN IDENT
JN-46	CH-22 So. ADS-15	28°57'	113°33'	PST/PDT	8/7	-	BLX

OTHER COMM Traffic 122.8
SETTLEMENT 3/4 mi So. POPULATION est 650
FROM Mexicali FREQ 115.0 TRACK 144°, 237 n.mi.
FROM S.Quintin FREQ 113.3 TRACK 113°, 156 n.mi.
FROM Sta Rosalia FREQ 112.6 TRACK 314°, 120 n.mi.
AV GAS Truck:80,100   CARDS? -   CASH TYPE Any
REPAIRS AVAILABLE Minor   TIEDOWNS? BYO

(15)
4856'x79' Paving
UPHILL 7'
1469'x34' Paving
UPHILL 5'
UPHILL 11'
ELEVATION 23' to 34' msl
(33)

When the wind isn't smoking out of the west this new runway at Bahia is a winner. But let wind come down Hurricane Canyon and you'll need logging chains for tiedowns to keep your airplane in the same County with you. Any number of times I've seen this part of the bay over thirty percent whitecap. The old strip, and the Munoz runway, are not in the direct flow.

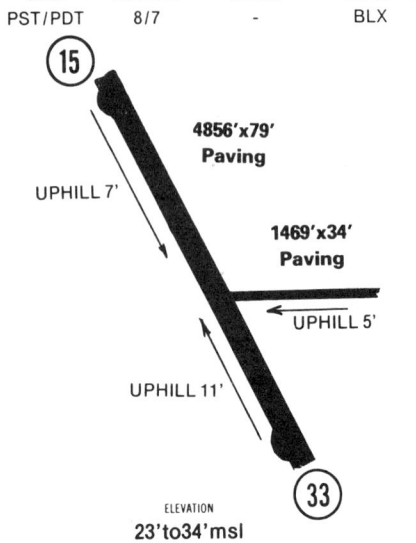

Desengaño   Baja Calif. Norte   *dess-enn-GONN-yoe*   243

JET CHART	WAC	SECTIONAL	LATITUDE	LONGITUDE	US TIME	FOR GMT ADD	ICAO IDENT	TOWN IDENT
JN-46	ADS-15o.	TPC H-22B	29°08'	113°57'	PST	8	-	-DÑO-

OTHER COMM Traffic 121.5
SETTLEMENT None   POPULATION 0
FROM Bahia los Angeles FREQ airport TRACK 285°, 24n.mi.
FROM Rancho Sta Ynez FREQ airport TRACK 122°, 61n.mi.
FROM San Quintin FREQ 113.3 TRACK 115°, 133n.mi.
FUEL -   CARDS -   CASH? -
REPAIRS -   TIEDOWN Noway

Existing now just as a ghost town for the dunebuggy set or a landmark for pilots, this distinctively shaped runway complex has seen better days. In the thirties hundreds of pounds of gold were flown out almost every month.

But these days it takes a gold mine to start a gold mine so everything stays dormant. Maybe if gold gets to a thousand dollars an ounce things may change.

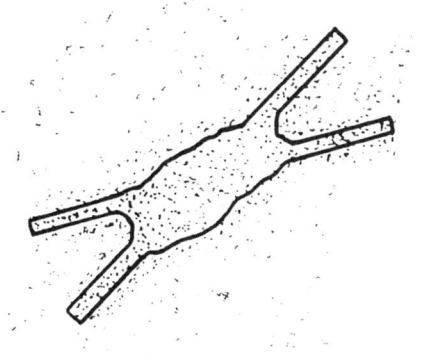

Unusable at present

ELEVATION
Est 2500'

244 Puerto Refugio

This lonely tucked away baylet at the north tip of Guardian Angel Island sees almost no airplanes flying by to enjoy the scene. Yachtsmen get here a whole lot and the fishermen describe the fishing in words which glow in the dark. Most pilots see only the white bird-poopoo island a mile SW, properly called Roca Vela, or sail rock.

One might think that with such an attractive bay, the uninhabited Guardian Angel Island would be well-populated at least by the transient fishermen, or possibly a scattering of weekend cabins. In the US that would be the case, however in Mexico, all islands are the responsibility of the Secretary of Navy. He has not been quick to permit development of any kind.

One finds, actually, that the armed, blue uniformed sailors who check our papers at Bahia de los Angeles or Bahia Kino are under orders to discourage any visits to islands except by permission. Antero Diaz at Bahia los Angeles can make those arrangements.

As soon as you ask around about Puerto Refugio the fishing tales will seem just too good to be true. I've been hearing them for years and have spent many an hours circling overhead searching for even 700' of reasonably smooth surface to land and wet a line but no luck so far. I'll keep you posted in the PREPS.

Punta Final — Baja Calif. Norte — *POON-tah fee-NAL* — 245

JET CHART	WAC	SECTIONAL	LATITUDE	LONGITUDE	US TIME	FOR GMT ADD	ICAO IDENT	TOWN IDENT
JN-46	CH-22 No. ADS-15	TPC H-22B	29°45'	114°18'	PST	8	-	-PFL-

OTHER COMM Traffic 122.8
SETTLEMENT North end **POPULATION** 0 to 145
FROM Mexicali **FREQ** 115.0 **TRACK** 149°, 182 n.mi.
FROM Tijuana **FREQ** 116.5 **TRACK** 127°, 219 n.mi.
FROM Punta Peñasco **FREQ** 112.1 **TRACK** 190°, 107 n.mi.
FUEL - **CARDS** - **CASH?** -
REPAIRS - **TIEDOWN** BYO

Avoid residents' tiedowns.

Some say the prettiest beach on the peninsula, closeness of little bays and really deep water makes this an explorers' and fishermen's delight. Several dozen leased lots with everything from simple ramadas to luxury vacation homes dot the beach and slopes.

Owned by a grand lady Doña Josefina Zúñiga of Rancho Santa Ynez, the lot rents are about twenty dollars a month at last report. Great place to relax.

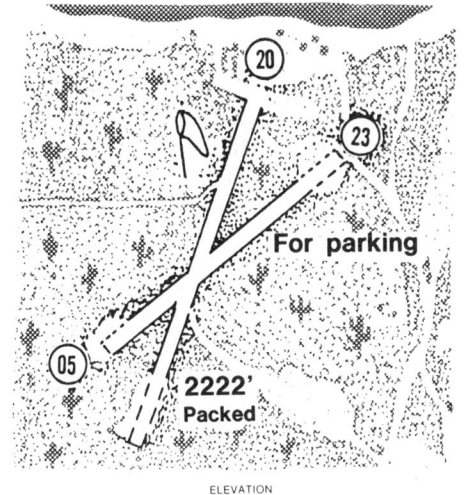

2222' Packed

ELEVATION 19'

246 Alfonsina's   Baja Calif. Norte   *all-fonn-SEE-nuss*

JET CHART	WAC	SECTIONAL	LATITUDE	LONGITUDE	US TIME	FOR GMT ADD	ICAO IDENT	TOWN IDENT
JN-46	CH-22 No. ADS-15	TPC H-22B	29°49'	114°24'	PST	8	-	-ALF-

OTHER COMM Traffic 122.85
SETTLEMENT Leased lots E side   POPULATION 50
FROM Mexicali   FREQ 115.0   TRACK 152°, 174n.mi.
FROM Pta Peñasco FREQ 112.1 TRACK 195°, 103 n.mi.
FROM San Quintin FREQ 113.3 TRACK 106°, 91N.mi.
FUEL 100   CARDS -   CASH? Yes
REPAIRS -   TIEDOWN BYO

HOTEL	RATE	WHERE	TEL
Casa Alfonsina	-$	Here	-

Popular cabin sites on the open Bahia de San Luís Gonzaga, this one is unique for the shrimp boat parking lot just offshore: you can sometimes buy or swap for some. Keep in mind they aren't really supposed to deal with you and limit your quantities to say fifty pounds.

Land is available here for lease, you will notice a couple dozen weekend homes with the usual plane parking mat, boat ramp, expanded mobile home.

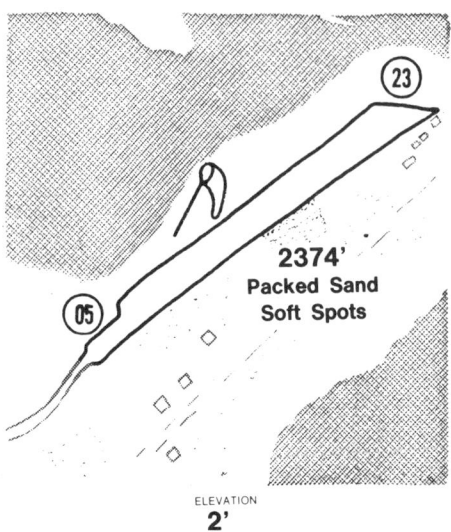

2374'
Packed Sand
Soft Spots

ELEVATION
2'

Papa Fernandez' Baja Calif. Norte POP-ah fair-NON-dess 247

JET CHART	WAC	SECTIONAL	LATITUDE	LONGITUDE	US TIME	FOR GMT ADD	ICAO IDENT	TOWN IDENT
JN-46	CH-22 No. ADS-15	TPC H-22B	29°50'	114°23'	PST	8	-	-PPF-

OTHER COMM Traffic 122.85
SETTLEMENT 1/4 mile East   POPULATION about 50
FROM Mexicali   FREQ 115.0   TRACK 149°, 174n.mi.
FROM San Quintín FREQ 113.3 TRACK 105°, 92n.mi.
FROM Punta Peñasco FREQ 112.1 TRACK 194°, 104 n.mi.
FUEL Some 80/87   CARDS -   CASH? Any
REPAIRS Minor   TIEDOWN BYO

Used by pilots who know exactly where the ruts are this week, strangers could have problems.

READER REPORT Runway 5/23 isn't too hot but 14/32 still okay. We go there in our early model Cessna 210. T Ryan, Arizona

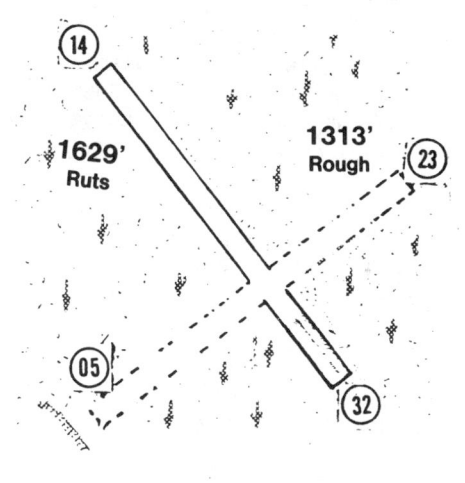

1629' Ruts
1313' Rough

ELEVATION
33'

248 el Huerfanito Baja Calif. Norte   *ell wair-fonn-EET-toe*

JET CHART	WAC	SECTIONAL	LATITUDE	LONGITUDE	US TIME	FOR GMT ADD	ICAO IDENT	TOWN IDENT
JN-46	CH-22 No. ADS-15	TPC H-22B	30°14'	114°37'	PST	8	-	-HFO-

OTHER COMM Traffic 122.85
SETTLEMENT Adjacent NE   POPULATION Usually zero
FROM Punta Peñasco FREQ 112.1 TRACK 206°,96Dme
FROM Mexicali   FREQ 115.0   TRACK 153°,157n.mi.
FROM San Quintin FREQ 113.3 TRACK 095°,73n.mi.
FUEL -   CARDS -   CASH? -
REPAIRS -   TIEDOWN BYO

A fishing/enjoying camp on the Sea of Cortés where people have built concrete block weekend cabins. The runways straddle the San Felipe-Punta Final road giving everyone two ways to come and go.

On my recent looks this runway appears marginal for nosewheels, in a taildragger the approach end of 28 seems the least worst.

1824' Rough Some brush

550' Ruts Maybe

ELEVATION
18' to 24'

Puertecitos   Baja Calif. Norte   *pwair-toe-SEE-toce*   **249**

JET CHART	WAC	SECTIONAL	LATITUDE	LONGITUDE	US TIME	FOR GMT ADD	ICAO IDENT	TOWN IDENT
JN-46	CH-22 No. ADS-15	TPC H-22B	30°22'	114°39'	PST	8	-	-PTO-

OTHER COMM Traffic 122.8
SETTLEMENT Adjacent   POPULATION 300
FROM Mexicali   FREQ 115.0   TRACK 148°, 142n.mi.
FROM Punta Peñaso FREQ 112.1   TRACK 211°, 86Dme
FROM San Quintin   FREQ 113.3   TRACK 085°, 69n.mi.
FUEL 80   CARDS -   CASH? Any
REPAIRS Minor   TIEDOWN BYO

HOTEL	RATE	WHERE	TEL
Casa Orozco	-$	Here	-

Runway 16/34: 2018' Graded
Runway 20/02: 1230' Packed
ELEVATION 17'

Has the waterski boats, bayside homes, and overall sun and fun of a miniature Newport Beach. Rafael Orozco has the Master Lease on this pretty place with great skindiving, a healthy hotspring, and a nice breeze.

If, after you've stayed and looked it over you would like a lot, Rafael will lease one to you. Rates are low.

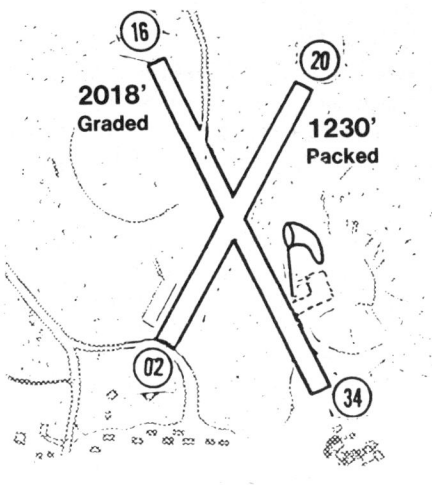

249 A Coloradito   Baja Calif. Norte   *coe-loe-rah-DEE-toe*

JET CHART	WAC	LATITUDE	LONGITUDE	US TIME	FOR GMT ADD	ICAO IDENT	TOWN IDENT
JN-46	CH-22 No. ADS-15	30°28'	114°39'	PST/PDT	8/7	-	DTO-

OTHER COMM Traffic 124.1
SETTLEMENT Adjacent SE POPULATION 0 to 60
FROM Pta Penasco FREQ 112.1 TRACK 215°, 78.8Dme
FROM San Felipe FREQ Airport TRACK 147°, 31 n.mi.
FROM San Quintin FREQ 113.3 TRACK 078°, 67.2n.mi.
AVIATION FUEL —   CARDS —   CASH TYPE —
REPAIRS? —   TIEDOWNS? BYO

Sea of Cortes beachfront lots by the hundred and a nearby palentologist's idea of heaven a mile West combine to make an interesting assortment for residents with a trailer or house here. Pleasant setting, can be windy in March or April.

2187'x47'
Packed Dirt
Gravel Overburden

ELEVATION
31 to 42' msl

cah-DANE-yuh

Baja Calif. Norte **Cadena** 249B

JET CHART	WAC	LATITUDE	LONGITUDE	US TIME	FOR GMT ADD	ICAO IDENT	TOWN IDENT
JN-46	CH-22 No. ADS-15	30°25'	114°38'	PST/PDT	8/7	-	NYA-

FROM **Pta Penasco** FREQ 112.1 TRACK 213°, 80.3Dme
FROM **Mexicali** FREQ 115.0 TRACK 157°, 185 n.mi.
FROM **Tijuana** FREQ 116.5 TRACK 122°, 174n.mi.

The coastline from San Felipe south is sprouting with drive-in or fly-in beachfront properties being developed for Gringos and Mexicans who want a cottage along the Sea of Cortes. Rents are modest, ten year renewable leases are the rule, and they are strictly controlled by the Mexican Government to prevent any possible misunderstandings.

Probably before you reads these words I will have measured this runway and have the data available to tell you through the PREPS.

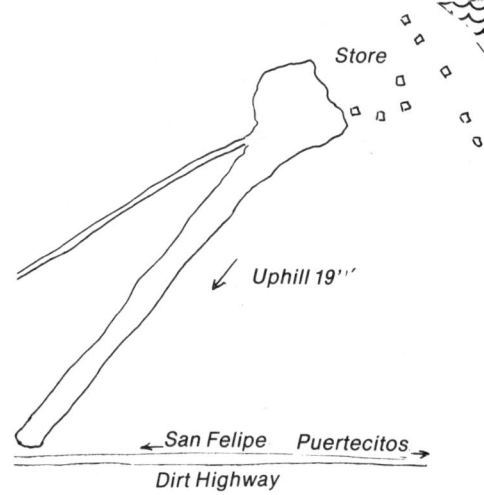

250 San Felipe Municipal   Baja Calif. Norte   *sahn fay-LEE-pay*

JET CHART	WAC	SECTIONAL	LATITUDE	LONGITUDE	US TIME	FOR GMT ADD	ICAO IDENT	TOWN IDENT
JN-46	CH-22 No. ADS-15	TPC H-22B	30°57'	114°51'	PST	8	-	SFE

OTHER COMM Traffic 122.8
CITY 3 miles N   POPULATION 5,000
FROM Mexicali   FREQ 115.0   TRACK 152°, 100n.mi.
FROM Punta Peñasco FREQ 112.1 TRACK 239°, 73Dme
FROM Tijuana   FREQ 116.5   TRACK 118°, 142 n.mi.
FUEL -   CARDS -   CASH? Yes
REPAIRS Minor-BYO   TIEDOWN

HOTEL	RATE	WHERE	TEL
Econohotel	$$	Near	tvl agt
Motel el Cortés	$	Central	-
Arnold's del Mar	$	Central	-

A nice new paved runway to start San Felipe on the way toward lots of good building, more boats to enjoy that Sea of Cortés. This one points into the strong winds which were once a bother. Now there is a marina, a good runway and hotels abuilding, crankup and go, enjoy.

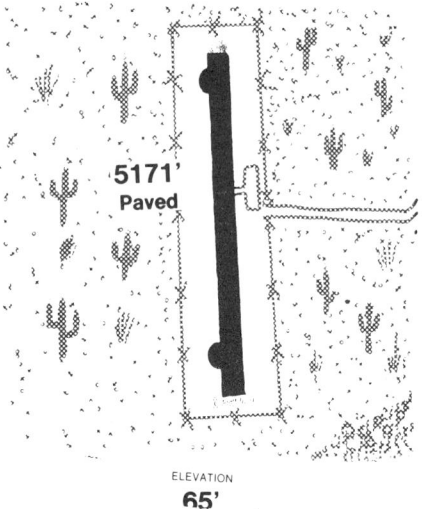

5171'
Paved

ELEVATION
65'

Make it a Perfect Landing...
...in SAN FELIPE

5 Quick Minutes from the new San Felipe Airport on Airport Road....................

LOS ANGELES 238 AIR MILES
PALM SPRINGS 198 AIR MILES
PHOENIX 230 AIR MILES
TUCSON 220 AIR MILES
SAN DIEGO 180 AIR MILES

STAY AT THE BEAUTIFUL

castel®
RESORT HOTEL
San Felipe

- Private beach resort.
  - 120 air-conditioned guest rooms with king or double-double beds, fully carpeted, telephones, poolside views, weekend discotheque, swimming pool with swim-up bar, dining room, cocktail lounge, tennis, gift shop.
  - Special rates mid-week

for reservations call toll-free:
Nationwide 1-(800)-854-2026, California 1-(800)-542-6028, San Diego (714) 459-0251

252 San Felipe-Downtown Baja Calif. Norte   *sahn fay-LEE-pay*

JET CHART	WAC	SECTIONAL	LATITUDE	LONGITUDE	US TIME	FOR GMT ADD	ICAO IDENT	TOWN IDENT
JN-46	CH-22 No. ADS-15	TPC H-22B	31°01'	114°51'	PST	8	-	SFE

OTHER COMM Traffic 122.8
CITY Adjacent NE   POPULATION 7,000
FROM Mexicali   FREQ 115.0   TRACK 152°,100n.mi.
FROM Punta Peñasco FREQ 112.1 TRACK 240°,73n.mi.
FROM Punta Final FREQ airport TRACK 326°,80n.mi.
FUEL 80; some 100?   CARDS -   CASH? Yes
REPAIRS Minor   TIEDOWN BYO

HOTEL	RATE	WHERE	TEL
Hotel Riviera	$$	So. of town	7-11-44
Motel el Cortés	$$	Central	7-10-55
Econohotel	$$	Near	tvl agt

From observation over the years it is a matter of land use. If someone builds a house or settlement in the middle of a closed airport it stays closed. Otherwise, planes coming and going often keep an airport open for years after it was 'closed'.

It will be interesting to what happens here.

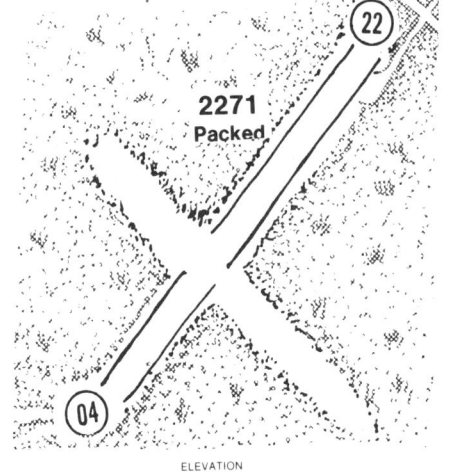

2271 Packed

ELEVATION
142'

Playa Blanca   Baja Calif. Norte   PLY-ah BLONK-ah   253

JET CHART	WAC	SECTIONAL	LATITUDE	LONGITUDE	US TIME	FOR GMT ADD	ICAO IDENT	TOWN IDENT
JN-46	CH-22 No. ADS-15	TPC H-22B	31°06'	114°52'	PST	8	-	-BCA-

OTHER COMM Traffic 122.85
SETTLEMENT 2 miles S   POPULATION 800
FROM Mexicali   FREQ 115.0   TRACK 152°, 94n.mi.
FROM Tijuana   FREQ 116.5   TRACK 117°, 137 n.mi.
FROM Punta Peñasco FREQ 112.1 TRACK 244°, 73Dme
FUEL -   CARDS -   CASH? -
REPAIRS -   TIEDOWN BYO

A long dormant runway on a real estate development just north of San Felipe, this runway is was, for a time when it was new, destination for Aeromexico's Twin Otters which for a short time served several whistle-stop destinations in Baja California. Now this is the closest place to Mexicali where you can at least get to the beach easily.

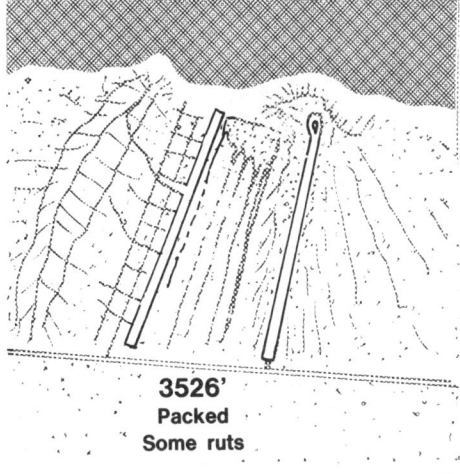

3526'
Packed
Some ruts

ELEVATION
80' to 92'

MEXICALI, B.C.N.
VOR/DME PISTA 28

254

ENERO 30 DE 1980/147

RADIO 127.6	TWR 118.2	ELEV 72'
		VAR MAG 14° E
		MXL

Caution For Information Only Not for Aerial Navigation

DME
MXL
115.0

FALLIDA: VIRE A LA **IZQUIERDA** E INTERCEPTE EN ASCENSO EL **RADIAL 126°** Y PROSIGA EN TRAYECTORIA DE APROXIMACION HASTA LA ALTITUD MINIMA DE ESPERA, DE ACUERDO CON INSTRUCCIONES DEL **A.T.C.**

CATEGORIA	DIRECTO PISTA 28 MDA 525'(448')	CATEGORIA	CIRCULANDO MDA
A		A	680'(608')-1
B	1	B	680'(608')-1
C		C	680'(608')-1¾
D	1½	D	680'(608')-2¼

SCT-DGAC-SENEAM   MXL-VD-1

SUNRISE & SUNSET – GMT   SALIDA y PUESTA del SOL – GMT

15th of	JAN	FEB	MAR	APR	MAY	JUN	JUL	AUG	SEPT	OCT	NOV	DEC	
SUNRISE	1443	1424	1351	1311	1242	1232	1244	1304	1324	1345	1411	1435	SALIDA
SUNSET	2457	0126	0148	0210	0232	0250	0249	0226	0147	0108	2440	2436	PUESTA
15° de	ENE	FEB	MAR	ABR	MAY	JUN	JUL	AGO	SEP	OCT	NOV	DIC	

To get local time just subtract 'GMT ADD'
PARA OBTENER TIEMPO LOCAL SUSTRIAGA 'GMT ADD'

Mexicali Internacional Baja Calif. Norte   *meh-hee CAH-lee*   **255**

JET CHART	WAC	SECTIONAL	LATITUDE	LONGITUDE	US TIME	FOR GMT ADD	ICAO IDENT	TOWN IDENT
JN-46	CG-18	ADS-15 Los Angeles	32°38'	115°16'	PST	8	MMML	MXL

tca to: 8,000'msl CENTER VorDme RADIUS 18mi
APPROACH 127.6 TOWER 118.2 GROUND 118.2
OTHER COMM FSS 122.6, Calexico 122.8
CITY 11 miles W POPULATION 320,000
LOCAL Vor FREQ 115.0 WHERE On airport HOURS 24
B'CAST FREQ 790 WHERE 15 mi WSW HOURS Daylight
FROM Palm Springs FREQ 115.5 TRACK 125°, 94Dme
FROM San Felipe FREQ Airport TRACK 152°, 103n.mi.
FROM Punta Peñasco FREQ 112.1 TRACK 295°, 115 n.mi.
FUEL 80, 100, JP CARDS Visa, MC CASH? Yes
REPAIRS Minor TIEDOWN BYO

HOTEL	RATE	WHERE	TEL
Lucerna	$$	Central	-
Holiday Inn	$$	Central	-

AOE 9am-5pm
8531'
Paved
Isolated

Busiest by far of all the internacional airports, recent rearrangements have cut the usual worst case delays from over two hours by about half.

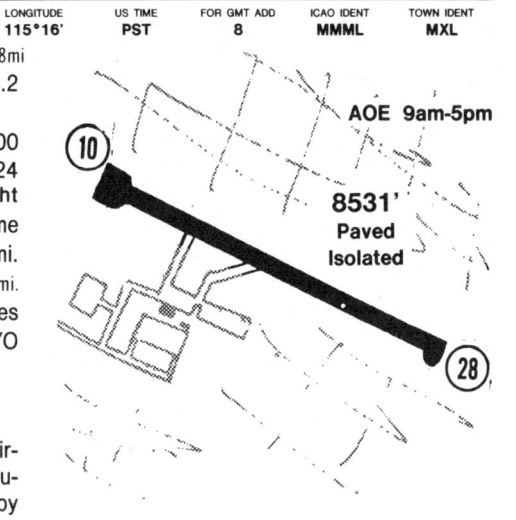

ELEVATION
77'

256 Calexico Int'l California *cah-LEXX-ee-coe*

JET CHART	WAC	SECTIONAL	LATITUDE	LONGITUDE	US TIME	FOR GMT ADD	ICAO IDENT	TOWN IDENT
JN-46	CG-18 So. ADS-15	Los Angeles	32°40'	115°32'	PST/PDT	8/7	ICAO	CXL

OTHER COMM Calexico Unicom 122.8 at office
CITY Adjacent East   POPULATION 60,000
LOCAL B'cast FREQ 1490 WHERE 2 miles N HOURS Daylight
FROM Thermal   FREQ 116.2   TRACK 134°, 66Dme
FROM Mexicali   FREQ 115.0   TRACK 266°, 13n.mi.
FROM Punta Peñasco FREQ 112.1 TRACK 294°, 127 n.mi.
FUEL 80,100,JP   CARDS Major   CASH? Yes
REPAIRS Major   TIEDOWN BYO rope

By far the busiest single airport of entry the US has, it is not unusual to see one or two hundred aircraft returning to the US on a Sunday afternoon.

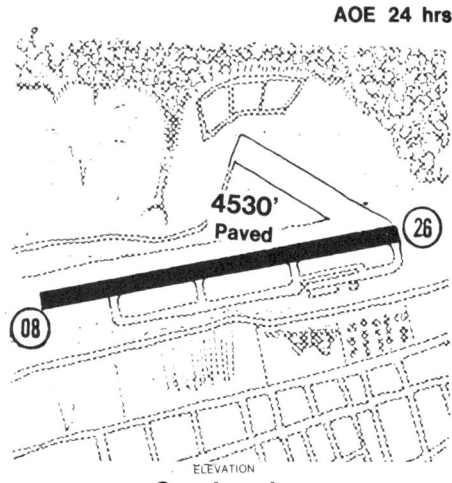

AOE 24 hrs

4530' Paved 26 08

ELEVATION
Sea Level

"WALK INTO MEXICO"

The historic De Anza Hotel is a well-known and treasured landmark. Old world charm, informal atmosphere, superb food and modest rates are just a few reasons why so many pilots are making the De Anza Hotel a regular stopover.

Conveniently located, the Hotel is within a 15 - 20 minute walk from the airport, although taxi cabs are readily available. The De Anza Hotel is just north of the port of entry to Baja California, Mexico.
A short three block walk from the Hotel's front door takes you into bustling Mexicali, Mexico, for tourist shopping and sightseeing.

The De Anza Hotel Coffee Shop is a favorite with everyone on both sides of the border serving breakfast and lunch until 3:30 P.M.

In the evening, Alicia's Supper Room and Cocktail Lounge is open, offering a fine variety of Mexican and American cuisine served in a colorful Mexican courtyard atmosphere.

On your next trip south, plan to stop at the De Anza Hotel, Calexico, California where you'll find friendly, south of the border hospitality, good food, comfortable air-conditioned rooms, and an inviting olympic-sized pool awaiting you.

"TE ESPERAMOS"

233 4th STREET • CALEXICO, CALIFORNIA 92231 • (714) 357-1112

VOR-A

IMPERIAL COUNTY (IPL)
IMPERIAL, CALIFORNIA
AL-790 (FAA)
Amdt 1 — 258

LOS ANGELES CENTER
128.6 291.7
IMPERIAL TOWER * #
120.2
GND CON
121.7

IMPERIAL
115.9 IPL
Chan 106

1700 NoPT
254° (10)
R-074
(IAF) IPL 10 DME

• 2562

MSA IPL 25 NM
120° / 2200
285° / 6600

MISSED APPROACH
Climbing right turn to 2000 direct IPL VORTAC and hold.

VORTAC
One minute Holding Pattern
074° / 254°
2000
IPL 5.7 DME
313° / 254°
1700

ELEV −56
△53
3304 x 100
12°
☆-4
313° 5.7 NM from VORTAC
TDZE −56
MIRL Rwy 14-32
−11

CATEGORY	A	B	C	D
CIRCLING	440-1 496 (500-1)	440-1 496 (500-1)	440-1½ 496 (500-1½)	500-2 556 (600-2)

FAF to MAP 5.7 NM

Knots	60	90	120	150	180
Min:Sec	5:42	3:48	2:51	2:17	1:54

VOR-A 32°50'N – 115°34'W
IMPERIAL, CALIFORNIA
IMPERIAL COUNTY (IPL)
129

SUNRISE & SUNSET – GMT   SALIDA y PUESTA del SOL – GMT

15th of	JAN	FEB	MAR	APR	MAY	JUN	JUL	AUG	SEPT	OCT	NOV	DEC	
SUNRISE	1444	1425	1352	1312	1243	1233	1244	1305	1325	1346	1412	1436	SALIDA
SUNSET	2458	0127	0149	0211	0233	0251	0251	0227	0148	0109	2441	2437	PUESTA
15° de	ENE	FEB	MAR	ABR	MAY	JUN	JUL	AGO	SEP	OCT	NOV	DIC	

To get local time just subtract 'GMT ADD'
PARA OBTENER TIEMPO LOCAL SUSTRIAGA 'GMT ADD'

Imperial County California

JET CHART	WAC	SECTIONAL	LATITUDE	LONGITUDE	US TIME	FOR GMT ADD	ICAO IDENT	TOWN IDENT
JN-46	CG-18	LA	32°45	115°30	PST/PDT	8/7	-	IPL

APPROACH - ADS-15/ER 120.2   GROUND 121.7
CITY 1 mile S   POPULATION 34000
LOCAL VorDme   FREQ 115.9   WHERE 6 mi SE   HOURS 24
FROM Mexicali   FREQ 115.0   TRACK 282°,16Dme,
FROM Hermosillo   FREQ 112.8   TRACK 302°,317 n.mi.
FROM Tijuana   FREQ 116.5   TRACK 065°,74Dme,
FUEL 80,100   CARDS Major   CASH? Yes
REPAIRS Yes   TIEDOWN Yes

HOTEL	RATE	WHERE	TEL
Airporter Inn	$$	here	-

    Sure is convewnient for Southern Californians to have this airport as an IFR or VFR alternate when coastal clouds move in along our coastline. Airporter is a hundred yards away with other motels down the road a piece. puzzle is why the tower.

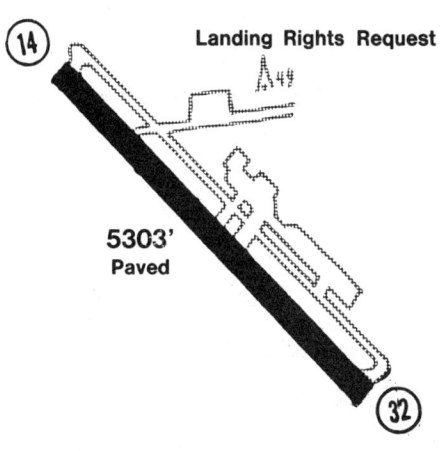

Landing Rights Request

5303'
Paved

ELEVATION
-56'

260 San Luís Rio Colorado, Sonora   *loo-EECE REE-oh coe=loe-RAH-doe*

JET CHART	WAC	SECTIONAL	LATITUDE	LONGITUDE	US TIME	FOR GMT ADD	ICAO IDENT	TOWN IDENT
JN-46	CG-18 So. ADS-15	Phoenix	32°27	114°48	MST	7	-	-

OTHER COMM Traffic 118.1
CITY 0.7 miles NE   POPULATION 8500
B'CAST FREQ 1270   WHERE 2 mi NE   HOURS Daylight
FROM Pto Peñasco   FREQ 112.1   TRACK 305°, 99Dme,
FROM Yuma   FREQ 116.8   TRACK 214°, 14Dme,
FROM Mexicali   FREQ 115.0   TRACK 078°, 21Dme,
FUEL Some 80   CARDS -   CASH? Yes
REPAIRS Minor   TIEDOWN BYO

Almost completely overlooked, this duster strip is a handy camping place for those who want to get a very early start, say about dawn.

You clear the border the night before, camp here, and set your travel alarm. You can be up, coffeed, packed, and ready as the eastern sky begins to gray just before it becomes pink. Seeing the sun's rays inching across the land as you are climbing to altitude is a wonderful way to start a day.

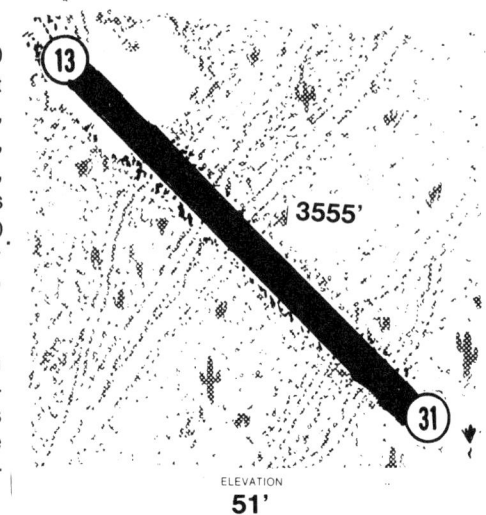

3555'

ELEVATION
51'

from the photo album **Interesting Picture** 261

While measuring the runway at el Arco in Baja California del Norte one day I asked my passenger Bob Manger to take my camera and shoot a picture of me as I was passing one of the piles of copper ore they whitewash there and use for runway markers.

Months later I discovered there were two images on that negative. Here you are able to pick out a second measuring wheel fainly seen just ahead of my 'real' measuring wheel, and a second image of me just in front of the 'real' me. Bob shot three and only this one has the extra image. Weird.

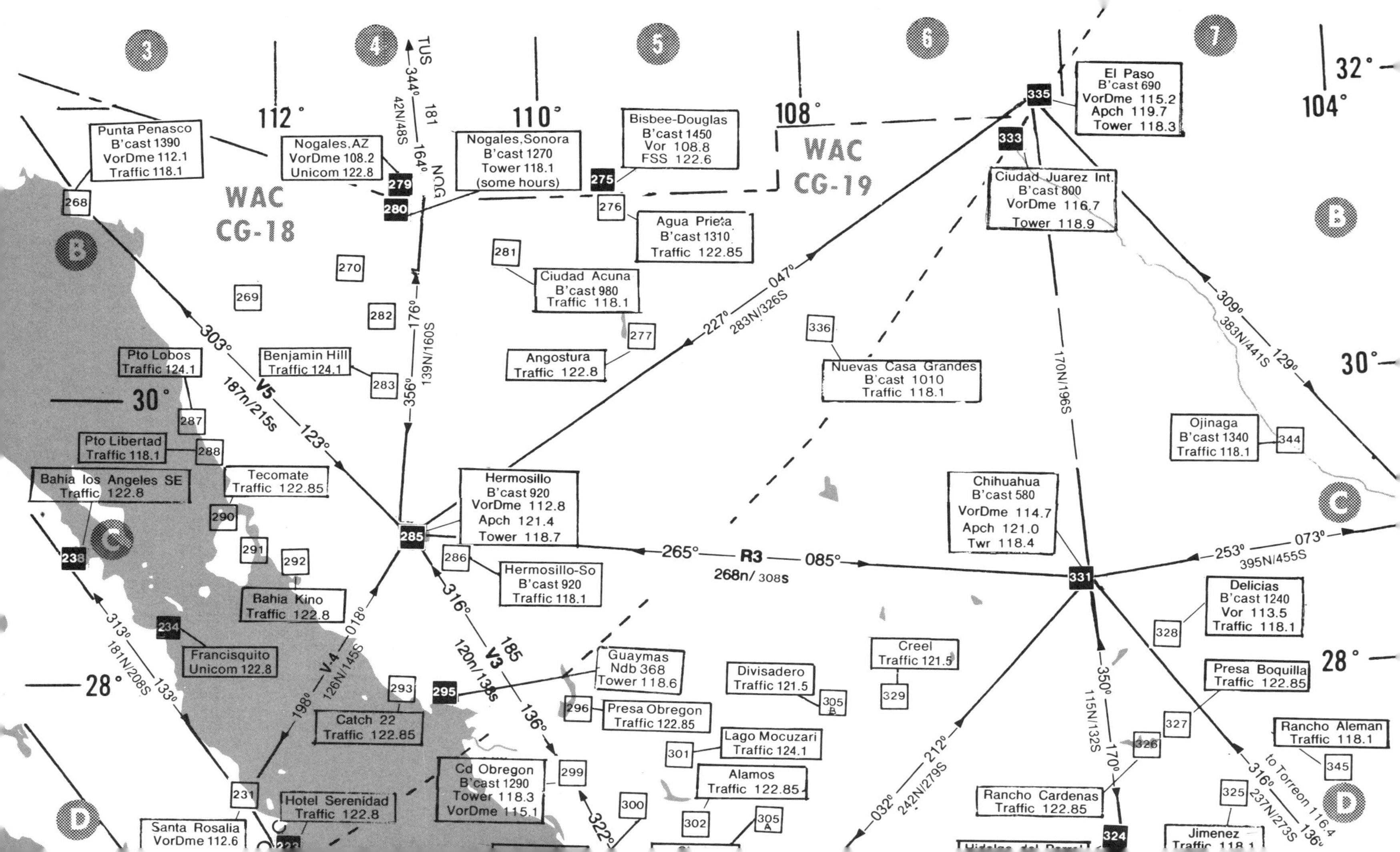

112°
110°
108°
104°
32°
30°
28°
WAC CG-18
WAC CG-19
TUS 344° 164° 181 42N/48S NOG
Punta Penasco B'cast 1390 VorDme 112.1 Traffic 118.1
Nogales,AZ VorDme 108.2 Unicom 122.8
Nogales,Sonora B'cast 1270 Tower 118.1 (some hours)
Bisbee-Douglas B'cast 1450 Vor 108.8 FSS 122.6
Agua Prieta B'cast 1310 Traffic 122.85
El Paso B'cast 690 VorDme 115.2 Apch 119.7 Tower 118.3
Ciudad Juarez Int. B'cast 800 VorDme 116.7 Tower 118.9
Ciudad Acuna B'cast 980 Traffic 118.1
Angostura Traffic 122.8
Nuevas Casa Grandes B'cast 1010 Traffic 118.1
Ojinaga B'cast 1340 Traffic 118.1
Benjamin Hill Traffic 124.1
Pto Lobos Traffic 124.1
Pto Libertad Traffic 118.1
Bahia los Angeles SE Traffic 122.8
Tecomate Traffic 122.85
Hermosillo B'cast 920 VorDme 112.8 Apch 121.4 Tower 118.7
Hermosillo-So B'cast 920 Traffic 118.1
Chihuahua B'cast 580 VorDme 114.7 Apch 121.0 Twr 118.4
Delicias B'cast 1240 Vor 113.5 Traffic 118.1
Bahia Kino Traffic 122.8
Francisquito Unicom 122.8
Guaymas Ndb 368 Tower 118.6
Divisadero Traffic 121.5
Creel Traffic 121.5
Presa Obregon Traffic 122.85
Lago Mocuzari Traffic 124.1
Alamos Traffic 122.85
Catch 22 Traffic 122.85
Cd Obregon B'cast 1290 Tower 118.3 VorDme 115.1
Hotel Serenidad Traffic 122.8
Santa Rosalia VorDme 112.6
Presa Boquilla Traffic 122.85
Rancho Aleman Traffic 118.1
Rancho Cardenas Traffic 122.85
Jimenez Traffic 118.1
to Torreon 116.4
303° V5 187n/215s 123°
176° 139N/160S 356°
227° 283N/326S 047°
170N/196S
309° 383N/441S 129°
265° R3 268n/308s 085°
253° 395N/455S 073°
316° 185 V3 120n/138s 136°
018° V-4 126N/145S 198°
313° 181N/208S 133°
350° 115N/132S 170°
032° 242N/279S 212°
316° 237N/273S 136°
322°
268 269 270 275 276 277 279 280 281 282 283 285 286 287 288 290 291 292 293 295 296 299 300 301 302 305 A 305 B 324 325 326 327 328 329 331 333 335 336 344 345 231 234 238

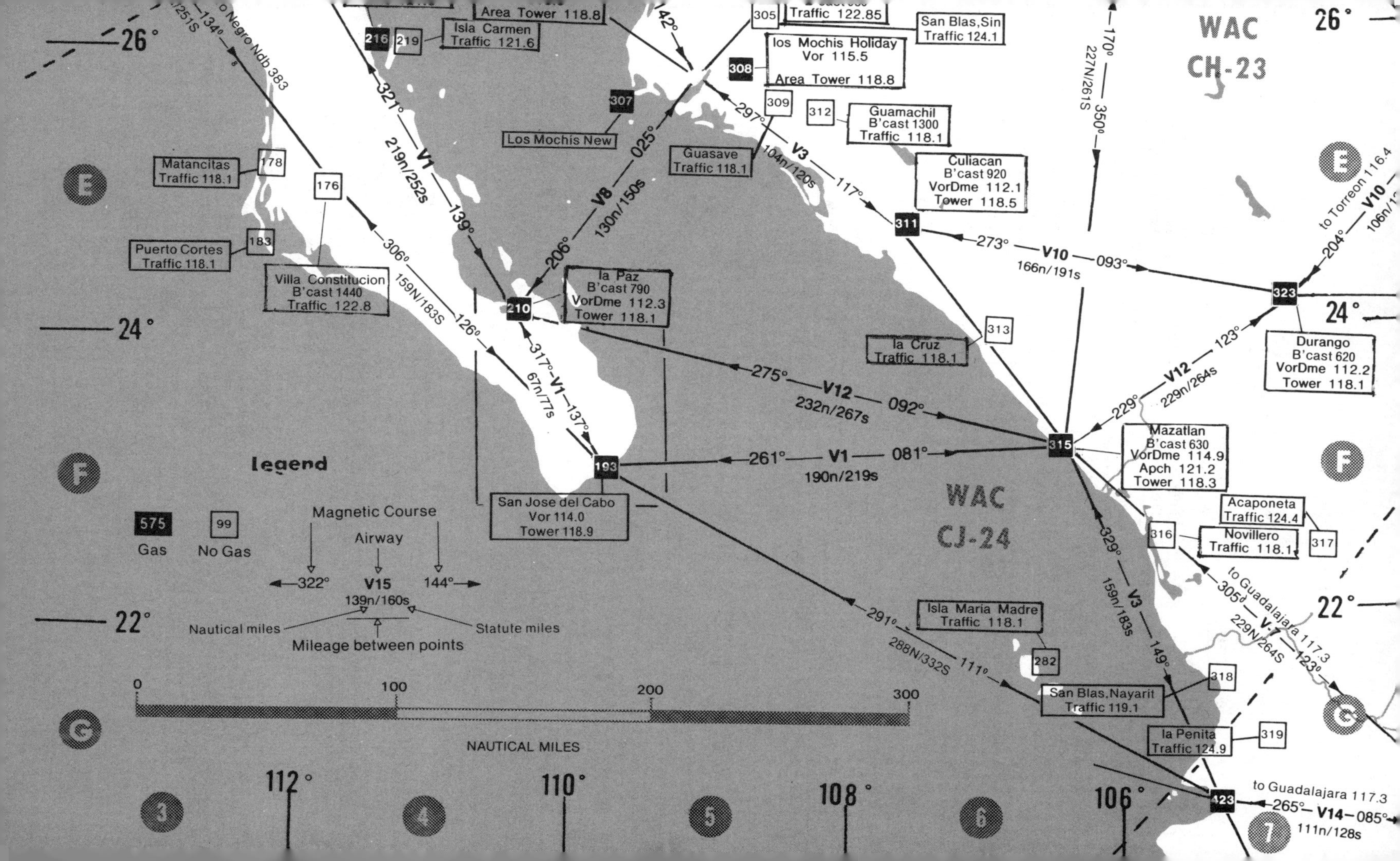

WAC CH-23
WAC CJ-24
26°
24°
22°
112°
110°
108°
106°
Area Tower 118.8
Isla Carmen Traffic 121.6
Traffic 122.85
San Blas,Sin Traffic 124.1
los Mochis Holiday Vor 115.5 Area Tower 118.8
Los Mochis New
Guasave Traffic 118.1
Guamachil B'cast 1300 Traffic 118.1
Culiacan B'cast 920 VorDme 112.1 Tower 118.5
Matancitas Traffic 118.1
Puerto Cortes Traffic 118.1
Villa Constitucion B'cast 1440 Traffic 122.8
la Paz B'cast 790 VorDme 112.3 Tower 118.1
la Cruz Traffic 118.1
Durango B'cast 620 VorDme 112.2 Tower 118.1
Mazatlan B'cast 630 VorDme 114.9 Apch 121.2 Tower 118.3
Acaponeta Traffic 124.4
Novillero Traffic 118.1
San Jose del Cabo Vor 114.0 Tower 118.9
Isla Maria Madre Traffic 118.1
San Blas,Nayarit Traffic 119.1
la Penita Traffic 124.9
to Torreon 116.4
to Guadalajara 117.3
o Negro Ndb 383
V1 219n/252s 321° 139°
V8 130n/150s 206° 025°
V3 104n/120s 297° 117°
V10 166n/191s 273° 093°
V12 232n/267s 275° 092°
V1 190n/219s 261° 081°
V12 229n/264s 229° 123°
V1 67n/77s 317° 137°
159N/183S 306° 126°
288N/332S 291° 111°
V3 159n/183s 329° 149°
V7 229N/264S 305° 123°
V14 111n/128s 265° 085°
227N/261S 170° 350°
V10 106n 204°
134° 251S
142°
216 219 305 308 307 309 312 311 313 323 178 176 183 210 193 315 316 317 282 318 319 423
Legend
575 Gas
99 No Gas
Magnetic Course
Airway
322° V15 144°
139n/160s
Nautical miles
Statute miles
Mileage between points
0 100 200 300
NAUTICAL MILES

Northwest Area Index

Sequence:
Place,Ident,Page

Acaponeta,ACP,317
Agua Prieta,APA,276
Alamos,ALA,302
Angostura,ARA,277

Bahia Escondida,DID-,292B
Bahia Kino,KIO-,292
Bahia Vermillion,292A
Benjamin Hill,BJN-,283
Bisbee Douglas IFR,IFR,274
Bisbee Douglas Int'l,DUG,275

Cananea,CNA,281
Catch 22,C22-,293
Chihuahua,CUU,331
Chihuahua IFR,CUU,330
Choix,Chih.,CHX,305A
Ciudad Juarez IFR,CJS,332
Ciudad Juarez Int'l,CJS,333
Ciudad Obregon,CEN,299
Ciudad Obregon IFR,CEN,298
Creel,CRL,329
Culiacan,CUL,311
Culiacan IFR,CUL,310

Delicias,DEL,328
Desemboque,DES,289
Dexter Products,337
Divisadero,DRO-,305B
Durango,DGO,323
Durango IFR,DGO,322

EL Paso IFR,ELP,334
EL Paso Int'l,ELP,335

El Fuerte,FRT,304
El Llano,PNT,319

Fifth of February,CEN2-,297
Fresnillo,FRS,356

Guamuchil,GCH,312
Guasave,GUS-,309
Guaymas IFR,GYM,294
Guaymas Int'l,GYM,295

Hermosillo IFR,HMO,284
Hermosillo Int'l,HMO,285
Hermosillo South,HMO2-,286
Hidalgo del Parral,HPC,324
Hidalgo,Presa,DLG-,303
Holiday-los Mochis,LMM,308

Isla Maria Madre,IMM,321

Jimenez,CJM,325
Juanito-Creel,CRL,329

La Cruz,CRU-,313
La Penita,PNT-,319
Lago Mocuzari,CUZ-,301
Los Mochis Holiday,LMM,308
Los Mochis IFR,LMM,306
Los Mochis New,LMM,307

Magdalena,Son,STO-,282
Mazatlan,MZT,315
Mazatlan IFR,MZT,314
Mocuzari,Lago,CUZ-,301

Navajoa,NVJ,300
Nogales IFR,278
Nogales Int'l,AZ,OLS,279
Nogales Int'l,Sonora,NOG,280
Northwest Area,262
Northwest Briefing,265
Northwest Index,264
Novillero,NOV-,316
Nuevas Casas Grandes,NCG,336

Parral,HPC,324
Penita,la,PNT,319
Presa Altar,ATR-,270
Presa Boquilla,BOQ-,327
Presa Hidalgo,DLG-,303
Presa Obregon,OBR-,296
Puerto Libertad,LBT-,288
Puerto Lobos,LOB-,287
Punta Penasco,PPE,268
Punta Tormento,MTO-,291

Rancho Cardenas,326
Rancho Manjares,CAB,269

San Blas,Nayarit,SBS,318
San Blas,Sinaloa,BLA-,305

Tecomate,ECO-,290
Tepic,TEP,320
Tucson IFR,TUS,272
Tucson Int'l,TUS,273

Yuma IFR,YUM,266
Yuma Int'l,YUM,267

Northwest introduction

Area includes: The mainland west from El Paso, and from Mexico's northern border south almost to Puerto Vallarta.
Best Known for: Guaymas' shrimp and sportfishing, Mazatlan's tropical splendiforous weather, delightful Copper Canyon.
But it also has: Miles of white sand beach at Bahia Kino, bass fishing at all the dams (look for 'Presa' in the area index), delightful Alamos, the almost secret El Fuerte, and the charms of San Blas.
Cities: Hermosillo, Nogales, Cd.Obregon, Culiacan, Tepic.
Climate: deserty north, sub-tropics south, then mile high conditions in what is called the Sierra Madre, or Mother of Mountains.
Weather: temperate in the north, warmly comfortable south of Los Mochis, more so in San Blas. High Country is summer warm, can bluster in winter.
Special notes: Fronts can arrive in this area from SW through NW then wait in the Sierra Madre to die out. If that takes awhile everything west can have low ceilings and rain showers with problems in the mountain ridges.
Shopping tips: seldom-visited Seri Indians at Desemboque produce distinctive wood carvings sold everywhere else for two or three times local price. We had a lime-buying spree one day in El Fuerte. A tourist lady insisted on three dollars worth of limes and asked my help to translate. She then needed help to carry forty pounds of limes.

Mazatlan and Guaymas are the number one seafood places in most people's minds. To get you started, the Shrimp Bucket in Mazatlan is a popular spot, as is the Del Mar in Guaymas.

The good restaurant of the week in Los Mochis varies a bit. To know which is good this time ask Octavio Serrano when you arrive at the airport. He's the flight instructor with the bushy mustache. The Serranos have been in Mochis just about a century now. If anyone knows he's the one.

Ace-in-the-hole: The ride from Culiacan to Durango is a pretty one up that canyon, but in summer the smart money makes that run, or any other across the Sierra Madre, to be out of the mountains by ten a.m. Any later there are winds around those high peaks ranging from uncomfortable to hazardous. You can always enjoy another day wherever you are then get an early start tomorrow. Easy way to be sure there will be a tomorrow.

The old Mazatlan airport was handily near everything; you can still see signs of it if you look closely

ILS RWY 21R

Amdt 3

YUMA MCAS–YUMA INTERNATIONAL (YUM)
AL-511 (FAA)
YUMA, ARIZONA

YUMA APP CON 120.0 314.0
YUMA TOWER* 119.3 382.8
GND CON 121.9 340.2
CLNC DEL *2225 118.0
ATIS * 118.8 273.2

BARD 116.8 BZA Chan 115

LOCALIZER 108.3 I-YUM

MSA BZA 25 NM — 4800

ELEV 213
TDZE 193

MISSED APPROACH
Climb to 800, then climbing right turn to 4000 direct BZA VORTAC and hold.

One Minute Holding Pattern
075° / 255° 3000
GS 3.00°
TCH 54

CATEGORY	A	B	C	D
S-ILS 21R		393-½ 200 (200-½)		
S-LOC 21R	600-½ 407 (500-½)		600-¾ 407 (500-¾)	
CIRCLING	660-1 447 (500-1)	680-1 467 (500-1)	680-1½ 467 (500-1½)	780-2 567 (600-2)

Category D S-LOC 21R visibility increased ¼ mile for inoperative MM.

OPTICAL LANDING SYSTEM AVAILABLE RWYS 3R and 21 L/R.
HIRL Rwys 3L-21R, 3R-21L, 8-26 and 17-35.

FAF to MAP 4.9 NM					
Knots	60	90	120	150	180
Min:Sec	4:54	3:16	2:27	1:58	1:38

ILS RWY 21R 32°39'N – 114°36'W YUMA, ARIZONA
YUMA MCAS–YUMA INTERNATIONAL (YUM)

SUNRISE & SUNSET – GMT   SALIDA y PUESTA del SOL – GMT

15th of	JAN	FEB	MAR	APR	MAY	JUN	JUL	AUG	SEPT	OCT	NOV	DEC	
SUNRISE	1440	1421	1348	1308	1239	1230	1241	1301	1322	1342	1408	1433	SALIDA
SUNSET	2454	0123	0146	0208	0229	0247	0247	0223	0145	0105	2437	2433	PUESTA
15° de	ENE	FEB	MAR	ABR	MAY	JUN	JUL	AGO	SEP	OCT	NOV	DIC	

To get local time just subtract 'GMT ADD'
PARA OBTENER TIEMPO LOCAL SUSTRIAGA 'GMT ADD'

Yuma International   Arizona   YOO-mah   267

JET CHART	WAC	SECTIONAL	LATITUDE	LONGITUDE	US TIME	FOR GMT ADD	ICAO IDENT	TOWN IDENT
JN-46	CG 18 So. ADS-15	Phoenix	32°40'	114°36'	MST	7	-	YUM

APPROACH 120.0   TOWER 119.3   GROUND 121.9
OTHER COMM -
CITY Adjacent NW   POPULATION 45,000
LOCAL VorDme FREQ 116.8 WHERE 7Dme N HOURS 24
B'CAST FREQ 560   WHERE -   HOURS Daylight
FROM Pta Peñasco FREQ 112.1 TRACK 311°,95Dme
FROM Mexicali   FREQ 115.0   TRACK -,-
FUEL 80, 100, JP CARDS Major CASH? Any
REPAIRS Major   TIEDOWN BYO ropes

HOTEL	RATE	WHERE	TEL
Stardust	$$$	Town	Courtesy

The epitome of courtesy in Customs men, Ray Darling, has retired from here but his manner lives on in the excellent service from linemen, Customs, and hotels. Makes this an attractive stop whether or not you are going or coming from the US.

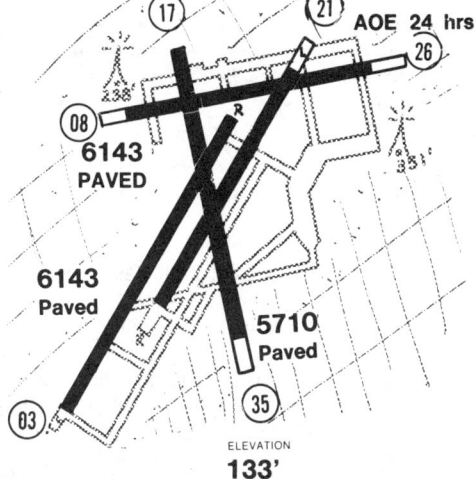

6143 PAVED
6143 Paved
5710 Paved
AOE 24 hrs
ELEVATION 133'

268 Punta Peñasco, Sonora

POON-tah penn-YASK-oh

| JET CHART JN-46 | WAC CH-22 | SECTIONAL ADS-15 | TPC H-22B | LATITUDE 31°23' | LONGITUDE 113°30' | US TIME MST | FOR GMT ADD 7 | ICAO IDENT - | TOWN IDENT PPE |

TCA Scheduled 1984
OTHER COMM Traffic 118.1
CITY 4 miles SW   POPULATION 27,000
LOCAL VorDme   FREQ 112.1   WHERE Here   HOURS 24
B'CAST FREQ 1390   WHERE 2.3 mi SW   HOURS Daylight
FROM Hermosillo   FREQ 112.8   TRACK 303°, 189 n.mi.
FROM Mexicali   FREQ 115.0   TRACK 115°, 115 n.mi.
FROM Yuma   FREQ 116.8   TRACK 131°, 101 n.mi.
FUEL Seldom 80   CARDS -   CASH? Pesos
REPAIRS -   TIEDOWN BYO

5034' x 99' Paved
3194' PACKED
ELEVATION 49'

Several decent local hotels.

Populated by campers from California and Arizona, people come here for the fishing and to see other people who come here for the fishing.

For some reason confiscated dope airplanes are everywhere. In backyards, service stations, junkyards; but I haven't seen even one at the airport.

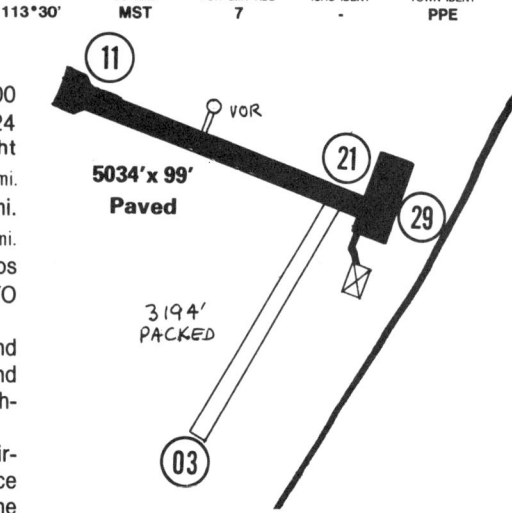

Rancho Manjarés, Sonora

RONN-choe monn-hah-RESS

269

JET CHART	WAC	SECTIONAL	LATITUDE	LONGITUDE	US TIME	FOR GMT ADD	ICAO IDENT	TOWN IDENT
JN-46	CH-22 No. ADS-15	TPC H-22B	30°43'	112°13'	MST	7	-	-JUL-

OTHER COMM Traffic 118.1
CITY Caborca 4 miles F   POPULATION 31,000
B'CAST FREQ 970   WHERE 8 mi E   HOURS Daylight
FROM Nogales   FREQ 108.2   TRACK 228°, 84Dme
FROM Punta Peñasco FREQ 112.1 TRACK 108°, 78Dme
FROM Hermosillo   FREQ 112.8   TRACK 317°, 114 n.mi.
FUEL 80, 100?   CARDS -   CASH? Pesos
REPAIRS Minor   TIEDOWN BYO

HOTEL	RATE	WHERE	TEL
el Camino	$	Central	2-04-66
Amelia	$	Central	?

Julián Manjarés owns this airport and the dusters (fumigators in Spanish) which operate from it. Always a lot of help to all US pilots, he once quietly joined a search by paying his pilots himself and sent six of his planes out searching for two days.

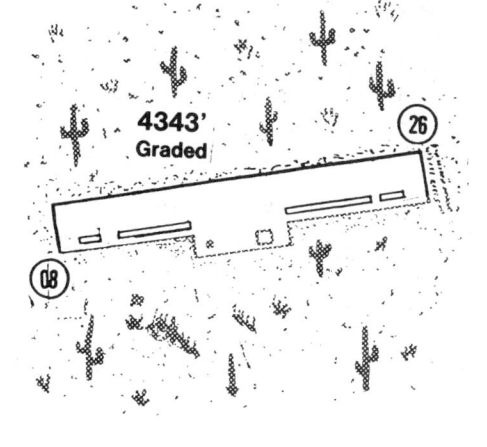

4343'
Graded

26
08

ELEVATION
997'

270 Presa Altar, Sonora *PRESS-ah all-TARR*

JET CHART	WAC	SECTIONAL	LATITUDE	LONGITUDE	US TIME	FOR GMT ADD	ICAO IDENT	TOWN IDENT
JN-46	CH-22 No. ADS-15	TPC H-22B	30°51'	111°34'	MST	7	-	-ATR-

OTHER COMM Traffic 122.85
SETTLEMENT 3 miles NE   POPULATION 150
FROM Nogales   FREQ 108.2   TRACK 214°, 50Dme
FROM Hermosillo   FREQ 112.8   TRACK 335°, 109 n.mi.
FROM Punta Peñaso FREQ 112.1   TRACK 094°, 105 n.mi.

Whenever the government agency for hydraulics builds a dam they put in a good runway for the engineers to come and go during construction. This was such an airport. Built by Recursos Hidraulicos for their then DC-3, it continues in occasional use by fishermen, farmers in the area, and who knows who else.

Surrounded by cotton fields, this could be an opportunity for your children to learn that Levis do not grow on bushes. At least not here.

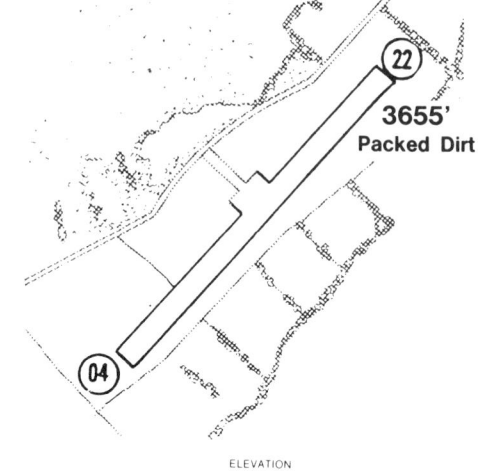

3655' Packed Dirt

ELEVATION
2097'

Intentionally Left Blank
Intencionalmente Dejada en Blanco

378

Amc
VOR/DME-B

AL-430 (FAA)

TUCSON INTERNATIONAL
TUCSON, ARIZONA

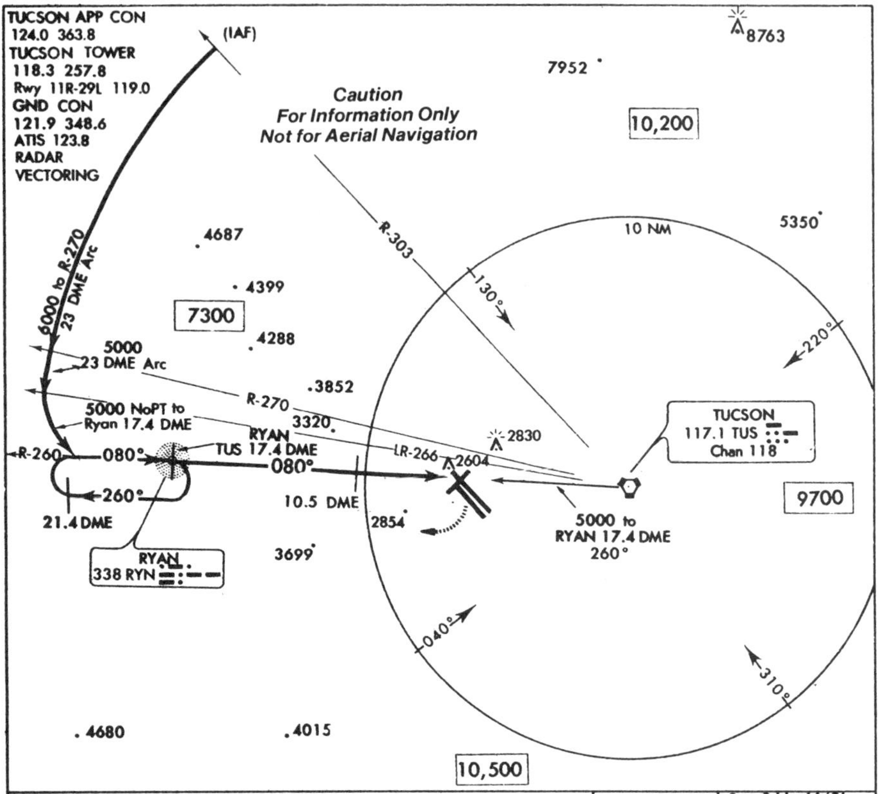

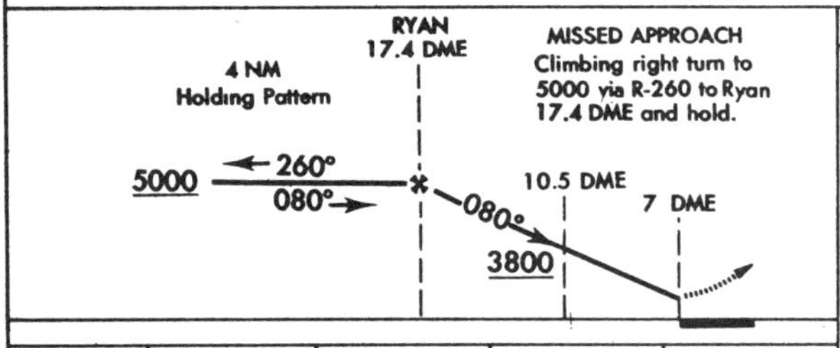

CATEGORY	A	B	C	D
CIRCLING	3120-1	490 (500-1)	3180-1½ 550 (600-1½)	3180-2 550 (600-2)

ELEV 2630

Rwy 3 ldg 6149′
Rwy 21 ldg 6500′
Rwy 11L ldg 10,902′
Rwy 29L ldg 7337′
Rwy 11R ldg 6975′

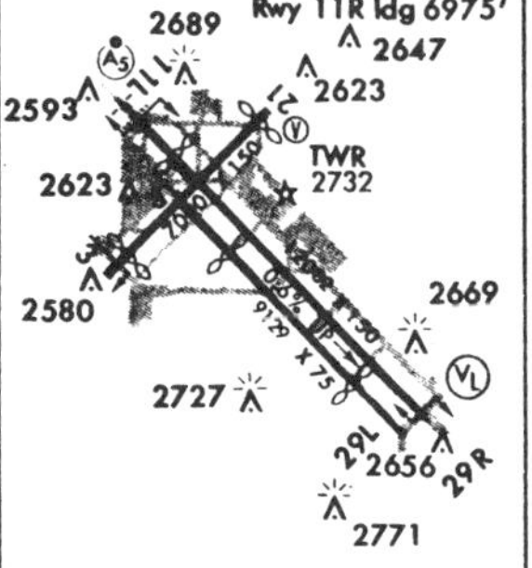

REIL Rwy 21
HIRL Rwy 11L-29R
MIRL Rwy 3-21

Knots	60	90	120	150	180
Min:Sec					

Tucson Inernational Arizona TOOS-onn 273

JET CHART	WAC	SECTIONAL	LATITUDE	LONGITUDE	US TIME	FOR GMT ADD	ICAO IDENT	TOWN IDENT
JN-46	CH-22 No. ADS-15	Phoenix	32°08'	110°57'	MST	7	-	TUS

APPROACH 124.0 TOWER 118.3 GROUND 121.9
OTHER COMM ATIS 123.8 FSS 122.7
CITY 6 miles North POPULATION 105,000
LOCAL VorDme FREQ 117.1 WHERE 7 miles E HOURS 24
B'CAST FREQ 990 WHERE - HOURS Daylight
FROM Phoenix FREQ 115.6 TRACK 135°,91Dme
FROM Nogales,Son. FREQ 265 TRACK 357°,55n.mi.
FROM Hermosillo FREQ 112.8 TRACK 352°,183 n.mi.
FUEL All CARDS All Major CASH? Yes
REPAIRS Major TIEDOWN Yes

HOTEL	RATE	WHERE	TEL
Rontel	$$	Here	294-3471
Holiday Inn So.	$$	3 miles N	622-5871
La Quinta Inn	$$	N side	622-6491

FSS, Customs, and an airport hotel are handy. Now if they'd shoo away those 1011s, 747s, DC-10s, it would be perfect.

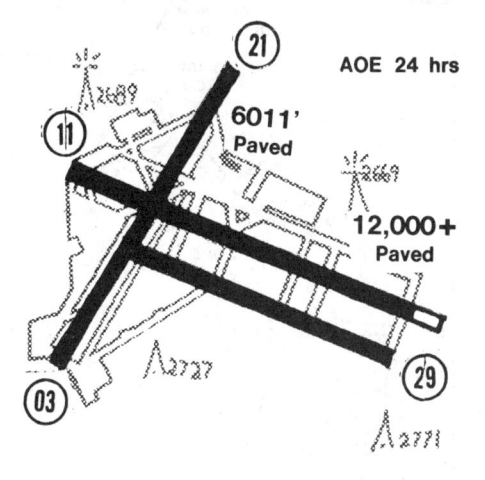

AOE 24 hrs
6011' Paved
12,000+ Paved

ELEVATION
2631'

VOR/DME RWY 17

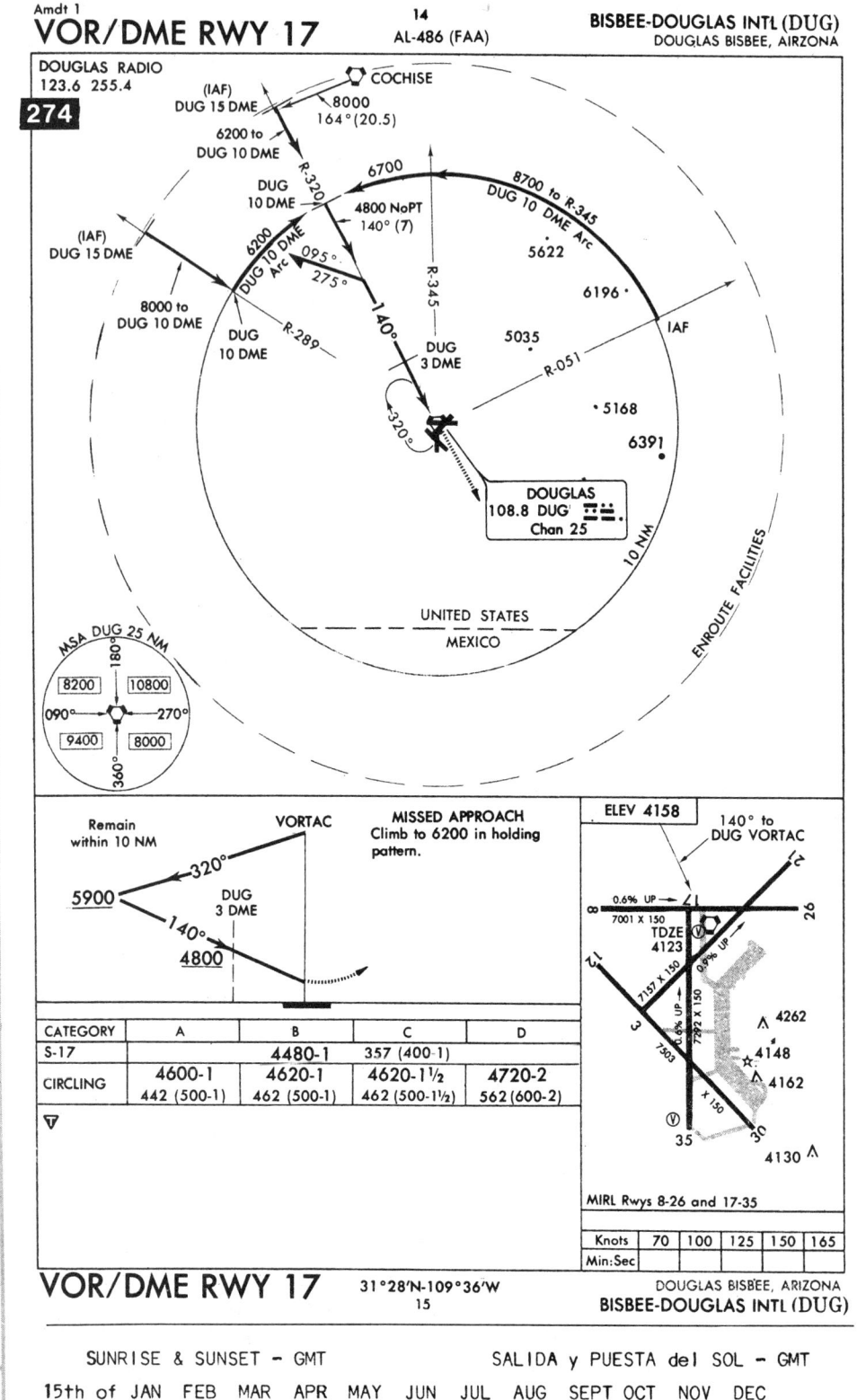

Amdt 1   14   AL-486 (FAA)   **BISBEE-DOUGLAS INTL (DUG)**
DOUGLAS BISBEE, AIRZONA

DOUGLAS RADIO 123.6 255.4

274

COCHISE   8000   164° (20.5)

(IAF) DUG 15 DME
6200 to DUG 10 DME
DUG 10 DME
R-320
6700
8700 to R-345
DUG 10 DME Arc
4800 NoPT 140° (7)
5622
6196
(IAF) DUG 15 DME
8000 to DUG 10 DME
6200
DUG 10 DME Arc
095°
275°
R-289
R-345
140°
R-051
IAF
DUG 10 DME
DUG 3 DME
5035
5168
6391
-320°
DOUGLAS 108.8 DUG Chan 25
10 NM
UNITED STATES / MEXICO
ENROUTE FACILITIES

MSA DUG 25 NM
180° | 8200 | 10800
090° | | 270°
| 9400 | 8000
360°

MISSED APPROACH
Climb to 6200 in holding pattern.

VORTAC
Remain within 10 NM
320°
5900
140°
DUG 3 DME
4800

ELEV 4158   140° to DUG VORTAC
0.6% UP
7001 X 150
TDZE 4123
7157 X 150
0.6% UP
7292 X 150
4262
4148
4162
7303
3
0.6% UP
V
35
4130
MIRL Rwys 8-26 and 17-35

CATEGORY	A	B	C	D
S-17		4480-1	357 (400-1)	
CIRCLING	4600-1 442 (500-1)	4620-1 462 (500-1)	4620-1½ 462 (500-1½)	4720-2 562 (600-2)

Knots	70	100	125	150	165
Min:Sec					

VOR/DME RWY 17   31°28'N-109°36'W   DOUGLAS BISBEE, ARIZONA
15   **BISBEE-DOUGLAS INTL (DUG)**

SUNRISE & SUNSET - GMT   SALIDA y PUESTA del SOL - GMT

15th of   JAN   FEB   MAR   APR   MAY   JUN   JUL   AUG   SEPT   OCT   NOV   DEC
SUNRISE   1418   1400   1328   1250   1222   1213   1224   1243   1302   1321   1346   1410   SALIDA
SUNSET   2437   0105   0126   0146   0207   0224   0224   0202   0124   2447   2419   2416   PUESTA
15 de   ENE   FEB   MAR   ABR   MAY   JUN   JUL   AGO   SEP   OCT   NOV   DIC
To get local time just subtract 'GMT ADD'
PARA OBTENER TIEMPO LOCAL SUSTRIAGA 'GMT ADD'

Bisbee-Douglas   Arizona

JET CHART	WAC	SECTIONAL	LATITUDE	LONGITUDE	US TIME	FOR GMT ADD	ICAO IDENT	TOWN IDENT
JN-46	CG-19 ADS-15	Phoenix	31°28'	109°37'	MST	7	-	DUG

275

OTHER COMM FSS 122.6
CITY 7 mi. SSE
POPULATION 24,000
LOCAL VorDme   FREQ 108.8   WHERE here   HOURS 24
B'CAST FREQ 1450   WHERE -   HOURS Daylight
FROM Hermosillo   FREQ 112.8   TRACK 015°, 160 n.mi.
FROM Nogales   FREQ 265*   TRACK 065°, 71 n.mi.,
FROM Chihuahua   FREQ 114.1   TRACK 299°, 249 n.mi.
FUEL 80, 100   CARDS -   CASH? Yes
REPAIRS Some   TIEDOWN BYO ropes

HOTEL	RATE	WHERE	TEL
Travelodge	$$	E side	364-8434

AOE 8-5 free

Not well publicized airport of entry, Douglas and Agua Prieta straddle the border in the grand tradition of El Paso/Juárez, Nogales/Nogales, and others. Handy off the beaten track place to clear on those busy holiday weekends when everyone with an airplane is waiting in long lines to clear Customs back into the U.S.

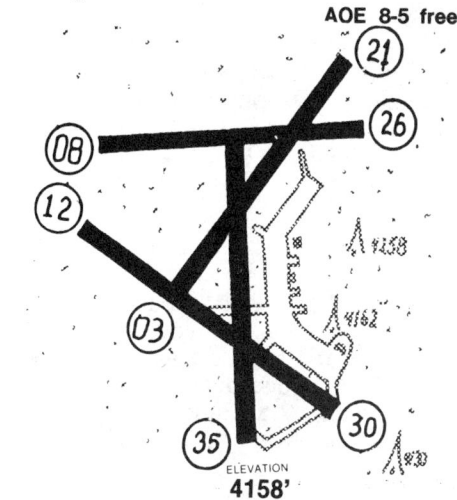

ELEVATION 4158'

276 Agua Prieta, Sonora

JET CHART	WAC	SECTIONAL	LATITUDE	LONGITUDE	US TIME	FOR GMT ADD	ICAO IDENT	TOWN IDENT
JN-46	CH-22 ADS-15	Phoenix	31°18'	109°38'	MST	7	–	APA

OTHER COMM

CITY POPULATION

B'CAST FREQ 1310 WHERE 5.6 mi E HOURS Daylight
FROM Nogales FREQ 108.2 TRACK 084° 61.9 Dme
FROM Douglas FREQ 108.8 TRACK 183° 9.3 Dme
FROM Hermosillo FREQ 112.8 TRACK 016° 151 n.mi.
FUEL CARDS – CASH? –
REPAIRS TIEDOWN
HOTEL RATE WHERE TEL

Remarks: Gateway to Eastern Arizona for carborne people. You and I need to go back and forth via airports of entry only. DUG is one but so far APA is not; many local people land at one side then cab to the other for shorter visits.

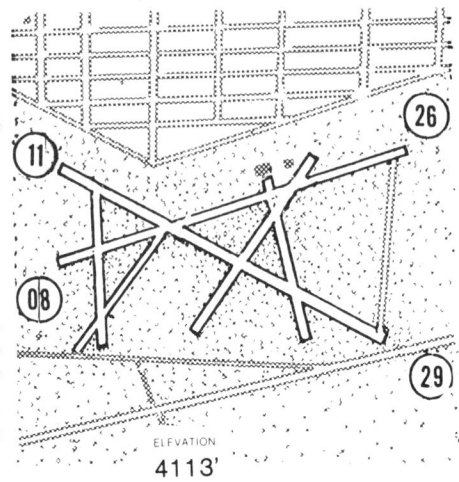

ELEVATION 4113'

Angostura, Sonora   *ang-oh-STOO-rah*   277

JET CHART	WAC	SECTIONAL	LATITUDE	LONGITUDE	US TIME	FOR GMT ADD	ICAO IDENT	TOWN IDENT
JN-46	CH-22 No. ADS-15	TPC H-22B	30°35'	109°22'	MST	7	-	ARA

OTHER COMM Traffic 122.8-
SETTLEMENT SE side   **POPULATION** 0 to 150
FROM Nogales   **FREQ** 108.2   **TRACK** 113°, 91Dme
FROM Hermosillo   **FREQ** 112.8   **TRACK** 034°, 125 n.mi.
FROM Bisbee   **FREQ** 108.8   **TRACK** 158°, 54Dme
FUEL -   **CARDS** -   **CASH?** -
REPAIRS -   **TIEDOWN** BYO

    Isolated fishing club camp: good bass fishing along this river and so close to the US. Friday afternoon arrivers can fish early Saturday and be home in time for the Eastern ballgames.

READER REPORT Things have quieted down a lot since the government let the water level way down a few times and the fish didn't learn to walk. J.Fowler, New Mexico

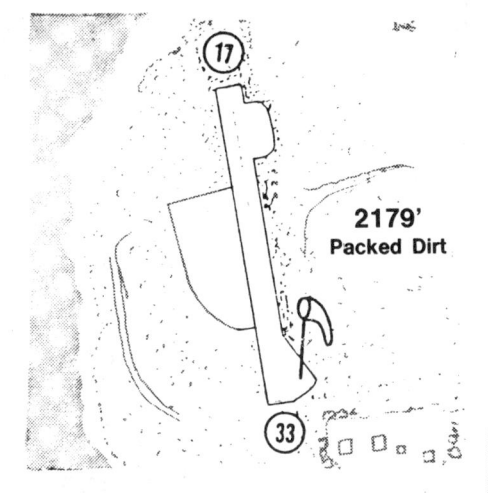

2179'
Packed Dirt

ELEVATION
2499'

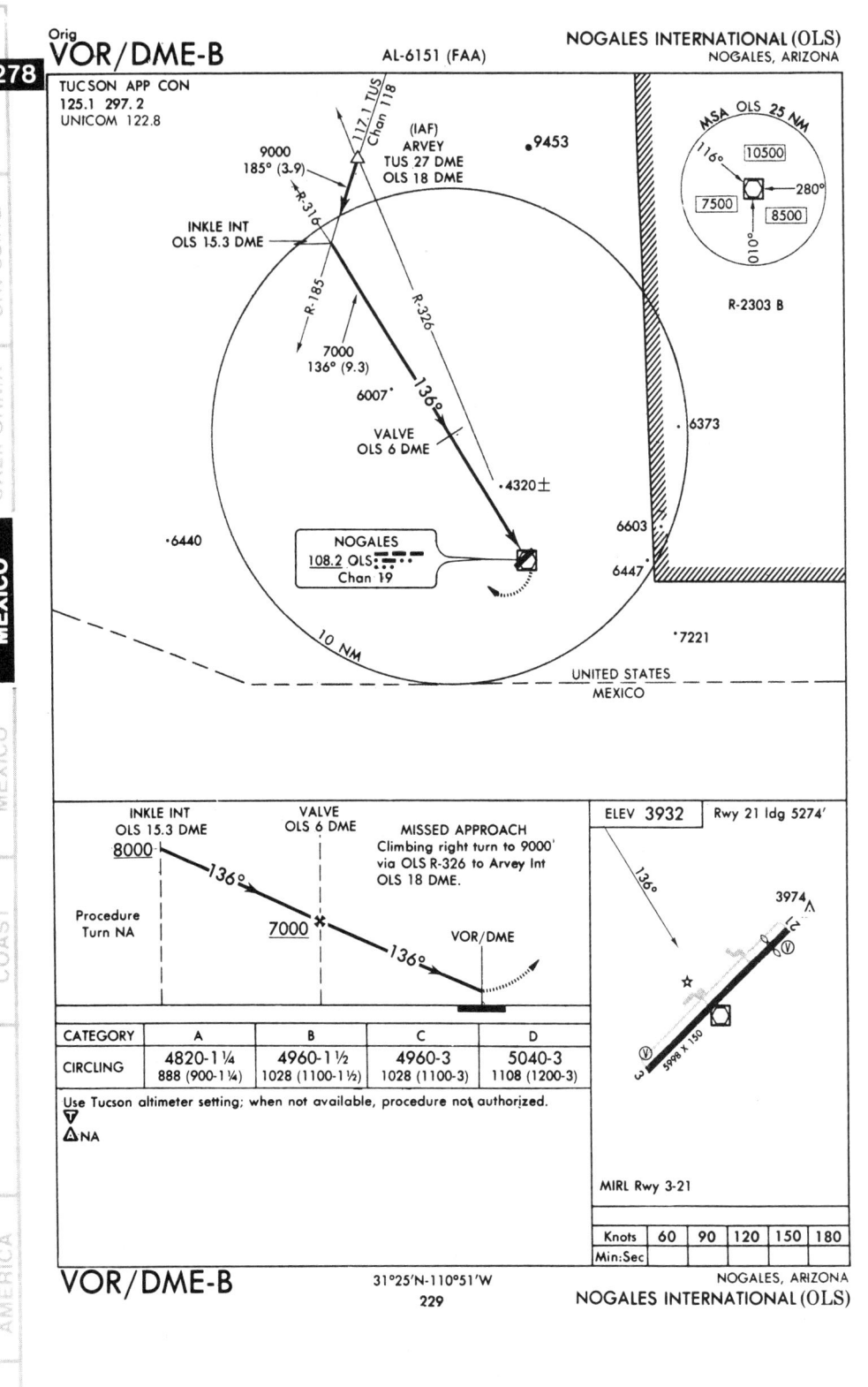

VOR/DME-B — NOGALES INTERNATIONAL (OLS)
NOGALES, ARIZONA

AL-6151 (FAA)

TUCSON APP CON 125.1 297.2
UNICOM 122.8

ARVEY (IAF) TUS 27 DME / OLS 18 DME — 117.1 TUS Chan 118

9000 185° (3.9)

INKLE INT OLS 15.3 DME

R-316 R-185 R-326

7000 136° (9.3)

6007
•9453
•4320±
•6440
•6373
•6603
•6447
•7221

VALVE OLS 6 DME — 136°

NOGALES 108.2 OLS Chan 19

R-2303 B

10 NM

UNITED STATES / MEXICO

MSA OLS 25 NM: 10500 (116°), 8500 (280°), 7500, 010°

INKLE INT OLS 15.3 DME — 8000
VALVE OLS 6 DME — 7000
136° / 136°
VOR/DME

Procedure Turn NA

MISSED APPROACH: Climbing right turn to 9000' via OLS R-326 to Arvey Int OLS 18 DME.

ELEV 3932   Rwy 21 ldg 5274'
3974
5998 X 150
MIRL Rwy 3-21

CATEGORY	A	B	C	D
CIRCLING	4820-1¼ 888 (900-1¼)	4960-1½ 1028 (1100-1½)	4960-3 1028 (1100-3)	5040-3 1108 (1200-3)

Use Tucson altimeter setting; when not available, procedure not authorized.
▽
△ NA

Knots	60	90	120	150	180
Min:Sec					

VOR/DME-B   31°25'N-110°51'W   NOGALES INTERNATIONAL (OLS) — NOGALES, ARIZONA

Nogales Arizona

noe-GALL-ess **279**

JET CHART	WAC	SECTIONAL	LATITUDE	LONGITUDE	US TIME	FOR GMT ADD	ICAO IDENT	TOWN IDENT
JN-46	CH-22 No. ADS-15	Phoenix	31°25'	110°51'	MST	7	-	OLS

OTHER COMM Unicom 122.8
CITY 6 miles SW   POPULATION 17,000
LOCAL VorDme   FREQ 108.2   WHERE Here   HOURS 24
FROM Tucson   FREQ 117.1   TRACK 172°, 42Dme
FROM Phoenix   FREQ 115.6   TRACK 142°, 136 n.mi.
FROM Hermosillo FREQ 112.8 TRACK 353°, 140 n.mi.
FUEL 80, 100   CARDS Major   CASH? Yes
REPAIRS Yes   TIEDOWN BYO

Not a busy Airport of Entry, my limited experience has shown long waits for Customs to arrive followed by an almost grilling question session. Tucson seems better.

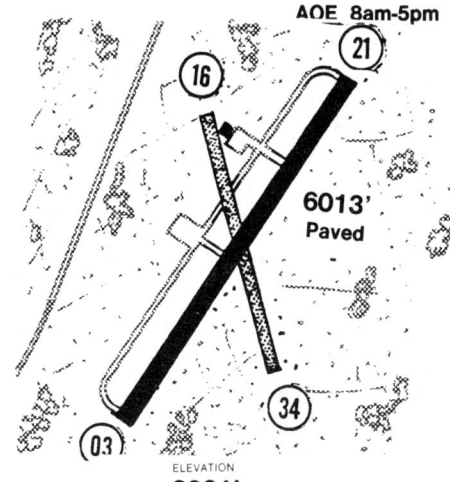

AOE 8am-5pm
21
16
6013' Paved
34
03
ELEVATION
3931'

280 Nogales Internacional, Sonora — *no-GOLL-ess*

JET CHART	WAC	SECTIONAL	LATITUDE	LONGITUDE	US TIME	FOR GMT ADD	ICAO IDENT	TOWN IDENT
JN-46	CH-22 No. ADS-15	TPC H-22B	31°14'	110°59'	MST	7	MMNG	NOG

APPROACH — TOWER 118.1   GROUND 118.1
CITY 5 miles N.   POPULATION 57,000
LOCAL Ndb FREQ 265   WHERE Here   HOURS Prior request
B'CAST FREQ 1270   WHERE 6 mi NW   HOURS Daylight
FROM Tucson   FREQ 117.1   TRACK 177°, 55Dme
FROM Hermosillo   FREQ 112.8   TRACK 349°, 128 n.mi.
FROM Nogales, Ariz.   FREQ 108.2   TRACK 195°, 13Dme
FUEL 80, 100   CARDS Visa, MC   CASH? Yes
REPAIRS Minor   TIEDOWN BYO

AOE 9am-4pm

16 / 34   5911' Paved

ELEVATION 4091'

Little-used internacional airport, nowadays pilots mostly checkout at Hermosillo because it is so quick. But anyone coming from north of there finds it easiest and shorter to pass through here. Be extra very doggoned sure on departure Northbound NOT to cross into US airspace until FSS tells you they have notified Customs. $500 US Customs fines are the reason.

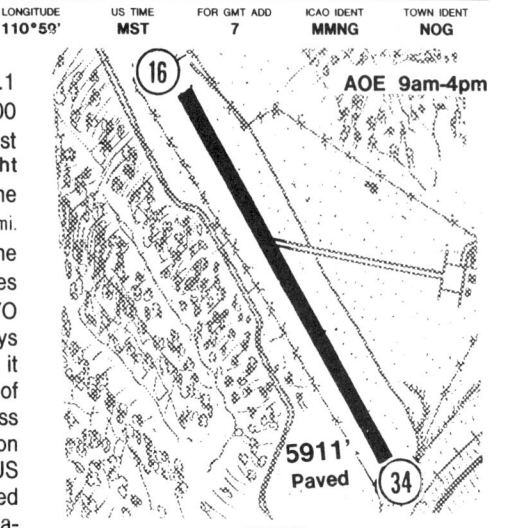

Cananea, Sonora   *cah-nah-NAY-ah*   281

JET CHART	WAC	SECTIONAL	LATITUDE	LONGITUDE	US TIME	FOR GMT ADD	ICAO IDENT	TOWN IDENT
JN-46	CH-22 No. ADS-15	TPC H-22B	31°00'	110°16'	MST	7	-	CNA

OTHER COMM Traffic 118.1-
CITY 2 miles SW
POPULATION 29,000
B'CAST FREQ 980   WHERE 2.5 mi SW   HOURS Daylight
FROM Nogales   FREQ 108.2   TRACK 119°, 38Dme
FROM Hermosillo   FREQ 112.8   TRACK 010°, 122 n.mi.
FROM Bisbee-Douglas FREQ 108.8 TRACK 223°, 44Dme
FUEL 100 Sometimes   CARDS -   CASH? Pesos
REPAIRS -   TIEDOWN BYO

HOTEL	RATE	WHERE	TEL
Motel Safari	$	1 mile SW	2-13-08

Runways: 20/02, 17/35, 09/27 — 4815' Gravel, 4319' Gravel, 4912' Gravel

ELEVATION 5191'

Copper mining country, evidently part of the same geologic structure the Arizona cities nearby are working. If you've never landed on gravel the drumming sound could be startling. Sounds like a very loud steady hum on initial touchdown, diminishing as your speed does on rollout.

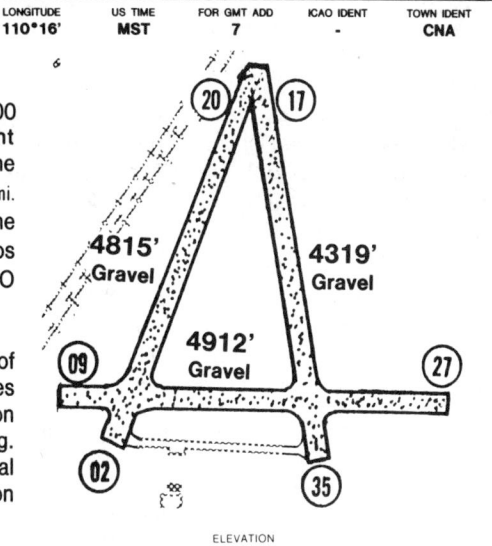

282   in Sonora: **Magdalena**

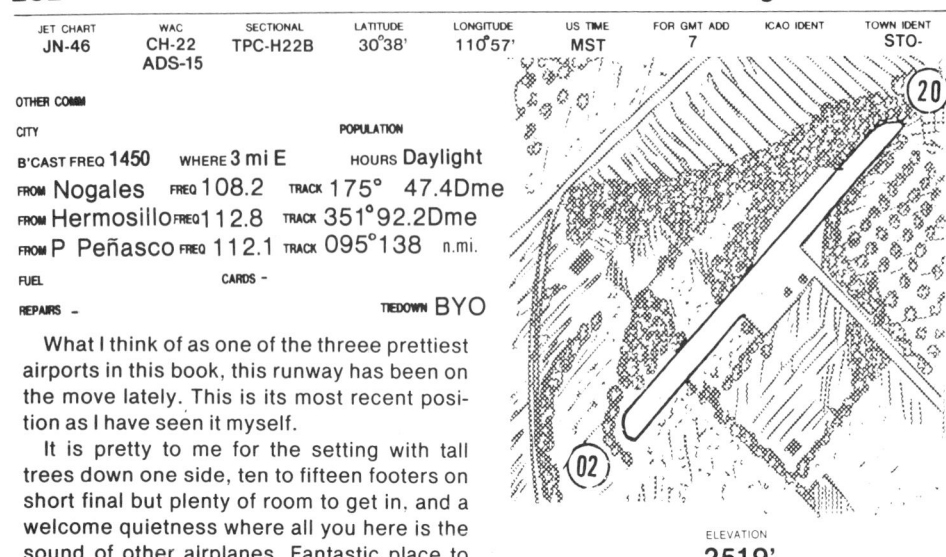

JET CHART	WAC	SECTIONAL	LATITUDE	LONGITUDE	US TIME	FOR GMT ADD	ICAO IDENT	TOWN IDENT
JN-46	CH-22 ADS-15	TPC-H22B	30°38'	110°57'	MST	7		STO-

OTHER COMM

CITY   POPULATION

B'CAST FREQ **1450**   WHERE **3 mi E**   HOURS **Daylight**
FROM **Nogales**   FREQ **108.2**   TRACK **175°**   **47.4Dme**
FROM **Hermosillo** FREQ **112.8**   TRACK **351°92.2Dme**
FROM **P Peñasco** FREQ **112.1**   TRACK **095°138**   n.mi.

FUEL   CARDS -

REPAIRS -   TIEDOWN **BYO**

What I think of as one of the threee prettiest airports in this book, this runway has been on the move lately. This is its most recent position as I have seen it myself.

It is pretty to me for the setting with tall trees down one side, ten to fifteen footers on short final but plenty of room to get in, and a welcome quietness where all you here is the sound of other airplanes. Fantastic place to eat lunch and just soak up contentment.

ELEVATION
2519'

benn-hah-MEEN heel   in Sonora: **Benjamin Hill**   283

JET CHART	WAC	LATITUDE	LONGITUDE	US TIME	FOR GMT ADD	ICAO IDENT	TOWN IDENT
JN-46	CH-22 * ADS-15	30°11'	111°08'	MST/MDT	7/6	-	BHL-

SETTLEMENT 1/4 mi. South POPULATION est 12,000
FROM Nogales FREQ 108.2 TRACK 179°, 75.4Dme
FROM Caborca FREQ Adf 970 TRACK 110°, 57n.mi.
FROM Hermosillo FREQ 112.8 TRACK 344°, 65.1Dme
AVIATION GAS-   CREDIT CARDS-   CASH TYPE-

Known mostly as the joining point for railroads from Mexicali and from Nogales, this has been a prominent point since the 1910-1920 revolution. It was a general of that war who gave the town its name.

Of most use to us for the stores, long distance phones, and pensiones or boarding house-style acommodations. Runway is used more for horse racing than for aeronautical purposes, hence the rugged starting gates.

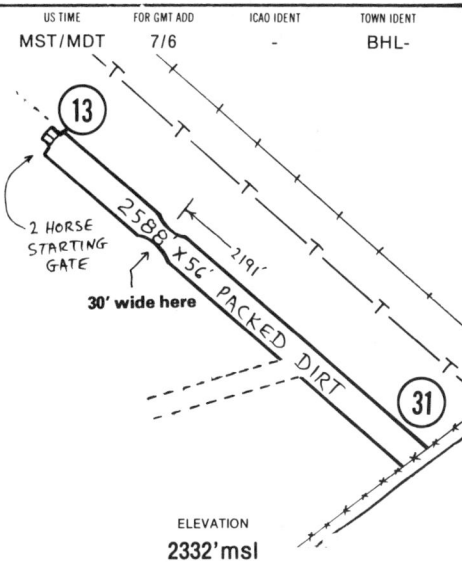

(runway diagram: 13 / 31, 2588' x 50' PACKED DIRT, 2191', 2 HORSE STARTING GATE, 30' wide here)

ELEVATION
2332' msl

HERMOSILLO, SON.
VOR/DME PISTA 05

284 — ENERO 30 DE 1980/147

RADIO			ELEV 630'
123.0 y 127.3	TWR	118.7	VAR MAG 12° E
	APP	121.4	HMO ·· ·· —
	ATIS	118.1	
	EMERG	121.5	

Caution — For Information Only — Not for Aerial Navigation

DME HMO 112.8

Holding: 241° / 043° at 4000', 260°, 0.8 / 0.8

Obstacles: 2289', 1640', 1312', 2017'

Circle: 5000' (NE), 3000' (SW)

Profile: 10 M.N. IZQ, D-8, 2000', 241°/4000', 043°, VOR/DME, 1340' (710'), ELEV 630'

FALLIDA: VIRE A LA **DERECHA** E INTERCEPTE EN ASCENSO EL **RADIAL 241°**, Y PROSIGA EN TRAYECTORIA DE APROXIMACION HASTA LA ALTITUD MINIMA DE ESPERA DE ACUERDO CON INSTRUCCIONES DEL **A.T.C.**

CATEGORIA	DIRECTO PISTA 05 MDA 1340' (710')	CATEGORIA	CIRCULANDO MDA
A	1	A	1340' (710') – 1
B	1	B	1340' (710') – 1
C	2	C	1340' (710') – 2
D	2 ½	D	1640' (1010') – 3

CAMBIOS: ELEV DEL AEROPUERTO y MINIMOS PARA CIRCULAR

SCT – DGAC – SENEAM   HMO-VD-2

SUNRISE & SUNSET – GMT   **SALIDA y PUESTA del SOL – GMT**

15th of	JAN	FEB	MAR	APR	MAY	JUN	JUL	AUG	SEPT	OCT	NOV	DEC	
SUNRISE	1419	1403	1333	1258	1232	1224	1235	1252	1309	1325	1347	1410	SALIDA
SUNSET	2448	0113	0132	0150	0208	0224	0224	0204	0129	2454	2429	2428	PUESTA
15° de	ENE	FEB	MAR	ABR	MAY	JUN	JUL	AGO	SEP	OCT	NOV	DIC	

To get local time just subtract 'GMT ADD'
PARA OBTENER TIEMPO LOCAL SUSTRIAGA 'GMT ADD'

Hermosillo Internacional, Sonora

air-moe-SEE-yo **285**

JET CHART	WAC	SECTIONAL	LATITUDE	LONGITUDE	US TIME	FOR GMT ADD	ICAO IDENT	TOWN IDENT
JN-46	CH-22 ADS-15	TPC H-22B	29°06'	111°03	MST	7	MMHO	HMO

- TCA TO: 20,000'   RADIUS 50 n.mi.   HOURS 1300-0300Z
- APPROACH 121.4   TOWER 118.7   GROUND 118.7
- CITY 8 miles E   POPULATION 325,000
- LOCAL VorDme   FREQ 112.8   WHERE here   HOURS 24
- B'CAST FREQ 920   WHERE 7 mi E   HOURS Daylight
- FROM Tucson   FREQ 117.1   TRACK 173°, 182 n.mi.
- FROM Punta Peñasco FREQ 112.1 TRACK 123°, 187 n.mi.
- FROM Cd. Obregón   FREQ 115.1 TRACK 316°, 121 n.mi.
- FUEL 80,100,JP   CARDS Visa,MC,etc   CASH? Yes
- REPAIRS Yes   TIEDOWN BYO

AOE 8am to 5pm

HOTEL	RATE	WHERE	TEL
San Alberto	$	Central	2-18-00
Internacional	$$	Central	3-89-66
Motel Valle Grande	$$	2 mi NE	4-45-75

3608' Paved
7541' Paved
ELEVATION 615'

Busy internacional airport where general aviation traffic funnels in from Denver, Phoenix, LA, Las Vegas, etc. Personnel loading seems to vary by expected workload. Result is that it is consistently the fastest, easiest place to clear into or out of México.

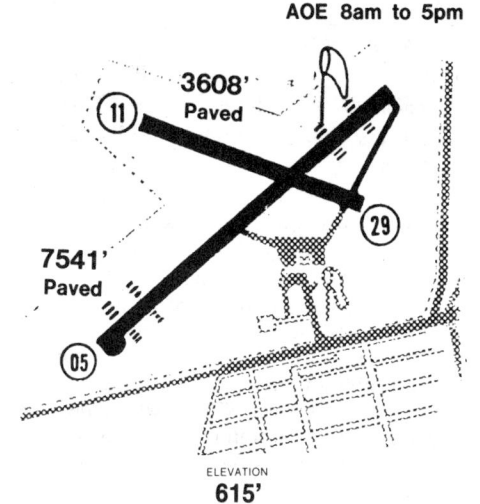

286 Hermosillo South, Sonora

air-moe-SEE-yoh

JN CHART	WAC	SECTIONAL	LATITUDE	LONGITUDE	US TIME	FOR GMT	ICAO	TOWN ID
JN-46	CH-22 ADS-15	TPC H22B	29°01'	110°55'	MST	+7	-	HMO

CITY IS 4 mi East POPULATION 400,000
COMM Monitor Tower 118.1
B'cast 920   WHERE 5 mi NW WHOURS Daylight
LOCAL VorDme   FREQ 112.8   WHERE 8.6 mi West
FROM Guaymas FREQ Adf 368 TRACK 012°, 64 n.mi.
FROM Nogales FREQ 108.2   TRACK 167°, 132 n.mi.
REPAIRS -   TIEDOWNS BYO

A depository for seized airplanes. usually involving dope problems. A practice attributed to Attorny General John Mitchell and leftover from the Nixon years seems to be that the US State Department will process no requests from US citizens seeking return of aircraft stolen from them and being held by foreign governments. Often, when the time has elapsed the aircraft location in its orignal color and painted-on registration number is no longer known.

Very Permanent Parking

UPHILL 13'

PWAIR-toe LOW-boce in Sonora: **Puerto Lobos New** 287

JET CHART	WAC	LATITUDE	LONGITUDE	US TIME	FOR GMT ADD	ICAO IDENT	TOWN IDENT
JN-46	CH-22 North ADS-15	28°15'	111°23'	MST	+7	-	LOE-

OTHER COMM Traffic 124.4

SETTLEMENT Town 0.5 mi SW

POPULATION est 300

REPAIRS? -   TIEDOWNS? BYO

**3243'x116'
Graded, Packed Dirt
Uphill 20' East**

An attractive new runway for those who'd like to stop here on the Sonoran West Coast for some fishing or swimming. So many miles of beach that one could swim swimsuit optionally with little evesdropping. I sure won't squeal.

Many boats in the settlement, a pilot eager to fish could make a deal and be out here on the Sea of Cortes fishing quote early unquote the next morning. Do keep in mind that early to you could be very extremely quite much too early to someone accustomed to a more leisurely pace.

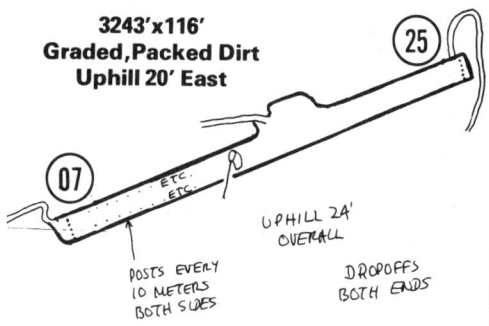

POSTS EVERY 10 METERS BOTH SIDES

UPHILL 24' OVERALL

DROPOFFS BOTH ENDS

ELEVATION
114' to 134' msl

288 Puerto Libertad New, Sonora

PWAIR-toe lee-bare-TODD

JET CHART	WAC	SECTIONAL	LATITUDE	LONGITUDE	US TIME	FOR GMT ADD	ICAO IDENT	TOWN IDENT
JN-46	CH-22 No. ADS-15	TPC H-22B	29°55'	112°40'	MST	7	-	-LBT-

OTHER COMM Traffic 118.1

TOWN 1 mi WSW POPULATION est 500

AVIATION FUEL Not yet   CARDS -   CASH TYPE --------

REPAIRS? -   TIEDOWNS? BYO

FROM Pta Penasco   FREQ 112.1   TRACK 140°, 98.9 Dme
FROM Caborca   FREQ 970   TRACK 198°, 57.6 n.mi.
FROM Hermosillo   FREQ 112.8   TRACK 300°, 71.6 Dme

A port city under construction here on the Sonoran NW coast. Hard to tell at this time what purpose; there are two skeletal steel towers and lots of tennis courts and sports fields in the building area. Check the PREPS for later information.

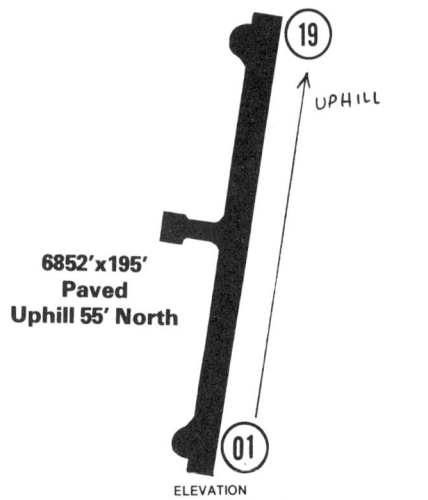

**6852' x 195'
Paved
Uphill 55' North**

Runway 19 / 01 — UPHILL

ELEVATION
212' to 267' msl

el Desemboque, Sonora — *ell dess-emm-BOKE-ay* — 289

JET CHART	WAC	SECTIONAL	LATITUDE	LONGITUDE	US TIME	FOR GMT ADD	ICAO IDENT	TOWN IDENT
JN-46	CH-22 No. ADS-15	TPC H-22B	29°31'	112°24'	MST	7	-	-DES-

OTHER COMM Traffic 122.85
SETTLEMENT 1 mile SE   POPULATION 350
FROM Punta Peñasco FREQ 112.1 TRACK 138°, 128 n.mi.
FROM Hermosillo FREQ 112.8 TRACK 277°, 75Dme
FROM Nogales FREQ 108.2 TRACK 196°, 141 n.mi.
FUEL -   CARDS -   CASH? -
REPAIRS -   TIEDOWN BYO

Home and headquarters for the Seri indians who once terrorized this part of the state of Sonora; they even kept the Spaniards at bay for a couple hundred years. Rumored to have practiced cannibalism, they have now settled down to making beautiful iron carvings. With those carvings selling in the two to five hundred dollar range there are some who would say the Seris haven't changed much.

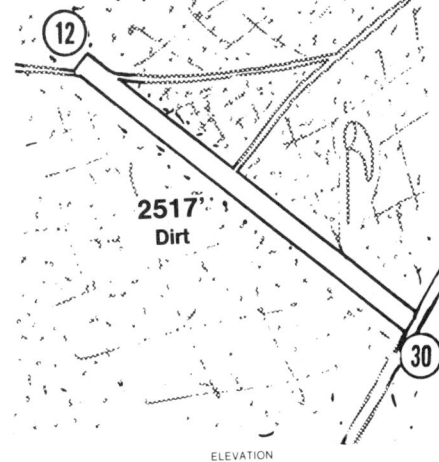

2517' Dirt

ELEVATION **65'**

290 Tecomate, Sonora   *tekk-oh-MOTT-ay*

JET CHART	WAC	SECTIONAL	LATITUDE	LONGITUDE	US TIME	FOR GMT ADD	ICAO IDENT	TOWN IDENT
JN-46	CH-22 No. ADS-15	TPC H-22B	29°11'	112°24'	MST	7	-	ECO-

OTHER COMM Traffic 122.85
SETTLEMENT 1 house 1/8 mile NW POPULATION 0 to 2
FROM Punta Peñasco FREQ 112.1 TRACK 144°, 143 n.mi.
FROM Hermosillo FREQ 112.8 TRACK 264°, 72Dme
FROM Nogales FREQ 108.2 TRACK 199°, 156 n.mi.
FUEL -   CARDS -   CASH? -
REPAIRS -   TIEDOWN BYO

Doubly isolated fishing warden camp, bring cigarettes or cigars or fresh bread or anything. The lonely guys stationed here are delighted with whatever and will make you marvelously welcome.

Legally the island is off limits except by writing México City for prior permission which is routinely refused. Shhhhh!

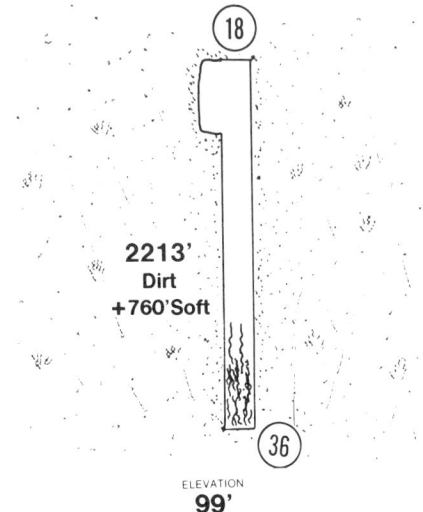

2213'
Dirt
+760' Soft

ELEVATION
99'

Punta Tormento, Sonora

POON-tah tore-meNN-toe **291**

JET CHART	WAC	SECTIONAL	LATITUDE	LONGITUDE	US TIME	FOR GMT ADD	ICAO IDENT	TOWN IDENT
JN-46	CH-22 No. ADS-15	TPC H-22B	29°01'	112°11'	MST	7	-	-MTO-

OTHER COMM Traffic 122.85
SETTLEMENT None   POPULATION Variable to 0
FROM Punta Peñasco FREQ 112.1 TRACK 142°, 159 n.mi.
FROM Hermosillo FREQ 112.8 TRACK 255°, 61 Dme
FUEL -   CARDS -   CASH? -
REPAIRS -   TIEDOWN BYO

See Tecomate

On the treacherous Infiernillo (Hell) Channel between Tiburón and the Sonora coast, this entire island is restricted against unauthorized visits.

Reason: the island is a game preserve. Worse yet, crews hired to build game wardens' homes killed off the island's game. But look for good news before long.

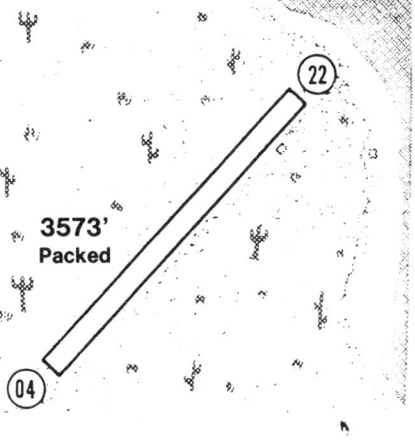

3573'
Packed

ELEVATION
11 to 39'

ADS-15

292 Bahía Kino, Sonora *bah-EE-yah KEE-noe*

JET CHART	WAC	SECTIONAL	LATITUDE	LONGITUDE	US TIME	FOR GMT ADD	ICAO IDENT	TOWN IDENT
JN-46	CH-22 No.	TPC H-22B	28°53'	111°58'	MST	-	-	KIO-

OTHER COMM Traffic 122.8-
CITY 1.5 miles W   POPULATION 4,000
FROM Punta Peñasco FREQ 112.1 TRACK 139°, 174 n.mi.
FROM Hermosillo FREQ 112.8 TRACK 244°, 51Dme
FROM Nogales   FREQ 108.2 TRACK 187°, 163 n.mi.
FUEL 100 Sometimes   CARDS -   CASH? Yes
REPAIRS -   TIEDOWN BYO

HOTEL	RATE	WHERE	TEL
Posada del Mar	$$	3 miles SE	122.8
Condos Jacqueline	$$	5 miles SSE	714-728-1144

Long sweeps of white sand beaches, nice weekend cabins, a good hotel or kitchen-equipped condos give you a wide choice of how to stay and enjoy this Sonoran area.

READER REPORT Enjoyed Condominiums Jacqueline on the beach within walking distance of a store and not that far from the hotel and its dining room.—P Gibson, Kansas

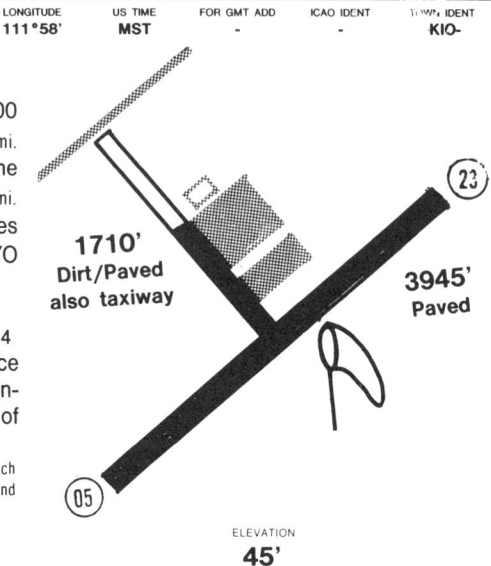

1710'
Dirt/Paved
also taxiway

3945'
Paved

ELEVATION
45'

Bahia Vermillon, Sonora bah-EE-yah bare-MEE-yoan 292 A

OTHER COMM Traffic 124.4

SETTLEMENT 1 empty house Adjacent South POPULATION 0 to 1
FROM **Hermosillo** FREQ 112.8 TRACK 188%, 54Dme
FROM **Guaymas** FREQ ADF368 TRACK 292%, 30n.mi.
FROM **Santa Rosalia** FREQ 112.6 TRACK 017%, 76Dme
AVIATION FUEL - CARDS - CASH TYPE -
REPAIRS? None TIEDOWNS? BYO

The second night we camped here sunset bathed the bay, and the hills in a bright orange which was unforgettable. Red Mountain, half a mile north, was all but incandescent. Altho we couldn't find anyone to ask what the place is called, nor did the marine charts help, we found it easy to come up with an appropriate name for this tiny, unforgettable bay.

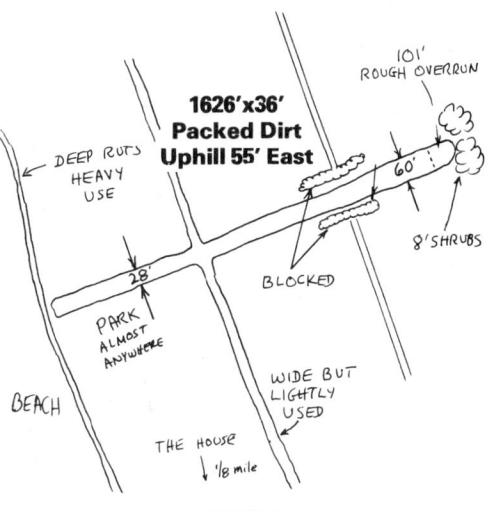

**1626'x36'
Packed Dirt
Uphill 55' East**

ELEVATION
14' to 69' msl

292B Bahia Escondida, Sonora

bah-EE-yah ess-cone-DEE-dah

JET CHART	WAC	LATITUDE	LONGITUDE	US TIME	FOR GMT ADD	ICAO IDENT	TOWN IDENT
JN-46	CH-22 No. ADS-15	28°13'	111°21'	MST	+7	-	DID-

OTHER COMM Traffic 124.4

SETTLEMENT Isolated   POPULATION 0 to 0

FROM Hermosillo   FREQ 112.8   TRACK 186%, 55Dme
FROM Guaymas   FREQ ADF368   TRACK 291%, 28n.mi
FROM Guaymas   FREQ ADF368   TRACK 291%, 28n.mi.
FROM Sta Rosalia   FREQ 112.6   TRACK 019%, 75Dme

AVIATION FUEL -   CARDS -   CASH TYPE ---------
REPAIRS? None   TIEDOWNS? BYO

Presently X'ed to prevent anyone from enjoying a very pretty little bay on a piece of coastline which has lots of interesting geography. To this writer that bay just begs to be explored out of an airplane. Keep your eye on the mail; soon as I can land and measure you will read about it in the PREPS.

Catch 22, Sonora

293

JET CHART	WAC	SECTIONAL	LATITUDE	LONGITUDE	US TIME	FOR GMT ADD	ICAO IDENT	TOWN IDENT
JN-46	CH-22 No. ADS-15	TPC H-22C	27°59'	111°05'	MST	7	-	-C22-

OTHER COMM Traffic area 122.85
SETTLEMENT Settled both sides   POPULATION Hundreds
FROM Guaymas   FREQ 368   TRACK 269°,9n.mi.
FROM Hermosillo   FREQ 112.8   TRACK 173°,67Dme

THIS IS NOT AN AIRPORT. Built for the movie only. The landowners have not registered this as an airport and are inhospitable to aircraft landing here. There is no such thing as 'prior permission' or knowing someone. THIS IS NOT AN AIRPORT.

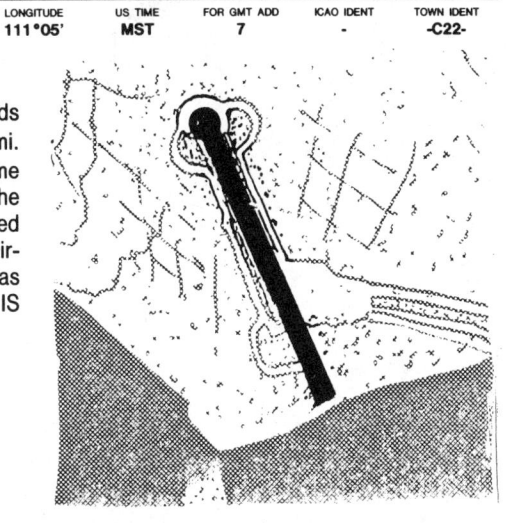

ELEVATION

GUAYMAS, SON.

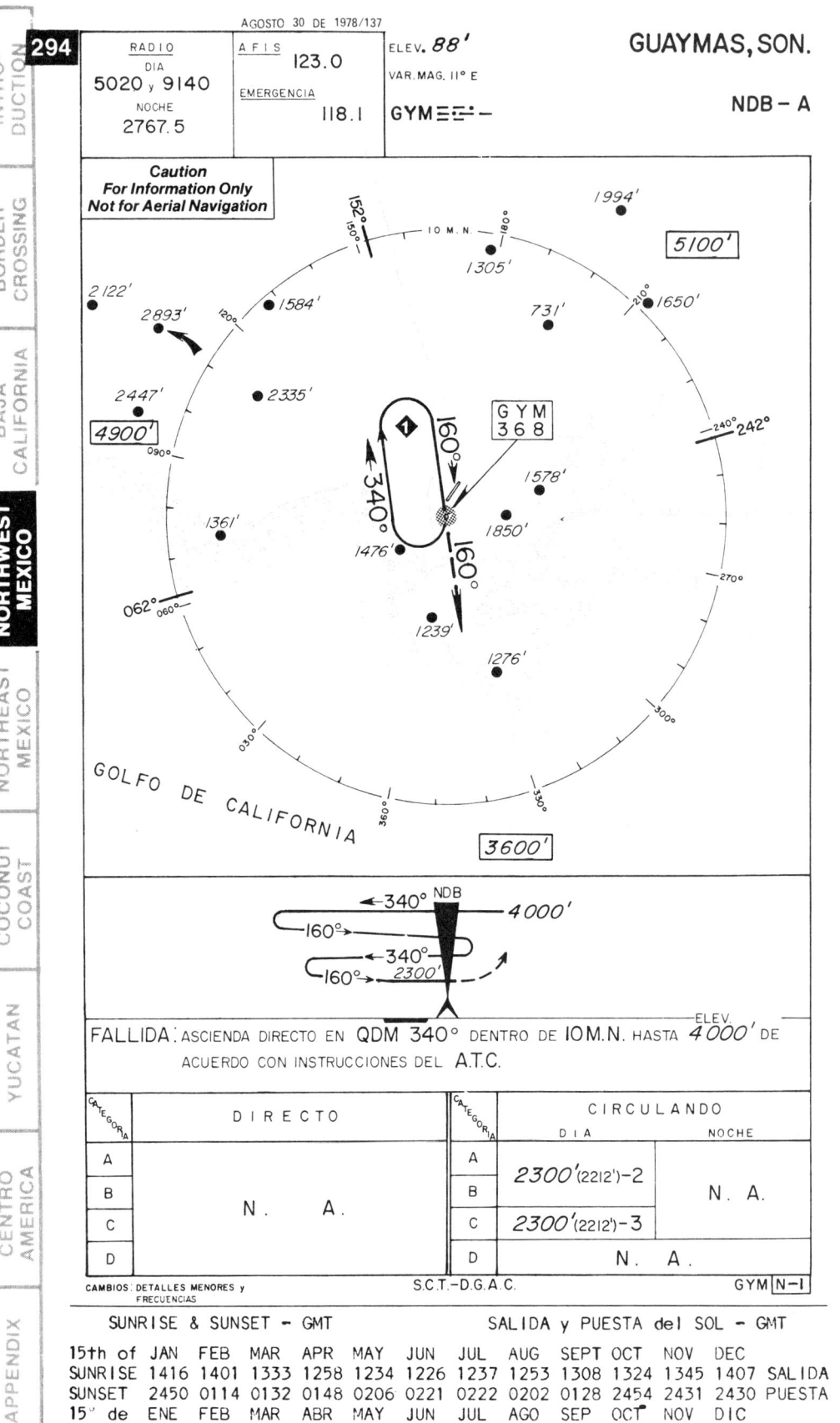

NDB - A

294 — AGOSTO 30 DE 1978/137

RADIO	AFIS 123.0	ELEV. 88'
DIA 5020 y 9140	EMERGENCIA 118.1	VAR. MAG. 11° E
NOCHE 2767.5		GYM ▬▬

Caution
For Information Only
Not for Aerial Navigation

Obstacles/spot elevations on plan view:
- 1994'
- 1305'
- 731'
- 1650' (210°)
- 5100'
- 2122'
- 2893'
- 1584'
- 2447'
- 2335'
- 4900'
- 1361'
- 1578'
- 1476'
- 1850'
- 1239'
- 1276'
- 242° (240°)
- 3600'

GYM 368

Holding pattern: 340° / 160°

Radials shown: 152°/150°, 180°, 210°, 240°/242°, 270°, 300°, 330°, 360°, 030°, 062°/060°, 090°, 120°

GOLFO DE CALIFORNIA

Profile view:
- 340° NDB — 4000'
- 160°
- 340°
- 160° — 2300'

FALLIDA: ASCIENDA DIRECTO EN QDM 340° DENTRO DE 10 M.N. HASTA 4000' DE ACUERDO CON INSTRUCCIONES DEL A.T.C.

CATEGORIA	DIRECTO	CATEGORIA	CIRCULANDO DIA	NOCHE
A		A	2300'(2212')-2	N. A.
B	N. A.	B		
C		C	2300'(2212')-3	
D		D	N. A.	

CAMBIOS: DETALLES MENORES y FRECUENCIAS

S.C.T.-D.G.A.C.

GYM N-1

SUNRISE & SUNSET - GMT   SALIDA y PUESTA del SOL - GMT

15th of	JAN	FEB	MAR	APR	MAY	JUN	JUL	AUG	SEPT	OCT	NOV	DEC	
SUNRISE	1416	1401	1333	1258	1234	1226	1237	1253	1308	1324	1345	1407	SALIDA
SUNSET	2450	0114	0132	0148	0206	0221	0222	0202	0128	2454	2431	2430	PUESTA
15 de	ENE	FEB	MAR	ABR	MAY	JUN	JUL	AGO	SEP	OCT	NOV	DIC	

Guaymas Internacional, Sonora

WYE-muss **295**

JET CHART	WAC	SECTIONAL	LATITUDE	LONGITUDE	US TIME	FOR GMT ADD	ICAO IDENT	TOWN IDENT
JN-46	CH-22 No. ADS-15	TPC H-22C	27°57'	110°56'	MST	7	MMGM	GWY

APPROACH - TOWER 118.6 GROUND 118.6
CITY 3 miles SE POPULATION 135,000
LOCAL Ndb FREQ 368 WHERE here HOURS usually on
B'CAST FREQ 1240 WHERE 4 mi SE HOURS Daylight
FROM Hermosillo FREQ 112.8 TRACK 165°, 69Dme
FROM Cd. Obregón FREQ 115.1 TRACK 288°, 67Dme
FROM Santa Rosalia FREQ 112.6 TRACK 048°, 83n.mi.
FUEL 80, 100, JP CARDS Visa, MC, etc. CASH? Yes
REPAIRS Minor TIEDOWN BYO

HOTEL	RATE	WHERE	TEL
Triana	$$	S. Carlos	LD#2
Playa Cortés	-	Old City	2-01-22
Leo's Inn	-$$	Near Town	-

Seaport known as the shrimp capital of México for all the boats bring in from other places. Undeniably the port is busy, the city seasoned, there is plenty to keep you occupied a few days.

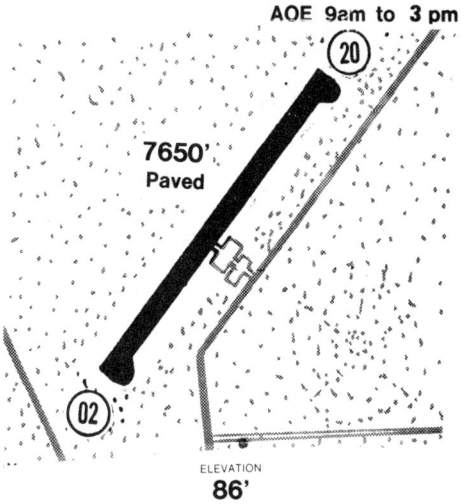

AOE 9am to 3 pm
7650' Paved
ELEVATION 86'

296 Presa Obregón, Sonora   *PRESS-ah obe-ray-GOAN*

JET CHART	WAC	SECTIONAL	LATITUDE	LONGITUDE	US TIME	FOR GMT ADD	ICAO IDENT	TOWN IDENT
JN-46	CH-22 No. ADS-15	TPC H-22A	27°48'	109°54'	MST	7	-	-OBR-

OTHER COMM Traffic 122.85
SETTLEMENT Scattered   POPULATION 250
FROM Hermosillo   FREQ 112.8   TRACK 132°, 99Dme
FROM Cd. Obregón FREQ 115.1   TRACK 341°, 25Dme
FUEL -   CARDS -   CASH? -
REPAIRS -   TIEDOWN BYO

Lots of trash on the runway.

Built by the Hydraulic Resources department when they built the dam, this runway is fading away. Appears to have more beer cans that anything else. Don't look for it in next year's edition.

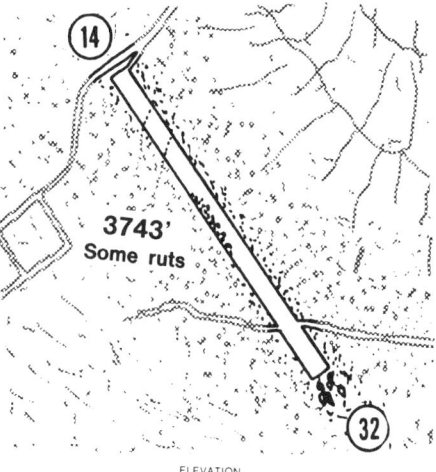

3743'
Some ruts

ELEVATION
135'

Fifth of February, Sonora

297

JET CHART	WAC	SECTIONAL	LATITUDE	LONGITUDE	US TIME	FOR GMT ADD	ICAO IDENT	TOWN IDENT
JN-46	CH-22So ADS-15	TPC H-22C	27°26	109°55	MST	7	-	-CEN2-

OTHER COMM Traffic 118.1
CITY 0.5 mile N   POPULATION 107,000
B'CAST FREQ 810   WHERE 5 mi NW   HOURS Daylight
FROM Cd Obregón   FREQ 115.1   TRACK 279°,5Dme,
FROM Guaymas   FREQ 368   TRACK 106°,62n.mi.,
FROM Santa Rosalia FREQ 112.6 TRACK 072°,126n.mi.,
FUEL Emergency 80   CARDS -   CASH? Pesos
REPAIRS Minor   TIEDOWN BYO

HOTEL	RATE	WHERE	TEL
Valle Grande	$$	Central	4-09-40
Costa de Oro	$$	Central	4-17-75

3156'x59' Paving

ELEVATION 180'

Hometown duster airport for the lush Obregón valley farms; these people are busy when they are busy and really prefer that most of us use the big airport. Not unfriendly, just busy.

All of the usual city things apply: good telephone service, several decent places to eat. Also a pleasant city to walk around after dinner.

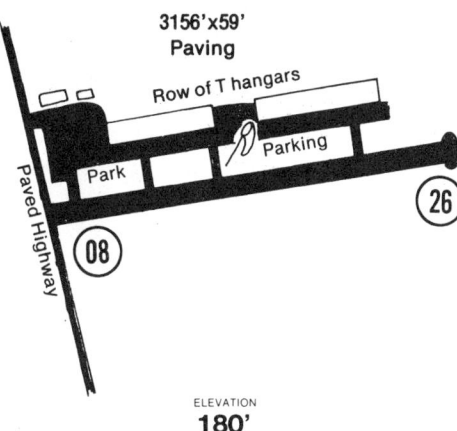

CD. OBREGON, SON.
VOR PISTA 35

298 SEPTIEMBRE-3-1981/160

RADIO AMSA 131.0	TWR 118.3	ELEV. 243'
		VAR. MAG. 11° E
		CEN ≡ · ‒

Caution For Information Only Not for Aerial Navigation

4900'
5800'
DME CEN 115.1
4000'
175° / 355°
220° / 040°
3000'

10 M.N 2100' DER. ←175° 4000'
355° 860' (617')
VOR ELEV. 243'

FALLIDA VIRE A LA IZQUIERDA E INTERCEPTE EN ASCENSO EL RADIAL 175° Y PROSIGA EN TRAYECTORIA DE APROXIMACION HASTA LA ALTITUD MINIMA DE ESPERA.

CATEGORIA	DIRECTO PISTA 35 MDA 860' (617')		CATEGORIA	CIRCULANDO MDA	
	DIA	NOCHE		DIA	NOCHE
A	1 (1600 M)		A	1140' (897') – 1¼ (2 000 M)	
B		N.A.	B		N.A.
C	N.A.		C	N.A.	
D			D		

CAMBIOS ELEV. HAA.   SCT-DGAC-SENEAM   CEN-V-3

SUNRISE & SUNSET – GMT   SALIDA y PUESTA del SOL – GMT

15th of	JAN	FEB	MAR	APR	MAY	JUN	JUL	AUG	SEPT	OCT	NOV	DEC	
SUNRISE	1410	1356	1328	1254	1230	1223	1234	1250	1304	1319	1339	1401	SALIDA
SUNSET	2446	0110	0127	0143	0200	0215	0216	0157	0124	2450	2427	2427	PUESTA
15° de	ENE	FEB	MAR	ABR	MAY	JUN	JUL	AGO	SEP	OCT	NOV	DIC	

To get local time just subtract 'GMT ADD'
PARA OBTENER TIEMPO LOCAL SUSTRIAGA 'GMT ADD'

Ciudad Obregón, Sonora

see-oo-DOD obe-ree-GOAN **299**

JET CHART	WAC	SECTIONAL	LATITUDE	LONGITUDE	US TIME	FOR GMT ADD	ICAO IDENT	TOWN IDENT
JN-46	CH-22 ADS-15	TPC H-22C	27°23'	109°50'	MST	7	MMCN	CEN

tca to: **4,000'msl** CENTER AT **VorDme** RADIUS **10 mi.**

APPROACH - TOWER **118.3** GROUND **118.3**
CITY **7 miles NW** POPULATION **110,000**
LOCAL **VorDme** FREQ **115.1** WHERE **Here** HOURS **24**
B'CAST FREQ **1290** WHERE **7 mi NW** HOURS **Daylight**
FROM **Hermosillo** FREQ **112.8** TRACK **136°, 120** n.mi.
FROM **Los Mochis** FREQ **115.5** TRACK **322°, 104**
FUEL **80, 100, JP** CARDS **Visa, MC** CASH? **Pesos**
REPAIRS **Minor** TIEDOWN **BYO**

HOTEL	RATE	WHERE	TEL
Motel el Valle	$$	Central	4-09-40
M. Costa del Oro	$	Central	4-17-75

Jet service airport for a busy agricultural city, this location was chosen to be far enough away that noise would not be a problem to the city itself.

READER REPORT The avgas crew here has to be the fastest around. They consistently have us refuelled and ready even before we've filed our next flight plan. The Wilkinsons, Idaho

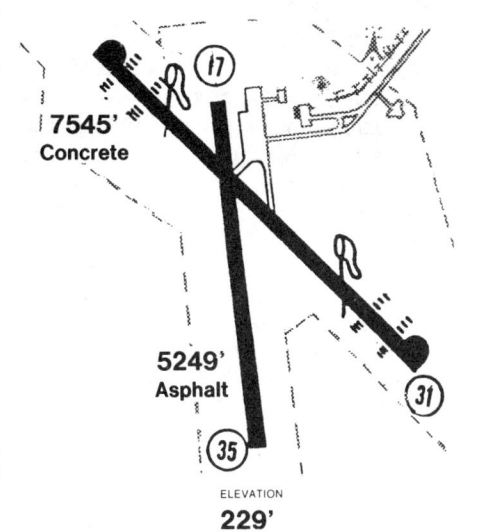

7545'
Concrete

5249'
Asphalt

ELEVATION
229'

300 Navajoa, Sonora

novv-ah-HOE-ah

JET CHART	WAC	SECTIONAL	LATITUDE	LONGITUDE	US TIME	FOR GMT ADD	ICAO IDENT	TOWN IDENT
JN-46	CH-22 So. ADS-15	TPC H-22C	27°04'	109°26'	MST	7	-	NVJ

OTHER COMM Traffic 118.1
CITY Adjacent W POPULATION 66,000
B'CAST FREQ 980 WHERE 1 mi NW HOURS Daylight
FROM Cd Obregon FREQ 115.1 TRACK 125°, 29Dme
FROM Los Mochis FREQ 115.5 TRACK 330°, 78n.mi.
FUEL 80/87 Emergency CARDS - CASH? Pesos
REPAIRS Minor TIEDOWN BYO

HOTEL	RATE	WHERE	TEL
el Rancho	$$	2 miles N	2-00-04
Motel el Rio	$$	1.5 miles N	2-03-31

Dove and duck season sees some powerful big iron parked on this runway as eager hunters arrive from the East, from Texas, just about everywhere you can imagine.

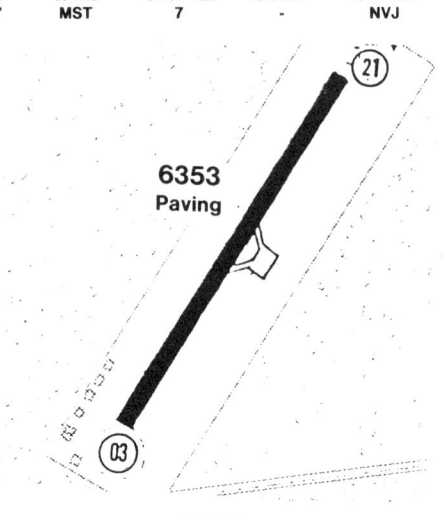

6353
Paving

ELEVATION
129'

Lago Mocuzari, Sonora

LAH-go moe-coo-SAH-ray 301

JN CHART	WAC	SECTIONAL	LATITUDE	LONGITUDE	US TIME	FOR GMT	ICAO	TOWN ID
JN-46	CH-22 ADS-15	-	27°13'	109°07'	MST	+7	-	MOC –

OTHER COMM Traffic 124.1
SETTLEMENT 0.6 miles NE
POPULATION est 1500
FROM Los Mochis   FREQ 115.5   TRACK 343°, 82.4 Dme
FROM Cd Obregon   FREQ 115.1   TRACK 094°, 105 n.mi.
FROM Navojoa   FREQ 1270 Khz   TRACK 049°, 19.2 n.mi.
REPAIRS -   TIEDOWNS BYO

A well-known fishing hole, Mocuzari is one of the many lakes which the government stocked and maintains as a bass lake both for tourism and as a source of protein for local residents.

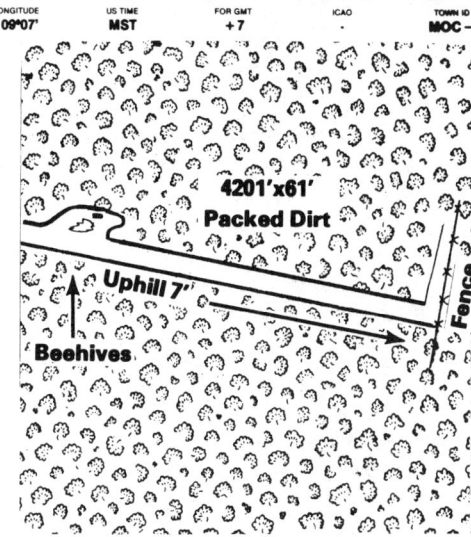

302 Alamos, Sonora

AH-lah-moce

JET CHART	WAC	SECTIONAL	LATITUDE	LONGITUDE	US TIME	FOR GMT ADD	ICAO IDENT	TOWN IDENT
JN-46	CH-22 So. ADS-15	-	27°03'	108°56'	MST	7	-	ALA

OTHER COMM Traffic 122.85
CITY Adjacent South **POPULATION** 30,000
FROM Cd. Obregón **FREQ** 115.1 **TRACK** 105°, 52n.mi.
FROM Los Mochis **FREQ** 115.° **TRACK** 350°, 71n.mi.
FROM Navajoa **FREQ** Airport **TRACK** 084°, 25n.mi.
FUEL - **CARDS** - **CASH?** -
REPAIRS Alt shop **TIEDOWN** BYO

HOTEL	RATE	WHERE	TEL
Casa Tesoros	$$$	Central	8-00-10
Hotel Portales	$$	Central	8-01-11

Preserved as a living example of Spanish Colonial architecture, mines once employed 30,000 resentful indians who would, in a series of uprisings lasting until 1927, finally stop mining altogether. Today a picturesque sleepy town where The Good Life is found at Casa de los Tesoros with gracious dining, quiet surroundings, and guests who enjoy it.

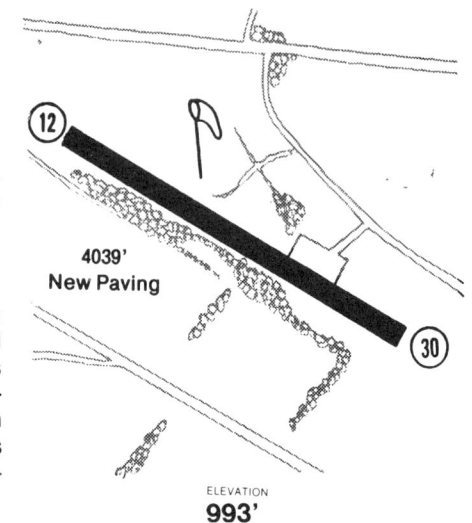

4039'
New Paving

ELEVATION
993'

Presa Hidalgo   Sinaloa   *PRESS-ah ee-DALL-go*   303

JET CHART	WAC	SECTIONAL	LATITUDE	LONGITUDE	US TIME	FOR GMT ADD	ICAO IDENT	TOWN IDENT
JN-46	CH-23 So. ADS-15	TPC H-23D	26°31'	108°33'	MST	7	-	-DLG-

OTHER COMM Traffic 122.85
CITY 9 miles SSW   POPULATION 5,600
LOCAL B'cast FREQ 950 WHERE 5 miles SW HOURS Days
FROM Cd Obregón   FREQ 115.1   TRACK 119°,87Dme
FROM los Mochis   FREQ 115.5   TRACK 018°,46n.mi.
FROM Culiacán   FREQ 112.1   TRACK 320°,121 n.mi.
FUEL -   CARDS -   CASH? -
REPAIRS -   TIEDOWN BYO

HOTEL	RATE	WHERE	TEL
Fishing resort	-	1 mile S	-
Posada Hidalgo	$$	in town	yes

Be fair to say this is the only dry land airport located inside a lake. As my eye sees it, this surface is about 30' below the road crossing the dam. If this surface is not available to you then just slip over to el Fuerte's paved runway then cab back here to fish.

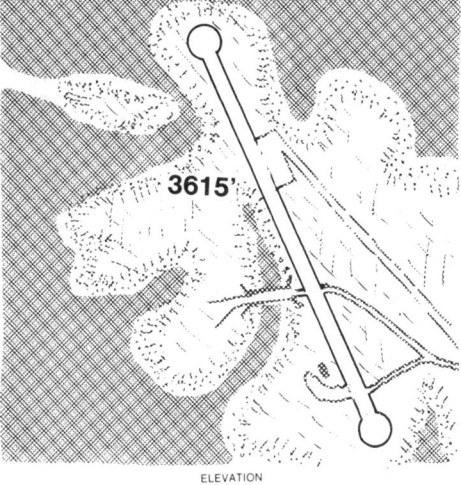

3615'

ELEVATION
325'

304 el Fuerte   Sinaloa   *ell FWARE-tay*

JET CHART	WAC	SECTIONAL	LATITUDE	LONGITUDE	US TIME	FOR GMT ADD	ICAO IDENT	TOWN IDENT
JN-46	CH-23 So. ADS-15	TPC H-23D	26°24'	108°36'	MST	7	-	-FRT-

OTHER COMM Traffic 122.85
CITY 1 mile W   POPULATION 5,600
B'CAST FREQ 950   WHERE 1 mi W   HOURS Daylight
FROM Cd Obregón   FREQ 115.1   TRACK 125°, 89Dme
FROM los Mochis   FREQ 115.5   TRACK 019°, 40n.mi.
FROM Culiacán   FREQ 112.1   TRACK 319°, 117 n.mi.
FUEL -   CARDS -   CASH? -
REPAIRS -   TIEDOWN BYO

HOTEL	RATE	WHERE	TEL
Posada Hidalgo	$$	Central	yes
San Francisco	-$	Central	maybe

AUTHORS REPORT We passed through here last July; the officials apologized that they couldn't offer fuel service. Marvina and Arnold, California

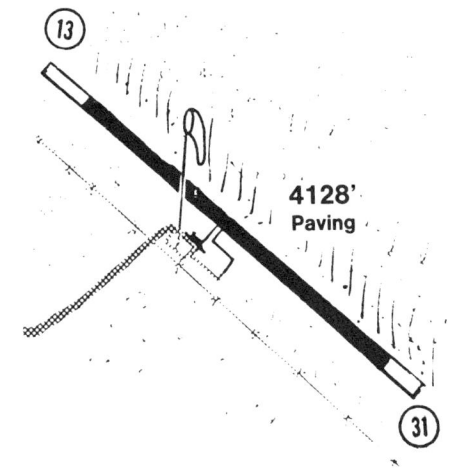

4128' Paving

ELEVATION
245'

San Blas, Sinaloa — sahn BLOSS seen-ah-LOW-ah — 305

OTHER COMM Traffic 124.1
TOWN 0.5 mile North
POPULATION est 4000
FROM Los Mochis   FREQ 115.5   TRACK 029°, 18.3Dme
FROM Cd Obregon   FREQ 115.1   TRACK 132°, 98Dme
FROM Culiacan   FREQ 112.1   TRACK 307°, 110n.mi.

AVIATION FUEL ·   CREDIT CARDS ·   CASH TYPE ·

Handy place to get over to the store for supplies without the need for a cab or flight plans or other distractions. Two landmarks: the huge power lines a few feet West and the railroad going through town. P.S. Yes, the windsock is starched and stands out rigidly no matter what the wind.

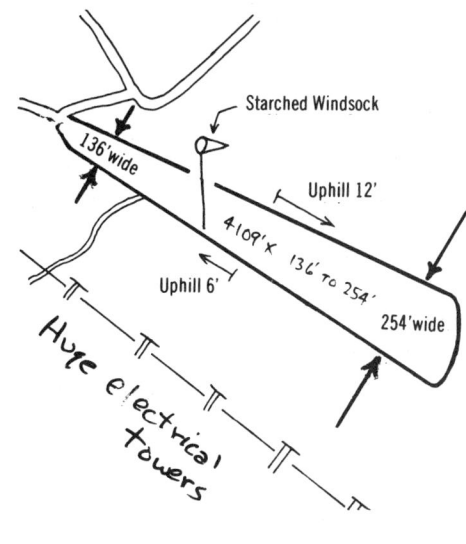

Sketch notes: Starched Windsock; 136' wide; Uphill 12'; 4109' x 136' to 254'; Uphill 6'; 254' wide; Huge electrical towers

305A Choix, Sinaloa *pronounced 'choice'*

JET CHART	WAC	LATITUDE	LONGITUDE	US TIME	FOR GMT ADD	ICAO IDENT	TOWN IDENT
JN-46	CH-23 So. ADS-15	26°43'	108°20'	MST	+7	-	CHX

OTHER COMM Traffic 118.1

TOWN 1 mi East   POPULATION est 30,000
FROM Cd Obregon   FREQ 115.1 TRACK 108°, 89Dme
FROM Los Mochis   FREQ 115.5   TRACK 026°, 63Dme
FROM Culiacan   FREQ 112.1   TRACK 323°, 124n.mi.
AVIATION FUEL Emergency Turbosina   CARDS -   CASH TYPE Pesos
REPAIRS? -   TIEDOWNS? BYO

2403'x55' to 65'
Graded, Packed

An interesting small city situated inside the bend of a river where it just can't be missed. The Ndb on 214 is reliable and strong out to nearly 200 miles altho for some reason it operates without identification. Peculiar fuel situation because government turbine powered helicopters are most of the traffic.

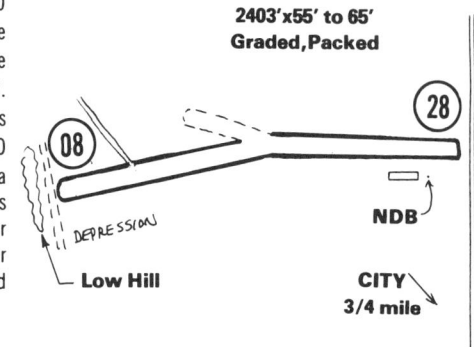

Divisadero, Chihuahua   *dee-vees-ah-DAIR-oh*   **305B**

JET CHART	WAC	LATITUDE	LONGITUDE	US TIME	FOR GMT ADD	ICAO IDENT	TOWN IDENT
JN-46	CH-23 North	27°31′	107°54′	MST	+7	-	DRO-
Interim Data	ADS-15						

OTHER COMM Traffic 121.5

SETTLEMENT Hotel 0.5mi NE   POPULATION est 50 to 100

FROM Los Mochis   FREQ 115.5 TRACK 019°, 117n.mi.

FROM Cd Obregon   FREQ 115.1 TRACK 075°, 105n.mi.

FROM Chihuahua   FREQ 114.1 TRACK 216°, 128n.mi.

AVIATION FUEL -   CARDS -   CASH TYPE -

REPAIRS? -   TIEDOWNS? BYO

A spectacular runway all but hanging from the edge of the famous Barrancas de Cobre, or Copper Canyon badlands. Runway appears to have gotten rundown with grass and soft spots. When it is usable this hotel is a very interesting place to stay on the teetery edge of a 3,000′ deep canyon. Certainly the definition of precarious. I'll land and measure when the runway is better then report to you via the PREPS on exact length and condition.

Data Incomplete—see PREPS

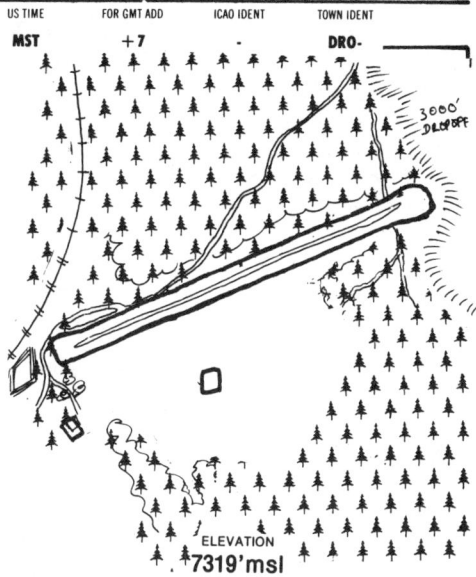

ELEVATION 7319′ msl

Los Mochis IFR *waiting for the new approach to be issued*

Intentionally Left Blank
Intencionalmente Dejada en Blanco

Los Mochis New — Sinaloa

loce MOE-cheece — 307

JN CHART	WAC	SECTIONAL	LATITUDE	LONGITUDE	US TIME	FOR GMT	ICAO	TOWN ID
JN-46	CH-22 ADS-15	TPC H22C	25°39'	109°05'	MST	+7	-	LMM

• TCA Scheduled 1983

APPROACH - TOWER - GROUND -
OTHER COMM Traffic 118.1
CITY 9 mi ENE   POPULATION 155,000

LOCAL NAVAID	TYPE	FREQ	WHERE	HOURS
B'CAST FREQ 650			WHERE 7 mi ENE	HOURS Daylight
FROM Cd.Obregon		FREQ 115.1	TRACK 147°, 113n.mi.	
FROM Culiacan		FREQ 112.1	TRACK 289°, 102n.mi.	
FROM Chihuahua		FREQ 114.1	TRACK 211°, 252n.mi.	

AVIATION GAS -   CREDIT CARDS -   CASH TYPE -
REPAIRS AVAILABLE -   TIEDOWNS? BYO

HOTEL	RATES	WHERE	TEL
El Dorado		Central	Tvl Agt
Holiday Inn	$	3 East	Tvl Agt
Sta Anita		Central	Tvl Agt

↑ CITY ≈ 8 miles

Under Construction
Data Incomplete
Keep checking the PREPS.

308 los Mochis Holiday Sinaloa   *loce MOE-cheece*

JET CHART	WAC	SECTIONAL	LATITUDE	LONGITUDE	US TIME	FOR GMT ADD	ICAO IDENT	TOWN IDENT
JN-46	CH-23 So ADS-15	TPC H-23D	25°48	108°57	MST	7	-	LMM

APPROACH -   TOWER 118.8   GROUND -
CITY 3 miles W   POPULATION 220,000
LOCAL Vor   FREQ 115.5   WHERE 2 mi NE   HOURS 24
FROM Cd Obregón   FREQ 115.1   TRACK 142°, 107 n.mi.
FROM Chihuahua   FREQ 114.1   TRACK 211°, 241 n.mi.
FROM Culiacán   FREQ 112.1   TRACK 296°, 101 n.mi.
FUEL -   CARDS -   CASH? Yes
REPAIRS -   TIEDOWN $3/day + BYO

HOTEL	RATE	WHERE	TEL
Holiday Inn	$$$	Adjacent	tvl agt
el Dorado	$$	Central	2-01-79
Santa Anita	$$	Central	2-00-46

Presently the terminal for the twice a day DC-3 flights to la Paz, those operations are expected to move over to the new Internacional airport now under liesurely construction a few miles West of town. The future of this site after that airport opens is uncertain.

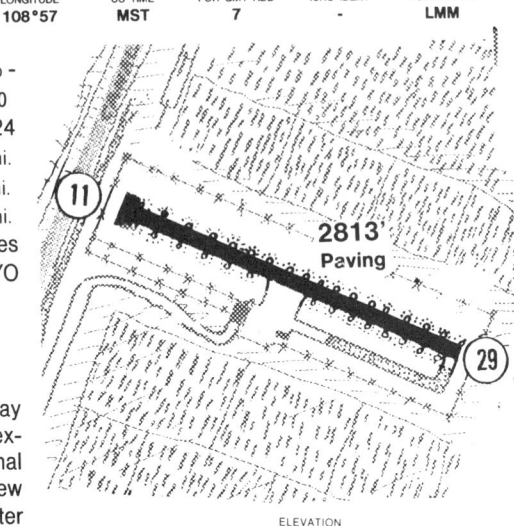

2813' Paving

ELEVATION
69'

Guasave   Sinaloa
wah-SAHH-vay   **309**

JN CHART	WAC	SECTIONAL	LATITUDE	LONGITUDE	US TIME	FOR GMT	ICAO	TOWN ID
JN-46	CH-23 ADS-15	TPC H23D	25°08'	108°26'	MST	+7	.	GUV

OTHER COMM Traffic 118.1
B'cast 610   WHERE ·   HOURS Daylight
FROM Culiacan   FREQ 112.1   TRACK 302°, 74Dme
FROM Los Mochis   FREQ 115.5   TRACK 104°, 31Dme
FROM Choix FREQ Ndb 214   TRACK 187°, 66n.mi.
AVIATION FUEL ·   CREDIT CARDS ·   CASH TYPE ·
REPAIRS AVAILABLE Minor   TIEDOWNS? BYO

One of the many new airports springing up here in the lush tropical coast of Sinaloa state. Airplanes seen here while measuring were either new or nearly new six place Cessnas both singles and twins. Fulltime guard/customs man lives in the residence at the SW corner of the runway.

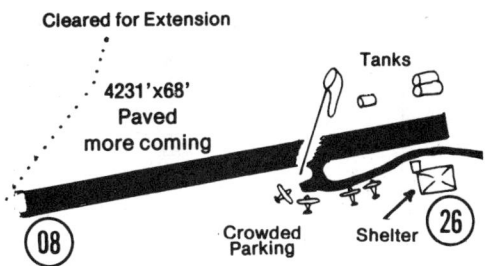

CULIACAN, SIN.
VOR PISTA 02

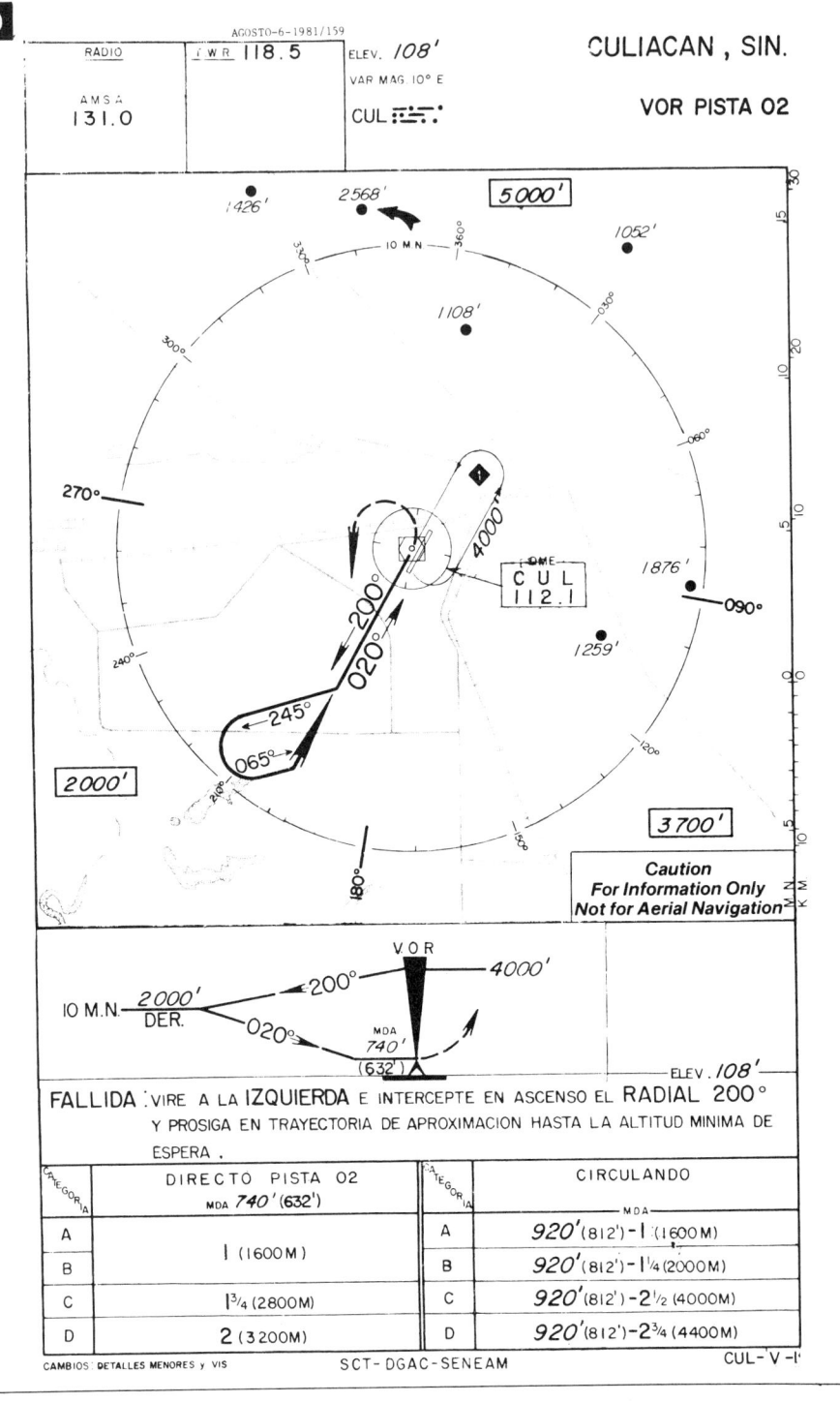

RADIO	TWR 118.5	ELEV. 108'
AMSA 131.0		VAR MAG. 10° E
		CUL ·-··

310 AGOSTO-6-1981/159

Chart elevations/notes: 1426', 2568', 1052', 1108', 1876', 1259', 5000', 4000', 2000', 3700'
CUL DME 112.1
Radials shown: 270°, 200°, 020°, 245°, 065°, 180°, 090°, 120°, etc.

Caution: For Information Only — Not for Aerial Navigation

Profile: VOR — 4000' — 200° — 2000' DER. — 10 M.N. — 020° — MDA 740' (632') — ELEV. 108'

FALLIDA: VIRE A LA **IZQUIERDA** E INTERCEPTE EN ASCENSO EL RADIAL 200° Y PROSIGA EN TRAYECTORIA DE APROXIMACION HASTA LA ALTITUD MINIMA DE ESPERA.

CATEGORIA	DIRECTO PISTA 02 MDA 740' (632')	CATEGORIA	CIRCULANDO MDA
A	1 (1600M)	A	920' (812') - 1 (1600M)
B	1 (1600M)	B	920' (812') - 1¼ (2000M)
C	1¾ (2800M)	C	920' (812') - 2½ (4000M)
D	2 (3200M)	D	920' (812') - 2¾ (4400M)

CAMBIOS: DETALLES MENORES y VIS   SCT-DGAC-SENEAM   CUL-V-1

SUNRISE & SUNSET - GMT   SALIDA y PUESTA del SOL - GMT

15th of	JAN	FEB	MAR	APR	MAY	JUN	JUL	AUG	SEPT	OCT	NOV	DEC	
SUNRISE	1356	1343	1318	1247	1225	1220	1229	1244	1255	1307	1326	1346	SALIDA
SUNSET	2442	0104	0118	0132	0146	0200	0201	0144	0114	2443	2422	2423	PUESTA
15° de	ENE	FEB	MAR	ABR	MAY	JUN	JUL	AGO	SEP	OCT	NOV	DIC	

To get local time just subtract 'GMT ADD'
PARA OBTENER TIEMPO LOCAL SUSTRIAGA 'GMT ADD'

Culiacán Sinaloa   cool-ee-ah-CONN   311

JET CHART	WAC	SECTIONAL	LATITUDE	LONGITUDE	US TIME	FOR GMT ADD	ICAO IDENT	TOWN IDENT
JN-46	CH-23	ADS-15 / TPC H-23D	24°46'	107°28'	MST	7	MMCL	CUL

tca to: **4,000'msl** center at **VorDme** radius **10 mi.**
APPROACH —   TOWER **118.5**   GROUND **118.5**
CITY **6 miles NE**   POPULATION **80,000**
LOCAL **VorDme** FREQ **112.1** WHERE **Here** HOURS **24**
B'CAST FREQ **920** WHERE **6.4 mi NE** HOURS **Daylight**
FROM **los Mochis** FREQ **Vor** TRACK **115.5, 117° 104 n.mi.**
FROM **Mazatlán** FREQ **114.9** TRACK **313°, 117 n.mi.**
FROM **Durango** FREQ **112.2** TRACK **277°, 161 n.mi.**
FUEL **80, 100**   CARDS **Visa, MC, etc**   CASH? **Yes**
REPAIRS **Some**   TIEDOWN **BYO**

HOTEL	RATE	WHERE	TEL
Executive	$$	Central	2-78-00
Motel San Luís		Central	3-16-00
Tres Rios	$$	Near town	2-30-30

Excellent soil and a fine growing season with nearly tropical climate gives Culiacán a fantastic agriculture potential. Sugar cane joins dozens of other crops which make for hard working prosperous farmers and farm laborers.

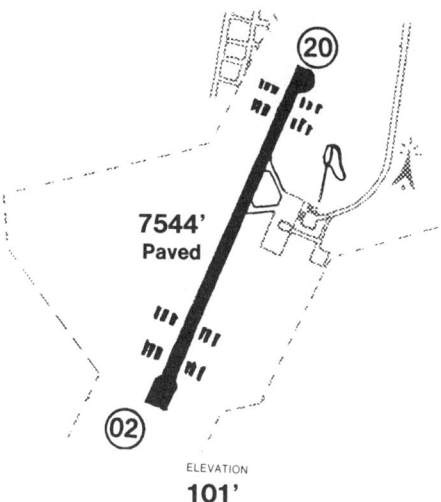

Runway 20 / 02
7544' Paved
ELEVATION **101'**

312 Guamuchil   Sinaloa   *wah-moo-CHEEL*

JET CHART	WAC	SECTIONAL	LATITUDE	LONGITUDE	US TIME	FOR GMT ADD	ICAO IDENT	TOWN IDENT
JN-46	CH-23 So. ADS-15	TPC H-23D	25°27'	108°05'	MST	7	-	GCH-

OTHER COMM Traffic 118.1
CITY 0.5 miles N   POPULATION 27,000
B'CAST FREQ 1300 WHERE 1 mi NNE HOURS Daylight
FROM los Mochis   FREQ 115.5   TRACK 108°, 53n.mi.
FROM Culiacán   FREQ 112.1   TRACK 309°, 54n.mi.
FUEL Some 80   CARDS -   CASH? Pesos
REPAIRS Minor   TIEDOWN BYO

HOTEL	RATE	WHERE	TEL
Motel York	$	North side	2-36

During my last measurement stop the runway was in poor condition. The army lieutenant whose men were inspecting in and outbound traffic - these hills are famous for dope - apologized for runway condition but said he believes a new runway will soon be built a mile or so north. Meantime do be careful here.

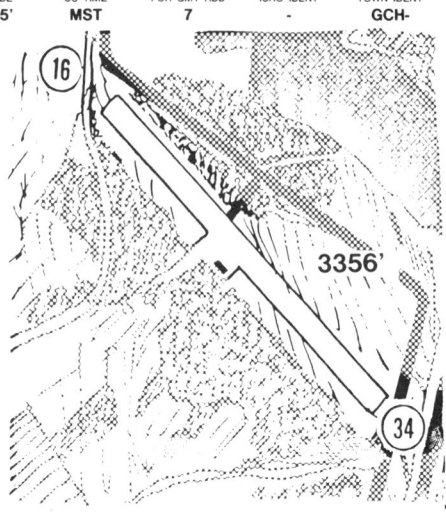

3356'

ELEVATION
70' to 80'

la Cruz   Sinaloa   lah CROOSE   313

JET CHART	WAC	SECTIONAL	LATITUDE	LONGITUDE	US TIME	FOR GMT ADD	ICAO IDENT	TOWN IDENT
JN-46	CJ-24 No. ADS-15	TPC J-24A	23°56'	106°53'	MST	7	-	-CRU-

OTHER COMM Traffic 118.1
CITY 0.1 miles S   POPULATION 3,500
FROM Culiacán   FREQ 112.1   TRACK 140°,60Dme
FROM Mazatlán   FREQ 114.9   TRACK 316°,59Dme
FUEL -   CARDS -   CASH? -
REPAIRS None   TIEDOWN BYO

Near enough to Mazatlán to give you a choice should you need it, this is an interesting little West Coast town. Couple stores to pump up your camping supplies.

READER REPORT This is a mobile runway: the cropdusters move it around to suit their needs. C. Powell, Washington

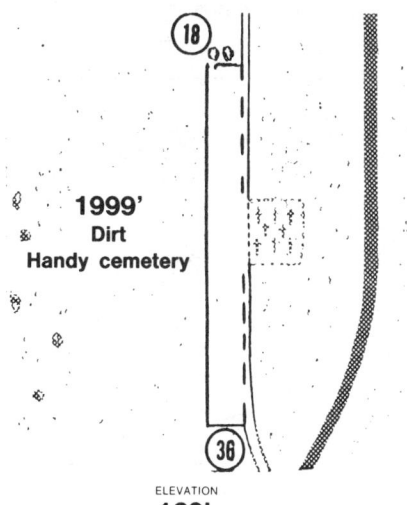

1999'
Dirt
Handy cemetery

ELEVATION
163'

MAZATLAN, SIN.
VOR/NDB PISTA 26

RADIO		
AMSA 131.0 y CMA 130.0	TWR	118.3
	APP	121.2
	EMER	121.5
	ATIS	114.9

ELEV. 33'
VAR. MAG. 10° E
MZT ≡ ≡ ··

Caution – For Information Only – Not for Aerial Navigation

AGOSTO-6-1981/159

DME MZT 114.9
MZ 285

FALLIDA: ASCIENDA EN **RADIAL 262°**, CON VIRAJE DE GOTA A LA **IZQUIERDA** DENTRO DE **10 M.N.** HASTA LA ALTITUD MINIMA DE ESPERA.

CATEGORIA	DIRECTO PISTA 26 MDA 500' (467')	CATEGORIA	CIRCULANDO — MDA —
A	1 (1600M)	A	720'(687')-1 (1600M)
B	1 (1600M)	B	720'(687')-1 (1600M)
C	1¼ (2000M)	C	720'(687')-2 (3200M)
D	1½ (2400M)	D	720'(687')-2¼ (3600M)

CAMBIOS: DETALLES MENORES
SCT-DGAC-SENEAM
MZT-V-1

SUNRISE & SUNSET – GMT   SALIDA y PUESTA del SOL – GMT

15th of	JAN	FEB	MAR	APR	MAY	JUN	JUL	AUG	SEPT	OCT	NOV	DEC	
SUNRISE	1348	1337	1313	1244	1223	1218	1228	1241	1251	1301	1318	1338	SALIDA
SUNSET	2440	0100	0114	0125	0138	0151	0153	0137	0108	2439	2420	2421	PUESTA
15° de	ENE	FEB	MAR	ABR	MAY	JUN	JUL	AGO	SEP	OCT	NOV	DIC	

To get local time just subtract 'GMT ADD'
PARA OBTENER TIEMPO LOCAL SUSTRIAGA 'GMT ADD'

Mazatlán Sinaloa

moss-ott-LONN

315

JET CHART	WAC	SECTIONAL	LATITUDE	LONGITUDE	US TIME	FOR GMT ADD	ICAO IDENT	TOWN IDENT
JN-46	CJ-24 ADS-15	TPC J-24A	23°09'	106°15'	MST	7	MMZT	MZT

- TCA TO: 20,000' RADIUS 50 n.mi. HOURS 24
- APPROACH 121.2 TOWER 118.3 GROUND 118.3
- CITY 16 miles NW POPULATION 260,000
- LOCAL VorDme FREQ 114.9 WHERE Here HOURS 24
- B'CAST FREQ 630 WHERE 11 mi NW HOURS Daylight
- FROM Culiacán FREQ 112.1 TRACK 137°, 117 n.mi.
- FROM Puerto Vallara FREQ 112.6 TRACK 329°, 159 n.mi.
- FROM Durango FREQ 112.2 TRACK 229°, 112 n.mi.
- FUEL 80,100,JP CARDS Visa,MC,etc CASH? Pesos
- REPAIRS Minor TIEDOWN BYO

HOTEL	RATE	WHERE	TEL
Camino Real	$$	5 miles N	Tvl agt
Playa Mazatlán	$$E	3 miles N	-
Hotel de Cima	-$$E	2 miles N	1-41-19

Warm balmy air even in winter, miles of brilliant white sand along a low surf shore, fun places to see and things to do, make Mazatlán special. An easy ride from LA or El Paso: you could be parasailing the same day in a spectacular sunset.

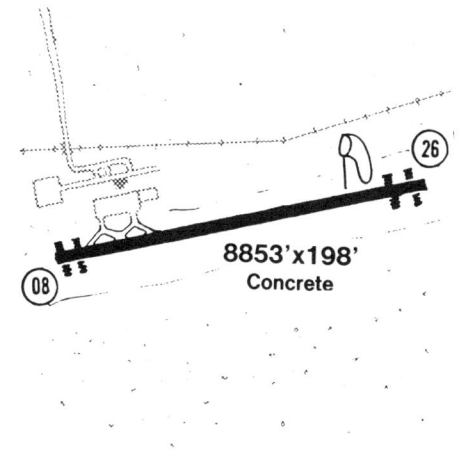

8853'x198'
Concrete

ELEVATION
17'

316 Novillero   Sinaloa   *no-vee-YAIR-oh*

JET CHART	WAC	SECTIONAL	LATITUDE	LONGITUDE	US TIME	FOR GMT ADD	ICAO IDENT	TOWN IDENT
JN-46	CJ-24 No. ADS-15	TPC J-24A	22°33'	105°45'	CST	6	-	-NOV-

OTHER COMM Traffic 123.2   *see page 93
CITY West   POPULATION NA
FROM Mazatlán 114.9   FREQ 132°   TRACK 45.4 Dme,
FROM Pto Vallarta 112.6   FREQ 337°   TRACK 115.2 n.mi.
FROM SJ del Cabo 114.0   FREQ 087°   TRACK 222 n.mi.,
FUEL -   CARDS -   CASH? -
REPAIRS -   TIEDOWN BYO

Incomplete data: additional information about this airport will be furnished.

Still Under Construction in mid-1982

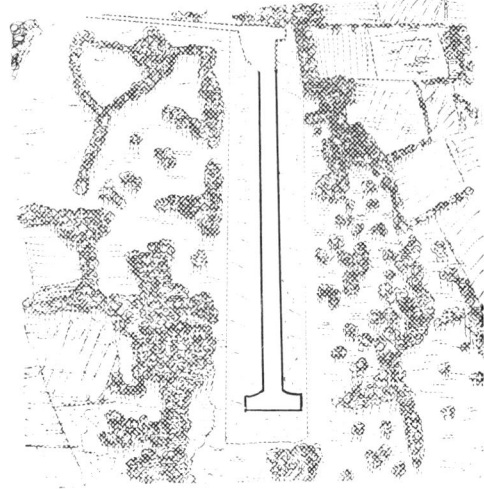

Acaponeta   Sinaloa   ah-cah-pone-ETT-tah   317

JN CHART	WAC	SECTIONAL	LATITUDE	LONGITUDE	US TIME	FOR GMT	ICAO	TOWN ID
JN-46	CJ-24 ADS-15	TPC J24A	22°28'	105°22'	MST	+7	-	ACP

OTHER COMM Traffic 124.4
CITY 4 miles NE
B'cast 1400
FROM Mazatlan   FREQ 114.9
FROM Vallarta   FREQ 112.6
FROM Durango   FREQ 112.2

POPULATION 80,000+
WHERE 4 mi NE HOURS Daylight
TRACK 119°, 63.8Dme
TRACK 347°, 107n.mi.
TRACK 191°, 129n.mi.

AVIATION GAS -   CREDIT CARDS -   CASH TYPE -
REPAIRS AVAILABLE -   TIEDOWNS? BYO

09 — 3926'x65' Paved — 27

A large, medium-old (about 240 years) Mexican city snuggled up against the Sierra Madre. Airport is well away from any taxi or bus patterns so plan to either BYO wheels or arrange ahead.

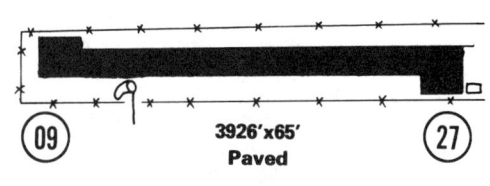

ELEVATION
291'msl

318 San Blas, Sinaloa

sahn BLAH-ss

JET CHART	WAC	SECTIONAL	LATITUDE	LONGITUDE	US TIME	FOR GMT ADD	ICAO IDENT	TOWN IDENT
JN-46	CJ-24 No.	TPC J-24A	21°34'	105°17'	MST	7	-	SBS

OTHER COMM Traffic 118.1
FROM Mazatlán **FREQ** 114.9 **TRACK** 139°, 110 n.mi.
FROM Puerto Vallarta **FREQ** 112.6 **TRACK** 350°, 53Dme
FROM Tepic **FREQ** airport **TRACK** 273°, 22n.mi.
FUEL -   **CARDS** -   **CASH?** -
REPAIRS -   **TIEDOWN** BYO

HOTEL	RATE	WHERE	TEL
Casa Morales	$$	South side	23

A tour of the mangrove swamps will answer any question about whether there are alligators. You will be able to report having seen them very close from a flimsy boat.

READER REPORT Stayed at the Flamingo Hotel and ate at McDonald's Restaurant in town; both very good.—W Hopper, California

READER REPORT We stopped here and paid the overnight parking fee but during the night someone very professionally stole more than $13,000 worth of equipment from our locked Cessna P337. Apparently this has happened before to others.--WF Crawford, Illinois.

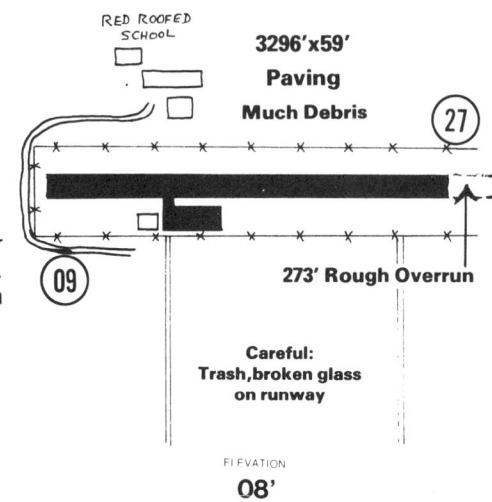

RED ROOFED SCHOOL

3296'x59'
Paving
Much Debris

27

09

273' Rough Overrun

Careful:
Trash, broken glass
on runway

ELEVATION
08'

la Penita, Sinaloa

lah penn-YEE-tah   **319**

JN CHART	WAC	SECTIONAL	LATITUDE	LONGITUDE	US TIME	FOR GMT	ICAO	TOWN ID
JN-46	CJ-24 ADS-15	TPC J24A	21°04'	105°14'	CST	+6	-	PNT

OTHER COMM Traffic 124.9
TOWN 2 miles South

FROM Pto.Vallarta	FREQ 112.6	TRACK 358°, 23.2Dme
FROM Mazatlan	FREQ 114.9	TRACK 145°, 138n.mi.
FROM Tepic	FREQ ADF 620	TRACK 207°, 30.4n.mi.

AVIATION GAS -   CREDIT CARDS -   CASH TYPE -

Called in some eidtions of the WACs 'El Llano' and by some controllers at Mazatlan 'el Rincon', Penita seems the more popular name used overall. Difficult to impossible to get over the fence to go direct to the beach, best go around.

Lady airport guard is a real tigres; you are in better hands than with Allstate.

READER REPORT Swimming and sunbathing are superb here. We find the Motel San Carlos with some housekeeping units very nice. Restaurants, Villa Nueva and Beachcomber in that order. The Runnings, Washington

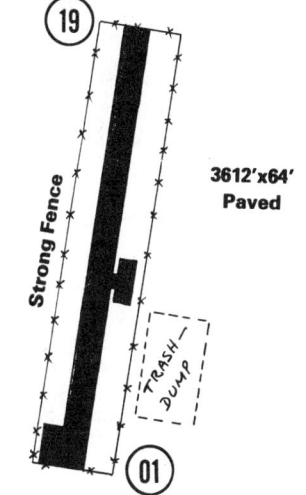

Runway diagram: 19/01, 3612' x 64' Paved, Strong Fence, Trash Dump

320 Tepic Nayarit *tay-PEEK*

JET CHART	WAC	SECTIONAL	LATITUDE	LONGITUDE	US TIME	FOR GMT ADD	ICAO IDENT	TOWN IDENT
JN-46	CJ-24 ADS-15	TPC J-24A	21°28'	104°53'	MST	7	-	TEP

tca to: VFR CENTER AT Airport RADIUS 5 mi.
APPROACH - TOWER 118.8 GROUND 118.8
CITY 1 mile NW POPULATION 45,000
B'CAST FREQ 620 WHERE 6 mi NE HOURS Daylight
FROM Mazatlán FREQ 114.9 TRACK 130°, 126 n.mi.
FROM Guadalajara FREQ 117.3 TRACK 297°, 106 n.mi.
FROM Puerto Vallarta FREQ 112.6 TRACK 015°, 52Dme
FUEL 80,100 CARDS Visa,MC,etc CASH? Pesos
REPAIRS Minor TIEDOWN BYO

HOTEL	RATE	WHERE	TEL
Hotel Corita	$E	Central	2-04-77

5248' Paved
ELEVATION 3145'

Higher elevation can still be tropical, as you see from the sugarcane fields on two sides of this airport and the huge cane processing mills going toward a surprisingly colonial style city. Combination of ancient buildings and occasional Huichol or Coro Indians from the mountains nicely keep up your interest in seeing what's next.

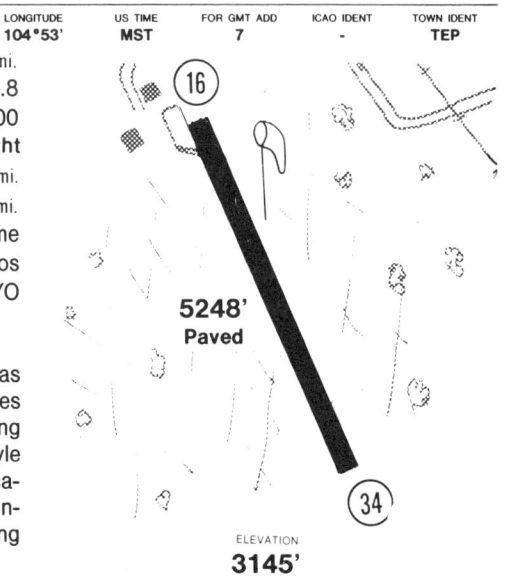

Isla María Madre Nayarit *EES-lah mah-REE-yah MODD-ray* 321

JET CHART	WAC	SECTIONAL	LATITUDE	LONGITUDE	US TIME	FOR GMT ADD	ICAO IDENT	TOWN IDENT
JN-46	CJ-24 No. ADS-15	TPC J-24A	21°40'	106°32'	MST	7	-	-

OTHER COMM Traffic 122.85
SETTLEMENT Prison Island   POPULATION ?
FROM Mazatlán   FREQ 114.9   TRACK 182°,92Dme
FROM Puerto Vallarta FREQ 112.6   TRACK 302°,94Dme
FUEL -   CARDS -   CASH? -
REPAIRS -   TIEDOWN BYO

HOTEL	RATE	WHERE	TEL
Carcel	Free	here	-

A prison island far enough off the Jalisco/Nayarit coast to discourage swimming over for an afternoon. This is the only airport in this book the author has not personally visited to measure and evaluate. Maybe later.

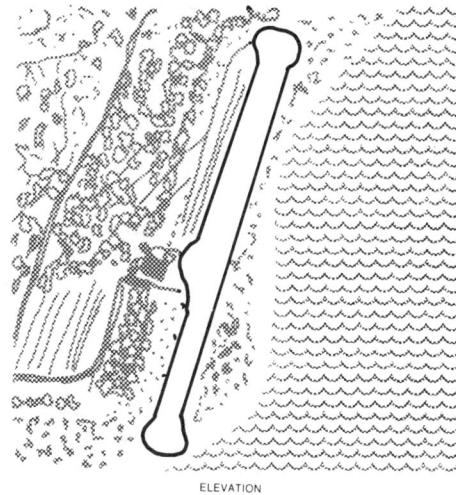

ELEVATION
12'

DURANGO, DGO.
VOR/DME PISTA 03

RADIO	TWR	ELEV. 6 093'
AMSA 131.0	118.1	VAR. MAG. 9° E
		DGO

AGOSTO-6-1981/159

Caution
For Information Only
Not for Aerial Navigation

DME DGO 112.2

FALLIDA: ASCIENDA EN RADIAL 024° CON VIRAJE DE GOTA A LA IZQUIERDA DENTRO DE 10 M.N. HASTA LA ALTITUD MINIMA DE ESPERA.

CATEGORIA	DIRECTO PISTA 03 MCA 6 560'(467')	CATEGORIA	CIRCULANDO MDA
A	1 (1600M)	A	6 900'(807')-1 (1600M)
B	1 (1600M)	B	6 900'(807')-1¼ (2000M)
C	1¼ (2000M)	C	6 900'(807')-2¼ (3600M)
D	1½ (2400M)	D	6 900'(807')-2½ (4000M)

CAMBIOS: VIS y DETALLES MENORES   SCT-DGAC-SENEAM   DGO-VD-2

SUNRISE & SUNSET — GMT   SALIDA y PUESTA del SOL — GMT

15th of	JAN	FEB	MAR	APR	MAY	JUN	JUL	AUG	SEPT	OCT	NOV	DEC	
SUNRISE	1343	1331	1307	1236	1215	1209	1219	1233	1244	1255	1313	1333	SALIDA
SUNSET	2431	2453	0107	0119	0133	0147	0148	0132	0102	2432	2412	2412	PUESTA
15 de	ENE	FEB	MAR	ABR	MAY	JUN	JUL	AGO	SEP	OCT	NOV	DIC	

To get local time just subtract 'GMT ADD'
PARA OBTENER TIEMPO LOCAL SUSTRIAGA 'GMT ADD'

Durango   Durango   *doo-RON-go*   323

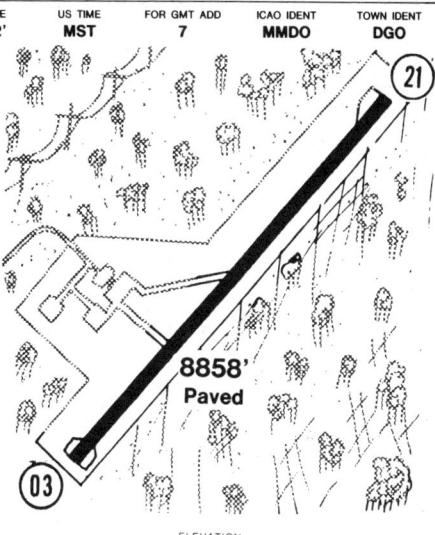

JET CHART	WAC	SECTIONAL	LATITUDE	LONGITUDE	US TIME	FOR GMT ADD	ICAO IDENT	TOWN IDENT
JN-46	CH-23 ADS-15	TPC H-23D	24°08'	104°32'	MST	7	MMDO	DGO

tca to: **10,000'msl**   CENTER AT **VorDme**   RADIUS **10**

APPROACH	—	TOWER **118.1**	GROUND **118.1**
CITY	**9 miles SW**	POPULATION	**210,000**
B'CAST FREQ **620**	WHERE **8 mi NW**	HOURS **Daylight**	
LOCAL **VorDme**	FREQ **112.2**	WHERE **Here**	HOURS **24**
FROM **Torreón**	FREQ **116.4**	TRACK **204°, 106** n.mi.	
FROM **Mazatlán**	FREQ **114.9**	TRACK **049°, 112** n.mi.	
FROM **Culiacán**	FREQ **112.1**	TRACK **093°, 166** n.mi.	
FUEL **80, 100**	CARDS **Visa, MC, etc**	CASH? **Pesos**	
REPAIRS **Minor**		TIEDOWN **BYO**	

HOTEL	RATE	WHERE	TEL
el Presidente	$$	Central	1-03-53
Casablanca	$	Central	1-35-99
Posada Duran	$	Central	1-24-12

Pancho Villa's birthplace city is also a mining center and shows the Spanish colonial influence in the cathedral and plaza. Clear skies and dependable sunlight make for good movie locations,

Runway: 21 / 03   **8858' Paved**
ELEVATION **6088'**

324 Hidalgo del Parral   Chihuahua   *ee-DALL-go dell pah-RALL*

JET CHART	WAC	SECTIONAL	LATITUDE	LONGITUDE	US TIME	FOR GMT ADD	ICAO IDENT	TOWN IDENT
JN-46	CH-23 So. ADS-15	TPC H-23D	26°55'	105°46'	CST	6	-	HPC

OTHER COMM Traffic 122.8
CITY 7 miles East
POPULATION 71,000
B'CAST FREQ 1400   WHERE 7 mi E   HOURS Daylight
FROM Chihuahua FREQ 114.1 TRACK 163°, 108 n.mi.
FROM Torreón FREQ 116.4 TRACK 292°, 150 n.mi.
FROM Durango FREQ 112.2 TRACK 329°, 180 n.mi.
FUEL 80, 100   CARDS -   CASH? Yes
REPAIRS Minor   TIEDOWN -

HOTEL	RATE	WHERE	TEL
Hotel Acosta	$	Central	2-21
Motel Camino Real	$	near town	7-00
Hotel Parral	$	On Plaza	4-20

Interesting colonial city with almost no tourist activity, early mining activities are still important today. One church with ore cast into its walls and benches, another which was built by a mysterious indian. It is the one without a dome. Good place for an occasional long weekend.

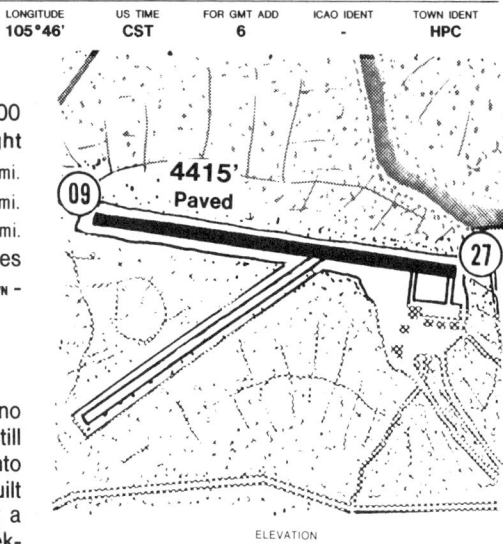

ELEVATION
5991'

4415' Paved
09 / 27

Jimenez Chihuahua

hee-MENN-ess **325**

JET CHART	WAC	SECTIONAL	LATITUDE	LONGITUDE	US TIME	FOR GMT ADD	ICAO IDENT	TOWN IDENT
JN-46	CH-23 So.	TPC H-23D	27°08'	104°57'	CST	6	-	-JIM-

OTHER COMM Traffic 118.1
SETTLEMENT 2 miles E   POPULATION 3,800
FROM Torreon   FREQ 116.4   TRACK 307°, 125 n.mi.
FROM H. del Parral FREQ airport TRACK 065°, 46 n.mi.
FUEL -   CARDS -   CASH? -
REPAIRS -   TIEDOWN BYO

México's cotton belt is all around, as are meteorite remnants. Large and small examples have found regularly from the early 1600s until last week. Wear a strong hat.

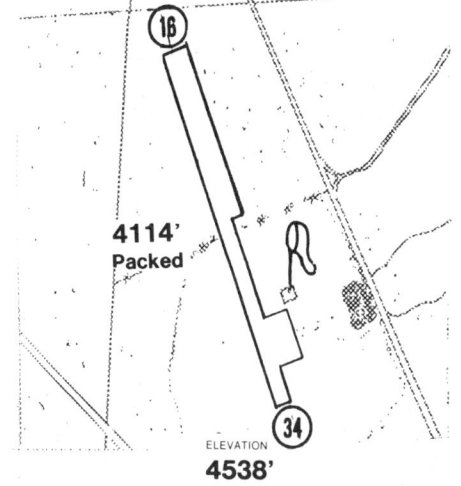

16
4114'
Packed
34
ELEVATION
4538'

326 Rancho Cárdenas   Chihuahua   ... CARR-den-uss

JET CHART	WAC	SECTIONAL	LATITUDE	LONGITUDE	US TIME	FOR GMT ADD	ICAO IDENT	TOWN IDENT
JN-46	CH-23 So.	TPC H-23D	27°29'	105°31'	CST	6	-	-

OTHER COMM Traffic 118.1
SETTLEMENT Adjacent   POPULATION Ranch
FROM Chihuahua   FREQ 114.1   TRACK 152°, 82Dme,
FROM Torreón   FREQ 116.4   TRACK 305°, 162 n.mi.,
FROM Culiacán   FREQ 112.1   TRACK 316°, 193 n.mi.,
FUEL -   CARDS -   CASH? -
REPAIRS -   TIEDOWN BYO

Formerly the ranch of a popular ex-President of Mexico, Lazaro Cardenas. Best known to us as the one who promulgated several socially oriented laws such as the one which requires non-resident vehicles to carry liability insurance written by a Mexican company.

This is now just a running down airport on the shore of a famous bass fishing lake. If you're flying a nosewheel aircraft particularly, you might want to look this over very very carefully.

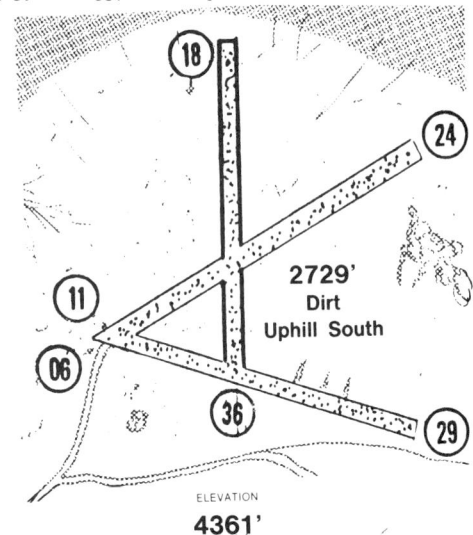

2729'
Dirt
Uphill South

ELEVATION
4361'

Presa Boquilla Chihuahua   *PRESS-ah(dam) bo-KEE-yah*   **327**

JET CHART	WAC	SECTIONAL	LATITUDE	LONGITUDE	US TIME	FOR GMT ADD	ICAO IDENT	TOWN IDENT
JN-46	CH-23 So.	TPC H-23D	27°35'	105°24'	CST	6	-	-BOQ-

OTHER COMM Traffic 122.85
CITY 3 miles SW   POPULATION 27,000
LOCAL B'cast FREQ 960 WHERE 10 miles SE HOURS Days
FROM Chihuahua   FREQ 114.1   TRACK 145°, 79Dme
FROM Torreón   FREQ 116.4   TRACK 308°, 162 n.mi.
FROM Culiacán   FREQ 112.1   TRACK 027°, 202 n.mi.

When Toronto, Canada supplied the bass, crappies, and bluegill to start this lake going it was decided to name the lake 'Toronto'. But people insist on calling it Boquilla. Sorry northern neighbor.

Not overly developed as yet, there is certainly good good fishing to one who brings his own flotation, etc.

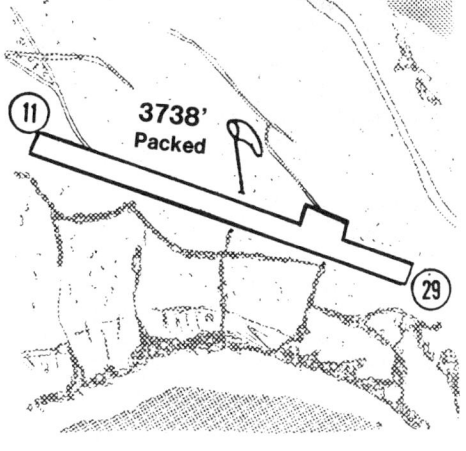

3738' Packed

ELEVATION
4251'

328   Chihuahua   **las Delicias**

JET CHART	WAC	SECTIONAL	LATITUDE	LONGITUDE	US TIME	FOR GMT ADD	ICAO IDENT	TOWN IDENT
JN-46	CH-23 No.	TPC H-23A	28°13'	105°27'	CST	6	-	DEL

OTHER COMM Traffic 118.1
CITY 2.5 miles SW   POPULATION 19,000
LOCAL VorDme   FREQ 113.5   WHERE here   HOURS 24
B'CAST FREQ 1240   WHERE Here   HOURS Daylight
FROM Chihuahua   FREQ 114.1   TRACK 135°,41Dme
FROM Marfa   FREQ 115.9   TRACK 199°,143n.mi.
FUEL Some 80 octane   CARDS -   CASH? Pesos
REPAIRS Minor   TIEDOWN BYO

     Brandy Town, México! The well known el Presidente brand comes from here, sold throughout the Republic. The irrigation for those vinyards also supplies water for grain and cotton. Research continues hopefully to rediscover the Aztecs' secret of growing colored cottons.

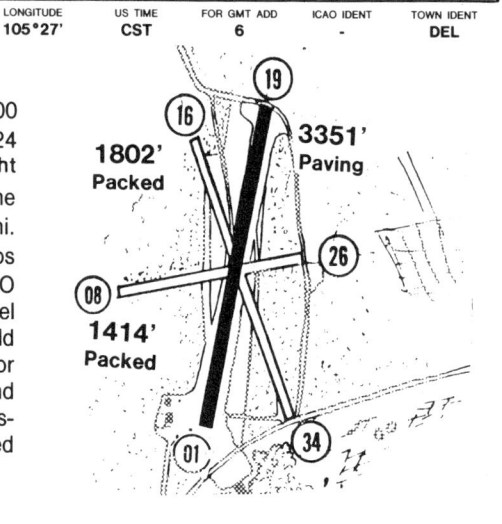

1802' Packed   **3351'** Paving
1414' Packed

ELEVATION
3884'

creel in Chihuahua: **Creel-Juanito** 329

JET CHART	WAC	SECTIONAL	LATITUDE	LONGITUDE	US TIME	FOR GMT ADD	ICAO IDENT	TOWN IDENT
JN-46	CH-23No. ADS-15	TPC CH-23D	27° 43'	107° 39'	CST	6		CRL

FROM Los Mochis FREQ 115.5 TRACK 019°, 132.4 n.mi.
FROM Chihuahua FREQ 114.1 TRACK 222°, 110.9 n.mi.
FROM Hermosillo FREQ 112.8 TRACK 102°, 198 n.mi.

HOTEL	RATE	WHERE	TEL
Copp.Can.Lodge	$$	6mi SW	Mochis
Motel Parador	$$	Central	No.5

Nearest Creel airport to the center of Tarahumara culture here in the high country, this runway suffers from semi-perpetual heavy turbulent crosswinds particularly after 8am local time. Called 'Juanito' to distinguish it from other Creel area airports, this has since been replaced by a paved airport reportedly nearby but not seen and measured by the author. The PREPS will document later finds.

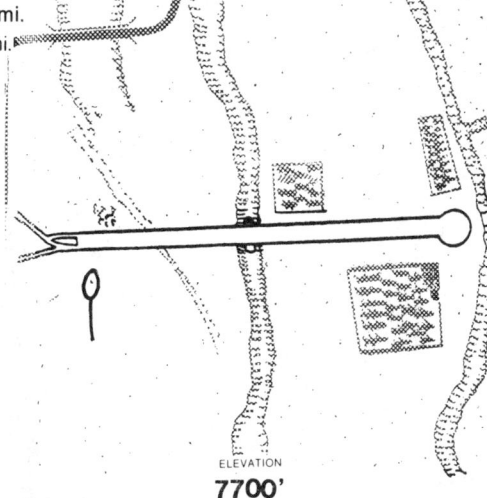

ELEVATION 7700'

CHIHUAHUA, CHIH.
VOR/DME PISTA 18

330

RADIO	TORRE 118.4	ELEV. 4462'
DIA Y NOCHE		VAR. MAG. 10° E
123.0 y 6603	APROXIMACION 121.0	CUU

MAYO 30 - 1978/136

CUU 114.1 DME 88
CUU 362

7700'
10700'
9500'
8000'

FALLIDA: SI NO ESTABLECE CONTACTO VISUAL CON LA PISTA, ASCIENDA DIRECTO HASTA ALCANZAR 5600' DENTRO DE 9 M.N. Y VIRE A LA DERECHA PARA CRUZAR EL VOR-DME/CUU DE ACUERDO CON INSTRUCCIONES DEL A.T.C.

NUDOS	60	80	100	120	140	160	180	200
VOR/CUU A APROX FALLIDA 5 M.N.	4:59	3:44	2:59	2:29	2:08	1:52	1:39	1:29

Caution For Information Only Not for Aerial Navigation

CATEGORIA	DIRECTO PISTA 18	CATEGORIA	CIRCULANDO MDA
A		A	5680' (1218') – 1¼
B	N.A.	B	5680' (1218') – 1½
C		C	5680' (1218') – 3
D		D	

CAMBIOS: MINIMOS   S.C.T - D.G.A.C   CUU VD-I

SUNRISE & SUNSET – GMT / SALIDA y PUESTA del SOL – GMT

15th of	JAN	FEB	MAR	APR	MAY	JUN	JUL	AUG	SEPT	OCT	NOV	DEC	
SUNRISE	1358	1342	1313	1238	1212	1205	1215	1233	1248	1304	1326	1349	SALIDA
SUNSET	2428	2453	0112	0129	0147	0203	0203	0143	0109	2434	2410	2408	PUESTA
15° de	ENE	FEB	MAR	ABR	MAY	JUN	JUL	AGO	SEP	OCT	NOV	DIC	

Chihuahua   Chihuahua   *chee-WAH-wah*   331

JET CHART	WAC	SECTIONAL	LATITUDE	LONGITUDE	US TIME	FOR GMT ADD	ICAO IDENT	TOWN IDENT
JN-46	CH-23 No.	TPC H-23A	28°42'	106°00'	CST	6	MMCU	CUU

•TCA TO: 20,000'   RADIUS 50 n.mi.   HOURS
APPROACH 121.0   TOWER 118.3   GROUND 118.3
CITY 6 miles SW   POPULATION 350,000
LOCAL VorDme FREQ 114.1 WHERE Here HOURS 24
B'CAST FREQ 580   WHERE 8 mi SW   HOURS Daylight
FROM El Paso   FREQ 115.2   TRACK 162°, 184 n.mi.
FROM Mazatlán   FREQ 114.9   TRACK 353°, 340 n.mi.
FROM Marfa   FREQ 115.9   TRACK 216°, 146 n.mi.
FUEL 80, 100, JP   CARDS Visa,MC,etc   CASH? Yes
REPAIRS Major   TIEDOWN BYO ropes

HOTEL	RATE	WHERE	TEL
el Presidente	$$	Central	2-66-83
Tierra Blanca	$	Central	2-54-26
Hotel Fremont	$	Central	2-68-83

3600' Paved   8523' Paved

ELEVATION **4444'**

Capital of the state of the same name, Chihuahua is the nerve center of a recently emphasized concentration on farming and cattle.

READER REPORT Leo Lopez Sr., in a real sense the founder of aviation in Chihuahua established a memorial museum when his friend Charles Lindbergh passed away in the seventies. IT is located in the Leo Lopez FBO buildings. The Watsons, Texas

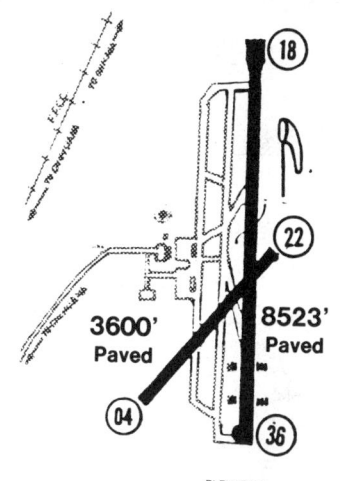

332

AGOSTO 30 DE 1978/137

RADIO	TORRE 118.9	ELEV. *3842'*	CD. JUAREZ, CHIH.
DIA y NOCHE		VAR. MAG. 11° E	
6603.0 y 131.0		CJS ▬▬ ▬ ▬	VOR/DME PISTA 03

Caution
For Information Only
Not for Aerial Navigation

8200'   6200'

5988' 5823'
270°
4085'   DME 114 CJS 116.7
4127' 240°
     028° 195° 8000'
        D-8   4029' 4022'
     208°
7000'

VOR/DME
10 M.N. DER. ←195°   8000'
6000' 028°→ 4540' (698')
ELEV. 3842'

FALLIDA: VIRE A LA **DERECHA** E INTERCEPTE EN ASCENSO EL **RADIAL 195°**, Y PROSIGA EN TRAYECTORIA DE APROXIMACION HASTA LA ALTITUD MINIMA DE ESPERA, DE ACUERDO CON INSTRUCCIONES DEL A.T.C.

CATEGORIA	DIRECTO PISTA 03 MDA 4540' (698')	CATEGORIA	CIRCULANDO MDA
A	1	A	4640' (798') - 1
B	1	B	4640' (798') - 1¼
C	2	C	4640' (798') - 2¼
D	2½	D	4640' (798') - 2¾

CAMBIOS: PROCEDIMIENTO NUEVO.   S.C.T.-D.G.A.C.   CJS VD-1

SUNRISE & SUNSET - GMT   SALIDA y PUESTA del SOL - GMT

15th of	JAN	FEB	MAR	APR	MAY	JUN	JUL	AUG	SEPT	OCT	NOV	DEC	
SUNRISE	1405	1347	1315	1237	1209	1200	1211	1230	1249	1308	1333	1358	SALIDA
SUNSET	2424	2452	0113	0134	0155	0212	0212	0149	0112	2434	2406	2403	PUESTA
15 de	ENE	FEB	MAR	ABR	MAY	JUN	JUL	AGO	SEP	OCT	NOV	DIC	

To get local time just subtract 'GMT ADD'
PARA OBTENER TIEMPO LOCAL SUSTRIAGA 'GMT ADD'

Ciudad Juárez Int'l — Chihuahua — *see-oo-DOD WHAR-ess* — 333

JET CHART	WAC	SECTIONAL	LATITUDE	LONGITUDE	US TIME	FOR GMT ADD	ICAO IDENT	TOWN IDENT
JN-46	CH-23 No.	El Paso	31°39'	106°27'	CST	6	MMCS	CJS

tca to 10,000'msl CENTER VorDme RADIUS 10mi
APPROACH -   TOWER 118.9   GROUND 118.9
CITY 5 miles NW   POPULATION 550,000
LOCAL Vor FREQ 116.7 WHERE here HOURS 24
B'CAST FREQ 800 WHERE 5 mi NE HOURS 24
FROM Chihuahua FREQ 114.1 TRACK 342°, 173 n.mi.
FROM El Paso FREQ 115.2 TRACK 203°, 15Dme
FROM Boquilla Dam FREQ Airport TRACK -, 337° 248n.mi.
FUEL 80, 100, JP CARDS Visa, MC, etc CASH? Yes
REPAIRS Minor TIEDOWN BYO ropes

HOTEL	RATE	WHERE	TEL
Camino Real	$$	Central	3-00-47
Rodeway Inn	$$	-	3-18-10

Today an important gateway between the two nations, it is variously known both as a wide-open town where anything can happen, and as a law abiding city where Texas Sunday school classes come for outings. As any place else, this city is pretty much what you make it.

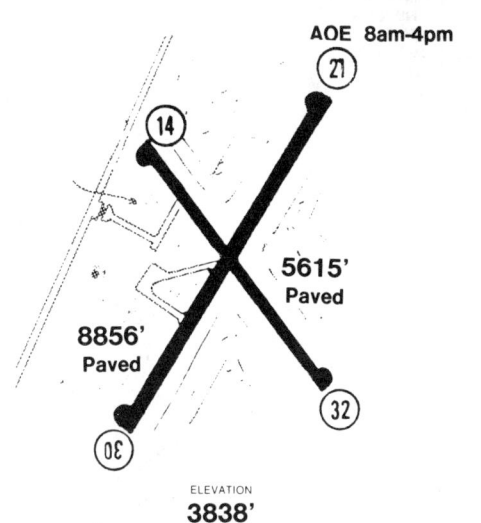

AOE 8am-4pm

8856' Paved
5615' Paved

ELEVATION 3838'

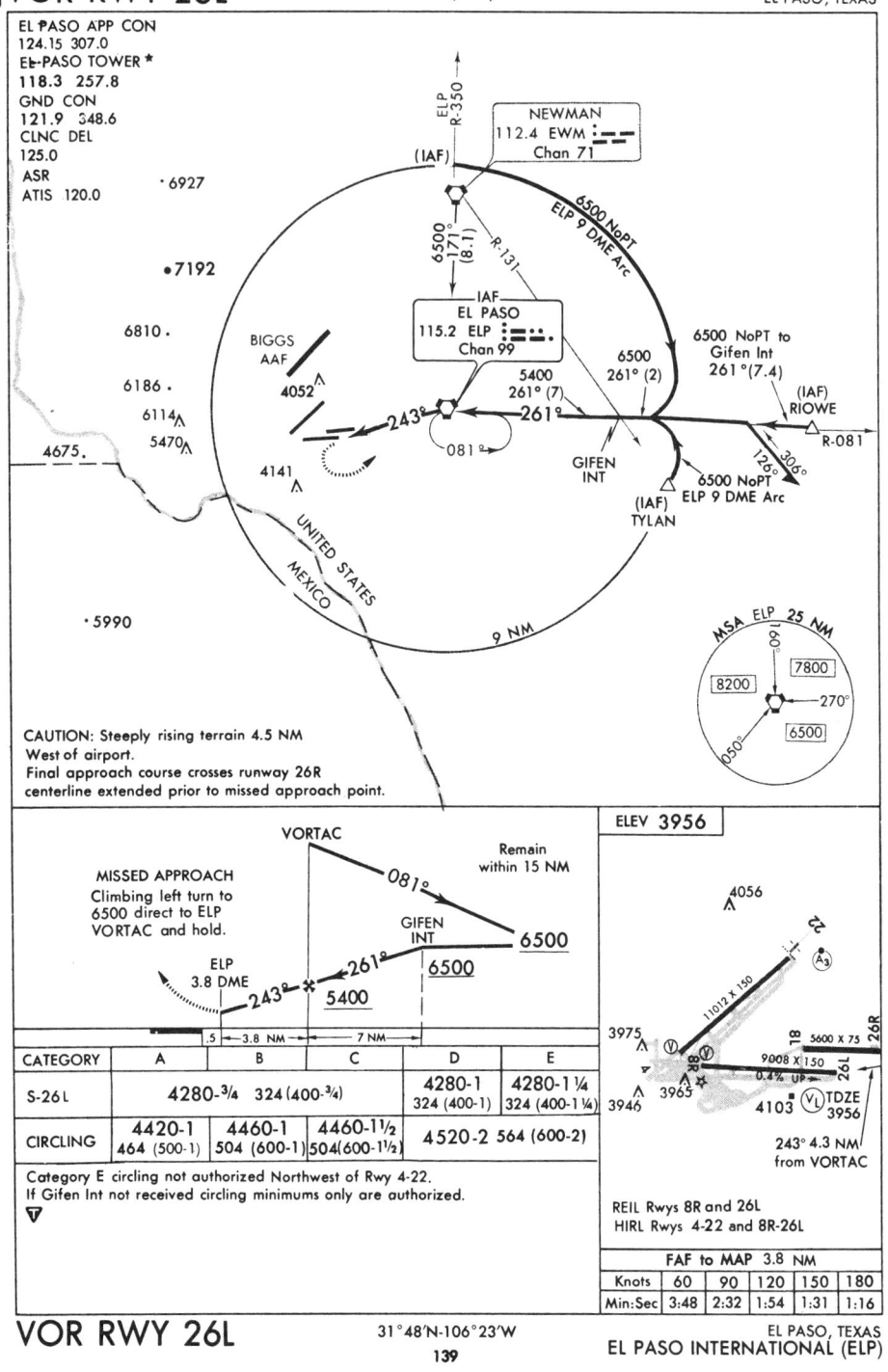

VOR RWY 26L — EL PASO INTERNATIONAL (ELP)
EL PASO, TEXAS

Amdt 27 · 334 · AL-134 (FAA)

EL PASO APP CON 124.15 307.0
EL PASO TOWER * 118.3 257.8
GND CON 121.9 348.6
CLNC DEL 125.0
ASR
ATIS 120.0

Plan View (depicted)

- NEWMAN 112.4 EWM Chan 71
- EL PASO 115.2 ELP Chan 99 (IAF)
- ELP R-350
- 6500 NoPT (ELP 9 DME Arc)
- 171° (8.1), R-131
- 243°
- 261° (2), 261° (7), 5400
- 6500 NoPT to Gifen Int 261° (7.4)
- RIOWE (IAF), R-081, 126°, 306°
- TYLAN (IAF), 6500 NoPT ELP 9 DME Arc
- GIFEN INT
- BIGGS AAF 4052
- 081°
- Spot elevations: 6927, 7192, 6810, 6186, 6114, 5470, 4675, 4141, 5990
- UNITED STATES / MEXICO, 9 NM

MSA ELP 25 NM: 8200 / 7800 / 6500 (270°) / (050°)

CAUTION: Steeply rising terrain 4.5 NM West of airport. Final approach course crosses runway 26R centerline extended prior to missed approach point.

Profile

MISSED APPROACH: Climbing left turn to 6500 direct to ELP VORTAC and hold.

VORTAC 081° — Remain within 15 NM — 6500
GIFEN INT 261° — 6500
243° — 5400
ELP 3.8 DME — .5 — 3.8 NM — 7 NM

Minimums

CATEGORY	A	B	C	D	E
S-26L	4280-¾ 324 (400-¾)			4280-1 324 (400-1)	4280-1¼ 324 (400-1¼)
CIRCLING	4420-1 464 (500-1)	4460-1 504 (600-1)	4460-1½ 504 (600-1½)	4520-2 564 (600-2)	

Category E circling not authorized Northwest of Rwy 4-22.
If Gifen Int not received circling minimums only are authorized.

Airport Diagram

ELEV 3956
Spot elevations: 4056, 3975, 3965, 3946, 4103
Runways: 11012 x 150, 9008 x 150, 5600 x 75
Runways 4/22, 8R/26L, 18/36
TDZE 3956
243° 4.3 NM from VORTAC
REIL Rwys 8R and 26L
HIRL Rwys 4-22 and 8R-26L

FAF to MAP 3.8 NM

Knots	60	90	120	150	180
Min:Sec	3:48	2:32	1:54	1:31	1:16

31°48'N–106°23'W

SUNRISE & SUNSET – GMT / SALIDA y PUESTA del SOL – GMT

15th of: JAN · FEB · MAR · APR · MAY · JUN · JUL · AUG · SEPT · OCT · NOV · DEC
SUNRISE: 1406 · 1347 · 1315 · 1236 · 1208 · 1159 · 1210 · 1230 · 1249 · 1308 · 1333 · 1358 SALIDA
SUNSET: 2424 · 2451 · 0113 · 0134 · 0155 · 0212 · 0212 · 0149 · 0111 · 2433 · 2406 · 2403 PUESTA
15° de: ENE · FEB · MAR · ABR · MAY · JUN · JUL · AGO · SEP · OCT · NOV · DIC

To get local time just subtract 'GMT ADD'
PARA OBTENER TIEMPO LOCAL SUSTRIAGA 'GMT ADD'

El Paso Texas

JET CHART	WAC	SECTIONAL	LATITUDE	LONGITUDE	US TIME	FOR GMT ADD	ICAO IDENT	TOWN IDENT
JN-46	CH-23 No.	El Paso	31°48'	106°23'	CST	6	KELP	ELP

APPROACH **119.7** TOWER **118.3** GROUND **121.9**
OTHER COMM **ATIS 120.0 Cpt 125.0, VOT 111.0**
CITY **W thru S** POPULATION **200,000**
LOCAL **VorDme** FREQ **115.2** WHERE **6 miles E** HOURS **24**
B'CAST FREQ **690** WHERE **8.3 mi NE** HOURS **24**
FROM **Cd Juárez** FREQ **116.7** TRACK **351°,11Dme**
FROM **Hermosillo** FREQ **112.8** TRACK **044°,294 n.mi.**
FROM **Chihuahua** FREQ **114.1** TRACK **343°,184 n.mi.**
FUEL **80, 100, JP** CARDS **Major** CASH? **Yes**
REPAIRS **Major** TIEDOWN **Yes**

HOTEL	RATE	WHERE	TEL
Rodeway Inn	$$	Nearby	Courtesy Car
Mesa Inn	$$	Nearby	Courtesy car
Howard Johnson	$$	Close	Courtesy car

READER REPORT Us country boys sure would like to see El Paso style service everyplace we go. Seems like anything we want is right close and they have it for you almost before you get the words out. D. Corlett, Colorado

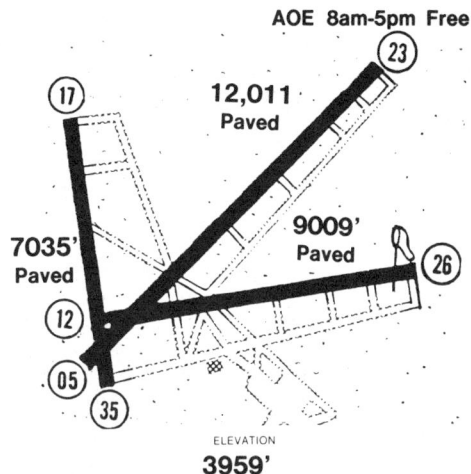

AOE 8am-5pm Free

12,011 Paved
9009' Paved
7035' Paved

ELEVATION
3959'

335

336 Nuevas Casas Grandes Chihuahua noo-EVV-uss COSS-uss GRON-dess

JET CHART	WAC	SECTIONAL	LATITUDE	LONGITUDE	US TIME	FOR GMT ADD	ICAO IDENT	TOWN IDENT
JN-46	CH-23 No. ADS-15	TPC H-23A	30°24'	107°53	CST	6	MMCG	CGS

OTHER COMM Traffic 118.1
CITY 3.5 miles E POPULATION 35,000
B'CAST FREQ 1010 WHERE 6.5 mi SW HOURS Daylight
FROM Cd Juárez FREQ 116.7 TRACK 211°,106n.mi.
FROM Chihuahua FREQ 114.1 TRACK 303°,140 n.mi.
FROM Nogales FREQ 108.2 TRACK 096°,166 n.mi.
FUEL Some 100 CARDS - CASH? Pesos
REPAIRS - TIEDOWN BYO

HOTEL	RATE	WHERE	TEL
Rodeway Inn	$$	N side	-

Ruins 4.5 miles south of town suggest a more northern limit to Aztec influence than had been previously confirmed. The architecture of adobe pyramids similar to the stone ones at Chichen-Itzá or Palenque, and a fine pottery found in the digs goes far beyond the pueblo indians of this area.

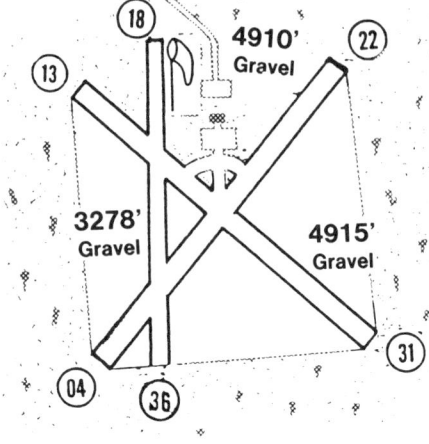

ELEVATION 4845'

THE BICKERTON 3-SPEED
...The finest folding bike made

Ready transportation you can tote in a bag...easy to asssemble and weighs only 23 pounds.

The Bickerton is ideal for the small plane pilot. Quick-action clamps allow for quick assembly without tools in just minutes. Chain requires no oil. This is a precision-made bicycle designed by a former Rolls Royce engineer. It will accommodate anyone up to 6' 5". All aluminum construction makes this the lightest folding bicycle in the world.

$388.00 plus shipping
California residents add 6% Sales Tax

DECKER PRODUCTS
P. O. Box 16992
Irvine, California 92714
(714) 770-8050

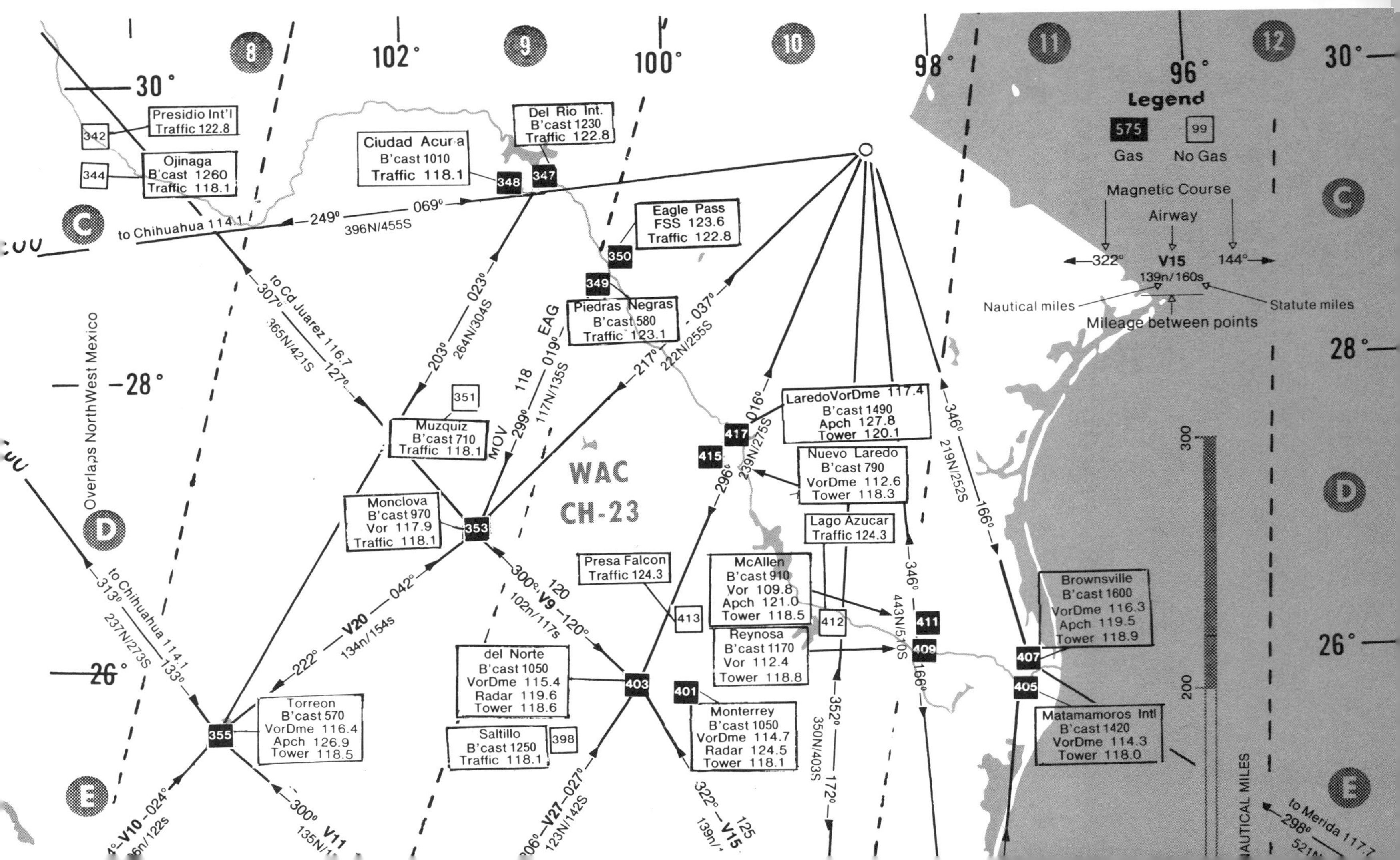

Legend
575 Gas
99 No Gas
Magnetic Course
Airway
322°
V15
144°
139n/160s
Nautical miles
Statute miles
Mileage between points
WAC CH-23
Overlaps NorthWest Mexico
Presidio Int'l Traffic 122.8
Ojinaga B'cast 1260 Traffic 118.1
Ciudad Acuña B'cast 1010 Traffic 118.1
Del Rio Int. B'cast 1230 Traffic 122.8
Eagle Pass FSS 123.6 Traffic 122.8
Piedras Negras B'cast 580 Traffic 123.1
Muzquiz B'cast 710 Traffic 118.1
Monclova B'cast 970 Vor 117.9 Traffic 118.1
LaredoVorDme 117.4 B'cast 1490 Apch 127.8 Tower 120.1
Nuevo Laredo B'cast 790 VorDme 112.6 Tower 118.3
Lago Azucar Traffic 124.3
Presa Falcon Traffic 124.3
McAllen B'cast 910 Vor 109.8 Apch 121.0 Tower 118.5
Reynosa B'cast 1170 Vor 112.4 Tower 118.8
del Norte B'cast 1050 VorDme 115.4 Radar 119.6 Tower 118.6
Saltillo B'cast 1250 Traffic 118.1
Monterrey B'cast 1050 VorDme 114.7 Radar 124.5 Tower 118.1
Torreon B'cast 570 VorDme 116.4 Apch 126.9 Tower 118.5
Brownsville B'cast 1600 VorDme 116.3 Apch 119.5 Tower 118.9
Matamamoros Intl B'cast 1420 VorDme 114.3 Tower 118.0
to Chihuahua 114.1
249° 069° 396N/455S
to Cd Juarez 116.7
307° 127° 365N/421S
203° 023° 264N/304S
EAG 019° 117N/135S
MOV 299° 118
217° 037° 222N/255S
016° 239N/275S
296°
346° 166° 219N/252S
346° 166° 443N/510S
352° 172° 350N/403S
300° V9 120° 120 102n/117s
222° V20 042° 134n/154s
to Chihuahua 114.1 313° 133° 237N/273S
V10 024°
300° V11 135N/
V27 027° 123N/142S
322° V15 125 139n/
to Merida 117.7 298° 521N
NAUTICAL MILES
300
200
30°
28°
26°
96°
98°
100°
102°

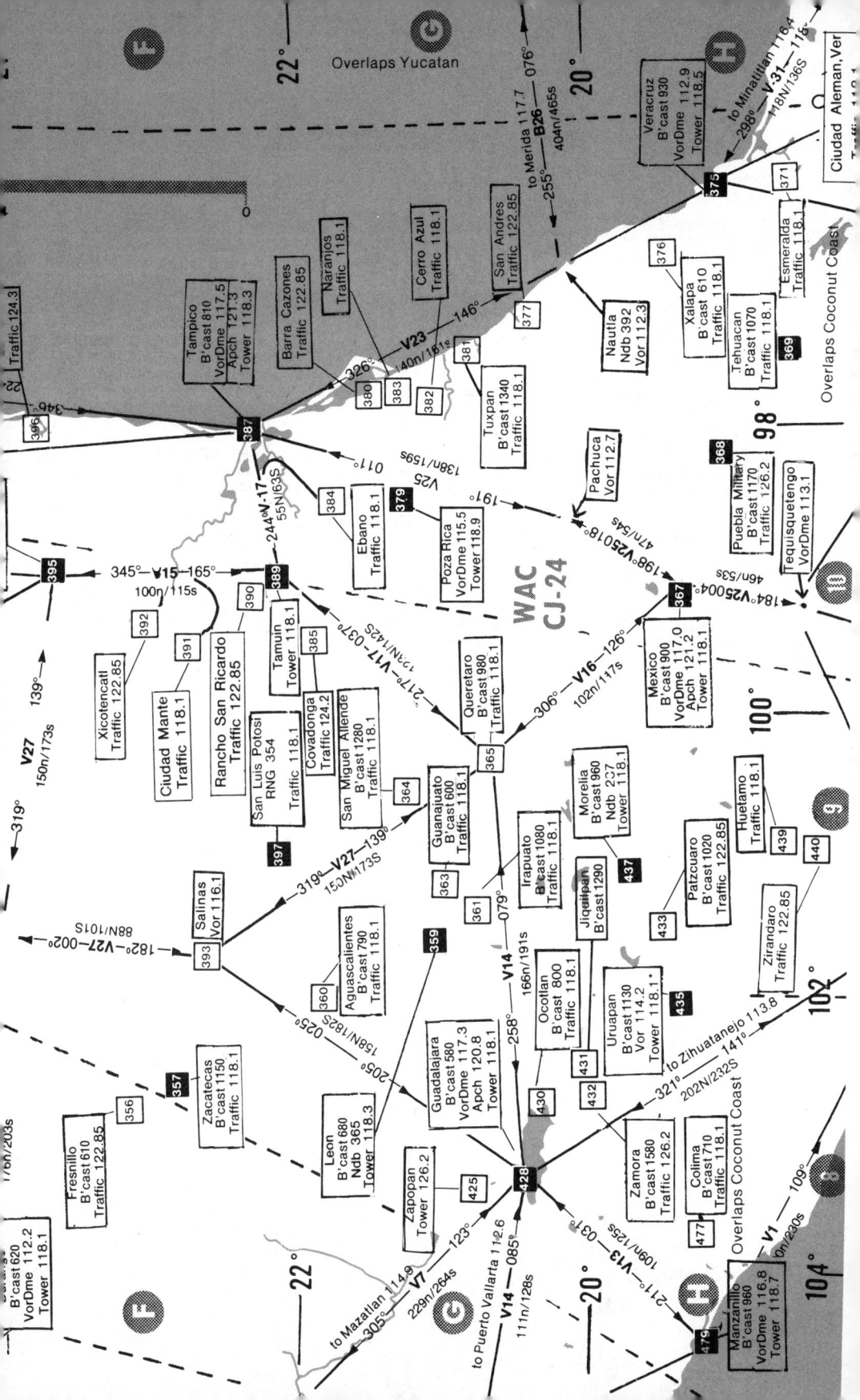

WAC CJ-24

Navigation Chart Data

Overlaps Yucatan

Veracruz B'cast 930, VorDme 112.9, Tower 118.5
to Minatitlan 116.4 — V31 — 115°
118N/136S
298° to Ciudad Aleman, Ver

B26 to Merida 117.7, 076°, 40n/46.5s, 255°

Naranjos Traffic 118.1
Cerro Azul Traffic 118.1
San Andres Traffic 122.85
Nautla Ndb 392, Vor 112.3
Xalapa B'cast 610, Traffic 118.1
Esmeralda Traffic 118.1
Tehuacan B'cast 1070, Traffic 118.1

Tampico B'cast 810, VorDme 117.5, Apch 121.2, Tower 118.3
Traffic 124.3
Barra Cazones Traffic 122.85
345° V15 — 346°
V23 146°
326° 140n/161s
380 383 382 377 381 376 375 371 369 368

Tuxpan B'cast 1340, Traffic 118.1
Pachuca Vor 112.7
Puebla Military B'cast 1170, VorDme 126.2
Tequisquetengo VorDme 113.1
198-V25-018° 47n/54s
184-V25-004° 46n/53s

Ebano Traffic 118.1
Poza Rica VorDme 115.5, Tower 118.9
384 379 367
011° V25 138n/159s
244-V-17 55N/63S
191°

Xicotencatl Traffic 122.85
Ciudad Mante Traffic 118.1
Rancho San Ricardo Traffic 122.85
Tamuin Traffic 118.1
Covadonga Traffic 124.2
San Miguel Allende B'cast 1280, Traffic 118.1
San Luis Potosi RNG 354, Traffic 118.1
Queretaro B'cast 980, Traffic 118.1
Mexico B'cast 900, VorDme 117.0, Apch 121.2, Tower 118.1

395 392 391 390 389 385 397 365
345° V15 165° 100n/115s
217° V17 037° 123N/142S
306° V16 126° 102n/117s

139° 319° V27 150n/173s

Guanajuato B'cast 600, Traffic 118.1
Irapuato B'cast 1080, Traffic 118.1
Morelia B'cast 960, Ndb 237, Tower 118.1
Huetamo Traffic 118.1
Patzcuaro B'cast 1020, Traffic 122.85
Jiquilpan B'cast 1290
Zirandaro Traffic 122.85

363 361 364 437 433 439 440
319° V27 139° 150N/173S
079°

Salinas Vor 116.1
Aguascalientes B'cast 790, Traffic 118.1
Ocotlan B'cast 800, Traffic 118.1
Uruapan B'cast 1130, Vor 114.2, Tower 118.1*
393 360 430 431 432 435
182°-V27-002° 88N/101S
258° V14 166n/191s
025° 205° 158N/182S
321° to Zihuatanejo 113.8, 141°, 202N/232S

Fresnillo Traffic 122.85
Zacatecas B'cast 1150, Traffic 118.1
Leon B'cast 680, Ndb 365, Tower 118.3
Zapopan Tower 126.2
Guadalajara B'cast 580, VorDme 117.3, Apch 120.8, Tower 118.1
Zamora B'cast 1580, Traffic 126.2
Colima B'cast 710, Traffic 118.1

357 356 425 428 477
176n/203s
B'cast 620 VorDme 112.2, Tower 118.1
Manzanillo B'cast 960, VorDme 116.8, Tower 118.7
479
109° V1 0n/230s
217° V13 109° 123S
031°
123° 085° V14 111n/128s
to Mazatlan 114.9, 305°, 229n/264s
to Puerto Vallarta 112.6
V7
Overlaps Coconut Coast

Northeast Index

Sequence:
Place, Ident, Page

Allende, San Miguel, SMA, 364
Aquascalientes, AGS, 360

Barra Cazones, CAZ-, 380
Brownsville IFR, BRO, 406
Brownsville Int'l, BRO, 407

Celaya, CYA, 362
Cerro Azul, CER-, 382
Ciudad Acuna Int'l, CAC, 348
Ciudad Aleman, ALM-, 372
Ciudad Mante, CDM, 391
Ciudad Victoria, CVM, 395
Ciudad Victoria IFR, CVM, 394
Covadonga, OVA-, 385

Del Rio IFR, DRT, 346
Del Rio Int'l, DRT, 347

Eagle Pass Int'l, EPS, 350
Ebano, EBN-, 384
Esmeralda, ESM-, 371

Guanajuato, GTO, 363

Irapuato, IPO, 361
Isla, Veracruz, ILA-, 370

La Pesca, PSA-, 396
Lago Azucar, AZU-, 412
Laredo IFR, LRD, 416
Laredo Int'l, LRD, 417

Leon, LEO, 359
Leon IFR, LEO, 358

Matamoros Int'l, MAM, 405
Matamoros IFR, MAM, 404
McAllen IFR, MFE, 410
McAllen Int'l, MFE, 411
Mexico City, MEX, 367
Mexico IFR, MEX, 366
Monclova, MOV, 353
Monclova IFR, MOV, 352
Monterrey, MTY, 401
Monterrey IFR, MTY, 400
Monterrey del Norte, ADN, 403
Monterrey del Norte IFR, ADN, 402
Muzquiz, MUZ-, 351

Naranjos, NAR-, 383
Northeast Area Chart, 338
Northeast Area, intro, 341
Northeast Index, 340
Nuevo Laredo IFR, NLD, 414
Nuevo Laredo Int'l, NLD, 415

Ojinaga, OJA, 344

Piedras Negras Int'l, PNG, 349
Poza Rica, PZA, 379
Poza Rica IFR, PZA, 378
Presa Falcon, LCN-, 413
Presidio IFR, DIO, 343

Presidio, TX Int'l, DIO-, 342
Puebla, PEB, 368

Queretero, QET, 365

Rancho Aleman, ALM-, 345
Rancho San Ricardo, SRC, 390
Reynosa IFR, REX, 408
Reynosa Int'l, REX, 409

Salinas, SNS, 393
Saltillo, IYO, 398
San Andreas, 377
San Luis Potosi, SLP, 397
San Miguel Allende, SMA, 364

Tampico, TAM, 387
Tampico IFR, TAM, 386
Tamuin, TMN, 389
Tamuin IFR, TMN, 388
Tehuacan, TCN, 369
Torreon, TRC, 355
Torreon IFR, TCR, 354
Tuxpan, TUX, 381

Veracruz, VER, 375
Veracruz IFR, VER, 374

Xalapa, JAL, 376
Xicotencatl, XIC, 392

Zacatecas, ZAC, 357

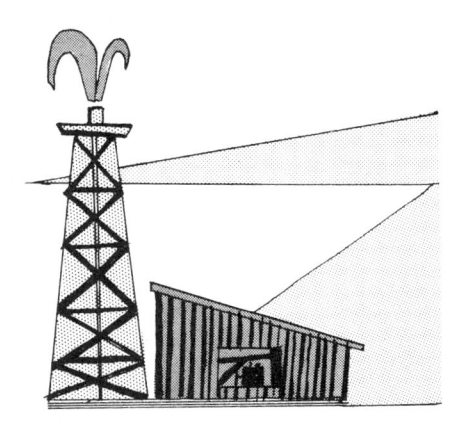

Northwest Briefing

Area includes: East half of Mexico from northern border to the capital.
Best known for: Mexico City megapolis, Tampico's old oil country, cattle spreads around Torreon.
Also has: Beer capital Monterrey, coffee city Xalapa, colonial Guanajuato, steel city San Luis Potosi.
Altitudes: from tropical sea level to Popocatapetl (Popo) and Iztaccihuatl (called Izzy) volcanoes SE of the capital just under 18.000'.
Climate: everything from the windy north plains to tropical warm to snow in the mountains around the capital.
Special note: Mexico City's smog level pushes the big airport into IFR conditions daily by about 9 am. Full radar and transponder environment at all times.
Shopping: Mexico City, with its 12,000,000+ population is a shopper's paradise. It is usually called simply 'Mexico' to note its being a cross section of the entire Republic. You will find virtually everything made anyplace in the country is available here, somewhere. Everything.
Must see: The capital's fantastic archeological museum in Chapultapec Park, Veracruz' historical port, coffee growing in Xalapa -it is impossible to miss once you are there- vast silver mines in Zacatecas, San Miguel Allende's art just about anyplace in town.
Remarks: Fast growing Mexico is in the running for largest city in the world. Over two hundred indian groups meld together to make one nation. There is a curious mixture of differing ways, looks, and costume which makes visiting any place a continuing delight no matter where or how often.
Ace-in-the-hole: Suggest using IFR cautiously; aside from the capital itself controllers may not be accustomed to heavy traffic.

NDB-A
Orig

AL-6548 (FAA)

PRESIDIO LELY INTL
PRESIDIO, TEXAS

ALBUQUERQUE CENTER
132.55 343.6

MARFA
115.9 MRF

5179

7300
197°
(45.3)

5315

4951

IAF
PRESIDIO
251 PRS

104°

284°   059°
       239°
       104°

3573

10 NM

UNITED STATES
MEXICO

CAUTION: Steeply rising terrain all quadrants.

• 6263

MIN SAFE ALT 25 NM 8800

ELEV 2932

MISSED APPROACH
Climbing right turn to 5900
in PRS NDB holding pattern.

NDB

Remain within 10 NM

104°

5900

284°

CATEGORY	A	B	C	D
CIRCLING		4440-3	1508 (1600-3)		NA

Use Marfa, TX altimeter setting.
▽
△ NA

LIRL Rwy 17-35

4500 X 75

17

35

284°
to NDB

Knots	60	90	120	150	180
Min:Sec					

NDB-A   29°38'N-104°22'W

PRESIDIO, TEXAS
PRESIDIO LELY INTL

Presidio, Texas — A new international airport — 343

OTHER COMM Traffic 122.8
AOE? Airport of Entry   HOURS 0830-1700   NOTICE 1 Hr
CITY 1 mile South   POPULATION est 4,500
NDB FREQ 251   WHERE Here   HOURS 24
FROM Chihuahua   FREQ 114.1   TRACK 048°97.1Dme
FROM Marfa   FREQ 115.9   TRACK 198°,43.3Dme
FROM Cd.Juarez   FREQ 116.7   TRACK 125°,162n.mi.
AVIATION GAS ·   CARDS? ·   TYPE CASH ·
REPAIRS AVAILABLE Some   TIEDOWNS? BYO ropes

Having this fuel-equipped international airport near to Texas' Big Bend is a right handy combination. The only fly in the ointment right now is the **One Hour Prior Notice** required to enter the U.S. here. That means one hour before entering U.S. Airspace. Mostly you'd be best off calling from your hotel the morning of the day you'll be coming in. Use the numbers in the Customs Guide For Private Flyers, reprinted toward the front of this book.

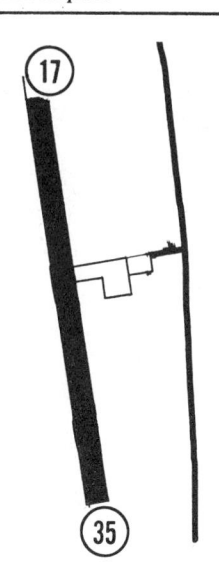

344   Ojinaga   Chihuahua   *oh-he-NOGG-ah kwa-WHEE-lah*

OTHER COMM Traffic 118.1
CITY Adjacent NW
B'cast 1340
FROM Chihuahua   FREQ 114.1
FROM Marfa   FREQ 115.9
AVIATION GAS ·
REPAIRS AVAILABLE Some

POPULATION est 45,000
WHERE 2 mi N HOURS Daylight
TRACK 050°, 92.4 Dme
TRACK 198°, 49.0 Dme
CREDIT CARDS ·
CASH TYPE ·
TIEDOWNS? BYO

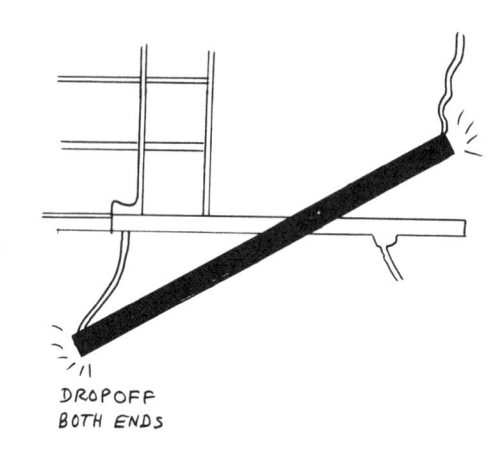

DROPOFF BOTH ENDS

Rancho Alemán Chihuahua *ah-lay-MONN* 345

JET CHART	WAC	SECTIONAL	LATITUDE	LONGITUDE	US TIME	FOR GMT ADD	ICAO IDENT	TOWN IDENT
JN-46	CH-23 So.	TPC H-23D	27°29'	104°42'	CST	6	-	-ALM-

OTHER COMM Traffic 118.1
SETTLEMENT Isolated   POPULATION –
FROM Chihuahua FREQ 114.1 TRACK 125°, 103 n.mi.
FROM Torreón FREQ 116.4 TRACK 318°, 135 n.mi.
FUEL –   CARDS –   CASH? –
REPAIRS –   TIEDOWN BYO

5286' Paved

ELEVATION
4658'

Personal ranch of Miguel Alemán, the ex-president who is working even harder since retirement. He is responsible for the effective tourism programs which have in the past twenty years helped the country and its foreign exchange. Somehow he doesn't look any different today than in those nineteen forties and fifties photographs. Amazing man.

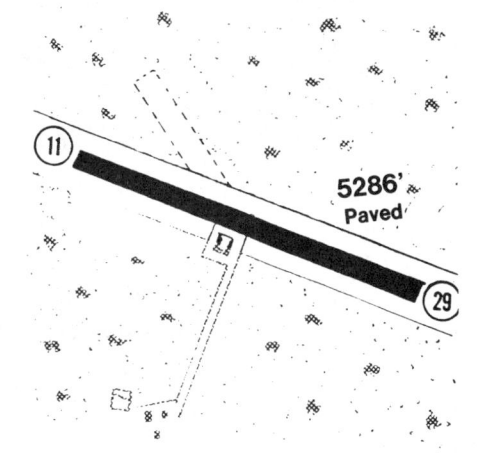

VOR-A — DEL RIO INTERNATIONAL, DEL RIO, TEXAS

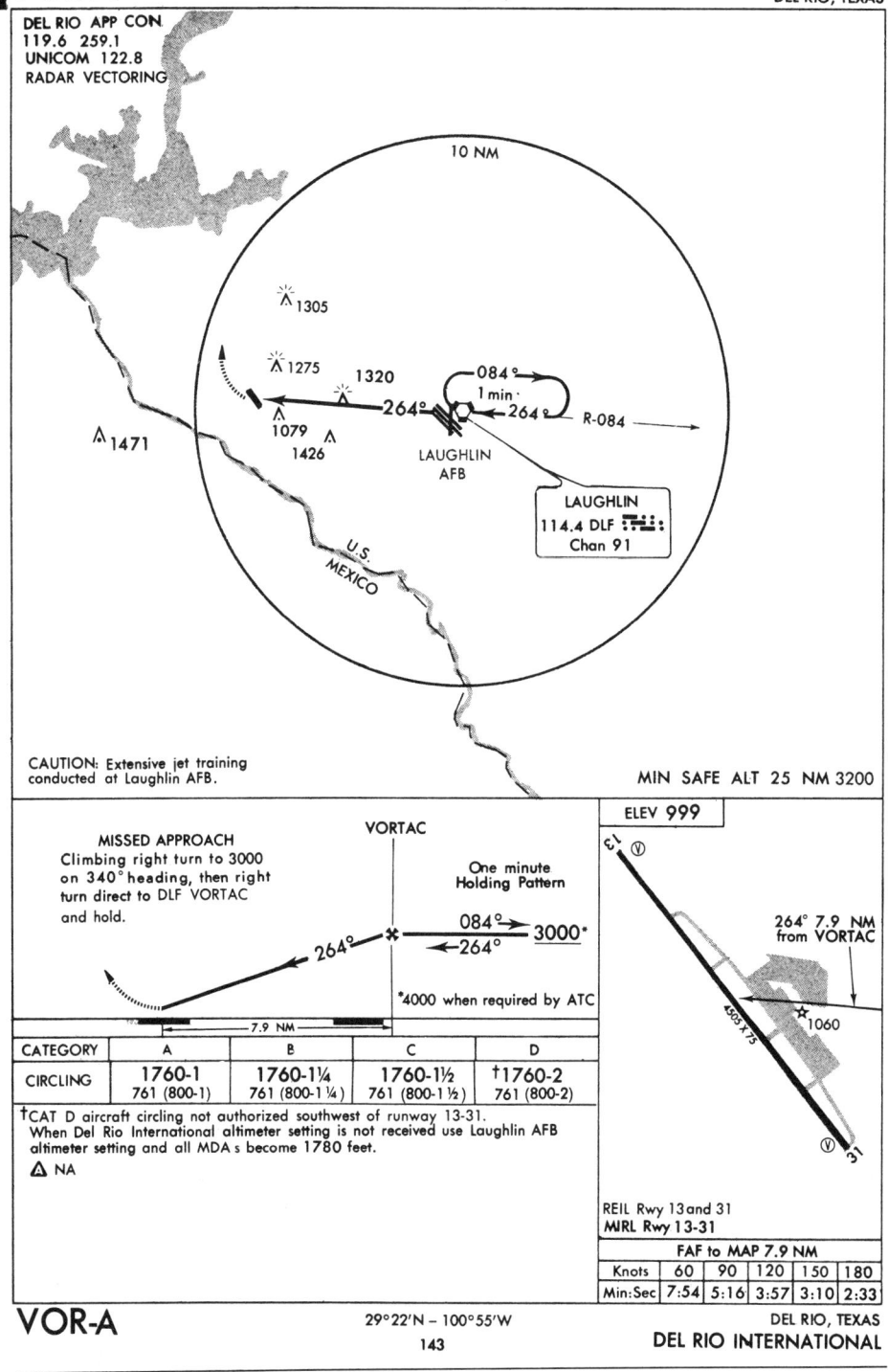

Amdt 8 | 112 | AL-5268 (FAA)

DEL RIO APP CON 119.6 259.1
UNICOM 122.8
RADAR VECTORING

Holding: 084°/264°, 1 min, at LAUGHLIN VORTAC
R-084

LAUGHLIN 114.4 DLF Chan 91

CAUTION: Extensive jet training conducted at Laughlin AFB.

MIN SAFE ALT 25 NM 3200

MISSED APPROACH: Climbing right turn to 3000 on 340° heading, then right turn direct to DLF VORTAC and hold.

One minute Holding Pattern: 084° → 3000* ← 264°

*4000 when required by ATC

7.9 NM

ELEV 999
264° 7.9 NM from VORTAC
4305 X 75
1060

CATEGORY	A	B	C	D
CIRCLING	1760-1 761 (800-1)	1760-1¼ 761 (800-1¼)	1760-1½ 761 (800-1½)	†1760-2 761 (800-2)

†CAT D aircraft circling not authorized southwest of runway 13-31.
When Del Rio International altimeter setting is not received use Laughlin AFB altimeter setting and all MDAs become 1780 feet.
⚠ NA

REIL Rwy 13 and 31
MIRL Rwy 13-31

FAF to MAP 7.9 NM

Knots	60	90	120	150	180
Min:Sec	7:54	5:16	3:57	3:10	2:33

29°22'N – 100°55'W

SUNRISE & SUNSET – GMT / SALIDA y PUESTA del SOL – GMT

15th of	JAN	FEB	MAR	APR	MAY	JUN	JUL	AUG	SEPT	OCT	NOV	DEC
SUNRISE	1339	1322	1253	1217	1151	1143	1154	1211	1228	1245	1307	1330
SUNSET	2407	2432	2451	0110	0128	0144	0145	0124	2449	2413	2348	2347
15º de	ENE	FEB	MAR	ABR	MAY	JUN	JUL	AGO	SEP	OCT	NOV	DIC

To get local time just subtract 'GMT ADD'
PARA OBTENER TIEMPO LOCAL SUSTRIAGA 'GMT ADD'

Del Rio International — Texas — *dell REE-yoe* — 347

JET CHART	WAC	SECTIONAL	LATITUDE	LONGITUDE	US TIME	FOR GMT ADD	ICAO IDENT	TOWN IDENT
JN-46	CH-23 No.	TPC H-23A	29°22'	100°56'	CST	6	-	DRT

OTHER COMM Unicom 122.8
CITY 1 mile SE **POPULATION** 27,000
LOCAL VorDme **FREQ** 114.4 **WHERE** 8 miles E **HOURS** 24
B'CAST FREQ 1230 **WHERE** - **HOURS** Daylight
FROM P. Negras **FREQ** Airport **TRACK** -,326° 49 n.mi.
FROM Chihuahua **FREQ** 114.1 **TRACK** 070°, 262 n.mi.
FROM Torreón **FREQ** 116.4 **TRACK** 018°, 264 n.mi.
FUEL 80, 100 **CARDS** Major **CASH?** Yes
REPAIRS Major **TIEDOWN** BYO ropes

AOE 8am-5pm Free

HOTEL	RATE	WHERE	TEL
Holiday Inn	$$	1.5 mi NW	775-7591
La Siesta	$	Free trans	775-3521

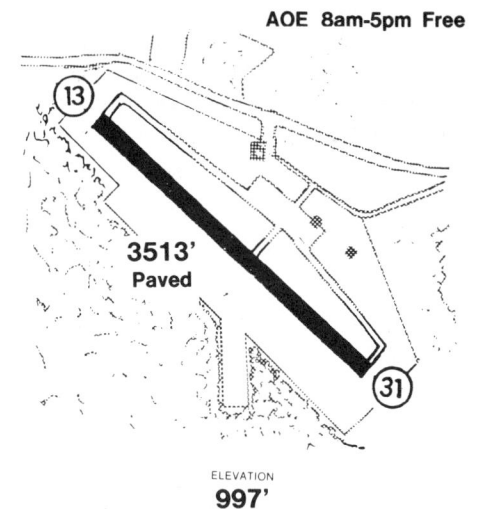

3513' Paved

ELEVATION **997'**

348   Cd. Acuña Int'l   Coahuila   *ah-COON-yah*

JET CHART	WAC	SECTIONAL	LATITUDE	LONGITUDE	US TIME	FOR GMT ADD	ICAO IDENT	TOWN IDENT
JN-46	CH-23 No.	San Antonio	29°20'	100°59'	CST	6	-	CAC

AOE 9am-4pm

OTHER COMM   Traffic 118.1-
CITY   1 mile SE
B'CAST FREQ **1010**   WHERE **2.5 mi SW**   POPULATION **19,000**   HOURS **Daylight**
FROM   Laughlin   FREQ **114.4**   TRACK **250°,10Dme**
FROM   Junction   FREQ **116.0**   TRACK **209°,98n.mi.**
FROM   Sabinas   FREQ **610**   TRACK **356°,89n.mi.**
FUEL   80 often   CARDS   -   CASH? Pesos
REPAIRS   Minor   TIEDOWN BYO

5545' Paving

Almost a hideout among the internacional airports: no one realizes they can clear into and out of México here. Let's just keep it to ourselves so you and I can clear faster here than at the heavily trafficked airports.

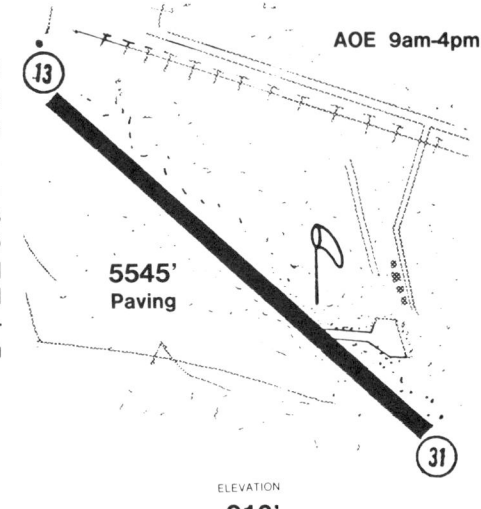

ELEVATION
913'

Piedras Negras Internacional   Coahuila   pee-EDD-russ NEGG-russ   349

JET CHART	WAC	SECTIONAL	LATITUDE	LONGITUDE	US TIME	FOR GMT ADD	ICAO IDENT	TOWN IDENT
JN-46	CH-23 No.	San Antonio	28°37'	100°32'	CST	6	MMPG	PNG

OTHER COMM Radio 123.1-
CITY 4 miles NE   POPULATION 51,000
B'CAST FREQ 580   WHERE 5 mi NNE   HOURS Daylight
FROM Cotulla   FREQ 115.8   TRACK 268°, 76Dme
FROM San Antonio FREQ 116.8   TRACK 232°, 126 n.mi.
FROM Monclova   FREQ 117.9   TRACK 017°, 113n.mi.
FUEL 80, 100   CARDS Visa,M   CASH? Yes
REPAIRS Minor   TIEDOWN BYO

HOTEL	RATE	WHERE	TEL
Autel Rio	$	Central	2-01-80
Motel 57	$	South side	2-12-20

AOE 9am-4pm

5303' Paved

ELEVATION
971'

Opposite Eagle Pass, this new oil town will boom along even bigger as the energy crunch grows. Made more popular as a city by the good highway to México City, as an airport of entry you will find it straight forward and efficient.

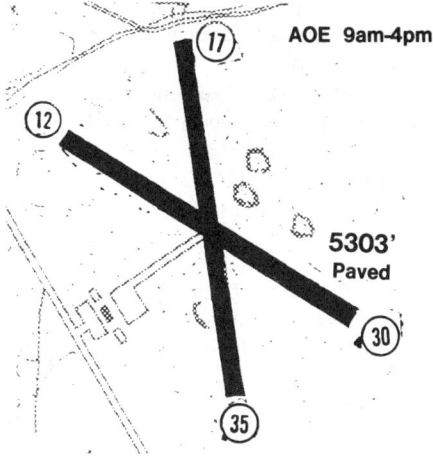

350 Eagle Pass Int'l Texas

JET CHART	WAC	SECTIONAL	LATITUDE	LONGITUDE	US TIME	FOR GMT ADD	ICAO IDENT	TOWN IDENT
JN-46	CH-23 No.	TPC H-23B	28°42'	100°29'	CST	6	-	EPS

OTHER COMM FSS 123.6 Unicom 122.8
CITY Adjacent W POPULATION 35,000
LOCAL B'cast FREQ 1270 WHERE 1 mile No. HOURS Days
FROM P. Negras FREQ Airport TRACK 025°5.5n.mi.,
FROM Monclova FREQ 117.9 TRACK 020,118n.mi.
FROM del Norte FREQ 115.4 TRACK 345°,170n.mi.
FUEL 80,100 CARDS Major CASH? Yes
REPAIRS Yes TIEDOWN Yes
Several motels.
Call FSS with a Customs ETA a good half hour before landing, an hour is even better. Use Unicom for backup if you can't get through to Fuss.

READER REPORT This is a hometown airport at its best. You are not overwhelmed with bizjets or other heavy iron in hte pattern. Downtown is just a short walk away. We like it. A. Morgan, Oklahoma

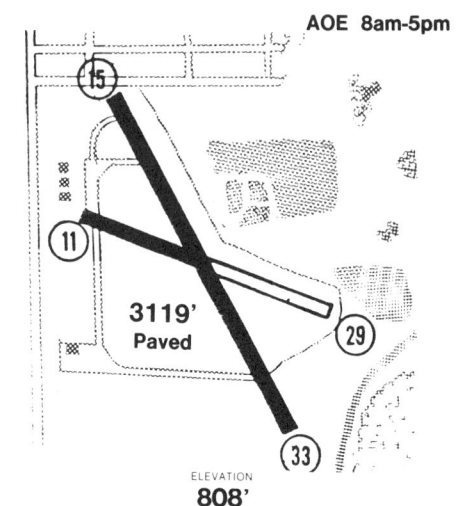

AOE 8am-5pm

3119' Paved

ELEVATION
808'

Muzquiz Coahuila *MOOSE-keece* 351

JET CHART	WAC	SECTIONAL	LATITUDE	LONGITUDE	US TIME	FOR GMT ADD	ICAO IDENT	TOWN IDENT
JN-46	CH-23 No.	TPC H-23C	27°50'	101°31'	CST	6	-	-MUZ-

OTHER COMM Traffic 118.1
CITY 2 miles N
B'CAST FREQ 710   WHERE 7 mi SE
POPULATION 13,000
HOURS Daylight
FROM P. Negras   FREQ -   TRACK 219°, 71 n.mi.
FROM Monclova   FREQ 117.9   TRACK 346°, 54 n.mi.
FROM Torreón   FREQ 116.4   TRACK 027°, 171 n.mi.
FUEL Some 80   CARDS -   CASH? Pesos
REPAIRS Minor   TIEDOWN BYO

HOTEL	RATE	WHERE	TEL
Motel Chulavista	$	Central	11-20
Hotel Gil Cantú	$	Central	13-30

One you never hear about since so few tourists visit here. Smallish city but very interesting for the old world charm.

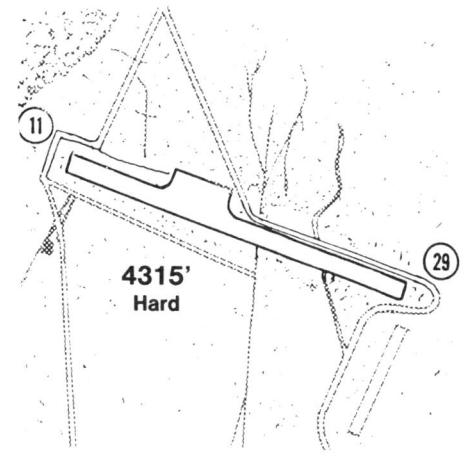

4315'
Hard

ELEVATION
1314'

352

RADIO	TWR

JULIO 9-1981/158

ELEV. *1850'*
VAR. MAG. 9° E

MOV ≡≡ −

MONCLOVA, COAH.

VOR PISTA 24

Caution For Information Only Not for Aerial Navigation

7000'

MOV 117.9

6000'

8600'

VOR 6000' — 058° — 4000' 10 M.N. IZQ
238°
2360' (510')
ELEV 1850'

FALLIDA: VIRE A LA **DERECHA** E INTERCEPTE EN ASCENSO EL **RADIAL 058°**, Y PROSIGA EN TRAYECTORIA DE APROXIMACION HASTA LA ALTITUD MINIMA DE ESPERA, O PARA ABANDONAR LA ESTACION.

CATEGORIA	DIRECTO PISTA 24 MDA 2360' (510')	CATEGORIA	CIRCULANDO MDA
A	1 (1600 M)	A	2660' (810') - 1 (1600 M)
B		B	
C	N. A.	C	N. A.
D		D	

CAMBIOS: DETALLES MENORES y VIS   SCT-DGAC-SENEAM   MOV-V-1

SUNRISE & SUNSET − GMT   SALIDA y PUESTA del SOL − GMT

15th of	JAN	FEB	MAR	APR	MAY	JUN	JUL	AUG	SEPT	OCT	NOV	DEC	
SUNRISE	1336	1322	1255	1221	1157	1151	1201	1217	1231	1245	1305	1327	SALIDA
SUNSET	2414	2437	2454	0109	0126	0141	0142	0123	2450	2417	2355	2354	PUESTA
15° de	ENE	FEB	MAR	ABR	MAY	JUN	JUL	AGO	SEP	OCT	NOV	DIC	

To get local time just subtract 'GMT ADD'
PARA OBTENER TIEMPO LOCAL SUSTRIAGA 'GMT ADD'

Monclova   Coahuila   *moan-CLO-vah*   **353**

JET CHART	WAC	SECTIONAL	LATITUDE	LONGITUDE	US TIME	FOR GMT ADD	ICAO IDENT	TOWN IDENT
JN-46	CH-23 So.	Bro'ville	26°57'	101°28'	ST	6	MMMV	MOV

OTHER COMM Traffic 118.1
CITY 2 miles S   POPULATION 113,000
LOCAL Vor   FREQ 117.9   WHERE Here   HOURS 24
B'CAST FREQ 970 WHERE 1 mi So.   HOURS Daylight
FROM N. Laredo   FREQ 112.6   TRACK 246°, 105 n.mi.
FROM P.Negras FREQ B'cast TRACK 920, 016° 113 n.mi.
FROM Torreón   FREQ 116.4   TRACK 042°, 134 n.mi.
FUEL 80, 100   CARDS Visa, M, etc   CASH? Pesos
REPAIRS Minor   TIEDOWN BYO

HOTEL	RATE	WHERE	TEL
Gil Cantú	$	On plaza	3-04-11
Chulavista			
Monclova	$$	N side	3-02-11

This was the capital of the State of Coahuila (kwah-WHEE-lah) when one of the north counties was what we now call Texas. Principle steel mills produce a significant percentage of the country's needs. Tours easily arranged.

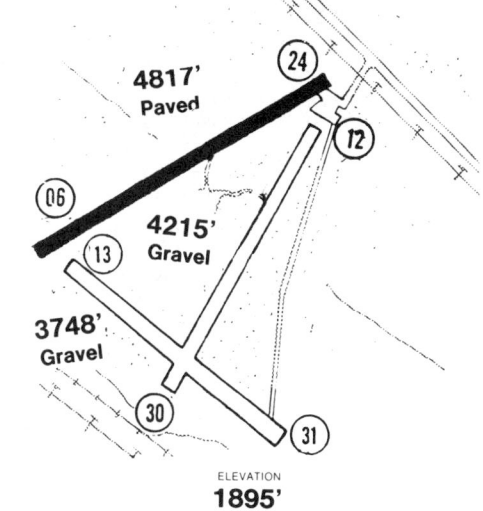

Runways: 4817' Paved (24/06), 4215' Gravel (12/30), 3748' Gravel (13/31)

ELEVATION **1895'**

354

RADIO	TWR	ELEV **3707'**	**TORREON, COAH.**
AMSA **123.0**	**118.5**	VAR. MAG 9° E TRC ≡·−·	**VOR PISTA 30**

**Caution
For Information Only
Not for Aerial Navigation**

7300'
11300'
9900'
12300'

DME TRC 116.4

5313'
5169'
4532'
5372'
5641'
5352'
6402'
5208'

ELEV 3707'

VOR 8000' — 122° — 6000' IZQ. 10 M.N.
302°
4140' (433')

FALLIDA: ASCIENDA EN RADIAL 307° CON VIRAJE DE PROCEDIMIENTO A LA DERECHA DENTRO DE 10 M.N. HASTA LA ALTITUD MINIMA DE ESPERA.

CATEGORIA	DIRECTO PISTA 30 MDA 4140' (433')	CATEGORIA	CIRCULANDO MDA
A	1 (1600 M)	A	4140' (433') - 1 (1600 M)
B	1 (1600 M)	B	4380' (673') - 1 (1600 M)
C	1¼ (2000 M)	C	4380' (673') - 2 (3200 M)
D	1½ (2400 M)	D	4400' (693') - 2¼ (3600 M)

CAMBIOS VIS y DETALLES MENORES   SCT – DGAC – SENEAM   TRC-V-2

SUNRISE & SUNSET – GMT   SALIDA y PUESTA del SOL – GMT

15th of JAN FEB MAR APR MAY JUN JUL AUG SEPT OCT NOV DEC
SUNRISE 1341 1328 1302 1230 1208 1202 1212 1226 1239 1252 1311 1332 SALIDA
SUNSET 2424 2447 0102 0116 0131 0145 0147 0129 2458 2426 2405 2405 PUESTA
15° de ENE FEB MAR ABR MAY JUN JUL AGO SEP OCT NOV DIC

To get local time just subtract 'GMT ADD'
PARA OBTENER TIEMPO LOCAL SUSTRIAGA 'GMT ADD'

Torreón Chihuahua   *tore-ee-YOAN*   **355**

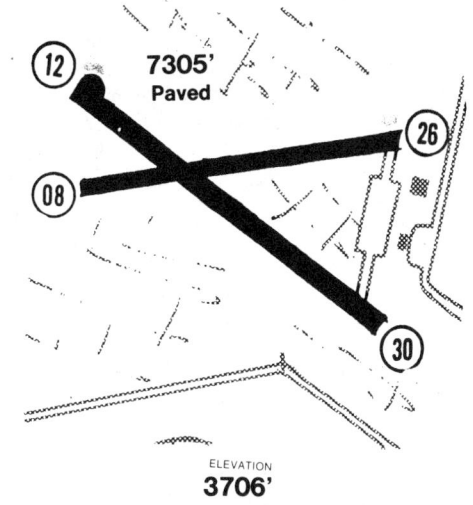

JET CHART	WAC	SECTIONAL	LATITUDE	LONGITUDE	US TIME	FOR GMT ADD	ICAO IDENT	TOWN IDENT
JN-46	CH-23 So.	TPC H-23D	25°34'	103°25'	CST	6	MMTC	TRC

tca to: **8,000'msl** CENTER AT **VorDme** RADIUS **10 mi.**
APPROACH **126.9** TOWER **118.5** GROUND **118.5**
CITY **3 miles SW** POPULATION **89,000**
LOCAL **VorDme** FREQ **116.4** WHERE **here** HOURS **24**
B'CAST FREQ **570** WHERE **6 mi NE** HOURS **Daylight**
FROM **Monclova** FREQ **117.9** TRACK **222°, 134 n.mi.**
FROM **Chihuahua** FREQ **114.1** TRACK **131°, 224** n.mi.
FROM **Durango** FREQ **112.2** TRACK **024°, 106** n.mi.
FUEL **80, 100, JP** CARDS **Visa, MC, etc** CASH? **Pesos**
REPAIRS **Some** TIEDOWN **BYO**

HOTEL	RATE	WHERE	TEL
Palacio Real	$$	On Plaza	6-00-00
Calvete	$	Central	6-10-10
Paraiso	$$	Central	6-11-22

A city which isn't that forward about tootling its own whistle, you need to dig a bit to discover the city is big in wheat, cotton, grapes and wine, copper, lead, mercury, and of course ore reduction.

7305' Paved

ELEVATION
3706'

356 Fresnillo   Zacatecas   *fress-NEE-yoe*

JET CHART	WAC	SECTIONAL	LATITUDE	LONGITUDE	US TIME	FOR GMT ADD	ICAO IDENT	TOWN IDENT
JN-46	CJ-24 No.	TPC J-24B	23°10'	102°50'	ST	6	-	FRS

OTHER COMM   Traffic 122.85
CITY   6 miles N   POPULATION 45,000
LOCAL   Ndb FREQ 392/1698 WHERE here HOURS on request
B'CAST FREQ 610   WHERE 4.2 mi NW   HOURS Daylight
FROM   Concepción Oro FREQ 117.1 TRACK 222°, 95 n.mi.
FROM   Durango   FREQ 112.2   TRACK 109°, 109 n.mi.
FROM   Guadalajara   FREQ 117.3   TRACK 001°, 161 n.mi.
FUEL -   CARDS -   CASH? -
REPAIRS -   TIEDOWN BYO

     Several local hotels in the city
     This airport is well isolated, arrange your transportation ahead or hope the airport watchman's car is running this time. Hot springs in town are mentioned by town boosters. I haven't been able to get off the airport to check them out.

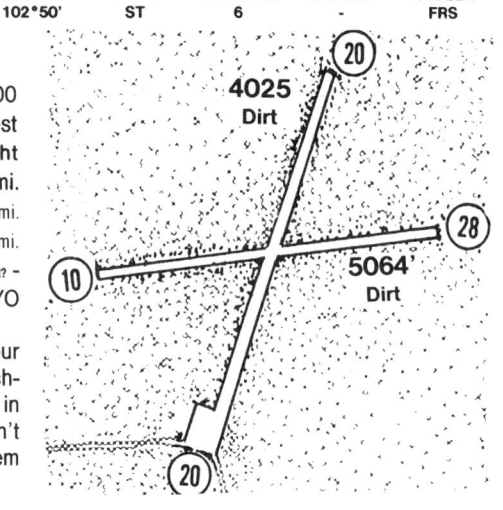

ELEVATION
7010'

Zacatecas   Zacatecas   sock-ah-TAKE-uss   357

JET CHART	WAC	SECTIONAL	LATITUDE	LONGITUDE	US TIME	FOR GMT ADD	ICAO IDENT	TOWN IDENT
JN-46	CJ-24 No.	TPC J-24A	22°54'	102°41'	CST	6	-	ZAC

OTHER COMM Traffic 118.1
B'CAST FREQ 1150 WHERE 10 mi SW   HOURS Daylight
FROM Concepción FREQ 117.1 TRACK 211°, 901n.mi.,
FROM Salinas   FREQ 116.1 TRACK 272°, 51n.mi.,
FROM Durango   FREQ 112.2 TRACK 115°, 126Dme,
FUEL 80,100?   CARDS Visa,MC   CASH? Pesos
REPAIRS Minor   TIEDOWN BYO

One of the richest silver cities of the Spanish Colonial time, the cerro grande with VW-sized holes lets you be driven in to clamber around ancient mining passages and interesting subterranean geology. If you are claustrophobic, do some silver shopping while others enjoy this part.

The city's baroque colonial architecture is very beautiful: get a local tour guide to show you some of the many outstanding examples of 1500s architecture.

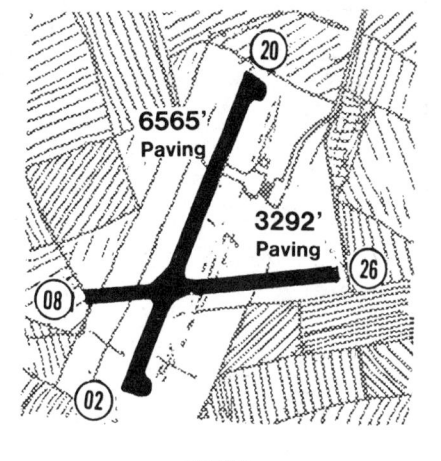

6565' Paving
3292' Paving

ELEVATION
7021'

LEON, GTO
NDB/ADF PISTA 09

SEPTIEMBRE 30 - 1978/138

RADIO	TORRE 118.3	ELEV. 6027'
DIA Y NOCHE 123.0		VAR. MAG. 8° E
		LEO ---

358

Caution
For Information Only
Not for Aerial Navigation

Altitudes shown on plan view: 12000', 10000', 11000'

Terrain/obstacle elevations: 7054', 9679', 9843', 9843', 8366', 7874', 7607', 8695', 9351', 9351', 8530', 6298', 8530'

NDB: LEO 365

Approach headings: 090°, 050°, 230°, 275°, 095°, 10000'

Profile view:
- NDB
- 10 M.N. 8000' IZQ.
- 275° ← 10000'
- 095° → 6940' (913')
- ELEV. 6027'

FALLIDA: VIRE A LA **DERECHA** E INTERCEPTE EN ASCENSO EL QDM 095°, Y PROSIGA EN TRAYECTORIA DE APROXIMACION HASTA LA ALTITUD MINIMA DE ESPERA, DE ACUERDO CON INSTRUCCIONES DEL A.T.C.

CATEGORIA	DIRECTO PISTA 09 MDA 6940' (913')	CATEGORIA	CIRCULANDO MDA
A	1 ¼	A	7040' (1013') — 1 ¼
B		B	7040' (1013') — 1 ½
C	2 ¾	C	7240' (1213') — 3
D	N. A.	D	N. A.

CAMBIOS: AJUSTE DE MINIMOS   S.C.T. — D.G.A.C.   LEO N-1

SUNRISE & SUNSET — GMT   SALIDA y PUESTA del SOL — GMT

15th of	JAN	FEB	MAR	APR	MAY	JUN	JUL	AUG	SEPT	OCT	NOV	DEC	
SUNRISE	1326	1316	1254	1227	1208	1204	1213	1224	1233	1241	1256	1315	SALIDA
SUNSET	2425	2444	2455	0105	0116	0128	0130	0116	2449	2422	2404	2407	PUESTA
15° de	ENE	FEB	MAR	ABR	MAY	JUN	JUL	AGO	SEP	OCT	NOV	DIC	

León Guanajuato *lee-OAN* 359

JET CHART	WAC	SECTIONAL	LATITUDE	LONGITUDE	US TIME	FOR GMT ADD	ICAO IDENT	TOWN IDENT
JN-46	CJ-24 No	TPC J-24B	21°04	101°34	CST	6	MMLO	LEO

tca to: **10,000'msl** CENTER AT **Ndb** RADIUS **10 mi.**
APPROACH — TOWER **118.3** GROUND **118.3**
CITY **7 mi NW** POPULATION **200,000**
LOCAL **Ndb** FREQ **365** WHERE **here** HOURS **24**
B'CAST FREQ **680** WHERE **9.2 mi NW** HOURS **Daylight**
FROM **Salinas** FREQ **116.1** TRACK **164°, 101 n.mi.**
FROM **Guadalajara** FREQ **117.3** TRACK **062°, 104 n.mi.**
FROM **Querétaro** FREQ **115.7** TRACK **284°, 73Dme.**
FUEL **80, 100, JP** CARDS — CASH? **Pesos**
REPAIRS **Minor** TIEDOWN **BYO**

HOTEL	RATE	WHERE	TEL
H. Condesa	$	Central	3-11-20
H. León	$+	Central	4-10-50
H. Señorial	$	Central	3-59-30

The city which is a definition of the word 'bustling': people in this shoe capital have plenty to do and sure do keep moving. Nearly all the shoes produced in the Republic are made here.

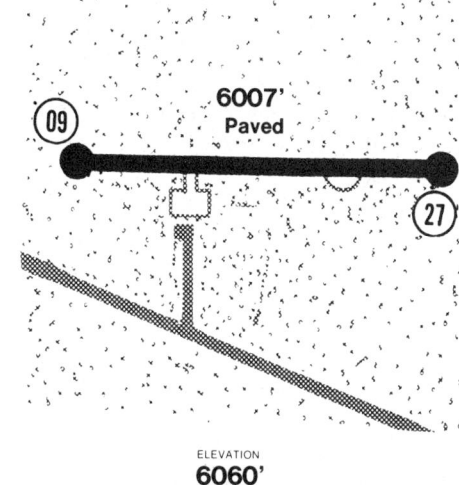

6007' Paved

ELEVATION **6060'**

360 Aguascalientes   Aguascalientes   *ah-woss-call-ee-ENT-tess*

JET CHART	WAC	SECTIONAL	LATITUDE	LONGITUDE	US TIME	FOR GMT ADD	ICAO IDENT	TOWN IDENT
JN-46	CJ-24 No.	TPC J-24A	21°51'	102°17'	CST	6	-	AGS

OTHER COMM Traffic 118.1
CITY Adjacent No.   POPULATION 275,000
B'CAST FREQ 790   WHERE 2 mi NE   HOURS Daylight
FROM Salinas   FREQ 116.1   TRACK 199°, 60 n.mi.
FROM Guadalajara   FREQ 117.3   TRACK 027°, 99Dme
FUEL 80, 100   CARDS -   CASH? Pesos
REPAIRS Minor   TIEDOWN BYO

HOTEL	RATE	WHERE	TEL
Motel Medrano	$$	1 mi No.	5-55-00
Hotel Paris	$	Central	5-11-21

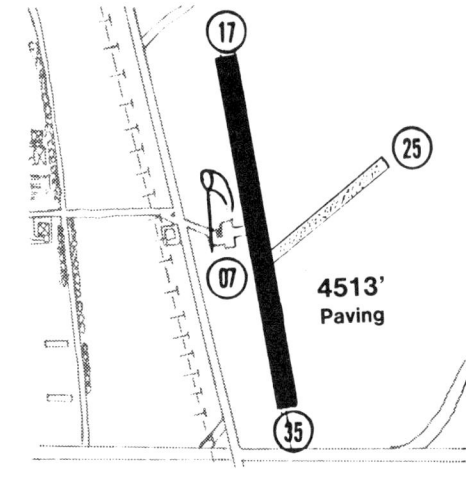

4513'
Paving

ELEVATION
6205'

Irapuato   Guanajuato   ear-ah-PWOTT-toe   361

JET CHART	WAC	SECTIONAL	LATITUDE	LONGITUDE	US TIME	FOR GMT ADD	ICAO IDENT	TOWN IDENT
JN-46	CJ-24 No.	TPC J-24B	20°42'	101°17'	CST	6	-	IPO

OTHER COMM Traffic 118.1
CITY 1 mile NW   POPULATION 62,000
LOCAL XEBO FREQ 1330 WHERE 4 mi WSW HOURS daylight
B'CAST FREQ 1080   WHERE -   HOURS Daylight
FROM Guadalajara FREQ 117.3 TRACK 074°,116 n.mi.
FROM Querétero   FREQ 115.7   TRACK 265°,52Dme
FUEL -   CARDS -   CASH? -
REPAIRS -   TIEDOWN BYO

HOTEL	RATE	WHERE	TEL
las Minas	$$E	Central	6-23-80
Hotel Florida	$E	Central	6-10-68

Raising strawberries the size of eggs, this is part of the agriculturally rich Bajío (bah-HEE-oh) area which stretches across NE from Guadalajara. Flying low you see mile after mile of intensely red soil. Family farmers are able to make a nice living on five acres.

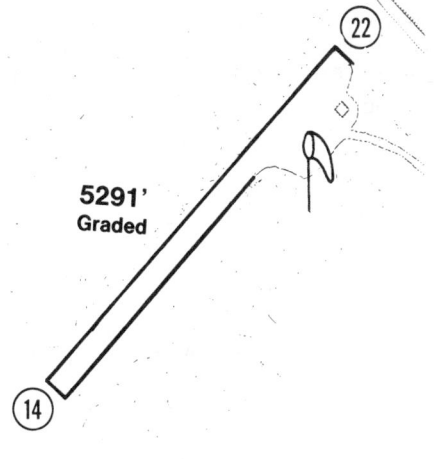

22
5291'
Graded
14
ELEVATION
5658'

362 Celaya New — Guanajuato — *say-LYE-yah*

JET CHART	WAC	SECTIONAL	LATITUDE	LONGITUDE	US TIME	FOR GMT ADD	ICAO IDENT	TOWN IDENT
JN-46	CJ-24 No.	TPC J-24B	20°33'	100°54'	CST	6	-	CYA

OTHER COMM Traffic 118.1
CITY 5 miles E   **POPULATION** 145,000
B'CAST FREQ 840 **WHERE** 14 mi SW **HOURS** Daylight
FROM Guadalajara **FREQ** 117.3 **TRACK** 080°,135 n.mi.
FROM Querétero **FREQ** 115.7 **TRACK** 253°,30Dme
FROM León **FREQ** 365 **TRACK** 121°,49n.mi.
FUEL 80 maybe   **CARDS** -   **CASH?** Pesos
REPAIRS Minor   **TIEDOWN** BYO

HOTEL	RATE	WHERE	TEL
Hotel Isabel	$E	Central	2-20-95
Hotel Gomez	-$	Central	2-00-51

Buzz town thoroughly at five hundred feet agl and hope that a car will come way out here.

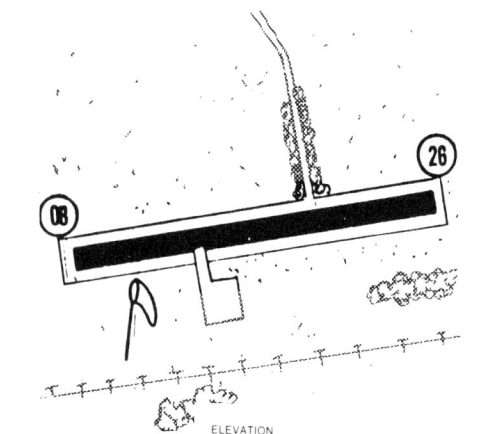

ELEVATION

Intentionally Left Blank
Intencionalmente Dejada en Blanco

Guanajuato   Guanajuato   *wonn-ah-WHOT-toe*   363

JET CHART	WAC	SECTIONAL	LATITUDE	LONGITUDE	US TIME	FOR GMT ADD	ICAO IDENT	TOWN IDENT
JN-46	CJ-24 No.	TPC J-24B	20°55'	101°21'	ST	6	-	GTO

OTHER COMM Traffic 118.1
CITY 6 miles NE   POPULATION 80,000
B'CAST FREQ 600   WHERE -   HOURS Daylight
FROM Querétero   FREQ 115.7   TRACK 278°, 58Dme
FROM México City   FREQ 117.0   TRACK 296°, 157 n.mi.
FROM Guadalajara   FREQ 117.3   TRACK 078°, 112 n.mi.

FUEL -   CARDS -   CASH? -
REPAIRS None   TIEDOWN BYO

HOTEL	RATE	WHERE	TEL
Real de Minas	$$E	Central	2-14-60
Castillo Sta Cecilia	$$E	NE SIDE	2-04-85
San Diego G/VG	$E	Central	2-13-00

Intensely a colonial city, these rich mines made it an instant city. Today the downtown street subways, ceramics and homespun fabrics at the central market, and many places vital to the independence of México are well worth seeing.

READER REPORT One evening we dined at the Motel Guanajuato and it was definitely five star. Also has a view overlooking the whole city. The McCaslins, California

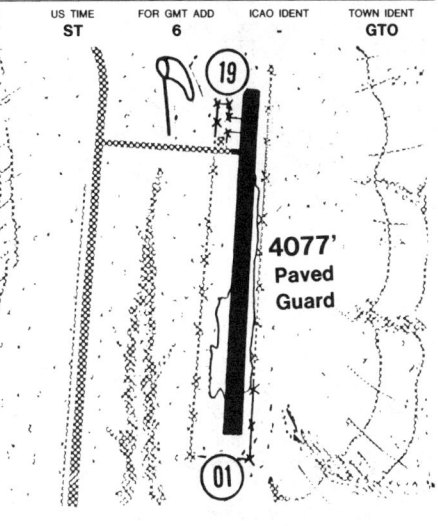

4077'
Paved
Guard

ELEVATION
6516'

364 San Miguel Allende Guanajuato *sahn mee-GELL ah-YENN-day*

JET CHART	WAC	SECTIONAL	LATITUDE	LONGITUDE	US TIME	FOR GMT ADD	ICAO IDENT	TOWN IDENT
JN-46	CJ-24 No.	TPC J-24B	20°55'	100°42'	CST	6	-	SMA

OTHER COMM Traffic 118.1
CITY 3 miles W POPULATION 37,000
B'CAST FREQ 1280 WHERE 2.4 mi W HOURS Daylight
FROM San Luís Potosí FREQ 354 TRACK 152°, 78n.mi.
FROM Querétero FREQ 115.7 TRACK 302°, 25Dme
FROM Salinas FREQ 116.1 TRACK 143°, 125n.mi.
FUEL - CARDS - CASH? -
REPAIRS - TIEDOWN BYO

HOTEL	RATE	WHERE	TEL
San Francisco	$$	Central	2-00-72
Atascadero	$$	1 mi E	2-02-06
la Huerta	$	Central	2-03-60

One of the few really private airports in the Republic, you are the guests of a man who, after seven years, still hasn't decided exactly what to do with the runway. Box of good cigars couldn't hurt.

READER REPORT This city is a jewel of Mexican architecture. We stayed at the Meson de San Antonio for under $30 double with meals. G Claire, California

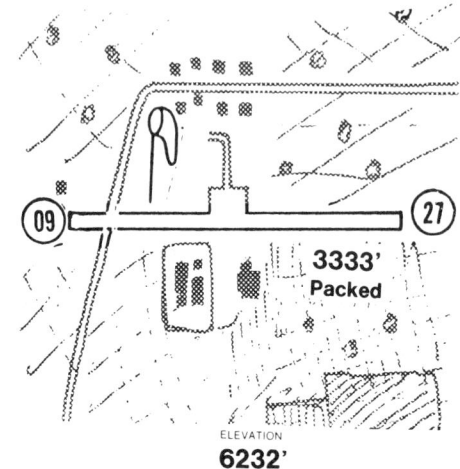

3333'
Packed

ELEVATION
6232'

Queretaro — Guanajuato

care-RETT-tah-roe

365

JET CHART	WAC	SECTIONAL	LATITUDE	LONGITUDE	US TIME	FOR GMT ADD	ICAO IDENT	TOWN IDENT
JN-46	CJ-24 No.	TPC J-24B	20°37'	100°22'	CST	6	MMTQ	QET

- OTHER COMM Traffic 118.1
- CITY 2 miles So.   POPULATION 196,000
- LOCAL VorDme   FREQ 115.7   WHERE here   HOURS 24
- B'CAST FREQ 980   WHERE 2.6 mi SW   HOURS Daylight
- FROM México   FREQ 117.0   TRACK 306°, 102 n.mi.
- FROM Salinas   FREQ 116.1   TRACK 138°, 150 n.mi.,
- FROM Tamuín   FREQ 113.3   TRACK 217°, 123 n.mi.,
- FUEL -   CARDS -   CASH? -
- REPAIRS -   TIEDOWN BYO

READER REPORT There is a new operation here with 100/130 avgas and Jet Fuel plus communications on 132.1. You can now telephone also, number is 463-42521. T.Braunsted and J.Hunt, Texas

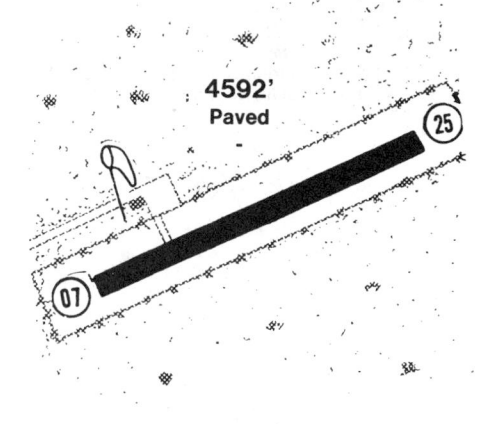

4592'
Paved

ELEVATION
6493'

MEXICO, D.F.
VOR/DME PISTAS 23 I/D

RADIO				
127.3 y 123.0	CD 122.1	TMA 119.7	ELEV 7341'	
	GND 121.0, 121.9	ATIS 127.0	VAR MAG 8° E	
	TWR 118.1, 118.7	FIS 126.9	MEX ▬·▬· ▬·· ▬	
	APP 121.2	EMER 121.5		

Caution – For Information Only – Not for Aerial Navigation

12 100'
14 800'
19 400'

DME MEX 117.0
LOM MW 255

Radials/bearings shown: 310°, 330°, 360°, 030°, 040°, 060°, 090°, 120°, 180°, 220°, 232°, 270°, 300°
Courses: 232°, 072°, 020°
Altitudes at fixes: 11 000', 8 800', 9 600', 7 717', 7 643', 7 750', 7 937', 7 710', 7 989'
Spot elevations: 9 876', 8 924', 8 924', 8 629', 9 416', 8 233', 8 039', 8 462', 8 399', 8 071', 8 268', 9 318', 9 350', 10 630', 11 385'

INT. CARACOL D-5.5 VOR/MEX

Profile

VOR/DME — 11 000' — 072° — CARACOL D-5.5 VOR/MEX — D-7 — 9 600' — 10 M.N. IZQ.
232° — 8 800' — 7 960' (619') — 5.5
ELEV 7341'

FALLIDA: ASCIENDA DIRECTO AL **NDB/MW**, VIRE A LA **IZQUIERDA** Y CONTINUE ASCENSO EN **RADIAL 200°** SOBRE EL **VOR/DME-MEX**, (IAS MAX. **210 KTS.** HASTA **11 000'**).

CATEGORIA	DIRECTO PISTA 23 I/D MDA 7960' (619')	CATEGORIA	CIRCULANDO MDA
A	1 (1600 M)	A	8080' (739') - 1 (1600 M)
B	1 (1600 M)	B	8080' (739') - 1 (1600 M)
C	1 ¾ (2800 M)	C	8080' (739') - 2 (3200 M)
D	2 (3200 M)	D	8080' (739') - 2 ¼ (3600 M)

CAMBIOS: ALTITUD ESPERA. SCT – DGAC – SENEAM MEX-VD-3

SUNRISE & SUNSET – GMT   SALIDA y PUESTA del SOL – GMT

15th of	JAN	FEB	MAR	APR	MAY	JUN	JUL	AUG	SEPT	OCT	NOV	DEC	
SUNRISE	1313	1304	1244	1218	1200	1157	1206	1216	1223	1230	1244	1302	SALIDA
SUNSET	2418	2435	2445	2453	0104	0115	0117	0104	2439	2413	2357	2400	PUESTA
15° de	ENE	FEB	MAR	ABR	MAY	JUN	JUL	AGO	SEP	OCT	NOV	DIC	

To get local time just subtract 'GMT ADD'
PARA OBTENER TIEMPO LOCAL SUSTRIAGA 'GMT ADD'

México Distrito Federal *MEH-hee-coe* 367

JET CHART	WAC	SECTIONAL	LATITUDE	LONGITUDE	US TIME	FOR GMT ADD	ICAO IDENT	TOWN IDENT
JN-46	CJ-24 So.	TPS J-24C	19°27'	99°03'	CST	6	MMMX	MEX

- TCA TO: 20,000' RADIUS 50 n.mi. HOURS 24
- APPROACH 121.2 TOWER 118.1 GROUND 121.9
- OTHER COMM ASR 119.7, Clearance 122.1, ATIS 117.0
- CITY All sides POPULATION 12,000,000+
- LOCAL VorDme FREQ 117.0 WHERE here/24 HOURS
- B'CAST FREQ 900 WHERE 9 mi SW HOURS 24
- FROM Querétero FREQ 115.7 TRACK 126°, 102 n.mi.
- FROM Acapulco FREQ 115.9 TRACK 006°, 166 n.mi.
- FROM Pachuca FREQ 112.7 TRACK 198°, 47 n.mi.
- FUEL 80, 100, JP CARDS Visa, Mc CASH? Yes
- REPAIRS Major TIEDOWN BYO ropes

HOTEL	RATE	WHERE	TEL
Holiday Inn	$$$	Central	5-33-35-00
Geneva	$	Central	5-25-15-00

And hundreds more.

When conquered by 400 Spaniards in 1521 this was probably the third largest city in the world after then-unknown Tokyo and Canton.

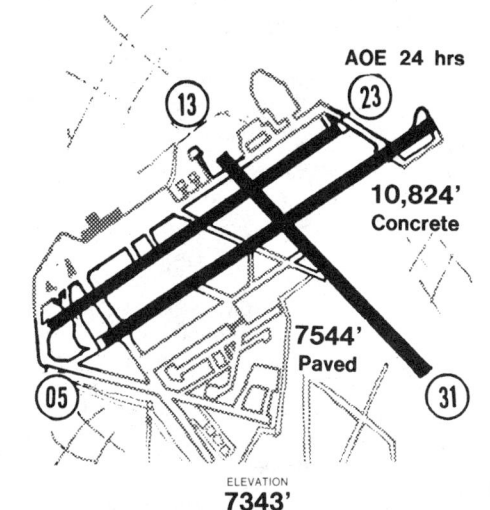

AOE 24 hrs
10,824' Concrete
7544' Paved
ELEVATION 7343'

368 Puebla Military   Puebla   *poo-EBB-lah*

JET CHART	WAC	SECTIONAL	LATITUDE	LONGITUDE	US TIME	FOR GMT ADD	ICAO IDENT	TOWN IDENT
JN-46	CJ-24 So.	TPC J-24C	19°02'	98°11'	CST	6	-	PEB

tca to: **9,000' msl**   CENTER AT **Airport**   RADIUS **5 mi.**

APPROACH -   TOWER **126.2**   GROUND **126.2**
CITY **Adjacent W**   POPULATION **210,000**
B'CAST FREQ **1170**   WHERE **1.4 mi NW**   HOURS **Daylight**
FROM **México**   FREQ **117.0**   TRACK **108°, 56Dme**
FROM **Pachuca**   FREQ **112.7**   TRACK **150°, 74n.mi.**
FROM **Tequisquetengo** FREQ **113.1** TRACK **064°, 65Dme**
FUEL **Emegency 100**   CARDS -   CASH? **Pesos**
REPAIRS **Minor**   TIEDOWN **BYO**

HOTEL	RATE	WHERE	TEL
Hotel Lastra	$	Central	-
H. Royalty	$	On square	Yes
H. Señorial	$	Central	Yes

     Military airports seem not to be a problem if you are at all pleasant. I use this one because it is the only airport serving Puebla. Without it I'd miss a very attractive city with a great bunch of Glider Club members.

5255' Paved

ELEVATION **7117'**

Tehuacán Puebla
tay-wah-CONN **369**

JET CHART	WAC	SECTIONAL	LATITUDE	LONGITUDE	US TIME	FOR GMT ADD	ICAO IDENT	TOWN IDENT
JN-46	CJ-24 So.	TPC J-24C	18°28'	97°25'	CST	6	-	TCN

OTHER COMM Traffic 118.1
CITY 3 mi SE
POPULATION 77,000
B'CAST FREQ 1070   WHERE 2 mi E   HOURS Daylight
FROM México   FREQ 117.0   TRACK 112°, 109 n.mi.
FROM Oaxaca   FREQ 112.0   TRACK 328°, 100 n.mi.
FROM Tequisquetengo FREQ 113.1 TRACK 088°, 106 n.mi.
FUEL 80, 100   CARDS -   CASH? Pesos
REPAIRS Minor   TIEDOWN BYO

HOTEL	RATE	WHERE	TEL
Hotel México	$	Central	2-00-19
Spa Peñafiel	$	1.5 mi NW	2-01-90

You could get spoiled by all the attention you receive at either of these two spa hotels. In a city whose name is used throughout the Republic to mean mineral water, yes they do have it.

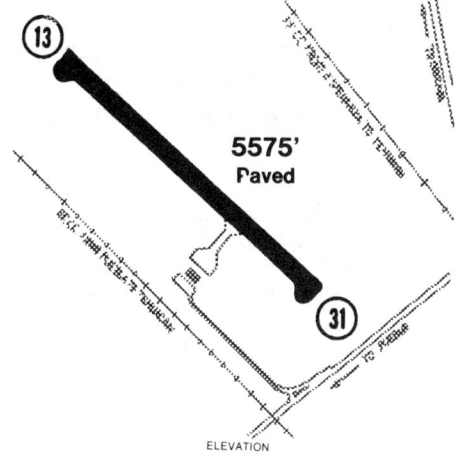

13
5575'
Paved
31

ELEVATION
5510'

370   Isla, Veracruz   EES-lah

JN CHART	WAC	SECTIONAL	LATITUDE	LONGITUDE	US TIME	FOR GMT	ICAO	TOWN ID
JN-46	CJ-25	TPC J25D	18°06'	95°32'	CST	+6	·	ILA –

OTHER COMM 118.1
SETTLEMENT Adj East   POPULATION est 4,000
FROM Minatitlan   FREQ 116.4   TRACK 268°, 56.3Dme
FROM Veracruz   FREQ 112.4   TRACK 141°, 73.1Dme
FROM Tehuacan   FREQ ADF 1070   TRACK 093°, 110n.mi.
AVIATION GAS Emergency 80   CREDIT CARDS -   CASH TYPE Pesos
REPAIRS AVAILABLE -   TIEDOWNS? BYO

A busy tropical town out by itself, the runway seems to be here because the aerial applicator needs it. For a real treat take your Spanish/English dictionary in hand and go to town to buy a something. The Fanta company's limon (ask for FONN-ta lee-MOAN) tastes something like 7up, would be easy. For a real challenge, find and buy an oil spout.

Runway diagram: Runway 18/36, 4151' x 39', hard packed. Populated pasture to west. Gate and drainage ditch on east side.

ELEVATION

Esmeralda Veracruz   *ess-mare-ALL-dah*   371

JET CHART	WAC	SECTIONAL	LATITUDE	LONGITUDE	US TIME	FOR GMT ADD	ICAO IDENT	TOWN IDENT
JN-46	CJ-25 So.	TPC J-25D	18°16'	96°03'	CST	6	-	-ESM-

OTHER COMM Traffic 118.1
SETTLEMENT isolated   **POPULATION** -
FROM Veracruz   **FREQ** 112.9   **TRACK** 165°,54n.mi.
FROM Minátitlan **FREQ** 116.4   **TRACK** 280°,89Dme
FUEL -   **CARDS** -   **CASH?** -
REPAIRS -   **TIEDOWN** BYO

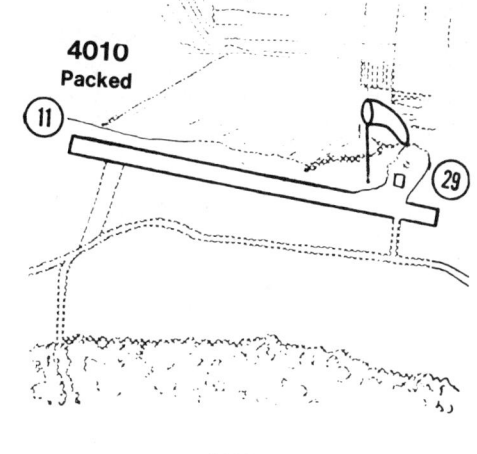

4010
Packed

⑪ ㉙

ELEVATION
203'

This is a rare opportunity for you to get out in the backwoods of agricultural flying in México. The men operating out of here are doing all the agflying things, but with unique crop/pest/application profiles.

If you should arrive overhead when they are going hot and heavy either pass on by this time and come back later, or plan to land along and park completely out of their way. When things get quiet will be time to poke around and ask questions. They will appreciate your consideration.

372 Ciudad Alemán Veracruz *see-oo-DOD ah-lay-MONN*

JET CHART	WAC	SECTIONAL	LATITUDE	LONGITUDE	US TIME	FOR GMT ADD	ICAO IDENT	TOWN IDENT
JN-46	CK-25 So.	TPC J-25D	18°12'	96°05'	CST	6	-	CDA

OTHER COMM Traffic 118.1
SETTLEMENT 8 miles S   POPULATION 3,500
FROM Veracruz   FREQ 112.9   TRACK 168°, 57n.mi.
FROM Minatitlan FREQ 116.4   TRACK 271°, 92Dme
FROM Ixtepec   FREQ 113.7   TRACK 324°, 121n.mi.
FUEL 100 maybe   CARDS -   CASH? Pesos
REPAIRS Minor   TIEDOWN BYO

4304'x91'
Paved

You can't get much closer to the farming jungle country of Veracruz state than right here near the gigantic dam which stabilizes times of heavy rainfall and deeply dry seasons. Hard to believe these tropic areas could get very dry, but on a relative basis they sure do.

AUTHOR REPORT The Governor of the State of Veracruz spends a lot of time here, hence the Aerocommanders and similar light twins on the ramp.

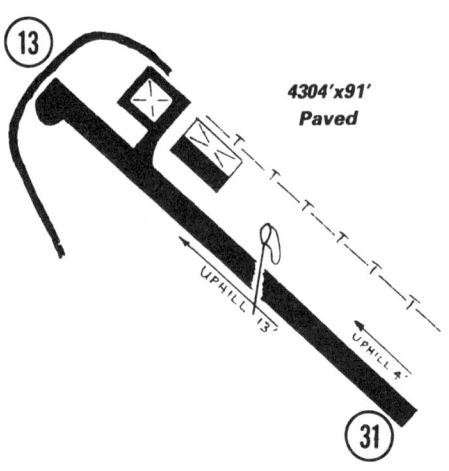

ELEVATION
148'msl

Measuring at San Pedrito

love story to an airplane

For those who aren't exactly sure what a round engined Cessna 195 looks like, here is my old trusty N1537D waiting for me again at Baja California's Rancho San Pedrito over SW of La Paz a ways.

I was fortunate in choosing this airplane when it was time to buy my first one: I couldn't have found a better combination for right then. All metal, four plus seats (don't believe five), easy parts availability, rated 300 hp all day long on 67 octane fuel.

I was a tad on the oily side with a specific oil consumption of two quarts per hour while also burning one liter of fuel per minute (15.9 gph). Both rates came down later: oil to three to four to five hours on a quart thanks to a Carl Baker chromed engine. Then Stu Carson showed me his DC-3 techniques on leaning out, fuel went down to a tad over twelve an hour.

Best of all, this airplane took on me with my two hundred hour flying time and patiently let me learn to fly. It showed me how three axis trim was handier than the autopilot I couldn't afford anyway. Its crosswind gear let me get into and out of airports I needed to measure but winds were often a problem. The full ball bearing cable pulleys were a delight to feel; I almost get goosebumps sitting here thinking what a seductive feel that airplane control had.

And this 195 taught me the delights of Big Airplane feel. Later in the right seat of Al Wagner's DC-3 I'd learn just how similar the 195 was to The Big Taildragger. Only in the -3 did I get close to losing my allegiance to the round engined Cessna.

But eventually it happened: an attack of sanity took over. I was no longer paying the same twenty-two cents a gallon for fuel of twelve years before, Carl Baker was getting out of the Jacobs engine business, Shell had stopped selling oil in gallon cans.

Fortunately Martin Litton was ready to give 37D a good home. He'd wanted her for twelve years; he actually had a standing offer all that time. In 1975 I finally accepted it and Martin came and flew it home. I didn't watch him leave.

VERACRUZ, VER.
VOR/DME PISTA 36

RADIO	TWR 118.5	ELEV. 95'
CMA 127.3	TMA/APP 120.4	VAR.MAG. 7° E

Caution For Information Only Not for Aerial Navigation

MMR-108 ALT. 5 000' SUP. TERR.

DME VER 1129

FALLIDA: ASCIENDA EN RADIAL 360° CON VIRAJE DE PROCEDIMIENTO A LA DERECHA DENTRO DE 10 M.N. HASTA LA ALTITUD MINIMA DE ESPERA.

CATEGORIA	DIRECTO PISTA 36 MDA 600' (505')	CATEGORIA	CIRCULANDO MDA
A	1 (1600 M)	A	600 (505')-1 (1600 M)
B		B	
C	1½ (2400 M)	C	800' (705')-2 (3200 M)
D		D	800' (705')-2¼ (3600 M)

CAMBIOS: V15-4 DETALLES MENORES   SCT-DGAC-SENEAM   VER VD-1

SUNRISE & SUNSET - GMT   SALIDA y PUESTA del SOL - GMT

15th of JAN FEB MAR APR MAY JUN JUL AUG SEPT OCT NOV DEC
SUNRISE 1301 1253 1233 1207 1150 1146 1155 1205 1212 1219 1232 1250 SALIDA
SUNSET 2407 2424 2434 2442 2452 0103 0105 2452 2427 2402 2346 2349 PUESTA
15° de   ENE FEB MAR ABR MAY JUN JUL AGO SEP OCT NOV DIC

To get local time just subtract 'GMT ADD'
PARA OBTENER TIEMPO LOCAL SUSTRIAGA 'GMT ADD'

Veracruz   Veracruz   *vair-ah-CRUCE* | 375 |

JET CHART	WAC	SECTIONAL	LATITUDE	LONGITUDE	US TIME	FOR GMT ADD	ICAO IDENT	TOWN IDENT
JNC-46	CJ-25 So.	TPC J-25C	19°08'	96°12'	CST	6	MMVR	VER

•TCA TO: 20,000'   RADIUS 50 n.mi.   HOURS 1300-0100Z
APPROACH 120.4   TOWER 118.5   GROUND 118.5
OTHER COMM Center 126.9
CITY 5 miles NE   POPULATION 276,000
LOCAL VorDme   FREQ 112.9   WHERE here   HOURS 24
B'CAST FREQ 930   WHERE 5.1 mi NE   HOURS Daylight
FROM Tampico   FREQ 117.5   TRACK 146°, 211 n.mi.
FROM Otumba   FREQ 115.0   TRACK 067°, 117 n.mi.
FROM Minátitlan FREQ 116.4 TRACK 298°, 118 n.mi.
FUEL 80,100,JP   CARDS Visa,MC   CASH? Yes
REPAIRS Minor   TIEDOWN BYO

HOTEL	RATE	WHERE	TEL
H.Veracruz	$$	Central	2-00-80
Gran H. Diligencia	$$	Central	2-01-80

This principle port for the city of México is a pleasant place to stay, to get good weather briefings, or to join the Spring Fiesta. Interesting tours include the coffee city of Xalapa, Fortín de las Flores, bass fishing in Presa Alemán.

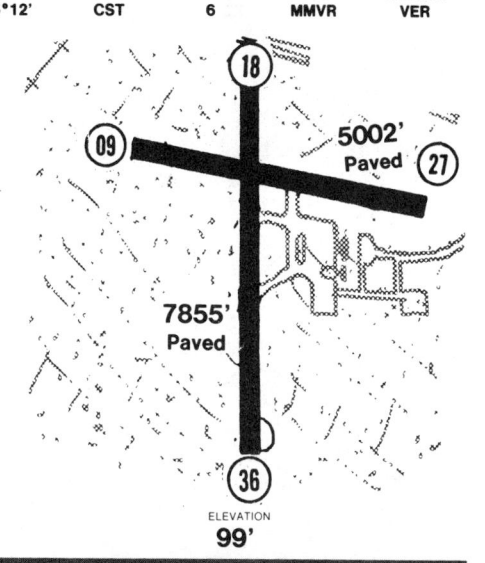

Runways: 09/27 5002' Paved; 18/36 7855' Paved
ELEVATION 99'

376 Xalapa   *also spelled 'Jalapa'*   Veracruz   hah-LOPP-ah

JET CHART	WAC	SECTIONAL	LATITUDE	LONGITUDE	US TIME	FOR GMT ADD	ICAO IDENT	TOWN IDENT
JNC-46	CJ-25 So.	TPC J-25D	19°38'	96°51'	CST	6	-	JAL

OTHER COMM Traffic 118.1
CITY 11 miles NW   POPULATION 155,000
B'CAST FREQ 610   WHERE 8 mi SW   HOURS Daylight
FROM Veracruz   FREQ 112.9   TRACK 292°,39Dme
FROM Nautla   FREQ 112.3   TRACK 173°,44Dme
FROM Pachuca   FREQ 112.7   TRACK 102°,116n.mi.
FUEL -   CARDS -   CASH? -
REPAIRS -   TIEDOWN BYO

HOTEL	RATE	WHERE	TEL
H. Maria Victoria	$	Central	7-56-00
H. Salmones	$	Central	7-54-31
H. México	-$	Central	7-50-30

Balmy tropical city just high enough to avoid mugginess. Coffee plants grow everywhere. Restaurant Jardin's coffee menu has over fifty ways they normally serve it. But they will follow your instructions if you have a new idea.

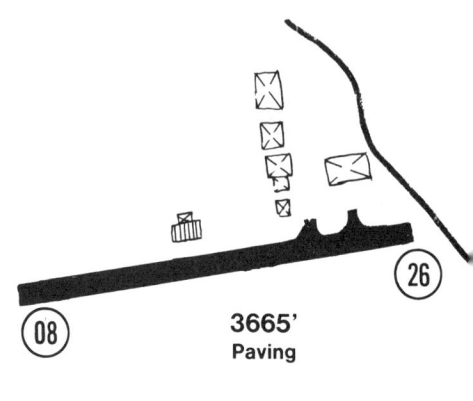

3665'
Paving

ELEVATION
2881'

San Andrés Veracruz
sohn onn-DRACE 377

JET CHART	WAC	SECTIONAL	LATITUDE	LONGITUDE	US TIME	FOR GMT ADD	ICAO IDENT	TOWN IDENT
JN-46	CJ-24 No.	TPC J-24B	20°27'	97°11'	CST	6	-	-

OTHER COMM Traffic 118.1
SETTLEMENT 4 mile No.   POPULATION 5500

FROM	FREQ	TRACK
FROM Nautla	FREQ 112.3	TRACK 295°, 28Dme,
FROM Tampico	FREQ 117.5	TRACK 153°, 116 n.mi.

FUEL -   CARDS -   CASH? -
REPAIRS -   TIEDOWN BYO

Here in México's petroleum belt there are many many burning gas wells. Over the years it has seemed to me those in this particular area create the most haze. Fortunately the river's hairpin loop is a distinctive landmark. Then if you haveDme there are several facilities now available to help avoid navigation difficulties.

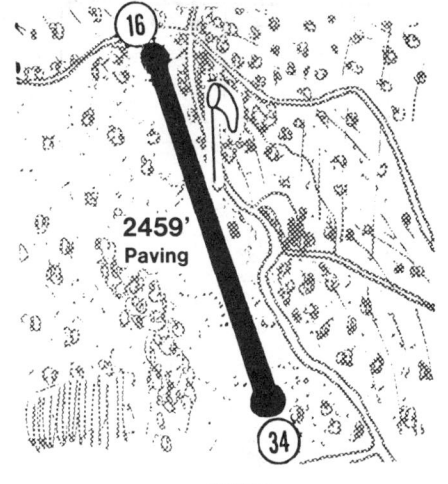

2459'
Paving

ELEVATION
100'

POZA RICA, VER.
VOR/DME PISTA 26

DICIEMBRE 24-1981/165

RADIO	TWR 118.9	ELEV. 453'
AMSA 131.0		VAR MAG 7° E
		PZA ·−−· −−· ··

PRECAUCION

NO UTILIZAR COMO INSTRUMENTO DE REFERENCIA EL RADIOALTIMETRO EN APROXIMACION, DEBIDO A CONDICIONES OROGRAFICAS. TODA INFORMACION DEBERA REFERIRSE AL ALTIMETRO BAROMETRICO
ELEV 453'

FALLIDA: VIRE A LA **DERECHA** E INTERCEPTE EN ASCENSO EL **RADIAL 283°**, Y PROSIGA CON VIRAJE DE GOTA A LA **IZQUIERDA** DENTRO DE **10 M.N.** HASTA LA ALTITUD MINIMA DE ESPERA.

CATEGORIA	DIRECTO PISTA 26 MDA 1080'(627')	CATEGORIA	CIRCULANDO MDA
A	1 (1600 M)	A	1200' (747') - 1 (1600 M)
B		B	1200' (747') - 1 1/4 (2000 M)
C	1 3/4 (2800 M)	C	1200' (747') - 2 1/4 (3600 M)
D	—	D	—

CAMBIOS FREC. AMSA   SCT-DGAC-SENEAM   PZA-VD-2

Poza Rica, Veracruz

poe-sah-REE-cah

379

JN CHART	WAC	SECTIONAL	LATITUDE	LONGITUDE	US TIME	FOR GMT	ICAO	TOWN ID
JN-46	CJ-24	TPC J24B	20°36'	97°28'	CST	+6	·	PZA

tca to: **2,500'msl** CENTER AT **VorDme** RADIUS **10 mi.**
APPROACH 118.9 TOWER 118.9 GROUND 118.9
CITY IS **4 mi South** POPULATION ·
LOCAL **VorDme** FREQ 115.5 HOURS **24**
B'cast **1480** WHERE **5 mi SE** HOURS **Daylight**
FROM **Tampico** FREQ 117.5 TRACK 159°, 103.2 n.mi.
FROM **Nautla** FREQ 112.3 TRACK 294°, 46.1Dme
AVIATION GAS **80,100** CARDS **VISA, MC** CASH **Pesos**
REPAIRS AVAILABLE **Some** TIEDOWNS? **BYO**

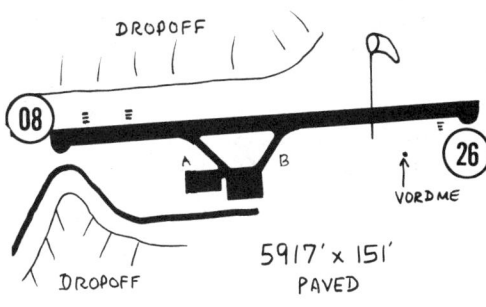

Part of the real Oil Country of Mexico, this newish airport gets a lot of Pemex traffic and very few English speaking pilots. While passing here one day I gave a position report and discovered the controller on duty had memorized a 'cleared to land' sentence in English which sounded really good. But he used the same exact response to any call on any subject as long as pilot calling spoke English. Wasn't my first similar experience.

380   **Barra Cazones**   Veracruz   *BAH-rah ah-SOAN-ess*

JET CHART	WAC	SECTIONAL	LATITUDE	LONGITUDE	US TIME	FOR GMT ADD	ICAO IDENT	TOWN IDENT
JN-46	CJ-24 No.	TPC J-24B	20°45'	97°11'	ST	6	-	-CAZ-

OTHER COMM   Traffic 122.85
SETTLEMENT   1/2 mile SW   POPULATION 300
FROM Tampico   FREQ 117.5   TRACK 151°, 99Dme
FROM Nautla   FREQ 112.3   TRACK 315°, 41N.mi.
FROM Poza Rica   FREQ 205   TRACK 040°, 20n.mi.
FUEL -   CARDS -   CASH? -
REPAIRS -   TIEDOWN BYO

Several basic hostelries across the river SW; generally a dugout canoe will meet you whether with or without reservations. Excellent fishing; intrusion of agriculture is diminishing hunting.

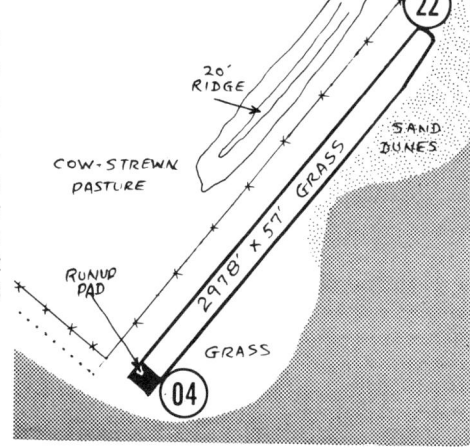

ELEVATION
10' to 15'

Tuxpan Veracruz

tukes-PONN 381

JET CHART	WAC	SECTIONAL	LATITUDE	LONGITUDE	US TIME	FOR GMT ADD	ICAO IDENT	TOWN IDENT
JN-46	CJ-24 No.	TPC J-24B	20°57'	97°22'	CST	6	MMTX	TUX

OTHER COMM Traffic 118.1
CITY 1.5 mi West   POPULATION 77,000
LOCAL Ndb   FREQ 262   WHERE here   HOURS Request
B'CAST FREQ 1340   WHERE 4 mi E   HOURS Daylight
FROM Tampico   FREQ 117.5   TRACK 153°,83Dme
FROM Tamuín   FREQ 113.3   TRACK 123°,103n.mi.
FROM Nautla   FREQ 112.3   TRACK 315°,57Dme
FUEL -   CARDS -   CASH? -
REPAIRS Minor   TIEDOWN BYO

HOTEL	RATE	WHERE	TEL
Motel Quinta Mitsi	$	SE	12

Port city for the Poza Rica oil fields, prowling around town will produce interesting sidelights. There is always Coca Cola, but try some of the Crespo soft drinks for a real taste delight. That's a start, now go to it.

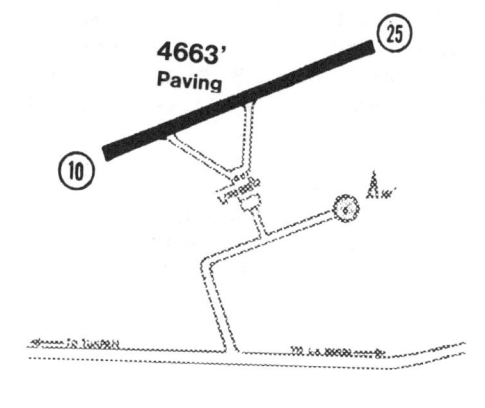

4663' Paving

ELEVATION
9'

382 Cerro Azul   Veracruz   SAIR-oh ah-SOOL

JET CHART	WAC	SECTIONAL	LATITUDE	LONGITUDE	US TIME	FOR GMT ADD	ICAO IDENT	TOWN IDENT
JN-46	CJ-24 No.	TPC J-24B	21°09'	97°45'	CST	6	-	-CER-

OTHER COMM Traffic 118.1-
CITY 3 miles N   POPULATION -
FROM Tampico   FREQ 117.5   TRACK 168°,68Dme
FROM Nautla   FREQ 112.3   TRACK 309°,80Dme
FROM Pachuca   FREQ 112.7   TRACK 032°,81n.mi.
FUEL -   CARDS -   CASH? -
REPAIRS -   TIEDOWN BYO

Here in the petroleum country visibilities are often a problem particularly when a winter low pressure area sits out there in the Gulf. We've waited through a week of hundred foot ceilings. A good time to explore.

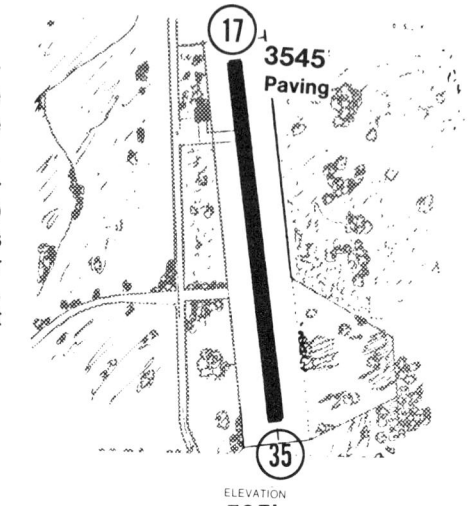

ELEVATION
595'

Naranjos Veracruz *narr-ONN-hoce* 383

JET CHART	WAC	SECTIONAL	LATITUDE	LONGITUDE	US TIME	FOR GMT ADD	ICAO IDENT	TOWN IDENT
JN-46	CJ-24 No.	TPC J-24B	21°20'	97°42'	CST	6	-	-NAR-

OTHER COMM Traffic 118.1
FROM Tampico   FREQ 117.5   TRACK 165°,58Dme
FROM Pachuca   FREQ 112.7   TRACK 029°,91n.mi.
FROM Nautla   FREQ 112.3   TRACK 314°,86Dme

Oil country atmosphere: lots of fumes and haze.

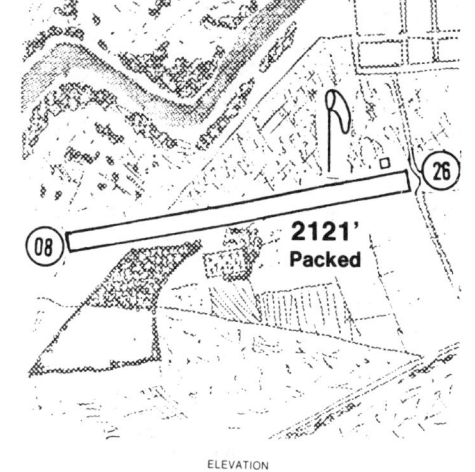

2121'
Packed

ELEVATION
312'

384 Ebano San Luis Potosi *ay-BONN-oh*

JET CHART	WAC	SECTIONAL	LATITUDE	LONGITUDE	US TIME	FOR GMT ADD	ICAO IDENT	TOWN IDENT
JN-46	CJ-24 No.	TPC J-24B	22°13'	98°24'	CST	6	-	-EBN-

OTHER COMM Traffic 118.1
CITY adjacent S POPULATION 9,000
FROM Tampico FREQ 117.5 TRACK 072°, 34Dme
FROM Tamuin FREQ 113.3 TRACK 239°, 29n.mi.
FUEL Some 80 CARDS - CASH? Pesos
REPAIRS - TIEDOWN BYO

Ag airport on the western outskirts of Tampico, not much else happening but a good alternate if you need one.

ELEVATION
177'

Covadonga — San Luis Potosi — *coe-vah-DONG-gah* — 385

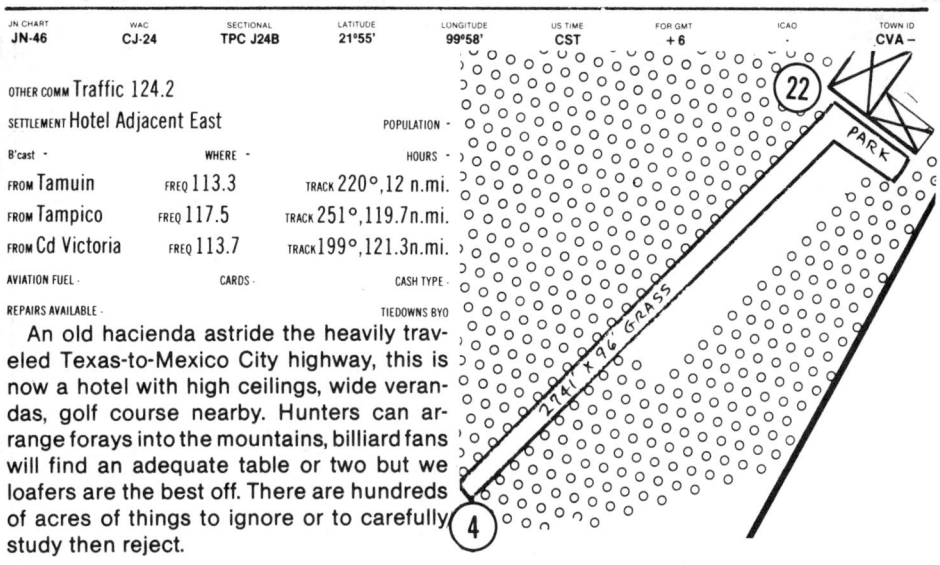

JN CHART	WAC	SECTIONAL	LATITUDE	LONGITUDE	US TIME	FOR GMT	ICAO	TOWN ID
JN-46	CJ-24	TPC J24B	21°55'	99°58'	CST	+6	-	CVA –

OTHER COMM Traffic 124.2
SETTLEMENT Hotel Adjacent East
POPULATION -

B'cast -   WHERE -   HOURS -
FROM Tamuin   FREQ 113.3   TRACK 220°, 12 n.mi.
FROM Tampico   FREQ 117.5   TRACK 251°, 119.7 n.mi.
FROM Cd Victoria   FREQ 113.7   TRACK 199°, 121.3 n.mi.
AVIATION FUEL -   CARDS -   CASH TYPE -
REPAIRS AVAILABLE -   TIEDOWNS BYO

An old hacienda astride the heavily traveled Texas-to-Mexico City highway, this is now a hotel with high ceilings, wide verandas, golf course nearby. Hunters can arrange forays into the mountains, billiard fans will find an adequate table or two but we loafers are the best off. There are hundreds of acres of things to ignore or to carefully study then reject.

VOR/DME RWY 13

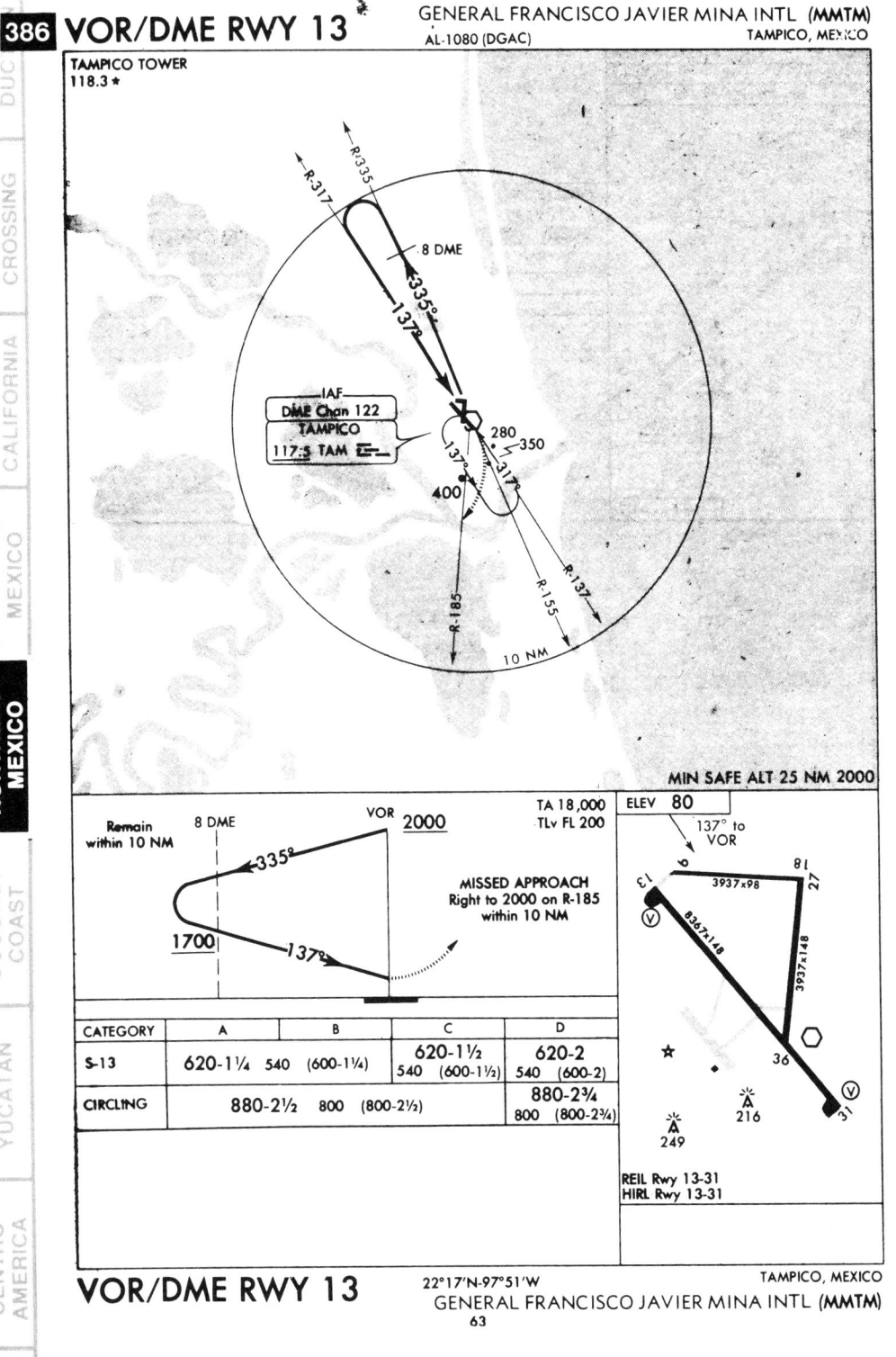

386 | GENERAL FRANCISCO JAVIER MINA INTL (**MMTM**)
AL-1080 (DGAC) | TAMPICO, MEXICO

TAMPICO TOWER 118.3 *

DME Chan 122
TAMPICO
117.5 TAM

IAF

MIN SAFE ALT 25 NM 2000

Remain within 10 NM — 8 DME — VOR 2000
335°
1700
137°

TA 18,000
TLv FL 200

MISSED APPROACH
Right to 2000 on R-185 within 10 NM

ELEV 80
137° to VOR

3937x98
8367x148
3937x148

REIL Rwy 13-31
HIRL Rwy 13-31

CATEGORY	A	B	C	D
S-13	620-1¼ 540 (600-1¼)		620-1½ 540 (600-1½)	620-2 540 (600-2)
CIRCLING	880-2½ 800 (800-2½)			880-2¾ 800 (800-2¾)

VOR/DME RWY 13 | 22°17'N-97°51'W | TAMPICO, MEXICO
GENERAL FRANCISCO JAVIER MINA INTL (**MMTM**)

*Caution
For Information Only
Not for Aerial Navigation*

Tampico   Tamaulipas   tom-PEE-koe   387

JET CHART	WAC	SECTIONAL	LATITUDE	LONGITUDE	US TIME	FOR GMT ADD	ICAO IDENT	TOWN IDENT
JN-46	CJ-24 No.	TPC J-24B	22°18'	97°52'	CST	6	MMTM	TAM

- TCA TO: 20,000'   RADIUS 50 n.mi.   HOURS 24
APPROACH 121.3   TOWER 118.3   GROUND 118.3
OTHER COMM ILS 109.3
CITY 4 mi SW   POPULATION 215,000
LOCAL VorDme   FREQ 117.5   WHERE here   HOURS 24
B'CAST FREQ 810   WHERE 5 mi SSW   HOURS 24
FROM Bro'ville   FREQ 116.3   TRACK 178°, 209 n.mi.
FROM Cd Victoria   FREQ 113.7   TRACK 136°, 105 n.mi.
FROM Veracruz   FREQ 112.9   TRACK 326°, 211 n.mi.
FUEL 80, 100, JP   CARDS Visa, MC   CASH? Yes
REPAIRS Minor   TIEDOWN BYO

HOTEL	RATE	WHERE	TEL
Camino Real	$$	N side	3-11-01
Inglaterra	$	Central	2-56-78
Impala	$	Central	2-09-90

Oil and port city, seafood is so plentiful even standup lunch counters offer stuffed crab or lobster broiled in butter.

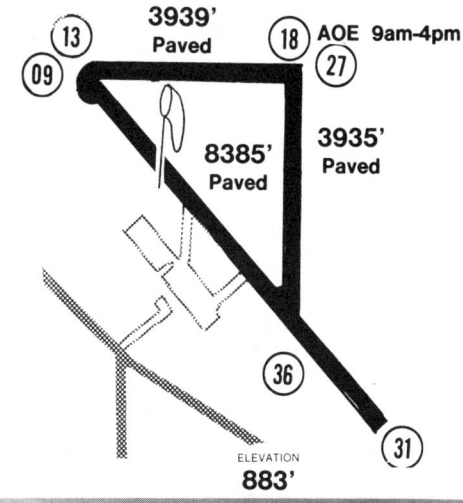

3939' Paved   AOE 9am-4pm
8385' Paved
3935' Paved
ELEVATION 883'

388

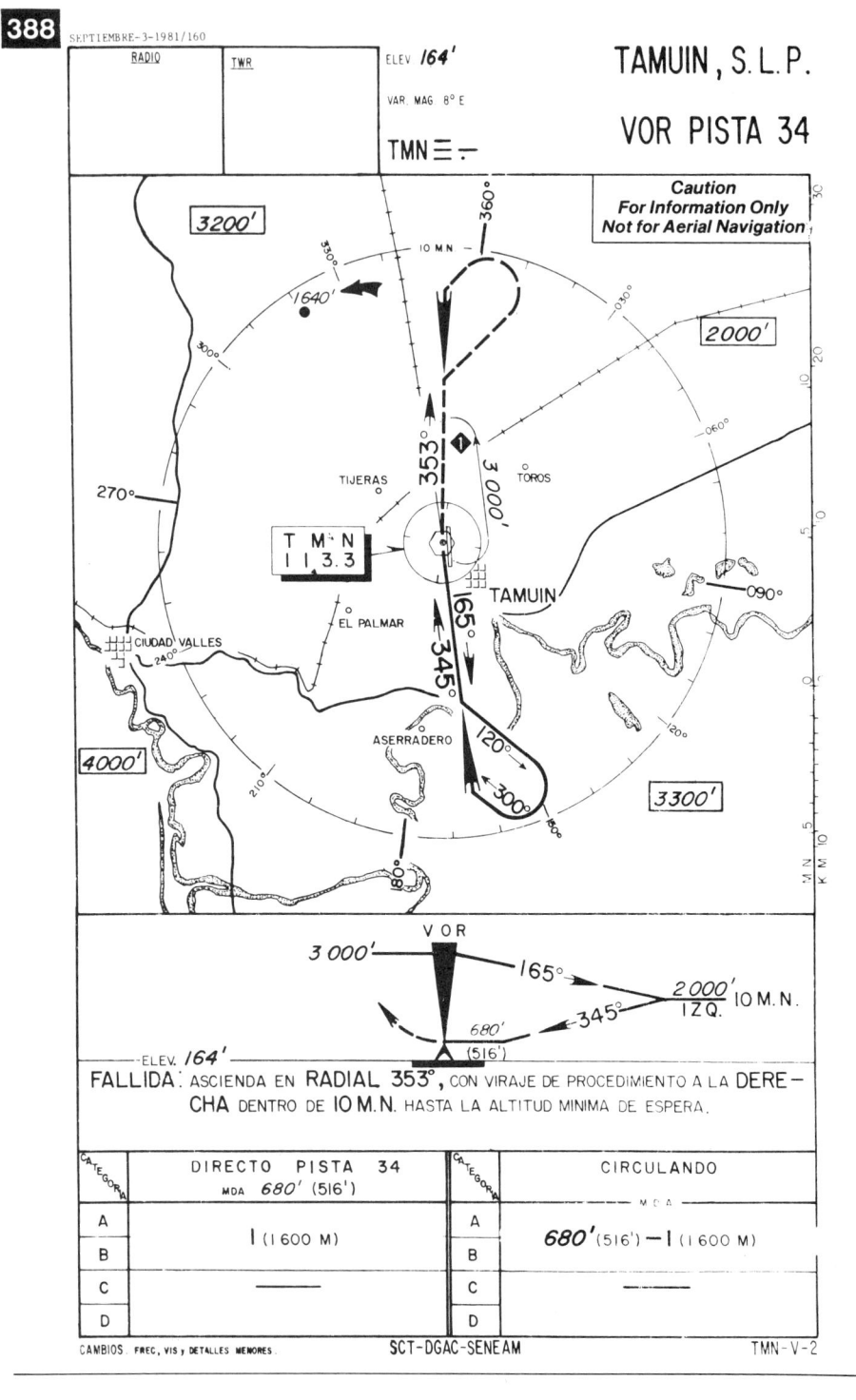

SEPTIEMBRE-3-1981/160

TAMUIN, S.L.P.
VOR PISTA 34

RADIO	TWR	ELEV 164'
		VAR. MAG. 8° E

TMN ≡ .−

Caution
For Information Only
Not for Aerial Navigation

FALLIDA: ASCIENDA EN RADIAL 353°, CON VIRAJE DE PROCEDIMIENTO A LA DERE- CHA DENTRO DE 10 M.N. HASTA LA ALTITUD MINIMA DE ESPERA.

CATEGORIA	DIRECTO PISTA 34 MDA 680' (516')	CATEGORIA	CIRCULANDO MDA
A	1 (1 600 M)	A	680' (516') − 1 (1 600 M)
B		B	
C	—	C	—
D		D	

CAMBIOS: FREC, VIS y DETALLES MENORES.   SCT-DGAC-SENEAM   TMN-V-2

SUNRISE & SUNSET − GMT   SALIDA y PUESTA del SOL − GMT

15th of	JAN	FEB	MAR	APR	MAY	JUN	JUL	AUG	SEPT	OCT	NOV	DEC	
SUNRISE	1315	1305	1243	1214	1154	1150	1159	1211	1221	1230	1246	1305	SALIDA
SUNSET	2411	2431	2443	2454	0106	0119	0120	0105	2437	2409	2351	2353	PUESTA
15° de	ENE	FEB	MAR	ABR	MAY	JUN	JUL	AGO	SEP	OCT	NOV	DIC	

To get local time just subtract 'GMT ADD'
PARA OBTENER TIEMPO LOCAL SUSTRIAGA 'GMT ADD'

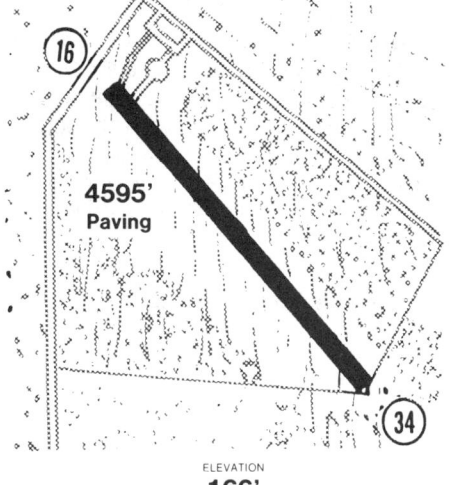

Tamuín   San Luis Potosi   *tah-moo-EEN*   **389**

JET CHART	WAC	SECTIONAL	LATITUDE	LONGITUDE	US TIME	FOR GMT ADD	ICAO IDENT	TOWN IDENT
JN-46	CJ-24 No.	TPC J-24B	22'03'	98°48'	CST	6	-	TMN

APPROACH -   TOWER 118.1   GROUND 118.1
CITY 1 mile SE   POPULATION 15,000
LOCAL Vor   FREQ 113.3   WHERE here   HOURS 24
FROM Cd Victoria   FREQ 113.7   TRACK 165°,100 n.mi.
FROM Tampico   FREQ 117.5   TRACK 244°,55Dme
FROM Pachuca   FREQ 112.7   TRACK 011°,138n.mi.
FUEL 80,100   CARDS -   CASH? Pesos
REPAIRS Minor   TIEDOWN BYO
Several clean local hotels reported

4595' Paving

ELEVATION **166'**

390 Rancho San Ricardo   San Luis Potosi

JET CHART	WAC	SECTIONAL	LATITUDE	LONGITUDE	US TIME	FOR GMT ADD	ICAO IDENT	TOWN IDENT
JN-46	CJ-24 No.	TPC J-24B	22°13'	98°58'	CST	6	-	-

OTHER COMM Traffic 122.85
SETTLEMENT North end   POPULATION Ranch
FROM Tamuín   FREQ 113.3   TRACK 308°, 14n.mi.,
FROM Tampico   FREQ 117.5   TRACK 258°62Dme,
FROM Cd Victoria   FREQ 113.8   TRACK 172°, 90Dme,

This ranch just outside Tampico is a good emergency alternate to keep in mind but unless you are expected you might not get too much of a welcome otherwise.

Caution-Pedestrians

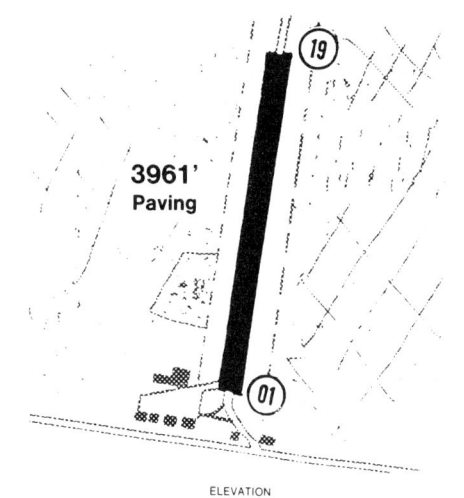

3961'
Paving

ELEVATION
1031'

Ciudad Mante   Tamps.   *see-oo-DOD MONN-tee*   391

JET CHART	WAC	SECTIONAL	LATITUDE	LONGITUDE	US TIME	FOR GMT ADD	ICAO IDENT	TOWN IDENT
JN-46	CJ-24 No.	TPC J-24B	22°45'	99°00'	CST	6	MMDM	-CDM-

OTHER COMM Traffic 118.1
CITY 0.5 miles E   POPULATION 99,000
FROM Tamuin   FREQ 113.3   TRACK 337°,43n.mi.
FROM Cd Victoria   FREQ 113.7   TRACK 173°,58Dme
FROM Tampico   FREQ 117.5   TRACK 286°,69Dme
FUEL Some 80   CARDS -   CASH? Pesos
REPAIRS Minor   TIEDOWN BYO

HOTEL	RATE	WHERE	TEL
Hotel Mante	$E		2-09-90
los Arcos Courts	$E	Not tried	2-08-70

A mostly fumigador strip in farm country; if you had a serious problem and needed some minor help, this runway is around.

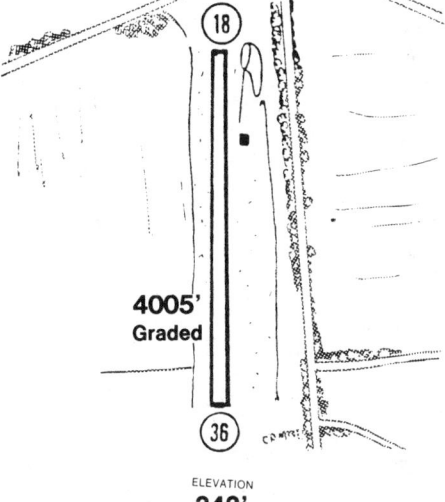

4005' Graded

ELEVATION
342'

392 Xicotencatl   Tamps.   *see-coat-enn-COTT-ull*

JET CHART	WAC	SECTIONAL	LATITUDE	LONGITUDE	US TIME	FOR GMT ADD	ICAO IDENT	TOWN IDENT
JN-46	CJ-24 No.	TPC J-24B	22°58'	98°58'	CST		-	XIC

OTHER COMM Traffic 118.1
CITY Adjacent No.   POPULATION 5500
FROM Cd Victoria FREQ 113.7 TRACK 168°,45Dme,
FROM Tampico   FREQ 117.5 TRACK 297°,74Dme,
FUEL Some 80   CARDS -   CASH? Yes
REPAIRS Minor   TIEDOWN BYO

These agricultural boom towns are everywhere as the government opens more thousands of hectarias of land for food production. Farm sizes are 100 to 500 acres; These will need to be consolidated for more efficient labor and equipment use.

The fly in the ointment is México's agrarian law which restricts large holdings. Intended to assure everyone a piece of land, population increases indicate some compromise may be necessary to provide enough food for everyone.

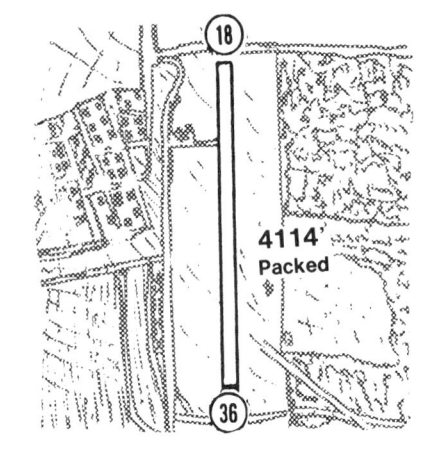

4114' Packed
Runway 18/36

ELEVATION
482'

Salinas San Luis Potosi sah-LEEN-uss 393

JET CHART	WAC	SECTIONAL	LATITUDE	LONGITUDE	US TIME	FOR GMT ADD	ICAO IDENT	TOWN IDENT
JN-46	CJ-24 No.	TPC J-24B	22°37'	101°45'	CST	6	-	SLS

OTHER COMM Traffic 118.1
SETTLEMENT East side   POPULATION 3500
LOCAL Vor FREQ 116.1 WHERE 6 mi NW HOURS 24
FROM Torreón FREQ 116.4 TRACK 142°,199 n.mi.,
FROM Concepción FREQ 115.8 TRACK 179°,94n.mi.,
FROM Guadalajara FREQ 117.3 TRACK 025°,153 n.mi.
FUEL -   CARDS -   CASH? -
REPAIRS -   TIEDOWN BYO

If the word 'windswept' doesn't occur to you here it never will. This wide open cattle country teeters on the verge of drought almost continuously. If it weren't for the salt works just East, some years there wouldn't be much going on. The lake in the lower right is transitory: years will often go by when it is continuously full, in other like periods it will be a desert.

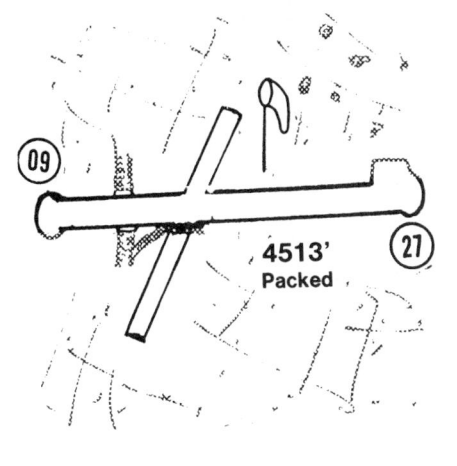

4513' Packed

ELEVATION
6191

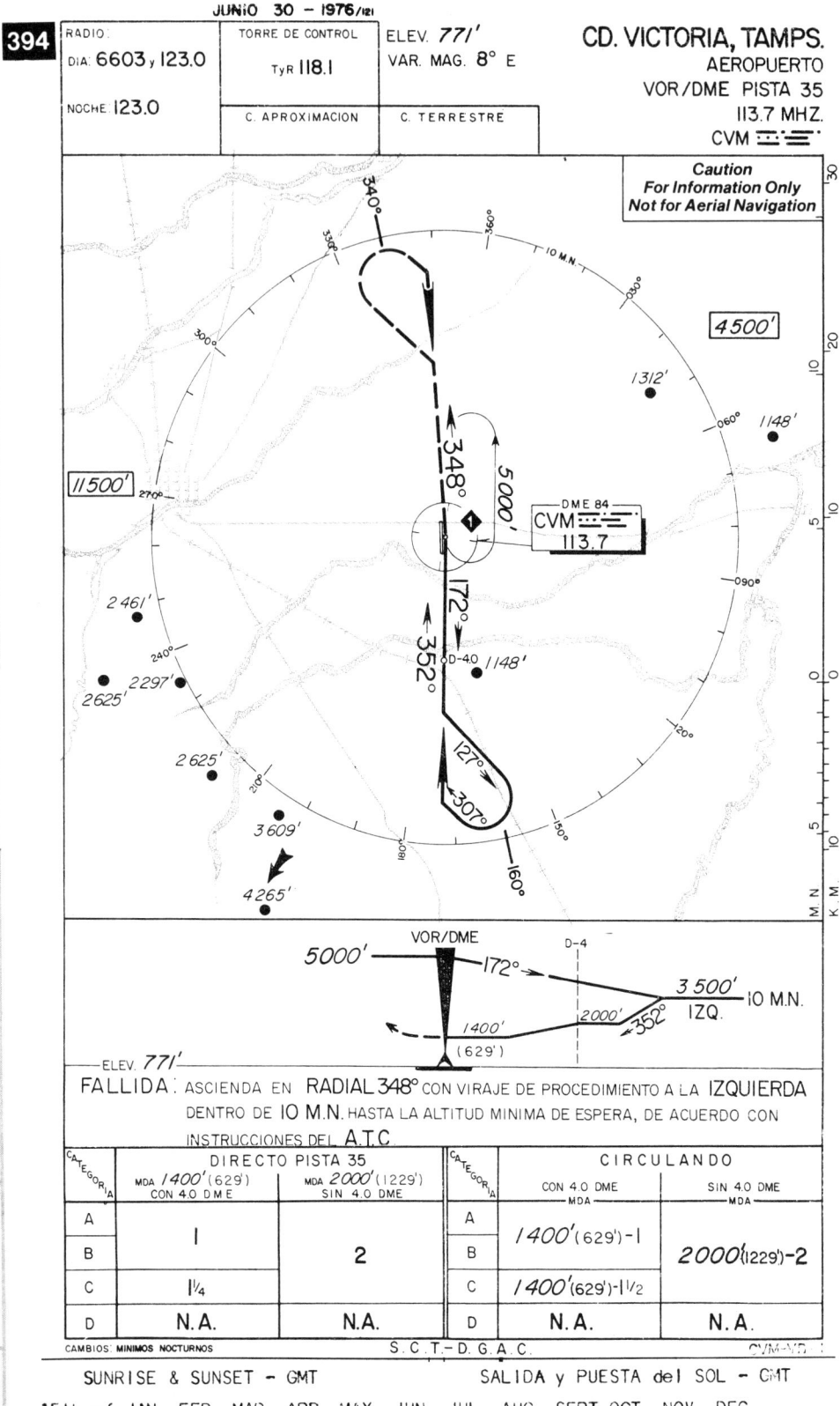

CD. VICTORIA, TAMPS.
AEROPUERTO
VOR/DME PISTA 35
113.7 MHZ.
CVM

394

JUNIO 30 - 1976/121

RADIO	TORRE DE CONTROL	ELEV. 771'
DIA: 6603 y 123.0	TyR 118.1	VAR. MAG. 8° E
NOCHE 123.0	C. APROXIMACION / C. TERRESTRE	

Caution: For Information Only — Not for Aerial Navigation

FALLIDA: ASCIENDA EN RADIAL 348° CON VIRAJE DE PROCEDIMIENTO A LA IZQUIERDA DENTRO DE 10 M.N. HASTA LA ALTITUD MINIMA DE ESPERA, DE ACUERDO CON INSTRUCCIONES DEL A.T.C.

CATEGORIA	DIRECTO PISTA 35 MDA 1400'(629') CON 4.0 DME	MDA 2000'(1229') SIN 4.0 DME	CATEGORIA	CIRCULANDO CON 4.0 DME MDA	SIN 4.0 DME MDA
A	1	2	A	1400'(629')-1	2000'(1229')-2
B	1	2	B	1400'(629')-1	2000'(1229')-2
C	1¼	2	C	1400'(629')-1½	2000'(1229')-2
D	N.A.	N.A.	D	N.A.	N.A.

CAMBIOS: MINIMOS NOCTURNOS   S.C.T.-D.G.A.C.

SUNRISE & SUNSET - GMT   SALIDA y PUESTA del SOL - GMT

15th of	JAN	FEB	MAR	APR	MAY	JUN	JUL	AUG	SEPT	OCT	NOV	DEC	
SUNRISE	1320	1308	1244	1214	1153	1148	1157	1211	1222	1233	1250	1310	SALIDA
SUNSET	2410	2431	2444	2457	0110	0123	0125	0109	2439	2410	2350	2351	PUESTA
15° de	ENE	FEB	MAR	ABR	MAY	JUN	JUL	AGO	SEP	OCT	NOV	DIC	

Ciudad Victoria Tamps.   *see-oo-DODD beek-TORE-ee-yah*   **395**

JET CHART	WAC	SECTIONAL	LATITUDE	LONGITUDE	US TIME	FOR GMT ADD	ICAO IDENT	TOWN IDENT
JN-46	CJ-24 No.	TPC J-24B	23°43'	98°58'	CST	6	MMCV	CVM

tca to: 5,000'msl   CENTER AT Vor   RADIUS 5 mi.
APPROACH -   TOWER 118.1   GROUND 118.1
CITY 6 miles W   POPULATION 110,000
LOCAL VorDme   FREQ 113.7   WHERE here   HOURS 24
B'CAST FREQ 580   WHERE 12 mi W   HOURS Daylight
FROM Tampico   FREQ 117.5   TRACK 316°, 105 n.mi.
FROM Reynosa   FREQ 112.4   TRACK 186°, 144n.mi.
FROM S. Luís Potosí   FREQ 354   TRACK 040°, 145n.mi.
FUEL 80   CARDS -   CASH? Pesos
REPAIRS -   TIEDOWN BYO

HOTEL	RATE	WHERE	TEL
Sierra Gorda	$E	Central	2-20-80
Hotel Everest	$E	Central	2-40-50

With the airport so far from town, best way to get a cab is to call Turners 2-20-86 from your last stop with an ETA and ask them to send a taxi out there for you.

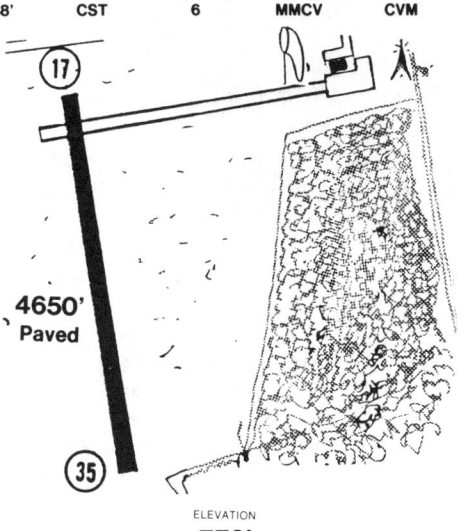

4650' Paved

ELEVATION
773'

396 la Pesca Tamps.   *lah PESS-cah*

JET CHART	WAC	SECTIONAL	LATITUDE	LONGITUDE	US TIME	FOR GMT ADD	ICAO IDENT	TOWN IDENT
JN-46	CJ-24 No.	TPC J-24B	23°48'	97°52'	CST	6	-	-PSA-

OTHER COMM Traffic 124.3
CITY 0.5 mi SW   POPULATION est 4,000

B'castFREQ ·	WHERE ·	HOURS ·
FROM Matamoros	114.3	TRACK 180°,119.4 n.mi.
FROM Cd Victoria	FREQ 113.7	TRACK 077°,60.6 Dme
FROM Tampico	FREQ 117.5	TRACK 351°,91.0Dme

AVIATION FUEL ·   CARDS ·   CASH TYPE ·
REPAIRS ·   TIEDOWNS? BYO

Texans' favorite fishing hole; they can easily get out on the Gulf through the rebuilt harbor entrance channel. You see interesting sights on those inner lagoons as various kinds of commercial fishermen use boats and equipment peculiarly adapted to the exact fish they go for.

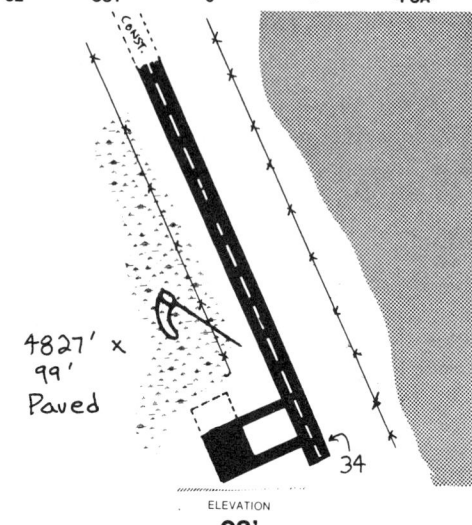

4827' x 99' Paved

34

ELEVATION
08'

San Luís Potosí San Luis Potosi *sahn loo-EECE poe-toe-SEE* 397

JET CHART	WAC	SECTIONAL	LATITUDE	LONGITUDE	US TIME	FOR GMT ADD	ICAO IDENT	TOWN IDENT
JN-46	CJ-24 No.	TPC J-24B	22°11'	100°59'	CST	6	MMSP	SLP

OTHER COMM Traffic 118.1
CITY Adjacent S POPULATION 280,000
LOCAL RNG FREQ 354 WHERE 2 miles NW HOURS days
B'CAST FREQ 540 WHERE 4 mi SE HOURS Daylight
FROM Salinas FREQ 116.1 TRACK 119°,56 Dme
FROM Queretero FREQ 115.7 TRACK 330°,100 n.mi.
FROM Guadalajara FREQ 117.3 TRACK 042°,162 n.mi.
FUEL 80, 100 CARDS - CASH? Pesos
REPAIRS Minor TIEDOWN BYO

HOTEL	RATE	WHERE	TEL
Cactus Motel	$	Central	2-18-71
Panorama	$	Central	2-17-77

Big steel city and capital of the state of the same name, an important gold, silver, lead and copper mining area. Most interesting sight is the baroque church a block from the main plaza, one example of really fine colonial architecture.

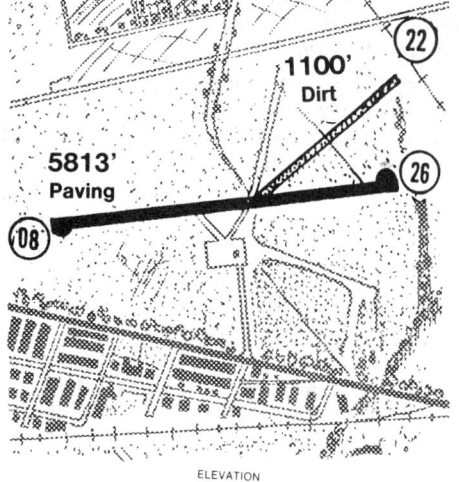

ELEVATION
7001'

398 Saltillo Coahuila *sall-TEE-yoh*

JET CHART	WAC	SECTIONAL	LATITUDE	LONGITUDE	US TIME	FOR GMT ADD	ICAO IDENT	TOWN IDENT
JN-46	CH-23 So.	Bro'ville	25°33'	100°56'	CST	6	MMIO	IYO

OTHER COMM Traffic 118.1
CITY 10 miles SW POPULATION 65,000
B'CAST FREQ 1250 WHERE 6 mi SW HOURS Daylight
FROM Monterrey FREQ 114.7 TRACK 243°, 48Dme
FROM Monclova FREQ 117.9 TRACK 153°, 90n.mi.
FROM Conc. de Oro FREQ 115.8 TRACK 012°, 87n.mi.
FUEL 80 CARDS – CASH? Pesos
REPAIRS Minor TIEDOWN BYO

HOTEL	RATE	WHERE	TEL
Camino Real	$$$	SE side	3-81-90
Arizpe Sainz	$	Central	LD#1
Rodeway Inn	$$	SE side	2-10-10

Called the 'air conditioned city' by jealous neighbors in smoggy Monterrey or hot hot Monclova and Torreón, the combination of elevation and breeze does make a pleasant climate.

Runway 17/35: 5615' Paving
Runway 03/21: 4085' Paving
ELEVATION 4611'

Nature's Contours

While coming west over Texas' Big Bend country one hot afternoon, airplane jiggling enough that I could only enjoy half cups of coffee, this view appeared outside my window.

Far as the eye could see the ground was covered with contour lines. Natural contour lines. Later I would carefully trace one or two along the ground just to be sure it wasn't a furrow plowed by some farmer with infinite patience. Nope, each line tied back to itself, so they are contour lines. But I'm left with the big problem.

With being so pre-occupied and taking pictures and all I forgot to notice where I was. Can anyone help?

MONTERREY, N.L.
VOR PISTA 29

SEPTIEMBRE 30 - 1978/138

RADIO		
DIA 5617, 131.0 y 127.3	TORRE	118.1
	APROXIMACION	121.4
NOCHE 3405, 131.0 y 127.3	TMA	119.6

ELEV. 1269'
VAR. MAG. 8° E
MTY ≡ · — —

Caution
For Information Only
Not for Aerial Navigation

FALLIDA: VIRE A LA **DERECHA** E INTERCEPTE EN ASCENSO EL **RADIAL 106°**, Y PROSIGA EN TRAYECTORIA DE APROXIMACION HASTA LA ALTITUD MINIMA DE ESPERA, DE ACUERDO CON INSTRUCCIONES DEL **A.T.C.**

CATEGORIA	DIRECTO PISTA 29 MDA 1780' (511')	CATEGORIA	CIRCULANDO — MDA —
A	1	A	1 880' (611') - 1
B	1	B	1 880' (611') - 1
C	1¼	C	1 880' (611') - 1¾
D	1¾	D	1 880' (611') - 2¼

CAMBIOS: AJUSTE DE MINIMOS   S.C.T.-D.G.A.C.   MTY V-1

SUNRISE & SUNSET - GMT   SALIDA y PUESTA del SOL - GMT

15th of	JAN	FEB	MAR	APR	MAY	JUN	JUL	AUG	SEPT	OCT	NOV	DEC	
SUNRISE	1328	1315	1249	1217	1154	1148	1158	1213	1226	1239	1258	1319	SALIDA
SUNSET	2411	2433	2449	0103	0118	0132	0134	0116	2445	2413	2351	2351	PUESTA
15° de	ENE	FEB	MAR	ABR	MAY	JUN	JUL	AGO	SEP	OCT	NOV	DIC	

Monterrey — Nuevo Leon — *moan-tah-RAY* — 401

JET CHART	WAC	SECTIONAL	LATITUDE	LONGITUDE	US TIME	FOR GMT ADD	ICAO IDENT	TOWN IDENT
JN-46	CH-23 So.	Bro'ville	25°46'	100°06'	ST	6	MMMY	MTY

- •TCA TO: 20,000'   RADIUS 50 n.mi.   HOURS 1300-0300Z
- APPROACH 119.6   TOWER 118.1   GROUND 118.1
- OTHER COMM Radar 119.6 or 124.5 ILS 111.1 292°
- CITY 8 miles SW   POPULATION 1,200,000
- LOCAL VorDme   FREQ 114.7   WHERE here   HOURS 24
- B'CAST FREQ 1050   WHERE 13 mi SW   HOURS 24
- FROM Laredo   FREQ 117.4   TRACK 190°, 112 n.mi.
- FROM McAllen   FREQ 109.8   TRACK 249°, 104 n.mi.
- FROM Cd Victoria   FREQ 113.7   TRACK 322°, 139 n.mi.
- FUEL 80, 100, JP   CARDS Visa, MC, etc   CASH? Yes
- REPAIRS Minor   TIEDOWN BYO

HOTEL	RATE	WHERE	TEL
Ancira	$$	On Plaza	LD #15
Ramada Inn	$$	On mountain	52-22-70
Hotel Monterrey	$	Central	43-51-20

The big airport in a bustling city, sure you are treated well here but mostly the other airport, del Norte, is for General Aviation.

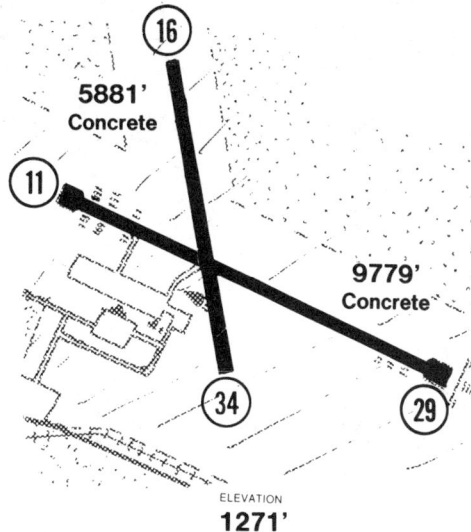

Runways: 16/34 5881' Concrete; 11/29 9779' Concrete
ELEVATION 1271'

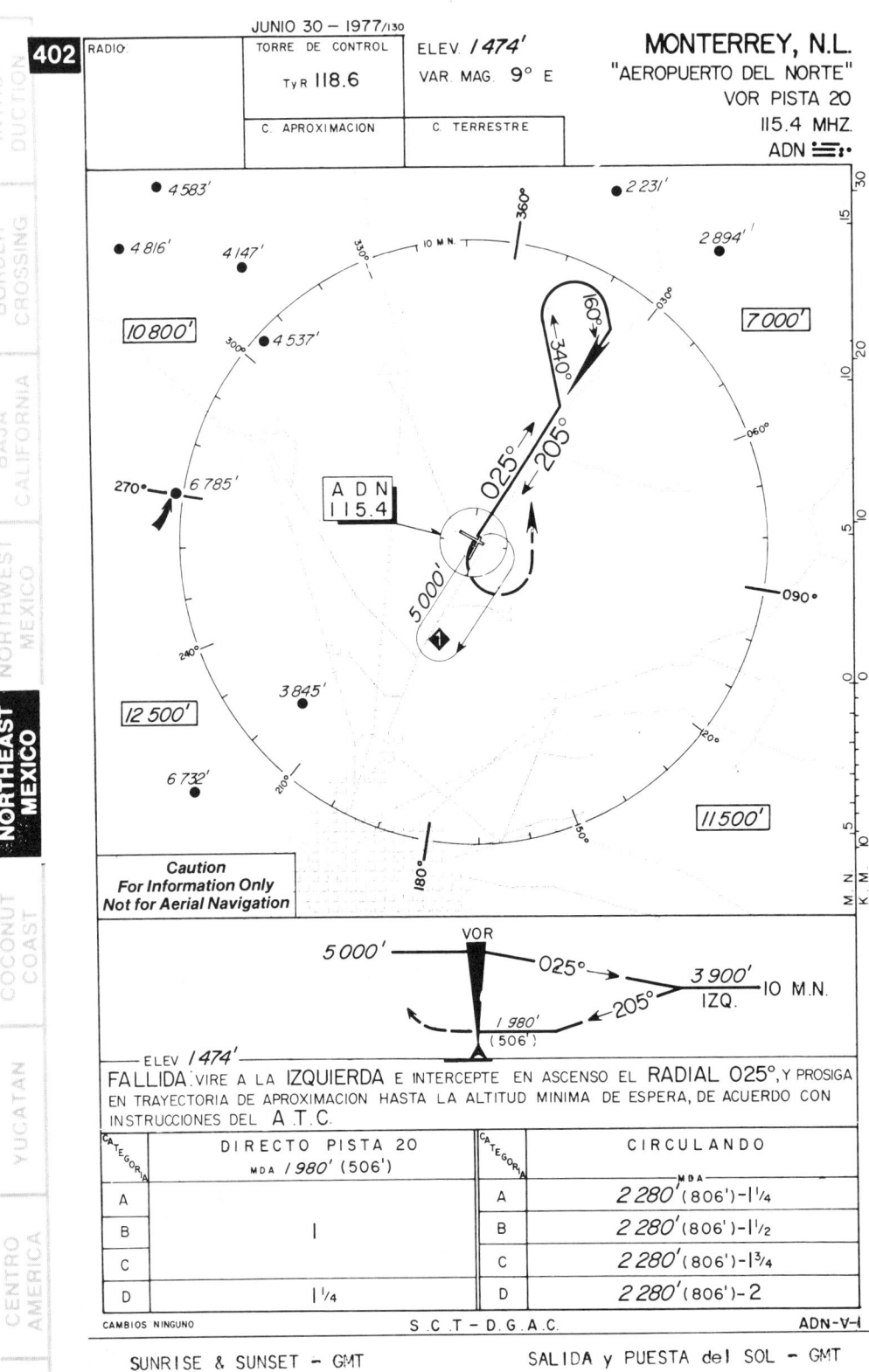

MONTERREY, N.L.
"AEROPUERTO DEL NORTE"
VOR PISTA 20
115.4 MHZ.
ADN

402

RADIO:	TORRE DE CONTROL	ELEV. *1474'*
	TyR 118.6	VAR. MAG. 9° E
	C. APROXIMACION	C. TERRESTRE

JUNIO 30 – 1977/130

Caution
For Information Only
Not for Aerial Navigation

FALLIDA: VIRE A LA IZQUIERDA E INTERCEPTE EN ASCENSO EL **RADIAL 025°**, Y PROSIGA EN TRAYECTORIA DE APROXIMACION HASTA LA ALTITUD MINIMA DE ESPERA, DE ACUERDO CON INSTRUCCIONES DEL A.T.C.

CATEGORIA	DIRECTO PISTA 20 MDA *1980'* (506')	CATEGORIA	CIRCULANDO MDA
A		A	2 280' (806')-1¼
B	1	B	2 280' (806')-1½
C		C	2 280' (806')-1¾
D	1¼	D	2 280' (806')-2

CAMBIOS NINGUNO   S.C.T - D.G.A.C.   ADN-V-I

SUNRISE & SUNSET – GMT   SALIDA y PUESTA del SOL – GMT

15th of	JAN	FEB	MAR	APR	MAY	JUN	JUL	AUG	SEPT	OCT	NOV	DEC	
SUNRISE	1329	1316	1250	1217	1154	1148	1158	1213	1226	1239	1259	1320	SALIDA
SUNSET	2411	2434	2449	0104	0119	0133	0134	0116	2445	2413	2352	2352	PUESTA
15° de	ENE	FEB	MAR	ABR	MAY	JUN	JUL	AGO	SEP	OCT	NOV	DIC	

del Norte Nuevo Leon   *dell NORR-tay*   **403**

JET CHART	WAC	SECTIONAL	LATITUDE	LONGITUDE	US TIME	FOR GMT ADD	ICAO IDENT	TOWN IDENT
JN-46	CH-23 So.	Bro'ville	25°52'	100°14'	ST	6	-	ADN

• TCA TO: 20,000'   RADIUS 50 n.mi.   HOURS 1300-0300Z
APPROACH 119.6   TOWER 118.6   GROUND 118.6
OTHER COMM Radar 119.6
CITY 6 miles SW   POPULATION 1,200,000
LOCAL Vor   FREQ 115.4   WHERE Here   HOURS 24
B'CAST FREQ 1050   WHERE 14 mi So.   HOURS 24
FROM Laredo   FREQ 117.4   TRACK 196°, 110 n.mi.
FROM McAllen   FREQ 109.8   TRACK 252°, 109 n.mi.
FROM Cd Victoria FREQ 113.7   TRACK 321°, 148 n.mi.
FUEL 80, 100   CARDS Visa, MC, etc   CASH? Yes
REPAIRS Some   TIEDOWN BYO

HOTEL	RATE	WHERE	TEL
Ambassador	$$	Central	42-20-40
Holiday Inn	$$	Near here	52-18-08
Chipinque	$$	12 miles SE	56-80-44

You're treated like home around here; things go easily since everyone speaks General Aviation.

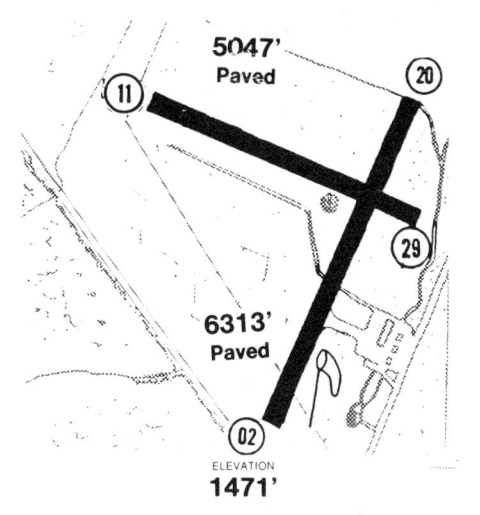

5047' Paved (11)—(20)
6313' Paved (02)—(29)
ELEVATION 1471'

404	RADIO	TORRE 118.0	ELEV. 27'	MATAMOROS, TAMPS.

AGOSTO 30 DE 1978/137

DIA Y NOCHE 123.0

VAR. MAG. 8° E

MAM

VOR PISTA 33

Caution
For Information Only
Not for Aerial Navigation

DME 90
MAM 114.3

FALLIDA: ASCIENDA EN RADIAL 313° CON VIRAJE DE GOTA A LA DERECHA DENTRO DE 10 M.N. HASTA LA ALTITUD MINIMA DE ESPERA, DE ACUERDO CON INSTRUCCIONES DEL A.T.C.

CATEGORIA	DIRECTO PISTA 33 MDA 540' (513')	CATEGORIA	CIRCULANDO MDA
A	1	A	740' (713') - 1
B	1	B	740' (713') - 1
C	1¼	C	740' (713') - 2
D	1¾	D	740' (713') - 2½

CAMBIOS: ELEVACION y MINIMOS   S.C.T. - D.G.A.C.   MAM V-1

SUNRISE & SUNSET - GMT   SALIDA y PUESTA del SOL - GMT

15th of	JAN	FEB	MAR	APR	MAY	JUN	JUL	AUG	SEPT	OCT	NOV	DEC	
SUNRISE	1318	1305	1239	1207	1144	1138	1148	1203	1215	1228	1248	1309	SALIDA
SUNSET	2400	2423	2438	2453	0108	0122	0123	0106	2434	2402	2341	2341	PUESTA
15° de	ENE	FEB	MAR	ABR	MAY	JUN	JUL	AGO	SEP	OCT	NOV	DIC	

Matamoros Tamps. *mott-ah-MORE-oce* 405

JET CHART	WAC	SECTIONAL	LATITUDE	LONGITUDE	US TIME	FOR GMT ADD	ICAO IDENT	TOWN IDENT
JN-46	CH-23 No.	Bro'ville	25°46'	97°32'	CST	6	MMMA	MAM

·tca to: 3,000'msl CENTER AT VorDme RADIUS 5 mi.
·tca to: 5,000'msl CENTER AT VorDme RADIUS 20 mi.
APPROACH — TOWER 118.0 GROUND 118.0
OTHER COMM FSS 122.2
CITY 6 miles N POPULATION 198,000
LOCAL VorDme FREQ 114.3 WHERE here HOURS 24?
B'CAST FREQ 1420 WHERE 8 mi No. HOURS Daylight
FROM Bro'ville FREQ 116.3 TRACK 209°, 15Dme
FROM Cd Victoria FREQ 113.7 TRACK 024°, 146 n.mi.
FROM Tampico FREQ 117.5 TRACK 358°, 209 n.mi.
FUEL 80, 100 CARDS Visa, MC CASH? Yes
REPAIRS Minor TIEDOWN BYO

HOTEL	RATE	WHERE	TEL
Holiday Inn	$$	Central	2-43-50

Other hotels in town

Not a really busy internacional airport, you could go through here in good time, especially when the Saturday morning or Sunday afternoon crushes are going.

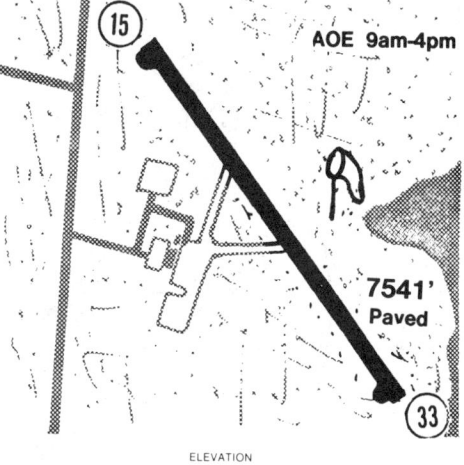

AOE 9am-4pm
7541' Paved
ELEVATION 21'

ILS RWY 13R

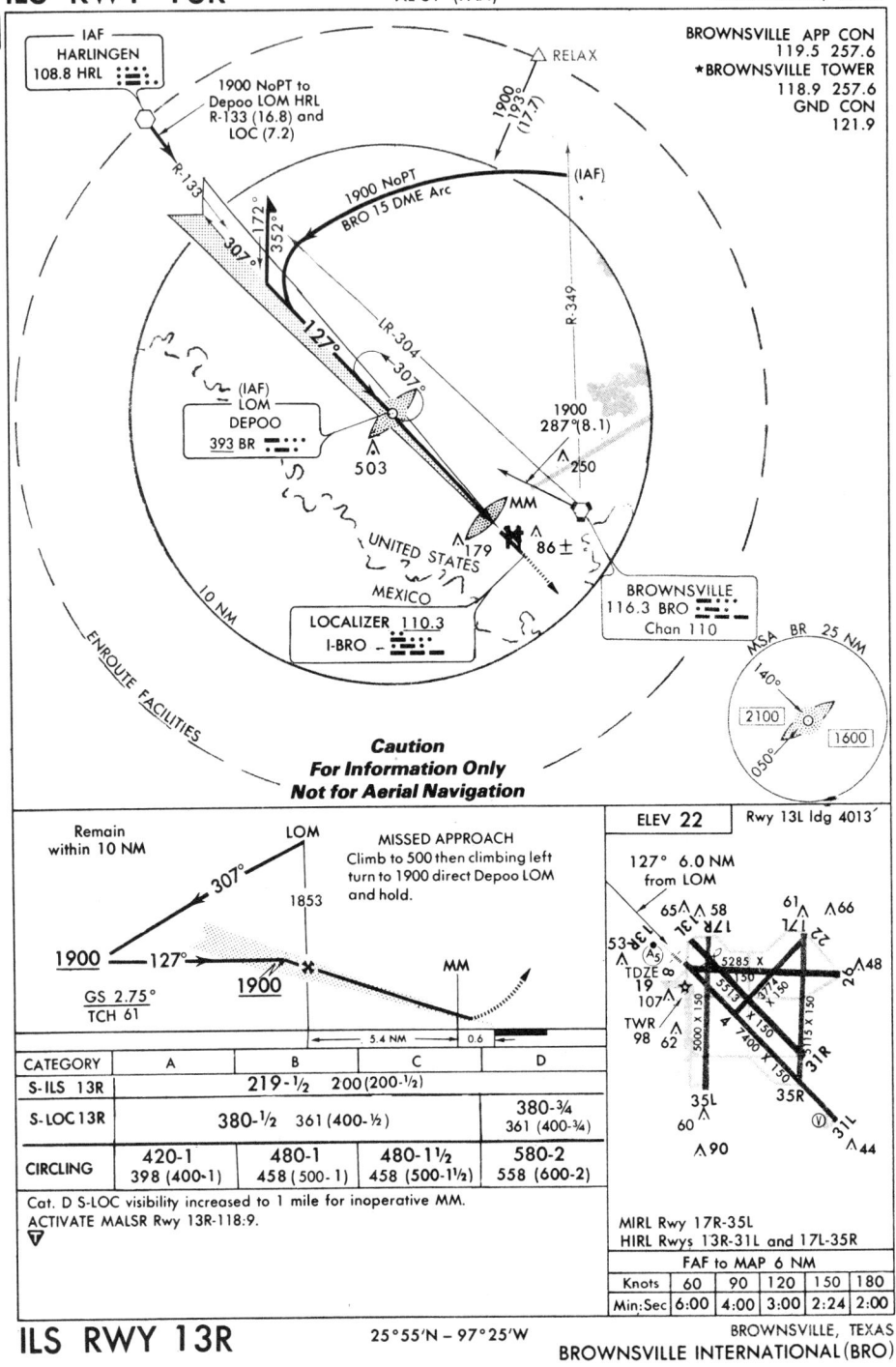

Amdt 7 AL-61 (FAA)

BROWNSVILLE INTERNATIONAL (BRO)
BROWNSVILLE, TEXAS

BROWNSVILLE APP CON 119.5 257.6
***BROWNSVILLE TOWER** 118.9 257.6
GND CON 121.9

IAF HARLINGEN 108.8 HRL

1900 NoPT to Depoo LOM HRL R-133 (16.8) and LOC (7.2)

RELAX
1900 193° (17.7)
1900 NoPT BRO 15 DME Arc (IAF)
R-133
307°
172°
352°
127°
LR-304
307°
R-349
1900 287° (8.1)
(IAF) LOM DEPOO 393 BR
503
250
MM
179
86±
UNITED STATES
MEXICO
LOCALIZER 110.3 I-BRO
BROWNSVILLE 116.3 BRO Chan 110

10 NM
ENROUTE FACILITIES

MSA BR 25 NM
140° / 2100 / 1600 / 050°

Caution For Information Only Not for Aerial Navigation

Remain within 10 NM
LOM
307°
1853
1900 — 127°
1900
GS 2.75°
TCH 61
5.4 NM | 0.6
MM

MISSED APPROACH
Climb to 500 then climbing left turn to 1900 direct Depoo LOM and hold.

ELEV 22   Rwy 13L ldg 4013'
127° 6.0 NM from LOM

CATEGORY	A	B	C	D
S-ILS 13R	219-½	200 (200-½)		
S-LOC 13R	380-½ 361 (400-½)			380-¾ 361 (400-¾)
CIRCLING	420-1 398 (400-1)	480-1 458 (500-1)	480-1½ 458 (500-1½)	580-2 558 (600-2)

Cat. D S-LOC visibility increased to 1 mile for inoperative MM.
ACTIVATE MALSR Rwy 13R-118.9.

MIRL Rwy 17R-35L
HIRL Rwys 13R-31L and 17L-35R

FAF to MAP 6 NM

Knots	60	90	120	150	180
Min:Sec	6:00	4:00	3:00	2:24	2:00

ILS RWY 13R

25°55'N – 97°25'W

BROWNSVILLE, TEXAS BROWNSVILLE INTERNATIONAL (BRO)

SUNRISE & SUNSET – GMT   SALIDA y PUESTA del SOL – GMT

15th of   JAN FEB MAR APR MAY JUN JUL AUG SEPT OCT NOV DEC
SUNRISE 1318 1304 1238 1206 1143 1137 1147 1202 1215 1228 1247 1308 SALIDA
SUNSET   2359 2422 2438 2452 0108 0122 0123 0105 2434 2402 2340 2340 PUESTA
15° de   ENE FEB MAR ABR MAY JUN JUL AGO SEP   OCT NOV DIC

To get local time just subtract 'GMT ADD'
PARA OBTENER TIEMPO LOCAL SUSTRIAGA 'GMT ADD'

Brownsville Texas — 407

JET CHART	WAC	SECTIONAL	LATITUDE	LONGITUDE	US TIME	FOR GMT ADD	ICAO IDENT	TOWN IDENT
JN-46	CH-23 So.	TPC H-23C	25°55'	97°23'	CST	6	-	BRO

APPROACH 119.5 TOWER 118.9 GROUND 121.9
OTHER COMM FSS 122.2 Unicom 123.0
CITY 4 miles W POPULATION 55,100
LOCAL VorDme FREQ 116.3 WHERE 2.3miles NE HOURS 24
B'CAST FREQ 1600 WHERE 1.5 mi No. HOURS Daylight
FROM Tampico FREQ 117.5 TRACK 177°, 219 n.mi.
FROM Matamoros FREQ 114.3 TRACK 155°, 28Dme
FROM del Norte FREQ 115.4 TRACK 073°, 140 n.mi.
FUEL 80, 100, JP CARDS Major CASH? Yes
REPAIRS Major TIEDOWN Yes

HOTEL	RATE	WHERE	TEL
Hotel la Quinta	$$	-	-
Cameron Motel	$	-	-

AOE
8am-5pm
Free

ELEVATION
21'

The relaxed attitude most think is The West sure is going here. Came through for Customs one day and the inspector took an hour to arrive. She wasn't the least surprised we were sitting by the airplane having a late lunch.

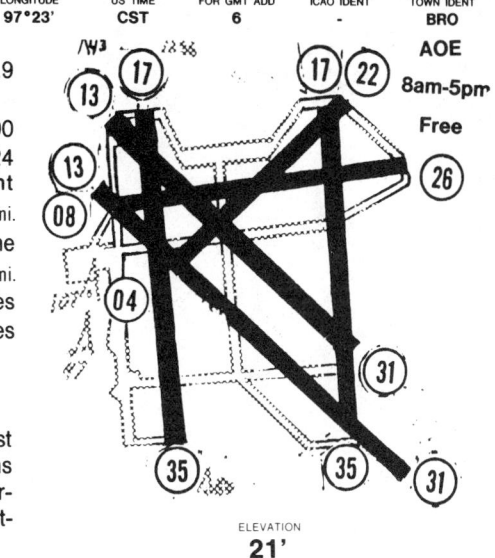

REYNOSA, TAMPS.
VOR PISTA-31

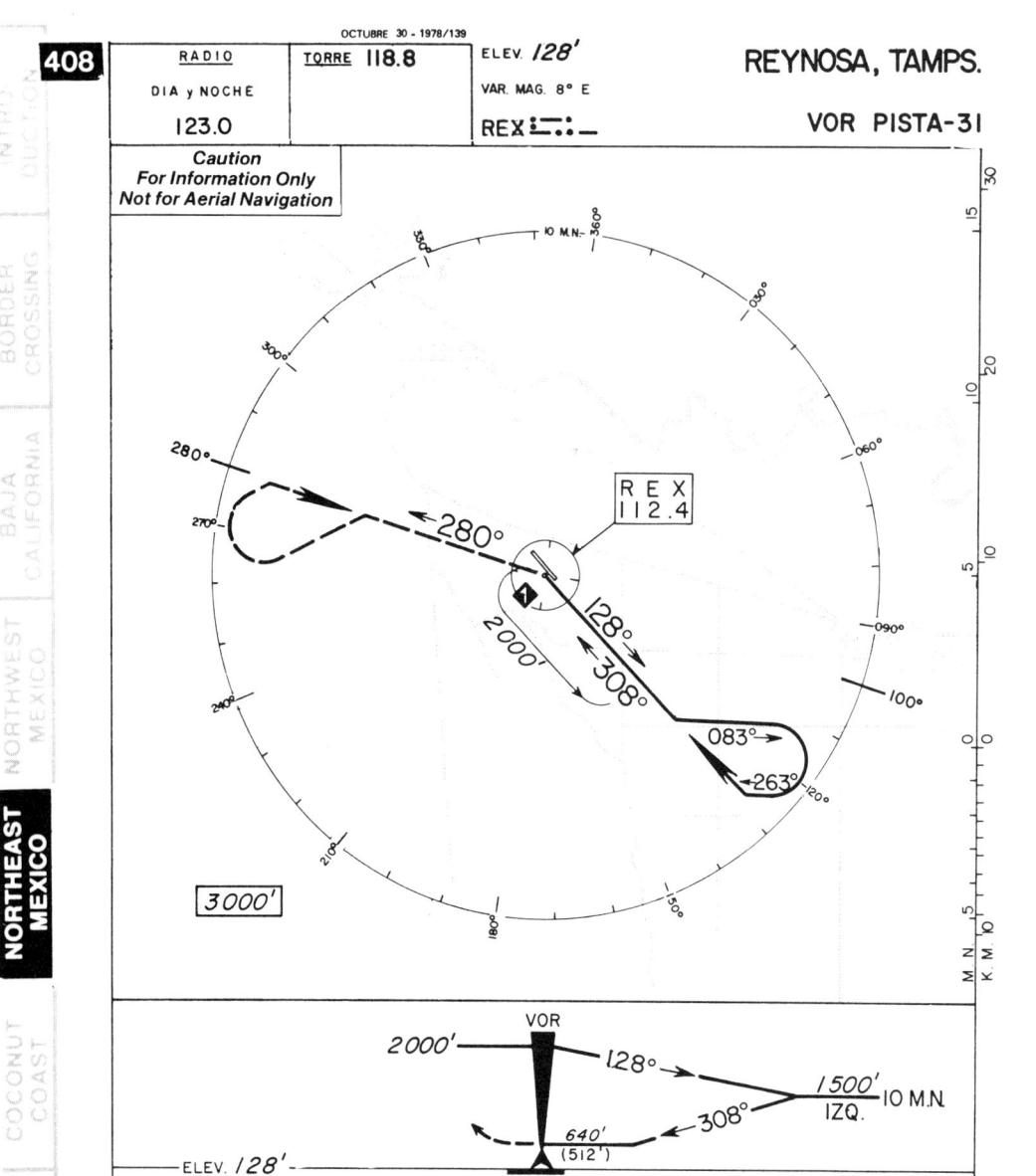

RADIO DIA y NOCHE 123.0
TORRE 118.8
ELEV. 128'
VAR. MAG. 8° E
REX —·—

OCTUBRE 30 - 1978/139 — 408

Caution — For Information Only — Not for Aerial Navigation

REX 112.4

FALLIDA: ASCIENDA EN RADIAL 280° CON VIRAJE DE PROCEDIMIENTO A LA IZQUIERDA DENTRO DE 10 M.N. HASTA LA ALTITUD MINIMA DE ESPERA, DE ACUERDO CON INSTRUCCIONES DEL A.T.C.

CATEGORIA	DIRECTO PISTA 31 MDA 640' (512')	CATEGORIA	CIRCULANDO MDA
A	1	A	640' (512') - 1
B	1	B	680' (552') - 1
C	1¼	C	680' (552') - 1½
D	1¾	D	740' (612') - 2¼

CAMBIOS: AJUSTE DE MINIMOS — S.C.T. – D.G.A.C. — REX V-1

SUNRISE & SUNSET - GMT / SALIDA y PUESTA del SOL - GMT

	JAN	FEB	MAR	APR	MAY	JUN	JUL	AUG	SEPT	OCT	NOV	DEC	
SUNRISE	1314	1303	1241	1213	1153	1149	1158	1210	1219	1228	1244	1303	SALIDA
SUNSET	2410	2430	2442	2452	0104	0117	0119	0104	2436	2408	2350	2352	PUESTA
15° de	ENE	FEB	MAR	ABR	MAY	JUN	JUL	AGO	SEP	OCT	NOV	DIC	

To get local time just subtract 'GMT ADD'
PARA OBTENER TIEMPO LOCAL SUSTRIAGA 'GMT ADD'

Reynosa Internacional

Tamps.   *ray-NO-sah*   **409**

JET CHART	WAC	SECTIONAL	LATITUDE	LONGITUDE	US TIME	FOR GMT ADD	ICAO IDENT	TOWN IDENT
JN-46	CH-23 So.	Bro'ville	26°01'	98°14'	CST	6	MMRX	REX

tca to: 4,000' msl   CENTER Vor   RADIUS 20 mi*

APPROACH —   TOWER 118.8   GROUND 118.8

CITY 4 miles NW   POPULATION 165,000

LOCAL Vor   FREQ 112.4   WHERE here   HOURS 24

B'CAST FREQ 1170   WHERE 6 mi NW   HOURS Daylight

FROM Corpus Christi FREQ 115.5 TRACK 204°, 110 n.mi.
FROM Cd. Victoria   FREQ 113.7 TRACK 186°, 144 n.mi.
FROM Monterrey   FREQ 114.7 TRACK 074°, 102 n.mi.

FUEL 80, 100   CARDS Visa, M   CASH? Yes

REPAIRS Minor   TIEDOWN BYO

HOTEL	RATE	WHERE	TEL
Virrey	$$	Central	2-25-30

AOE 9am-4pm

6191 Paved

ELEVATION **123'**

Busy internacional airport, fuel and clearing goes quickly. Inbound to México have your passports handy to get tourist cards, outbound be sure the pilot has everyone's tourist permits and the aircraft General Declaration. Tips, if you feel like it, a dollar per person who helps you.

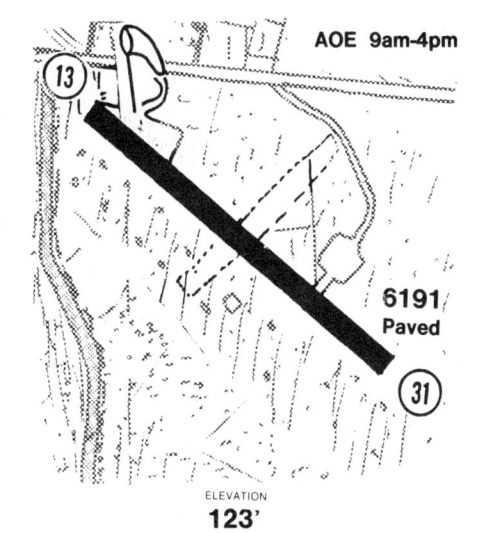

LOC BC RWY 31

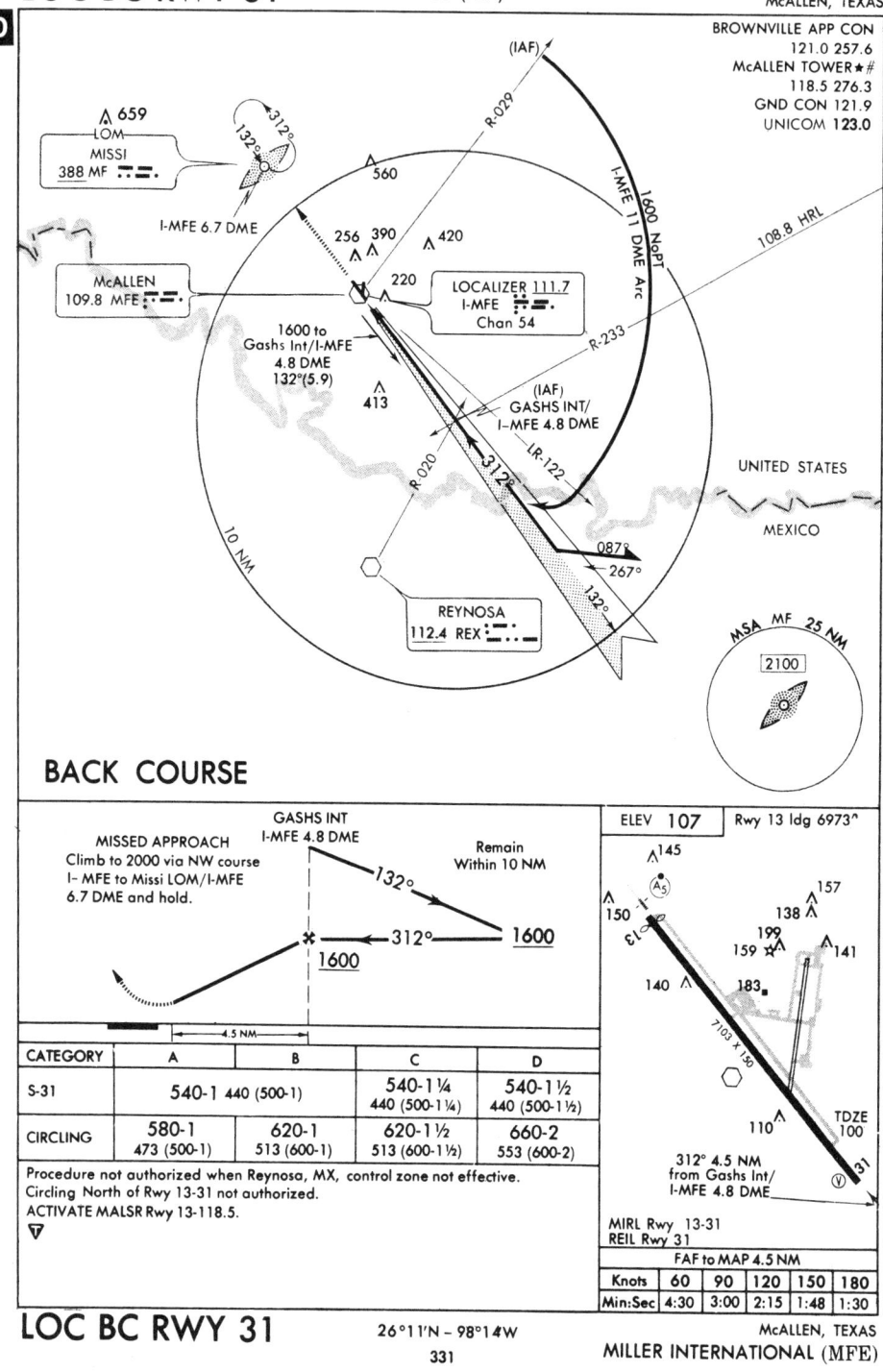

Amdt 2
288
AL-985 (FAA)

MILLER INTERNATIONAL (MFE)
McALLEN, TEXAS

BROWNVILLE APP CON 121.0 257.6
McALLEN TOWER ★ # 118.5 276.3
GND CON 121.9
UNICOM 123.0

MISSI LOM 388 MF
I-MFE 6.7 DME
McALLEN 109.8 MFE
LOCALIZER 111.7 I-MFE Chan 54
REYNOSA 112.4 REX
1600 to Gashs Int/I-MFE 4.8 DME 132°(5.9)
(IAF) I-MFE 11 DME Arc NoPT
(IAF) GASHS INT/I-MFE 4.8 DME
R-029, R-233, R-020, LR-122
108.8 HRL
UNITED STATES / MEXICO
MSA MF 25 NM: 2100

BACK COURSE

MISSED APPROACH: Climb to 2000 via NW course I-MFE to Missi LOM/I-MFE 6.7 DME and hold.

GASHS INT I-MFE 4.8 DME
Remain Within 10 NM
132° — 312° — 1600
1600
4.5 NM

ELEV 107 Rwy 13 ldg 6973'
TDZE 100
312° 4.5 NM from Gashs Int/ I-MFE 4.8 DME
MIRL Rwy 13-31
REIL Rwy 31

CATEGORY	A	B	C	D
S-31	540-1 440 (500-1)	540-1 440 (500-1)	540-1¼ 440 (500-1¼)	540-1½ 440 (500-1½)
CIRCLING	580-1 473 (500-1)	620-1 513 (600-1)	620-1½ 513 (600-1½)	660-2 553 (600-2)

Procedure not authorized when Reynosa, MX, control zone not effective.
Circling North of Rwy 13-31 not authorized.
ACTIVATE MALSR Rwy 13-118.5.

FAF to MAP 4.5 NM

Knots	60	90	120	150	180
Min:Sec	4:30	3:00	2:15	1:48	1:30

LOC BC RWY 31
26°11'N - 98°14'W
331

McALLEN, TEXAS
MILLER INTERNATIONAL (MFE)

SUNRISE & SUNSET - GMT   SALIDA y PUESTA del SOL - GMT

15th of	JAN	FEB	MAR	APR	MAY	JUN	JUL	AUG	SEPT	OCT	NOV	DEC	
SUNRISE	1322	1308	1242	1209	1146	1140	1150	1205	1218	1232	1251	1312	SALIDA
SUNSET	2402	2425	2441	2456	0112	0126	0127	0109	2437	2405	2343	2343	PUESTA
15° de	ENE	FEB	MAR	ABR	MAY	JUN	JUL	AGO	SEP	OCT	NOV	DIC	

To get local time just subtract 'GMT ADD'
PARA OBTENER TIEMPO LOCAL SUSTRIAGA 'GMT ADD'

McAllen Texas

JET CHART	WAC	SECTIONAL	LATITUDE	LONGITUDE	US TIME	FOR GMT ADD	ICAO IDENT	TOWN IDENT
JN-46	CH-23 So.	Bro'ville	26°11'	98°14'	CST	6	KMFE	MFE

411

APPROACH 121.0 TOWER 118.5 GROUND 121.9
OTHER COMM Approach on 119.5 if tower is off
CITY Adjacent N POPULATION 43,000
LOCAL Vor FREQ 109.8 WHERE here HOURS 24
B'CAST FREQ 910 WHERE 8 mi NW HOURS Daylight
FROM Del Norte FREQ 115.4 TRACK 068°, 109n.mi.
FROM Monterrey Int'l FREQ 114.7 TRACK 064°, 103 n.mi.
FROM Tampico FREQ 117.5 TRACK 346°, 233 n.mi.
FUEL 80,100,JP CARDS Major CASH? Yes
REPAIRS Yes TIEDOWN Yes

HOTEL	RATE	WHERE	TEL
Hilton Inn	$$	across st.	-
Best Western	$$	Central	-
Rodeway Inn	$$	2 miles N	-

Hard to beat as a place to clear into the US, each time I've been through here the Customs guys have been courteous, helpful, and in general excellent examples of their calling.

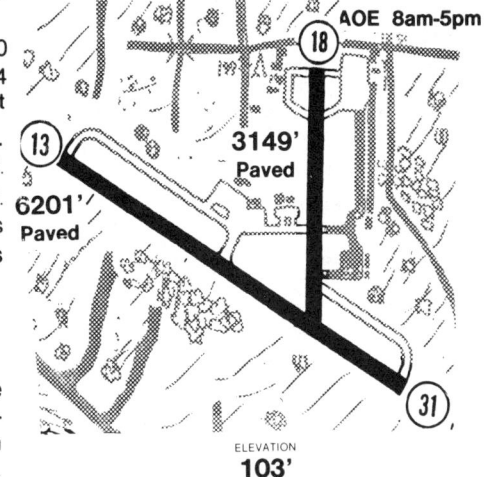

AOE 8am-5pm
18
3149' Paved
6201' Paved
13
31
ELEVATION 103'

412 Lago Azucar, Tamaulipas *LAH-go ah-soo-CARR*

JN CHART	WAC	SECTIONAL	LATITUDE	LONGITUDE	US TIME	FOR GMT	ICAO	TOWN ID
JN-46	CH-23	TPC H23C	26°14'	98°55'	CST	+6		AZU –

OTHER COMM Traffic 124.3

RANCH South 0.75 mi

POPULATION 1 Ranch

FROM McAllen FREQ 109.8 TRACK 265°, 36.9Dme

FROM N.Laredo FREQ 112.6 TRACK 145°, 80.0Dme

FROM Monterrey FREQ 114.7 TRACK 057°, 69.7Dme

AVIATION FUEL -   CREDIT CARDS -   CASH TYPE -

REPAIRS AVAILABLE -   TIEDOWNS? BYO

DATA INCOMPLETE - SEE UPDATING PREPS

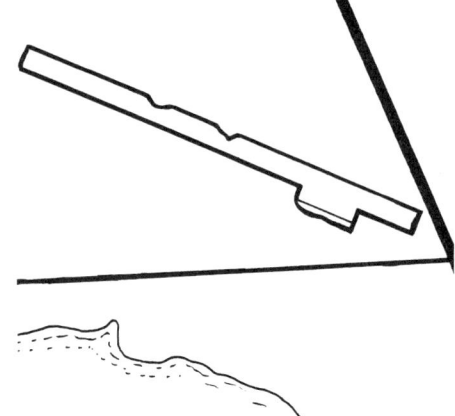

Presa Falcon, Tamaulipas   *PRESS-ah fall-CONE*   413

JN CHART	WAC	SECTIONAL	LATITUDE	LONGITUDE	US TIME	FOR GMT	ICAO	TOWN ID
JN-46	CH-23	TPC H23C	26°31'	99°08'	CST	+6	-	FAL –

OTHER COMM Traffic 124.5
SETTLEMENT Isolated
FROM Nuevo Laredo   FREQ 112.6   TRACK 339°,
FROM McAllen   FREQ 109.8   TRACK 283°, 52.4 Dme
FROM Monterrey   FREQ 114.7   TRACK 039°, 68.8 Dme
AVIATION FUEL Emergency 80   CARDS-   CASH TYPE Dlls or Pesos
REPAIRS AVAILABLE Minor   TIEDOWNS? BYO

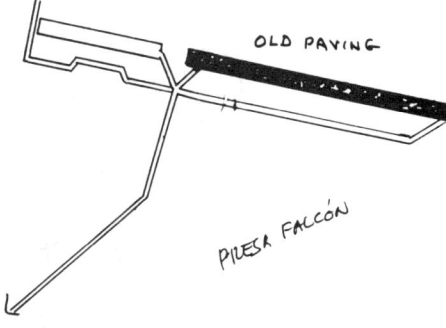

DATA INCOMPLETE - SEE UPDATING PREPS

OLD PAVING

PRESA FALCON

FEBRERO 29–1976/120

RADIO:	TORRE DE CONTROL	ELEV. *486'*	**NVO. LAREDO, TAMPS.**
DIA: 5617 y 127.3	TyR 118.3	VAR. MAG 9° E	AEROPUERTO INTERNACIONAL
NOCHE 3404 y 127.3	C. APROXIMACION	C. TERRESTRE	VOR PISTA 14 112.6 MHZ. NLD — · —

414

NLD 112.6 DME 73

FALLIDA: VIRE A LA **DERECHA**, E INTERCEPTE EN ASCENSO EL **RADIAL 320°**, Y PROSIGA EN TRAYECTORIA DE APROXIMACION HASTA LA ALTITUD MINIMA DE ESPERA O DE ACUERDO CON INSTRUCCIONES DEL **C.T.A.**

CATEGORIA	DIRECTO PISTA 14 MDA 1020' (534')	CATEGORIA	CIRCULANDO
A	1	A	1020' (534')–1
B	1	B	1100' (614')–1
C	1	C	1100' (614')–1 1/2
D	1 1/4	D	1200' (714')–2

CAMBIOS: NINGUNO.   S.C.T.–D.G.A.C.   NLD-V-1

SUNRISE & SUNSET – GMT   SALIDA y PUESTA del SOL – GMT

15th of JAN   FEB   MAR   APR   MAY   JUN   JUL   AUG   SEPT OCT   NOV   DEC
SUNRISE 1329 1315 1247 1213 1149 1142 1152 1209 1223 1238 1259 1320 SALIDA
SUNSET 2405 2429 2446 0102 0119 0134 0135 0116 2443 2409 2346 2345 PUESTA
15° de ENE   FEB   MAR   ABR   MAY   JUN   JUL   AGO   SEP   OCT   NOV   DIC

Nuevo Laredo Tamps.   noo-EVV-oh lah-RAY-doe   415

JET CHART	WAC	SECTIONAL	LATITUDE	LONGITUDE	US TIME	FOR GMT ADD	ICAO IDENT	TOWN IDENT
JN-46	CH-23 So.	TPC H-23C	27°26'	99°34'	CST	6	MMNL	NLD

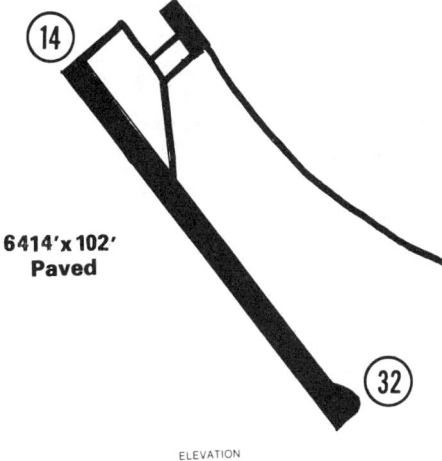

tca to: 2,000'msl   CENTER Vor   RADIUS 5mi*
APPROACH -   TOWER 118.3   GROUND 118.3
OTHER COMM Texas' Cotulla FSS 122.2
CITY 5 mi NE   POPULATION 28,000
LOCAL VorDme   FREQ 112.6   WHERE here   HOURS 24
B'CAST FREQ 790   WHERE 5.4 mi NW   HOURS Daylight
FROM Saltillo   FREQ Airport   TRACK 022°, 137n.mi.
FROM Monclova   FREQ 117.9   TRACK 070°, 105n.mi.
FUEL 80,100   CARDS Visa, Mc   CASH? Yes
REPAIRS -   TIEDOWN BYO

HOTEL	RATE	WHERE	TEL
Motel el Rio	$	So side	2-36-00
Hacienda Motel	$	So side	2-66-66

6414' x 102'
Paved

ELEVATION
414'

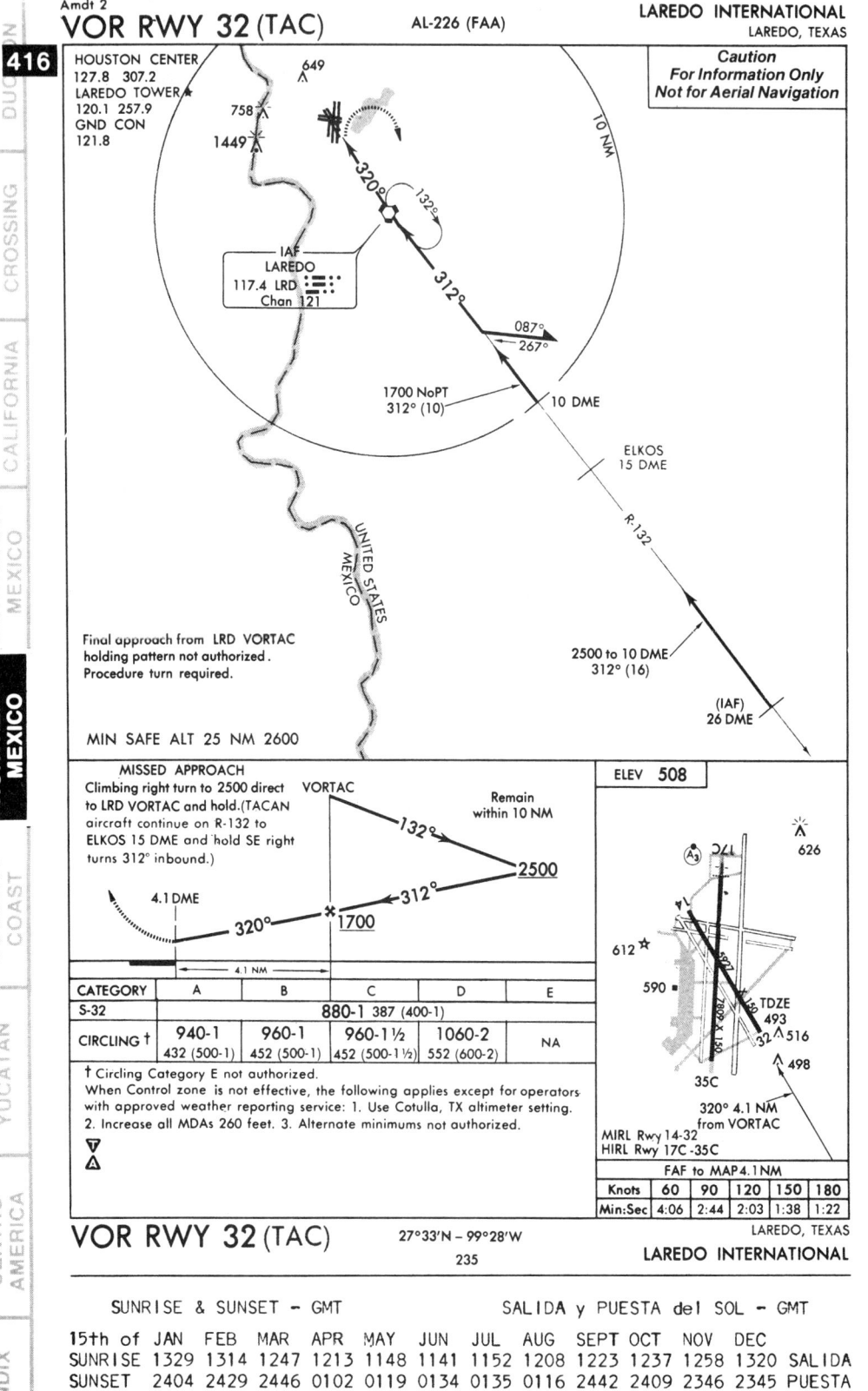

VOR RWY 32 (TAC) — LAREDO INTERNATIONAL, LAREDO, TEXAS

Amdt 2 AL-226 (FAA)

Caution: For Information Only — Not for Aerial Navigation

HOUSTON CENTER 127.8 307.2
LAREDO TOWER 120.1 257.9
GND CON 121.8

IAF LAREDO 117.4 LRD Chan 121

1700 NoPT 312° (10) — 10 DME
ELKOS 15 DME
R-132
2500 to 10 DME 312° (16)
(IAF) 26 DME

087° / 267°
320° / 132° / 312°

649
758
1449

Final approach from LRD VORTAC holding pattern not authorized. Procedure turn required.

MIN SAFE ALT 25 NM 2600

MISSED APPROACH
Climbing right turn to 2500 direct to LRD VORTAC and hold. (TACAN aircraft continue on R-132 to ELKOS 15 DME and hold SE right turns 312° inbound.)

VORTAC — Remain within 10 NM
132° — 2500
312°
4.1 DME — 320° — 1700
4.1 NM

ELEV 508
TDZE 493
612, 590, 626, 516, 498
320° 4.1 NM from VORTAC
MIRL Rwy 14-32
HIRL Rwy 17C-35C

CATEGORY	A	B	C	D	E
S-32			880-1 387 (400-1)		
CIRCLING †	940-1 432 (500-1)	960-1 452 (500-1)	960-1½ 452 (500-1½)	1060-2 552 (600-2)	NA

† Circling Category E not authorized.
When Control zone is not effective, the following applies except for operators with approved weather reporting service: 1. Use Cotulla, TX altimeter setting. 2. Increase all MDAs 260 feet. 3. Alternate minimums not authorized.

FAF to MAP 4.1 NM
Knots	60	90	120	150	180
Min:Sec	4:06	2:44	2:03	1:38	1:22

VOR RWY 32 (TAC) 27°33'N – 99°28'W
235
LAREDO, TEXAS — LAREDO INTERNATIONAL

SUNRISE & SUNSET – GMT   SALIDA y PUESTA del SOL – GMT

15th of JAN FEB MAR APR MAY JUN JUL AUG SEPT OCT NOV DEC
SUNRISE 1329 1314 1247 1213 1148 1141 1152 1208 1223 1237 1258 1320 SALIDA
SUNSET   2404 2429 2446 0102 0119 0134 0135 0116 2442 2409 2346 2345 PUESTA
15° de   ENE FEB MAR ABR MAY JUN JUL AGO SEP OCT NOV DIC

To get local time just subtract 'GMT ADD'
PARA OBTENER TIEMPO LOCAL SUSTRIAGA 'GMT ADD'

Laredo International   Texas   *lah-RAY-doe*   **417**

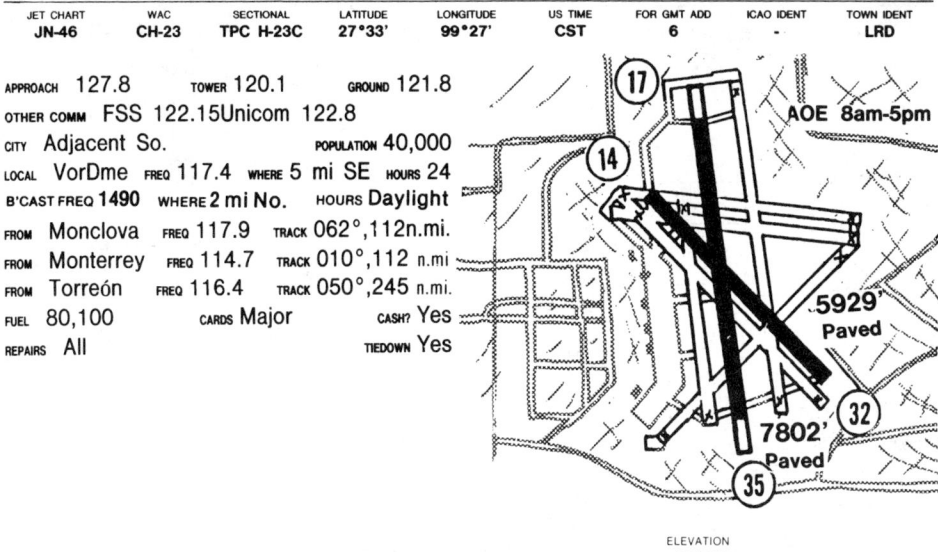

JET CHART	WAC	SECTIONAL	LATITUDE	LONGITUDE	US TIME	FOR GMT ADD	ICAO IDENT	TOWN IDENT
JN-46	CH-23	TPC H-23C	27°33'	99°27'	CST	6	-	LRD

APPROACH 127.8   **TOWER** 120.1   **GROUND** 121.8
OTHER COMM FSS 122.15 Unicom 122.8
CITY Adjacent So.   **POPULATION** 40,000
LOCAL VorDme   **FREQ** 117.4   **WHERE** 5 mi SE   **HOURS** 24
B'CAST FREQ 1490   **WHERE** 2 mi No.   **HOURS** Daylight
FROM Monclova   **FREQ** 117.9   **TRACK** 062°, 112 n.mi.
FROM Monterrey   **FREQ** 114.7   **TRACK** 010°, 112 n.mi.
FROM Torreón   **FREQ** 116.4   **TRACK** 050°, 245 n.mi.
FUEL 80, 100   **CARDS** Major   **CASH?** Yes
REPAIRS All   **TIEDOWN** Yes

AOE 8am-5pm
5929' Paved
7802' Paved

ELEVATION
508'

Overlaps NorthWest Mexico

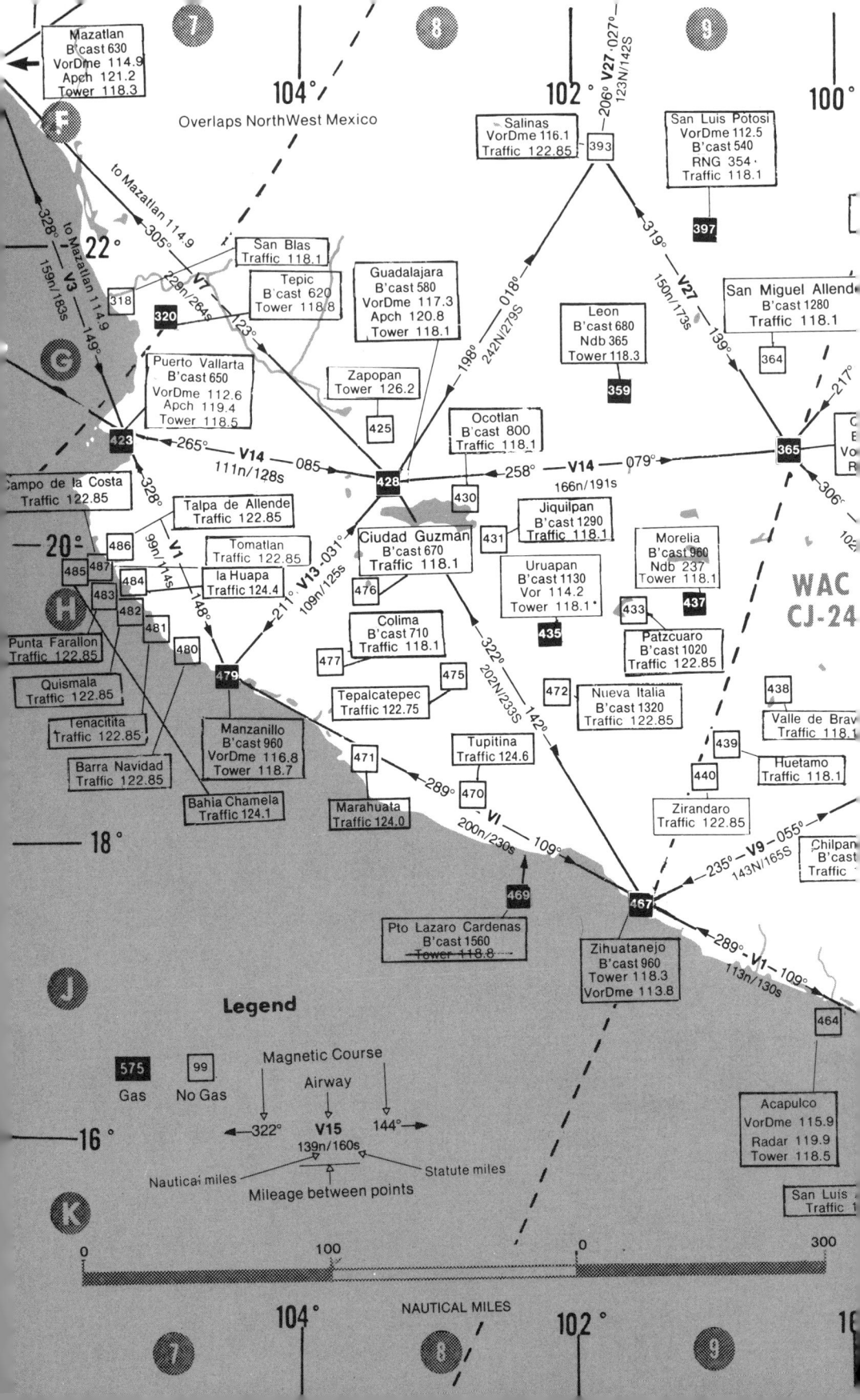

Mazatlan
B'cast 630
VorDme 114.9
Apch 121.2
Tower 118.3

Salinas
VorDme 116.1
Traffic 122.85

San Luis Potosi
VorDme 112.5
B'cast 540
RNG 354·
Traffic 118.1

San Blas
Traffic 118.1

Tepic
B'cast 620
Tower 118.8

Guadalajara
B'cast 580
VorDme 117.3
Apch 120.8
Tower 118.1

Leon
B'cast 680
Ndb 365
Tower 118.3

San Miguel Allende
B'cast 1280
Traffic 118.1

Puerto Vallarta
B'cast 650
VorDme 112.6
Apch 119.4
Tower 118.5

Zapopan
Tower 126.2

Ocotlan
B'cast 800
Traffic 118.1

Campo de la Costa
Traffic 122.85

Talpa de Allende
Traffic 122.85

Jiquilpan
B'cast 1290
Traffic 118.1

Morelia
B'cast 960
Ndb 237
Tower 118.1

Tomatlan
Traffic 122.85

Ciudad Guzman
B'cast 670
Traffic 118.1

Uruapan
B'cast 1130
Vor 114.2
Tower 118.1*

la Huapa
Traffic 124.4

Patzcuaro
B'cast 1020
Traffic 122.85

Punta Farallon
Traffic 122.85

Colima
B'cast 710
Traffic 118.1

Quismala
Traffic 122.85

Tepalcatepec
Traffic 122.75

Nueva Italia
B'cast 1320
Traffic 122.85

Valle de Bravo
Traffic 118.1

Tenacitita
Traffic 122.85

Manzanillo
B'cast 960
VorDme 116.8
Tower 118.7

Tupitina
Traffic 124.6

Huetamo
Traffic 118.1

Barra Navidad
Traffic 122.85

Bahia Chamela
Traffic 124.1

Marahuata
Traffic 124.0

Zirandaro
Traffic 122.85

Pto Lazaro Cardenas
B'cast 1560
Tower 118.8

Zihuatanejo
B'cast 960
Tower 118.3
VorDme 113.8

Chilpan
B'cast
Traffic

Acapulco
VorDme 115.9
Radar 119.9
Tower 118.5

San Luis
Traffic 1

Legend

575 Gas
99 No Gas

Magnetic Course
Airway
←322° **V15** 144°→
139n/160s
Nautical miles — Statute miles
Mileage between points

0 — 100 — 300
NAUTICAL MILES

WAC CJ-24

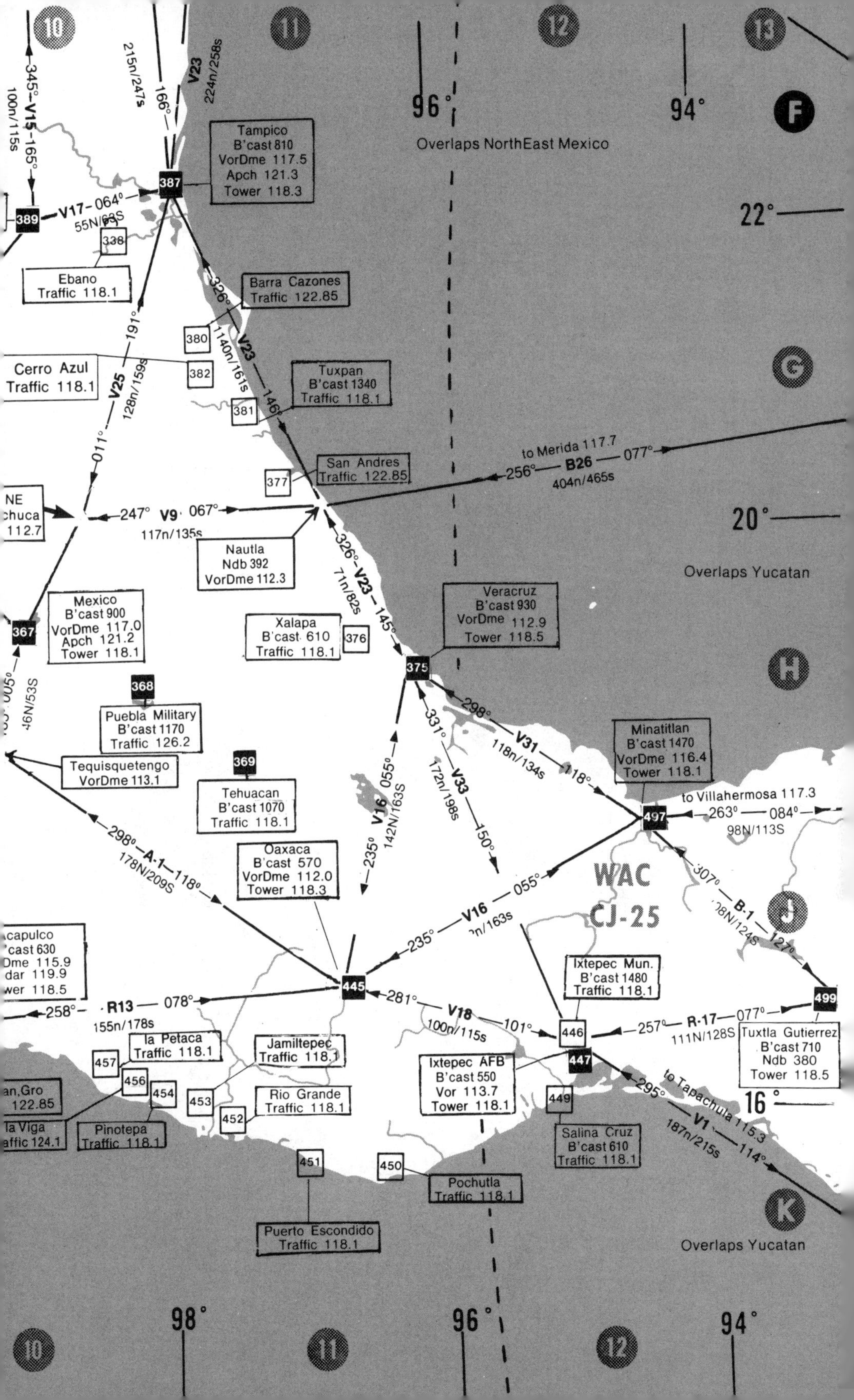

10
11
12
13
F
G
H
J
K
96°
94°
22°
20°
16°
98°
Overlaps NorthEast Mexico
Overlaps Yucatan
Overlaps Yucatan
WAC CJ-25
Tampico B'cast 810 VorDme 117.5 Apch 121.3 Tower 118.3
387
389
V17-064°
55N/63S
345°-V15-165°
100n/115s
215n/247s
166°
V23 224n/258s
338
Ebano Traffic 118.1
Barra Cazones Traffic 122.85
326°
380
382
Cerro Azul Traffic 118.1
V25
191°
128n/159s
011°
1140n/161s
V23
146°
Tuxpan B'cast 1340 Traffic 118.1
381
San Andres Traffic 122.85
377
to Merida 117.7
256°-B26-077°
404n/465s
NE chuca 112.7
247° V9 067°
117n/135s
Nautla Ndb 392 VorDme 112.3
326°-V23-145°
71n/82s
Veracruz B'cast 930 VorDme 112.9 Tower 118.5
375
Mexico B'cast 900 VorDme 117.0 Apch 121.2 Tower 118.1
367
Xalapa B'cast 610 Traffic 118.1
376
368
Puebla Military B'cast 1170 Traffic 126.2
Tequisquetengo VorDme 113.1
369
Tehuacan B'cast 1070 Traffic 118.1
298°
V31
118n/134s
118°
331°
V33
172n/198s
150°
055°
V16
142N/163S
235°
Minatitlan B'cast 1470 VorDme 116.4 Tower 118.1
497
to Villahermosa 117.3
263°-084°
98N/113S
307°
B-1
127°
298°-A-1-118°
178N/209S
Oaxaca B'cast 570 VorDme 112.0 Tower 118.3
235°-V16-055°
Acapulco B'cast 630 VorDme 115.9 Radar 119.9 Tower 118.5
445
258°-R13-078°
155n/178s
281°-V18-101°
100n/115s
Ixtepec Mun. B'cast 1480 Traffic 118.1
446
447
257°-R-17-077°
111N/128S
499
Tuxtla Gutierrez B'cast 710 Ndb 380 Tower 118.5
la Petaca Traffic 118.1
457
456
454
Jamiltepec Traffic 118.1
453
452
Rio Grande Traffic 118.1
Ixtepec AFB B'cast 550 Vor 113.7 Tower 118.1
449
Salina Cruz B'cast 610 Traffic 118.1
to Tapachula 115.3
295°-V1-114°
187n/215s
an,Gro 122.85
la Viga Traffic 124.1
Pinotepa Traffic 118.1
451
450
Pochutla Traffic 118.1
Puerto Escondido Traffic 118.1

420 Coconut Coast Index

Sequence:
Place,Ident,Page

Acapulco,ACA,463
Acapulco IFR,ACA,462
Acapulco Map,ACA,461
Aleman,GRO,460
Altamirano,ALT,441
Apatzingan,AZG,474
Arcelia,ARC,442

Bahia Chamela,ELA-,485
Barra N ividad,BRR-,480
Briefing ,Coconut Coast,421

Campo de la Costa,CST-,487
Chilpancingo,CHG,443
Ciudad Guzman,CGZ,476
Coconut Coast Area,418
Coconut Coast Briefing,421
Coconut Coast Index,420
Colima,IMA,477

Guadalajara,GDL,429
Guadalajara IFR,GDL,428

Huapa,UAP-,484
Huetamo, M,439

Iguala New,IGA,455
Ixtepec,IZT,446

Ixtepec Hurricane Damage,448
Ixtepec Military,IZT,447

Jamiltepec,JAM,453
Jiquilpan,JQL,431

La Petaca,PET-,457
La Viga,FIG-,456

Manzanillo,ZLO,479
Manzanillo IFR,ZLO,478
Marihuata,UAT-,471
Morelia,MLM,437
Morelia IFR,MLM,436

Nueva Italia,NAT-,472

Oaxaca,OAX,445
Oaxaca IFR,OAX,444
Ocotlan,OCO-,430
Ometepec,OMT,458

Patzcuaro,PTZ,433
Pie de la Cuesta,PIE-,464
Pinotepa,PNO,454
Pochutla,SPO,450
Puerto Escondido,PES,451
Puerto Lazaro Cardenas,LZC,469
Puerto Vallarta,PVR,423

Puerto Vallarta IFR,PVR,422
Puerto Vallarta Map,424
Punta Farallon,FAR-,483

Quismala,QIS-,482

Renteria,473
Rio Grande,RGD,452

Salina Cruz,SCZ,449
San Louis Acatlan,SLT,459

Talpa de Allende,TLJ,425
Tenacitita,TNT,481
Tepalcatepec,TPC,475
Tomatlan,TOM,486
Tupitina,TUP-,470

Uruapan,UPN,435
Uruapan IFR,UPN,434

Valle de Bravo,438

Zamora,ZAM,432
Zapopan,ZAP,426
Zihuatanejo,ZIH,467
Zihuatanejo Bay,468
Zihuatanejo IFR,ZIH,466
Zihuatanejo Map,ZIH,465
Zirandaro,ZIR,440

Coconut Coast introduction

Area includes: the coast and foothills running eastward along the beach from Puerto Vallarta to Ixtepec and Tehuantepec.

Best known for: Acapulco and Vallarta beaches and fun things to see and do there.

But it also has: marvelously quiet Colima, highland tropics at Uruapan (oo-roo-AH-ponn), the hat city of Jiquilpan, Silver city at Taxco near Iguala, fifty or a hundred uncharted airports along the coast for camping, and more.

Cities included: Puerto Vallarta, Guadalajara, Manzanillo, Zihuatanejo, Acapulco.

Altitudes: sea level to 14,000+ foot high volcanos

Climate: coastline country usually warm almost never hot, foothills such as Uruapan delightful in the warm months, not bad in cool time of year.

Weather: cumulo nimbus clouds sit on the mountains many afternoons suggesting morning flights up or across. Have yet to see or hear of any day when there was less than VFR conditions along the coastline.

Shopping tips: museum quality lacquerware is made in the small settlements between Patzcuaro and Uruapan. Between Morelia and Uruapan are some very good to excellent copper handiskills. If you can't find the artesans themselves out there, you will be able to catch up with them at the larger of the two squares in Patzcuaro or in the stores on your left as you enter the smaller first square.

In Oaxaca the indians' daring and resourceful use of color in combinations makes that a place to get back to often. No matter how thoroughly you shop there, you missed something good.

Be sure to see: both seahorse statues in Vallarta. Talpa de Allende's cathedral, the open market in Guadalajara, those very good duster pilots along the interior valleys. Stop in at Renteria or Apatzingan or anyplace along there and watch their skill. Gosh, those guys are good.

Special notes: 1) fly around the coastline anytime of day but try to do your mountain valley stuff over 5,000' before noon when the winds aren't as fierce. 2) Remember to file flight plans with any airport which has facilities. No matter how modest 'the facilities', always file when asked or given the opportunity.

Club Med at Playa Blanca

Playa Carreyes

PTO. VALLARTA, JAL.
VOR/DME I PISTA 04

RADIO — DIA Y NOCHE: 127.3, 123.0
TORRE 118.5
ELEV. 19'
VAR MAG 9° E
PVR

SEPTIEMBRE 30 - 1978/138
422

DME 73 PVR 112.6

BAHIA DE BANDERAS

Caution
For Information Only
Not for Aerial Navigation

FALLIDA: VIRE A LA **IZQUIERDA**, E INTERCEPTE EN ASCENSO EL **RADIAL 216°** Y PROSIGA EN TRAYECTORIA DE APROXIMACION HASTA LA ALTITUD MINIMA DE ESPERA, DE ACUERDO CON INSTRUCCIONES DEL **A.T.C.**

CATEGORIA	DIRECTO PISTA 04 MDA 420'(407')	CATEGORIA	CIRCULANDO MDA
A	1	A	520'(501') – 1
B	1	B	520'(501') – 1
C		C	520'(501') – 1¼
D	1½	D	740'(721') – 2½

CAMBIOS: MINIMOS   S.C.T.- D.G.A.C.   PVR VD-1

SUNRISE & SUNSET – GMT   SALIDA y PUESTA del SOL – GMT

15th of	JAN	FEB	MAR	APR	MAY	JUN	JUL	AUG	SEPT	OCT	NOV	DEC	
SUNRISE	1341	1331	1310	1243	1224	1221	1229	1241	1249	1257	1312	1330	SALIDA
SUNSET	2441	0100	0111	0120	0131	0143	0146	0131	0105	2438	2421	2423	PUESTA
15° de	ENE	FEB	MAR	ABR	MAY	JUN	JUL	AGO	SEP	OCT	NOV	DIC	

Puerto Vallarta   Jalisco   PWAIR-toe vye-YARR-tah   **423**

JET CHART	WAC	SECTIONAL	LATITUDE	LONGITUDE	US TIME	FOR GMT ADD	ICAO IDENT	TOWN IDENT
JN-46 | CJ-24	ADS-15 |	TPC J-24A	20°42'	105°15'	CST	6	MMPR	PVR

- **TCA TO:** 20,000'   **RADIUS** 50 n.mi.   **HOURS** 1200-2400Z
- **APPROACH** 119.4   **TOWER** 118.5   **GROUND** 118.5
- **CITY** 6 miles S   **POPULATION** 38,000
- **LOCAL** VorDme   **FREQ** 112.6   **WHERE** Here   **HOURS** 24
- **B'CAST FREQ** 650   **WHERE** 5 mi So.   **HOURS** Daylight
- **FROM** Mazatlán   **FREQ** 114.9   **TRACK** 149°, 159 n.mi.
- **FROM** Guadalajara   **FREQ** 117.3   **TRACK** 265°, 111 n.mi.
- **FROM** Manzanillo   **FREQ** 116.8   **TRACK** 320°, 102 n.mi
- **FROM** Cabo San Lucas **FREQ** 114.0 **TRACK** 288°, 295n.mi.
- **FUEL** 80,100,JP   **CARDS** Visa, MC, etc   **CASH?** Yes
- **REPAIRS** Minor   **TIEDOWN** BYO

HOTEL	RATE	WHERE	TEL
Playa de Oro	$$$E	Nr airport	2-03-48
Hac. Lobos	$$	Near	Tvl Agt
Hotel Oceano	$E	in Old City	2-10-50

READER REPORT We arrived without reservations couldn't find a room anywhere. Finally the cab driver, Oscar Rodriguez took us to his home rather than see us sleep in the airplane. He would accept no payment of any kind; we did manage to convey a small gift to his wife.—M DeFleur, New Mexico

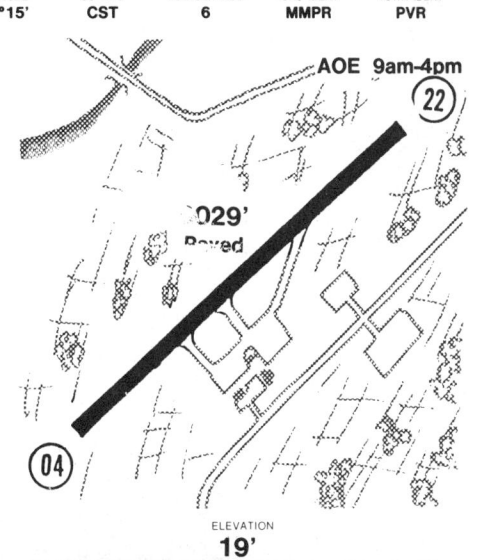

AOE 9am-4pm
22
'029'
Paved
04
ELEVATION
19'

MARINA →

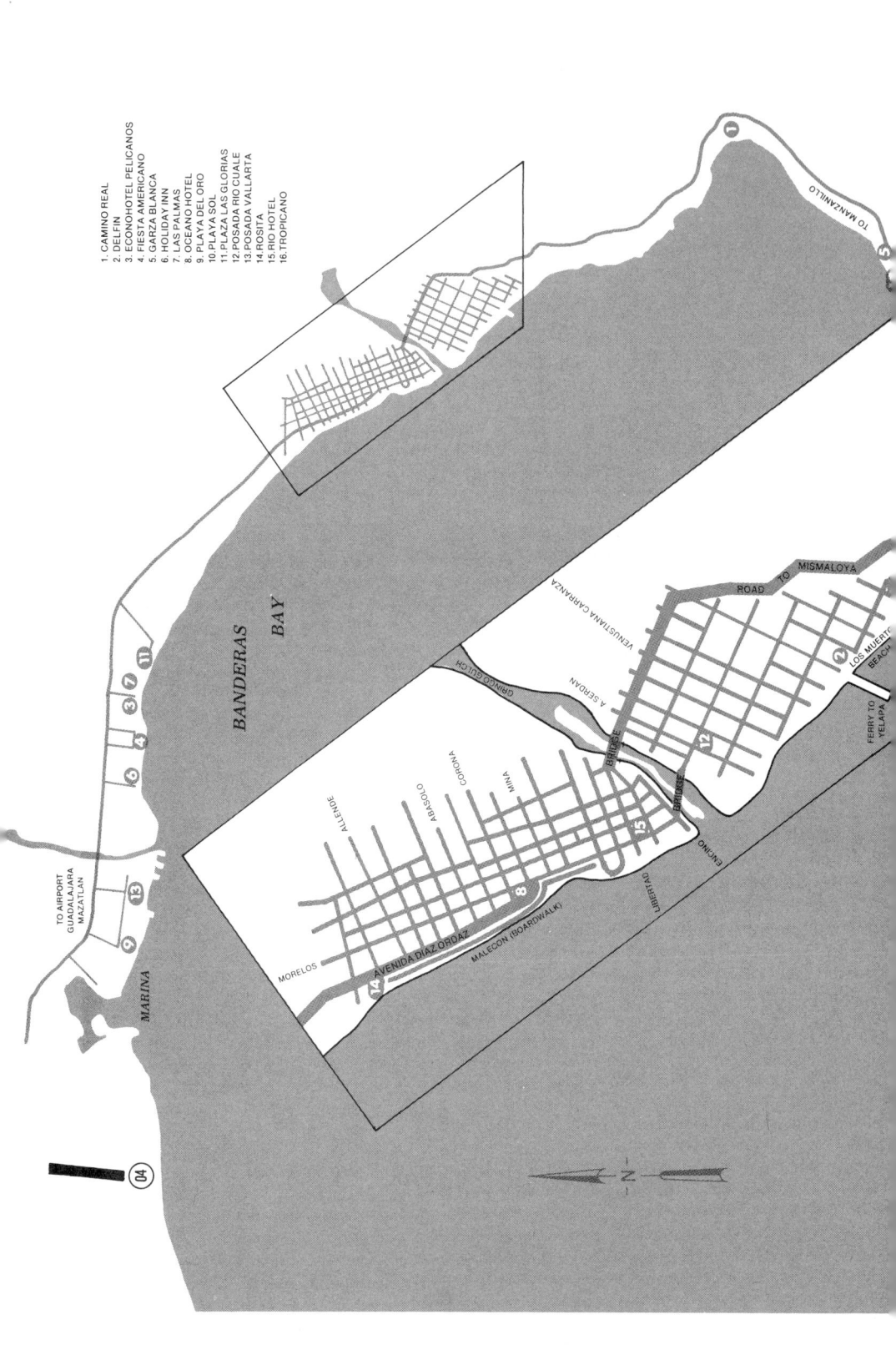

1. CAMINO REAL
2. DELFIN
3. ECONOHOTEL PELICANOS
4. FIESTA AMERICANO
5. GARZA BLANCA
6. HOLIDAY INN
7. LAS PALMAS
8. OCEANO HOTEL
9. PLAYA DEL ORO
10. PLAYA SOL
11. PLAZA LAS GLORIAS
12. POSADA RIO CUALE
13. POSADA VALLARTA
14. ROSITA
15. RIO HOTEL
16. TROPICANO

Talpa de Allende Jalisco   *TALL-pa day ah-YENN-day*   425

JET CHART	WAC	SECTIONAL	LATITUDE	LONGITUDE	US TIME	FOR GMT ADD	ICAO IDENT	TOWN IDENT
JN-46	CJ24 No.	TPC J-24A	20°24'	104°50'	CST	6	-	TLJ

OTHER COMM Traffic 118.1-
CITY 0.25 mi NE   POPULATION 17,000
FROM Pto Vallarta FREQ 112.6 TRACK 115°,29.7 Dme
FROM Guadalajara FREQ 117.3 TRACK 256°,85.5 Dme
FROM Manzanillo FREQ 116.8 TRACK 340°,76.3 Dme
FUEL -   CARDS -   CASH? -
REPAIRS -   TIEDOWN BYO

HOTEL	RATE	WHERE	TEL
Hotel Pelayo	-$	Central	-

Sleepy very old city in a Jalisco mountain valley; the colonial times aren't that far back. This is one of few opportunities to see what some regard as The True México: a small town all but untouched by outside influences. It is worth an afternoon to see and to learn. For an added inducement, the two special town holidays are February 2nd and September 19.

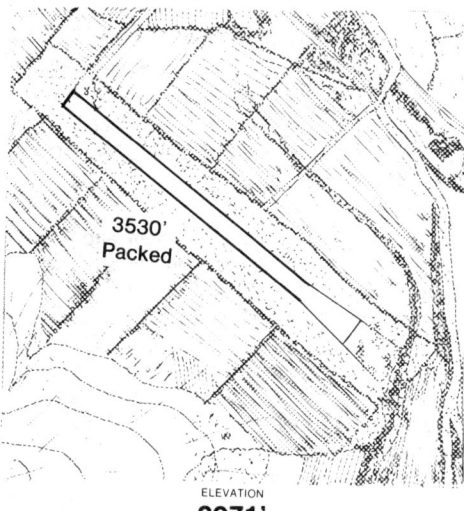

3530'
Packed

ELEVATION
3971'

426 Zapopán Military   Jalisco   *sopp-oh-PONN*

JET CHART	WAC	SECTIONAL	LATITUDE	LONGITUDE	US TIME	FOR GMT ADD	ICAO IDENT	TOWN IDENT
JN-46	CJ-24 No.	TPC J-24A	20°45'	103°28'	CST	-	-	ZAP

OTHER COMM Military tower 126.2
CITY 7 miles W   POPULATION 1,80,000
LOCAL Ndb FREQ 321   WHERE here HOURS On request
FROM Guadalajara FREQ 117.3 TRACK 317°,18Dme
FROM Puerto Vallarta FREQ 112.6 TRACK 078°,101 n.mi.
FUEL Emergency 100   CARDS -   CASH? Pesos
REPAIRS -   TIEDOWN BYO

If you really have a problem and need a place to land, no one is going to say much if you use a military facility to solve that part. Best rule is to first take care of the mechanical problem, then the administrative. If possible while in the air either flip on the ELT or better yet say, on 121.5, the place name and the word "Emergencia" a few times so they'll be alerted.

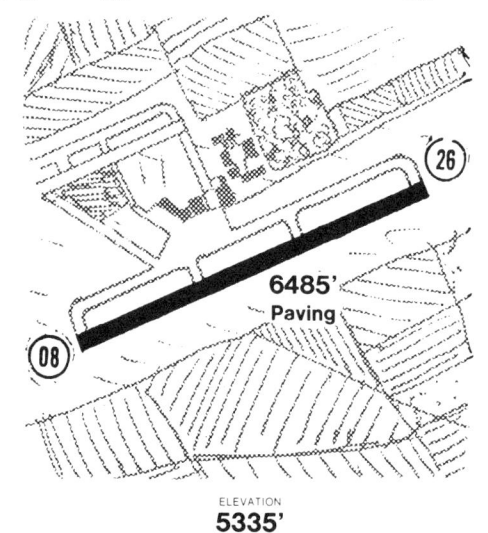

6485'
Paving

ELEVATION
5335'

you've already missed too many good trips

P.O. BOX 27310, ESCONDIDO, CALIF. 92027

Membership Application

Name _____
Spouse _____
Home Address _____
    City, State _____
    Zip/Nation _____
Home Phone _____
Office Phone _____
Aircraft Type _____ N Number _____
Own _____ Rent _____ Club _____
Pilot License No. _____ Total Time _____
Hours Last 6 Months _____ Landings _____
First Solo Date _____ Place _____

As a member I will be entitled to the following:

1. To participate, with the group, in conducted Expeditions. Each Expedition or trip to be announced well in advance so I can plan ahead for it.

2. From time to time discounts and other buying opportunities will be extended to me as a member of *Bush Pilots Internacional* for goods and services offered at lower costs than to those not members, and:

3. As a member I shall receive *The Bush Pilots Journal* presently published quarterly. I agree to assist by contributing reports or ideas of interest to other members, and:

4. As part of my membership I shall receive a membership certificate, decals, and other materials. I agree that all such insignia shall be for my own use and that of members of my family resident at my address and that no insignia of membership will be sold or given to others not members or given to others not members or families of members.

In agreement with the above, here is my check in the amount of $19.00 for my initiation fee and first year's dues.

Signed _____

Place _____ Date _____

GUADALAJARA, JAL.
ILS PISTA 28
LOC 111.3

ABRIL 30-1977/129

RADIO DIA Y NOCHE	TORRE 118.1	ELEV. 5 012'
127.3 y 123.0	EMERGENCIA 121.5	VAR.MAG. 9° E
	APROXIMACION 120.8	GDL

IGDL

MSA
335°	065°	155°	245°	335°
9 900'	9 700'	11 700'	9 700'

Caution For Information Only Not for Aerial Navigation

Spot elevations and navigation aids:
- 5 870'
- 6 199'
- 7000' (SNA 336)
- 10 000' 023°
- 285° DME 120 GDL 117.3
- MM, 5 837'
- LOM GD 385
- 6 430'
- 7 806'
- 6 788'
- 6 264'
- 6 362'
- ILS 282° 111.3 IGDL
- D-8 LOM 282°
- 147° / 327°
- D-13 7 120'
- 6 296'
- 6 232'
- 5 968'
- 6 490'
- 5 935'
- 9 000'
- D-17
- 9 774'
- 6 723'

Profile
- NDB/SNA 7.0 — ELEV. PISTA 28 5 008'
- VOR/GDL — 1.00
- MM GS 5 308'(300')
- LOM GS 7 330'(2 322') — 6.43 — 7.43
- 282° 7400' 8000'
- VIRAJE SOBRE EL LOM DER. 9000' D-13
- ELEV. 5 012'

APROXIMACION FALLIDA 1
(MULTIMOTORES Y TURBORREACTORES)

ASCIENDA DIRECTO EN ODM 285° A NDB/SNA (7.0 DME) CRUCE A 7000' MINIMO Y VIRE A LA DERECHA HACIA VOR/DME - GDL DE ACUERDO CON INSTRUCCIONES DEL ATC.
SE REQUIERE DE UN GRADIENTE DE ASCENSO MINIMO DE 206 PIES/M.N.

NUDOS	100	120	140	160	180	200
PIES/MIN	343	412	480	549	617	686

DE NO CUMPLIR CON ESTE GRADIENTE DE ASCENSO EFECTUESE LA APROXIMACION FALLIDA 2.

APROXIMACION FALLIDA 2
(1 Y 2 MOTORES)

ASCIENDA EN RUMBO 282° ALCANCE 400' Y VIRE INMEDIATAMENTE A LA DERECHA, INTERCEPTE EL RADIAL 023° DEL VOR/DME - GDL Y PROSIGA ASCENSO CON VIRAJE DE PROCEDIMIENTO A LA DERECHA DENTRO DE 10 M.N. HASTA LA ALTITUD-MINIMA DE ESPERA DE ACUERDO CON INSTRUCCIONES DEL A.T.C.
EN CASO DE FALLA DEL VOR, VIRE A LA DERECHA PARA INTERCEPTAR EL ODM 102° DEL LOM/GD Y ASCIENDA EN TRAYECTORIA DE APROXIMACION.

NUDOS	60	80	100	120	140	160	180	200
G.S 3° 00'	3 18	4 24	5 30	6 36	7 42	8 48	9 54	10 60
LOM A APROX.FALLIDA 7.43	7 06	5 19	4 16	3 33	3 03	2 40	2 22	2 08

APROXIMACION DIRECTA PISTA 28
DH 5308'(300') DH 5358'(350') MDA 5560'(552')

	ILS COMPLETO	SIN MM y OM	SIN ALS	SIN MM/OM/ALS	SIN GS	SIN MM/GS	SIN GS/ALS/MM
A	RVR 40	RVR 40	RVR 50		1½		
B	3/4	3/4	1				
C							
D							

NO REGULAR 1¼ | DH 5458'(450') 1½ | MDA 5560'(552') 1½

CIRCULANDO
	MDA
A	5 680'(668')-1
B	5 800'(788')-1¼
C	5 800'(788')-1½
D	5 960'(948')-2
NO REGULAR	6 000'(988')-2

CAMBIOS: RVR y DETALLES MENORES — S C T - D G A C — GDL ILS-I

SUNRISE & SUNSET - GMT   **SALIDA y PUESTA del SOL - GMT**

15th of	JAN	FEB	MAR	APR	MAY	JUN	JUL	AUG	SEPT	OCT	NOV	DEC
SUNRISE	1332	1322	1301	1234	1216	1212	1221	1232	1240	1248	1302	1321	SALIDA
SUNSET	2433	2451	0102	0111	0122	0134	0136	0122	2456	2429	2412	2415	PUESTA
15 de	ENE	FEB	MAR	ABR	MAY	JUN	JUL	AGO	SEP	OCT	NOV	DIC	

Guadalajara   Jalisco   *wah-dah-lah-HAH-rah*   **429**

JET CHART	WAC	SECTIONAL	LATITUDE	LONGITUDE	US TIME	FOR GMT ADD	ICAO IDENT	TOWN IDENT
JN-46	CJ-24	ADS-15 TPC J-24A	20°31'	103°19'	¢CST	6	MMGL	GDL

•TCA TO: 20,000'   RADIUS 50 n.mi.   HOURS 24
APPROACH 120.8   TOWER 118.1   GROUND 118.1
CITY 7 miles N   POPULATION 1,850,000
LOCAL VorDme   FREQ 117.3   WHERE here   HOURS 24
B'CAST FREQ 580   WHERE 11 Mi NW   HOURS Daylight
FROM Puerto Vallarta FREQ 112.6 TRACK 085°, 111 n.mi.
FROM Mazatlán   FREQ 114.9   TRACK 125°, 229 n.mi.
FROM Acapulco   FREQ 115.9   TRACK 307°, 299 n.mi.
FUEL 80,100,JP   CARDS Visa,M,etc   CASH? Yes
REPAIRS Yes   TIEDOWN BYO Ropes

HOTEL	RATE	WHERE	TEL
Tapatio Princess	$$	4 miles N	35-60-50
H Fenix	$$	Central	14-75-14
H de Mendoza	-	Cntrl	13-46-46

READER REPORT Was overcharged $25 U.S. due to a math error on part of the gas attendant. Two days later on return to the airport the Commandante promptly set it straight, with apologies. Very nice.—The Neilsons, Oregon

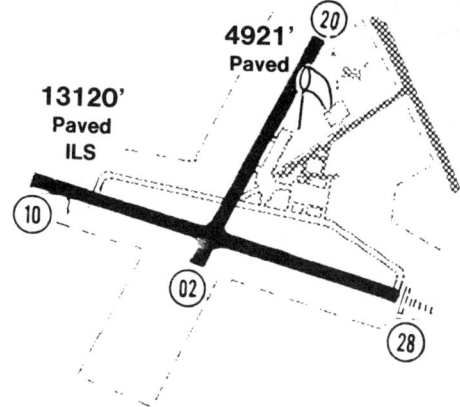

4921' Paved
13120' Paved ILS

ELEVATION
5007'

430 Ocotlán   Jalisco   *oh-coat-LONN*

JET CHART	WAC	SECTIONAL	LATITUDE	LONGITUDE	US TIME	FOR GMT ADD	ICAO IDENT	TOWN IDENT
JN-46	CJ-24 No.	TPC J-24A	20°22'	102°47'	CST	6	-	-OCO

OTHER COMM Traffic 118.1
CITY 1 mile S   POPULATION 15,000
B'CAST FREQ 800   WHERE 3 Mi SW   HOURS Daylight
FROM Guadalajara   FREQ 117.3   TRACK 102°, 32Dme
FROM Morelia   FREQ 237   TRACK 280°, 97n.mi.
FUEL -   CARDS -   CASH? -
REPAIRS -   TIEDOWN BYO

4917'
Paving

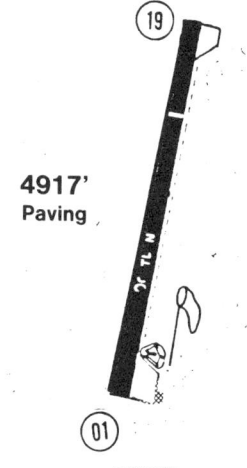

ELEVATION
4994'

Jiquilpán Michoacan   hee-keel-PONN 431

JET CHART	WAC	SECTIONAL	LATITUDE	LONGITUDE	US TIME	FOR GMT ADD	ICAO IDENT	TOWN IDENT
JN-46	CJ-24 No.	TPC J-24C	19°59'	102°45'	CST	6	-	JQL

OTHER COMM Traffic 118.1
CITY 3 miles E   POPULATION 19,000
B'CAST FREQ 1290   WHERE 2 mi E   HOURS Daylight
FROM Guadalajara   FREQ 117.3   TRACK 125°, 52Dme
FROM Uruapan   FREQ 114.2   TRACK 302°, 53n.mi.

Handy for a picnic or just to see what the country looks like. Expect an indian or two to be curious whether visible or not.

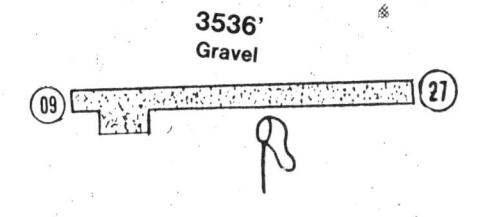

3536'
Gravel

(09) ──────────────── (27)

ELEVATION
5848'

432 Zamora Michoacan *sah-MORE-ah*

JET CHART	WAC	SECTIONAL	LATITUDE	LONGITUDE	US TIME	FOR GMT ADD	ICAO IDENT	TOWN IDENT
JN-46	CJ-24 No.	TPC J-24C	20°01'	102°17'	CST	6	-	ZAM

OTHER COMM Traffic 118.1
CITY 1 mile S POPULATION 18,000
B'CAST FREQ 1580 WHERE 7 mi ESE HOURS Daylight
FROM Guadalajara FREQ 117.3 TRACK 109°,66Dme
FROM Morelia FREQ Ndb TRACK 237 ,290°64n.mi.
FUEL - CARDS - CASH? -
REPAIRS - TIEDOWN BYO

If you are nervous about these soldiers, don't be. Best way to get over it is to take a few minutes with a Spanish-English dictionary to struggle through a conversation with the sergeant. You find once communication is established, however basic, you change from strangers to individuals. Try it.

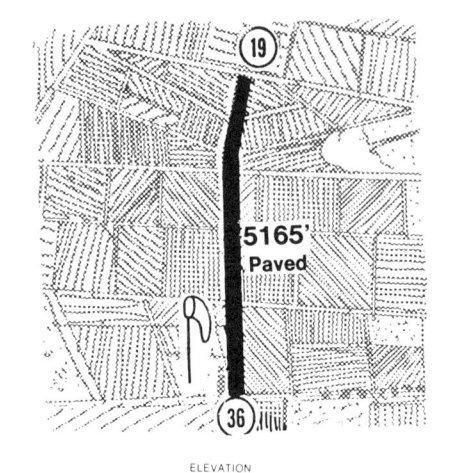

5165' Paved

ELEVATION
5677'

Patzcuaro		Michoacan				*POTTS-coo-arr-oh*			**433**
JET CHART	WAC	SECTIONAL	LATITUDE	LONGITUDE	US TIME	FOR GMT ADD	ICAO IDENT		TOWN IDENT
JN-46	CJ-24 So.	TPC J-24B	19°32'	101°35'	CST	6	-		PTZ

OTHER COMM Traffic 122.85

CITY 2.5 mi SW POPULATION 66,000
B'CAST FREQ 1020 WHERE 5 mi ESE HOURS Daylight
FROM Morelia FREQ 237 TRACK 233°,24n.mi.
FROM Guadalajara FREQ 117.3 TRACK 114°,117 n.mi.
FROM Uruapan FREQ 114.2 TRACK 061°,28n.mi.
FUEL - CARDS - CASH? -
REPAIRS None TIEDOWN BYO

HOTEL	RATE	WHERE	TEL
Posada don Vasco	$$	N side	Yes
San Rafael	$	Big Plaza	Spanish
Posada Basilica	-$	Central	Spanish

3461' Gravel Cattle

ELEVATION
6889'

One of the unique cities: the styles of art, of fishing, of Sunday afternoon band concerts, are all a blend of the Tarascan Indian culture, with additions accepted from the Mexican culture only where a definite benefit would come to the indians.

READER REPORT Posada San Rafael: if I ever turn up missing, look for me here first. Patzcuaro is serene.—O Anderson, Michigan

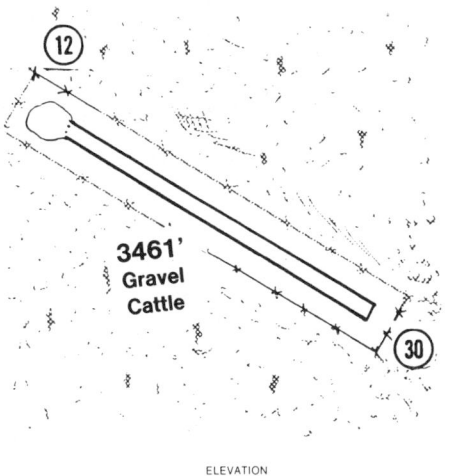

434 JULIO 9-1981/158

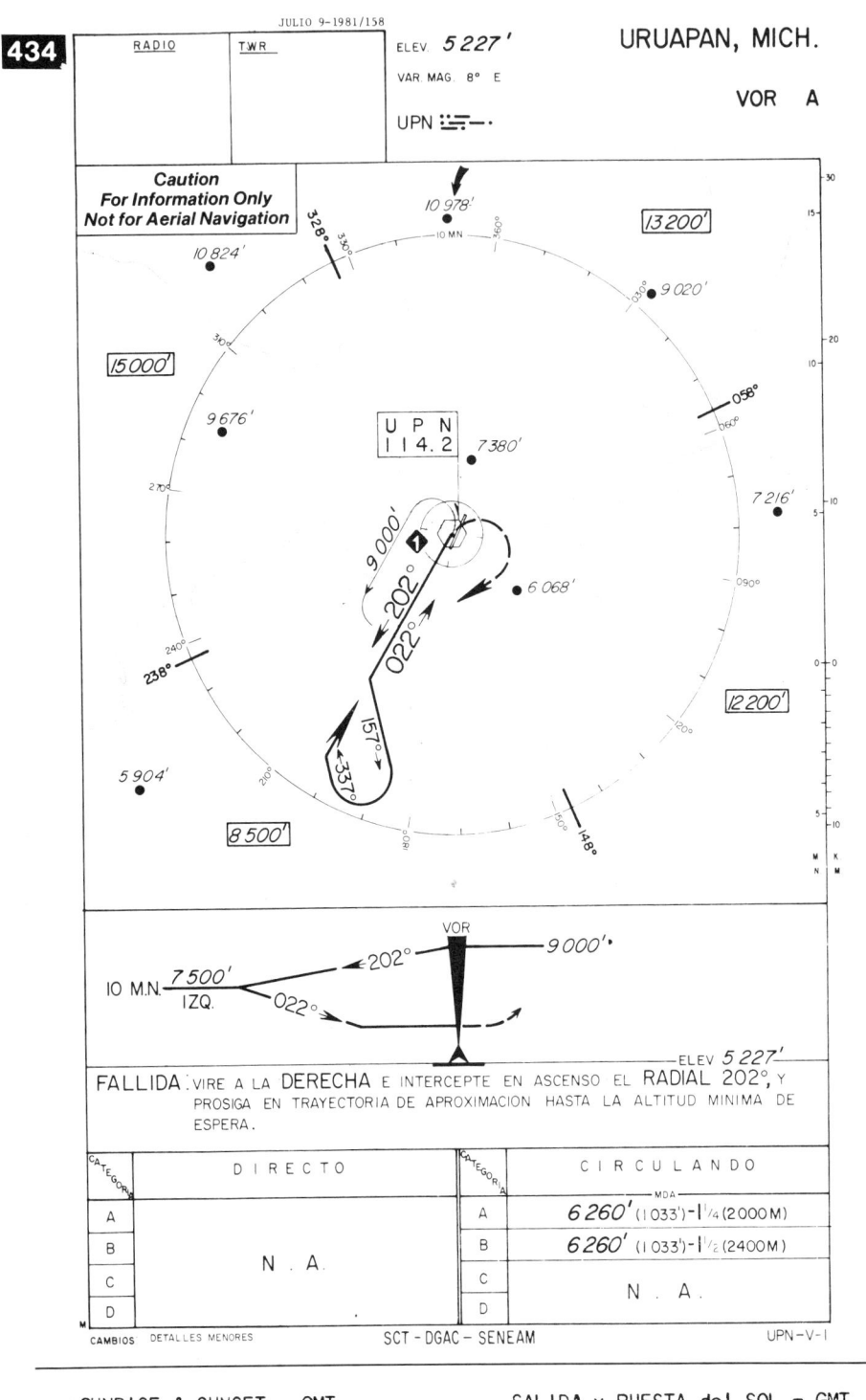

RADIO	TWR

ELEV. **5 227'**
VAR. MAG. 8° E
UPN ··−·· −−·−·

URUAPAN, MICH.

VOR A

*Caution
For Information Only
Not for Aerial Navigation*

UPN 114.2

Altitudes noted on chart: 10 978', 13 200', 10 824', 9 020', 15 000', 9 676', 7 380', 7 216', 9 000', 6 068', 12 200', 5 904', 8 500', 148°

Radials/bearings: 328°, 058°, 238°, 157°, 337°, 202°, 022°

10 M.N. 7 500' IZQ. — 022° / 202° — 9 000' — VOR — ELEV 5 227'

FALLIDA: VIRE A LA **DERECHA** E INTERCEPTE EN ASCENSO EL **RADIAL 202°**, Y PROSIGA EN TRAYECTORIA DE APROXIMACION HASTA LA ALTITUD MINIMA DE ESPERA.

CATEGORIA	DIRECTO	CATEGORIA	CIRCULANDO MDA
A		A	6 260' (1 033') - 1¼ (2000 M)
B	N.A.	B	6 260' (1 033') - 1½ (2400 M)
C		C	N.A.
D		D	

CAMBIOS: DETALLES MENORES SCT - DGAC - SENEAM UPN-V-1

SUNRISE & SUNSET - GMT   SALIDA y PUESTA del SOL - GMT

15th of   JAN FEB MAR APR MAY JUN JUL AUG SEPT OCT NOV DEC
SUNRISE   1325 1316 1256 1230 1212 1209 1218 1228 1235 1242 1256 1314 SALIDA
SUNSET   2430 2447 2457 0105 0115 0127 0129 0116 2451 2425 2409 2412 PUESTA
15° de   ENE FEB MAR ABR MAY JUN JUL AGO SEP OCT NOV DIC

To get local time just subtract 'GMT ADD'
PARA OBTENER TIEMPO LOCAL SUSTRAIGA 'GMT ADD'

Uruapan Michoacan

oo-roo-OPP-onn

435

JET CHART	WAC	SECTIONAL	LATITUDE	LONGITUDE	US TIME	FOR GMT ADD	ICAO IDENT	TOWN IDENT
JN-46	CJ-24 So.	TPC J-24C	19°24'	102°02'	CST	6	-	UPN

APPROACH —   TOWER 118.1   GROUND 118.1
CITY 1 mile NW   POPULATION 109,000
LOCAL Vor   FREQ 114.2   WHERE Here   HOURS 24
B'CAST FREQ 1130 WHERE 6 mi ENE HOURS Daylight
FROM Guadalajara FREQ 117.3 TRACK 123°,99Dme
FROM Manzanillo   FREQ 116.8 TRACK 031°,109 n.mi.
FROM Morelia   FREQ Ndb 237 TRACK 237°,52n.mi.
FUEL 80,100   CARDS Visa,MC   CASH? Pesos
REPAIRS Minor   TIEDOWN BYO

HOTEL	RATE	WHERE	TEL
Hotel Hernandez	$	On plaza	Yes
Pie de la Sierra	$	2 mi W	Yes
Motel	$	3/4 mi NW	-
H. Victoria	$	Central	-

For some reason I can't remember the name of that motel between the airport and city. Haven't stayed there, that might be the reason, but reports say it is clean and okay.

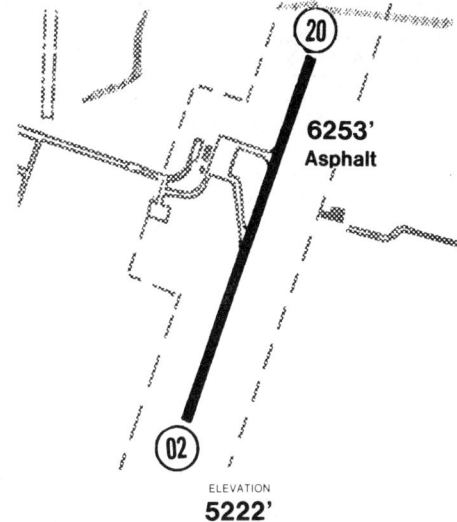

20

6253'
Asphalt

02

ELEVATION
5222'

ENERO 30 DE 1980/147

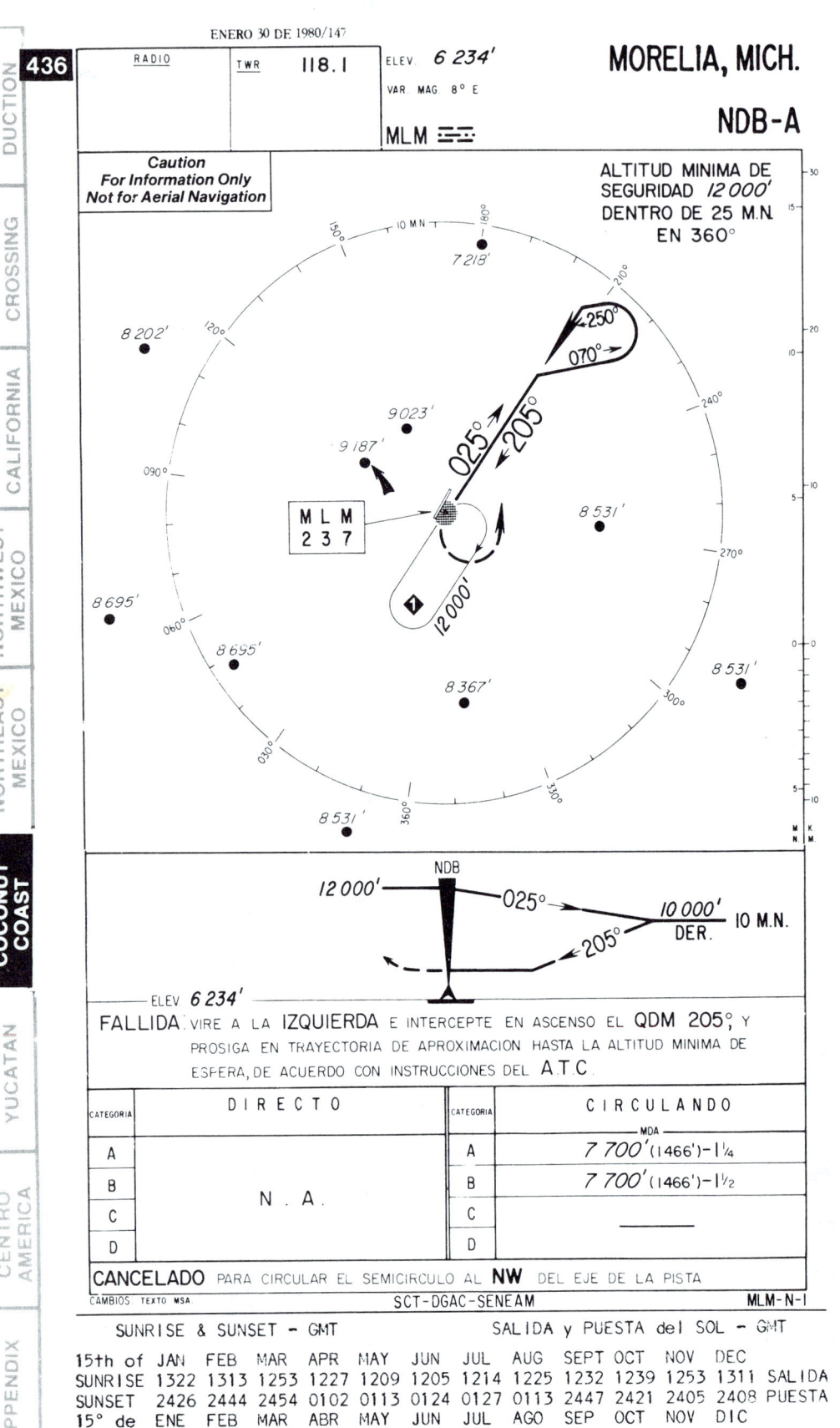

RADIO	TWR	118.1	ELEV	6 234'
			VAR. MAG.	8° E

MLM ▄▄▄

MORELIA, MICH.
NDB-A

436

Caution — For Information Only — Not for Aerial Navigation

ALTITUD MINIMA DE SEGURIDAD *12 000'* DENTRO DE 25 M.N. EN 360°

MLM 237

FALLIDA: VIRE A LA **IZQUIERDA** E INTERCEPTE EN ASCENSO EL QDM 205°, Y PROSIGA EN TRAYECTORIA DE APROXIMACION HASTA LA ALTITUD MINIMA DE ESFERA, DE ACUERDO CON INSTRUCCIONES DEL A.T.C.

ELEV 6 234'

CATEGORIA	DIRECTO	CATEGORIA	CIRCULANDO — MDA
A		A	7 700' (1466') - 1¼
B	N. A.	B	7 700' (1466') - 1½
C		C	—
D		D	—

CANCELADO PARA CIRCULAR EL SEMICIRCULO AL **NW** DEL EJE DE LA PISTA

CAMBIOS TEXTO MSA   SCT-DGAC-SENEAM   MLM-N-1

SUNRISE & SUNSET – GMT   SALIDA y PUESTA del SOL – GMT

15th of	JAN	FEB	MAR	APR	MAY	JUN	JUL	AUG	SEPT	OCT	NOV	DEC	
SUNRISE	1322	1313	1253	1227	1209	1205	1214	1225	1232	1239	1253	1311	SALIDA
SUNSET	2426	2444	2454	0102	0113	0124	0127	0113	2447	2421	2405	2408	PUESTA
15° de	ENE	FEB	MAR	ABR	MAY	JUN	JUL	AGO	SEP	OCT	NOV	DIC	

Morelia   Michoacan

moe-RAY-lee-ah

437

JET CHART	WAC	SECTIONAL	LATITUDE	LONGITUDE	US TIME	FOR GMT ADD	ICAO IDENT	TOWN IDENT
JN-46	CJ-24 No.	TPC J-24C	19°43'	101°13'	CST	6	-	MLM

tca to: **12,000'msl**   CENTER AT **Ndb**   RADIUS **5 mi.**

APPROACH —   TOWER **118.1**   GROUND **118.1**
CITY **1 mile SE**   POPULATION **260,000**
LOCAL **Ndb**   FREQ **237**   WHERE **here**   HOURS **days**
B'CAST FREQ **960**   WHERE **7 mi ESE**   HOURS **Daylight**
FROM **Guadalajara**   FREQ **117.3**   TRACK **105°, 128** n.mi.
FROM **Uruapan**   FREQ **114.2**   TRACK **057°, 52** n.mi.
FROM **México**   FREQ **117.0**   TRACK **270°, 116** n.mi.
FUEL **80, 100**   CARDS **Visa, MC**   CASH? **Pesos**
REPAIRS **Minor**   TIEDOWN **BYO**

HOTEL	RATE	WHERE	TEL
Villa Montana	$$	Hills	2-25-88
Virrey Mendosa	$$	Central	2-06-33

Most aristocratic of Mexican cities, the small size of Morelos belies its historic value to the Republic.

A treasure city in setting and architecture. Most beautiful is the Cathedral, whose full magnificence is difficult to adequately express.

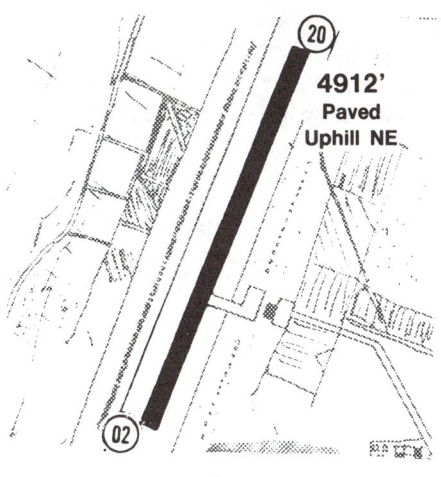

4912'
Paved
Uphill NE

ELEVATION
6232' to 6240'

438 Valle de Bravo   Mexico

VAH-yay day BRAH-voe

JET CHART	WAC	SECTIONAL	LATITUDE	LONGITUDE	US TIME	FOR GMT ADD	ICAO IDENT	TOWN IDENT
JN-46	CJ-24 No.	TPC J-24C	19°11'	100°14'	CST	6	-	-

OTHER COMM Traffic 126.2
CITY 1 mi SE   POPULATION Army Base
FROM México   FREQ 117.0   TRACK 249°, 68Dme,
FROM Tequisquetengo FREQ 113.1 TRACK 290°, 63Dme,
FROM Uruapan   FREQ 114.2   TRACK 087°, 103n.mi.,
FUEL -   CARDS -   CASH? -
REPAIRS -   TIEDOWN BYO

Located well inside Restricted Area MMR-103, only emergency landings are suggested. Soldiers show considerable attention to any arriving aircraft.

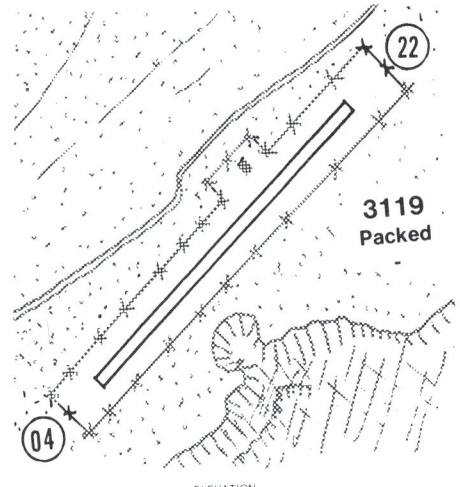

3119 Packed

ELEVATION 5671'

Huetamo   Michoacan   *way-TOMM-oh*   **439**

JET CHART	WAC	SECTIONAL	LATITUDE	LONGITUDE	US TIME	FOR GMT ADD	ICAO IDENT	TOWN IDENT
JN-46	CJ-24 So.	TPC J-24C	18°38'	100°55'	CST	6	-	HTM

OTHER COMM Traffic 118.1
SETTLEMENT 1/2 mi S   POPULATION 2,000
FROM Uruapan   FREQ 114.2   TRACK 117°, 79n.mi.
FROM Zihuatanejo FREQ 113.8 TRACK 020°, 70Dme
FUEL 80, 100   CARDS -   CASH? Pesos
REPAIRS Minor   TIEDOWN BYO

    Town airport located on the edge of the restricted area; you will see a true Mexican town. Plan to wander around the markets, buy some of this and that, and watch the people. They will enjoy it too, if your camera doesn't intrude.

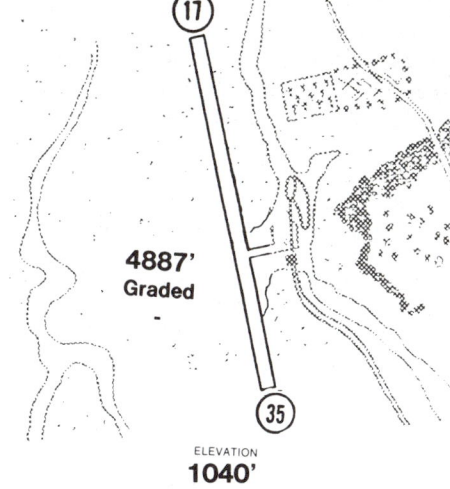

17 / 35
4887' Graded
ELEVATION 1040'

440 Zirándaro Guerrero *sear-ONN-dah-roe*

JET CHART	WAC	SECTIONAL	LATITUDE	LONGITUDE	US TIME	FOR GMT ADD	ICAO IDENT	TOWN IDENT
JN-46	CJ-24 So.	TPC J-24C	18°29'	101°00'	CST	6	-	ZIR

OTHER COMM Traffic 118.1
SETTLEMENT 0.5 mile N   POPULATION 2500
FROM Zihuatanejo FREQ 113.8 TRACK 021°,60Dme,
FROM Tequisquetengo FREQ 113.1 TRACK 255°,100 n.mi.
FROM Acapulco FREQ 115.9 TRACK 318°,126 n.mi.
FUEL -   CARDS -   CASH? -
REPAIRS -   TIEDOWN BYO

Farm town on the Rio Balsas, good supply point if you are camping and want to pick up the necessities without getting cabs and all. For the rest, this is a chance to see México off the beaten path. Just don't try to do anything serious for the twelve days before Christmas. You'd be lucky to even find a bartender sober.

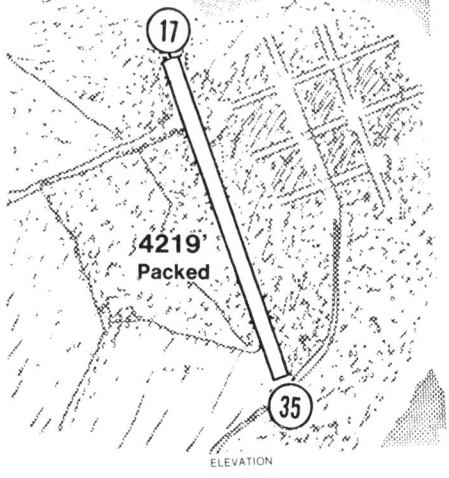

4219'
Packed

ELEVATION
1131'

Altimarano Guerrero   *all-tah-meer-AH-no*   **441**

JET CHART	WAC	SECTIONAL	LATITUDE	LONGITUDE	US TIME	FOR GMT ADD	ICAO IDENT	TOWN IDENT
JN-46	CJ-24 So.	TPC J-24C	18°22'	100°42'	CST	6	-	ALT

OTHER COMM Traffic 118.1
CITY 2 mi SW   POPULATION 14,000
B'CAST FREQ 1530   WHERE 6 mi SE   HOURS Daylight
FROM Zijuatanejo   FREQ 113.8   TRACK 042°, 65Dme
FROM Uruapan   FREQ 114.2   TRACK 121°, 103n.mi.
FROM Tequisquetengo   FREQ 113.1   TRACK 82Dme,
FUEL Some 80 octane   CARDS -   CASH? Pesos
REPAIRS Minor   TIEDOWN BYO

Busy agricultural town along the Rio Balsas with lots of fumigadores and aitraxis: watch for local traffic. Suggest a tidy left traffic pattern, standard downwind entry. Leaving, using the normal normal right forty five degree crosswind turn will make your movements predictable to all.

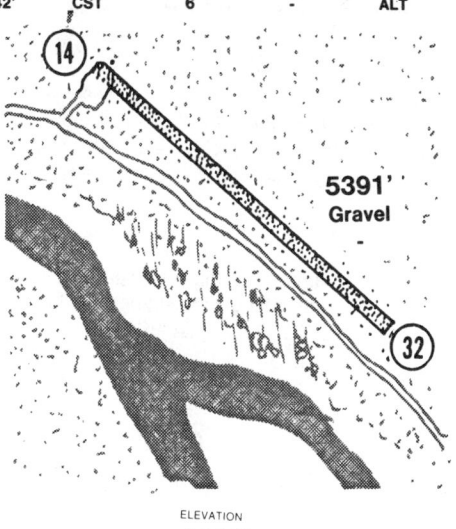

5391' Gravel

ELEVATION
1113'

442 Arcelia Guerrero *arr-SAY-lee-yah*

JET CHART	WAC	SECTIONAL	LATITUDE	LONGITUDE	US TIME	FOR GMT ADD	ICAO IDENT	TOWN IDENT
JN-46	CJ-24	TPC J-24C	18°18'	100°17'	CST	6	-	ARC

OTHER COMM Traffic 122.85
SETTLEMENT 5 Mi North   POPULATION 6,500
FROM Tequisquetengo FREQ 113.1 TRACK 240°, 63Dme,
FROM Zihuatanejo FREQ 113.8 TRACK 050°, 80Dme,
FROM Acapulco FREQ 115.9 TRACK 334°, 98Dme,
FUEL -   CARDS -   CASH? -
REPAIRS -   TIEDOWN BYO

Nearest airport to the extensive ruins of 'los Monos', that archeological zone is eight to ten miles WSW of town just off Highway 51.

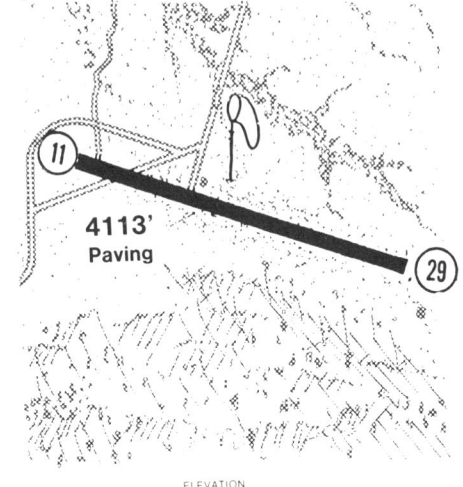

4113'
Paving

11
29

ELEVATION
1310'

Chilpancingo Guerrero   cheel-ponn-SING-go   443

JET CHART	WAC	SECTIONAL	LATITUDE	LONGITUDE	US TIME	FOR GMT ADD	ICAO IDENT	TOWN IDENT
JN-46	CJ-24 So.	TPC J-24C	17°34'	99°32'	CST	6	-	CHG

OTHER COMM Traffic 118.1
CITY 3 mi SW   POPULATION 65,000
B'CAST FREQ 1580   WHERE 4 mi SW   HOURS Daylight
FROM Acapulco   FREQ 115.9   TRACK 009°,50Dme
FROM Tequisquetengo FREQ 113.1 TRACK 188°,69Dme
FUEL 80, ~~100~~   CARDS Private stock   CASH? Pesos
REPAIRS Minor   TIEDOWN BYO

Several modest local hotels.

This airport is a problem to approach when the wind is from the coast. The canyons NW have antennas and power lines on those hills on each side. Best way I've found has been to make left traffic for 15 with baseleg over the microwave tower nearest the highway. Going by there with full flap and slow gets me down soon enough to not make a go around over the city. Might be better to accept a tailwind and land 32 if you are good with them.

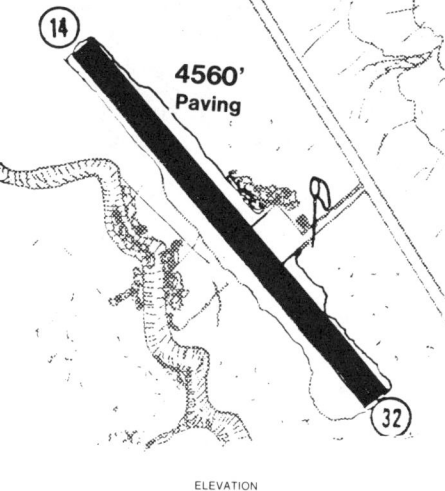

4560' Paving

ELEVATION
4513'

OAXACA, OAX.
VOR/DME PISTA 01

RADIO
DIA: 5617, 127.3 y 123.0
NOCHE: 3116, 127.3 y 123.0

TORRE 118.3

ELEV. 5012'
VAR. MAG. 7° E
OAX —·— ·— —·—

MAYO 30 - 1978/136

DME 57 OAX 112.0

Caution
For Information Only
Not for Aerial Navigation

FALLIDA: ASCIENDA DIRECTO EN RADIAL 003° HASTA ALCANZAR 6 500' DENTRO DE 5 DME VIRE A LA IZQUIERDA E INTERCEPTE EL RADIAL 190° Y PROSIGA EN TRAYECTORIA DE ASCENSO DE ACUERDO CON INSTRUCCIONES DEL A.T.C.

CATEGORIA	DIRECTO PISTA 01 MDA 5 780'(768')	CATEGORIA	CIRCULANDO MDA
A	1	A	5 880'(868')-1
B	1¼	B	5 880'(868')-1¼
C	2¼	C	5 880'(868')-2½
D	2¾	D	5 880'(868')-3

CAMBIOS: NINGUNO   S.C.T.- D.G.A.C.   OAX-VD-1

SUNRISE & SUNSET - GMT   **SALIDA y PUESTA del SOL - GMT**

15th of	JAN	FEB	MAR	APR	MAY	JUN	JUL	AUG	SEPT	OCT	NOV	DEC	
SUNRISE	1259	1253	1234	1211	1155	1153	1201	1210	1215	1219	1231	1248	SALIDA
SUNSET	2413	2429	2436	2442	2450	0101	0104	2452	2429	2405	2351	2355	PUESTA
15 de	ENE	FEB	MAR	ABR	MAY	JUN	JUL	AGO	SEP	OCT	NOV	DIC	

Oaxaca   Oaxaca   wah-HAH-kah   445

JET CHART	WAC	SECTIONAL	LATITUDE	LONGITUDE	US TIME	FOR GMT ADD	ICAO IDENT	TOWN IDENT
JNC-46	CJ-25 So.	TPC J-25D	17°00'	96°44'	CST	6	MMOX	OAX

tca to: **12,000'msl**   CENTER AT **VorDme**   RADIUS **10**
APPROACH —   TOWER **118.3**   GROUND **118.3**
CITY **5 miles N**   POPULATION **75,000**
LOCAL **VorDme** FREQ **112.0** WHERE **1 mile So.** HOURS **24**
B'CAST FREQ **570** WHERE **4 mi So.** HOURS **Daylight**
FROM **Acapulco** FREQ **115.9** TRACK **077°, 176** n.mi.
FROM **Minátitlan** FREQ **116.4** TRACK **235°, 142** n.mi.
FROM **Tequisquetengo** FREQ **113.1** TRACK **118°, 178** n.mi.
FUEL **80,100**   CARDS —   CASH? **Pesos**
REPAIRS **Minor**   TIEDOWN **BYO**

HOTEL	RATE	WHERE	TEL
el Presidente	$$	Central	6-06-11
Señorial	$	Plaza	6-39-33

Go shopping up the hill three or four blocks in all those open air markets. Bargain. It won't do a lot of good but you are told the indian ladies expect it and would be disappointed if you didn't. Likewise the indian ladies are told you expect it and would be disappointed if they didn't.

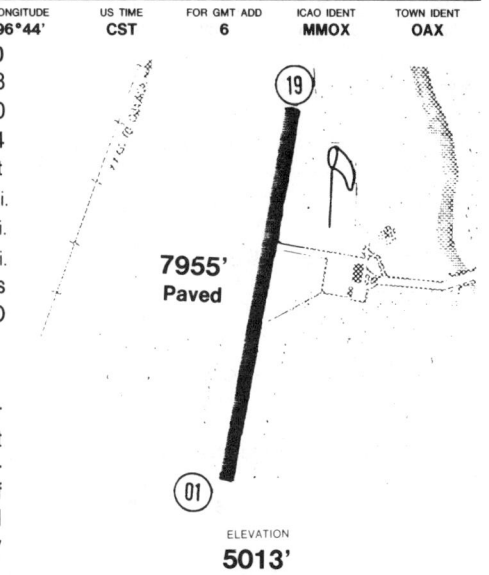

7955'
Paved

ELEVATION
5013'

446 Ixtepec Oaxaca   *ees-tay-PECK*

JET CHART	WAC	SECTIONAL	LATITUDE	LONGITUDE	US TIME	FOR GMT ADD	ICAO IDENT	TOWN IDENT
JN-46	CJ-25So.	TPC J-25D	16°34'	95°07'	CST	6	MMIT	IXT

OTHER COMM Traffic 118.1
CITY Adjacent N   POPULATION 7,500
LOCAL Ndb FREQ 365   WHERE 1 mile SW   HOURS ?
B'CAST FREQ 1480 WHERE 1.5 mi SW HOURS Daylight
FROM Ixtepec   FREQ 113.7   TRACK 346°, 6 n.mi.
FROM Oaxaca   FREQ 112.0   TRACK 094°, 97 n.mi.
FROM Tapachula FREQ 115.3   TRACK 294°, 187 n.mi.
FUEL Actually, no   CARDS -   CASH? -
REPAIRS -   TIEDOWN BYO

HOTEL	RATE	WHERE	TEL
Pan American	–$	Central	-
Calli	$	Tehuantepec	6-3

You may be told there is gasoline here; it has been a technique to collect landing/parking/whatever fees. There is fuel at the military airport, not here.

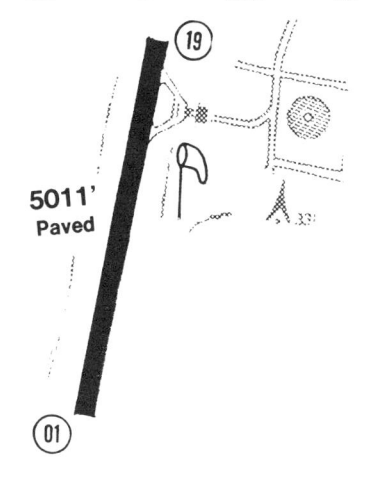

5011' Paved

ELEVATION **202'**

Ixtepec Military   Oaxaca   ess-tay-PECK   447

JET CHART	WAC	SECTIONAL	LATITUDE	LONGITUDE	US TIME	FOR GMT ADD	ICAO IDENT	TOWN IDENT
JN-46	CJ-25 So.	TPC J-25D	16°26'	95°08'	CST	6	-	IZT

APPROACH -   TOWER 118.1   GROUND 118.1
CITY Air Force   POPULATION est. 4,000
B'CAST FREQ 550   WHERE 8.5 mi NW   HOURS Daylight
FROM Ixtepec   FREQ 113.7   TRACK 211°,3n.mi.
FROM Minatitlan   FREQ 116.4   TRACK 194°,100 n.mi.
FROM Oaxaca   FREQ -   TRACK 103°,101n.mi.
FUEL 100 often   CARDS -   CASH? Pesos
REPAIRS -   TIEDOWN BYO

As at any military facility anywhere in the world calling on the skipper is a good idea. Sending in your respects is usually sufficient. Printed callings are handy for occasions such as this.

READER REPORT We landed here for gas and were presented with a printed bill for $75 dollars U.S. landing fee. We negotiated it down a whole lot. Anonymous, Washington

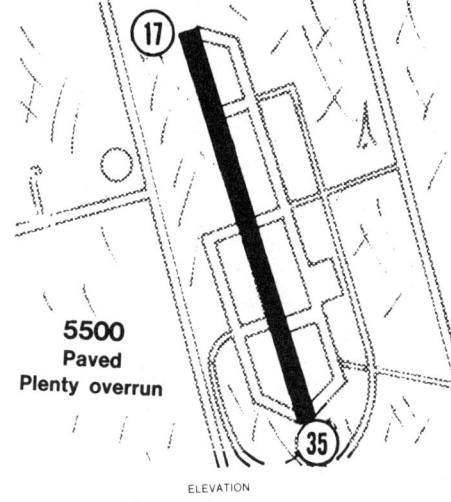

5500
Paved
Plenty overrun

ELEVATION
81'

448 Windy Tehuantepec

100 knots is possible in December and/January

One reason you don't see a lot of traffic along the Acapulco to/from Tapachula coastline route is that this halfway point at the southern side of the Isthmus of Tehuantepec is a weather factory. The strong winds flow southward from the Gulf of Mexico at the top of the picture, across the low Isthmus. There can be mischief afoot for the unwary pilot of a boat or airplane.

Ma Bell's overseas radio system from Oakland, California, honors this area with an hourly weather report and forecast for those with High Frequency (i.e. long distance) radio equipment.

I took picture on a smooth day last February 16 miles east of Salina Cruz and 15 SW of Ixtepec Military airport with the camera pointing, as usual, magnetic north. You can see that a past hurricane blew sand out of Laguna Superior and took it almost to the Pacific, at the bottom of the picture. Notice that the wind-driven sand buried houses, streets, barns, and undoubtedly people as well.

Some pilots try to avoid this area by taking an almost direct heading from Acapulco to/from Tapachula. And although it puts them sixty to sixty five nautical miles offshore here, they report about the same chop as we cowards who stick to the coastline.

Not That Bad

That's background. To put this in perspective, in the Bush Pilots we often go by here in mid to late January on our way to South America, then back a month later. Looking back on all of those trips, plus the many survey flights which have taken me by here over the years probably totals thirty to forty times flying by here. About the strongest wind, as wind, that I've personally experienced has been about fifty knots helping me come across southward from Villahermosa a time or. At sixty five hundred feet the chop is strong enough that I'd just as soon put off that half cup of coffee until I was well past Salina Cruz, say abeam of Pochutla. All the other times I've flown by here at or above sixty five there was some chop, unusual at that altitude of course, but if there is a conversation going on I missed noticing even that.

Salina Cruz Oaxaca   *sah-LEE-nah CROOZ*   449

JET CHART	WAC	SECTIONAL	LATITUDE	LONGITUDE	US TIME	FOR GMT ADD	ICAO IDENT	TOWN IDENT
JNC-46	CJ-25 So.	TPC J-25D	16°12'	95°12'	CST	6	-	SCZ

OTHER COMM Traffic 122.85
CITY 2 miles So.
B'CAST FREQ 610 WHERE 10 mi NW
POPULATION 15,000
HOURS Daylight

FROM Ixtepec   FREQ 113.7   TRACK 109°, 17 n.mi.
FROM Oaxaca   FREQ 112.0   TRACK 111°, 101 n.mi.
FROM Minátitlan   FREQ 916.4   TRACK 193°, 114 n.mi.

FUEL -   CARDS -   CASH? -
REPAIRS -   TIEDOWN BYO

Runway to serve the busy port and dry-dock city, the navy people can be difficult. Don't show too much curiosity about confiscated dope airplanes, you too could be royally chewed out for it.

No telephone to town so you either get the guard's help to grab a bus, or hitchhike. Either will be an adventure.

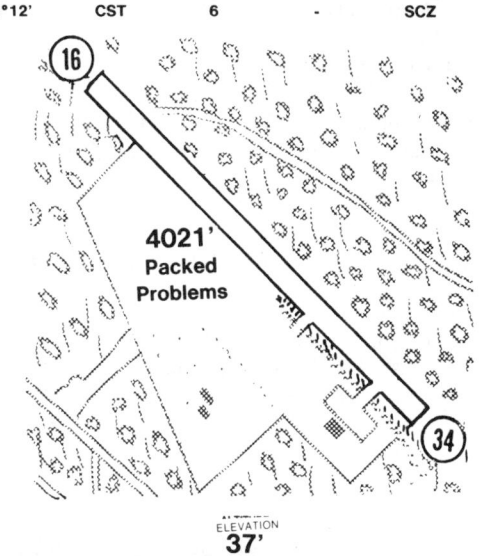

4021'
Packed
Problems

ELEVATION
37'

450 Pochutla   Oaxaca   *poe-CHOOT-lah*

JET CHART	WAC	SECTIONAL	LATITUDE	LONGITUDE	US TIME	FOR GMT ADD	ICAO IDENT	TOWN IDENT
JNC-46	CJ-25 So.	TPC J-25D	15°44'	96°28'	CST	6	-	SPO

OTHER COMM   Traffic 122.85
CITY   0.6 miles No.   POPULATION 3,500
FROM Oaxaca   FREQ 112.0   TRACK 161°,77Dme
FROM Ixtepec   FREQ 113.7   TRACK 235°,91n.mi.
FUEL -   CARDS -   CASH? -
REPAIRS -   TIEDOWN BYO

Nearest runway I can find to the pretty little bay at Puerto Angel (PWAIR-toe onn-HELL) on the Oaxaca coast, favorite winter resort area for people in the area.

Very big coffee planting area, the tiny bay at Puerto Angel ships that product via the coasting vessels. Lots of activity here: look for big changes in the next edition.

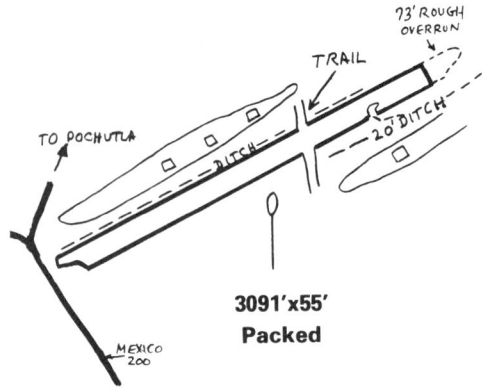

3091'x55' **Packed**

ELEVATION **501'**

Puerto Escondido   Oaxaca   PWAIR-toe ess-conn-DEED-oh   451

JET CHART	WAC	SECTIONAL	LATITUDE	LONGITUDE	US TIME	FOR GMT ADD	ICAO IDENT	TOWN IDENT
JN-46	CJ-24 So.	TPC J-24C	15°52'	97°05'	CST	6	-	PES

OTHER COMM   Traffic 118.1
CITY   3/4 mi SE   POPULATION 4,000
FROM   Acapulco   FREQ 115.9   TRACK 101°, 164 n.mi.
FROM   Oaxaca   FREQ 112.0   TRACK 189°, 71 Dme
FUEL   -   CARDS -   CASH? -
REPAIRS   None   TIEDOWN BYO

HOTEL	RATE	WHERE	TEL
Rcho Pescadero	$	Near	#43

This smallish resort area is about to explode with new development as the jetport brings more people to enjoy the balmy tropical beaches.

México City's twelve millions plus another six or eight not too far away say there is a huge nearby population looking for places to go in every price range. Puerto Escondido is about to come into its own.

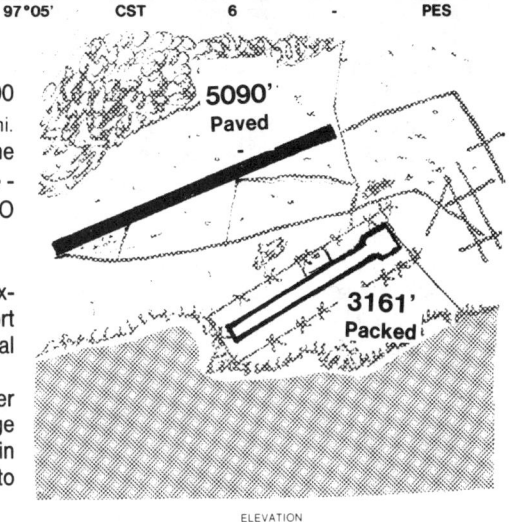

5090' Paved
3161' Packed

ELEVATION
88'

452 Rio Grande Oaxaca

REE-yoe GRONN-day

JET CHART	WAC	SECTIONAL	LATITUDE	LONGITUDE	US TIME	FOR GMT ADD	ICAO IDENT	TOWN IDENT
JN-46	CJ-24 So.	TPC J-24C	15°57'	97°27'	CST	6	-	RGD

OTHER COMM Traffic 118.1
CITY 3 mi NE POPULATION 5,500
FROM Acapulco FREQ 115.9 TRACK 102°, 142 n.mi.
FROM Oaxaca FREQ 112.0 TRACK 206°, 75Dme
FUEL Sometimes 80 CARDS - CASH? Pesos
REPAIRS Minor TIEDOWN BYO

Pleasant Coconut Coast airport near a small river just right for a cooling afternoon dip. Look things over carefully, there might be an unfilled hole which 'everyone knows is there.'

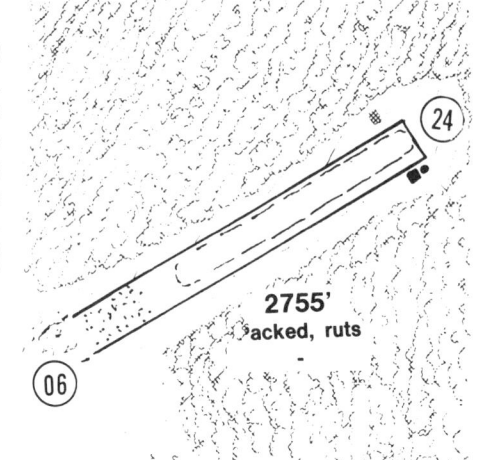

2755'
cracked, ruts

ELEVATION
215'

Jamiltepec Oaxaca *homm-eel-tee-PECK* 453

JET CHART	WAC	SECTIONAL	LATITUDE	LONGITUDE	US TIME	FOR GMT ADD	ICAO IDENT	TOWN IDENT
JN-46	CJ-24 So.	TPC J-24C	16°17'	97°50'	CST	6	-	JAM

OTHER COMM Traffic 118.1
CITY 1/4 mi N   POPULATION 4,350
FROM Acapulco   FREQ 115.9   TRACK 097°, 114 n.mi.
FROM Oaxaca   FREQ 112.0   TRACK 230°, 76Dme
FUEL -   CARDS -   CASH? -
REPAIRS -   TIEDOWN BYO

Your dollars will be curious pieces of paper here but for shopping, pesos only. If the shopkeeper slurs his words in telling you how much, ask him to write it, say: "ess-KREEB-ah-loh pore fah-VOR".

READER REPORT We spend about twenty minutes wandering around here but couldn't find either the town or airport in the tropical haze. We'll try it again next time. M. Pauling, Kansas

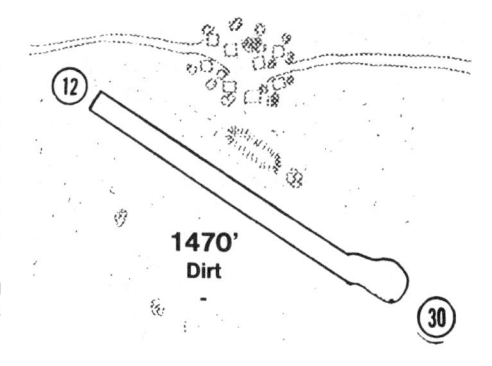

1470'
Dirt

ELEVATION
1515'

454 Pinotepa Oaxaca

peen-oh-TEPP-ah

JET CHART	WAC	SECTIONAL	LATITUDE	LONGITUDE	US TIME	FOR GMT ADD	ICAO IDENT	TOWN IDENT
JN-46	CJ-24 So.	TPC J-24C	16°20'	98°04'	CST	6	-	PNO

OTHER COMM Traffic 118.1
CITY Adjacent S   POPULATION 8,500
FROM Acapulco   FREQ 115.9   TRACK 096°, 101 n.mi.
FROM Oaxaca   FREQ 112.0   TRACK 237°, 85Dme
FROM Tequisquetengo FREQ 113.1 TRACK 146°, 156 n.mi.
FUEL Some 80 octane   CARDS -   CASH? Pesos
REPAIRS Minor   TIEDOWN BYO

2880'
Packed

ELEVATION
347

Few years ago Joan and Belmont Reid and I stayed here in backup tourist accommodations. Beds were a bit basic but okay, the theatre's sound system on the other side of the wall was of course set for Deafening. But Joan and Bel were, it turned out, the first married to each other couple ever to stay overnight in that House.

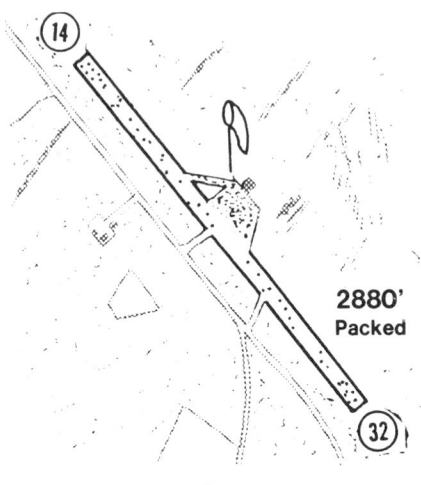

Iguala New   Guerrero   *ee-WAH-lah*   455

JET CHART	WAC	SECTIONAL	LATITUDE	LONGITUDE	US TIME	FOR GMT ADD	ICAO IDENT	TOWN IDENT
JN-46	CJ-24 So.	TPC J-24C	18°16'	99°30'	CST	6	-	IWA

OTHER COMM Traffic 118.1
CITY 7 mi NW   POPULATION 63,000
B'CAST FREQ 1430 WHERE 6 mi NNW HOURS Daylight
FROM Acapulco   FREQ 115.9   TRACK 002°,93Dme
FROM Tequisquetengo FREQ 113.1 TRACK 201°,29Dme
FUEL -   CARDS -   CASH? -
REPAIRS None   TIEDOWN BYO

HOTEL	RATE	WHERE	TEL
los Quintos	$$	Cuernavaca	2-88-00
Posada Misión	$$	Taxco	2-00-63

5514'
Paved

One of the gateways to the silver city of Taxco, this airport is well isolated. Be sure to call your intended hotel from the last stop to have wheels waiting. Friday market in town is a good source of pottery and baskets.

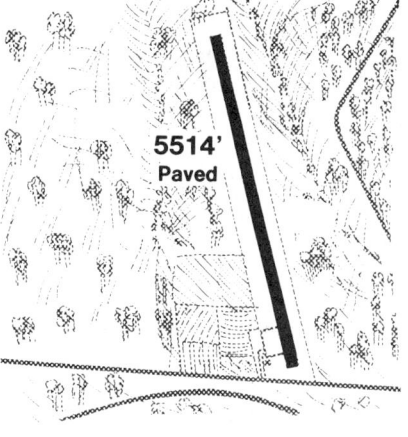

ELEVATION
2613'

456 la Viga or "La Figa" Guerrero *lah VEE-gah*

JN CHART	WAC	SECTIONAL	LATITUDE	LONGITUDE	US TIME	FOR GMT	ICAO	TOWN ID
JN-46	CJ-24	TPC J24C	16°26'	98°09'	CST	+6		FIG –

OTHER COMM Traffic 124.1
SETTLEMENT 0.8 mile NE
POPULATION est 800
FROM Acapulco FREQ 115.9 TRACK 093°, 94Dme
FROM Tequis'go FREQ 113.1 TRACK 148°, 150 n.mi.

Part of a very large farming operation, the good news is that goats here are still unsophisticated enough to run from an airplane. Long as they keep that up we can land with much less fuss.

AVIATION GAS - CREDIT CARDS - CASH TYPE -
REPAIRS AVAILABLE - TIEDOWNS? BYO

Approx 1.68 megaGoats

2782' x 80' to 122'
Hard Packed

la Petaca   Guerrero   *lah pay-TOCK-ah*   457

JET CHART	WAC	SECTIONAL	LATITUDE	LONGITUDE	US TIME	FOR GMT ADD	ICAO IDENT	TOWN IDENT
JN-46	CJ-24 So.	TPC J-24C	16°32'	98°31'	CST	6	-	-PET-

OTHER COMM Traffic 118.1
SETTLEMENT 6 mi N   POPULATION 3,500
FROM Acapulco   FREQ 115.9   TRACK 091°,73Dme
FROM Oaxaca   FREQ 112.0   TRACK 249°,107 n.mi.
FUEL 80 sometimes   CARDS -   CASH? Pesos
REPAIRS None   TIEDOWN BYO

Duster (fumigator) airport along the Coconut Coast. Pleasant place to walk over to the stream for a picnic, with permission of course. If you need help with your Spanish, show them this: Con su permiso, quieremos va, de pie, al corriente para comer nos comida.

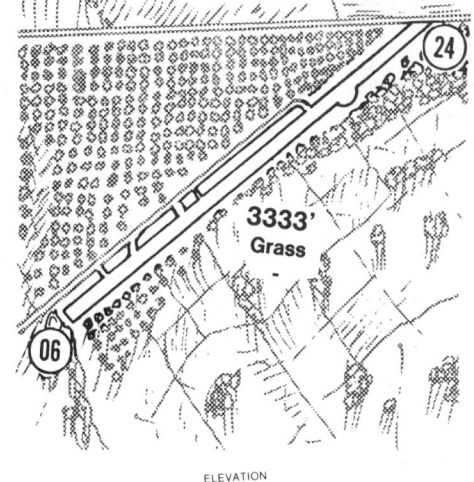

ELEVATION
291'

458 Ometepec Guerrero *oh-meh-teh-PECK*

JET CHART	WAC	SECTIONAL	LATITUDE	LONGITUDE	US TIME	FOR GMT ADD	ICAO IDENT	TOWN IDENT
JN-46	CJ-24 So.	TPC J-24C	16°42'	98°25'	CST	6	-	-

OTHER COMM Traffic 118.1
SETTLEMENT 1 mile SE POPULATION 5500
FROM Acapulco FREQ 115.9 TRACK 084°,78Dme,
FROM Oaxaca FREQ 112.0 TRACK 257°,98Dme,
FROM Tequisquetengo FREQ 113.1 TRACK 150°128 n.mi.
FUEL Some 80 CARDS - CASH? Pesos
REPAIRS - TIEDOWN BYO

South of here are two settlements originally madeup of the descendants of Bantu brought as slaves from Africa. Town of Scuilja people came from natural wattle areas of Africa while those in San Nicolás prefer theirs painted orange. As in any melting pot, those distinctions are fading and will soon be lost.

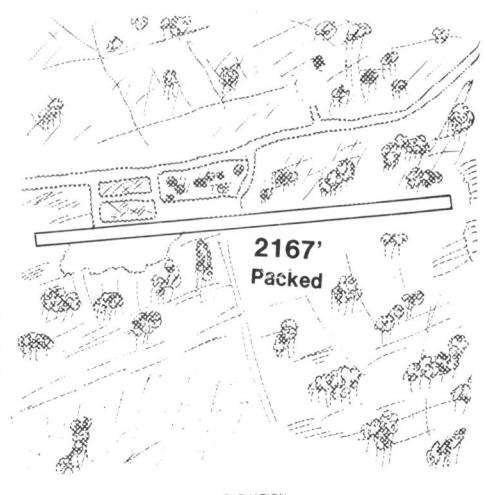

2167'
Packed

ELEVATION
1058'

San Luís Acatlán Guerrero *sahn loo-EECE ock-ott-LONN* 459

JET CHART	WAC	SECTIONAL	LATITUDE	LONGITUDE	US TIME	FOR GMT ADD	ICAO IDENT	TOWN IDENT
JN-46	CJ-24 So.	TPC J-24C	16°48'	98°45'	CST	6	-	SLT

OTHER COMM Traffic 118.1
CITY Adjacent E   POPULATION 7,000
FROM Acapulco   FREQ 115.9   TRACK 079°,59Dme
FROM Oaxaca   FREQ 112.0   TRACK 257°,118 n.mi.
FROM Tequisquetengo FREQ 113.1 TRACK 157°,117 n.mi.
FUEL -   CARDS -   CASH? -
REPAIRS None   TIEDOWN BYO

Throughout México you see cemeteries adjacent to airports. Whether that is just zoning or an attitude about air travel would be hard to say. Fortunately a Sierra Madre stream flows by the NE end for a pleasant picnicking spot in a very indian town.

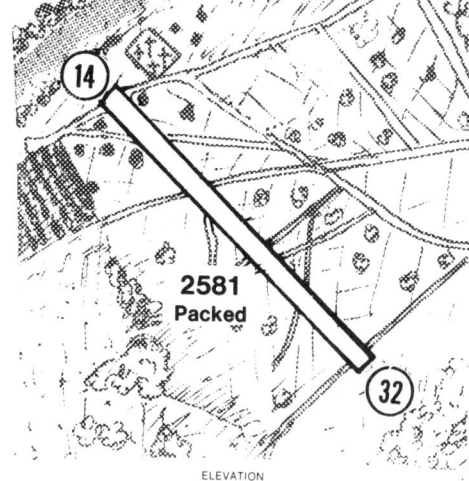

2581 Packed

ELEVATION
243'

460 Alemán   Guerrero   *ah-lay-MONN*

JET CHART	WAC	SECTIONAL	LATITUDE	LONGITUDE	US TIME	FOR GMT ADD	ICAO IDENT	TOWN IDENT
JN-46	CJ-24 So.	TPC J-24C	16°42'	99°30'	CST	6	-	ALE

OTHER COMM Traffic 122.85
SETTLEMENT Scattered farms   POPULATION -
FROM Acapulco   FREQ 115.9   TRACK 108°, 7Dme
FROM San Marcos FREQ 221 KHz TRACK 242°, 12n.mi.
FUEL -   CARDS -   CASH? -
REPAIRS -   TIEDOWN BYO

1540'
Paving?

Gradually fading runway where I once camped a lot to enjoy the climate and people. Settlement of former slaves nearby, quiet watchful pre-teen boys are eager to learn about others. You might get lucky and spend an hour or two laboriously plodding back and forth through your Spanish/English dictionary learning what crops they grow, where they are sold for how much. Asking a teenaged boy about school would embarass him.

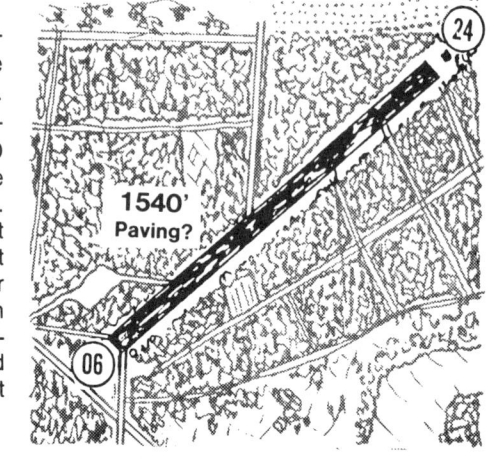

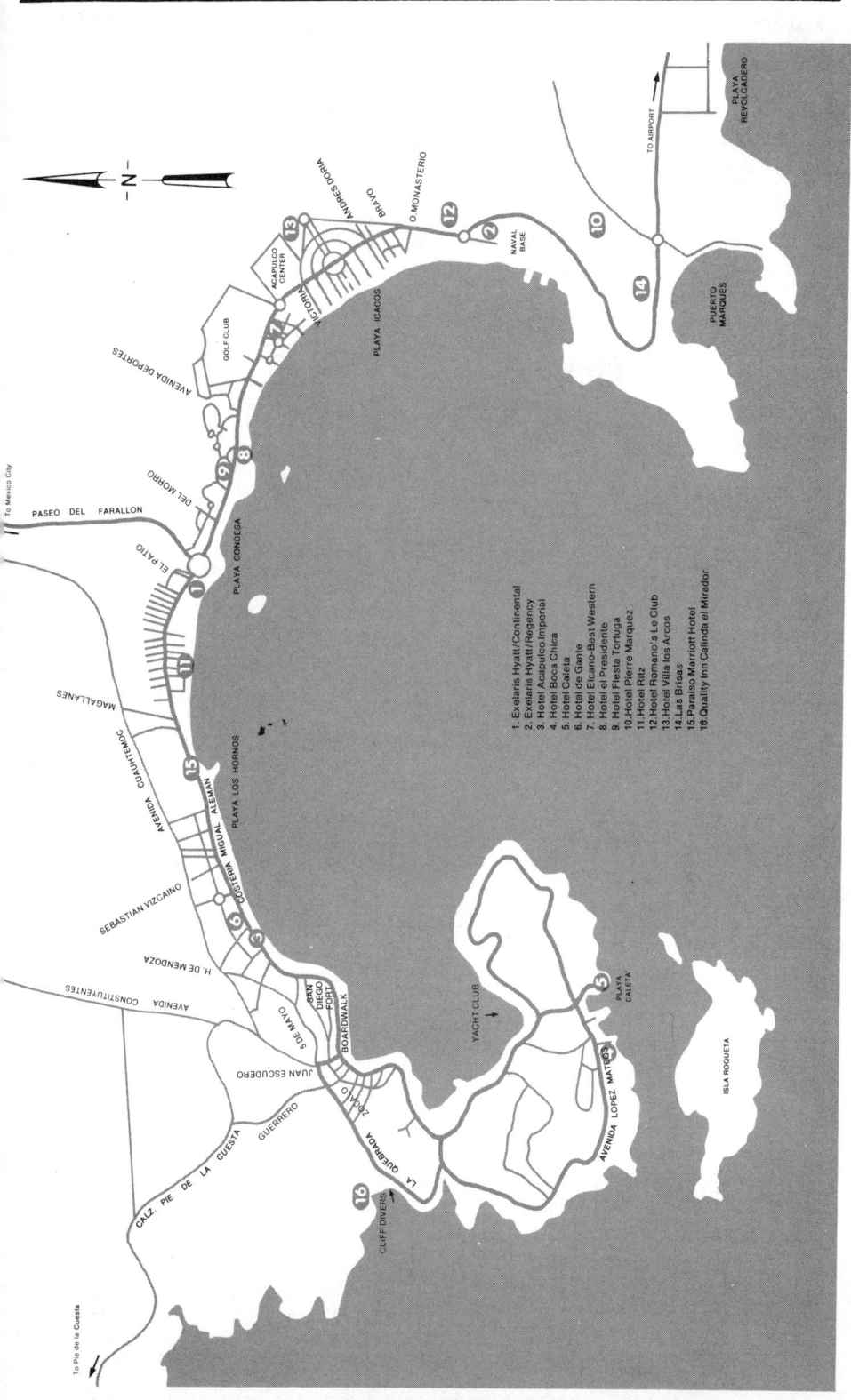

where at least some of the hundreds of hotels are **Acapulco**

1. Exelaris Hyatt/Continental
2. Exelaris Hyatt/Regency
3. Hotel Acapulco Imperial
4. Hotel Boca Chica
5. Hotel Caleta
6. Hotel de Gante
7. Hotel Elcano-Best Western
8. Hotel el Presidente
9. Hotel Fiesta Tortuga
10. Hotel Pierre Marquez
11. Hotel Ritz
12. Hotel Romano's Le Club
13. Hotel Villa los Arcos
14. Las Brisas
15. Paraiso Marriott Hotel
16. Quality Inn Calinda el Mirador

VOR RWY 28

GENERAL JUAN N. ALVAREZ INTL (MMAA)
AL-2506(DGAC)
ACAPULCO, MEXICO

ACAPULCO APPROACH CONTROL 119.9
ACAPULCO TOWER 118.5
ATIS 115.9

Caution
For Information Only
Not for Aerial Navigation

IAF
DME Chan 106
ACAPULCO
115.9 ACA

MISSED APPROACH
Climb on R-270
or as directed
by APP CON

VOR — TLv FL 200 — TA 18,000
3000
102°
282°
1500
Remain within 10 NM

ELEV 18

CATEGORY	A	B	C	D
S-28	520-1¼	504 (600-1¼)		520-1¾ 504 (600-1¾)
CIRCLING	520-1¾	502 (600-1¾)		580-2 562 (600-2)

REIL Rwy 10
HIRL Rwy 10-28 and 6-24

282° to VOR
ELEV 16

VOR RWY 28
16°45'N - 99°46'W
ACAPULCO, MEXICO
GENERAL JUAN N. ALVAREZ INTL (MMAA)

SUNRISE & SUNSET - GMT   SALIDA y PUESTA del SOL - GMT

15th of	JAN	FEB	MAR	APR	MAY	JUN	JUL	AUG	SEPT	OCT	NOV	DEC	
SUNRISE	1235	1229	1210	1147	1131	1129	1137	1146	1151	1155	1207	1224	SALIDA
SUNSET	2349	2405	2413	2418	2426	2437	2439	2428	2405	2341	2328	2332	PUESTA
15° de	ENE	FEB	MAR	ABR	MAY	JUN	JUL	AGO	SEP	OCT	NOV	DIC	

To get local time just subtract 'GMT ADD'
PARA OBTENER TIEMPO LOCAL SUSTRIAGA 'GMT ADD'

Acapulco Guerrero   ah-cah-POOL-co   463

JET CHART	WAC	SECTIONAL	LATITUDE	LONGITUDE	US TIME	FOR GMT ADD	ICAO IDENT	TOWN IDENT
JN-46	CJ-24 So.	TPC J-24C	16°45'	99°46'	CST	6	MMMA	ACA

•TCA TO: 20,000'   RADIUS 50 n.mi.   HOURS 24
APPROACH 119.9   TOWER 118.5   GROUND 118.5
OTHER COMM Radar available 119.9
CITY 10 mi W   POPULATION 300,000
LOCAL VorDme FREQ 115.9 WHERE Here HOURS 24
B'CAST FREQ 630 WHERE 10 mi NW HOURS Daylight
FROM Zihuatanejo FREQ 113.8 TRACK 109°, 113 n.mi.
FROM Tequisquetengo FREQ 113.1 TRACK 186°, 120 n.mi.
FROM Mexico City FREQ 117.0 TRACK 184°, 166 n.mi.
FUEL 80,100,JP   CARDS Visa,MC   CASH? Yes
REPAIRS Few   TIEDOWN BYO

HOTEL	RATE	WHERE	TEL
Princess	$$$$	Near	Tvl Agt
Imperial	$$$	Over bay	Tvl Agt
Club Pesca	$$	On bay	LD#13

Literally dozens of other hotels in a full range of services and rates, including most US chains. Ramada, Marriott, Holiday Inn, are all represented with deluxe resort hotels.

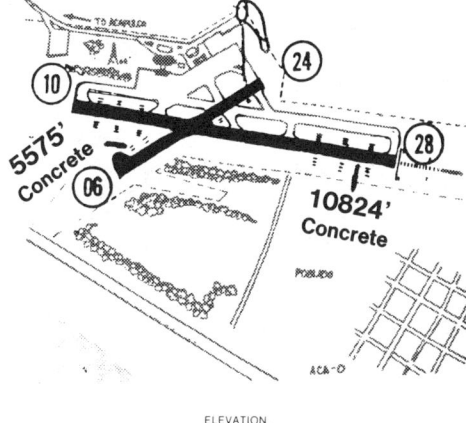

5575' Concrete
10824' Concrete

ELEVATION
17'

464 Pie de la Cuesta   Guerrero   *pee-AY day la KWESS-tah*

JET CHART	WAC	SECTIONAL	LATITUDE	LONGITUDE	US TIME	FOR GMT ADD	ICAO IDENT	TOWN IDENT
JN-46	CJ-24 So.	TPC J-24C	19°55'	99°59'	CST	6	-	-PIE-

OTHER COMM Military 126.2
CITY Military base   POPULATION est 5,000
FROM Acapulco   FREQ 115.9   TRACK 298°,17Dme
FROM Zihuatanejo FREQ 113.8   TRACK 107°,96Dme
FROM Tequisquetengo FREQ 113.1 TRACK 195°,115 n.mi.
FUEL -   CARDS -   CASH? -
REPAIRS -   TIEDOWN BYO

Acapulco's first airport back in the forties when that bay immediately south was just another pretty place, but with a natural deepwater harbor. Civil traffic is not welcomed but if you have a reason for stopping they won't get that upset either. The very steep beach here makes for a treacherous surf.

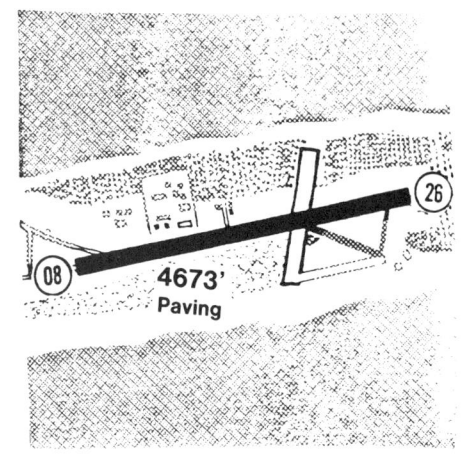

4673' Paving

ELEVATION
17'

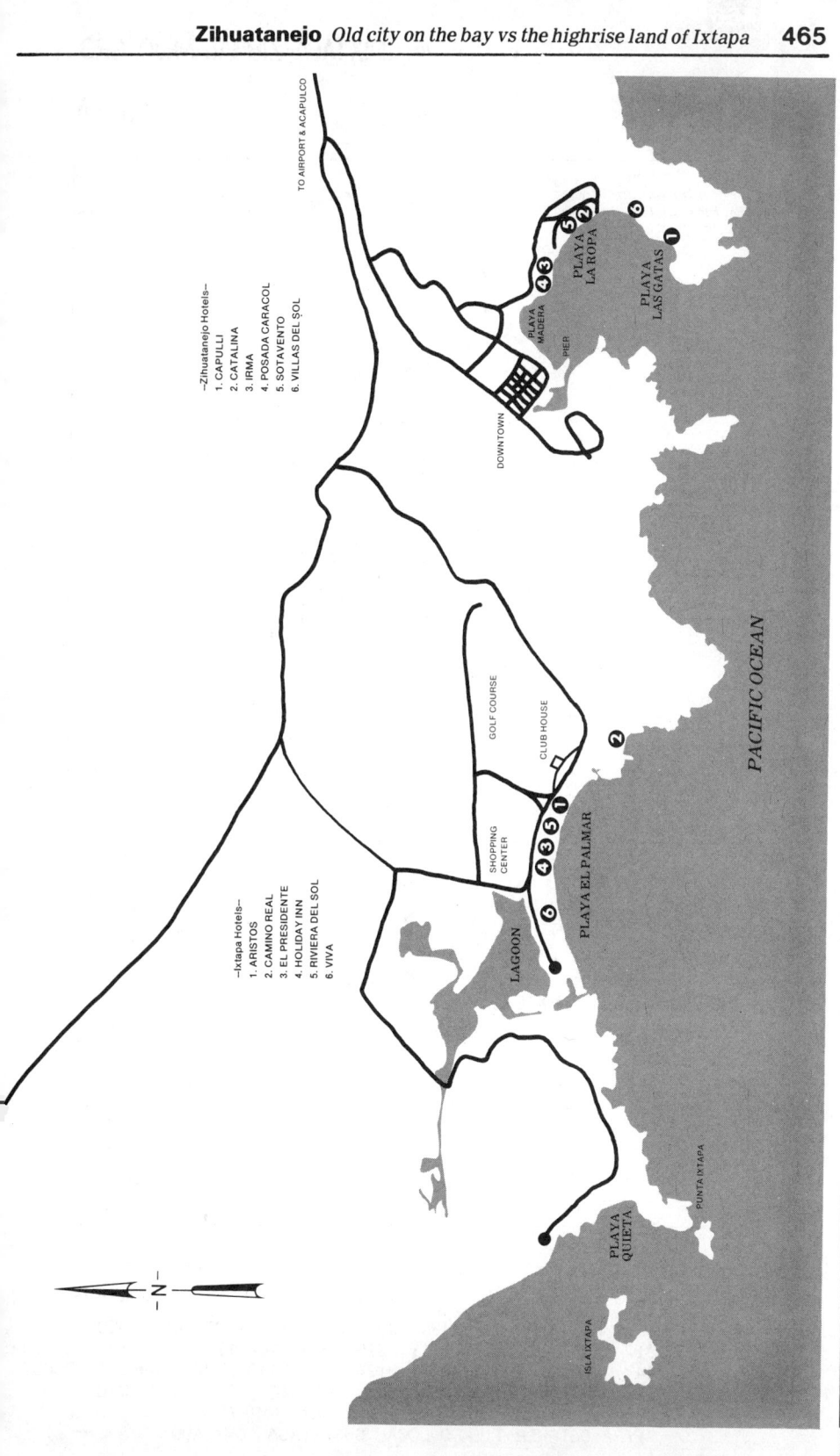

Zihuatanejo *Old city on the bay vs the highrise land of Ixtapa*   465

—Zihuatanejo Hotels—
1. CAPULLI
2. CATALINA
3. IRMA
4. POSADA CARACOL
5. SOTAVENTO
6. VILLAS DEL SOL

—Ixtapa Hotels—
1. ARISTOS
2. CAMINO REAL
3. EL PRESIDENTE
4. HOLIDAY INN
5. RIVIERA DEL SOL
6. VIVA

466

RADIO	TWR 118.3	ELEV 10'	IXTAPA-ZIHUATANEJO, GRO.
AMSA CMA 131.0 y 130.0		VAR MAG 8° E ZIH ▬ ▬ ·· ·· · ·	**VOR - A**

Caution
For Information Only
Not for Aerial Navigation

DME ZIH 113.8

10 000'
3 500'
4 000'
240° 125° 305° 170° 350°

VOR
4 000' — 125°
2 000' / 10 M.N.
305° DER.
ELEV 10'

FALLIDA: VIRE A LA **IZQUIERDA** E INTERCEPTE EN ASCENSO EL **RADIAL 125°**, Y PROSIGA EN TRAYECTORIA DE APROXIMACION HASTA LA ALTITUD MINIMA DE ESPERA.

CATEGORIA	DIRECTO	CATEGORIA	CIRCULANDO — MDA —
A		A	640' (630') - 1 (1600 M)
B	N.A.	B	800' (790') - 1¼ (2000 M)
C		C	960' (950') - 2¾ (4400 M)
D		D	960' (950') - 3 (4800 M)

CAMBIOS DETALLES MENORES y VIS.   SCT - DGAC - SENEAM   ZIH-V-2

SUNRISE & SUNSET - GMT   SALIDA y PUESTA del SOL - GMT

15th of JAN FEB MAR APR MAY JUN JUL AUG SEPT OCT NOV DEC
SUNRISE 1319 1312 1254 1229 1213 1211 1219 1228 1234 1239 1251 1308 SALIDA
SUNSET 2431 2447 2455 0102 0111 0121 0124 0112 2448 2424 2409 2413 PUESTA
15 de   ENE FEB MAR ABR MAY JUN JUL AGO SEP   OCT NOV DIC

To get local time just subtract 'GMT ADD'
PARA OBTENER TIEMPO LOCAL SUSTRIAGA 'GMT ADD'

Zihuatanejo Guerrero

see-whott-ah-NAY-hoe

467

JET CHART	WAC	SECTIONAL	LATITUDE	LONGITUDE	US TIME	FOR GMT ADD	ICAO IDENT	TOWN IDENT
JN-46	CJ-24 So.	TPC J-24C	17°37'	101°30'	CST	6	MMZH	ZIH

tca to: 4,000'msl CENTER AT VorDme RADIUS 10 mi.
APPROACH — TOWER 118.3 GROUND 118.3
CITY 8 mi NW POPULATION 21,000
LOCAL VorDme FREQ 113.8 WHERE here HOURS 24
B'CAST FREQ 960 WHERE 2 mi NW HOURS Daylight
FROM Manzanillo FREQ 116.8 TRACK 109°, 200 n.mi.
FROM Uruapan FREQ 114.2 TRACK 155°, 112 n.mi.
FROM Tequisquetengo FREQ 113.1 TRACK 235°, 143 n.mi.
FUEL 80,100,JP CARDS Visa,MC CASH? Yes
REPAIRS Minor TIEDOWN BYO

HOTEL	RATE	WHERE	TEL
Aristos Ixtapa	$$$	13 mi N	Tvl Agt
el Presidente	$$$	13 mi N	Tvl agt
Hotel Irma	$$	7 mi NW	4-20-25

Total development has changed a sleepy hideaway resort pueblo into two multi-hotel resort cities. One is Ixtapa, 'way west of town, and the original Zihuatanejo around the bay.

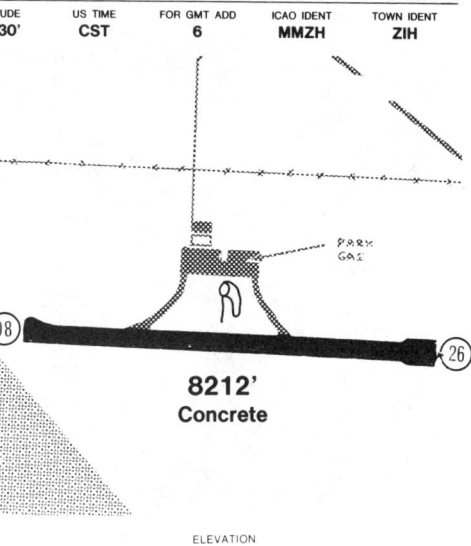

8212'
Concrete

ELEVATION
11'

468 Zihuatanejo Bay *see-wott-ah-NAY-hoe*

Times change. This picture from the 1968 edition marks the downtown airport. Today the Chevrolet dealer is at the left arrow!

Zihuatanejo, Manzanillo, and Acapulco are credited with entertaining the first Trans-Pacifiic tourists when Chinese vessels were making occasional if not regular trips to these three ports. For the skeptical, the indigenous dress of Ixtepec, further east, is an oriental-style dress called well before the Spaniards' arrival 'china poblana' or Chinese dress.

This Treasure Bay has been a favorite of mine since my' first trip. The quiet tropics atmosphere, air which feels like velvet caressing your skin, while an orderly three inch surf pounds against the white sandy beaches.

The haze over in the valley leading out to the airport at the right is not smog, at least not as we know it. Here in January the leaves are burned from sugarcane as the first step in the harvesting cycle. This isn't at all bad by comparison. Around eastern Guatemala and western Honduras visibility gets down to twenty or thirty miles or less at or below nine thousand during caneburning season.

Don't know if you can make it out in these reproduced pictures, there is a small highrise, say five storeys, almost dead center on the bayfront. I think that just might be the start of a march to turn this bay to the center of attention for all Zihuatanejo resorts. Let's watch and see what happens.

Looking north into Zihuatanejo bay, city seen to the left, airport out of the frame eight miles to the right.

Puerto Lázaro Cárdenas Michoacan *PWAIR-toe LAH-sarr-oh CARR-denn-uss* **469**

JET CHART	WAC	SECTIONAL	LATITUDE	LONGITUDE	US TIME	FOR GMT ADD	ICAO IDENT	TOWN IDENT
JN-46	CJ-24 So.	TPC J-24C	17°59'	102°13'	CST	6	-	-

OTHER COMM Traffic 118.8
CITY 1/2 mi NE   POPULATION 17,000+
B'CAST FREQ 1560 WHERE 4.5 mi SE   HOURS Daylight
FROM Manzanillo   FREQ 116.8   TRACK 109°,150 n.mi.
FROM Zihuatanejo FREQ 113.8   TRACK 289°,47Dme
FROM Uruapan   FREQ 114.2   TRACK 178°,85n.mi.
FUEL 100   CARDS VISA   CASH? Pesos
REPAIRS None   TIEDOWN BYO

Originally just an airport to serve the big big lake, the building of Puerto Lázaro Cárdenas as a seaport for Southwestern México was overdue. So far only the tiniest bit of the harbor area has been dredged. There is potential for steady expansion through the beginning of the next century.

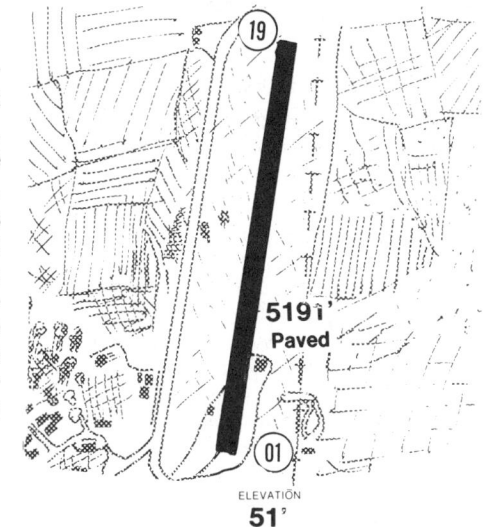

5191'
Paved
ELEVATION
51'

470	**Tupitina**	Guerrero					*too-pee-TEE-nah*
JET CHART	WAC	LATITUDE	LONGITUDE	US TIME	FOR GMT ADD	ICAO IDENT	TOWN IDENT
JN-46	CJ-24So.	18°05'	102°	CST	6	-	TPT-

OTHER COMM Traffic 124.6
SETTLEMENT 0.5 mile West   POPULATION est 1500
FROM Manzanillo   FREQ 116.8   TRACK 112°,122n.mi.
FROM Z'anejo   FREQ 113.8   TRACK 349°,29.0Dme
FROM Uruapan   FREQ 114.2   TRACK 199°,88.0n.mi.
AVIATION GAS-   __ CREDIT CARDS-   CASH TYPE
REPAIRS AVAILABLE -   TIEDOWNS? BYO

2397' x 80'
Paved, Curbed

ELEVATION
65' to 146' msl

You need to see this skijump airport a couple of times to believe it, then fly along level with it to be sure there is all the slope. Landing itself is easy: go for long. A touchdown much more than halfway to the uphill end will assure you of being able to taxi the rest of the way up to the tiny parking area.

A too-close highway, altho well below, would make me worry about my plane being here unattended overnight. Haven't talked to anyone about it yet, assume this was built as an airtaxi stop.

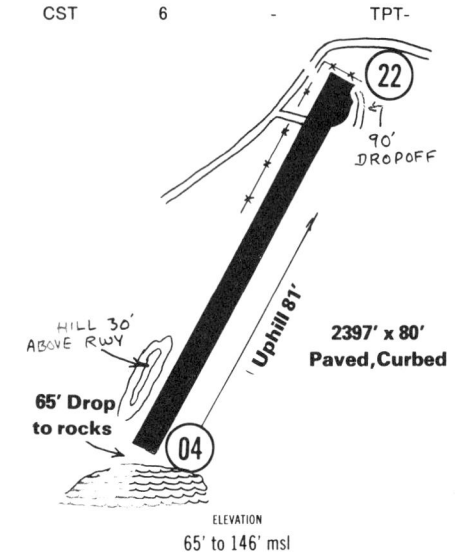

Marahuata   Guerrero   *marr-ah-WHOT-ah*   471

JN CHART	WAC	SECTIONAL	LATITUDE	LONGITUDE	US TIME	FOR GMT	ICAO	TOWN ID
JN-46	CJ-24	TPC J24C	18°17'	103°23'	CST	+6	·	HUA –

OTHER COMM Traffic 124.0
SETTLEMENT Adjacent   POPULATION est 100
FROM Manzanillo   FREQ 116.8   TRACK 118°, 85.8Dme
FROM Z'anejo   FREQ 113.8   TRACK 282°, 115.9Dme
FROM Uruapan   FREQ 114.2   TRACK 172°, 66.0n.mi.
AVIATION GAS -   CREDIT CARDS -   CASH TYPE -
REPAIRS AVAILABLE -   TIEDOWNS?BYO

3941'x100'
Paved
Easiest Parking On Runway

ELEVATION
12'msl

Another spectacularly beautiful Coconut Coast spot with an airport. If I were a scuba addict those rocky beaches a hundred fifty yards away would attract me like magnets. Clear approaches, altho it doesn't look like it at first.

I'll have hotel/accomodations info next time, meantime campers can have at it.

472 Nueva Italia (aka Francisco Sarabia)   Michoacan

JET CHART	WAC	SECTIONAL	LATITUDE	LONGITUDE	US TIME	FOR GMT ADD	ICAO IDENT	TOWN IDENT
JN-46	CJ-24 So.	TPC J-24C	10°09'	102°00'	CST	6	-	-NAT-

OTHER COMM   Traffic 118.1-
B'CAST FREQ 1320   WHERE 1.5 mi NE   HOURS Daylight
FROM Uruapan   FREQ 114.2   TRACK 162°, 14.2 n.mi.
FROM Zihuatanejo   FREQ 113.8   TRACK 334°, 97.5
FROM Guadalajara   FREQ 117.3   TRACK 137°, 111 n.mi.
FUEL Some 80   CARDS -   CASH? Pesos
REPAIRS Some   TIEDOWN BYO

A duster (fumigator in Spanish) strip in the productive valley. The guys here are serious pilots and good aerial applicators. You meet local boys from here throughout the rest of the Republic so you know they are well thought of elsewhere.

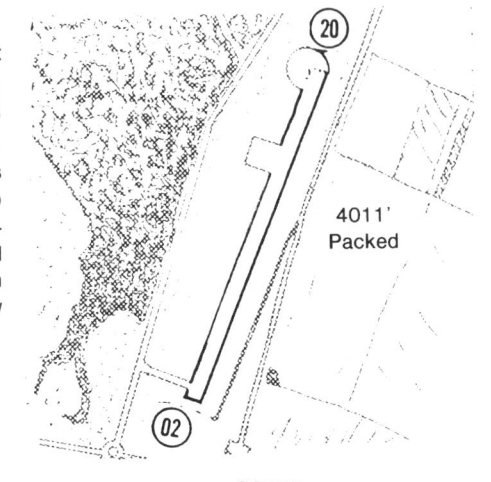

4011'
Packed

ELEVATION
1129'

Renteria Michoacan *renn-tair-REE-yah* 473

JET CHART	WAC	SECTIONAL	LATITUDE	LONGITUDE	US TIME	FOR GMT ADD	ICAO IDENT	TOWN IDENT
JN-46	CJ-24 So	TPC J-24C	19°04'	102°21'	CST	6	-	-

OTHER COMM Traffic 118.1-
CITY 1/2 mi West
POPULATION 7500

FROM Zihuatanejo FREQ 113.8 TRACK 322°,101n.mi.
FROM Uruapan FREQ 114.2 TRACK 215°,26n.mi.n.mi.
FROM Guadalajara FREQ 117.3 TRACK 103°,138n.mi.

FROM Guadalajara FREQ VorDme-

FUEL Some 80   CARDS -   CASH? Pesos
REPAIRS Some   TIEDOWN BYO

2571
PAcked

ELEVATION
1039'

Bustling cropduster (fumigador) airport in an important agricultural center of the Republic. Expect to pay a modest surcharge for fuel. It is their own private stock which they must purchase at the same pump prices anyone else pays.

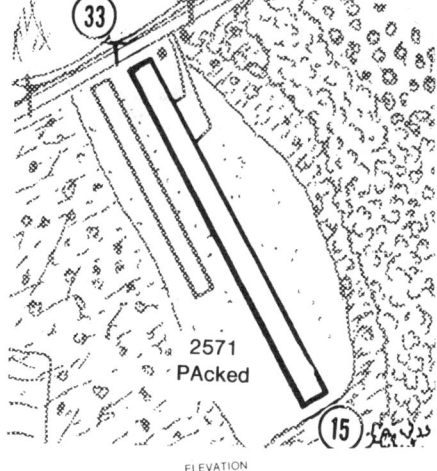

474 Apatzingan Michoacan *ah-POTT-sing-gonn*

JET CHART	WAC	SECTIONAL	LATITUDE	LONGITUDE	US TIME	FOR GMT ADD	ICAO IDENT	TOWN IDENT
JN-46	CJ-24 So.	TPC J-24D	19°12'	102°24'	CST	6	-	AZG

OTHER COMM Traffic 122.85
SETTLEMENT 3 mi SE **POPULATION** 15,000
B'CAST FREQ 970 **WHERE** 7 mi SE **HOURS** Daylight
FROM Uruapan **FREQ** 114.2 **TRACK** 221°, 28 n.mi.
FROM Zihuatanejo **FREQ** 113.8 **TRACK** 321°, 102 n.mi.
FUEL Some 80 **CARDS** - **CASH?** Pesos
REPAIRS Some **TIEDOWN** BYO

Enough traffic to keep your head out of the cockpit, a standard pattern is always your best protection.

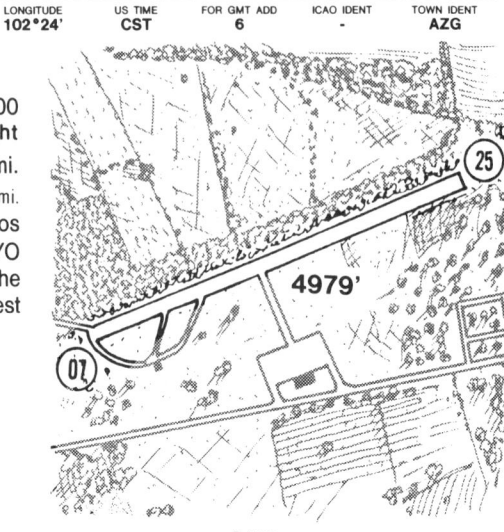

4979'

ELEVATION
1011'

Copyright © 1979 Arnold D Senterfitt

Tepalcatepec Michoacan *tay-pall-cah-tay-PECK* 475

JET CHART	WAC	SECTIONAL	LATITUDE	LONGITUDE	US TIME	FOR GMT ADD	ICAO IDENT	TOWN IDENT
JN-46	CJ-24 So.	TPC J-24D	19°11'	102°51'	CST	6	-	-TPL-

OTHER COMM Traffic 122.75
SETTLEMENT Adjacent NW   POPULATION 3,000
FROM Uruapan   FREQ 114.2   TRACK 245°, 48n.mi.
FROM Manzanillo   FREQ 116.8   TRACK 082°, 98Dme
FUEL -   CARDS -   CASH? -
REPAIRS -   TIEDOWN BYO

Duster, or in Spanish fumigator strip in a rich agricultural valley. These runways tend to be mobile, don't be surprised to find any of them different from trip to trip as the farmers change crops.

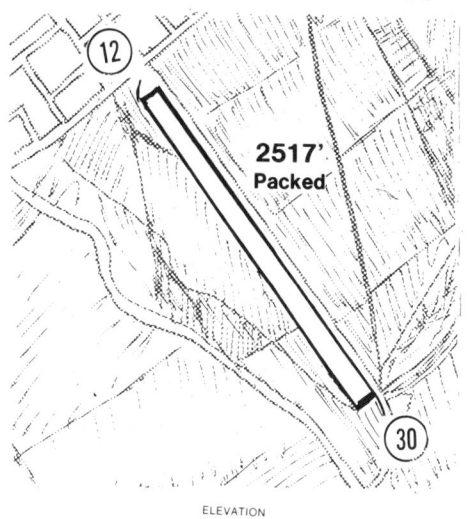

2517' Packed

ELEVATION
1149'

476 Ciudad Guzman Jalisco   *see-oo-DOD GOOSE-mon*

JET CHART	WAC	SECTIONAL	LATITUDE	LONGITUDE	US TIME	FOR GMT ADD	ICAO IDENT	TOWN IDENT
JN-46	CJ-24 No.	TPC J-24A	19°42'	103°30'	CST	6	-	CGZ

OTHER COMM Traffic 118.1
CITY 1.5 miles E   POPULATION 22,000
B'CAST FREQ 670   WHERE 1 mi So.   HOURS Daylight
FROM Guadalajara   FREQ 117.3   TRACK 185°, 51 Dme
FROM Puerto Vallarta FREQ 112.6 TRACK 109°, 117 n.mi.
FROM Manzanillo   FREQ 116.8   TRACK 050°, 72 Dme
OTHER COMM Traffic 118.1
FUEL 100 sometimes   CARDS -   CASH? Pesos
REPAIRS Minor   TIEDOWN BYO

2047'
Graded
Paving reported

ELEVATION
5012'

Colima   Colima   coe-LEE-ma   477

JET CHART	WAC	SECTIONAL	LATITUDE	LONGITUDE	US TIME	FOR GMT ADD	ICAO IDENT	TOWN IDENT
JN-46	CJ-24 So.	TPC J-24D	19°13'	103°43'	CST	6	-	IMA

OTHER COMM Traffic 118.1
CITY Adjacent NW   POPULATION 87,000
B'CAST FREQ 710   WHERE 1 mi No.   HOURS Daylight
FROM Manzanillo   FREQ 116.8   TRACK 060°,72Dme
FROM Zihuatanejo FREQ 113.8   TRACK 118°,159 n.mi.
FUEL   -   CARDS -   CASH? -
REPAIRS -   TIEDOWN BYO

HOTEL	RATE	WHERE	TEL
Costeño	$	2 mi SE	2-19-00
los Candiles	$	1 mi NE	2-32-12

A city which pre-dates the Spaniards arrival by at least a thousand years.

Today a quiet city with lush gardens and a big volcano in its backyard. You can fly in close to that plume at nearly 14,000' to test for active or not by sniffing for smoke. Last trip, not.

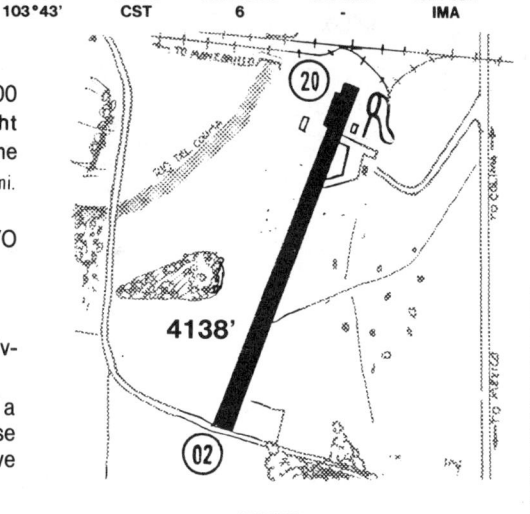

ELEVATION
1491'

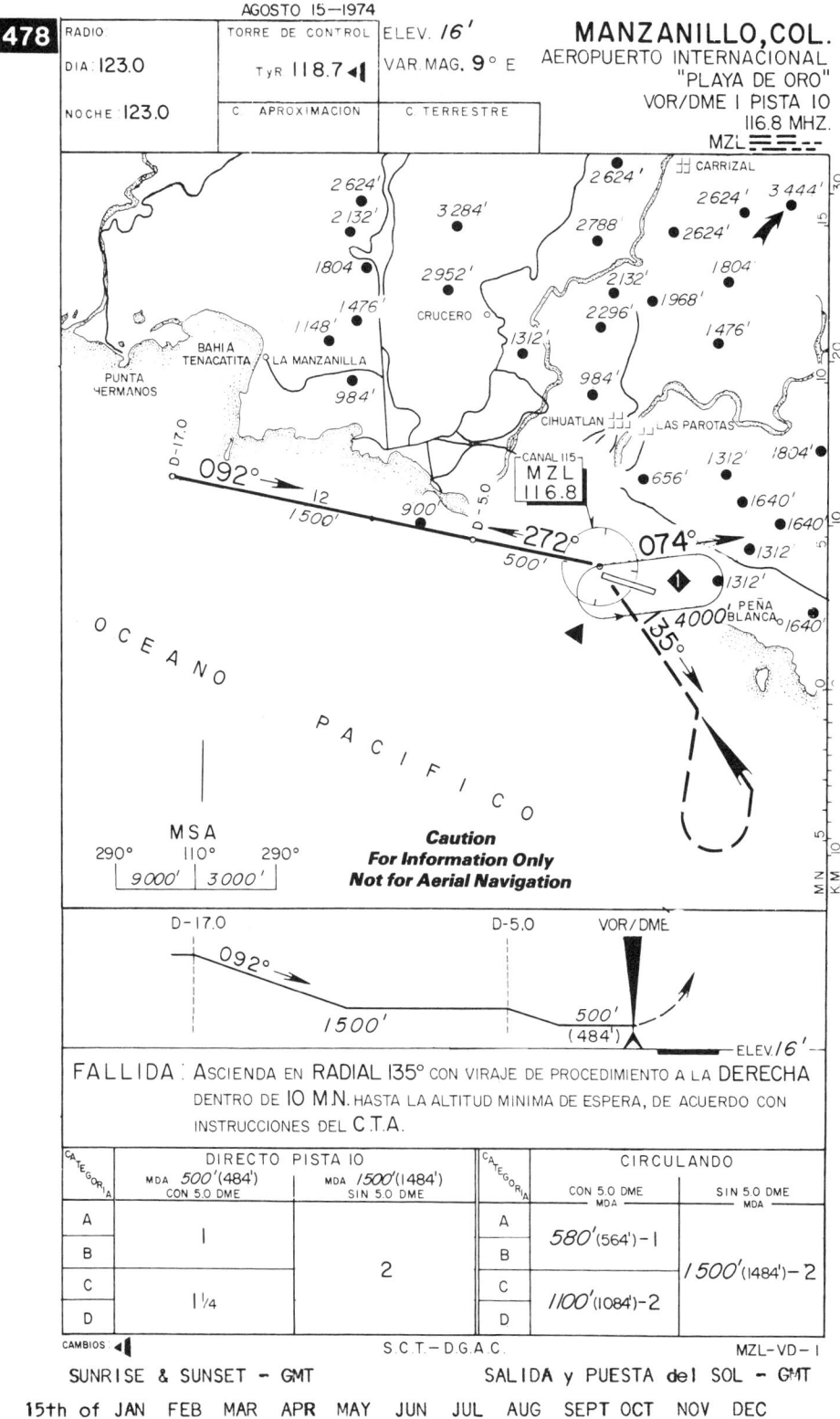

MANZANILLO, COL.
AEROPUERTO INTERNACIONAL "PLAYA DE ORO"
VOR/DME I PISTA 10
116.8 MHZ.
MZL

AGOSTO 15-1974

RADIO	TORRE DE CONTROL	ELEV. *16'*
DIA: 123.0	TyR 118.7	VAR. MAG. 9° E
NOCHE: 123.0	C. APROXIMACION	C. TERRESTRE

MSA
290°	110°	290°
9000'	3000'	

Caution
For Information Only
Not for Aerial Navigation

FALLIDA: ASCIENDA EN RADIAL 135° CON VIRAJE DE PROCEDIMIENTO A LA **DERECHA** DENTRO DE 10 M.N. HASTA LA ALTITUD MINIMA DE ESPERA, DE ACUERDO CON INSTRUCCIONES DEL C.T.A.

CATEGORIA	DIRECTO PISTA 10		CATEGORIA	CIRCULANDO	
	MDA 500'(484') CON 5.0 DME	MDA 1500'(1484') SIN 5.0 DME		CON 5.0 DME MDA	SIN 5.0 DME MDA
A	1	2	A	580'(564')-1	1500'(1484')-2
B			B		
C	1¼		C	1100'(1084')-2	
D			D		

CAMBIOS: ◀   S.C.T.–D.G.A.C.   MZL-VD-1

SUNRISE & SUNSET – GMT   SALIDA y PUESTA del SOL – GMT

15th of	JAN	FEB	MAR	APR	MAY	JUN	JUL	AUG	SEPT	OCT	NOV	DEC	
SUNRISE	1334	1326	1306	1240	1223	1220	1228	1239	1245	1252	1305	1323	SALIDA
SUNSET	2440	2458	0107	0115	0125	0137	0139	0126	0101	2435	2419	2422	PUESTA
15° de	ENE	FEB	MAR	ABR	MAY	JUN	JUL	AGO	SEP	OCT	NOV	DIC	

To get local time just subtract 'GMT ADD'
PARA OBTENER TIEMPO LOCAL SUSTRIAGA 'GMT ADD'

Manzanillo — Colima

monn-zonn-EE-yoe

479

JET CHART	WAC	SECTIONAL	LATITUDE	LONGITUDE	US TIME	FOR GMT ADD	ICAO IDENT	TOWN IDENT
JN-46	CJ-24 So.	TPC J-24D	19°09'	104°35'	CST	6	MMMZ	MZL

tca to: 4,000'msl **CENTER AT** VorDme **RADIUS** 10 mi.
APPROACH – **TOWER** 118.7 **GROUND** 118.7
CITY 15 mi SE **POPULATION** 55,000
LOCAL VorDme **FREQ** 116.8 **WHERE** Here **HOURS** 24
B'CAST FREQ 960 **WHERE** 18 mi SE **HOURS** Daylight
FROM Puerto Vallarta **FREQ** 112.6 **TRACK** 148°, 99Dme
FROM Guadalajarta **FREQ** 117.3 **TRACK** 211°, 109 n.mi.
FROM Zihuatanejo **FREQ** 113.8 **TRACK** 289°, 200 n.mi.
FUEL 80,100,JP **CARDS** Visa, Mc **CASH?** Yes
REPAIRS Minor **TIEDOWN** BYO

HOTEL	RATE	WHERE	TEL
las Hadas	$$$$	Santiago B.	Tvl Agt
Playa Santiago	$$	Santiago	Tvl Agt
Vida Delmar	$$	Near	Tvl Agt

One of the old cities of México, Manzanillo was an indian resort a thousand years before the Spaniards arrrived and one of the ports for trade with the Orient prior to 1000 AD.

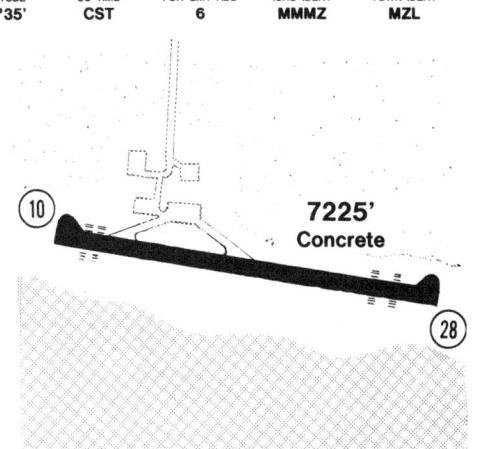

7225'
Concrete

ELEVATION
19'

480 Barra Navidad, Jalisco

BARR-ah novv-ee-DODD

JET CHART	WAC	SECTIONAL	LATITUDE	LONGITUDE	US TIME	FOR GMT ADD	ICAO IDENT	TOWN IDENT
JN-46	CJ-24 So. ADS-15	TPC J-24D	,J°14'	104°43'	CST	6	-	-BRR-

OTHER COMM Traffic 122.85
SETTLEMENT 4 mi SW   POPULATION 3,000
FROM Manzanillo   FREQ 116.8   TRACK 291°,10Dme
FROM Puerto Vallarta FREQ 112.6 TRACK 150°,82Dme
FUEL -   CARDS -   CASH? -
REPAIRS -   TIEDOWN BYO

HOTEL	RATE	WHERE	TEL
Melaque	-$	On beach	Yes

Fantastic beach at very modest prices, plus an alternate to having salt spray coat your airplane at Manzanillo. The hotels and beaches are at the left side of this picture, as is the town. It is a rare chance to find actual México in México: delightful.

READER REPORT We found the way to get a cab without walking out to the highway is to buzz the Melaque Hotel, the four or five storey one on the beach.—W Hopper, California

2893' Packed

ELEVATION **13'**

Tenacatita Jalisco   tenn-ah-cah-TEE-tah 481

JET CHART	WAC	SECTIONAL	LATITUDE	LONGITUDE	US TIME	FOR GMT ADD	ICAO IDENT	TOWN IDENT
JN-46	CJ-24 So. ADS-15	TPC J-24D	19°17'	104°54'	CST	6	-	TNT

OTHER COMM Traffic 122.85
SETTLEMENT 1/2 mi N   POPULATION 300
FROM P.Vallarta   FREQ 112.6   TRACK 154°,86Dme
FROM Manzanillo   FREQ 116.8   TRACK 106°,21Dme
FROM Guadalajara FREQ 117.3   TRACK 218°,116 n.mi.
REPAIRS -   TIEDOWN BYO
FUEL -   CARDS -   CASH? -
REPAIRS -   TIEDOWN

Excellent Coconut Coast camping with a jungle town less than a mile NE to add interest. Be sure to carry some anti-bug stuff; Cutters works well, but Off seems to attract hungry insects.

This runway is fading away; the new hotel immediately west has a set of two runways which we'll document in the PREPS. Meantime use this with great care; it is still a very nice camping place but trash and holes grow on unused runways.

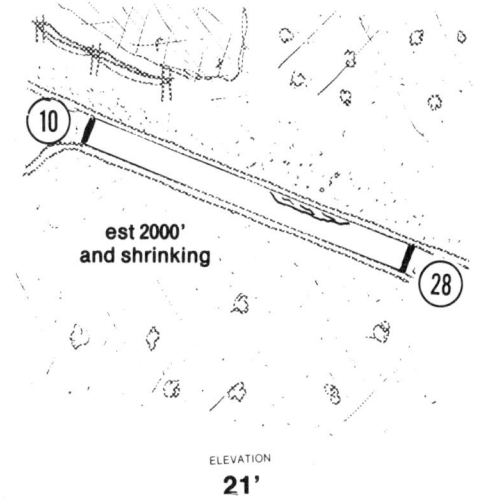

est 2000' and shrinking

10   28

ELEVATION
21'

482　Quismala　Jalisco　　　　　　　　　　　kees-MAH-lah

JET CHART	WAC	SECTIONAL	LATITUDE	LONGITUDE	US TIME	FOR GMT ADD	ICAO IDENT	TOWN IDENT
JN-46	CJ-24 So. ADS-15	TPC J-24D	19°22'	104°59'	CST	6	-	-

OTHER COMM　Traffic 122.85
SETTLEMENT　NE side　　　　　　POPULATION Ranch
FROM　Manzanillo　FREQ 116.8　TRACK 290°,26Dme,
FROM　Pto Vallarta　FREQ 112.6　TRACK 159°,81Dme,
FROM　Guadalajara　FREQ 117.3　TRACK 225°,117 n.mi.
FUEL　-　　　　　CARDS　-　　　　　CASH?
REPAIRS　-　　　　　　　　　　　TIEDOWN BYO

Visiting this Coconut Coast plantation makes you feel you are stepping backward in time to the middle 1800s. People work coconut harvesting and packing by hand, the peddler with his wares comes in a muledrawn cart and barters. Aside from your airplane, nothing in sight says twentieth century.

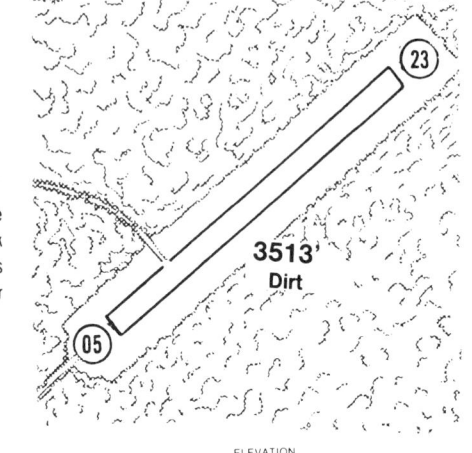

3513'
Dirt

05 / 23

ELEVATION
31'

Punta Farallón Jalisco   *POON-tah fare-ah-YOAN*   **483**

JET CHART	WAC	SECTIONAL	LATITUDE	LONGITUDE	US TIME	FOR GMT ADD	ICAO IDENT	TOWN IDENT
JN-46	CJ-24 So. ADS-15	TPC J-24D	19°23'	105°01'	CST	6	-	-FAR-

OTHER COMM Traffic 122.85
CITY Resorts 4 mi NE   POPULATION 800
FROM Manzanillo   FREQ 116.8   TRACK 290°,33Dme
FROM P. Vallarta   FREQ 112.6   TRACK 160°,78Dme
FUEL -   CARDS -   CASH? -
REPAIRS None   TIEDOWN BYO

HOTEL	RATE	WHERE	TEL
Club Med	$$$$	4 mi NE	Tvl Agt
Carreyes	$$$	3.8 mi NE	Tvl Agt

The nearest airport to Club Med's Playa Blanca, this swamp setting is hardly the place you want to park during a fun week. As an enroute lunch or lighthouse visit okay. Personally I'd never relax and enjoy either of the comfortable resorts if my airplane were here alone.

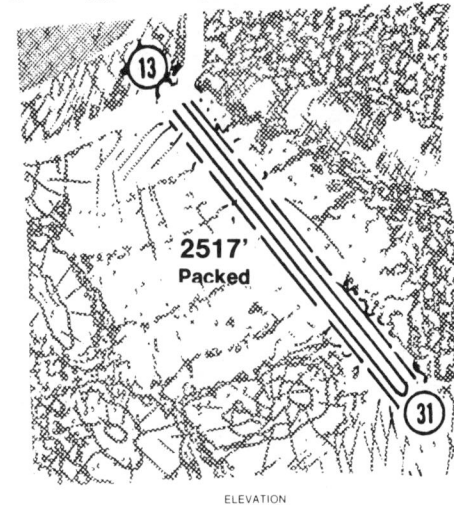

2517'
Packed

ELEVATION
28'

484 la Huapa Colima

lah WOPP-ah

JN CHART	WAC	SECTIONAL	LATITUDE	LONGITUDE	US TIME	FOR GMT	ICAO	TOWN ID
JN-46	CJ-24 ADS-15	TPC J25D	19°39'	105°11'	CST	+6	.	UAP –

OTHER COMM Traffic 124.4
SETTLEMENT 1 mile East   POPULATION est 300
FROM Pto Vallarta   FREQ 112.6   TRACK 165°,61.3Dme
FROM Manzanillo   FREQ 116.8   TRACK 304°,45.3Dme
FROM Colima   FREQ B'Cast700   TRACK 307°,37.1n.mi.
AVIATION FUEL ·   CREDIT CARDS ·   TYPE CASH ············
REPAIRS AVAILABLE No   TIEDOWNS? BYO

4520'x103'
Mature Paving

Mexico seems to be going in for huge farming operations as a means of efficiently solving their agricultural needs. This one has the flavor of both a corporate operation and of a government-controlled one. It is obviously efficient, the workers are in good nutrition and the farm equipment is in good condition and seems well driven. The idea seems to be working.

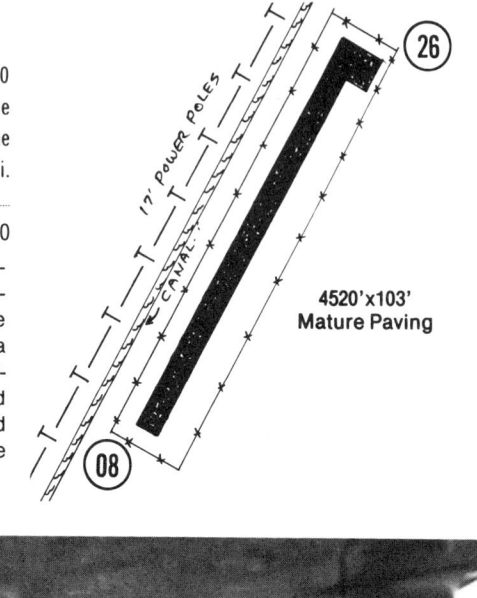

Bahia Chamela   Guerrero   *ba-EE-yah chah-MAY-lah*   485

JN CHART	WAC	SECTIONAL	LATITUDE	LONGITUDE	US TIME	FOR GMT	ICAO	TOWN ID
JN-46	CJ-24	TPC J24D	19°31'	105°03'	CST	+6	·	CHM –

SETTLEMENT Scattered
FROM Pto Vallarta   FREQ 112.6   TRACK 161°,71.1Dme
FROM Manzanillo   FREQ 116.8   TRACK 300°,34.4Dme
FROM Colima   FREQ Airpt   TRACK 274°,79n.mi.
HOTEL Under construction 0.5 mi SW

One of Mexico's spectacularly pretty bays, this one even has some islands just the right size for picnickers. Only a hundred yards out, close enough for any of us to easily swim out and enjoy. The hotel pointed on the diagram seems to be going up at the rate of a brick per week so we may have be able to enjoy this camping spot awhile longer.

486 Tomatlán Jalisco tome-ott-LON

JET CHART	WAC	SECTIONAL	LATITUDE	LONGITUDE	US TIME	FOR GMT ADD	ICAO IDENT	TOWN IDENT
JN-46	CJ-24 So. ADS-15	TPC J-24D	19°56'	105°16'	CST	6	-	TOM

OTHER COMM Traffic 122.85
SETTLEMENT NE end   POPULATION 2500
FROM Pto Vallarta FREQ 112.6 TRACK 171°,45Dme,
FROM Manzanillo FREQ 116.8 TRACK 311°,61Dme,
FROM Guadalajara FREQ 117.3 TRACK 243°,115 n.mi..
FUEL -   CARDS -   CASH? -
REPAIRS -   TIEDOWN BYO

Small indian town where our tomato originated. When I first measured it in the sixties, this runway was about the onliest way people could come visit. Now with the nearby highway from Vallarta serving the entire Coconut Coast, tourist traffic in town is up to three or four campers a year.

Hunters treasure towns with immediate foothills; to arrange a hunt for yourself just ask around at the store.

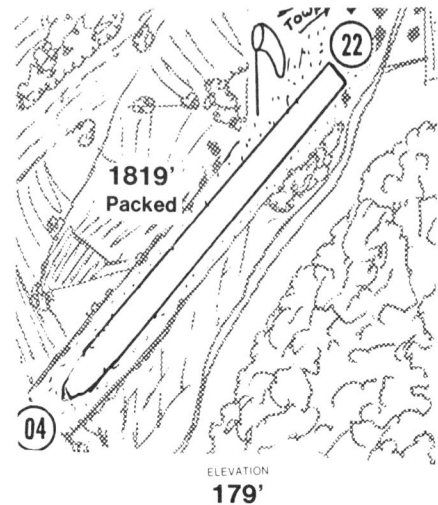

**1819'
Packed**

ELEVATION
179'

Campo de la Costa Jalisco *COM-po day lah CO-stah* 487

JET CHART	WAC	SECTIONAL	LATITUDE	LONGITUDE	US TIME	FOR GMT ADD	ICAO IDENT	TOWN IDENT
JN-46	CJ-24 So ADS-15	TPC J-24D	19°45'	105°05'	CST	6	-	-CST-

OTHER COMM Traffic 118.1
SETTLEMENT 1 mile N   POPULATION 5500
FROM Pto Vallarta FREQ 112.6 TRACK 160°57Dme,
FROM Manzanillo FREQ 116.8 TRACK 312°,46Dme,
FROM Guadalajara FREQ 117.3 TRACK 236°,110Dme,
FUEL -   CARDS -   CASH? -
REPAIRS -   TIEDOWN BYO

Lush farming area abounding in new techniques as México squeezes all possible productivity out of the soil to feed an increasing population. Here just below Vallarta there is cattle, farming, and the ocean; all are farmed equally.

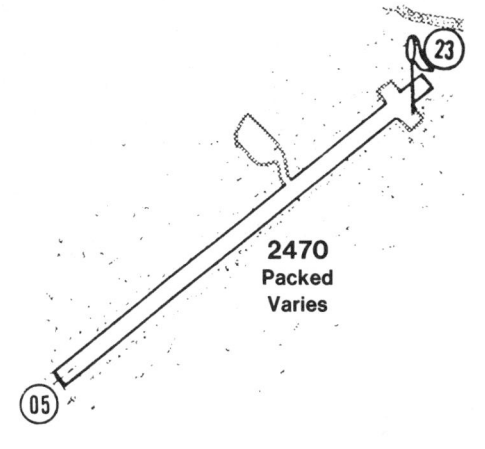

2470
Packed
Varies

ELEVATION
60'

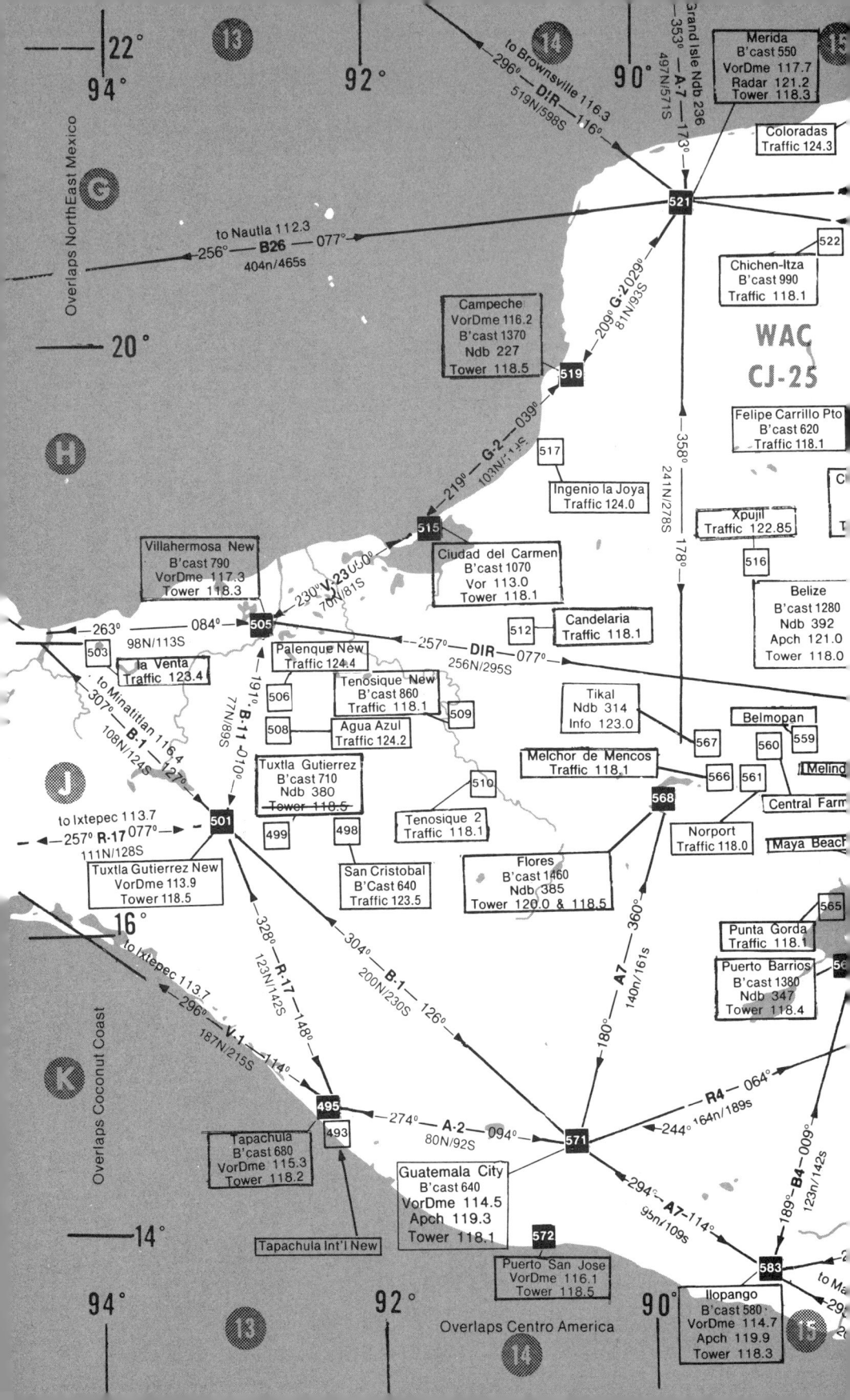

Aeronautical chart excerpt — Gulf of Mexico / Yucatán / Central America region.

Coordinate grid: 22°, 20°, 16°, 14° N latitude; 94°, 92°, 90° W longitude.

Region labels: Overlaps NorthEast Mexico; Overlaps Coconut Coast; Overlaps Centro America; WAC CJ-25.

Grid cells: G, H, J, K, 13, 14.

Airways / routes:
- to Brownsville 116.3 — 296° D!R 116° — 519N/598S
- Grand Isle Ndb 236 — 353° A-7 173° — 497N/571S
- to Nautla 112.3 — 256° B26 077° — 404n/465s
- 209° G-2 029° — 81N/93S
- 219° G-2 039° — 103N/115S
- 358° / 241N/278S / 178°
- 230° V-23 050° — 70N/81S
- 263° / 084° — 98N/113S
- 257° DIR 077° — 256N/295S
- to Minatitlan 116.4 — 307° B-1 127° — 108N/124S
- 191° B-11 010° — 77N/89S
- to Ixtepec 113.7 — 257° R-17 077° — 111N/128S
- 328° R-17 148° — 123N/142S
- to Ixtepec 113.7 — 296° V-1 114° — 187N/215S
- 304° B-1 126° — 200N/230S
- 360° A7 180° — 140n/161s
- 274° A-2 094° — 80N/92S
- 244° R4 064° — 164n/189s
- 294° A7 114° — 95n/109s
- 189° B4 009° — 123n/142s

Airport / Navaid boxes:

Merida — B'cast 550; VorDme 117.7; Radar 121.2; Tower 118.3

Coloradas — Traffic 124.3

Chichen-Itza — B'cast 990; Traffic 118.1

Campeche — VorDme 116.2; B'cast 1370; Ndb 227; Tower 118.5

Felipe Carrillo Pto — B'cast 620; Traffic 118.1

Ingenio la Joya — Traffic 124.0

Xpujil — Traffic 122.85

Ciudad del Carmen — B'cast 1070; Vor 113.0; Tower 118.1

Belize — B'cast 1280; Ndb 392; Apch 121.0; Tower 118.0

Villahermosa New — B'cast 790; VorDme 117.3; Tower 118.3

Candelaria — Traffic 118.1

la Venta — Traffic 123.4

Palenque New — Traffic 124.4

Tenosique New — B'cast 860; Traffic 118.1

Tikal — Ndb 314; Info 123.0

Belmopan

Agua Azul — Traffic 124.2

Melchor de Mencos — Traffic 118.1

Central Farm / Melinda / Maya Beach

Tuxtla Gutierrez — B'cast 710; Ndb 380; Tower 118.5

Tenosique 2 — Traffic 118.1

Norport — Traffic 118.0

San Cristobal — B'Cast 640; Traffic 123.5

Flores — B'cast 1460; Ndb 385; Tower 120.0 & 118.5

Tuxtla Gutierrez New — VorDme 113.9; Tower 118.5

Punta Gorda — Traffic 118.1

Puerto Barrios — B'cast 1380; Ndb 347; Tower 118.4

Tapachula — B'cast 680; VorDme 115.3; Tower 118.2

Tapachula Int'l New

Guatemala City — B'cast 640; VorDme 114.5; Apch 119.3; Tower 118.1

Puerto San Jose — VorDme 116.1; Tower 118.5

Ilopango — B'cast 580; VorDme 114.7; Apch 119.9; Tower 118.3

Waypoint/fix numbers visible: 515, 517, 519, 521, 522, 516, 512, 505, 503, 506, 508, 509, 510, 499, 498, 501, 495, 493, 567, 559, 560, 566, 561, 568, 565, 571, 572, 583.

Legend

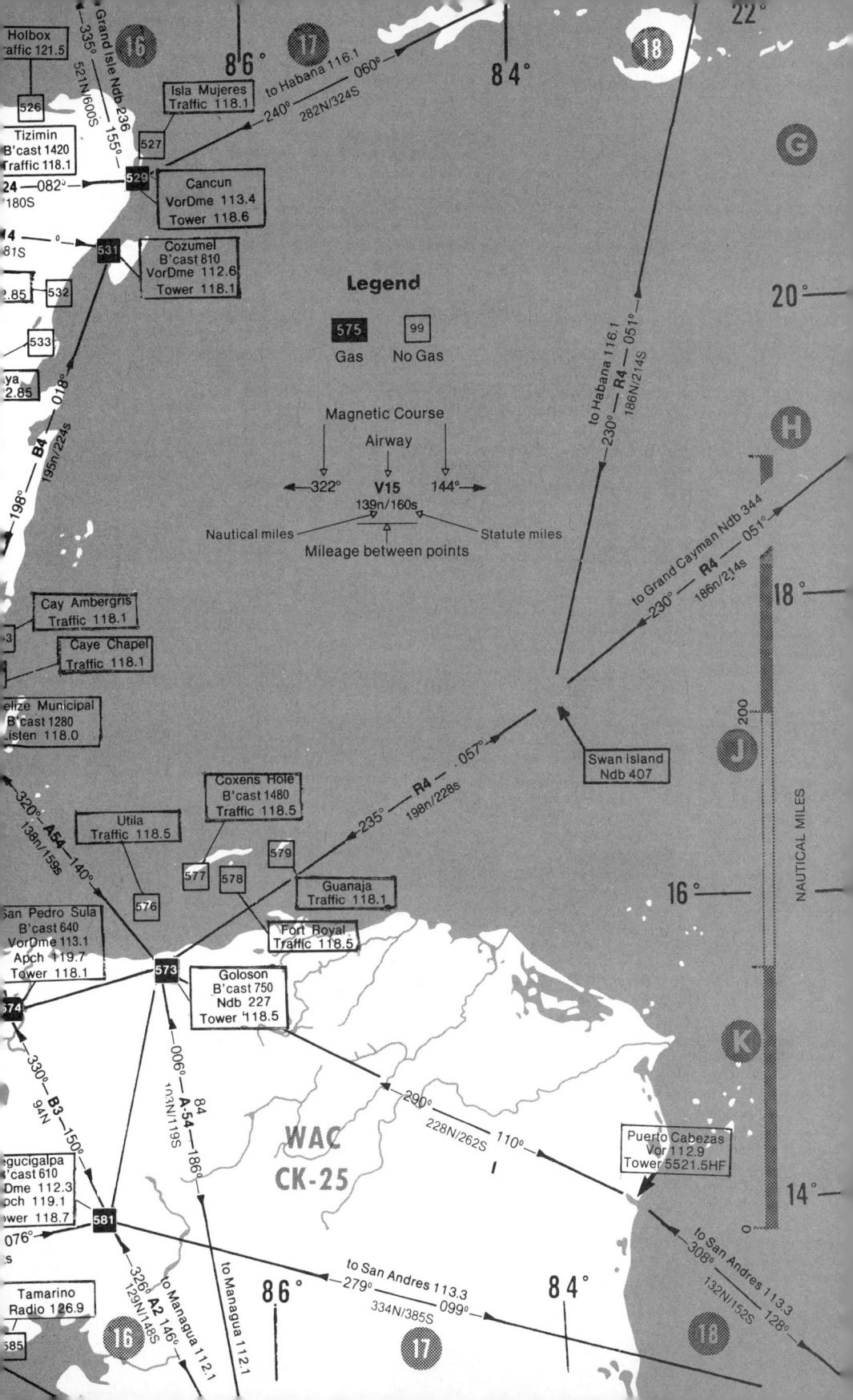

575 Gas   99 No Gas

Magnetic Course
Airway
← 322°   **V15**   144° →
139n/160s
Nautical miles   Mileage between points   Statute miles

WAC CK-25

490 Yucatan Index

Sequence:
Place,Ident,Page

Agua Azul,GUA-,509

Boca Paila,PEZ-,534

Campeche,CPE,519
Campeche IFR,CPE,518
Cancun IFR,CUN,528
Cancun Int'l,CUN,529
Candelaria,CDL-,513
Chetumal IFR,CTM,536
Chetumal Int'l,CTM,537
Chichen-Itza,CZA,522
Chichen-Itza Briefing,523
Ciudad del Carmen,CME,515
Ciudad del Carmen IFR,CME,514
Cozumel IFR,CZM,530
Cozumel Int'l,CZM,531

Emiliano Zapata,EZT,512

Felipe Carrill Pto.,535

Holbox,BOX-,526

Ingenio de la Joya,JOY-,517
Isla Mujeres,IMU,527

La Venta,LAV-,503
Las Coloradas,ADS-,525

Merida,MID,521
Merida IFR,MID,520
Minatitlan,MTT,497
Minatitlan IFR,MTT,496

Palenque Aerial View,PQE,506
Palenque Airport,PQE,508
Palenque's Airport,PQE,507

San Cristobal/Casas,SNC,498

Tapachula IFR,TAP,494
Tapachula Int'l,TAP,495

Tapachula Int'l New,TAP,493
Tapachula New IFR,TAP,492
Tenosique Jungle,YGL-,511
Tenosique New,TIQ,510
Tizimin,TZM,524
Tulum,TLM,532
Tulum Briefing,533
Tuxtla Gutierrez New,TGZ,501
Tuxtla Gutierrez New IFR,TGZ,500
Tuxtla Gutierrez Old,TGZ,499

Villahermosa IFR,VSA,504
Villahermosa New,VSA,505

Xpujil,XJL,516

Yucatan Area,489
Yucatan Area Chart,488
Yucatan Briefing,491
Yucatan Index,490

Crawl-in Bar for those who must, but who can't quite

Yucatan Briefing

Area includes: Isthmus of Tehuantepec, Yucatan peninsula, Western Caribbean.
Best known for: Cancun, Cozumel, Chichen-Itza.
But also has: mountain hideaway San Cristobal de las Casas, interesting city of Tuxtla Gutierrez, Villahermosa with oil wells, chocolate farms, and coffee plantations.
Cities: Minatitlan, Ixtepec, Campeche, Merida, Ciudad del Carmen, Tapachula.
Altitudes: low gradient tropics to mile high mountains.
Climate: mainly tropical, some more temperate in the mountains.
Weather: usual tropics cumulous; scattered to broken, bases two to three thousand late morning with afternoon rain in the mountains.
Special notes: Solid morning fog forms after dawn over the Yucatan peninsula generally east of Carmen. Tops not over 300'agl. Be patient, it dissipates an hour later.
Shopping tips: Mayan sandals may appear crude but are anatomically correct, feel good, often wear like iron. Hand embroidered clothing needs to be selected from machine made. Spanish for "is it hand made?" is "?HAY-cho pore MAHno?" (?Hecho por mano?)
Remarks: Yucatan is Maya country from one end to the other. Mayans are happy happy people. These five foot tall people can give the new visitor uncertainties because of their bubbling-over happiness. It is difficult for many of us to realize all that giggling is just because they are happy, they're not laughing at anyone.

My first experience was the lady desk clerk at Motel Linos in Carmen. She giggled, ended most sentences with a rising inflection, I wondered if there was a zipper problem. Took a quick trip to the room and back to steady me. Later I would learn most Mayans perpetually teeter on the verge of outright laughter. They are delighted at the day, their friends, the pretty place where they live, everything. Easy to feel good being around people like that.

On your must-see list you want to include Chichen-Itza where you land immediately next to the ancient Mayan city's archeological park. If the hole is still in the fence you can make an unofficial back entrance by turning to the right off the road about fifty yards from the parking area. If you do, it shows good taste to pay on the way out, having had a nice walk.

Legend is that virgins were sacrificed to the gods by tossing them seventy feet down to the water in the Sacred Well. System was that if they didn't come back they were acceptable to the gods. Temple of the warriors, ballcourt, pyramid of the sun, all are must-see. Allow yourself at least three days to see the whole park; it spreads out several miles.

Cancun and Isla Cozumel are the posh places with plenty to keep one busy and entertained. If you like the older cities, Merida is a delight with everyone in white pajama-like clothing, windmills in the city, unforgettable sights on the main square.

The frequent artesans' shows in the Palacio Gobierno, Government Palace, display the crafts of Yucatan. Best wool sweater I've had in a long time came from one of those shows. Passed up beautiful hammocks, hats, shoes, fantastic sandals I could use right now. Oh well, next trip.

This is an introduction to the Yucatan area, read everything you can before your first trip out here. You may discover that trying to make just one flight to Yucatan is like trying to eat just one peanut.

Ace-in-the-hole: However unlikely it may appear at first, all cities have clean commercial grade hotels in the $100 peso ($4-$5U.S.) range, decent restaurants, plus one or more English speaking someones ready to help a visitor with the language. May take a little patience to get them all lined up but it will happen. If your only word of Spanish is 'please' (por fah-VORE) you will get along just fine.

Ace-in-the-hole: When bad weather comes into the Minatitlan/Ixtepec area it can stick to the ground with ceilings near zero for a day or two at a time. Good time to catchup on your hangar flying with the local pilots.

Tapachula New IFR *approach not yet published*

Intentionally Left Blank
Intencionalmente Dejada en Blanco

Tapachula Int'l-New Chiapas   *topp-ah-CHOO-lah*   493

JN CHART	WAC	SECTIONAL	LATITUDE	LONGITUDE	US TIME	FOR GMT	ICAO	TOWN ID
JN-61	CK-25	TPC-K25A	14°53'	88°02'	CST	+6	-	TAP

APPROACH-　　　　　　　TOWER-　　　　　　　　　GROUND-

AOE? AOE　　　　　　　　　　　　HOURS 9am-1pm, 3pm-5pm
CITY 11 mi NE　　　　　　　　　POPULATION est 90,000
B'cast 680　　　　　　　　　　　WHERE 3mi NE HOURS Daylight
FROM P San Jose　　FREQ 116.1　　TRACK 297°, 103n.mi.
FROM T.Gutierrez　　FREQ 113.9　　TRACK 145°, 128n.mi.
FROM Ixtepec　　　　FREQ 113.7　　TRACK 113° 188n.mi.

AVIATION GAS -　　　　　CREDIT CARDS -　　　　　CASH TYPE -
REPAIRS AVAILABLE -　　　　　　　　　　　　　　TIEDOWNS? BYO

Paved New Airport

This is a new airport and was not open on my most recent visit. When it is open and in service the next issue of the updating PREPS will give you information to wite into the blanks left open here.

**Data Incomplete
see PREPS**

TAPACHULA, CHIS.
VOR PISTA 07

494

RADIO	TWR 118.2	ELEV 361'
AMSA 123.0		VAR MAG 6° E
		TAP

JULIO 9-1981/158

Caution: For Information Only — Not for Aerial Navigation

DME TAP 115.3

12 000'
16 000'
3 000'

VOLCAN TACANA 13,504' A 18.6 MN DEL VOR EN RADIAL 030°

2 624'
Δ 890'

251° 071° 206° 026° 240° 3 000'

VOR — 3 000'
10 M.N. 2 000' IZQ. 251° 071° 880' (519')
ELEV 361'

FALLIDA: VIRE A LA **DERECHA** E INTERCEPTE EN ASCENSO EL **RADIAL 251°** Y PROSIGA EN TRAYECTORIA DE APROXIMACION, HASTA LA ALTITUD MINIMA DE ESPERA.

CATEGORIA	DIRECTO PISTA 07 MDA 880' (519')	CATEGORIA	CIRCULANDO MDA
A	1 (1600 M)	A	980' (619') - 1 (1600 M)
B	1 (1600 M)	B	980' (619') - 1 (1600 M)
C	1½ (2400 M)	C	980' (619') - 1¾ (2800 M)
D		D	

CAMBIOS: DETALLES MENORES, VIS Y FRECUENCIAS S C T - D G A C - SENEAM TAP-V-

---

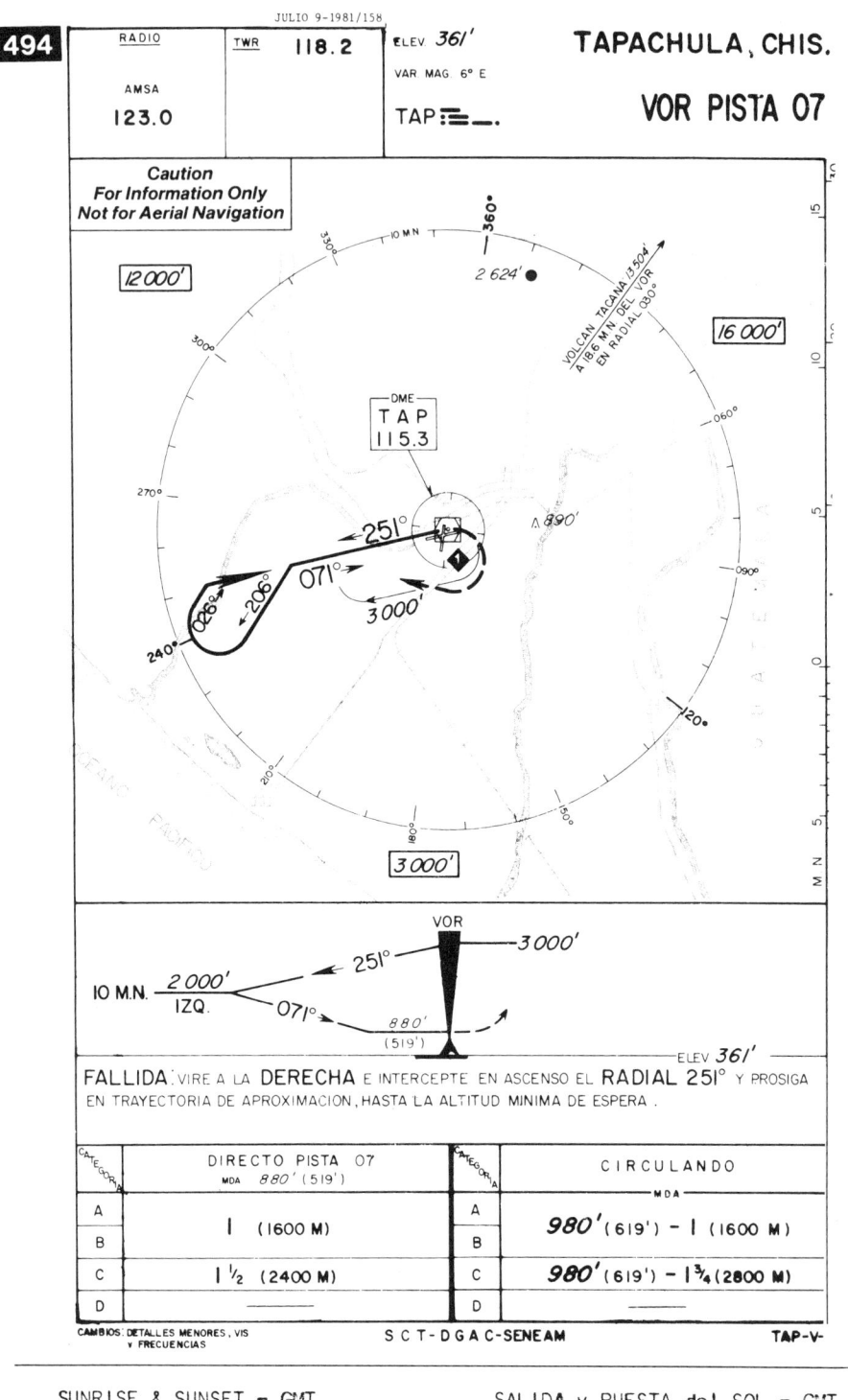

SUNRISE & SUNSET — GMT   SALIDA y PUESTA del SOL — GMT

15th of	JAN	FEB	MAR	APR	MAY	JUN	JUL	AUG	SEPT	OCT	NOV	DEC	
SUNRISE	1238	1233	1216	1155	1140	1139	1147	1154	1157	1200	1210	1226	SALIDA
SUNSET	2358	2413	2419	2423	2430	2439	2442	2432	2410	2349	2337	2341	PUESTA
15 de	ENE	FEB	MAR	ABR	MAY	JUN	JUL	AGO	SEP	OCT	NOV	DIC	

To get local time just subtract 'GMT ADD'
PARA OBTENER TIEMPO LOCAL SUSTRIAGA 'GMT ADD'

Tapachula Int'l Old, Chiapas

topp-ah-CHOO-lah

495

JET CHART	WAC	SECTIONAL	LATITUDE	LONGITUDE	US TIME	FOR GMT ADD	ICAO IDENT	TOWN IDENT
JNC-61	CK-25 No.	TPC K-25A	14°53'	92°18'	CST	6	MMTP	TAP

tca to: 3,000'msl CENTER AT VorDme RADIUS 10 mi.

APPROACH — TOWER 118.2 GROUND 118.2
OTHER COMM Enroute 126.9
CITY 3 miles NE POPULATION 115,000
LOCAL VorDme FREQ 115.3 WHERE here HOURS 24
B'CAST FREQ 680 WHERE 7 mi NE HOURS Daylight
FROM Ixtepec FREQ 113.7 TRACK 115°, 187n.mi.
FROM Guatemala FREQ 114.1 TRACK 274°, 105 n.mi.
FROM Pto San José FREQ 116.1 TRACK 296°, 94Dme
FUEL ~~80~~, 100 CARDS — CASH? Yes
REPAIRS Minor TIEDOWN BYO

HOTEL	RATE	WHERE	TEL
Lomas Real	$$	N side	14-40
H. San Francisco	-$	Central	14-54

AOE 9am-1, 3-5pm
3513'x148' Asphalt
5001'x148' Asphalt
ELEVATION 367'

This SW-most airport in México is about to perambulate a few more miles SW to be nearer a new port out near the beach.

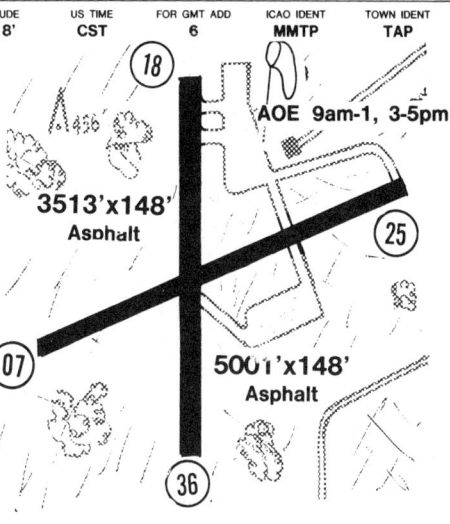

MINATITLAN, VER
VOR PISTA 02

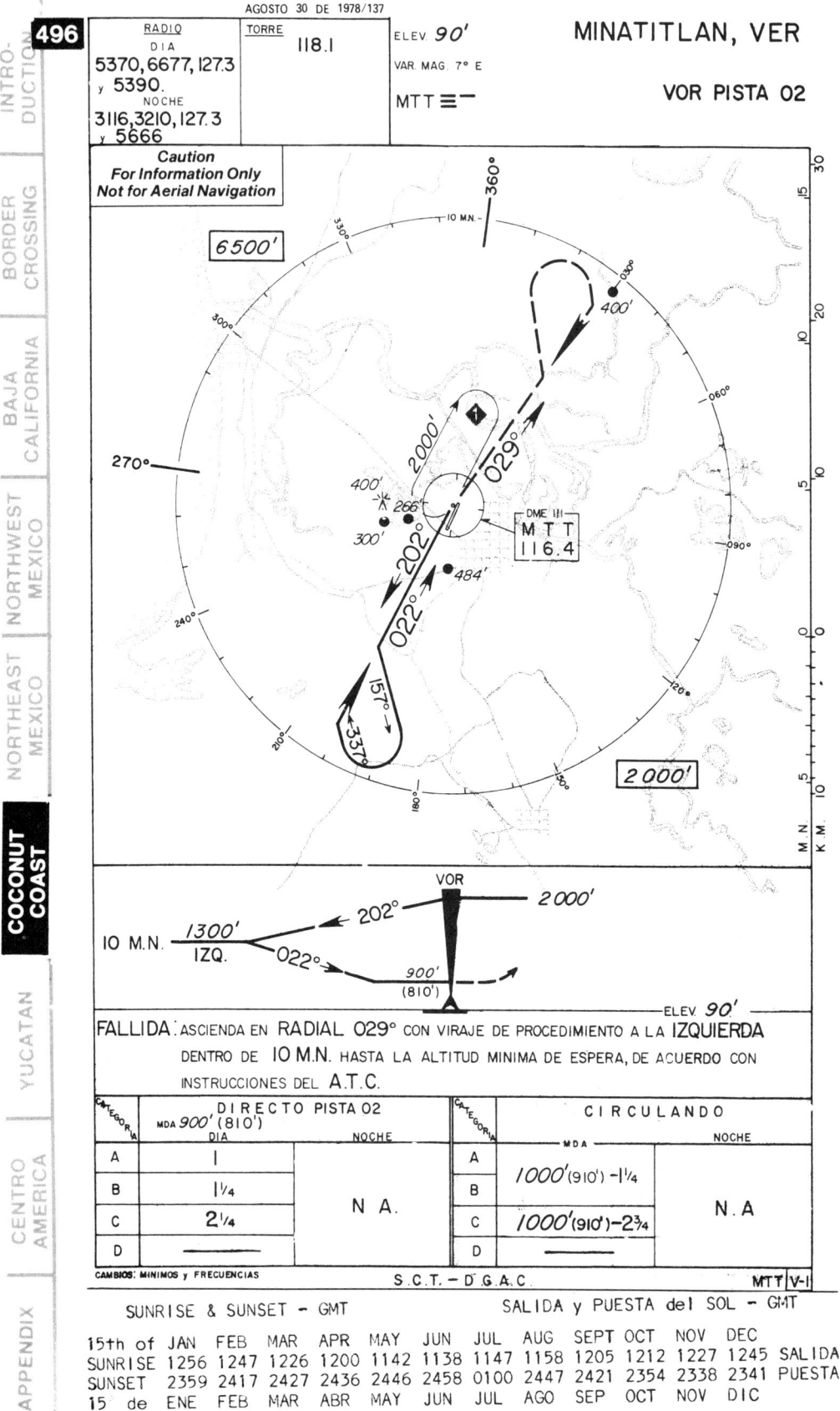

AGOSTO 30 DE 1978/137

RADIO	TORRE	ELEV. 90'
DIA: 5370, 6677, 127.3 y 5390	118.1	VAR. MAG. 7° E
NOCHE: 3116, 3210, 127.3 y 5666		MTT ≡ —

496

Caution — For Information Only — Not for Aerial Navigation

6500'

DME 111 MTT 116.4

2000'

FALLIDA: ASCIENDA EN RADIAL 029° CON VIRAJE DE PROCEDIMIENTO A LA IZQUIERDA DENTRO DE 10 M.N. HASTA LA ALTITUD MINIMA DE ESPERA, DE ACUERDO CON INSTRUCCIONES DEL A.T.C.

CATEGORIA	DIRECTO PISTA 02 MDA 900' (810') DIA	NOCHE
A	1	N.A.
B	1¼	N.A.
C	2¼	N.A.
D		N.A.

CATEGORIA	CIRCULANDO MDA	NOCHE
A	1000' (910') - 1¼	N.A.
B	1000' (910') - 1¼	N.A.
C	1000' (910') - 2¾	N.A.
D		N.A.

CAMBIOS: MINIMOS y FRECUENCIAS   S.C.T. - D.G.A.C.   MTT V-1

SUNRISE & SUNSET - GMT   SALIDA y PUESTA del SOL - GMT

15th of	JAN	FEB	MAR	APR	MAY	JUN	JUL	AUG	SEPT	OCT	NOV	DEC	
SUNRISE	1256	1247	1226	1200	1142	1138	1147	1158	1205	1212	1227	1245	SALIDA
SUNSET	2359	2417	2427	2436	2446	2458	0100	2447	2421	2354	2338	2341	PUESTA
15 de	ENE	FEB	MAR	ABR	MAY	JUN	JUL	AGO	SEP	OCT	NOV	DIC	

Minátitlan Veracruz *meen-OTT-teet-lonn* **497**

JET CHART	WAC	SECTIONAL	LATITUDE	LONGITUDE	US TIME	FOR GMT ADD	ICAO IDENT	TOWN IDENT
JNC-46	CJ-25 So.	TPC J-25C	17°59'	94°31'	CST	6	MMMT	MTT

•TCA Scheduled 1983

APPROACH –		TOWER 118.1	GROUND 118.1
CITY Adjacent SW		POPULATION 115,000	
LOCAL VorDme	FREQ 116.4	WHERE here	HOURS 24
B'CAST FREQ 1470	WHERE 2 mi SE		HOURS Daylight
FROM Veracruz	FREQ 112.9	TRACK 118°,118n.mi.	
FROM Oaxaca	FREQ 112.0	TRACK 055°,142 n.mi.	
FROM Villahermosa	FREQ 117.3	TRACK 264°,89Dme	
FUEL 80, 100		CARDS Visa,MC	CASH? Pesos
REPAIRS Minor			TIEDOWN BYO
HOTEL	RATE	WHERE	TEL
Trópico	$	Central	–

5577'
Paved
Uphill SW

ELEVATION
87' to 93'

Capital of Veracruz' oil areas, that refinery you saw over by the river is forty percent of the country's capacity and increasing. Not a tourist route city, there are only modest hotels and the Country Club. If you can wangle an invitation do it, their steaks are excellent or better.

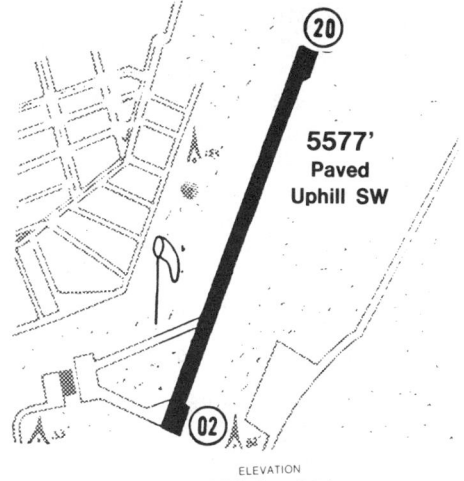

498 San Cristobal de las Casas Chiapas *sahn creece-toe-BALL day las COSS-*

JET CHART	WAC	SECTIONAL	LATITUDE	LONGITUDE	US TIME	FOR GMT ADD	ICAO IDENT	TOWN IDENT
JNC-46	CJ-25 So.	TPC J-25D	16°43'	92°38'	CST	6	-	SNC

OTHER COMM Traffic 118.1
CITY 1 mile N
B'cast 640
POPULATION 39,000
WHERE 1 mi No. HOURS Daylight
FROM T.Gutierrez   FREQ 113.9   TRACK 088°,41.3Dme
FROM V'hermosa   FREQ 117.3   TRACK 166°,77.5n.mi.
FROM Tapachula   FREQ 115.3   TRACK 344°,112n.mi.
AVIATION GAS Emergency 100   CREDIT CARDS -   CASH TYPE Pesos
REPAIRS AVAILABLE Minor   TIEDOWNS? BYO

HOTEL	RATE	WHERE	TEL
Molino Alboriada	$$A	SE	8-09-35
H.Español	$	Central	8-00-45

The one genuine Spanish Colonial city in México, this isolated city has the old world charm many of us seek. At the daily-except-Sunday indian markets you see and may buy the colorful Chamula clothing.

READER REPORT Molino de Alborada: time has stood still but the accomodations, food, and friendliness are unbeatable. Superb margaritas.—O Anderson, Michigan

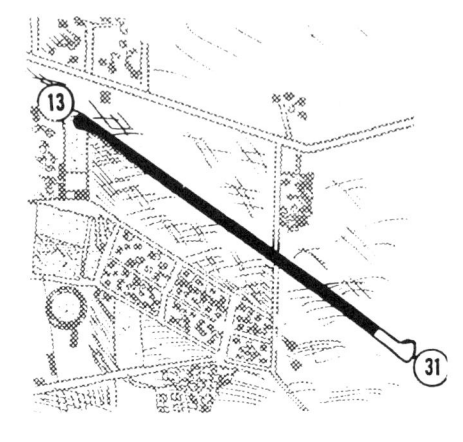

ELEVATION
7313'

Tuxtla Gutierrez Chiapas   TOOS-lah goo-teer-AIR-ess   499

JET CHART	WAC	SECTIONAL	LATITUDE	LONGITUDE	US TIME	FOR GMT ADD	ICAO IDENT	TOWN IDENT
JNC-46	CJ-25 So.	TPC J-25D	16°44'	93°10'	CST	6	MMTG	TGZ

APPROACH -   TOWER -   GROUND -
CITY 4 miles NE   POPULATION 110,000
LOCAL Ndb   FREQ 380   WHERE here   HOURS 24
B'CAST FREQ 710   WHERE 5 mi E   HOURS Daylight
FROM Minatitlan   FREQ 116.4   TRACK 127°, 108 n.mi.
FROM Tapachula   FREQ 115.3   TRACK 328°, 123 n.mi.
FROM San Cristobal FREQ Airport TRACK 085°, 31 n.mi.
FUEL 80, 100   CARDS -   CASH? Pesos
REPAIRS Minor   TIEDOWN BYO

HOTEL	RATE	WHERE	TEL
Hotel Umberto	$$	Central	2-20-80
H. Bonampak	$	W side	2-02-01
Motel S. Francisco	-$	E side	-

The new airport eight miles west now gets most of Tuxtla's traffic. In the PREPS we will keep you posted on whether landing here might be a problem.

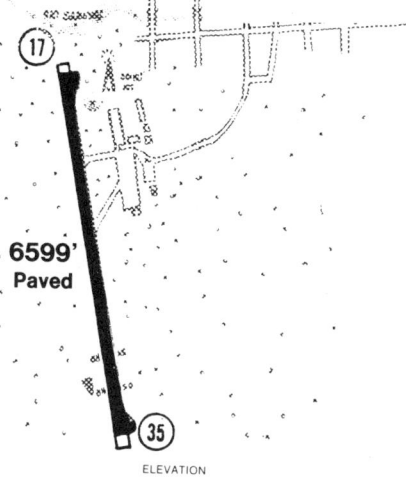

6599'
Paved

ELEVATION
1901'

TUXTLA GUTIERREZ, CHIS.
ILS PISTA 27
LOC 109.7
ITGZ

500

ENERO-30-1981/154

RADIO	TWR 118.5	ELEV 3451'
127.3 y 123.0	EMER 121.5	VAR MAG 6° E

TGZ ≡—..
ITGZ ≡≡—..

Caution
For Information Only
Not for Aerial Navigation

ILS/DME 272° 109.7 ITGZ

DME TGZ 113.9

270° / 072° / 272° / 269° / 252° / 6000' / 5500' / D-8 / D-6.4 ILS / INT PAYA

Elevations shown: 5577', 5085', 4265', 4003', 4069', 3675', 3871', 3820', 3840', 3871', 3773', 3773', 4134', 3544'

MM GS 3658' (200')
INT PAYA GS 5500' (2055') D-6.4 ILS
TDZ 3441'
ELEV 3451'
272° 5500'

NO UTILICE RADIOALTIMETRO DEBIDO A CONDICIONES OROGRAFICAS

0 / 47 / 5.82 / 6.29

FALLIDA: ASCIENDA EN **RADIAL** 270° CON VIRAJE DE GOTA A LA **IZQUIERDA** DENTRO DE **10 M.N.** HASTA LA ALTITUD MINIMA DE ESPERA O DE ACUERDO CON INSTRUCCIONES DEL **A.T.C.**

DIRECTO PISTA 27

	ILS DH 3741'(300') COMPLETO	SIN ALS	SIN MM DH 3791'(350') SIN ALS		LOC (SIN G.S.) MDA 4040'(589')	SIN ALS		CIRCULANDO MDA
A	3/4 (1200M)	1 (1600M)	3/4 (1200M)	1 (1600M)	3/4 (1200M)	1 (1600M)	A	4180'(729')-1 (1600M)
B							B	
C			1 (1600M)	1¼ (2000M)	1¼ (2000M)	1½ (2400M)	C	4180'(729')-2 (3200M)
D			1 (1600M)	1¼ (2000M)	1½ (2400M)	1¾ (2800M)	D	4180'(729')-2¼ (3600M)
NO REGULARES	DH 3791'(350') 1 (1600M)	1¼ (2000M)	DH 3791'(350') 1 (1800M)	1¼ (2000M)	1½ (2400M)	1¾ (2800M)	—	—

VELOCIDAD - NUDOS	60	80	100	120	140	160	180
G S 3°	318	425	531	637	743	849	955
PAYA A THR 6.29	6.17	4.43	3.46	3.08	2.41	2.21	2.05

CAMBIOS: AJUSTE DE MINIMOS

SCT-DGAC-SENEAM

TGZ-ILS-1

SUNRISE & SUNSET - GMT   SALIDA y PUESTA del SOL - GMT

15th of	JAN	FEB	MAR	APR	MAY	JUN	JUL	AUG	SEPT	OCT	NOV	DEC	
SUNRISE	1245	1239	1221	1157	1142	1140	1148	1157	1201	1206	1217	1234	SALIDA
SUNSET	2359	2415	2423	2428	2437	2447	2450	2438	2415	2352	2338	2342	PUESTA
15 de	ENE	FEB	MAR	ABR	MAY	JUN	JUL	AGO	SEP	OCT	NOV	DIC	

To get local time just subtract 'GMT ADD'
PARA OBTENER TIEMPO LOCAL SUSTRIAGA 'GMT ADD'

Tuxtla Gutierrez New   Chiapas   *TOOS-lah goo-tee-AIR-ess*   **501**

JN CHART	WAC	SECTIONAL	LATITUDE	LONGITUDE	US TIME	FOR GMT	ICAO	TOWN ID
JN-46	CJ-25	TPC J25D	16°46'	93°21'	CST	+6	.	TGZ

tca to: **8,000'msl** CENTER AT **VorDme**   RADIUS **10 mi.**
APPROACH 118.5   TOWER 118.5   GROUND 118.5
OTHER ILS 109.7 CAT1;272°Hdg,3°Slope
CITY 9 miles East   POPULATION est 200,000
LOCAL VorDme   FREQ 113.9   WHERE Here
B'cast 710   WHERE 11 mi.E HOURS Daylight
FROM V'hermosa   FREQ 117.3   TRACK 194°,80.8Dme
FROM Tapachula   FREQ 115.3   TRACK 325°,128n.mi.
FROM Ixtepec   FREQ 113.7   TRACK 072°102n.mi.
AVIATION GAS 80,100,JP   CREDIT CARDS Visa,MC   CASH TYPE Pesos
REPAIRS AVAILABLE Minor   TIEDOWNS? BYO Ropes

This new airport is so far out in the country from its city that it does appear to me it is in someone else's town. No kidding: just over the edge of the airport is a relatively large city whose name I haven't found out yet.

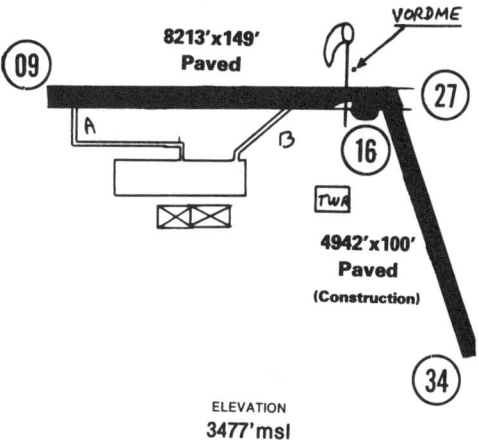

Runway 09/27: 8213'x149' Paved
Runway 16/34: 4942'x100' Paved (Construction)

ELEVATION 3477'msl

502 The Cap For All Seasons

for well-prepared members

Send your check for just

$12.00 per set of 2 caps

Postpaid

Baja Bush Pilots
P.O. Box 11950
Reno, Nevada 89510

or by VISA/MC for $3 more, telephone:
702-359-9814

other Bush Pilots information in this book:

a membership application on page 427   and a proud description of us on pages 18 & 19

la Venta Tabasco   *lah VENN-tah*   503

JET CHART	WAC	SECTIONAL	LATITUDE	LONGITUDE	US TIME	FOR GMT ADD	ICAO IDENT	TOWN IDENT
JN-46	CJ-25So.	TPC J-25D	18°05'	94°02'	CST	6	-	-LAV-

OTHER COMM Air taxis use 123.4
CITY All sides   POPULATION 10,500
FROM Minátitlan   FREQ 116.4   TRACK 071°29Dme,
FROM Villahermosa FREQ 117.3   TRACK 269°,61Dme
FUEL -   CARDS -   CASH? -
REPAIRS -   TIEDOWN BYO

Interesting camping here in oil country. The soldiers are often nearly pure indian, about five feet tall and learning Spanish. Talking to them via a Spanish/English dictionary is always interesting, sometimes hilarious. Plan ten words an hour tops.

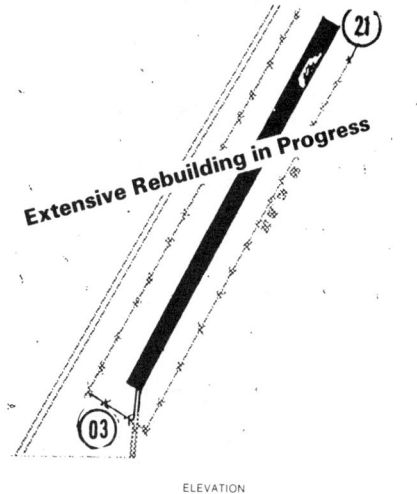

Extensive Rebuilding in Progress

ELEVATION
73'

MARZO 31 - 1980/148

504

RADIO	TWR	118.3	ELEV. **43'**	VILLAHERMOSA, TAB.
123.0 , 127.3			VAR. MAG. 6° E	**VOR PISTA 26**
			VSA ::: —	

**Caution
For Information Only
Not for Aerial Navigation**

DME
V S A
116.7

2000'

AEROPUERTO CERRADO
271°
425'
2000'
085°
040°
220°
265°
2700'

VOR
2000' 085°
        265° 1500' 10 M.N.
              IZQ
560'
(517')
ELEV. 43'

FALLIDA: ASCIENDA EN **RADIAL 271°**, CON VIRAJE DE GOTA A LA **IZQUIERDA** DENTRO DE **10 M.N.** HASTA LA ALTITUD MINIMA DE ESPERA, O DE ACUERDO CON INSTRUCCIONES DEL **ATC**.

CATEGORIA	DIRECTO PISTA 26 MDA 560' (517')	CATEGORIA	CIRCULANDO — MDA —
A	1	A	560' (517') - 1
B		B	
C	1 1/4	C	560' (517') - 1 1/2
D	1 3/4	D	600' (557') - 2

CAMBIOS: DETALLES MENORES   SCT-DGAC-SENEAM   VSA-V-3

Villahermosa New   Tabasco   *vee-yah-air-MOE-sah* | 505 |

JET CHART	WAC	SECTIONAL	LATITUDE	LONGITUDE	US TIME	FOR GMT ADD	ICAO IDENT	TOWN IDENT
JNC-46	CJ-25 So.	TPC J-25D	18°00'	92°47'	CST	6	MMVA	VSA

tca to: **2,000' msl** CENTER AT **VorDme**   RADIUS **10 mi.**
APPROACH —   TOWER **118.3**   GROUND **118.3**
LOCAL **VorDme**   FREQ **117.3**   WHERE **Here**   HOURS **24**
B'CAST FREQ **790**   WHERE **8 mi W**   HOURS **Daylight**
FROM **Minátitlan**   FREQ **116.4**   TRACK **082°, 101** n.mi.
FROM **Chetumal**   FREQ **113.0**   TRACK **255°, 257** n.mi.
FROM **Palenque**   FREQ **airport**   TRACK **296°, 55** n.mi.
FUEL **100**   CARDS —   CASH? **Pesos**
REPAIRS **Minor**   TIEDOWN **BYO**

HOTEL	RATE	WHERE	TEL
Maya Tabasco	$$	W side	2-11-11
Maria Dolores	$	Central	2-22-11
H.Olmeca	$	Central	2-00-22

Smack dab in the middle of the booming oil country, this city on the Grijalva River is surrounded by gas flares, oil well derricks, coffee plantations, cocoa fields, plus farms raising half a dozen fine spices.

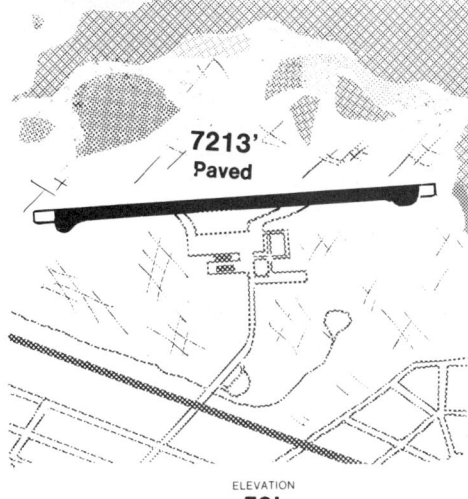

7213'
Paved

ELEVATION
59'

INTRO-DUCTION | BORDER CROSSING | BAJA CALIFORNIA | NORTHWEST MEXICO | NORTHEAST MEXICO | COCONUT COAST | YUCATAN | CENTRO AMERICA | APPENDIX

Ruiz discovered in the Temple of the Inscriptions a burial crypt with the remains of a royal personage including 9 stucco figures. It is accessible by going down a narrow sloping walkway. Grace tells me it is well worth seeing. She suggests you do your own homework at a local library beforehand to best understand why Palenque is important and unique.

After one look down that coffin sized stuffy passageway I was able to avoid it by finding something (anything) else to do.

Buses and cabs are readily available to bring you to the ruins. One tip: please don't try to 'do' Palenque in one day. Sure, it is possible to superficially expose yourself to it in that time, but take two or three days to poke around. Look for some ot those as yet undeveloped pyramids you see so easily from the air before landing. The jungle is full of unexplored ruins. The special memories you'll take home will make you glad for years that you took a little extra effort.

Cutaway drawing of Temple of the Inscriptions which Grace was able to enjoy while Arnold "found something else to do"

Palenque Briefing 507

The view outside your window while circling the ruins five to seven miles West of Palenque airport.

Apparently for over seven hundred years an important Mayan city until abandoned in the 12th century, the unique well-developed architecture of Palenque includes multi-story towers of The Palace, the temples of the Sun and of the Cross, and also of the Foliated Cross.

The Foliated Cross is of particular interest. The only other example of the work has been found on a sculptured panel in Angkor Vat, Cambodia. This is further evidence of pre-Columbian Mayan intercourse with the Orient.

Clarence Brock, on the left, helping the author measure.

508 Palenque Chiapas   pah-LENN-kay

JET CHART	WAC	SECTIONAL	LATITUDE	LONGITUDE	US TIME	FOR GMT ADD	ICAO IDENT	TOWN IDENT
JNC-46	CJ-25 So.	TPC J-25D	17°30'	91°59'	CST	6	-	PQE

OTHER COMM Traffic 124.4
CITY 1 mile So. POPULATION est 20,000
FROM S.Cristobal FREQ Adf640 TRACK 031°,61.6n.mi.
FROM V'hermosa FREQ 117.3 TRACK 114°,53.6Dme
FROM T.Gutierrez FREQ 113.9 TRACK 053°,53.6Dme
AVIATION GAS - CREDIT CARDS - CASH TYPE -
REPAIRS AVAILABLE - TIEDOWNS? BYO

HOTEL	RATE	WHERE	TEL
Chah Kah Cabañas	$	Nr ruins	-
Hotel Palenque	$	Central	5-0103

4938'x105' Paved
11'Dropoff
to Villahermosa
to Palenque
Wreck

WORDS ON FUSELAGE SAY:
ADIOS AIRLINES
And a 10'Marijuana Leaf logo
Actually, it was just a movie set!

FLEVATION
215'

The most complete Mayan ceremonial center yet found, these sophisticated architecture and murals do disturb the 'isolated jungle indian' theory. The foliated tree is too similar to one found in Angkor Vat, Cambodia. Also several statues have the exact form as Buddhist ones found in India. Obviously tourism is a very old industry.

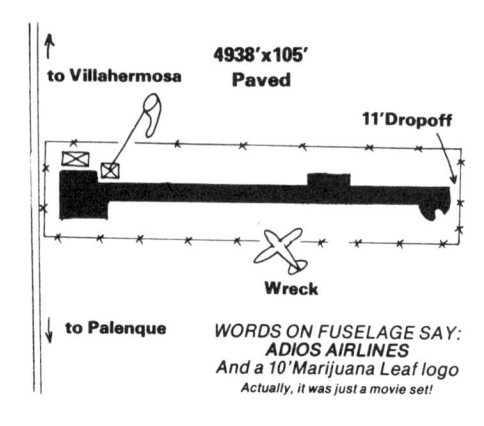

Agua Azul	Chiapas				*AH-wah ah-SOOL*			509
JN CHART JN-46	WAC CJ-25	SECTIONAL TPC J25D	LATITUDE 17°17'	LONGITUDE 92°09'	US TIME CST	FOR GMT +6	ICAO -	TOWN ID AZM

OTHER COMM Traffic 124.2
SETTLEMENT Adjacent South   POPULATION est 1200
FROM V'hermosa   FREQ 117.3   TRACK 131°, 56Dme
FROM Cd.Carmen   FREQ 113.0   TRACK 188°, 84.6Dme
FROM T.Gutierrez FREQ 113.4   TRACK 054°, 75.5Dme
AVIATION GAS -   CREDIT CARDS - CASH TYPE -
REPAIRS AVAILABLE No   TIEDOWNS? BYO

These tumbling waters form a two hundred foot wide, bright blue-green cataract. What a surprise to stumble across it in the Yucatecan jungle. Most tourists will be here, as we were, after an interesting two hour bus ride from Palenque and will lunch, then ride the bus back. If you decide to fly in, remember this is a One Way Strip (no go around possible) with poor braking on wet grass. Lot to be said for the bus ride.

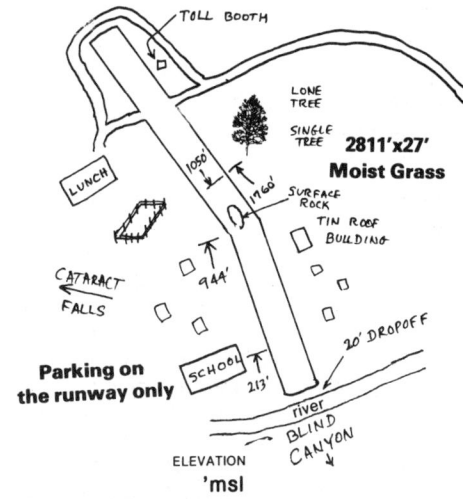

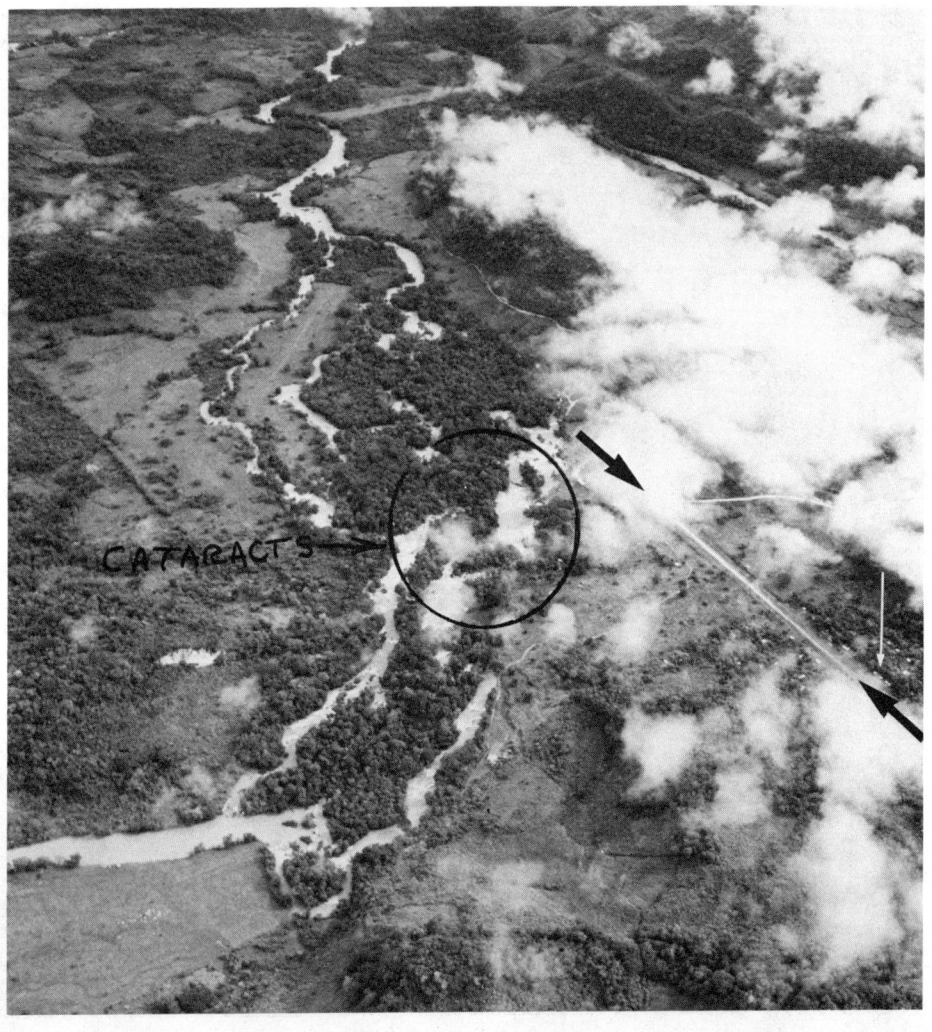

2811'x27'
Moist Grass

Parking on the runway only

ELEVATION 'msl

510 Tenosique New Chiapas *tenn-oh-SEE-kay*

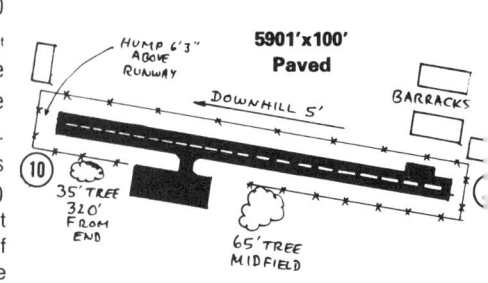

JET CHART	WAC	SECTIONAL	LATITUDE	LONGITUDE	US TIME	FOR GMT ADD	ICAO IDENT	TOWN IDENT
JNC-46	CJ-25 So.	TPC J-25D	17°28'	91°24'	CST	6	-	TIQ

OTHER COMM Traffic 124.9
CITY West 0.5 mi
POPULATION est 34,000
B'cast 860
WHERE 12 mi NW HOURS Daylight
FROM V'hermosa FREQ 117.3 TRACK 104°, 85.3Dme
FROM T.Gutierrez FREQ 113.9 TRACK 063°, 119Dme
FROM Palenque FREQ Apt TRACK 087°, 33.5n.mi.
AVIATION GAS Emergency 100 CREDIT CARDS - CASH TYPE Pesos
REPAIRS AVAILABLE Some TIEDOWNS? BYO

5901'x100' Paved

HUMP 6'3" ABOVE RUNWAY
DOWNHILL 5'
BARRACKS
35' TREE 320' FROM END
65' TREE MIDFIELD

Nice comfortable paved airport in Mexico at the corner of Guatemala's Department of Peten. I'm anxious to get back and explore this area including some days in dugout canoes on the Usumacinta River. Between fishing and exploring the archeology and getting to meet the Lacandon Maya, learning the right way to use a machete from the real experts, I have enough projects in mind to occupy many weeks.

ELEVATION
211'

Tenosique Jungle also called 'Yachilan'   Chiapas   tenn-oh-SEE-kay   511

JET CHART	WAC	SECTIONAL	LATITUDE	LONGITUDE	US TIME	FOR GMT ADD	ICAO IDENT	TOWN IDENT
JN-47	CJ-25	TPC J-25D	17°21'	91°20	CST	6	-	YGL-

OTHER COMM Traffic 123.4-
SETTLEMENT SE side   POPULATION 1 to 50
FROM Cd Carmen FREQ 193.3 TRACK 155°,82.1n.mi.
FROM V'hermosa FREQ 117.; TRACK 108°,91.6 Dme
FROM Flores Ndb FREQ 385 TRACK 282°,87.1n.mi.
FUEL -   CARDS -   CASH? -
REPAIRS -   TIEDOWN BYO machete also

On various editions of our ONCs and WACs this runway has been called 'Tenosique New', 'Lacondón', a couple of names I've forgotten. Each time it was shown to have a length of two to three thousand feet. Obviously it is a thousand or two shorter.

Point is, please please don't land on any runway anytime just because some chart or book (including this one) lists a comforting runway length. Look it over yourself and then decide for yourself.

PS I've yet to see the grass less than a foot high so I haven't landed to measuare; one of these days.

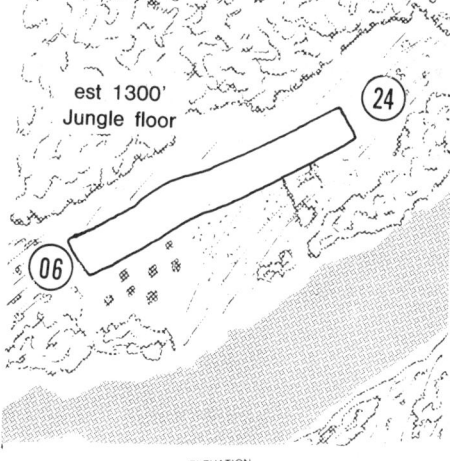

est 1300'
Jungle floor

06 / 24

ELEVATION
500'

512 Emeliano Zapata Chiapas   *ay-meel-ee-AH-noe sopp-OTT-tah*

JET CHART	WAC	SECTIONAL	LATITUDE	LONGITUDE	US TIME	FOR GMT ADD	ICAO IDENT	TOWN IDENT
JN-46	CK-25 So.	TPC J-25D	17°44'	91°47'	CST	6	-	EZT

OTHER COMM Traffic 123.4
CITY 1 mile E   POPULATION 6,000
FROM Villahermosa FREQ 117.3 TRACK 095°,72Dme
FROM Cd Carmen FREQ 113.0 TRACK 174°,55n.mi.
FUEL Emergency 80   CARDS -   CASH? Pesos
REPAIRS Minor   TIEDOWN BYO

    If I were going to collect towns, this would be the place to start. You land in a six hundred acre permanent pasture with grass six inches tall. Its you and the Brahma cows and their white cowbirds.

3870'
Turf Pasture

ELEVATION
80' to 97'

Candelaria Campeche   *conn-dell-ARR-ee-yah*   513

JET CHART	WAC	SECTIONAL	LATITUDE	LONGITUDE	US TIME	FOR GMT ADD	ICAO IDENT	TOWN IDENT
JN-46	CJ-25 No.	TPC J-25D	18°21'	91°01'	CST	6	-	-CDL-

OTHER COMM Traffic 118.1
CITY 2 miles W   POPULATION 2,000
FROM Villahermosa FREQ 117.3 TRACK 078°, 132 n.mi.
FROM Campeche FREQ 227 TRACK 192°, 122 n.mi.
FROM Isla Carmen FREQ 113.0 TRACK 118°, 62 n.mi.
FUEL -   CARDS -   CASH? -
REPAIRS -   TIEDOWN BYO

Interesting small town in the tropical state of Chiapas (chee-OPP-uss). The river plus railroad and highway make a good solid landmark.

Notice in this picture that the jungle south of the runway has receded a lot since last edition. Mexico is developing all possible jungle areas for desperately needed food production. I haven't heard what happened to the 'House of Tolerance' formerly located in the jungle SE of the runway.

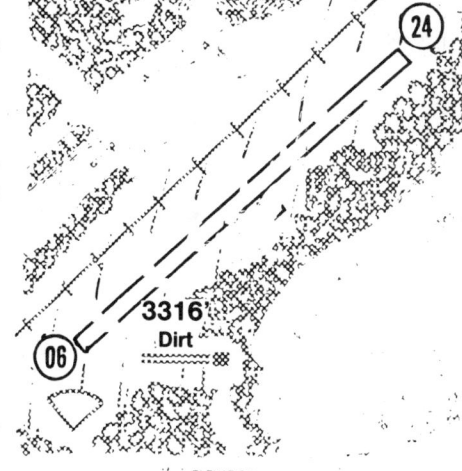

ELEVATION **209'**

RADIO	TORRE 118.1	ELEV 7'	CD. DEL CARMEN, CAMP.
DIA 5666 y 5915	EMERGENCIA	VAR. MAG. 6° E	
NOCHE 3116	121.5	CME ·-·-·	VOR PISTA 13

SEPTIEMBRE 30 - 1978/138

Caution — For Information Only — Not for Aerial Navigation

ALTITUD MINIMA DE SEGURIDAD 2000' DENTRO DE 25 M.N. EN 360°

CME 113.0

FALLIDA: ASCIENDA EN RADIAL 132°, Y PROSIGA CON VIRAJE DE PROCEDIMIENTO A LA IZQUIERDA DENTRO DE 10 M.N. HASTA LA ALTITUD MINIMA DE ESPERA, DE ACUERDO CON INSTRUCCIONES DEL A.T.C.

CATEGORIA	DIRECTO PISTA 13 MDA 420' (413')	CATEGORIA	CIRCULANDO MDA
A		A	520' (513') — 1
B	1	B	520' (513') — 1
C		C	520' (513') — 1¼
D	1½	D	560' (553') — 1¾

CAMBIOS: AJUSTE DE MINIMOS   S.C.T. — D.G.A.C.   CME V-1

SUNRISE & SUNSET - GMT   SALIDA y PUESTA del SOL - GMT

15th of	JAN	FEB	MAR	APR	MAY	JUN	JUL	AUG	SEPT	OCT	NOV	DEC	
SUNRISE	1242	1235	1215	1150	1133	1130	1138	1148	1154	1201	1214	1231	SALIDA
SUNSET	2350	2407	2416	2424	2433	2444	2447	2434	2409	2344	2329	2332	PUESTA
15° de	ENE	FEB	MAR	ABR	MAY	JUN	JUL	AGO	SEP	OCT	NOV	DIC	

Ciudad del Carmen Campeche *see-oo-DOD dell CARR-men* 515

JET CHART	WAC	SECTIONAL	LATITUDE	LONGITUDE	US TIME	FOR GMT ADD	ICAO IDENT	TOWN IDENT
JN-46	CJ-25 So.	TPC J-25D	18°40	91°48'	CST	6	MMCE	CME

tca to: **2,000'msl**   CENTER AT **Vor**   RADIUS **10 mi.**
APPROACH —   TOWER **118.1**   GROUND **118.1**
CITY **0.5 miles W**   POPULATION **84,000**
LOCAL **Vor**   FREQ **113.0**   WHERE **here**   HOURS **24**
B'CAST FREQ **1070**   WHERE **11 mi SE**   HOURS **Daylight**
FROM **Villahermosa**   FREQ **117.3**   TRACK **055°,79Dme**
FROM **Campeche**   FREQ **227**   TRACK **219°,103n.mi.**
FROM **Tuxtla Gutierrez** FREQ **380** TRACK **030°,143n.mi.**
FUEL **80 100,JP**   CARDS **—**   CASH? **Pesos**
REPAIRS **Minor**   TIEDOWN **BYO**

HOTEL	RATE	WHERE	TEL
Motel Linos	$	Nearest	-
Hotel Lli re	$	Central	2-05-88
Internacional	--$	Dockside	-

During a gas stop a few months ago gas men told me that with all the turboprop helos and oil exploring aircraft they are selling ten to twelve thousand gallons of JP (jet fuel) *per day* but less avgas than that per month.

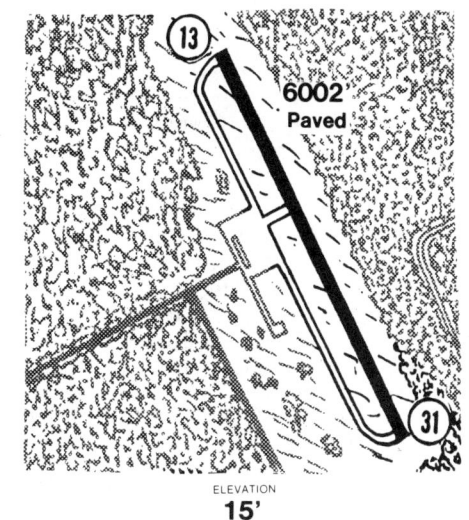

ELEVATION
15'

516 Xpujil   Quintana Roo   *sshh-poo-HEEL*

JET CHART	WAC	SECTIONAL	LATITUDE	LONGITUDE	US TIME	FOR GMT ADD	ICAO IDENT	TOWN IDENT
JN-47	CJ-25 So.	TPC J-25C	18°32'	89°24'	CST	6	-	XJL

OTHER COMM Traffic 121.5
SETTLEMENT SE end   POPULATION 17
FROM Chetumal   FREQ 113.0   TRACK 268°, 63 n.mi.,
FROM Cd del Carmen FREQ 113.0 TRACK 089°, 137 n.mi.,
FROM Tulum   FREQ airport   TRACK 224°, 154 n.mi.,
FUEL -   CARDS -   CASH? -
REPAIRS -   TIEDOWN BYO

Lonely archeological site, this runway gets so little care that pretty soon we're going to be competing with cars to use the highway.

Before it comes to that console yourself with the thought there isn't that much to see, the sites at Tulum and Chichen-Itzá offer more, plus have good runways. A good location aid for here is that the third microwave tower, counting from Chetumal, is just east.

Tip: the service station across the highway could be a starting point for people contact.

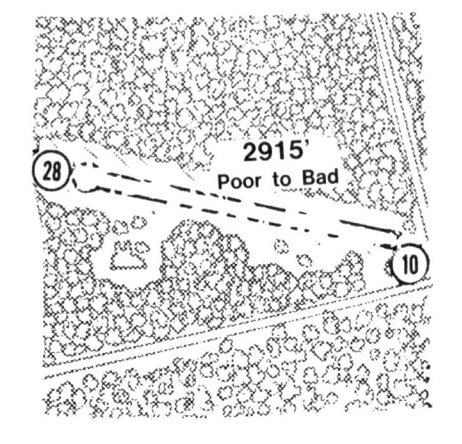

2915'
Poor to Bad

ELEVATION
847'

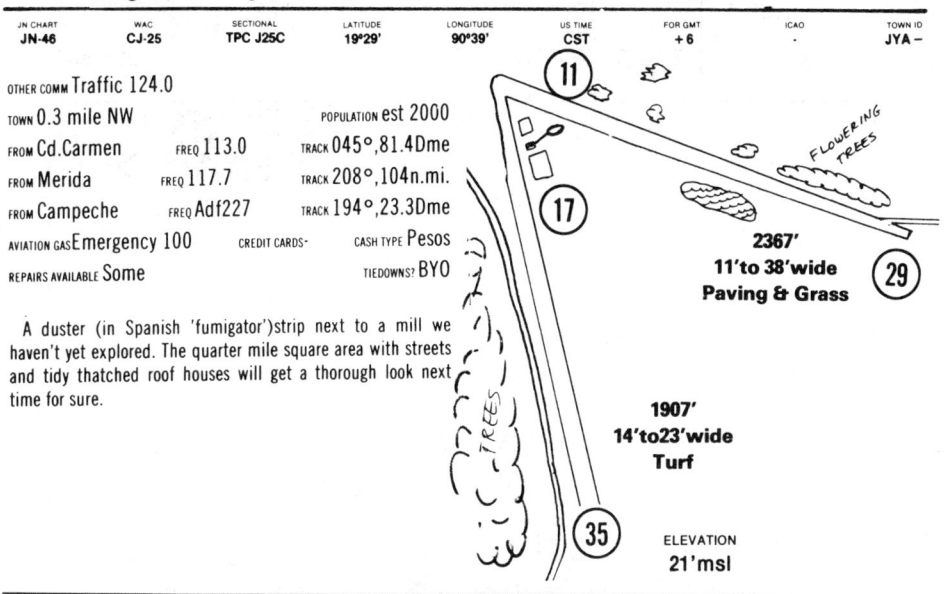

Ingenio la Joya Campeche   *enn-HENN-ee-oh lah HOY-yah*   517

JN CHART	WAC	SECTIONAL	LATITUDE	LONGITUDE	US TIME	FOR GMT	ICAO	TOWN ID
JN-46	CJ-25	TPC J25C	19°29'	90°39'	CST	+6	-	JYA –

OTHER COMM Traffic 124.0
TOWN 0.3 mile NW
FROM Cd.Carmen FREQ 113.0 TRACK 045°, 81.4Dme
FROM Merida FREQ 117.7 TRACK 208°, 104 n.mi.
FROM Campeche FREQ Adf227 TRACK 194°, 23.3Dme
AVIATION GAS Emergency 100 CREDIT CARDS - CASH TYPE Pesos
REPAIRS AVAILABLE Some TIEDOWNS? BYO

A duster (in Spanish 'fumigator') strip next to a mill we haven't yet explored. The quarter mile square area with streets and tidy thatched roof houses will get a thorough look next time for sure.

2367'
11' to 38' wide
Paving & Grass

1907'
14' to 23' wide
Turf

ELEVATION
21' msl

CAMPECHE, CAMP.
AEROPUERTO
NDB/ADF PISTA 32
227 KHZ.
CPE —·— ·—

518

SEPTIEMBRE 30 – 1974

RADIO	TORRE DE CONTROL	ELEV. 30'
DIA. 5666, 5915 y 127.3	TyR 118.5	VAR. MAG. 6° E
NOCHE: 3116 y 127.3	R 121.5	
	C. APROXIMACION	C. TERRESTRE

ALTITUD MINIMA DE SEGURIDAD 2000' DENTRO DE 25 M.N. EN 360°

GOLFO DE MEXICO

A MERIDA

CAMPECHE

CPE 227

A CHAMPOTON

SEYBAPLAYA

Caution: For Information Only Not for Aerial Navigation

NDB 2000' — 145° — 1300' — 10 M.N. IZQ.
325°
760' (730')
ELEV. 30'

FALLIDA: ASCIENDA EN QDM 145°, Y PROSIGA CON VIRAJE DE PROCEDIMIENTO A LA IZQUIERDA DENTRO DE 10 M.N. HASTA LA ALTITUD MINIMA DE ESPERA, DE ACUERDO CON INSTRUCCIONES DEL C.T.A.

CATEGORIA	DIRECTO PISTA 32 MDA 760' (730')	CATEGORIA	CIRCULANDO MDA
A	1 3/4	A	780' (750') –2
B		B	
C	—	C	—
D		D	

CAMBIOS: QDM DE APROXIMACION   S.C.T.– D.G.A.C.   CPE-N-1

SUNRISE & SUNSET – GMT   SALIDA y PUESTA del SOL – GMT

15th of   JAN FEB MAR APR MAY JUN JUL AUG SEPT OCT NOV DEC
SUNRISE 1239 1231 1210 1144 1126 1122 1131 1142 1149 1156 1210 1229 SALIDA
SUNSET   2343 2401 2411 2420 2430 2442 2444 2430 2405 2338 2322 2325 PUESTA
15° de   ENE FEB MAR ABR MAY JUN JUL AGO SEP OCT NOV DIC

To get local time just subtract 'GMT ADD'
PARA OBTENER TIEMPO LOCAL SUSTRIAGA 'GMT ADD'

Campeche Campeche   com-PECH-ay   519

JET CHART	WAC	SECTIONAL	LATITUDE	LONGITUDE	US TIME	FOR GMT ADD	ICAO IDENT	TOWN IDENT
JN-46	CJ-25 No.	TPC J-25C	19°50'	90°31'	CST	6	MMCP	CPE

tca to: **2,000'msl**   CENTER AT **Ndb**   RADIUS **10 mi.**

APPROACH —   TOWER **118.5**   GROUND **118.5**
CITY **1 mile W**   POPULATION **96,000**
LOCAL **Ndb**   FREQ **227**   WHERE **here**   HOURS **24**
B'CAST FREQ **1370**   WHERE **2 mi NW**   HOURS **Daylight**
FROM **Carmen**   FREQ **113.0**   TRACK **041°,104** Dme
FROM **Mérida**   FREQ **117.7**   TRACK **212°,84**Dme
FUEL **80, 100**   CARDS —   CASH? **Yes**
REPAIRS **Minor**   TIEDOWN **BYO**

HOTEL	RATE	WHERE	TEL
el Presidente	$$	Central	—
Baluartes	$	Central	6-33-11
Si Ho Playa	$	Central	6-29-89

Historically a city which Caribbean pirates used to practice raping and sacking, Campeche now is just an important fishing and shrimping port with miles of white sandy beaches.

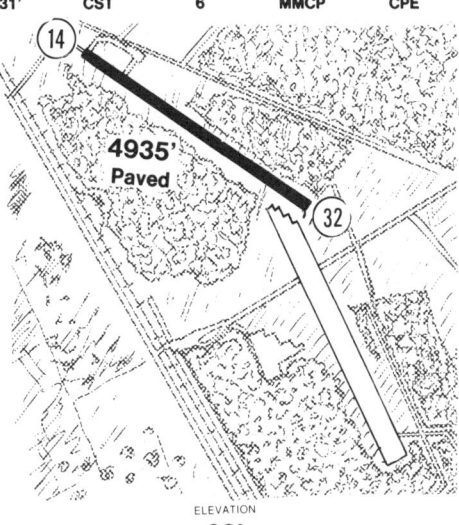

4935' Paved

ELEVATION **30'**

NDB RWY 35

LICENCIADO MANUEL CRECENCIO REJON INTL (MMMD)
(USAF) AL-1103 (DGAC)
MERIDA, MEXICO

520

MERIDA APP CON 121.2
MERIDA TOWER 118.3

IAF MERIDA
280 MID
A2

Caution
For Information Only
Not for Aerial Navigation

MIN SAFE ALT 25 NM 1900

TA 18,000 TLv FL 200

NDB 2000
160° Remain within 10 NM
1500
340°

MISSED APPROACH
Left to 2000 on track of 160° within 10 NM

ELEV 30

REIL Rwys 10-35
HIRL Rwys 10-28, 17-35

340° to NDB

CATEGORY	A	B	C	D
S-NDB-35	640-1¼ 610 (700-1¼)		640-1¾ 610 (700-1¾)	640-2¼ 610 (700-2¼)
CIRCLING	640-2½ 610 (700-2½)			740-2½ 710 (800-2½)

Circling not authorized over city

NDB RWY 35
20°56'N-89°39'W
LICENCIADO MANUEL CRECENCIO REJON INTL (MMMD)
100
MERIDA, MEXICO

SUNRISE & SUNSET – GMT   SALIDA y PUESTA del SOL – GMT

15th of JAN FEB MAR APR MAY JUN JUL AUG SEPT OCT NOV DEC
SUNRISE 1238 1228 1207 1139 1120 1117 1125 1137 1145 1153 1208 1227 SALIDA
SUNSET 2337 2356 2407 2417 2428 2440 2442 2428 2401 2334 2317 2319 PUESTA
15° de   ENE FEB MAR ABR MAY JUN JUL AGO SEP OCT NOV DIC

To get local time just subtract GMT ADD'
PARA OBTENER TIEMPO LOCAL SUSTRIAGA 'GMT ADD'

Mérida Yucatan

MARE-idd-ah

521

JET CHART	WAC	SECTIONAL	LATITUDE	LONGITUDE	US TIME	FOR GMT ADD	ICAO IDENT	TOWN IDENT
JNC-46	CJ-25 No.	TPC J-25B	20°56'	89°38'	CST	6	MMMD	MID

•TCA TO: 20,000'   RADIUS 50 n.mi.   HOURS 24
APPROACH 121.2   TOWER 118.3   GROUND 118.3
OTHER COMM ATIS 117.7   Radar Available
CITY 4 miles NE   POPULATION 325,000
LOCAL VorDme   FREQ 117.7   WHERE here   HOURS 24
B'CAST FREQ 550   WHERE 3.7 mi NNE   HOURS Daylight
FROM New Orleans FREQ 236   TRACK 171°, 494 n.mi.
FROM Bro'ville   FREQ 116.3   TRACK 117°, 520 n.mi.
FROM Guatemala   FREQ 114.1   TRACK 360°, 380 n.mi.
FUEL 80, 100, Jet   CARDS -   CASH? Yes
REPAIRS Some   TIEDOWN BYO

HOTEL	RATE	WHERE	TEL
Paseo Montejo	$$	N side	1-90-33
Casa Balam	$$	Central	1-94-74

Several comfortable hotels, good restaurants, and at least some night life are good reasons for the city as a basecamp. Set aside at least one of your afternoons for wandering around the squares shopping for whatever appeals to you.

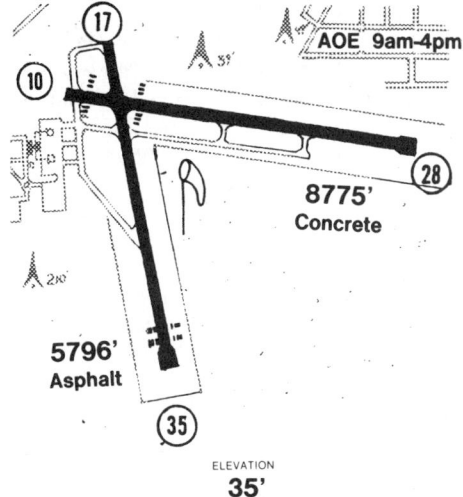

AOE 9am-4pm
8775' Concrete
5796' Asphalt
ELEVATION 35'

522 Chichen-Itzá Yucatan *CHEE-chin eet-SAH*

JET CHART	WAC	SECTIONAL	LATITUDE	LONGITUDE	US TIME	FOR GMT ADD	ICAO IDENT	TOWN IDENT
Jn-47	CJ-25 No.	TPC J-25B	20°41'	88°32'	CST	6	-	CZA

OTHER COMM Traffic 118.1
CITY 1 mile SW
B'CAST FREQ 990 WHERE 19 mi E
POPULATION 3,500
HOURS Daylight

FROM Mérida FREQ 117.7 TRACK 103°, 66n.mi.
FROM Cancún FREQ 113.4 TRACK 256°, 97Dme
FROM Chetumal FREQ 113.0 TRACK 350°, 134n.mi.

FUEL - CARDS - CASH? -
REPAIRS - TIEDOWN BYO

HOTEL	RATE	WHERE	TEL
Mayaland	$$	Central	Tvl Agt
Hacienda	$$	Nr Central	Tvl Agt

4035'
Paving Variable

ELEVATION
112'

This Archeological Zone houses one of the prettiest and certainly the most accessible ancient Mayan city in México. You can land right here and trot over to the hotel. (Please avoid climbing through the fence by the sacrificial well, go in the front and pay the quarter or fifty cents fee.)

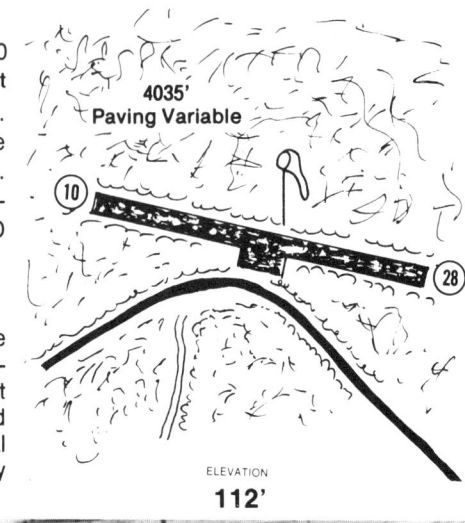

Chichen-Itza Briefing

Easily the best known and easiest to reach of the early Mayan cities, Chichen-Itza presents a perfect example of the rise, spectacular reign, and disintegration of Mayan influence.

In its salad years Chichen was both a religious center and a Mayan scientific center where astronomical observations rival today's in accuracy. Entire building complexes are found to be precisely oriented to coincide with sunrise at each of the year's principle seasons. Corn, the staple and god-like in its importance to the civilization, could thus be planted and tended with scientific accuracy.

Probably the best known feature is the Sacred Well, a natural limestone vertical well about two hundred feet across and seventy feet deep. Young virgins were sacrificed by being thrown off the south platform. It was felt they thus went to heaven, living on into eternity. Contributing to their disappearance is the fact that the water in this well is part of a Yucatan-wide underground river system. Flying over the area you see many duplicates of this Well.

El Castillo, the Toltec structure built to honor the Feathered Serpent, and seen over my shoulder in the middle picture, is Chichen's most imposing structure. About 80 feet high, the building on top houses a red jaguar. If you are lucky a guide might take you to visit this pyramid to see the original Mayan pyramid underneath.

In past visits I've noticed an eerie effect over at the ballcourt. Truck and bus tires on

Author inspecting chronicles of a thousand or more years ago

El Castillo over the author's shoulder, Chaac-mool on the left

the concrete highway would set up a high frequency s-s-s-s sound which, during quiet moments, would sound for all the world like crowds cheering at a sports event. Now that the highway has been moved north I wonder if that effect is still possible to hear.

Many tourists try to just drive out from Merida, see Chichen-Itza in a couple hours, and go on to another ruin. Record-setters have 'done' up to four ruins a day with little or no idea of what they've seen. You might want to stop here two or better, three nights. Guides will help you discover there are good, better, and best times to see various features. Don't hurry: you'll see more slow.

Hot Flash Mayan gardners use Toro mowers!

524 Tizimín   Yucatan   *teece-ee-MEEN*

JET CHART	WAC	SECTIONAL	LATITUDE	LONGITUDE	US TIME	FOR GMT ADD	ICAO IDENT	TOWN IDENT
JNC-47	CJ-25 No.	TPC J-25B	21°09'	88°09'	CST	6	-	TZM

OTHER COMM Traffic 118.1
CITY 0.5 mile E   POPULATION 9,500
B'CAST FREQ 1420   WHERE 2 mi So.   HOURS Daylight
FROM Mérida   FREQ 117.4   TRACK 078°,86Dme
FROM Cancún   FREQ 113.4   TRACK 274°,73Dme
FROM Cozumel   FREQ 112.6   TRACK 296°,79Dme
FUEL 80/87   CARDS -   CASH? Pesos
REPAIRS Minor   TIEDOWN BYO

HOTEL	RATE	WHERE	TEL
Pan American	-$	Central	-

3917'
Concrete

ELEVATION
215'

Off the beaten track, this small Yucatan city gives you an inside look at the working side of the peninsula. Commercial hotels, good but plain restaurants, stores for staples of interest to campers, no gouging cab fares. Last time the town policeman gave me a 6 a.m. ride to the airplane at regular rates. Cabbie wasn't up.

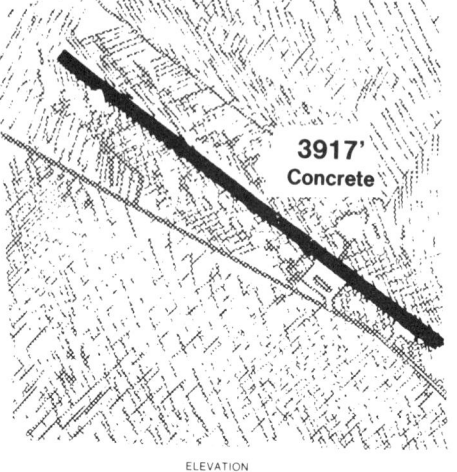

Coloradas, ¹ Yucatan   coe-loe-RAH-doss   525

JN CHART	WAC	SECTIONAL	LATITUDE	LONGITUDE	US TIME	FOR GMT	ICAO	TOWN ID
JN-47	CJ-25	TPC J25B	21°35'	88°04'	CST	+6	.	CDS-

OTHER COMM Traffic 124.3
TOWN Adjacent East   POPULATION est 4500
FROM Tizimin   FREQ Adf1420   TRACK 003°,30n.mi.
FROM Merida   FREQ 117.7   TRACK 060°,96.8Dme
FROM Cancun   FREQ 113.4   TRACK 294°,75.2Dme
AVIATION GAS-   CREDIT CARDS-   CASH TYPE -
REPAIRS AVAILABLE -   TIEDOWNS? BYO

3597'
41'to78'wide
Stone-hard Sand

Very productive salt evaporating operation on a magnificent sweep of coastline at the top of Yucatan. The beaches are crystal white, vaters warm, but the surf is a raging eight or nine inches tall. The customs man doesn't see much aircraft traffic. Be ready to show him all your papers. He's not unfriendly, just doing his job.

The 'Kiosco del Gallo', Kiosk of the Rooster, has available soft drinks in case you were flying along getting thirsty.

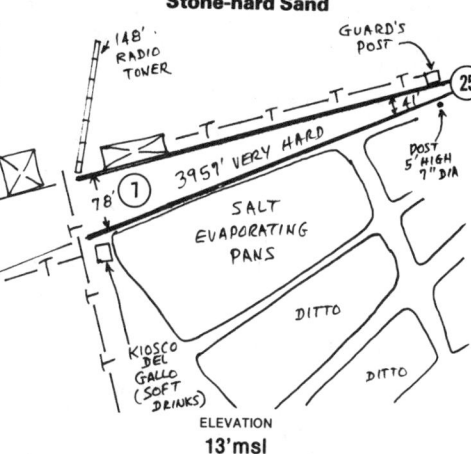

ELEVATION
13'msl

526 Holbox Yucatan *HOLE-bosh*

JN CHART	WAC	SECTIONAL	LATITUDE	LONGITUDE	US TIME	FOR GMT	ICAO	TOWN ID
JN-47	CJ-25	TPC J25B	21°31'	87°24'	CST	+6		HBX –

OTHER COMM Traffic 121.5
SETTLEMENT 0.6 mile NE   POPULATION est 2500
FROM Tizimin   FREQ Adf1420   TRACK 055°,48Dme
FROM Merida   FREQ 117.7   TRACK 064°,131n.mi.
FROM Cancun   FREQ 113.4   TRACK 312°,42.3Dme
AVIATION GAS-   CREDIT CARDS-   CASH TYPE -
REPAIRS AVAILABLE   TIEDOWNS? BYO

Once you see the waters around Holbox its hard to believe Cancun came in first for pretty resort real estate. The waters in this picture are in turquoise ranging from white to deep deep blue- green. Looks like a piece of Navajo indian jewelry miles and miles across.

Data Incomplete–See PREPS

ELEVATION
11'msl

Isla Mujeres Quintana Roo   *EES-lah moo-HAIR-ess*   527

JET CHART	WAC	SECTIONAL	LATITUDE	LONGITUDE	US TIME	FOR GMT ADD	ICAO IDENT	TOWN IDENT
JNC-47	CJ-25 No.	TPC J-25B	21°14'	86°44'	CST	6		IMU

OTHER COMM Traffic 118.1
CITY Adjacent N   POPULATION 7,500
FROM Cancún   FREQ 113.4   TRACK 025°, 14Dme
FROM Cozumel   FREQ 112.6   TRACK 011°, 44Dme
FROM Mérida   FREQ 117.7   TRACK 078°, 168 n.mi.

FUEL   CARDS —   CASH?
REPAIRS Minor   TIEDOWN BYO

HOTEL	RATE	WHERE	TEL
Posada del Mar	$$	W side	1-38-38*
*Mérida			

Always a sleeper, Mujeres has come into its own with a bang now that Cancún is taking hold. This quieter island has only one or two Mayan artifacts but beautiful seas and beaches.

At the north end you can tidepool to your hearts content (rugged shoes a must) with camera or stick for exciting fishlets. No spears please, those are reserved to commercial fishermen.

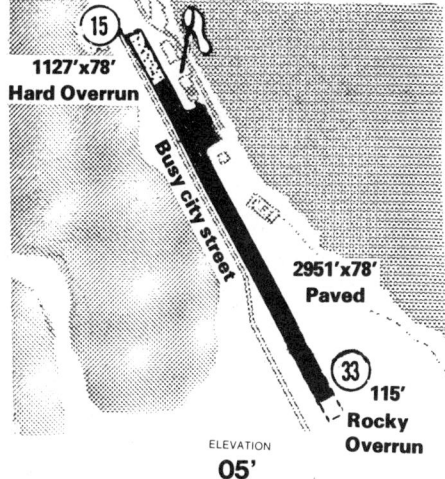

Runway 15: 1127'x78' Hard Overrun
Runway: 2951'x78' Paved
Runway 33: 115' Rocky Overrun
Busy city street
ELEVATION 05'

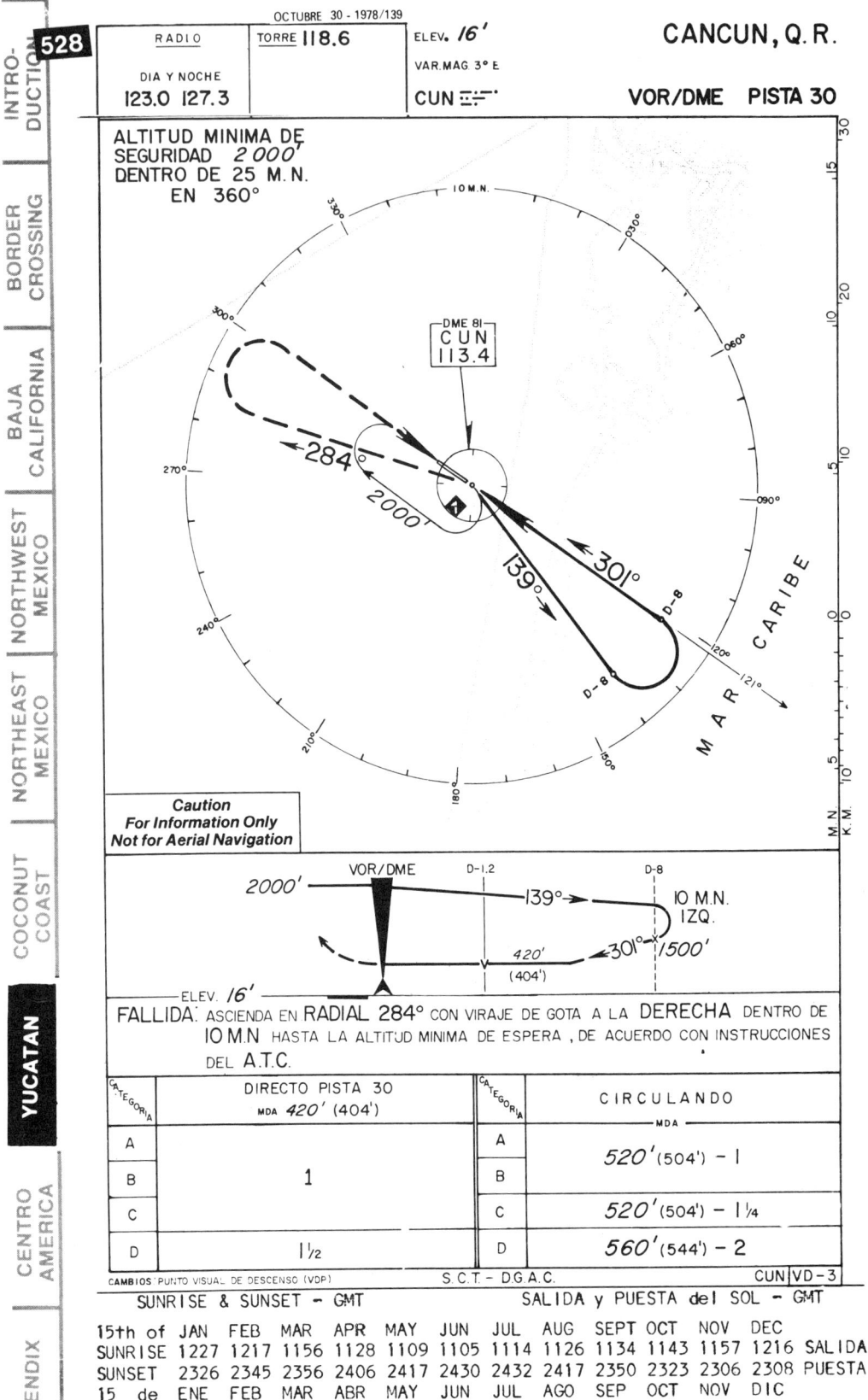

528	RADIO DIA Y NOCHE 123.0 127.3	OCTUBRE 30 - 1978/139 TORRE 118.6 CUN ≡	ELEV. *16'* VAR.MAG 3° E

CANCUN, Q.R.
VOR/DME PISTA 30

ALTITUD MINIMA DE SEGURIDAD *2000'* DENTRO DE 25 M.N. EN 360°

DME 81 CUN 113.4

284°   2000'   139°   301°   D-8

MAR CARIBE

Caution *For Information Only Not for Aerial Navigation*

VOR/DME — D-1.2 — 139° — D-8 — 10 M.N. IZQ.
2000' → 420' (404') → 301° → 1500'
ELEV. *16'*

FALLIDA: ASCIENDA EN RADIAL 284° CON VIRAJE DE GOTA A LA DERECHA DENTRO DE 10 M.N HASTA LA ALTITUD MINIMA DE ESPERA, DE ACUERDO CON INSTRUCCIONES DEL A.T.C.

CATEGORIA	DIRECTO PISTA 30 MDA *420'* (404')	CATEGORIA	CIRCULANDO MDA
A	1	A	*520'* (504') – 1
B		B	*520'* (504') – 1
C		C	*520'* (504') – 1¼
D	1½	D	*560'* (544') – 2

CAMBIOS: PUNTO VISUAL DE DESCENSO (VDP)   S.C.T. – D.G.A.C.   CUN | VD-3

SUNRISE & SUNSET – GMT   SALIDA y PUESTA del SOL – GMT

15th of JAN FEB MAR APR MAY JUN JUL AUG SEPT OCT NOV DEC
SUNRISE 1227 1217 1156 1128 1109 1105 1114 1126 1134 1143 1157 1216 SALIDA
SUNSET 2326 2345 2356 2406 2417 2430 2432 2417 2350 2323 2306 2308 PUESTA
15 de   ENE FEB MAR ABR MAY JUN JUL AGO SEP OCT NOV DIC

To get local time just subtract 'GMT ADD'
PARA OBTENER TIEMPO LOCAL SUSTRIAGA 'GMT ADD'

Cancún Int'l Quintana Roo conn-KOON 529

JET CHART	WAC	SECTIONAL	LATITUDE	LONGITUDE	US TIME	FOR GMT ADD	ICAO IDENT	TOWN IDENT
JN-47	CJ-25 No.	TPC J-25B	21°02'	86°53'	CST	6	MMUN	CUN

- TCA TO: 20,000'   RADIUS 50 n.mi.   HOURS 1300-0300Z
- APPROACH 120.4   TOWER 118.6   GROUND 118.6
- CITY $15 No.   POPULATION 20,000
- LOCAL VorDme   FREQ 113.4   WHERE here   HOURS 24
- FROM New Orleans   FREQ 236   TRACK 155°, 412 n.mi.
- FROM Key West   FREQ 332   TRACK B26&B4, 386 n.mi.
- FROM Mérida   FREQ 117.1   TRACK 084°, 183 n.mi.
- FUEL 80, 100   CARDS Visa, MC   CASH? Yes
- REPAIRS -   TIEDOWN BYO

AOE 9am-5pm

HOTEL	RATE	WHERE	TEL
Cancun Caribe	$$$$	Island	3-01-2
Club Med	$$$$	Nearer	Tvl Agt
Verano Beat	$$$	Peninsula	-
Many more			

8491'
Concrete
Vasi Rwy 12

ELEVATION
17'

Computer-selected as the best resort city in the world, the clear shallow water lagoons, balmy tropical air most months, and smog-free sun all do their share to making Cancún a complete resort city.

VOR RWY 5

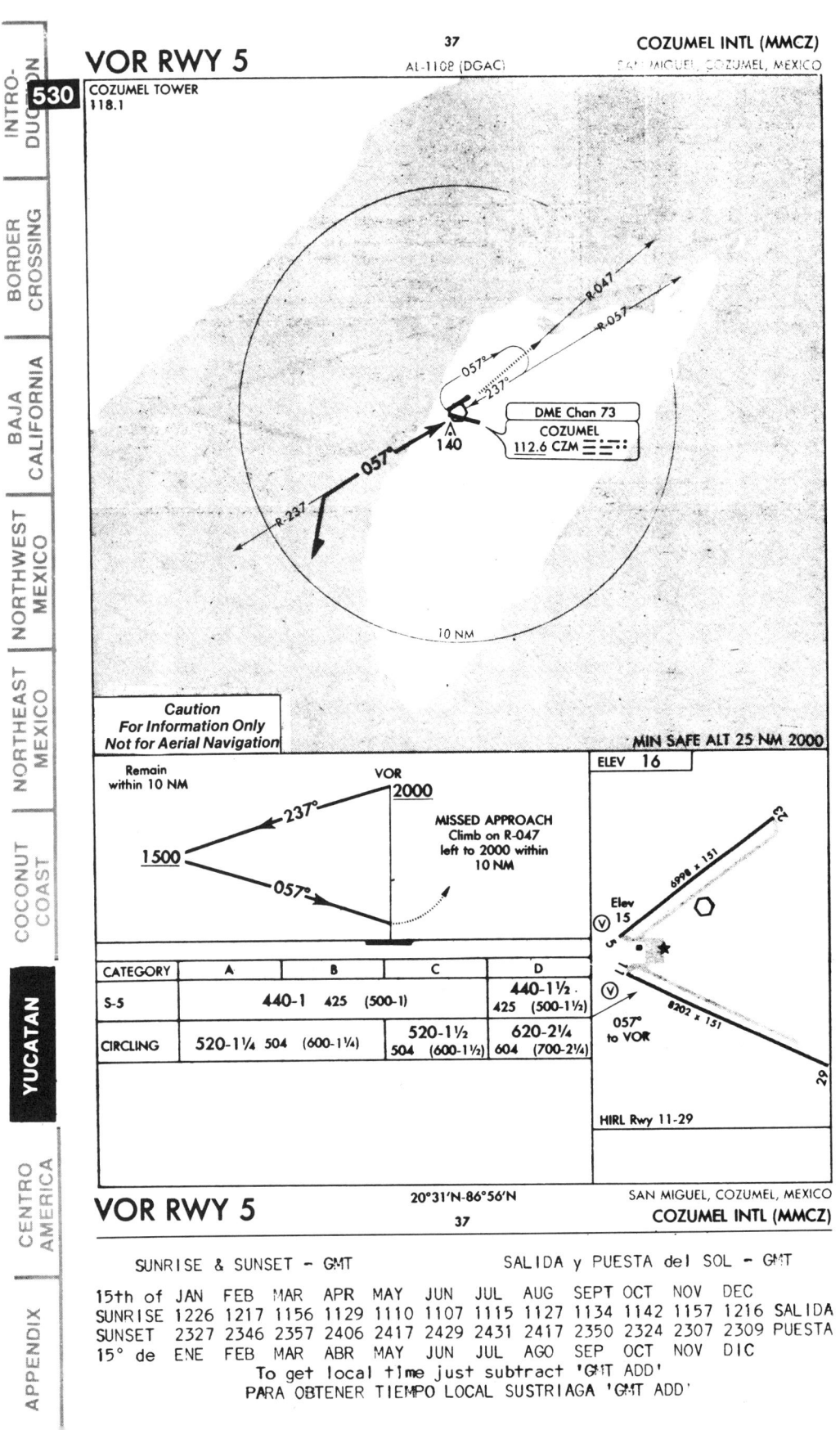

COZUMEL INTL (MMCZ)
SAN MIGUEL, COZUMEL, MEXICO

AL-1108 (DGAC)

COZUMEL TOWER 118.1

DME Chan 73
COZUMEL
112.6 CZM

Caution For Information Only Not for Aerial Navigation

MIN SAFE ALT 25 NM 2000

ELEV 16

Remain within 10 NM

VOR 2000

MISSED APPROACH
Climb on R-047 left to 2000 within 10 NM

Elev 15

6998 x 151

8202 x 151

057° to VOR

HIRL Rwy 11-29

CATEGORY	A	B	C	D
S-5	440-1 425 (500-1)			440-1½ 425 (500-1½)
CIRCLING	520-1¼ 504 (600-1¼)		520-1½ 504 (600-1½)	620-2¼ 604 (700-2¼)

20°31'N-86°56'N

VOR RWY 5

SAN MIGUEL, COZUMEL, MEXICO
COZUMEL INTL (MMCZ)

SUNRISE & SUNSET - GMT   SALIDA y PUESTA del SOL - GMT

15th of	JAN	FEB	MAR	APR	MAY	JUN	JUL	AUG	SEPT	OCT	NOV	DEC	
SUNRISE	1226	1217	1156	1129	1110	1107	1115	1127	1134	1142	1157	1216	SALIDA
SUNSET	2327	2346	2357	2406	2417	2429	2431	2417	2350	2324	2307	2309	PUESTA
15° de	ENE	FEB	MAR	ABR	MAY	JUN	JUL	AGO	SEP	OCT	NOV	DIC	

To get local time just subtract 'GMT ADD'
PARA OBTENER TIEMPO LOCAL SUSTRIAGA 'GMT ADD'

Cozumel Internacional   Quintana Roo   koce-oo-MELL   531

JET CHART	WAC	SECTIONAL	LATITUDE	LONGITUDE	US TIME	FOR GMT ADD	ICAO IDENT	TOWN IDENT
47	CJ25 No.	TPC J-25B	20°31'	86°56'	CST	6	MMCZ	CZM

tca to: **2,000'msl** center at **VorDme**   radius **10 mi.**

APPROACH	—	TOWER **118.1**	GROUND **118.1**

AOE **9am-4pm**

CITY **Adjacent SE**   POPULATION **52,000**
LOCAL **Ndb**   FREQ **281**   WHERE **Here**   HOURS **24**
LOCAL **VorDme**   FREQ **112.6**   WHERE **Here**   HOURS **24**
B'CAST FREQ **810**   WHERE —   HOURS **Daylight**
FROM **Cancún**   FREQ **113.4**   TRACK **185°,31Dme**
FROM **Grand Isle**   FREQ **236**   TRACK **150°,547n.mi.**
FROM **Key West**   FREQ **332**   TRACK **B26/B4,390n.mi.**
FUEL **80,100**   CARDS —   CASH? **Yes**
REPAIRS **Minor**   TIEDOWN **BYO**

HOTEL	RATE	WHERE	TEL
el Presidente	$$$	4 mi S	Tvl Agt
Cozumel-Caribe	$$	2 mi N	Tvl Agt

This twenty mile long Caribbean island has pretty green-blue water, acres of white sandy beaches, a selection of hotels from beach posh to the intown sleeping bag optional ones. Courtesy is king: one hotel has a bar sunken into the beach for the crawl in trade.

6997' Paved
8203' Paved

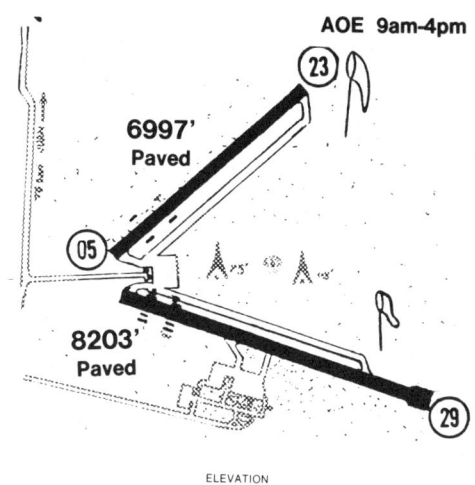

ELEVATION **17'**

532 Tulum   Quintana Roo   *too-LOOM*

JET CHART	WAC	SECTIONAL	LATITUDE	LONGITUDE	US TIME	FOR GMT ADD	ICAO IDENT	TOWN IDENT
JNC-47	CJ-25 No.	TPC J-25D	20°14'	87°27'	CST	6	-	TLM

OTHER COMM Traffic 122.85
SETTLEMENT 0.5 mile SE   POPULATION 600
FROM Cancún   FREQ 113.4   TRACK 21;°,59Dme
FROM Cozumel   FREQ 112.6   TRACK 235°,44Dme
FROM Chetumal   FREQ 113.0   TRACK 023°,114n.mi.
FUEL -   CARDS -   CASH? -
REPAIRS -   TIEDOWN BYO
       HOTEL   RATE   WHERE   TEL
Akumal $$$ 4 miles N   Tvl agt

5987' Paving

ELEVATION
15' to 48'

Loneliest of the Mayan cities, this has been called a Mayan beach house or Aztec lighthouse, neither correctly. Incomplete archeology seems to indicate a new, non-Maya religion was just taking hold as the Spaniards approached for the Conquest.

Cabs are available at the airport to take you to the archeological zone. Be handy to have a guidebook ahead of time for details as to the various buildings and towers.

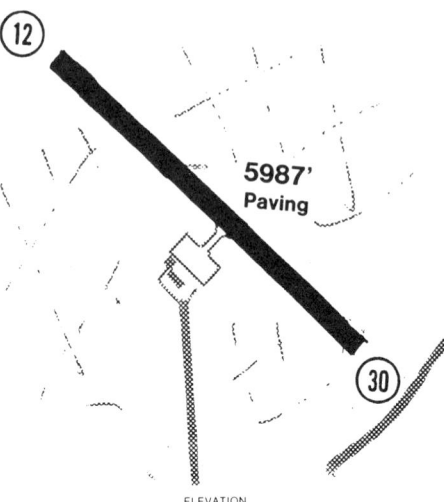

533

Jack Connolly is a little hard to spot on the south side of the Archeological Park. Notice the author stands next to the pretty one. Tulum 1971

534 Boca Paila   Quintana Roo   boe-cah pye-EE-lah

JET CHART	WAC	SECTIONAL	LATITUDE	LONGITUDE	US TIME	FOR GMT ADD	ICAO IDENT	TOWN IDENT
JNC-47	CJ-25 No.	TPC J-25B	20°01'	87°29'	CST	6	-	-PEZ-

OTHER COMM Traffic 122.85
SETTLEMENT Alongside runway E   POPULATION 45
FROM Cozumel   FREQ 112.6   TRACK 221°, 44Dme
FROM Mérida   FREQ 117.7   TRACK 109°, 142 n.mi.
FROM Chetumal FREQ 113.0   TRACK 024°, 102 n.mi.
FUEL -   CARDS -   CASH? -
REPAIRS -   TIEDOWN BYO

HOTEL	RATE	WHERE	TEL
Pez Maya resort	$$$	here	tvl agt

A large expanse of shallow water out to the reef a quarter mile away says Bonefish! Those same warm waters say 'lazy swimming' to lazy swimmers and the white sand under the slowly waving coco palms holds your own dugout canoe, awaiting your next adventure.

A smallish resort, there is parking off the runway for up to one airplane, depending on size.

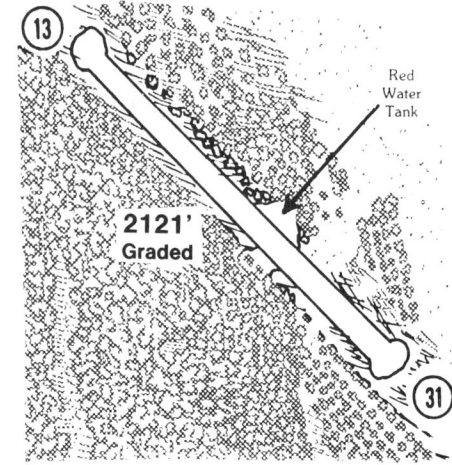

2121' Graded — Red Water Tank
Runway 13 / 31
ELEVATION **04'**

Felipe Carril Puerto   Quintana Roo   *fay-LEE-pay cah-REEL PWAIR-toe*   535

JN CHART	WAC	SECTIONAL	LATITUDE	LONGITUDE	US TIME	FOR GMT	ICAO	TOWN ID
JN-61	CJ-25	TPC J-25C	19°32'	88°05'	CST	6	·	CPU

OTHER COMM Traffic 118.1
CITY 2 mi NE
B'cast 620
POPULATION est 19,000
WHERE 1 mi NE   HOURS Daylight
FROM Chetumal   FREQ 113.0   TRACK 008°, 68n.mi.
FROM Cozumel   FREQ 112.6   TRACK 224°, 87.7Dme
FROM Chichen-I   FREQ Apt   TRACK 148°, 76.9n.mi

AVIATION GAS -   CREDIT CARDS -   CASH TYPE -

Inbound to take a picture and measure this airport, I lost a race to one of the larger healthier CB, cumulo nimbus, clouds I've seen in awhile. Tried to sit it out. After an hour the middle of the storm hadn't yet reached the airport. At an estimated rate of inches per hour I decided next time would be soon enough. See you in the 17th edition, Felipe Carrill Puerto.

DATA INCOMPLETE

CHETUMAL, Q.R.

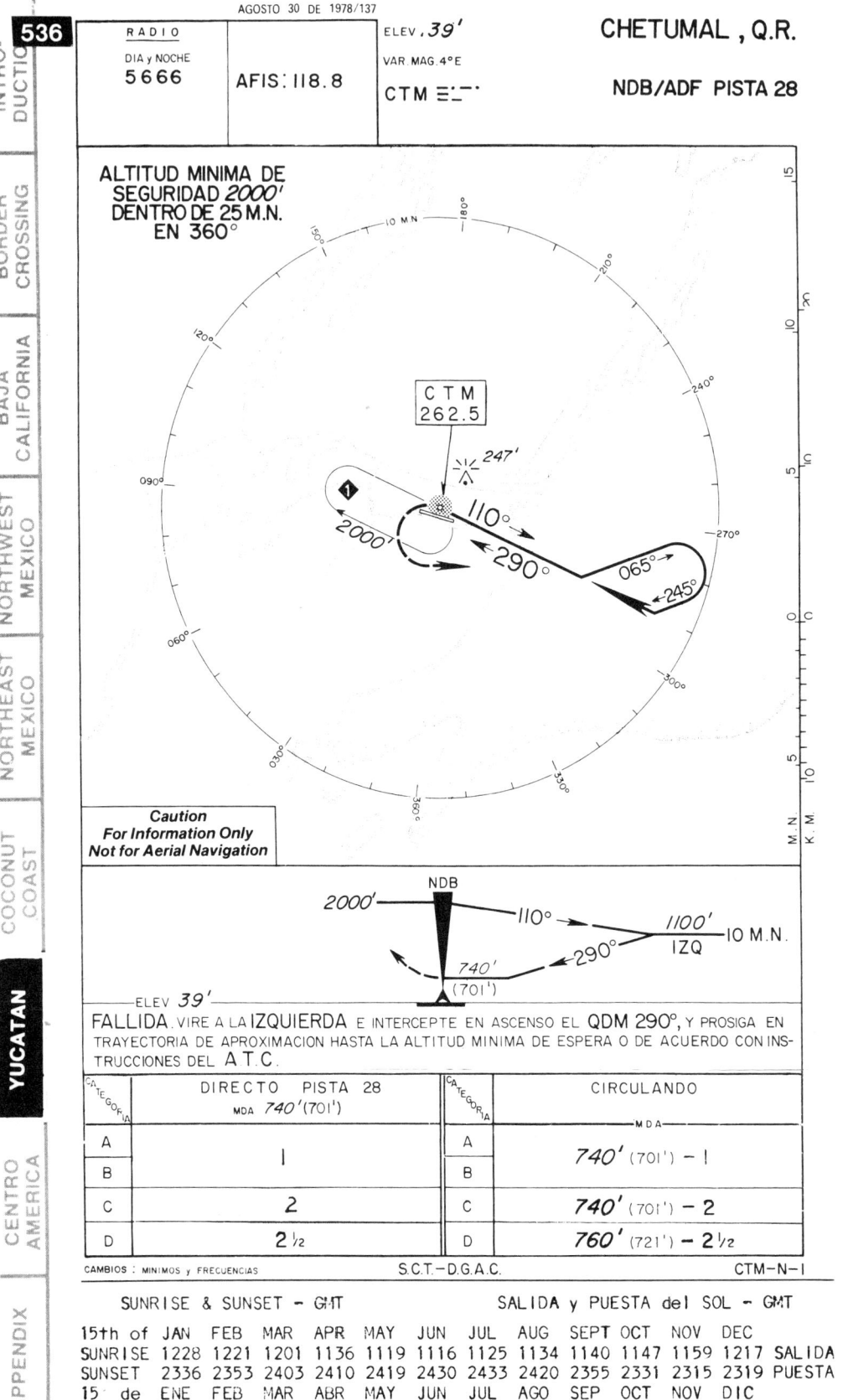

NDB/ADF PISTA 28

AGOSTO 30 DE 1978/137

RADIO DIA y NOCHE: 5666
AFIS: 118.8
ELEV. 39'
VAR. MAG. 4°E
CTM ≡·−··

ALTITUD MINIMA DE SEGURIDAD 2000' DENTRO DE 25 M.N. EN 360°

CTM 262.5
247'

Caution — For Information Only — Not for Aerial Navigation

NDB — 2000' — 110° — 1100' IZQ 10 M.N. — 290° — 740' (701')
ELEV. 39'

FALLIDA. VIRE A LA **IZQUIERDA** E INTERCEPTE EN ASCENSO EL **QDM 290°**, Y PROSIGA EN TRAYECTORIA DE APROXIMACION HASTA LA ALTITUD MINIMA DE ESPERA O DE ACUERDO CON INSTRUCCIONES DEL A.T.C.

CATEGORIA	DIRECTO PISTA 28 MDA 740'(701')	CATEGORIA	CIRCULANDO MDA
A	1	A	740' (701') − 1
B	1	B	740' (701') − 1
C	2	C	740' (701') − 2
D	2 ½	D	760' (721') − 2 ½

CAMBIOS: MINIMOS y FRECUENCIAS — S.C.T.−D.G.A.C. — CTM-N-I

SUNRISE & SUNSET − GMT   SALIDA y PUESTA del SOL − GMT

15th of   JAN FEB MAR APR MAY JUN JUL AUG SEPT OCT NOV DEC
SUNRISE 1228 1221 1201 1136 1119 1116 1125 1134 1140 1147 1159 1217 SALIDA
SUNSET   2336 2353 2403 2410 2419 2430 2433 2420 2355 2331 2315 2319 PUESTA
15 de   ENE FEB MAR ABR MAY JUN JUL AGO SEP OCT NOV DIC

Chetumal Int'l Quintana Roo

chett-oo-MALL **537**

JET CHART	WAC	SECTIONAL	LATITUDE	LONGITUDE	US TIME	FOR GMT ADD	ICAO IDENT	TOWN IDENT
JNC-47	CJ-25 So.	TPC J-25C	18°30'	88°19'	CST	6	MMCM	CTM

tca to: **2,000'msl**   CENTER AT **Vor**   RADIUS **5 mi.**
APPROACH -   TOWER **118.8**   GROUND **118.8**
CITY **1 mi E**   POPULATION **88,000**
LOCAL **Vor**   FREQ **113.0**   WHERE **here**   HOURS **24**
B'CAST FREQ **960**   WHERE **4 mi NE**   HOURS **Daylight**
FROM **Belice**   FREQ **392**   TRACK **176°, 57 n.mi.**
FROM **Cancún**   FREQ **113.4**   TRACK **207°, 176** n.mi.
FROM **Villahermosa**   FREQ **117.3**   TRACK **078°, 284 Dme**
FUEL **100**   CARDS -   CASH? **Yes**
REPAIRS **Minor**   TIEDOWN **BYO**

HOTEL	RATE	WHERE	TEL
el Presidente	$$	Central	2-05-42
Cont. Caribe	$$	Central	2-11-00

AOE 9am-12, 3-4pm

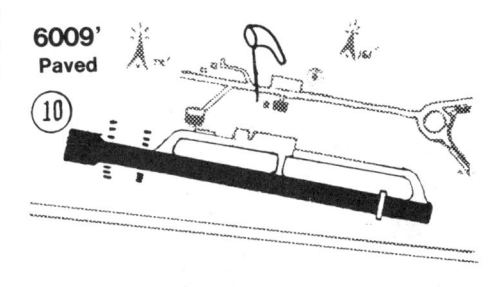

6009'
Paved
(10)

ELEVATION
22'

There are huge farms a few miles west of town where millions of jungle acres have been cleared to help with México's ever growing need for food. You can measure the constant battle between the jungle and farmers. Both want the land; it is a continual seesaw contest.

WAC CK-25

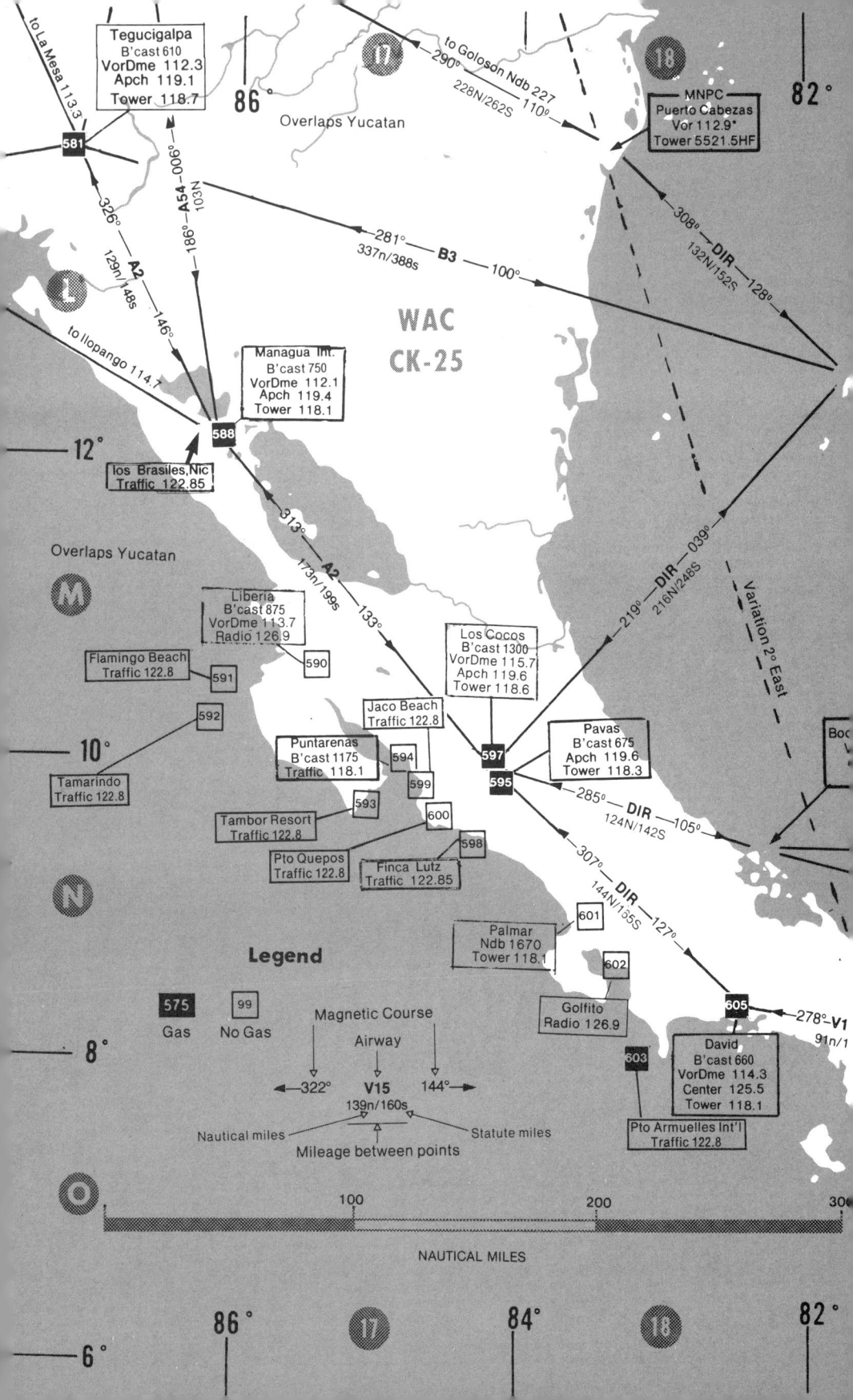

Tegucigalpa
B'cast 610
VorDme 112.3
Apch 119.1
Tower 118.7

to Goloson Ndb 227

MNPC
Puerto Cabezas
Vor 112.9°
Tower 5521.5HF

to La Mesa 1133

581 — Gas

326° A2 129n/148s
to Ilopango 114.7
A54 —006° 186° 103N
290° 228N/262S 110°

281° **B3** 100°
337n/388s

308° **DIR** 039°
132N/152S 128°

146°

Managua Int.
B'cast 750
VorDme 112.1
Apch 119.4
Tower 118.1

588

los Brasiles, Nic
Traffic 122.85

313° A2 173n/199s 133°

Overlaps Yucatan

219° **DIR** 039°
216N/248S

Variation 2° East

Liberia
B'cast 875
VorDme 113.7
Radio 126.9

590

Flamingo Beach
Traffic 122.8
591

Los Cocos
B'cast 1300
VorDme 115.7
Apch 119.6
Tower 118.6

597

Pavas
B'cast 675
Apch 119.6
Tower 118.3

595

592

Tamarindo
Traffic 122.8

Jaco Beach
Traffic 122.8

Puntarenas
B'cast 1175
Traffic 118.1
594
599

285° **DIR** 105°
124N/142S

Tambor Resort
Traffic 122.8
593

600

Pto Quepos
Traffic 122.8

Finca Lutz
Traffic 122.85

598

307° **DIR** 127°
144N/155S

Legend

575 Gas   99 No Gas

Magnetic Course
Airway
←322° **V15** 144°→
139n/160s
Nautical miles — Statute miles
Mileage between points

Palmar
Ndb 1670
Tower 118.1

601

602

Golfito
Radio 126.9

605

278°— **V1**
91n/1

David
B'cast 660
VorDme 114.3
Center 125.5
Tower 118.1

603

Pto Armuelles Int'l
Traffic 122.8

0 — 100 — 200 — 300

NAUTICAL MILES

Aeronautical Chart — Panama Region

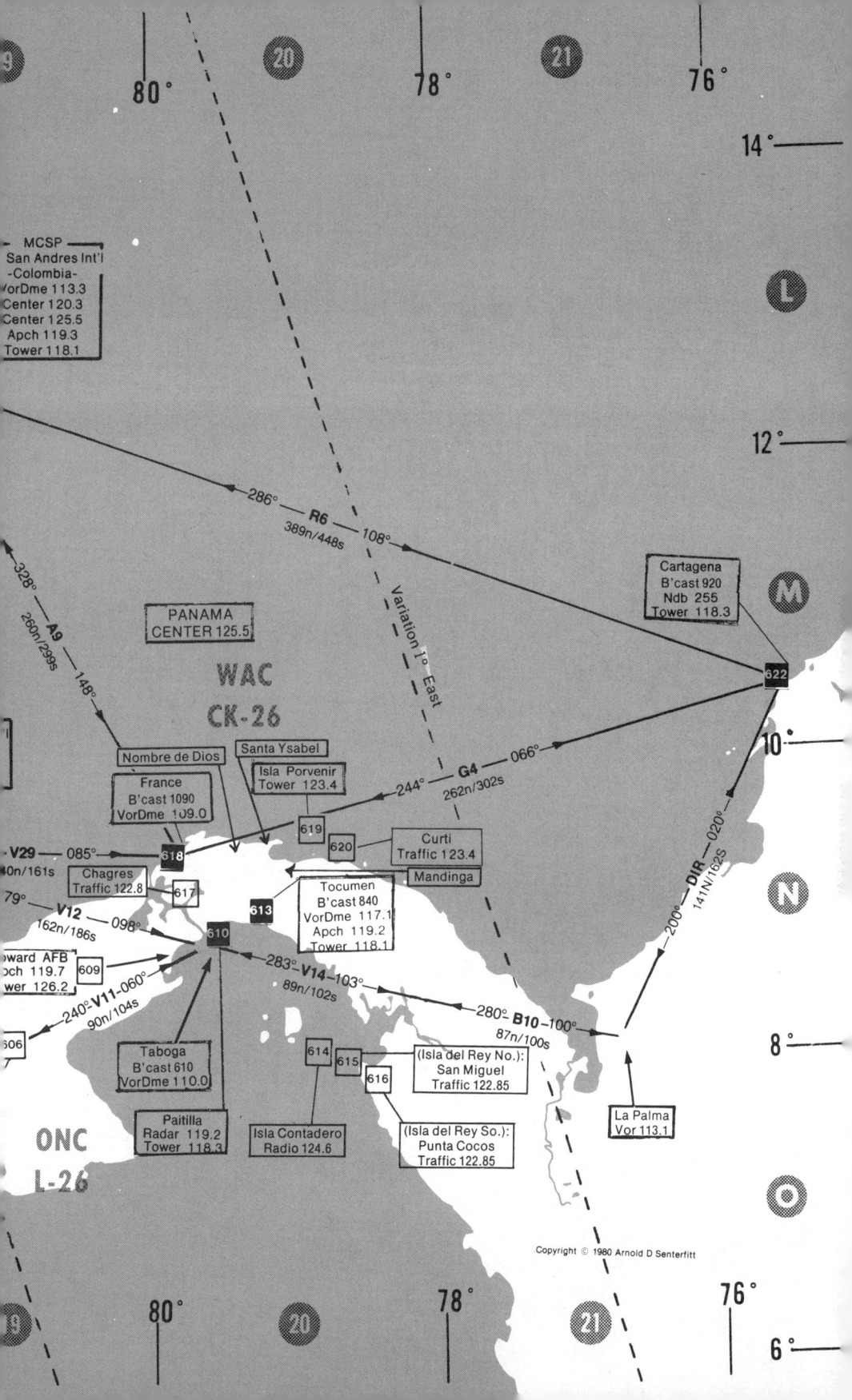

MCSP
San Andres Int'l
-Colombia-
VorDme 113.3
Center 120.3
Center 125.5
Apch 119.3
Tower 118.1

PANAMA CENTER 125.5

WAC CK-26

ONC L-26

Cartagena
B'cast 920
Ndb 255
Tower 118.3

France
B'cast 1090
VorDme 109.0

Isla Porvenir
Tower 123.4

Curti
Traffic 123.4

Chagres
Traffic 122.8

Tocumen
B'cast 840
VorDme 117.1
Apch 119.2
Tower 118.1

Howard AFB
Apch 119.7
Tower 126.2

Taboga
B'cast 610
VorDme 110.0

Paitilla
Radar 119.2
Tower 118.3

Isla Contadero
Radio 124.6

(Isla del Rey No.):
San Miguel
Traffic 122.85

(Isla del Rey So.):
Punta Cocos
Traffic 122.85

La Palma
Vor 113.1

Nombre de Dios
Santa Ysabel
Mandinga

Airways:
- 286°—R6—108° 389n/448s
- 328°—A9—148° 260n/299s
- 244°—G4—066° 262n/302s
- V29 085°
- V12 098° 162n/186s
- V11 240°—060° 90n/104s
- V14 283°—103° 89n/102s
- B10 280°—100° 87n/100s
- DIR 200°—020° 141n/162s

Variation 1° East

Copyright © 1980 Arnold D Senterfitt

540 Centro America Index

**Sequence:
Place,Ident,Page**

Arrive/Departure,550

Belice Int'l,ZDZ,557
Belice Municipal,ZDZ2-,558
Belize IFR,ZDZ,556
Belmopan,BMO-,559
Boarding Pass,548

Centro America Flt Plan,551
Centro America All Borders,542
Centro America Gen.Decl.,546
Centro America Perm. Form,545
Centro America Permission,544
Cartagena IFR,CTG,621
Cartagena Int'l,CTG,622
Cay Ambergris,MBR-,553
Caye Chapel,HPL-,554
Central Farm,CFM-,560
Centro America Area,538
Centro America Briefing,541
Centro America Index,540
Chagres,CAG,617
Corozal,552
Carti,CAW,620

David IFR,DAV,604
David Int'l,DAV,605

El Salvador Int'l,CAT,584

Finca Lutz,LUT-,598
Flamingo Beach,NGO-,591
Flores,FLS,568
Fort Royal,FTK-,578

Gamboa,CAG,617
Golfito Int'l,MRGF,602

Goloson Int'l,LCE,573
Guanaja,GJA,579
Guatemala City IFR,AUR,570
Guatemala City Int'l,AUR,571

Howard AFB,HOW,609
Howard IFR,HOW,608

Ilopango IFR,YSX,582
Ilopango Int'l,YSX,583
Incountry Tourist Offices,549
Isla Contadora,COZ,614
Isla Porvenir,PVR,619
Isla del Rey North,SMI,615
Isla del Rey South,PCO,616

Jaco Beach,JCO-,599

La Aurora IFR,AUR,570
La Aurora Int'l,AUR,569
La Mesa Int'l IFR,LMS,575
Liberia Int'l,MRLB,590
Los Brasiles,587
Los Cocos IFR,TIO,596

Managua IFR,MGA,588
Managua Int'l,MGA,589
Maya Beach,MAY-,563
Melchor de Mencos Int'l,MCH-,566
Melinda,MDA-,562

New France,FTD,618
Nombre de Dios,NDI,618B
Norport,NPT-,561

Orange Walk,555

Paitilla Int'l,MAG,610
Palmar,TIPM,601
Panama Shopping,611
Pavas Int'l,PAV,595
Porvenir,PVR,619
Punta Cocos,RYS-,616
Puerto Armuelles,ARM-,603
Puerto Barrios Int'l,BAR,569
Puerto Quepos,QPO-,600
Puerto San Jose Int'l,SGA,572
Punta Gorda,GOR-,565
Puntarenas,594

Rio Hato,R ,607
Roatan,COX-,577

San Jose:Cocos Int'l,TIO,597
San Miguel,RYN-,615
San Pedro Sula Int'l,LMS,574
Sandino IFR,MGA,568
Sandino Int'l,MGA,569
Santa Isabel,SIE,618A
Santiago,STG,606

Tamarindo,TAM-,592
Tamarino,585
Tambor,BOR-,593
Tegucigalpa IFR,TNT,580
Tegucigalpa Int'l,TNT,581
Tikal,TKL,567
Tocumen IFR,TCM,612
Tocumen Int'l,TCM,613

Utila,UTL-,576

Volcano,586

Waha Leaf,WAH-,564

Centro America introduction

Area includes: Countries south of Mexico: Belice, Guatemala, Honduras, El Salvador, Nicaragua, Costa Rica, Panama. Colombia is also represented by Crespo airport in Cartagena, a famous city from days of the Spanish Main.

Best known for: ancient Mayan city of Tikal, Panama Canal, Swiss-like Costa Rica.

But it also has: Caribbean islands of Roatan, Cay Ambergris, and Porvenir. There's excellent shopping in Guatemala, hundreds of miles of uniquely beautiful west coast beaches.

Cities: Guatemala City, Tegucigalpa, the beginning to be cosmopolitan ones San Jose Costa Rica and Panama City, we'll leave out San Salvador and Nicaragua City for now.

Altitudes: Ranging from Roatan's beaches to Guatemala's three mile high volcanoes.

Climate: Although the jungles will be on the warm side, they are surprisingly comfortable once you get inside the canopy of treetops. In the higher levels winters are cool but San Jose will fool you into carrying a sweater when it is windy from tradewinds. Not cold or even cool, they are shirt sleeve comfortable at the city's 3.000'.

Weather of note: the Caribbean side is usually clouded over and often downright uncomfortable in heavy chop. Prevailing winds are NE or SW, twenty knots about usual.

Special caution: the situations in Nicaragua, or in El Salvador, altho widely advertised to be unstable, are not that bad for an enroute fuel stop or an adventuresome overnight. The writers of scare headlines ignore the flocks of trucks, cars, and general aviation airplanes normally going and coming on a daily basis.

You know very well if a tourist got into the slightest trouble there'd be splashy headline stories here. In the Bush Pilots we've been to Nicaragua when things were supposedly very bad. Onliest thing we found terrible were cab rates, everyone was pretty much trying to get along.

Shopping tips: El Salvador has the reputation for the best in handicrafts but

Bush Pilots at Tikal's Majestic Temple One

Guatemala is head and shoulders above all the other Centro America nations for excellent work. The indians up in the mountain areas are busy and turnout quality clothing and articles. Our bedspread is made of two of what were called hand loomed heavy cotton table cloths. Grace sewed them together here; their extra weight helps in the cooler months.

As on all the articles, colors are fast, workmanship very good. Prices at the airport and in the mountain villages are surprisingly close. The artisans center near La Aurora airport has a good wide selection.

Costa Rica leather in chairs or luggage, is a good value, as is coffee. Last trip the controlled price in the Municipal market in San Jose was about eighty U.S. cents per pound.

Ace-in-the-hole: when you have trouble getting into San Jose direct from Managua, try my IFRR approach. Go over Puntarenas at or below 3,000 and follow the railroad tracks to San Jose under the ever-present cloud bank on that first ridge. Once past it you can climb. Getting past the ridge is the trick.

| COUNTRY | Neighbors | PERSONAL PAPERS |||
		Visa requirement	Tourist Permit	Get it where
Belice	Mexico Guatemala	No	Yes	At Airport of Entry
Colombia	Panama South America	No	Yes	Any Colombian Consular Office
Costa Rica	Nicaragua Panama	No	Yes	At Airport of Entry
El Salvador	Guatemala Honduras	Visa or Tourist Permit	Either, not both	At Airport of Entry
Guatemala	Mexico Belice Honduras El Salvador	Visa or Tourist Permit	Either, not both	At Airport of Entry
Honduras	Guatemala El Salvador Nicaragua	Visa or Tourist Permit	Either, not both	At Airport of Entry
Mexico	U.S.A. Belice Guatemala Texas	Only if on business	Yes, for tourists	Tourist Permit at Airport of Entry
Nicaragua	Honduras Costa Rica	Visa or Tourist Permit	Either, not both	A Consulate or Embassy
Panama	Costa Rica Colombia	Yes, or pay $10 fine		Any Panamanian Consular Office

FOR AIRCRAFT ENTRY

Need written permission?	If not, what is needed	Address for letters	Telex/TWX Telegraph Address	COUNTRY
No	Flight Plan	Chief Aviation Officer Box 367 Belice, Belice, C.A.	CIVILAR BELICE	**Belice**
No	Flight Plan 2 hours ahead		AEROCIVIL BOGOTA	**Colombia**
No	24 hr. notice and Flight Plan	DGAC* Box 5026 San Jose, C.R. C.A.	AEROCIVIL SAN JOSE	**Costa Rica**
Yes	At least 48 hr. notice	DGAC* Apto Ilopango San Salvador, El Salvador, C.A.	AEROCIVIL EL SALVADOR	**El Salvador**
24 hr. Notice: will reply if refused	Letter or wire	DGAC* Aeropuerto La Aurora Guatemala City, Guatemala, C.A.	AEROCIVIL GUATEMALA	**Guatemala**
Notice	Letter or wire	DGAC* Apartado Postal 250 Tegucigalpa, Honduras, C.A.	DIRGA TEGUCIGALPA	**Honduras**
Not if 15 or less seats; 8 if rented	Flight Plan	DGAC* Dpto Transport Int'l Universidad y Xola Mexico 12, D.F.	CIVILAIR MEXICO	**Mexico**
24 hr. Notice Confirm by Radio @ Frontier	Letter or wire	Ministerio de la Defensa Apartado 87 Managua, Nicaragua, C.A.	DIDAC MANAGUA or Telex 1369 AEROCIVIL NIC	**Nicaragua**
24 hr. notice	Flight Plan	DGAC* Apartado 7501 o 7615 Panama 5, R.P.	AEROCIVIL PANAMA or Telex 2057/0143/2618	**Panama**

*DGAC means Director General de Aviacion Civil

544 Centro America Prior Notification or Permission

Each Latin American country covered in this book requires that you give them some kind of prior notice of your arrival. In some cases just filing a flight plan from the last country is plenty, in others a full notice and a carried in hand response is required. We have assembled the All Border Data double page, shown both in the Border Crossing Section pages 42 and 43, and repeated on pages 542 and 543, covers this in detail. Lets talk about how to apply it.

Notification

It is not only a good idea, but it is vital that you comply with each country's needs for prior notification or permission. Notice on the chart I have listed both Post Office addresses for postal mail and Telex/Twx style addresses you may use for that system. There isn't any choice about *whether* to do it, the only choice is how. Start at least four weeks ahead.

Letters or Post Cards

At fifty cents or so per country this is the easiest way and the least expensive. You just fill in the Permission Form on page 545 and xerox copies on postcard weight paper, send one to each country's address on the All Border Data page, stick on the airmail postage, and mail them. Can't hurt to carry with you on the trip a xerox copy of both sides of each one you've sent so you have proof you did it.

Telex and Twx

Next up in cost. If you or your company this service you may send the required messages to the TWX addresses listed on the All Border Data page, 542. Last time I noticed the rates were about two dollars per country notified.

Same xerox idea: copy *AND* take along the originals so you will have inhand proof. Where permission from them for your flight is required per the All Border page, be sure your message authorizes a prepaid response by whatever means your Telex/Twx carrier uses. And xerox both the outgoing and incame messages.

Straight Wire

At thirty to forty dollars per country notified this method is reserved for those times when it is too late to let them know any other way that you are coming. Xerox copies of outgoing and incoming copies are harder to arrange since you may be sending the wire from a country Telegrafos outlet where xerox really is a foreign word. But try.

Visas/Tourist Permits

For countries other than Colombia and Panama, it is easiest to get either of these at your airport of entry than to scurry around ahead of time. For Colombia we generally plan to get tourist visas in San Jose, Costa Rica on the way to Colombia. I get my Panamanian one in San Diego only because I enjoy the view in that office.

If you forget to have extra passport photos along, you may get the required two pictures for the Colombian visa in San Jose. There are flocks of passport photo places in the city. The only problem we've ever had was in not phoning the Colombian Embassy the first time and found they routinely close on Saturdays. I Should have figured that out.

Carry A Passport

For both U.S. and Canadian citizens your best proof of citizenship is a passport. US citizens can get them in ten days to two weeks with a birth certificate and passport photos, usually starting with your County Recorder's office.

Are They Visas or Tourist Permits

For what it's worth my definition is if the permission gets stamped in my passport its a visa. But if it is a separate piece of paper I call it a tourist permit. Which one you get and where it is available is decided by the host country. In this book we assume we are talking only about tourist type visiting papers.

Mexico issues tourist permits to tourist tourists and visas to business tourists. Guatemala issues visas to both categories of visitor, as does Panama, etc. The Prior Permission Page says which one and where to get them.

1982 Unrest Situation

At this writing El Salvador isn't being visited much by those in the know, Nicaragua is inevitable for the 60 gallon Skylane heading south from Mexico to Panama. The prevailing NW winds of 12 to 20 knots make the stop in Managua on the northbound leg just about essential but only quite likely on the southbound leg. Guatemala isn't a serious problem to the general aviation tourist at this time. Some expect Salvador's situation to improve later in 1982.

The Latest and Best Information   At any time the absolute latest and best word on what to expect is available by calling Radio (126.9 or other) where you are or more candidly by talking face-to-face with Civil Aeronautics people where you are. Civil Aeronautics people know best of all what Civil Aeronautics people in neighboring countries are doing and how they are acting because they talk with them several times an hour or day. I've never had them lead me astray.

Permission Form

To notify Centro American countries that you are coming and when, just complete this form and xerox a copy for each country and mail them. Addresses are on the Prior Permission page. Check your Post Office for air mail postage; it is about fifty cents at this writing but changes are probable.

Allow at least three weeks and be sure to xerox a copy of each one before sending it. Keep that copy with you on your trip to show that you did do as required.

SOLICITUD DE PERMISO DE ATERRIZAJE
(Request for Permission to Land)

(Aircraft Registration) **MATRICULA**:

(Aircraft Type) **TIPO**:

Name of **PILOTO**:

Name of **COPILOTO**:

(Purpose) **MOTIVO**:

(Number of) **PASAJEROS**:

(Nationalities) **NACIONALIDAD**:

(Arrival Date) **FECHA**:

BBP 06-75

Note
Copyright holder's permission granted to photocopy this page for personal use, not for commercial purposes.

Copyright © 1975 Arnold D Senterfitt

546 General Declaration Courtesy of AOPA

GENERAL DECLARATION   Declaración General
(OUTWARD/INWARD)   *(Salida/Entrada)*

AGRICULTURE, CUSTOMS, IMMIGRATION, AND PUBLIC HEALTH
Agricultura, Aduanas, Migración y Salubridad Pública

OWNER OR OPERATOR
Dueño o operador

MARKS OF NATIONALITY AND REGISTRATION .... FLIGHT NO. ....
Marcas de nacionalidad y registro   *Vuelo Número*

DEPARTURE FROM .... ARRIVAL AT .... DATE ....
Punto de despacho   *Para entrar a*   *Fecha*
(Place and Country) *Lugar y país*   (Place and Country) *Lugar y país*

FLIGHT ROUTING *Ruta del vuelo*
("Place" Column always to list origin, every en-route stop and destination)
(La columna correspondiente a "Lugar" deberá contener siempre cada parada en ruta así como el destino final)

PLACE *Lugar*	TOTAL NUMBER OF CREW *Número total de la tripulación*	NUMBER OF PASSENGERS ON THIS STAGE *Número de pasajeros en este vuelo*	CARGO *Carga*
		DEPARTURE PLACE: *Lugar de salida*	
		Embarking *Al embarcarse*	
		Through on same flight *En tránsito en el mismo vuelo*	Cargo *Carga*
		ARRIVAL PLACE: *Lugar de destino:*	Manifests Attached *Manifestos de carga anexos*
		Disembarking *Al desembarcar*	
		Through on same flight *En tránsito en*	

Declaración de salud

Persons on board known to be suffering from illness other than airsickness or the effects of accidents, as well as those cases of illness disembarked during the flight:
Nombres de las personas a bordo que padezcan de alguna enfermedad que no sea el mareo, o que padezcan como resultado de algún accidente, así como aquellos casos de enfermos que hayan desembarcado durante el vuelo:

Any other condition on board which may lead to the spread of disease:
Cualquiera otra condición a bordo que pueda contribuir a la propagación de alguna enfermedad:

Details of each disinsecting or sanitary treatment (place, date, time, method) during the flight. If no disinsecting has been carried out during the flight give details of most recent disinsecting:
Detalles acerca de cada tratamiento contra insectos o tratamiento sanitario (lugar, fecha, hora y método) durante el vuelo. En caso de que no se haya llevado a cabo ningún tratamiento contra insectos durante el vuelo, anótense los datos del tratamiento contra insectos más reciente.

Signed, if required ....
Firma, en caso de requerirse   Crew Member Concerned
*Miembro de la tripulación
a quien concierna*

I declare that all statements and particulars contained in this General Declaration, and in any supplementary forms required to be presented with this General Declaration are complete, exact and true to the best of my knowledge and that all through passengers will continue/have continued on the flight.

Certifico que todos los datos y declaraciones contenidas en la presente Declaración General, así como los asentados en cualquiera otras formas suplementarias que sea necesario presentar con la presente Declaración General, son completas, exactas y verídicas según los datos a mi alcance y que todos los pasajeros en tránsito continuarán o continúan en el vuelo.

SIGNATURE ....
Firma

Authorized Agent or Pilot-in-Command
Agente autorizado o piloto Encargado.

Courtesy of AOPA

548 Boarding Pass? yes

In Centro America the administrators are airline oriented meaning general aviation gets much more help than needed. Part of that 'help' are boarding passes used at every airport where airlines come and go.

Speed things up: take this page to an instant printer. Have him run 25 copies then fill in the constant we've checked in the margin. It will save lots of time at each Centro America airport of entry or departure.

---

cut this line

Baja Bush Pilots
Embarcation/Disembarcation Card
TARJETA INTERNACIONAL
DE EMBARQUE/DESEMBARQUE

1. Mr. } Sr. }
   Mrs. } Sra. } _____
   Miss } Srta.} Name in full (Please print) Nombre y Apellido (En letras de molde
                 Maiden name (Apellido de soltera)

2. Date of birth
   Fecha de nacimiento _____
                        Day (Día)   Month (Mes)   Year (Año)

3. Place of birth
   Lugar de nacimiento _____

4. Nationality
   Nacionalidad _____

5. Occupation
   Ocupación _____

6. Home address
   Dirección habitual _____

7. For arriving passengers—Port of embarcation }
   For passengers leaving—Port of disembarcation } _____
   Pasajeros que llegan-Puerto de embarque   }
   Pasajeros que salen-Puerto de desembarque   } _____

8. For arriving passengers-Intended address   }
   For passengers leaving-last address   } _____
   Pasajeros que llegan-Dirección prevista   }
   Pasajeros que salen-Ultima dirección   } _____

9. Passport number
   Número del pasaporte _____

10. Place and date of issue
    Lugar y fecha de expedición _____

_____
Signature of passenger (Firma de pasajero)

REVERSE SIDE FOR OFFICIAL USE ONLY
EL REVERSO PARA USO OFFICIAL SOLAMENTE

Form BBP-E19

cut this line

Note
Copyright holder's permission granted to photocopy this page for personal use, not for commercial purposes.

Incountry Tourist offices

These incountry offices of tourism will be a help for the "who do I see for..," "where is.." or "can I.." questions which may come up. More oriented toward airlines passengers, the staffs at each of these offices will be helpful on any subject except general aviation. Airport civil aviation offices will handle those.

Belice City, Belice
   Secretary
   Belice Tourist Board

Costa Rica
   Instituto Costarricennse de Turismo
   Opposite the BIG square in San Jose
   Mail address: Apartado Postal (P O Box) 777
   San Jose, Costa Rica, C.A.
      Telephone 23-17-33

El Salvador
   Instituto Salvadoreno de Turismo
   Ruben Dario No. 619
   San Salvador, El Salvador. C.A.
   Mail: same
      Telephone 22-32-55

Guatemala
   Instituto Guatemalteco de Turismo
   6a (means 6th) Avenida 5-34, Zona 1
   Guatemala City, Guatemala, C.A.
   Mail: same
      Telephones 24015, 24118, 85262, 85311

Honduras
   Instituto Hondureno de Turismo
   Apartado Postal 154-C
   Tegucigalpa, Honduras, C.A.
   Mail: same
      Telephones: 22-80-34, 22-95-44, 22-11-83, 22-77-52

Nicaragua
   Dirrecion Nacional de Turismo
   Avenida Roosevelt y Calle Colon
   Managua, Nicaragua C.A.

Republica de Panama
   Instituto Pameno de Turismo
   Via Espana, opposite First City Nat'l Bank
   Mail: Apartado Postal 9525
   Panama 4, R.P.
      (Note: just R.P. - not C.A.)
      Telephone 25-8486

On every internacional arrival or departure to or from any Centro American country you will go through all same the steps, but the order in which you do them will vary not only by the country, but by port of entry.

For example in the country of Honduras, San Pedro Sula does things one way, Goloson another, and the capital Tegucigalpa has yet another system. But the importatnt thing is that they all do the same things, no matter in what order. Lets talk about the things.

General Declarations are used to organize the various points which offices need to know about you, your passengers, and the airplane. 'Office' in this case includes Civil Aviation (aviacion civil), Customs (aduana), Immigration (migracion), and Public Health (salud publico).

So many offices and people are involved you will need upwards of ten copies per country. To get enough take this book to an instant printer and have him make ten copies per country of pages 474 and 475 on NCR CFB (no carbon) paper. Fill the fixed things out ahead of time, then as you approach each office the men there will busily stampsignstampsigntearoffcopies and herd you onward.

Every country will want to see your flight plan from the last one. They will want you to fill out an ICAO flight plan such as the one on the opposite page. Each country prints theirs in a different size and paper color, different ink color, but the same flight plan. Don't bother getting copies of these before leaving, your size wouldn't fit their filing system.

Do get good filling in blanks and at circling your kind of survival gear for 'selva'(jungle) not 'polar' and passup 'botes' unless you are carrying a launch. The rest is self explaining. Just realize these will be used and be ready.

Migracion, among others, will want you to have tourist permits or visas. Generally the former are pieces of paper, the latter are stamped in your passport. Except for Colombia and Panama always get your tourist permit on arrival in a country. Guatemala permits are downstairs at La Aurora. At Pavas in San Jose the Migracion office is on the right just inside the glass door.

Crew are usually treated differently from passengers, at least part of the time. Up to two fully licensed (no fresh student permits please) pilots per aircraft will count as crew who do not pay exit taxes, in some cases they also don't pay tourist permits. Medicals may be checked.

Tech Stops

A peculiar to Centro America provision is the technical stop, an enroute pause for fuel, potty time, or anything not including passenger change. In the countries which recognize it you can stop briefly and go on. There are no fees, no entry procedures of any kind. Belice does not recognize techstops except by aircraft from other C.A. countries excepting Guatemala.

Departures

Leaving a country is usually the reverse of arriving in that you go through the same steps but with some slight changes. Sometimes you start with a new set of declarations, at other places you've been through that and will just take another six or eight to bail out.

Tourist permits need to be returned or stamped off, a departure flight plan filed and landing/parking fees paid. If you told the office how many days you'd be when you arrived you will pay straight rates and leave. In Costa Rica you must tell the administrator on arrival how many days you'll be to get the monthly rate. No fair asking for the monthly rate three weeks after arrival.

For the most part weather information is good along Centro America and the dispatchers I've encountered have been helpful every way they can. Nicaraguan controllers have other problems right now so be as understanding there as you can.

General aviation is treated a lot like the airlines because often the administrators only have one system. Once you are away from towers and the word 'internacional' things get back to US-normal. While at the big ones, things will go very well if you relax and listen. There will be any number of people helping you find the next step in the process. At Pavas tower there's even a procedure writen on the wall for you to follow. Can't beat that for heipful, and it is typical.

C.A. Flight Plan 551

FLIGHT PLAN - PLAN DE VUELO
DIRECCION GENERAL DE AERONAUTICA CIVIL

PRIORITY INDICATOR	
FILING TIME	
ADDRESSEE(S) INDICATOR(S)	
ORIGINATOR INDICATOR	
SPECIFIC IDENTIFICATION OF ADDRESSEE(S) AND/OR ORIGINATOR	
1 DESCRIPTION	(FPL
6 AIRCRAFT IDENTIFICATION	N180EE
8 FLIGHT RULES AND STATUS	VFR
9 NUMBER AND TYPE OF AIRCRAFT	C180
10 COM	VHF
NAV	VHF
SSR	
13 AERODROME OF DEPARTURE / TIME	MZBZ 1410Z (Belice)
FIR BOUNDARIES & ESTIMATED TIMES	
15 SPEED	120
LEVEL	9,500'
RUTA	
17 AERODROME OF DESTINATION / TIME	MRPV 1840Z
ALTERNATE AERODROME(S)	MNMG
18 OTHER INFORMATION	BELICE TO PAVAS - ALT: MANAGUA
19 ENDURANCE (FUEL)	6 hrs
PERSONS ON BOARD (POB)	2
EMERGENCY & SURVIVAL EQUIPMENT	R/(U)/121,5 / 243 / 500 / 8364
EQUIPMENT	POLAR / DESERTICO / MARITIMO / (SELVA) / CHALECOS / LUZ / (FLUORESCENTE)
DINGHIES	
BOTES / CUBIERTA	
RMK	
Name of pilot-in-command	SENTERFITT

BERTOHD 100B. XII-76

552 Corozal, Belice

core-oh-SALL

JET CHART	WAC	SECTIONAL	LATITUDE	LONGITUDE	US TIME	FOR GMT ADD	ICAO IDENT	TOWN IDENT
JN-47	CJ-25	TPC J-25C	18°24'	88°26	CST	6	-	-

OTHER COMM Traffic 118.1
SETTLEMENT 1/2 mile NE   POPULATION 5500
FROM Chetumal   FREQ 113.0   TRACK 223°, 9n.mi.,
FROM Belice   FREQ 392   TRACK 347°, 53n.mi.,
FROM Tikal   FREQ 314   TRACK 048°, 84n.mi.,
FUEL -   CARDS -   CASH? -
REPAIRS -   TIEDOWN BYO

Northern-most of Belice's airports, you will see some version of this 19' width in other Belice airports. The privately built runways seem to be about sixty to eighty percent of the wingspan of whichever airplane the owner learned to fly. With the great expense of paving he decided to sharpen his skills and save tens of kilobucks.

Town stores are handy if you need to stock up on supplies.

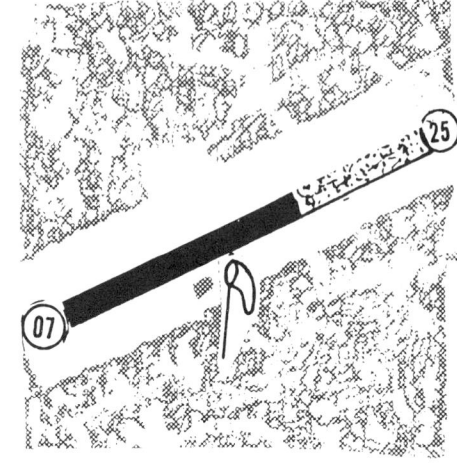

ELEVATION
45'

Cay Ambergris, Belice

key AMM-burr-griss   553

JET CHART	WAC	SECTIONAL	LATITUDE	LONGITUDE	US TIME	FOR GMT ADD	ICAO IDENT	TOWN IDENT
JNC-47	CJ-25 So.	TPC J-25C	17°54'	87°58	CST	6	-	MBR-

*AOE **on prior request**

OTHER COMM Traffic 118.1
CITY Adjacent   POPULATION 1,100
FROM Chetumal   FREQ 113.0   TRACK 147°, 40 n.mi.
FROM Belice Int'l   FREQ 392   TRACK 036°, 29 n.mi.
FROM Cancún   FREQ 113.4   TRACK 194°, 224 n.mi.
FUEL -   CARDS -   CASH? -
REPAIRS -   TIEDOWN BYO

HOTEL	RATE	WHERE	TEL
*Paradise House	$$$	N side	-
several others	-	-	-

2579'x33'
Graded Coral

ELEVATION
2' 6"

Most populous of the two cays with runways, the town here is San Pedro. Stores, billiards, schools, restaurants, bars, hotels but no gas stations. With only six cars on a mile of island who needs to go broke pumping a gallon almost every week.

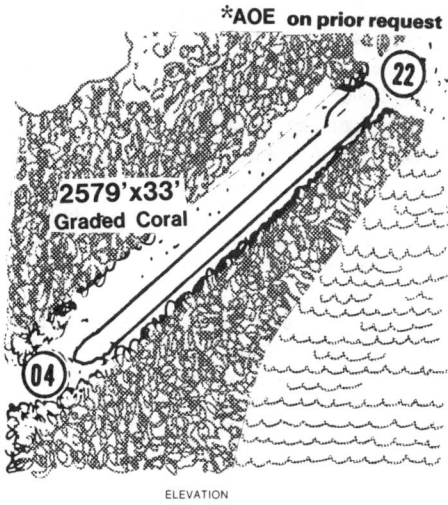

554 Caye Chapel, Belice   *key* CHAP-*ell*

JET CHART	WAC	SECTIONAL	LATITUDE	LONGITUDE	US TIME	FOR GMT ADD	ICAO IDENT	TOWN IDENT
JNC-47	CJ-25 So.	TPC J-25C	17°42'	88°01'	CST	6	-	-

OTHER COMM   Traffic 118.1
SETTLEMENT   E side   POPULATION 1 to 35
FROM   Belice   FREQ 392   TRACK 055°, 18n.mi.
FROM   Chetumal   FREQ 113.0   TRACK 156°, 51n.mi.
FROM   Cay Ambergris FREQ airport TRACK 186°, 13n.mi.
FUEL -   CARDS -   CASH? -
REPAIRS -   TIEDOWN BYO

HOTEL	RATE	WHERE	TEL
Caye Chapel		here	-
not always open	-	-	-

An on again off again hotel is located on this cay. I've camped when it was off and stayed when on, anything to be able to swim and enjoy these waters of the Western Caribbean.

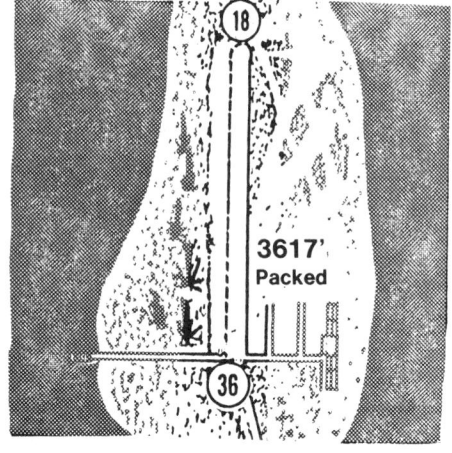

3617'
Packed

ELEVATION
4' 6"

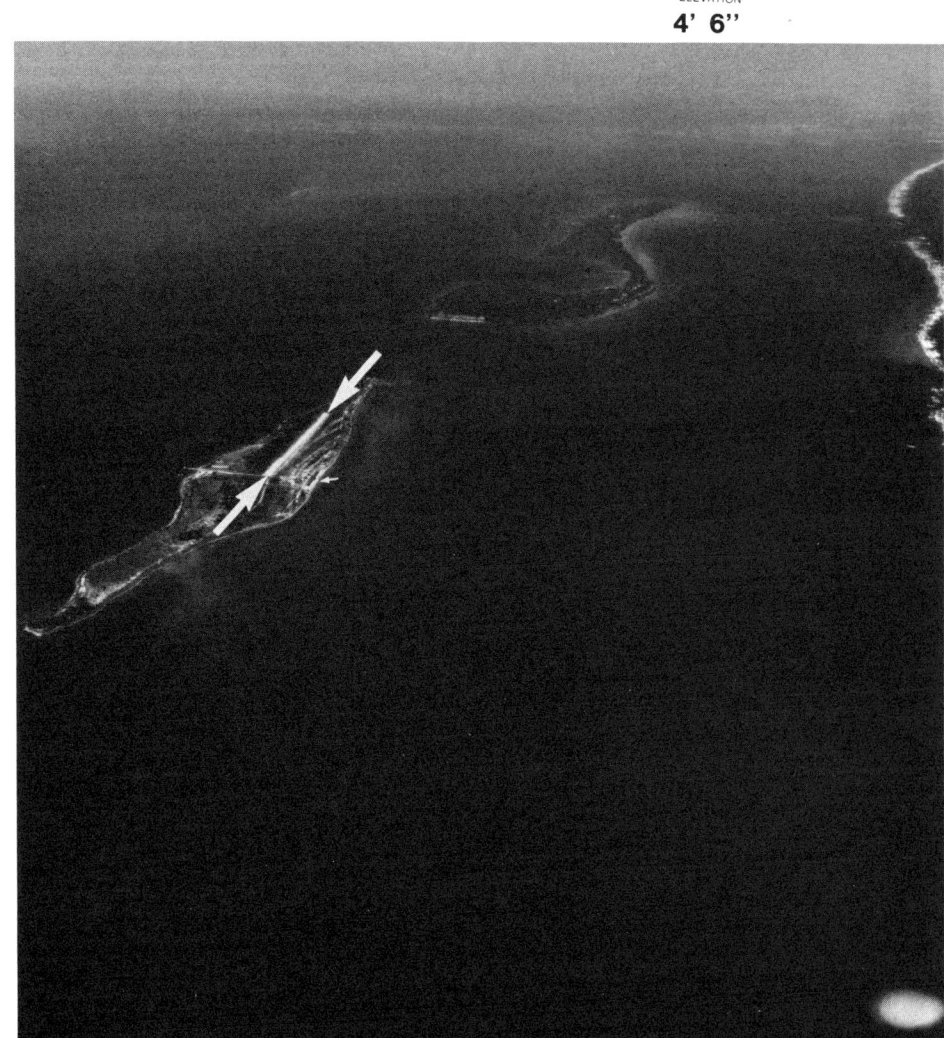

Orange Walk, Belice

555

JET CHART	WAC	SECTIONAL	LATITUDE	LONGITUDE	US TIME	FOR GMT ADD	ICAO IDENT	TOWN IDENT
JNC-47	CJ-25 So.	TPC J-25C	17°15'	88°47'	CST	6	-	-

OTHER COMM Traffic 118.1
CITY Adjacent NW
FROM Belice FREQ 392
FROM Chetumal FREQ 113.0
FROM Flores FREQ 385
POPULATION 3,800
TRACK 331°, 33n.mi.
TRACK 205°, 81n.mi.
TRACK 043°, 68n.mi.
FUEL - CARDS - CASH? -
REPAIRS - TIEDOWN BYO

Small city of Belice's interior, getting microscopically larger with the completion of the highway from Chetumal to Belice city. Stores for basic foods.

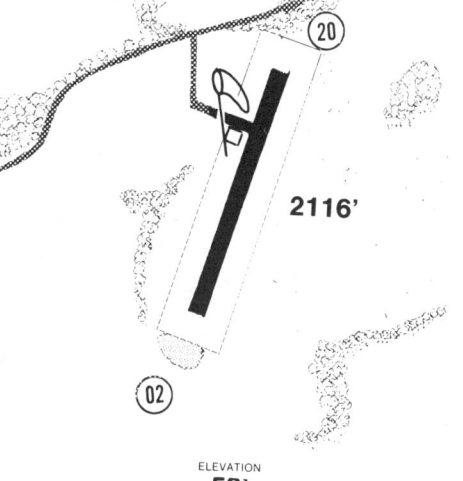

2116'

ELEVATION
53'

NDB 2 RWY 25

AL-1485 (CAD)

BELIZE INTL (MZBZ)
BELIZE

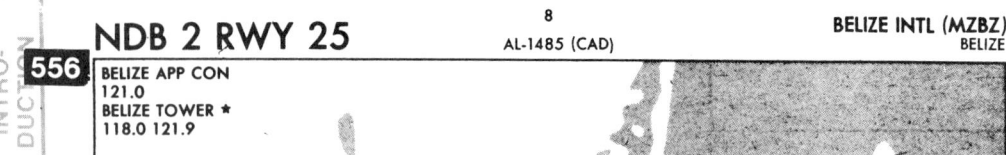

BELIZE APP CON
121.0
BELIZE TOWER ★
118.0 121.9

IAF
BELIZE
392 ZDZ
A2

2000

3500

190°
065°
245°
180°
065°
2500
10 NM

Caution
For Information Only
Not for Aerial Navigation

TLv FL 200	NDB	TA 19,000		ELEV 15

2500 — 065° — 1500 — 245°

MISSED APPROACH
To 2500 on 245°

Remain within 10 NM

TDZE 14
6300 x 150
140
245° to NDB

CATEGORY	A	B	C	D
S-25	620-1¼ 606	(700-1¼) ★	620-1¾ 606 (700-1¾)	620-2¼ 606 (700-2¼)
CIRCLING		NOT AUTHORIZED		

★ Night vis 1¾

NDB 2 RWY 25

17°32'N-88°18'W

BELIZE
BELIZE INTL (MZBZ)

SUNRISE & SUNSET – GMT   SALIDA y PUESTA del SOL – GMT

15th of JAN FEB MAR APR MAY JUN JUL AUG SEPT OCT NOV DEC
SUNRISE 1226 1219 1201 1137 1120 1118 1126 1135 1141 1146 1158 1215 SALIDA
SUNSET 2338 2354 2403 2409 2418 2428 2431 2419 2355 2331 2317 2320 PUESTA
15 de   ENE FEB MAR ABR MAY JUN JUL AGO SEP OCT NOV DIC
To get local time just subtract 'GMT ADD'
PARA OBTENER TIEMPO LOCAL SUSTRIAGA 'GMT ADD'

Belice International, Belice

bay-LEECE **557**

JET CHART	WAC	SECTIONAL	LATITUDE	LONGITUDE	US TIME	FOR GMT ADD	ICAO IDENT	TOWN IDENT
JNC-47	CJ-25 So.	TPC J-25C	17°32'	88°18'	CST	6	MZBZ	ZDZ

APPROACH 121.0 TOWER 118.0 GROUND 121.9 AOE 9am-12, 2-4pm
CITY 6 miles E POPULATION 67,000
B'CAST FREQ 1280 WHERE 8 mi E HOURS Daylight
FROM Chetumal FREQ 113.0 TRACK 176°57n.mi.,
FROM Cancún FREQ 113.4 TRACK 197°,237 n.mi.
FROM Bro'ville FREQ 116.3 TRACK 128°,728 n.mi.
FUEL 100, JP CARDS Shell Int'l CASH? Yes
REPAIRS - TIEDOWN BYO

HOTEL	RATE	WHERE	TEL
Ft George	$$	Central	22-41
Bellevue	$$	Central	3:-51
Bliss	$	Central	25-52

6297' Paved

ELEVATION **17'**

Principle city of a small newly independent nation previously called 'British Honduras'. Their neighbors Guatemala and México would still like to have this area back. Each considers Britain stole it when they weren't looking.

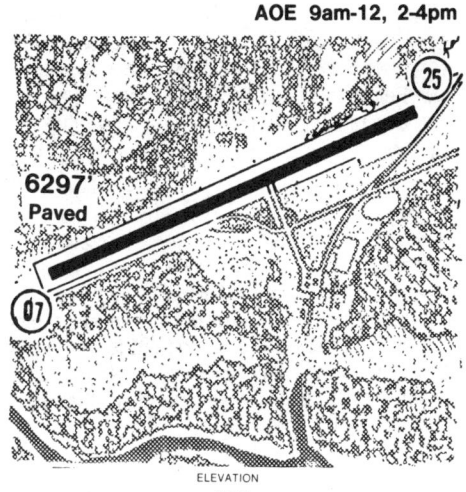

558 Belice Municipal, Belice

bay-LEECE

JET CHART	WAC	SECTIONAL	LATITUDE	LONGITUDE	US TIME	FOR GMT ADD	ICAO IDENT	TOWN IDENT
JNC-47	CJ-25 So.	TPC J-25C	17°31'	88°11'	CST	6	-	-ZDM-

APPROACH 121.0   TOWER -   GROUND -
CITY Adjacent So.   POPULATION 67,000
B'CAST FREQ 1280   WHERE 0.5 mi   HOURS Daylight
FROM Belice Int'l   FREQ 392   TRACK 095°, 6.5 n.mi.
FROM Chetumal   FREQ 113.0   TRACK 169°, 59 n.mi.
FUEL 100   CARDS -   CASH? Yes
REPAIRS Minor   TIEDOWN BYO

HOTEL	RATE	WHERE	TEL
Ft George	$$	Central	22-41
Bellevue	$$	Central	32-51
Bliss	$	Central	25-52

AOE On Request

(12) **1710'** (30)
Paved

ELEVATION
10 inches

This airport handy to downtown is an air-taxi base. Local people can be out to here very quickly from their offices. Runway's length plus swamps at each end could put it on the snug side for some airplanes.

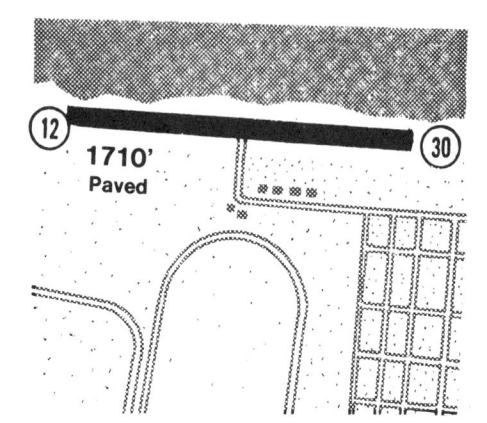

Belmopán, Belice *bell-moe-PONN* 559

JET CHART	WAC	SECTIONAL	LATITUDE	LONGITUDE	US TIME	FOR GMT ADD	ICAO IDENT	TOWN IDENT
JN-61	CJ-25	TPC J-25C	97°12'	88°54'	CST	6	-	-BMO-

OTHER COMM Traffic 118.1-
CITY New capitol 3/4 mi SW
POPULATION Varies
FROM Belice **FREQ** 392 **TRACK** 235°,39.8n.mi.
FROM Chetumal **FREQ** 113.3 **TRACK** 198°,84.8n.mi.
FROM Flores **FREQ** 385 **TRACK** 068°,58.9n.mi.
FUEL - **CARDS** - **CASH?** -
REPAIRS - **TIEDOWN** BYO

Site of the new capitol of the newly emerging nation of 'Belice', things have a raw frontier look, combined with the inevitable tropical takeover. Even in the large cleared areas you know someone is out at the edge steadily fighting back the jungle. Not much happening up here since most civil servants are slow to move out of Belice.

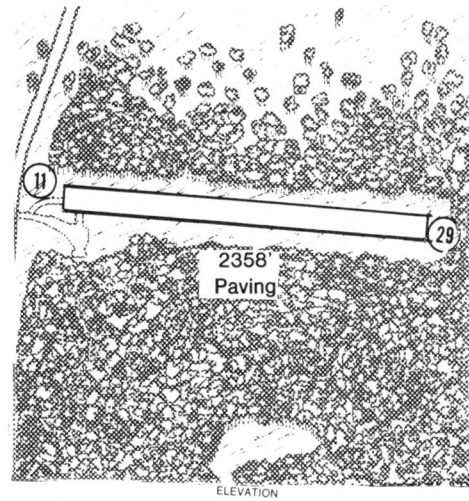

2358' Paving

ELEVATION **173'**

560 Central Farm, Belice

JET CHART	WAC	SECTIONAL	LATITUDE	LONGITUDE	US TIME	FOR GMT ADD	ICAO IDENT	TOWN IDENT
JN-61	CJ-25	TPC J-25C	17°12'	89°01'	CST	6	-	CFM-

OTHER COMM Traffic 118.1
SETTLEMENT 1/4 mile E   POPULATION 300
FROM Belice   FREQ 392   TRACK 240°, 46n.mi.,
FROM Flores   FREQ 385   TRACK 066°, 53n.mi.,
FROM Chetumal FREQ 113.0 TRACK 203°, 88n.mi.,
FUEL -   CARDS -   CASH? -
REPAIRS -   TIEDOWN BYO

If you've been looking for a place to try flying under the wires on takeoff or landing, pass on this one. They are country-height at the East end: there isn't enough room between the barbed wire fence and the sagging wires. When the grass is tall here it would be a good idea to try somewhere else. Surprising how much it will lengthen a takeoff roll.

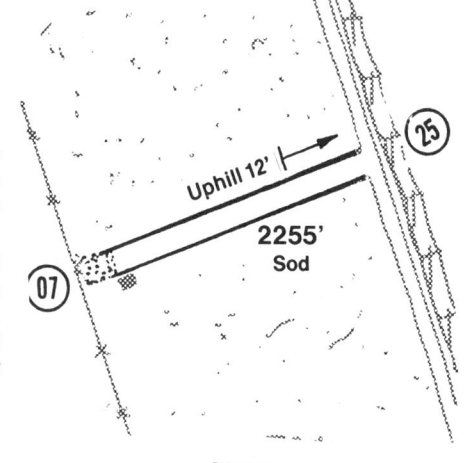

Uphill 12'
2255' Sod
07 / 25

ELEVATION
184'

Norport, Belice

NOR-port 561

JET CHART	WAC	SECTIONAL	LATITUDE	LONGITUDE	US TIME	FOR GMT ADD	ICAO IDENT	TOWN IDENT
JN-61	CJ-25 So	TPC J-25C	17°10'	89°04	CST	6	-	-NPT-

OTHER COMM Traffic 118.0-
CITY 2 mi W
POPULATION 5500
FROM Belice   FREQ Adf 392   TRACK 240°, 46 n.mi.
FROM Chetumal   FREQ 113.0   TRACK 203°, 88 n.mi.
FROM Flores   FREQ Adf 385   TRACK 068°, 53 n.mi.
FUEL -   CARDS -   CASH? -
REPAIRS -   TIEDOWN BYO

Nearby city is Cayo, this grass runway is usually mowed. After measuring we spend a few minutes at our next stop just pulling grass away from around the wheels and brakes. Might not be too great for retractables.

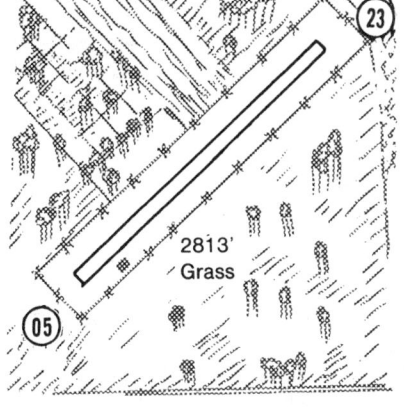

2813' Grass

ELEVATION **180'**

562   Melinda, Belice   *mell-INN-dah*

JET CHART	WAC	SECTIONAL	LATITUDE	LONGITUDE	US TIME	FOR GMT ADD	ICAO IDENT	TOWN IDENT
JNC-47	CJ-25 So.	TPC J-25C	17°00'	88°19'	CST	6	-	MEL-

OTHER COMM   Traffic 118.1
FROM Belice   FREQ 392   TRACK 178°, 33n.mi.
FROM Tikal   FREQ 314   TRACK 092°, 77n.mi.
FROM Poptun   FREQ 363   TRACK 068°, 77n.mi.
FUEL -   CARDS -   CASH? -
REPAIRS -   TIEDOWN BYO

HOTEL	RATE	WHERE	TEL
Pelican Beach	$$	Stann Creek	05-20-44

(Reported, not tried.)

Airport to serve Stann Creek; that city was begun in the 1700s, making it the first European settlement along this coastline. Now a charming local resort here in the southern part of Belice; a good road links it to the capital. Interesting caves nearby in the mountains while lots of agricultural development dots the surrounding level area.

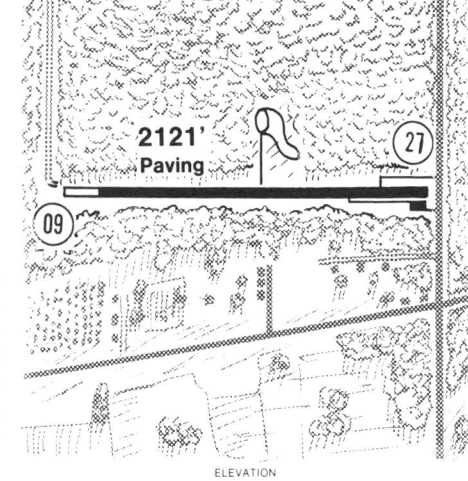

ELEVATION
65'

Maya Beach, Belice

MY-yah BEE-ch 563

JET CHART	WAC	SECTIONAL	LATITUDE	LONGITUDE	US TIME	FOR GMT ADD	ICAO IDENT	TOWN IDENT
JN-47	CJ-25 So.	TPC J-25C	16°37'	88°32'	CST	6	-	MAY-

OTHER COMM Traffic 118.1
SETTLEMENT E, across lagoon **POPULATION** est 300
FROM Belice **FREQ** 392 **TRACK** 196°, 55n.mi.
FROM Poptun **FREQ** 250 **TRACK** 071°, 64n.mi.
FROM Pto Barrios **FREQ** 347 **TRACK** 003°, 53n.mi.
FUEL - **CARDS** - **CASH?** -
REPAIRS - **TIEDOWN** BYO

Runway for those on the cay to the right, for their aircraft or for the airtaxis from Belice. A dock at the bottom of the picture is a good place to fish if you are camping.

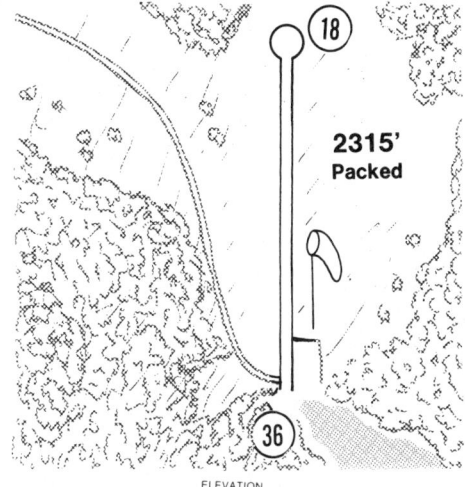

18
2315'
Packed
36

ELEVATION
23'

564 Waha Leaf, Belice

WAH-hah leaf

JET CHART	WAC	SECTIONAL	LATITUDE	LONGITUDE	US TIME	FOR GMT ADD	ICAO IDENT	TOWN IDENT
JN-61	CJ-25 So.	TPC J-25C	16°43'	88°41'	CST	6	-	WAH-

OTHER COMM Traffic 118.1
SETTLEMENT Adjacent SE   POPULATION 300
FROM la Mesa   FREQ 113.1   TRACK 323°, 87n.mi.,
FROM Poptun   FREQ 250   TRACK 056°, 49n.mi.,
FROM Belize   FREQ 392   TRACK 200°, 54n.mi.,
FUEL -   CARDS -   CASH? -
REPAIRS -   TIEDOWN BYO

2771' Packed
ELEVATION 219'

A beehive busy coconut plantation on the south edge of Belice's mountain range near the Guatemalan border. Don't think I've ever seen this airport listed on any of the charts but is certainly there. The workmen do seem confused each time we go in to recheck the airport. Maybe someone was supposed to say don't come back next edition and forgot.

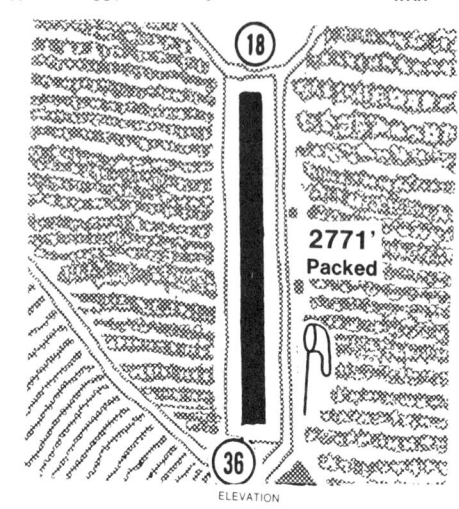

Punta Gorda, Belice

POON-tah GORE-dah   **565**

JET CHART	WAC	SECTIONAL	LATITUDE	LONGITUDE	US TIME	FOR GMT ADD	ICAO IDENT	TOWN IDENT
JNC-47	CJ-25 So.	TPC J-25C	16°06'	88°49'	CST	6	-	GOR-

OTHER COMM   Traffic 118.1
CITY   Adjacent E   POPULATION 2,800
FROM   Belice   FREQ 392   TRACK 196°, 92n.mi.
FROM   Poptun   FREQ 250   TRACK 104°, 38n.mi.
FUEL -   CARDS -   CASH? -
REPAIRS -   TIEDOWN BYO

Small town with stores, Texaco marine fuel dealer, but no avgas. Great place to camp and explore. Take your tape recorder, the lilting accents of the kids will give you enjoyment every time you rehear them.

For some fun ask a storekeeper for coconuts. They have trouble walking around town without getting bonked on the head and here you get to BUY some. His restraint is enjoyable to watch. Took me three trips to the airplane to carry a dollar's worth.

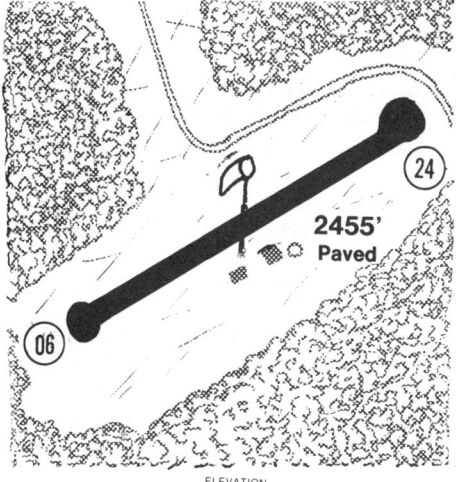

2455' Paved

ELEVATION **45'**

566 Melchor de Mencos, Guatemala *MELL-chore day MENN-cose*

JET CHART	WAC	SECTIONAL	LATITUDE	LONGITUDE	US TIME	FOR GMT ADD	ICAO IDENT	TOWN IDENT
JN-47	CJ-25 So.	TPC J-25C	17°05'	89°10'	CST	6	-	MCH-

OTHER COMM Traffic 118.1

CITY 4 sides POPULATION 3,900
FROM Belice   FREQ 392   TRACK 239°, 58n.mi.
FROM Chetumal FREQ 113.0 TRACK 206°, 100n.mi.
FROM Flores   FREQ 385   TRACK 072°, 44n.mi.
FUEL -   CARDS -   CASH? -
REPAIRS -   TIEDOWN BYO

AOE 9am-12, 3-5 pm

2315'
Huge Gravel Not smooth

ELEVATION
615'

Handy internacional airport: you can slip through here and over to Flores or Tikal very quickly, saves an hour each way to the mile high Guatemala City.

Although every time I've come through here before it was to park at the far end and take a bus, next time we will park at the south end. That will put us well within walking distance of the Customs House at the bridge shown in the lower right corner of the picture That's where the clearing takes place and from which the inspectors come to look.

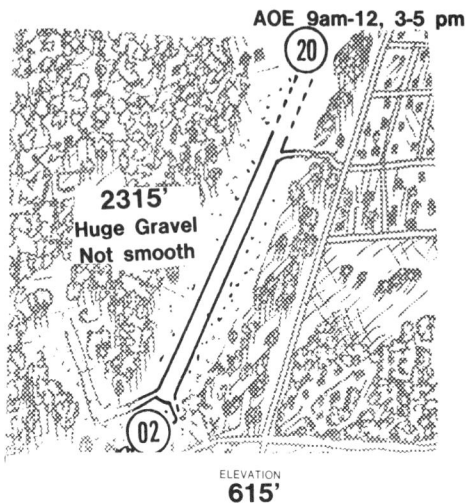

Tikal, Guatemala

tick-KALL 567

JET CHART	WAC	SECTIONAL	LATITUDE	LONGITUDE	US TIME	FOR GMT ADD	ICAO IDENT	TOWN IDENT
JNC-46	CJ-25 So.	TPC J-25C	17°14'	89°36'	CST	6	-	TKL

OTHER COMM Information 123.0
SETTLEMENT Ruins 1 mile W   **POPULATION** 200
LOCAL Ndb **FREQ** 314   **WHERE** here **HOURS** Days
FROM Flores **FREQ** 385   **TRACK** 037°, 29n.mi.
FROM Melchor **FREQ** Airport **TRACK** 285°, 28n.mi.
FROM Guatemala **FREQ** 114.1 **TRACK** 014°, 170 n.mi.
FUEL - **CARDS** -   **CASH?** -
REPAIRS -   **TIEDOWN** BYO
HOTEL   **RATE**   **WHERE**   **TEL**
Jungle Inn $$ E end   -
Jungle Lodge $ E End   -

CAUTION: PYRAMIDS ON FINAL

Oldest (300 A.D.) of the ancient Mayan ceremonial cities, this mile square complex also has the tallest pyramids (180' to 227' AGL) in Meso-America. Pyramids were used for ceremonies and for scientific studies.

READER REPORT This runway is good even after three days of rain. Water seems to go right through it.—A.Wyoscan, California

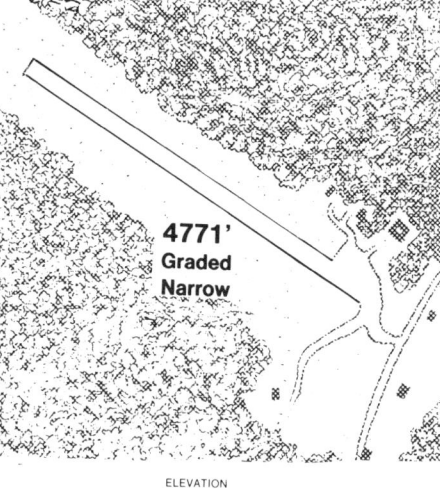

4771'
Graded
Narrow

ELEVATION
747'

568 Flores, Guatemala

FLOW-ress

JET CHART	WAC	SECTIONAL	LATITUDE	LONGITUDE	US TIME	FOR GMT ADD	ICAO IDENT	TOWN IDENT
JN-46	CJ-25 So.	TPC J-25C	16°55'	89°53	CST	6	MGFL	FLS

APPROACH 126.9 TOWER 120.0/118.5 GROUND 120.0/118.5
CITY Adjacent So.   POPULATION 6,500
B'CAST FREQ 1460   WHERE -   HOURS Daylight
FROM Melchor   FREQ airport   TRACK 252°, 43 n.mi.
FROM Guatemala   FREQ 114.1   TRACK 011°, 148 n.mi.
FROM Tikal   FREQ 314   TRACK 217°, 29 n.mi.
FUEL Emergency 100   CARDS -   CASH? Dollars
REPAIRS Minor   TIEDOWN BYO

HOTEL	RATE	WHERE	TEL
Maya Int'l	$$	Adjacent W	1-21
Hotel Peten	–$	On island	-
Monja Blanca	–$	Adjacent S	-

Runway 09/27, 3719' Graded
Elevation 285'

That pretty small island on the left names both itself and the area as 'Flores' although this airport is in Santa Elena. Flores itself is the seat of government for the whole Department of Petén, what you see as the square panhandle of Guatemala.

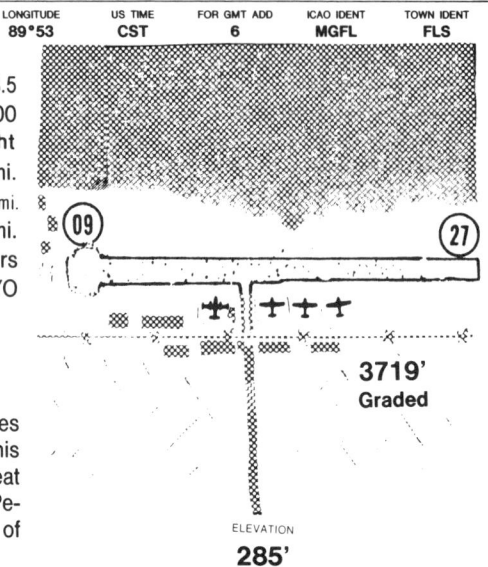

Puerto Barrios Int'l, Guatemala

PWAIR-toe BARR-ee-oce

569

JET CHART	WAC	SECTIONAL	LATITUDE	LONGITUDE	US TIME	FOR GMT ADD	ICAO IDENT	TOWN IDENT
JNC-61	CK-25 No.	TPC K-25A	15°44'	88°35'	CST	6	MGPB	BAR

APPROACH –   TOWER 118.4   GROUND 118.4
OTHER COMM Twr also 120.0; enroute 126.9
CITY Adjacent NW   POPULATION 65,000
B'CAST FREQ 1380   WHERE –   HOURS Daylight
FROM Tikal   FREQ 314   TRACK 140°,110n.mi.
FROM San Pedro Sula FREQ 113.1 TRACK 290°,39n.mi.
FROM Belice   FREQ 392   TRACK 182°,110n.mi.
FUEL Slow 100/130   CARDS –   CASH? Yes
REPAIRS –   TIEDOWN BYO

HOTEL	RATE	WHERE	TEL
Hotel del Norte	$	Bayside	–

that's it

Guatemala's only Caribbean port, you see lots of petroleum activity, both the platforms near the beach and the Exxon ships in this harbor.

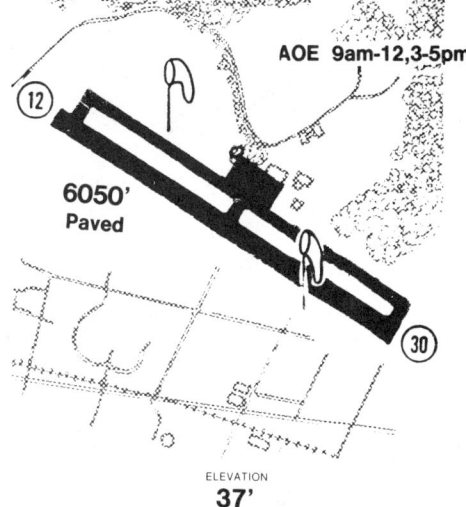

AOE 9am-12, 3-5pm

6050' Paved

ELEVATION **37'**

VOR/DME RWY 1

(USAF) AL-1085 (DGAC)

LA AURORA (MGGT)
GUATEMALA CITY, GUATEMALA

LA AURORA APP CON
119.3
LA AURORA TOWER
118.1 126.2
GND CON
121.9

CAUTION: Do not exceed 7.7 DME in procedure turn or distance limitation in holding pattern due to high terrain all quadrants just beyond buffer area. Do not exceed 170K IAS at or below 10,000'.

IAF
DME Chan 88
LA AURORA
114.1 AUR

11,000
10,900
15,000
10 NM

Also Missed Approach Holding

Caution
For Information Only
Not for Aerial Navigation

Remain within 7.7 DME
VOR
TA 19,000
ELEV 4951

8000
6.5 DME
2.2 DME
6900
009°
210°

MISSED APPROACH Climb on 009° right to VOR to 8000 in holding pattern

Rwy 19 ldg 9062'
TDZE 4880
REIL Rwys 1-19
009° to VOR

CATEGORY	A	B	C	D
S-1	5440-1¼ 560 (500-1¼)		5440-1½ 560 (500-1½)	5440-2 560 (500-2)
CIRCLING *	5660-2¼ 709 (800-2¼)			5660-2½ 709 (800-2½)

* Not authorized E of rwy centerline extended

VOR/DME RWY 1

14°35'N-90°32'W

GUATEMALA CITY, GUATEMALA
LA AURORA (MGGT)

SUNRISE & SUNSET – GMT   SALIDA y PUESTA del SOL – GMT

15th of	JAN	FEB	MAR	APR	MAY	JUN	JUL	AUG	SEPT	OCT	NOV	DEC	
SUNRISE	1230	1226	1209	1148	1134	1132	1140	1148	1150	1153	1203	1219	SALIDA
SUNSET	2352	2406	2412	2416	2422	2432	2435	2425	2403	2342	2330	2335	PUESTA
15 de	ENE	FEB	MAR	ABR	MAY	JUN	JUL	AGO	SEP	OCT	NOV	DIC	

To get local time just subtract 'GMT ADD'
PARA OBTENER TIEMPO LOCAL SUSTRIAGA 'GMT ADD'

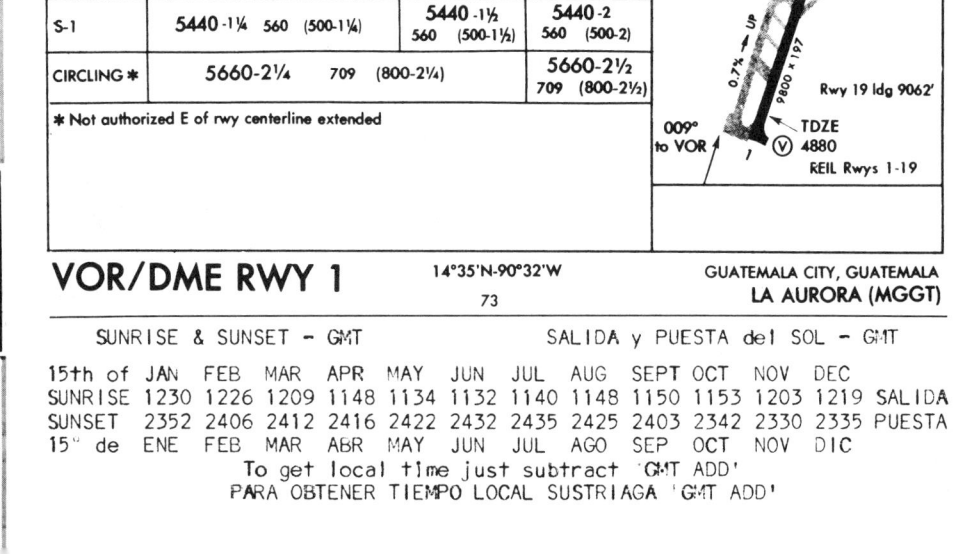

Guatemala, Guatemala

wott-eh-MAH-lah

571

JET CHART	WAC	SECTIONAL	LATITUDE	LONGITUDE	US TIME	FOR GMT ADD	ICAO IDENT	TOWN IDENT
JNC-61	CK-25 No.	TPC K-25A	14°35'	90°32'	CST	6	MGGT	AUR

APPROACH 119.3   TOWER 118.1   GROUND 121.9
OTHER COMM 126.9 Enroute, close-in only
CITY Adjacent No.   POPULATION 1,100,000
B'CAST FREQ 640   WHERE 4 mi NE   HOURS Daylight
LOCAL VorDme   FREQ 114.5   WHERE here   HOURS 24
FROM Tapachula   FREQ 115.3   TRACK 094°,105 n.mi.
FROM Tikal   FREQ 314   TRACK 194°,170n.mi.
FROM Ilopango   FREQ 114.7   TRACK 294°,95Dme
FUEL 100   CARDS -   CASH? Yes
REPAIRS Yes   TIEDOWN BYO

AOE 8am-12,3-5pm

The airport name is 'La Aurora'; transponder and twowqy radio are required. Notice that the airport is literally in a hole so your calls will be answered only when you are fairly close in. Be very watchful. I have been in the pattern here with several heavies including a Panam 747 AND other transports simultaneously.

READER REPORT Pan American Hotel, food great, splendid service, outstanding bar. That brief enough? *Answer:too brief, no signature.*

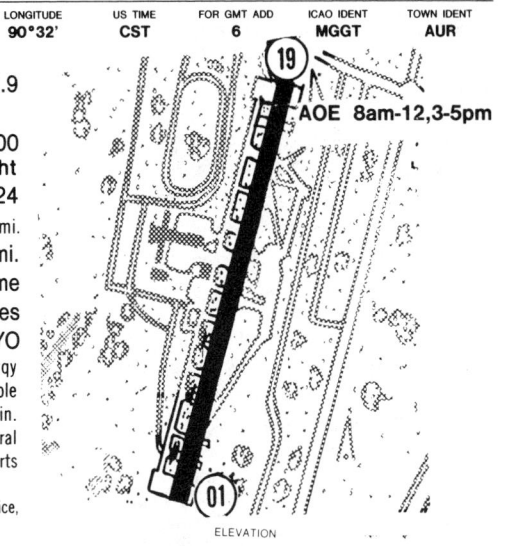

ELEVATION

572 Puerto San José, Guatemala   *PWAIR-toe sonn hoe-SAY*

JET CHART	WAC	SECTIONAL	LATITUDE	LONGITUDE	US TIME	FOR GMT ADD	ICAO IDENT	TOWN IDENT
JNC-61	CK-25 No.	TPC K-25A	13°57'	90°50'	CST	6	MGSJ	SGA

APPROACH -   TOWER 118.5   GROUND 118.5
OTHER COMM Enroute 126.9
CITY 1/2 mile SE   POPULATION 15,000
LOCAL VorDme FREQ 116.1 WHERE 1 mile SW HOURS 24
FROM Guatemala FREQ 114.1 TRACK 170°/205°,43Dme
FROM Tapachula FREQ 115.3 TRACK 116°,107 n.mi.
FROM Managua FREQ 112.1 TRACK 286°,289 n.mi.
FUEL 100   CARDS -   CASH? Yes
REPAIRS -   TIEDOWN BYO

AOE On request

5111'
Asphalt

ELEVATION 23'

Joint use military/civil airport you will appreciate when a Guatemalan highlands storm or hurricane discourages you from getting up to the capital. Bus and cab service to the capital is handy and efficient. Expect bad smog in the early Spring during the sugarcane leaf burning. VFR conditions with less than a mile visibility are not unusual at that time.

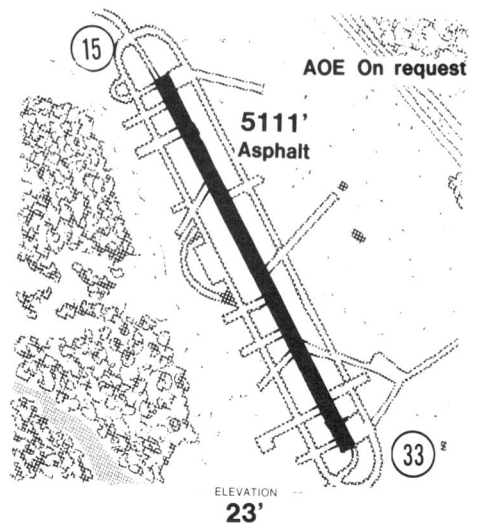

Goloson Int'l, Honduras

GO-loe-son   **573**

JET CHART	WAC	SECTIONAL	LATITUDE	LONGITUDE	US TIME	FOR GMT ADD	ICAO IDENT	TOWN IDENT
JNC-61	CK-25 No.	TPC K-25B	15°44'	86°52'	CST	6	MHLC	LCE

REPAIRS Minor   TIEDOWN BYO
APPROACH -   TOWER 118.5   GROUND 118.5
FUEL 100/130   CARDS -   CASH? Yes
B'CAST FREQ 750   WHERE -   HOURS Daylight
LOCAL Ndb FREQ 227 WHERE 1.5 mi. HOURS on request
FROM Chetumal FREQ 113.1 TRACK 148°, 187n.mi.
FROM Swan Island FREQ 407 TRACK 235°, 198n.mi.
FROM Tegucigalpa FREQ 113.0 TRACK 006°, 103 n.mi.

Handy internacional airport along Honduras' busy banana coast. Not yet tied up with heavy jet traffic, you do see plenty of DC-3s and air taxi aircraft heading for Bay Islands. Expect total fees of about $40 per aircraft for the entry procedures. When you come back here to check out of the country fees will be about $15.

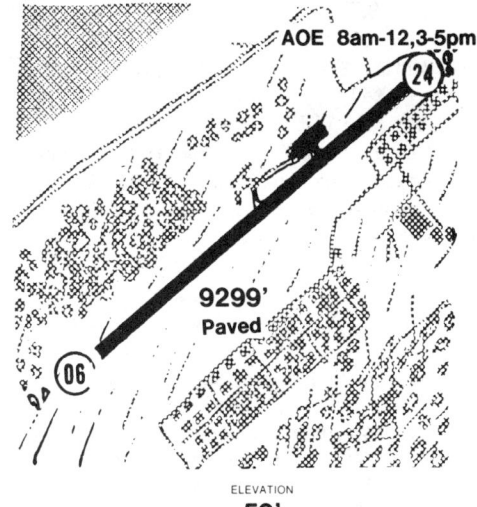

AOE 8am-12, 3-5pm
24
9299' Paved
06

ELEVATION
59'

574 San Pedro Sula, Honduras

sohn PAY-droe SOO-lah

JET CHART	WAC	SECTIONAL	LATITUDE	LONGITUDE	US TIME	FOR GMT ADD	ICAO IDENT	TOWN IDENT
JN-61	CK-25 No.	TPC K-25B	15°27'	87°55'	CST	6	MHLM	LMS

APPROACH 119.7 TOWER 118.1 GROUND 121.9
OTHER COMM Enroute 126.9
CITY 8 miles NW POPULATION 170,000
B'CAST FREQ 640 WHERE HOURS Daylight
LOCAL Vor FREQ 113.1 WHERE here HOURS On Test
FROM Belice FREQ 392 TRACK 163°, 126n.mi.
FROM Coxens Hole FREQ airport TRACK 231°, 98n.mi.
FROM Copan Ruins FREQ airport TRACK 056°, 80n.mi.
FUEL 100 CARDS - CASH? Dollars
REPAIRS Minor TIEDOWN BYO

HOTEL	RATE	WHERE	TEL
Gran Sula	$$	Central	52-32-83
Vitanza	$	2 mi. No.	52-31-40

AOE 9am-12, 3-4pm
9555' Paved
ELEVATION 93'

Excellent clear approaches, this full service airport will provide all entry/departure forms and facilities to enter or depart Honduras. Expect to practice your Spanish alot: even the English speaking controller loses that language when he's off mike.

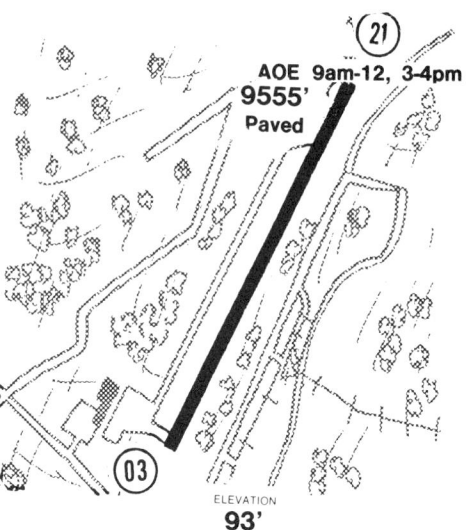

NDB RWY 21

(USAF) AL-3113 (DGAC)

LA MESA INTL (MHLM)
SAN PEDRO SULA, HONDURAS

LA MESA APP CON 119.7
LA MESA TOWER * 118.1

Caution
For Information Only
Not for Aerial Navigation

575

IAF TACAMICHE
370 LAL A2

MIN SAFE ALT 25 NM 8800

ELEV 90

Rwy 3 ldg 9055'
Rwy 21 ldg 9055'

226° 1.5 NM from NDB

TDZE 85

NDB 3300
052°
Remain within 10 NM
1600
232°
1100
0.5

MISSED APPROACH
Left climbing turn for 1 minute return to NDB at 1600

CATEGORY	A	B	C	D
S-21		760-2 675 (700-2)	NOT AUTHORIZED	760-2½ 675 (700-2½)
CIRCLING			NOT AUTHORIZED	

REIL aval Rwy 3-21
HIRL aval Rwys 3-21

FAF to MAP 0.5 NM

Knots	60	90	120	150	180
Min:Sec	0:30	0:20	0:15	0:12	0:10

NDB RWY 21

15°27'N-87°55'W

SAN PEDRO SULA, HONDURAS
LA MESA INTL (MHLM)

75

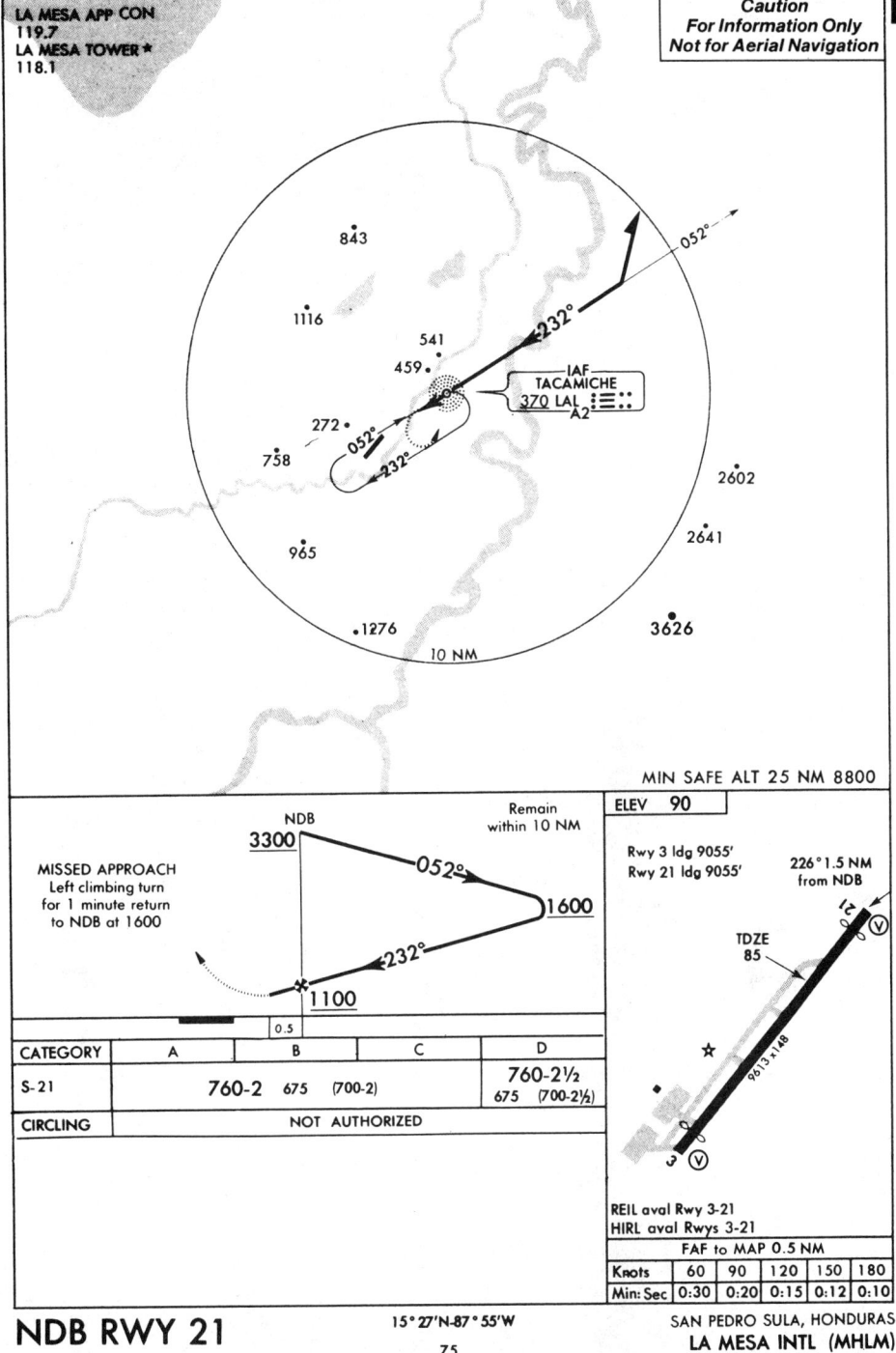

SUNRISE & SUNSET - GMT   SALIDA y PUESTA del SOL - GMT

15th of	JAN	FEB	MAR	APR	MAY	JUN	JUL	AUG	SEPT	OCT	NOV	DEC	
SUNRISE	1221	1216	1159	1137	1122	1120	1128	1136	1140	1143	1153	1210	SALIDA
SUNSET	2340	2355	2401	2406	2413	2423	2426	2415	2353	2331	2318	2323	PUESTA
15 de	ENE	FEB	MAR	ABR	MAY	JUN	JUL	AGO	SEP	OCT	NOV	DIC	

To get local time just subtract 'GMT ADD'
PARA OBTENER TIEMPO LOCAL SUSTRIAGA 'GMT ADD'

576 Utila, Honduras

oo-TILL-ah

JET CHART	WAC	SECTIONAL	LATITUDE	LONGITUDE	US TIME	FOR GMT ADD	ICAO IDENT	TOWN IDENT
JNC-47	CJ-25 So.	TPC J-25C	16°05'	86°53'	CST	6	-	-UTL-

OTHER COMM Traffic 118.1
SETTLEMENT 1/8 mile NNW
POPULATION
FROM San Pedro FREQ 113.1* TRACK 052°, 71n.mi.
FROM Goloson FREQ 227 TRACK 351°, 21n.mi.
FROM Belice FREQ 392 TRACK 133°, 119n.mi.
FUEL -   CARDS -   CASH? -
REPAIRS -   TIEDOWN BYO
Boarding houses

A hurricane went through the Bay Islands and messed up this runway a bit. I haven't been able to get over and check for current condition: check PREPS for later word.

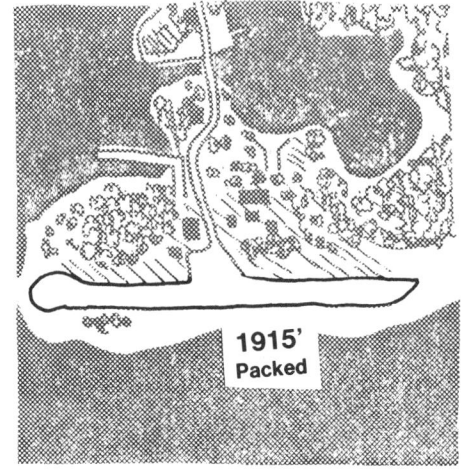

1915'
Packed

ELEVATION
15'

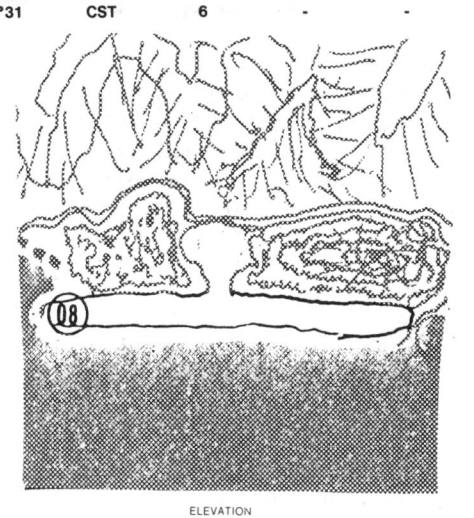

Coxens Hole on Isla Roatan, Honduras 577

JET CHART	WAC	SECTIONAL	LATITUDE	LONGITUDE	US TIME	FOR GMT ADD	ICAO IDENT	TOWN IDENT
JN-47	CJ-25 So	TPC J-25C	16°20	86°31	CST	6	-	-

OTHER COMM Traffic 118.5
CITY 1/2 mile West POPULATION 8,000
B'CAST FREQ 1480 WHERE - HOURS Daylight
FROM Goloson FREQ 227 TRACK 027°, 52n.mi.,
FROM San Pedro Sula FREQ 113.1 TRACK 052°, 94n.mi.,
FROM Belice FREQ 392 TRACK 120°, 125n.mi.,
FUEL - CARDS - CASH? -
REPAIRS - TIEDOWN BYO: Guards 'available'

HOTEL	RATE	WHERE	TEL
Anthonys Key	$$$	5 mi No	Tvl Agt
Roatán Lodge	$$	Pt Royal	Tvl Agt
Reef House	$$	Oak Ridge	Tvl Agt
H.Corral	---$	Central	-

Principle island of the lushly tropical Bay Islands group which stretch about forty miles east-west, in parallel with Honduras' north coast.

ELEVATION
12'

578 Fort Key on Isla Roatan, Honduras

JET CHART	WAC	SECTIONAL	LATITUDE	LONGITUDE	US TIME	FOR GMT ADD	ICAO IDENT	TOWN IDENT
JN-47	CJ-25 So.	TPC J-25C	16°24'	86°17'	CST	6	-	FTK-

OTHER COMM Traffic 118.1
SETTLEMENT Across baylet N   POPULATION 15
FROM Goloson   FREQ 227   TRACK 025°, 51n.mi.
FROM Belice   FREQ 392   TRACK 117°, 135n.mi.
FROM Chetumal   FREQ 113.0 TRACK 132°, 172n.mi.
FUEL -   CARDS -   CASH? -
REPAIRS -   TIEDOWN BYO
      HOTEL   RATE   WHERE   TEL
Fort Key resort $$ Across baylet

A snug runway for ones who want a unique vacation. Here in the isolated part of Roatán you may take advantage of clear warm waters either on this the leeward side, or cab over to the north side for frolicking water. The Cessna 206 based here will come to Coxens Hole to pick you up if you'd prefer.

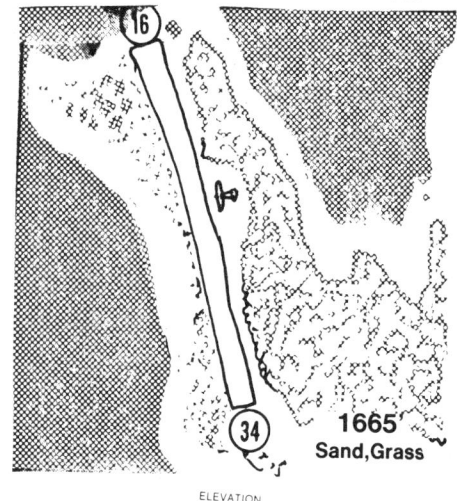

1665
Sand, Grass

ELEVATION
15'

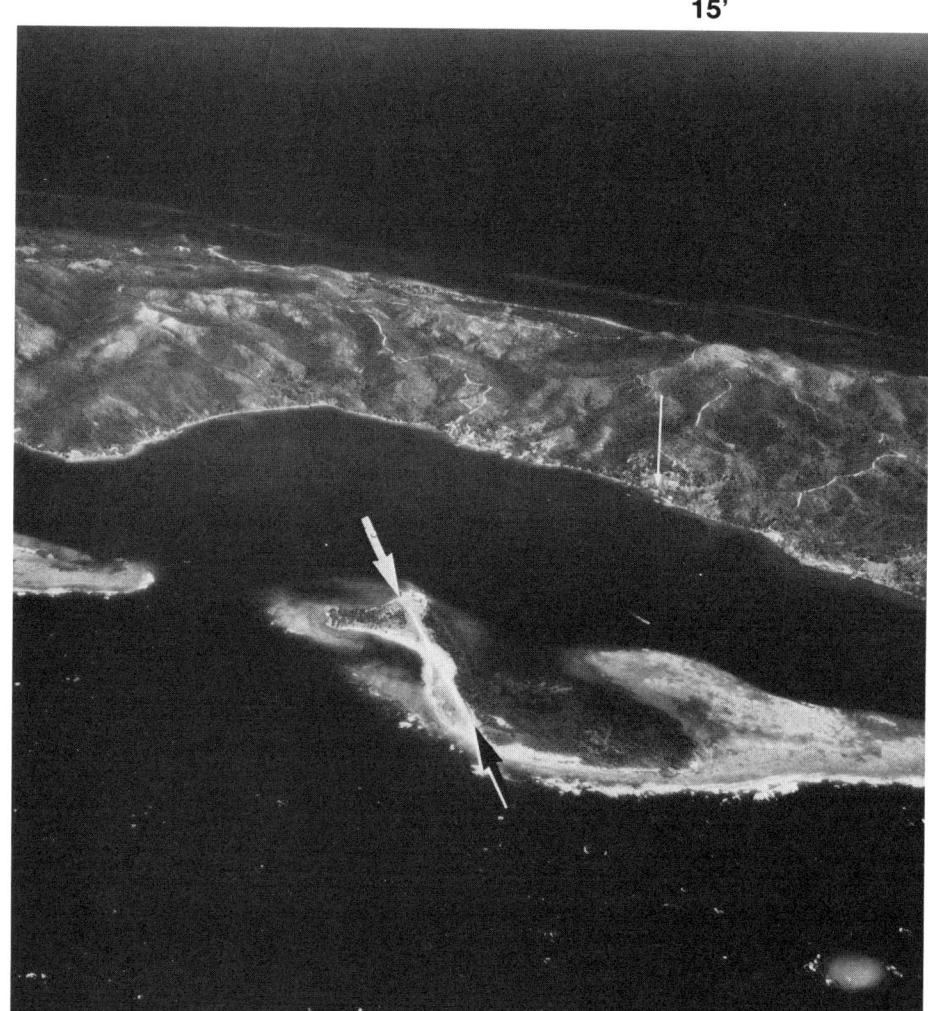

Guanaja, Honduras

wah-NAH-hah   579

JET CHART	WAC	SECTIONAL	LATITUDE	LONGITUDE	US TIME	FOR GMT ADD	ICAO IDENT	TOWN IDENT
JN-47	CJ-25 So.	TPC J-25C	16°27'	85°55'	CST	6	-	GJA

OTHER COMM Traffic 118.1
CITY On island   **POPULATION** 4,500
FROM Goloson   **FREQ** 227   **TRACK** 047°, 69n.mi.
FROM Puerto Castillo **FREQ** airport **TRACK** 003°, 27n.mi.
FROM Chetumal   **FREQ** 113.0   **TRACK** 127°, 185n.mi.
FUEL -   **CARDS** -   **CASH?** -
REPAIRS -   **TIEDOWN** BYO

Serious runway work is just starting here at the East end of the Bay Islands group. This piece of old volcano jutting up out of the Western Caribbean is about to see lots of development. The Scots background of many residents still comes out in their clear burr on certain words. Pretty place, hurry before the brochure writers get here.

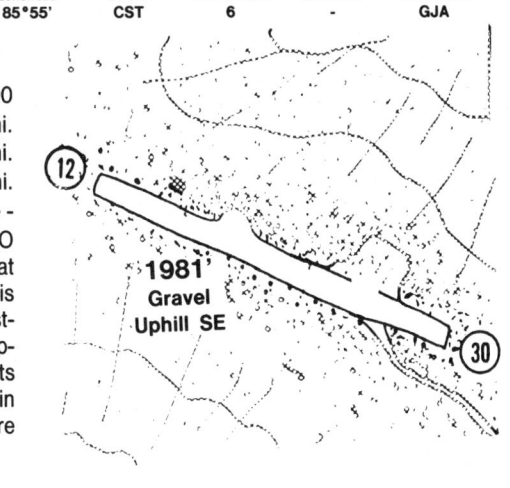

1981' Gravel Uphill SE

ELEVATION
27' to 45'

VOR/DME RWY 1

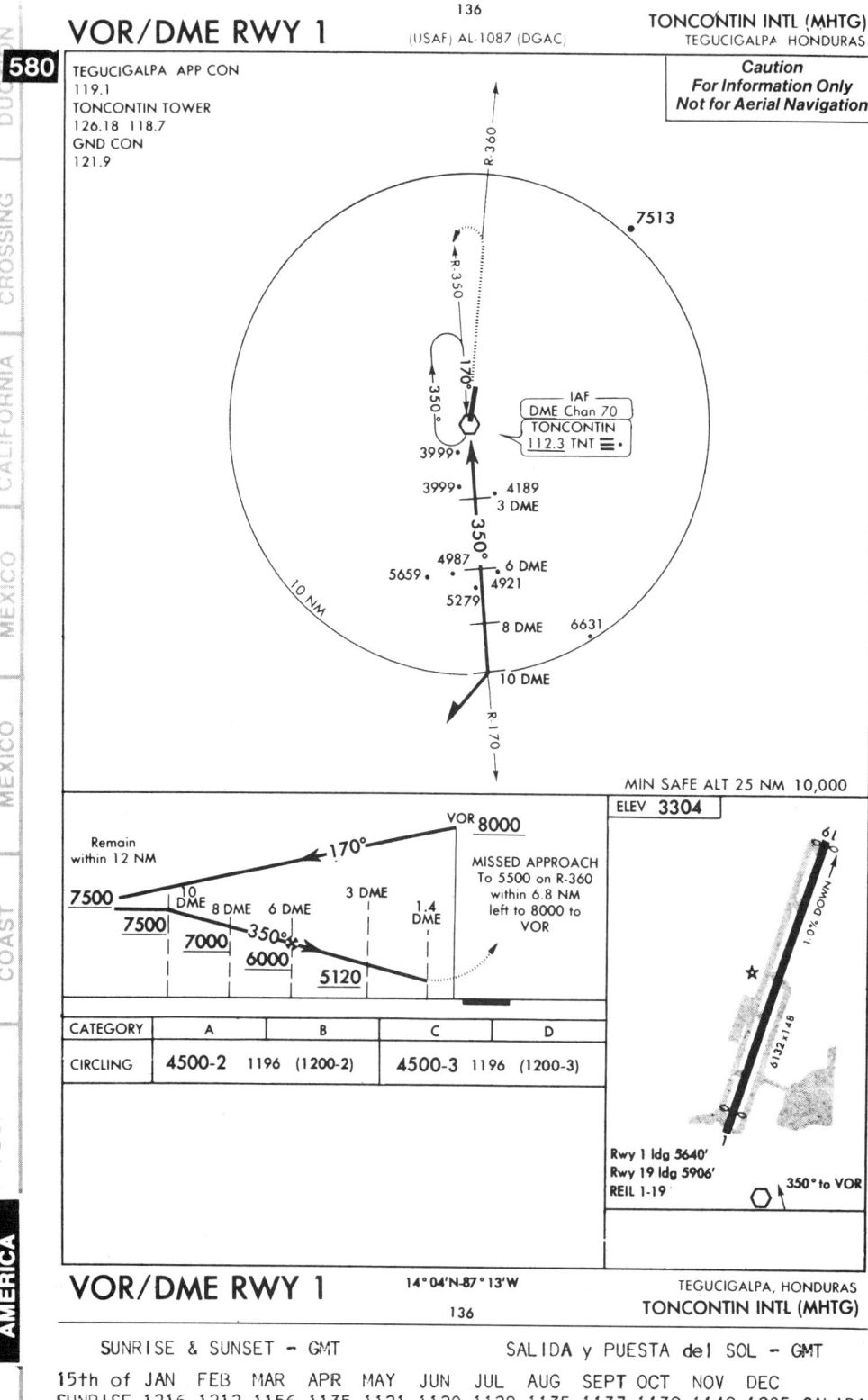

TONCONTIN INTL (MHTG)
TEGUCIGALPA HONDURAS

(USAF) AL-1087 (DGAC)

TEGUCIGALPA APP CON 119.1
TONCONTIN TOWER 126.18 118.7
GND CON 121.9

Caution — For Information Only — Not for Aerial Navigation

IAF
DME Chan 70
TONCONTIN
112.3 TNT

R-360, R-350, 350°, 170°
3999, 3999, 4189 (3 DME), 5659, 4987, 4921 (6 DME), 5279, 6631 (8 DME), 10 DME
7513
R-170
10 NM

MIN SAFE ALT 25 NM 10,000
ELEV 3304

Remain within 12 NM

VOR 8000
170°
7500 — 10 DME — 8 DME — 6 DME — 3 DME — 1.4 DME
7500 7000 6000 5120
350°

MISSED APPROACH
To 5500 on R-360 within 6.8 NM left to 8000 to VOR

CATEGORY	A	B	C	D
CIRCLING	4500-2 1196 (1200-2)		4500-3 1196 (1200-3)	

Rwy 1 ldg 5640'
Rwy 19 ldg 5906'
REIL 1-19
6132 x 148
1.0% DOWN
350° to VOR

14°04'N - 87°13'W

TEGUCIGALPA, HONDURAS
TONCONTIN INTL (MHTG)

VOR/DME RWY 1

SUNRISE & SUNSET — GMT   SALIDA y PUESTA del SOL — GMT

15th of	JAN	FEB	MAR	APR	MAY	JUN	JUL	AUG	SEPT	OCT	NOV	DEC	
SUNRISE	1216	1212	1156	1135	1121	1120	1128	1135	1137	1139	1149	1205	SALIDA
SUNSET	2339	2353	2359	2402	2408	2417	2421	2411	2350	2329	2317	2323	PUESTA
15° de	ENE	FEB	MAR	ABR	MAY	JUN	JUL	AGO	SEP	OCT	NOV	DIC	

To get local time just subtract 'GMT ADD'
PARA OBTENER TIEMPO LOCAL SUSTRIAGA 'GMT ADD'

Tegucigalpa, Honduras

tay-goo-see-GALL-pah

581

JET CHART	WAC	SECTIONAL	LATITUDE	LONGITUDE	US TIME	FOR GMT ADD	ICAO IDENT	TOWN IDENT
JNC-61	CK-25 No.	TPC K-25B	14°04'	87°13'	CST	6	MHTG	TNT

APPROACH 119.1 TOWER 118.7 GROUND 121.9
OTHER COMM Enroute 126.9
CITY 1 mile N POPULATION 295,000
B'CAST FREQ 610 WHERE - HOURS Daylight
LOCAL VorDme FREQ 112.3 WHERE here HOURS 24
FROM San Pedro Sula FREQ 113.1 TRACK 150°, 94 n.mi.
FROM Guatemala FREQ 114.1 TRACK 094°, 198 n.mi.
FROM Managua FREQ 112.1 TRACK 326°, 129 n.mi.
FUEL 80,100,JP CARDS - CASH? Yes
REPAIRS Some TIEDOWN BYO

HOTEL	RATE	WHERE	TEL
Honduras Maya	$$	N side	22-31-91
la Ronda	$	Central	22-81-51

AOE 9-12, 3-5pm

6112'
Asphalt

RESTRICTED MILITARY ONLY

ELEVATION
3311'

This capital city of Honduras is in a high valley, about the driest spot in the country. You jump over mountains to get in from any side so inbound VorDme is very quiet until 30 miles out. Communications the same, if you have been told to report fifty miles out do so, but don't expect an answer.

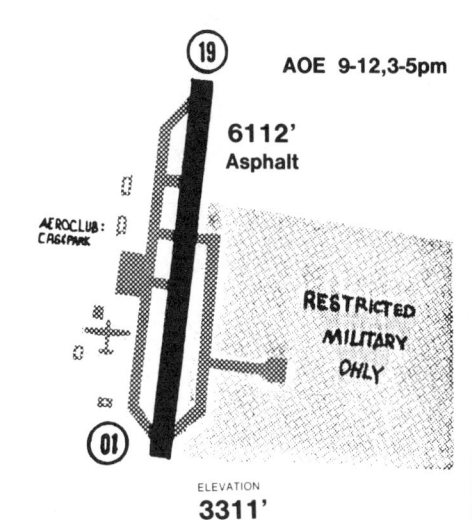

VOR RWY 15

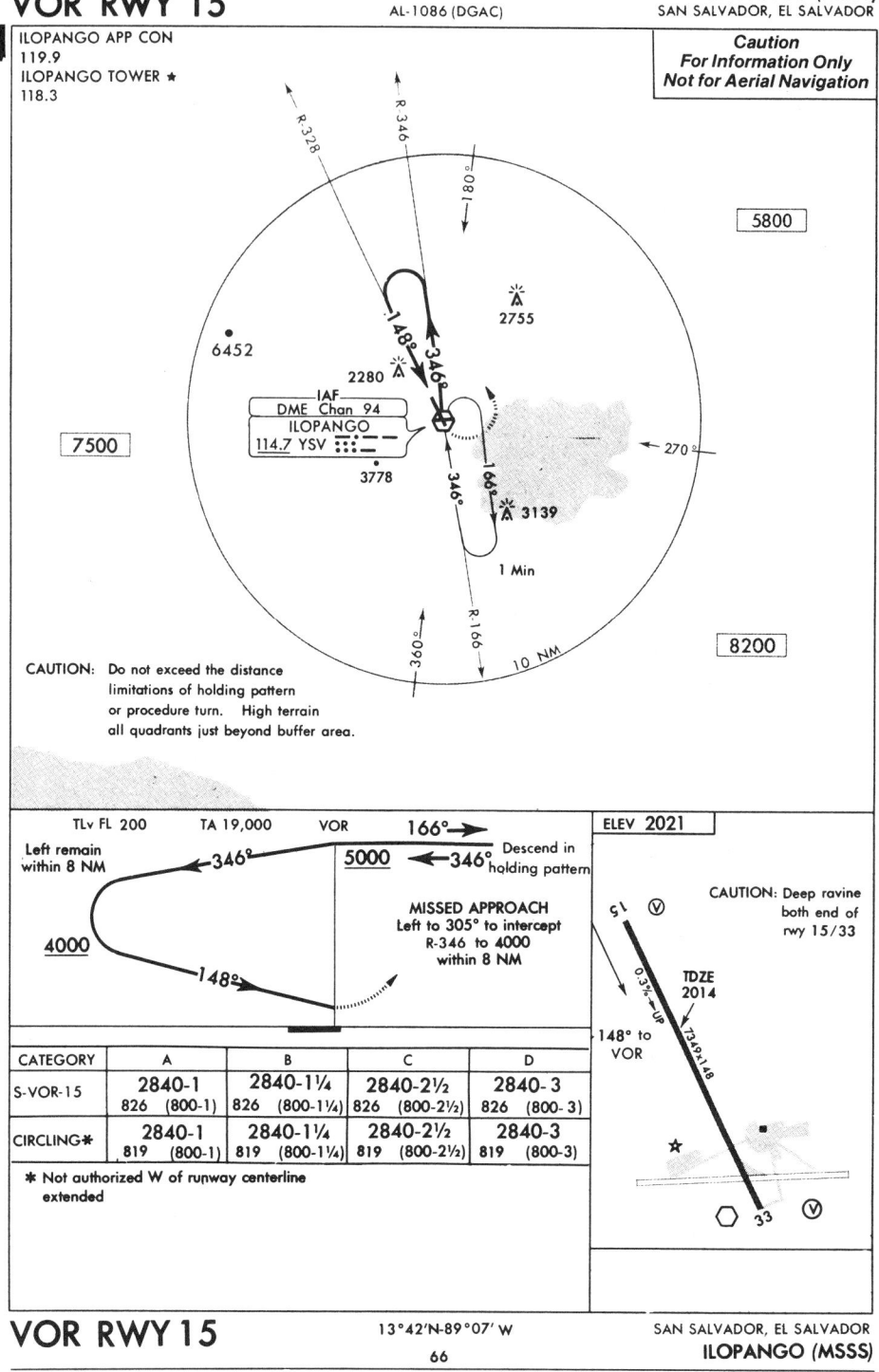

ILOPANGO (MSSS)
SAN SALVADOR, EL SALVADOR

AL-1086 (DGAC)

ILOPANGO APP CON 119.9
ILOPANGO TOWER ★ 118.3

Caution
For Information Only
Not for Aerial Navigation

IAF
DME Chan 94
ILOPANGO
114.7 YSV

5800
7500
8200

CAUTION: Do not exceed the distance limitations of holding pattern or procedure turn. High terrain all quadrants just beyond buffer area.

TLv FL 200   TA 19,000   VOR   166°→   ELEV 2021

Left remain within 8 NM   ←346°   5000   ←346° Descend in holding pattern

4000   148°

MISSED APPROACH
Left to 305° to intercept
R-346 to 4000
within 8 NM

CAUTION: Deep ravine both end of rwy 15/33

TDZE 2014

148° to VOR

CATEGORY	A	B	C	D
S-VOR-15	2840-1 826 (800-1)	2840-1¼ 826 (800-1¼)	2840-2½ 826 (800-2½)	2840-3 826 (800-3)
CIRCLING★	2840-1 819 (800-1)	2840-1¼ 819 (800-1¼)	2840-2½ 819 (800-2½)	2840-3 819 (800-3)

★ Not authorized W of runway centerline extended

VOR RWY 15   13°42'N-89°07'W   SAN SALVADOR, EL SALVADOR
ILOPANGO (MSSS)

SUNRISE & SUNSET - GMT   SALIDA y PUESTA del SOL - GMT

15th of JAN FEB MAR APR MAY JUN JUL AUG SEPT OCT NOV DEC
SUNRISE 1223 1219 1204 1143 1129 1128 1136 1143 1145 1147 1156 1211 SALIDA
SUNSET   2348 2401 2406 2409 2415 2424 2428 2418 2357 2337 2325 2331 PUESTA
15° de   ENE FEB MAR ABR MAY JUN JUL AGO SEP OCT NOV DIC

To get local time just subtract 'GMT ADD'
PARA OBTENER TIEMPO LOCAL SUSTRIAGA GMT ADD'

Ilopango, El Salvador   *eel-oh-PONN-goe*   **583**

JET CHART	WAC	SECTIONAL	LATITUDE	LONGITUDE	US TIME	FOR GMT ADD	ICAO IDENT	TOWN IDENT
JNC-61	CK-25 No.	TPC K-25A	13°42'	89°07'	CST	6	MSSS	YSX

APPROACH 119.9   TOWER 118.3   GROUND 121.9
OTHER COMM Enroute 126.9
CITY 4 miles NE   POPULATION 180,000
B'CAST FREQ 580   WHERE -   HOURS Daylight
LOCAL VorDme   FREQ 114.7   WHERE here   HOURS 24
FROM Guatemala   FREQ 114.1   TRACK 114°, 95Dme
FROM S. Pedro Sula   FREQ 113.1   TRACK 210°, 126n.mi.
FROM Managua   FREQ 112.1   TRACK 293°, 177 n.mi.
FUEL 100, JP   CARDS Shell Intl   CASH? Dollars
REPAIRS Yes   TIEDOWN BYO

HOTEL	RATE	WHERE	TEL
Camino Real	$$$	Central	-
Ramada	$$	Central	-

AOE 9am-12, 3-5pm
7331' Paved Uphill SE
Prior Permission Required Within 24 Hrs
ELEVATION 2020'

Small country of feisty people, evidenced by their famous Soccer War of a few years back. Larger Honduras tried pushing Salvadoreans around but found themselves invaded, unable to throw out the conquerers.

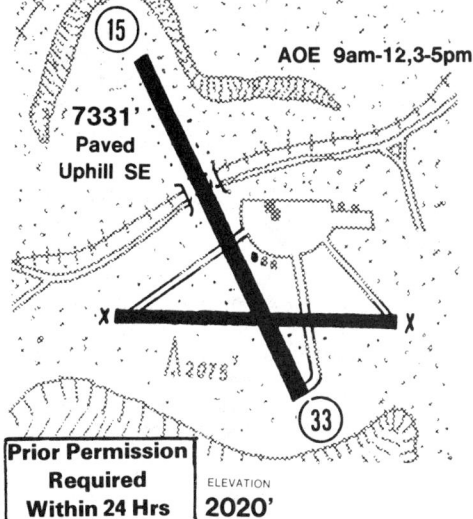

584 el Salvador Internacional, El Salvador *ell sal-vah-DORR*

JET CHART	WAC	LATITUDE	LONGITUDE	US TIME	FOR GMT	ICAO IDENT	PLACE IDENT
JN-61	CK-25Mo.	13°26'	89°03'	CST	+6	MSLP	CAT

APPROACH 119.9   TOWER 118.0   GROUND 121.7
CITY 20+mi N   POPULATION 800,000+
LOCAL VorDme   FREQ 117.5   WHERE Here
FROM Gtm.City FREQ 114.5 TRACK 122°, 111 n.mi.
FROM Tegucigalpa FREQ 112.3 TRACK 245°, 113 n.mi.
FROM Managua FREQ 112.1 TRACK 291°, 186 n.mi.
AVIATION GAS 100, JP   CREDIT CARDS -   CASH TYPE Yes
REPAIRS AVAILABLE Minor   TIEDOWNS? BYO Ropes

In a nation of volcanos it was necessary to go all the way out to the coastal shelf to find an airport site with good approaches and room to expand. The men here are courteous and helpful but it is necessary to re-verify your permission to land and have normal fuel service 24 hours before arrival.

Send your permissions as mentioned elsewhere, but then the day before arrival just let them know you really are coming.

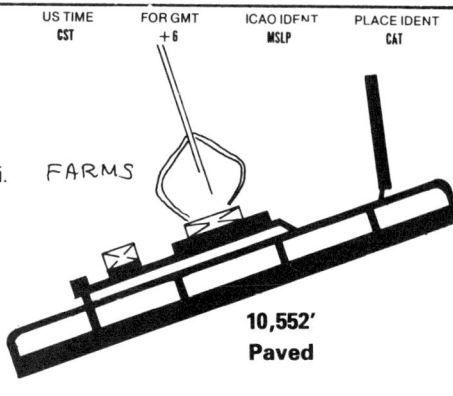

FARMS

10,552'
Paved

FARMS

Prior Permission Required Within 24 Hrs

ELEVATION
107' msl

Tamarino, El Salvador   *tom-ah-RENO*   585

JET CHART	WAC	SECTIONAL	LATITUDE	LONGITUDE	US TIME	FOR GMT ADD	ICAO IDENT	TOWN IDENT
JN-61	CK-25 No.	TPC K-25B	13°10'	87°54'	CST	6	-	-

OTHER COMM Traffic 118.1, Enroute 126.9
FROM Ilopango   FREQ 114.7   TRACK 109°, 77Dme
FROM Tegucigalpa   FREQ 112.3   TRACK 212°, 68Dme
FROM Managua   FREQ 112.1   TRACK 296°, 119 n.mi.
FUEL -   CARDS -   CASH? -
REPAIRS -   TIEDOWN BYO

A comforting runway to know about when you are making your first flights across the mouth of this Golfo de Fonseca. Land-borne pilots will be nervous those first few times they are seven miles out. Just keep in mind you could land here easily. You won't need to, but you could.

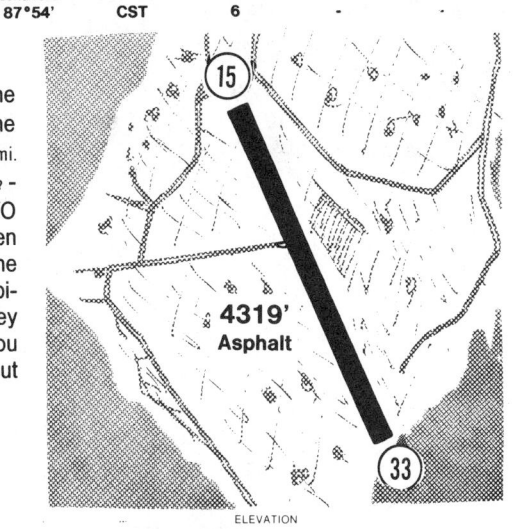

4319'
Asphalt

ELEVATION
26' to 37'

586 Active Volcano — Nicaragua

JET CHART	WAC	SECTIONAL	LATITUDE	LONGITUDE	US TIME	FOR GMT ADD	ICAO IDENT	TOWN IDENT
JN-61	CK-25 No.	TPC K-25B	12°42'	87°00'	-	-	-	-

OTHER COMM Traffic 122.9
FROM Tegucigalpa FREQ 112.3 TRACK 164°, 82Dme,
FROM Managua FREQ 112.1 TRACK 299°, 60Dme,
FROM Ilopango FREQ 114.7 TRACK 111°, 137 n.mi.

A very active volcano here in the northern part of Nicaragua, about ten or so miles from the coast. It is a very exciting your first time, and second, and so on. After a dozen times by this it hasn't lost a bit of the thrill in seeing all that steam boiling up out of the cone.

Two Cautions

Good idea to keep a sharp watch out for other traffic. You will be circling at about six thousand both to stay out of the almost perpetual clouds and to see: but so will everyone else. Second, the lee side will be very choppy at or below cone elevation. On our Bush Pilots trips by here we let down, see the volcano on a wide, left 720° turn, then after we're content, climb back up to smooth air.

Los Brasiles — Nicaragua

587

JET CHART	WAC	SECTIONAL	LATITUDE	LONGITUDE	US TIME	FOR GMT ADD	ICAO IDENT	TOWN IDENT
JN-61	CK-25	TPC K25B	12 11'	86 21	CST			BRS-

OTHER COMM
CITY Adjacent   **POPULATION**

LOCAL	FREQ	WHERE	HOURS
FROM Managua	FREQ 112.1	TRACK 281° 11.3Dme	
FROM Ilopango	FREQ 114.7	TRACK 115° 185.6 n.mi.	
FROM Liberia	FREQ 113.7	TRACK 329° 106.0 n.mi.	

FUEL   **CARDS** -   **CASH?** -
REPAIRS   **TIEDOWN**
     HOTEL **RATE** **WHERE** **TEL**

Remarks: we'll wait for a bit more settling down of the political situation before this airport will see much use. One day you will be entering on the forty five to land in downtown Managua by flying your plane over those two open volcano craters in the background. One is full of green water the other with blue.

ELEVATION
229'

VOR RWY 9

SANDINO (MNMG)
MANAGUA, NICARAGUA

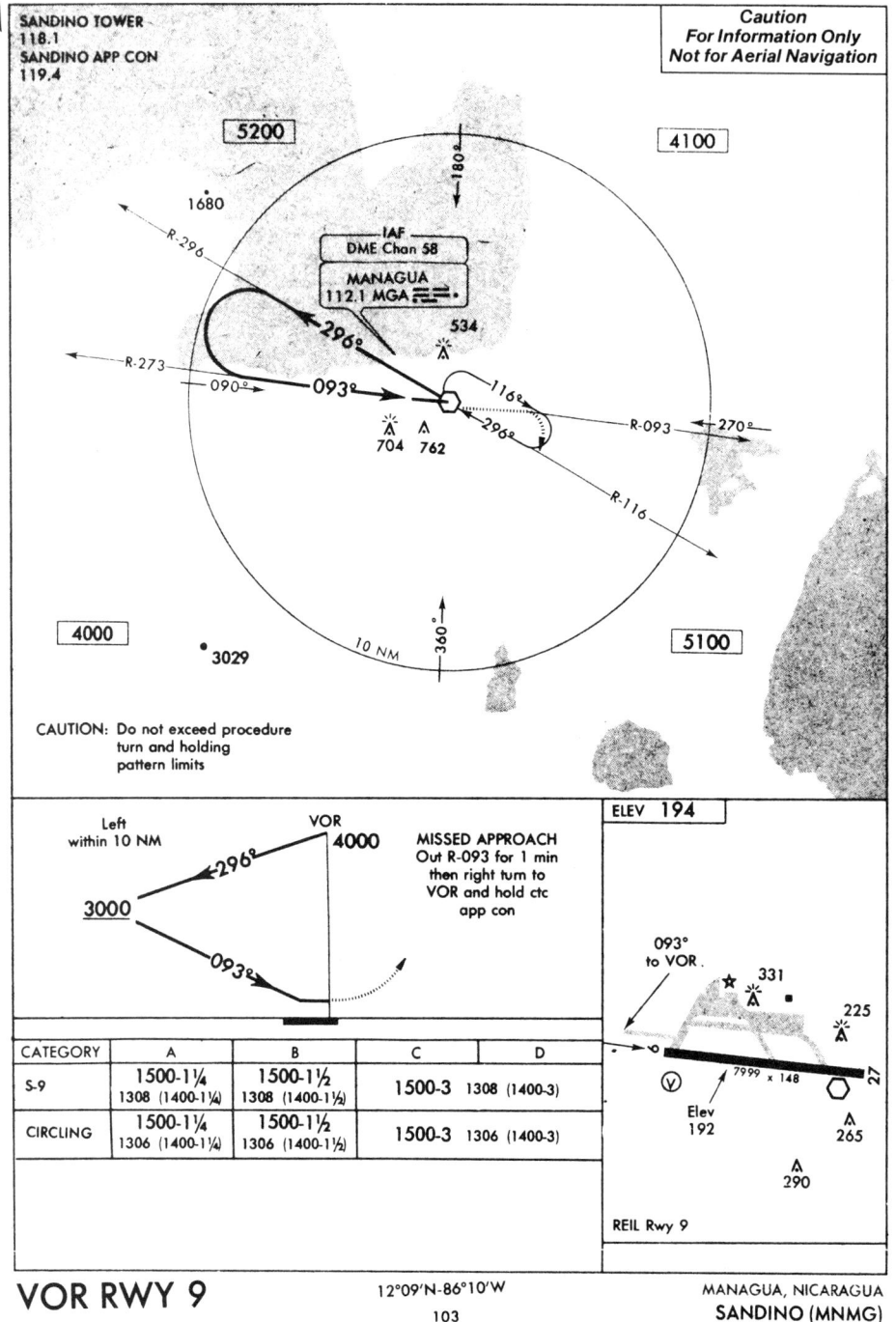

(USAF) AL-1088 (DAC)

SANDINO TOWER 118.1
SANDINO APP CON 119.4

Caution
For Information Only
Not for Aerial Navigation

IAF
DME Chan 58
MANAGUA
112.1 MGA

CAUTION: Do not exceed procedure turn and holding pattern limits

Left within 10 NM
VOR 4000
296°
3000
093°

MISSED APPROACH
Out R-093 for 1 min then right turn to VOR and hold ctc app con

ELEV 194

093° to VOR
331
225
7999 x 148
Elev 192
27
265
290

REIL Rwy 9

CATEGORY	A	B	C	D
S-9	1500-1¼ 1308 (1400-1¼)	1500-1½ 1308 (1400-1½)	1500-3 1308 (1400-3)	
CIRCLING	1500-1¼ 1306 (1400-1¼)	1500-1½ 1306 (1400-1½)	1500-3 1306 (1400-3)	

VOR RWY 9

12°09'N-86°10'W

MANAGUA, NICARAGUA
SANDINO (MNMG)

SUNRISE & SUNSET — GMT   SALIDA y PUESTA del SOL — GMT

15th of   JAN   FEB   MAR   APR   MAY   JUN   JUL   AUG   SEPT OCT   NOV   DEC
SUNRISE   1209 1206 1151 1132 1120 1120 1127 1133 1133 1134 1142 1157 SALIDA
SUNSET   2338 2351 2355 2356 2401 2410 2413 2404 2345 2326 2316 2322 PUESTA
15 de   ENE   FEB   MAR   ABR   MAY   JUN   JUL   AGO   SEP   OCT   NOV   DIC

To get local time just subtract 'GMT ADD'
PARA OBTENER TIEMPO LOCAL SUSTRIAGA 'GMT ADD'

Managua — Nicaragua

mah-NOGG-wah

589

JET CHART	WAC	SECTIONAL	LATITUDE	LONGITUDE	US TIME	FOR GMT ADD	ICAO IDENT	TOWN IDENT
JNC-61	CK-25 No.	TPC K-25B	12°09'	86°10'	CST	6	MNMG	MGA

APPROACH 119.4 TOWER 118.1 GROUND 118.1
CITY 6 miles W POPULATION 300,000
B'CAST FREQ 750 WHERE - HOURS Daylight
LOCAL VorDme FREQ 112.1 WHERE here HOURS 24
FROM Ilopango FREQ 114.7 TRACK 113°, 177 n.mi.
FROM Tegucigalpa FREQ 112.3 TRACK 146°, 129 n.mi.
FROM los Cocos FREQ 115.7 TRACK 313°, 173 n.mi.
FUEL 100, JP CARDS - CASH? Dollars
REPAIRS Minor TIEDOWN BYO

HOTEL	RATE	WHERE	TEL
Intercontinental	$$	Central	2-35-30
Hotel Carlos	$	Central	2-27-48
las Mercedes	$$	Nearest	37-10

AOE 9am-12, 3-5pm

8013' Paved

ELEVATION **197'**

Following the recent political problems you might want to wait a year until everything settles in. Too bad, the country has many attractive places to see and things to do.

On my most recent stop fuel was $3.20 US per gallon, a dollar more than the neighboring countries.

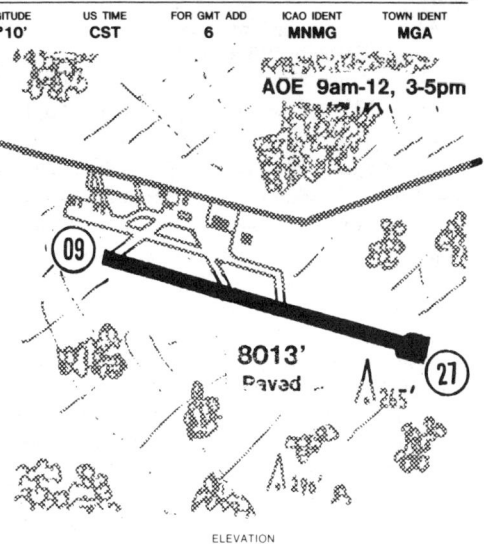

590 Llano Grande Int'l, Costa Rica YAH-no GRONN-day

JET CHART	WAC	SECTIONAL	LATITUDE	LONGITUDE	US TIME	FOR GMT ADD	ICAO IDENT	TOWN IDENT
JNC-61	CK-25 No.	TPC K-25C	10°36'	85°33'	CST	6	MRLB	-

OTHER COMM Enroute 126.9
CITY 5 miles NE POPULATION 27,000
B'CAST FREQ 875 WHERE - HOURS Daylight
LOCAL VorDme FREQ 113.7 WHERE Here
FROM Managua FREQ 112.1 TRACK 154°,99Dme
FROM Cocos FREQ 115.7 TRACK 292°,84Dme
FUEL July-Nov CARDS - CASH? -
REPAIRS - TIEDOWN BYO

HOTEL	RATE	WHERE	TEL
el Delfin	$	Central	-
el Bramadero	$	Central	-

AOE Prior Request

7211'
Asphalt

ELEVATION
235'

Only internacional airport in the lush NW part of Costa Rica, this one was also a staging area for the recent changes in the government of Nicauragua. These spectacular beaches are about to be thoroughly tapped by lots of tourists. Suggest you get cracking and see it ahead of the crowds. Blanco Tours in San José can do the arrangements for you.

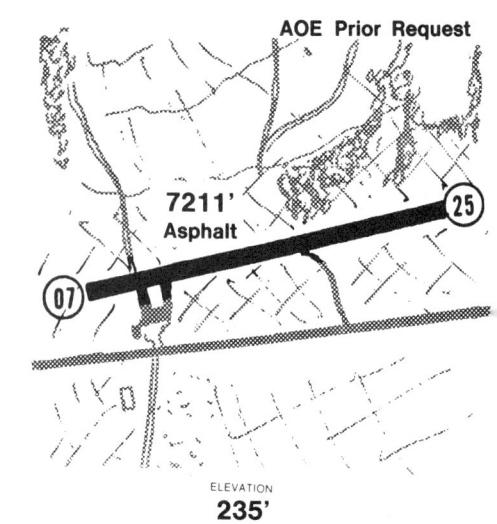

Flamingo, Costa Rica *fla-MING-goe*

JN CHART	WAC	SECTIONAL	LATITUDE	LONGITUDE	US TIME	FOR GMT	ICAO	TOWN ID
JN-61	CK-25	TPC K25C	10°26'	85°47'	CST	+6	-	MGO –

OTHER COMM Traffic 124.8
Scattered Beach Homes POPULATION est 400-1500
FROM Liberia   FREQ 113.7   TRACK 229°, 17.0Dme
FROM los Cocos FREQ 115.7   TRACK 282°95.4Dme
FROM Managua   FREQ 112.1   TRACK 163°, 105n.mi.
AVIATION GAS -   CREDIT CARDS -   CASH TYPE -
REPAIRS AVAILABLE None   TIEDOWNS? BYO

Hotel	Rate	Where	Tel
Portrero		0.5mi NE	Tvl Agt

2971'x17'
Sod & Packed Dirt

Almost hidden in the vastness of Potrero Bay are several hundred building lots fronting that black sand bay. Buyers eager to enjoy Costa Rica's coastline were just beginning to build before the recent Downturn began. That may slow things temporarily.

This runway is on the leeside of a ridge to the right. Your airplane will bounce around as tho it had a mind of its own during takeoff or landing during the late winter easterly winds.

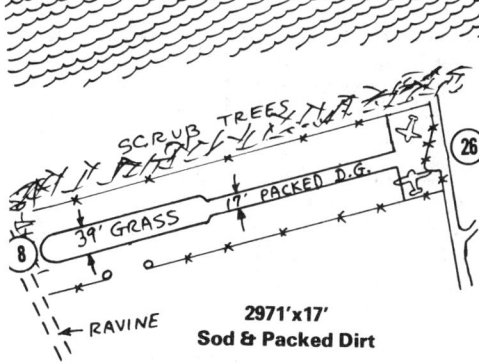

Intentionally left blank

Intencionalmente dejada en blanco

592 Tamarindo de Santa Cruz, Costa Rica *tomm-ah-REEN-doe*

JET CHART	WAC	LATITUDE	LONGITUDE	US TIME	FOR GMT ADD	ICAO IDENT	PLACE IDENT
JN-61	CR25-Sa.	10°19'	85°49'	CST	6	-	MRA-

OTHER COMM Traffic 124.8

CITY 5 mi SW
FROM Liberia   FREQ 113.7
FROM los Cocos FREQ 115.7
FROM Puntarenas FREQ Apt
AVIATION GAS -   CREDIT CARDS -
REPAIRS AVAILABLE -

POPULATION est 3500
TRACK 218°, 23.1Dme
TRACK 278° 95.6Dme
TRACK 283°, 65n.mi.
CASH TYPE -
TIEDOWNS? BYO

An isolated runway where the daily STOL transport brings customers to be picked up for the resort SW of here. Pretty pretty country, excellent farms, and judging by the spoor, well-fed cows by the jillion.

Can be windy; be sure to have your full tiedown kit: stakes, vice grips to get them out, ropes, 5 lb hand sledge, and vice grips to get them out, are all onboard this time.

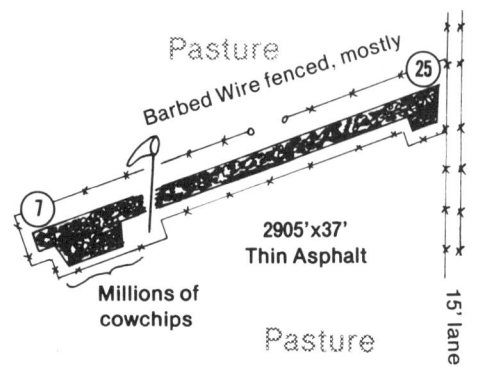

Pasture
Barbed Wire fenced, mostly
[7] [25]
2905'x37'
Thin Asphalt
Millions of cowchips
Pasture
15' lane

ELEVATION
46'msl

Tambor, Costa Rica

tomm-BORE 593

JN CHART	WAC	SECTIONAL	LATITUDE	LONGITUDE	US TIME	FOR GMT...	ICAO	TOWN ID
JN-61	CK-25	TPC K25C	9°44'	84°58'	CST	+6		TBR –

OTHER COMM Traffic 122.8
SETTLEMENT Resort West side
FROM Liberia FREQ 113.7 TRACK 142°, 62.4 Dme
FROM los Cocos FREQ 115.7 TRACK 246°, 45.9 Dme
FROM Puntarenas FREQ Apt TRACK 214°, 19.2 n.mi.

POPULATION est 100

AVIATION GAS - CREDIT CARDS - CASH TYPE -
REPAIRS AVAILABLE - TIEDOWNS? BYO

Hotel	Rate	Where	Tel
H.Tambor		Here	Tvl Agt

This jewel of a resort is located in a lush green peninsula directly across the bay from Puntarenas. In this picture you can see the chocolate brown sand beach in the foreground. Looks exactly the same in person. Comfortable, clean rooms, courteous service, and fine food make this a favorite Pacific Coast retreat.

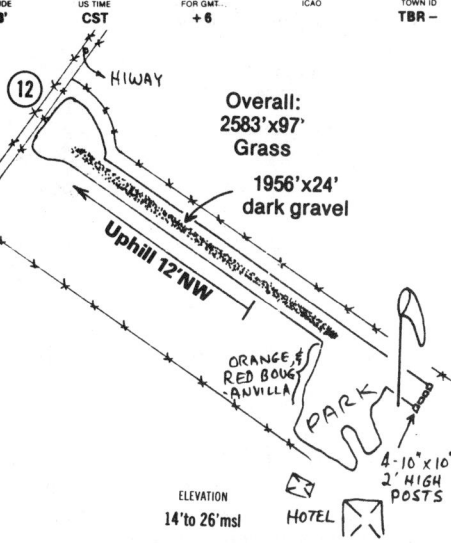

Overall: 2583'x97' Grass
1956'x24' dark gravel
Uphill 12' NW
ORANGE & RED BOUG - ANVILLA
PARK
4 - 10"x10" 2' HIGH POSTS
HOTEL
ELEVATION 14' to 26' msl

594 Puntarenas, Costa Rica

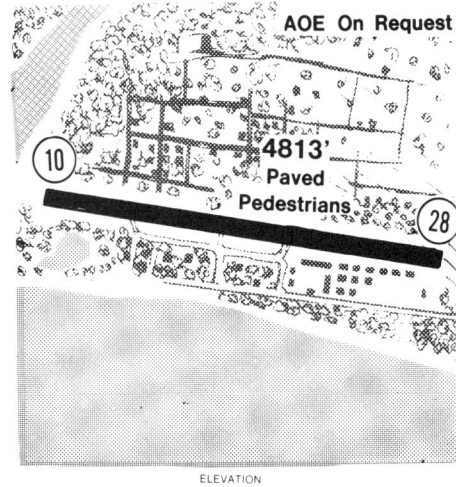

POON-tah RAY-nuss

JET CHART	WAC	SECTIONAL	LATITUDE	LONGITUDE	US TIME	FOR GMT ADD	ICAO IDENT	TOWN IDENT
JNC-61	CK-25 So.	TPC K-25C	09°59'	84°46'	CST	6	MRPT	-

OTHER COMM Traffic 118.1
CITY 3 miles W   POPULATION 15,00
B'CAST FREQ 1175   WHERE -   HOURS Daylight
FROM los Cocos   FREQ 115.7   TRACK 266°, 30Dme
FROM Managua   FREQ 112.1   TRACK 144°, 154 n.mi.
FROM Palmar   FREQ 1670   TRACK 304°, 98n.mi.
FUEL Emergency 100   CARDS -   CASH? Yes
REPAIRS -   TIEDOWN BYO

HOTEL	RATE	WHERE	TEL
Motel Colonial	$$	Central	61-00-11
Isla Jesusita	$$	Far	61-02-63
Hotel Cayuga	$$	-	61-03-44

Attractive port city on Costa Rica's West Coast. Ships destined for (inland) San José are actually heading here. An optional airport of entry if you can't figure out how to get through the passes to the capital. Pedestrians going across the runway may disturb you at first.

AOE On Request
4813'
Paved
Pedestrians

ELEVATION
11'

Pavas Int'l, Costa Rica

PAHH-vuss **595**

JET CHART	WAC	SECTIONAL	LATITUDE	LONGITUDE	US TIME	FOR GMT ADD	ICAO IDENT	TOWN IDENT
JNC-61	CK-25 So.	TPC K-25C	09°57'	84°09'	CST	6	MRPV	PAV

APPROACH 119.6 TOWER 118.3 GROUND 121.7
CITY Adjacent E POPULATION 400,000
B'CAST FREQ 675 WHERE - HOURS Daylight
LOCAL VorDme FREQ 115.7 WHERE 7 mi W HOURS 24
FROM Puntarenas FREQ airport TRACK Railroad, 38n.mi.
FROM Palmar FREQ 1670 TRACK 318°, 77n.mi.
FUEL 100 CARDS Shell Int'l CASH? Yes
REPAIRS Yes TIEDOWN BYO

HOTEL	RATE	WHERE	TEL
see listing	-	-	-

AOE 8am-12, 3-5pm

09 — 3232' Paved — 27

ELEVATION
3267'

Very handy general aviation airport for the pleasant city of San José. With plenty of air taxi, student training, and tourist traffic but the runway length says no jets.

Be very careful of the perpetual downdrafts: one short final to 09, the other at the upwind end of 09. 27 does not seem to have these problems.

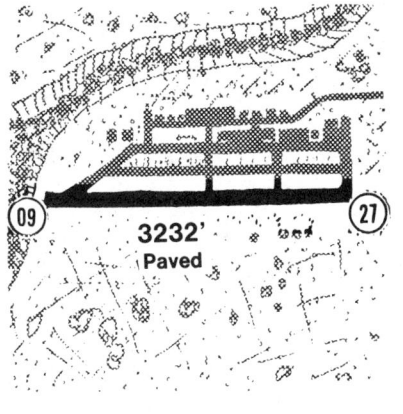

VOR/DME RWY 7

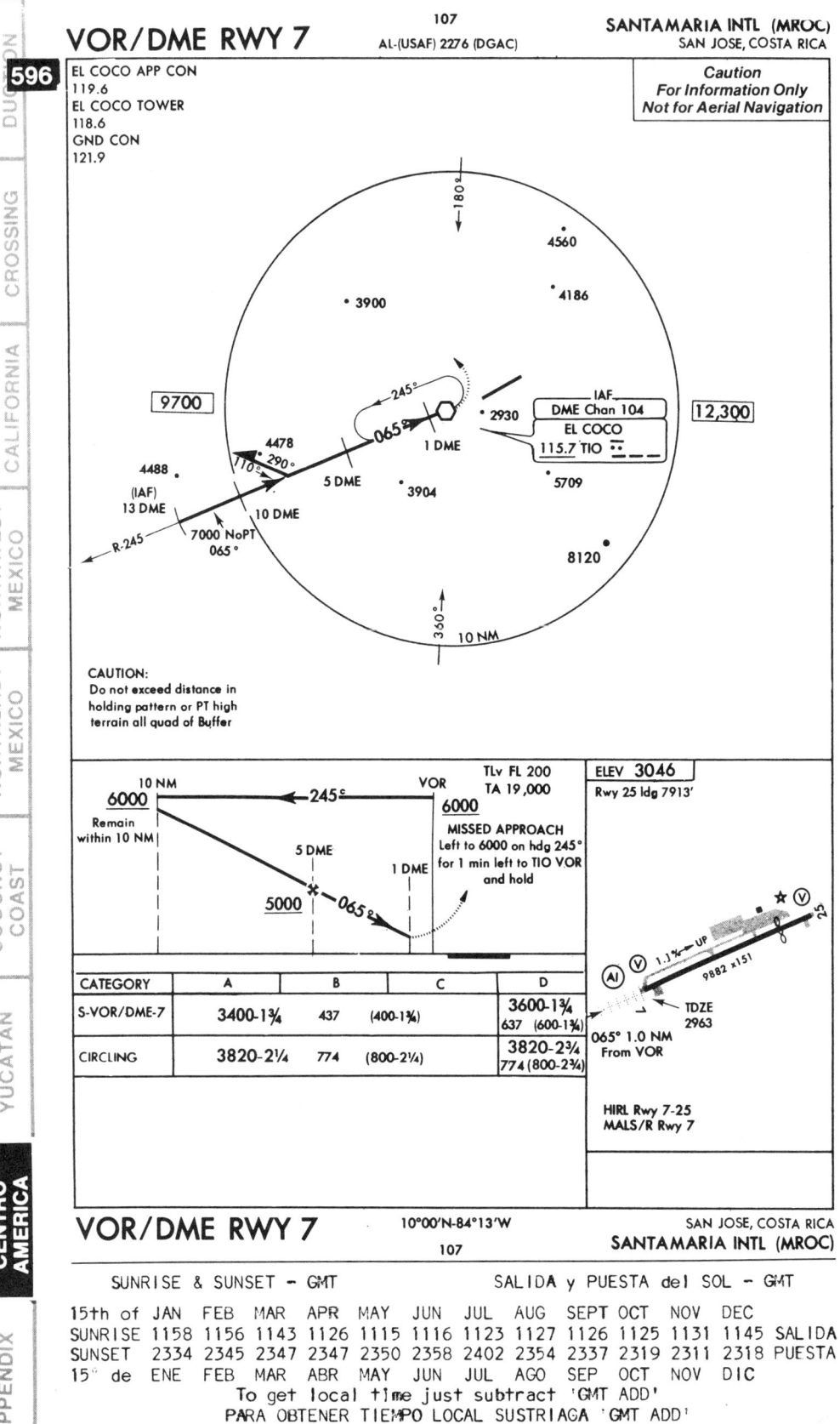

AL-(USAF) 2276 (DGAC) — 107

SANTAMARIA INTL (MROC)
SAN JOSE, COSTA RICA

EL COCO APP CON 119.6
EL COCO TOWER 118.6
GND CON 121.9

Caution
For Information Only
Not for Aerial Navigation

9700 | 12,300

IAF
DME Chan 104
EL COCO
115.7 TIO

R-245
(IAF) 13 DME
7000 NoPT 065°
10 DME
5 DME
1 DME
245°
065°
110°
290°
4478
4488
3900
4560
4186
2930
3904
5709
8120
180°
350°
10 NM

CAUTION: Do not exceed distance in holding pattern or PT high terrain all quad of Buffer

TLv FL 200
TA 19,000

ELEV 3046
Rwy 25 ldg 7913'

10 NM — 245° — VOR
6000 6000
Remain within 10 NM
5 DME 1 DME
5000 —065°—

MISSED APPROACH
Left to 6000 on hdg 245° for 1 min left to TIO VOR and hold

TDZE 2963
065° 1.0 NM From VOR

9882 x 151

HIRL Rwy 7-25
MALS/R Rwy 7

CATEGORY	A	B	C	D
S-VOR/DME-7	3400-1¾	437	(400-1¾)	3600-1¾ 637 (600-1¾)
CIRCLING	3820-2¼	774	(800-2¼)	3820-2¾ 774 (800-2¾)

VOR/DME RWY 7

10°00'N-84°13'W — 107

SAN JOSE, COSTA RICA
SANTAMARIA INTL (MROC)

SUNRISE & SUNSET – GMT   SALIDA y PUESTA del SOL – GMT

15th of	JAN	FEB	MAR	APR	MAY	JUN	JUL	AUG	SEPT	OCT	NOV	DEC
SUNRISE	1158	1156	1143	1126	1115	1116	1123	1127	1126	1125	1131	1145	SALIDA
SUNSET	2334	2345	2347	2347	2350	2358	2402	2354	2337	2319	2311	2318	PUESTA
15° de	ENE	FEB	MAR	ABR	MAY	JUN	JUL	AGO	SEP	OCT	NOV	DIC

To get local time just subtract 'GMT ADD'
PARA OBTENER TIEMPO LOCAL SUSTRIAGA 'GMT ADD'

SantaMaria Int'l, Costa Rica

it's called los Cocos

597

JET CHART	WAC	SECTIONAL	LATITUDE	LONGITUDE	US TIME	FOR GMT ADD	ICAO IDENT	TOWN IDENT
JNC-61	CK-25 So.	TPC K-25C	10°00'	84°13'	CST	6	MROC	TIO

APPROACH 119.6   TOWER 118.6   GROUND 121.4
CITY 10 miles E   POPULATION 400,000 this week
B'CAST FREQ 1300   WHERE -   HOURS Daylight
LOCAL VorDme   FREQ 115.7   WHERE here   HOURS 24
FROM Managua   FREQ 112.1   TRACK 133°,173 n.mi.
FROM Palmar   FREQ 1670   TRACK 318°,80n.mi.
FROM Puntarenas FREQ Airport TRACK Railroad,30n.mi.
FUEL 100, JP?   CARDS Shell Int'l   CASH? Yes
REPAIRS Minor   RATE   WHERE   TIEDOWN BYO
         HOTEL   TEL
see listing

AOE 8am-12, 2-4pm

9905'
Paved
Uphill NE

ELEVATION
3049'

Bustling full service airport with longhaul jet service to about anywhere, some air-taxis and a few general aviation with recently nervous pilots. After experiencing the severe, to them, downdrafts at Pavas, they tiptoe over to here. They'd rather put up with wingtip vortices and less than handy services in exchange for a nice long runway with no surprises.

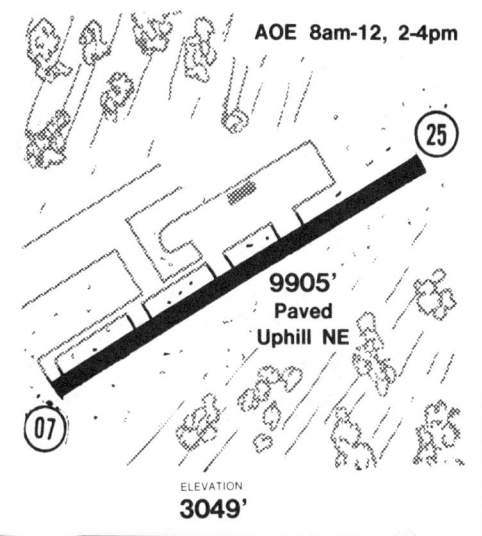

598 Finca Lutz, Costa Rica   *FEEN-cah LOOTS*

JET CHART	WAC	SECTIONAL	LATITUDE	LONGITUDE	US TIME	FOR GMT ADD	ICAO IDENT	TOWN IDENT
JN-61	CK-25 So.	TPC K-25C	09°24'	84°07'	EST	5	-	LUTZ-

OTHER COMM Traffic 123.1
SETTLEMENT Midfield   POPULATION Family ranch
FROM Cocos   FREQ 115.7   TRACK   Dme
FROM Liberia   FREQ   TRACK
FROM David   FREQ 114.3   TRACK   Dme
FUEL -   CARDS -   CASH? -
REPAIRS -   TIEDOWN BYO

*INCOMPLETE DATA

additional to be furnished

The coastline begs for at least a faceplate and fins and some underwater sightseeing. The rugged rocky leges falling into the sea, low surf level, and lush tropics with almost no development along that coast make it impossible to pass up. Give it one try and you'll be hooked.

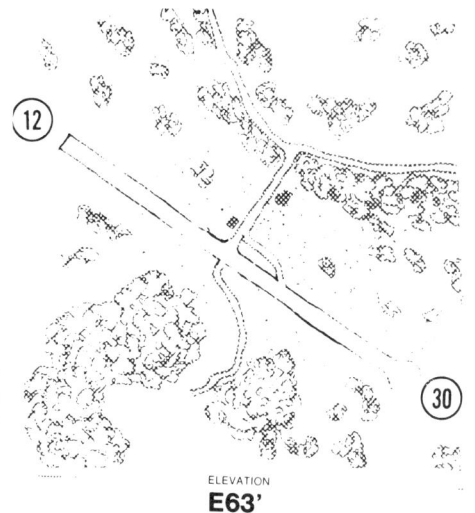

ELEVATION
E63'

Jaco Beach, Costa Rica

hah-COE beach   599

JN CHART	WAC	SECTIONAL	LATITUDE	LONGITUDE	US TIME	FOR GMT	ICAO	TOWN ID
JN-61	CK-25	TPC K25C	9°37'	84°38'	CST	+6	-	JCO -

OTHER COMM Traffic 124.8

FROM Pavas	FREQ Adf400	TRACK 221°, 34.9n.mi.
FROM Liberia	FREQ 113.7	TRACK 133°, 80.1Dme
FROM Cocos	FREQ 115.7	TRACK 223°, 32.3Dme
AVIATION GAS -	CREDIT CARDS -	CASH TYPE -

REPAIRS AVAILABLE No   TIEDOWNS? BYO; no rocks: BYO chocks

A beautiful beach resort all by itself on the Pacific side of Costa Rica. The hotel is set among the coconut palms on the left side of the picture. The farm, they're called fincas' there, is on the right.

The beach sand is not the crystal white you see elsewhere, mostly Costa Rica's west coast beaches are medium to light brown in color. The water is warm and the surf just the right size to enjoy without being intimidated.

During my measuring session a Cessna 320 dropped in: three businessmen coming down from San Jose for lunch. Manager says that happens a lot.

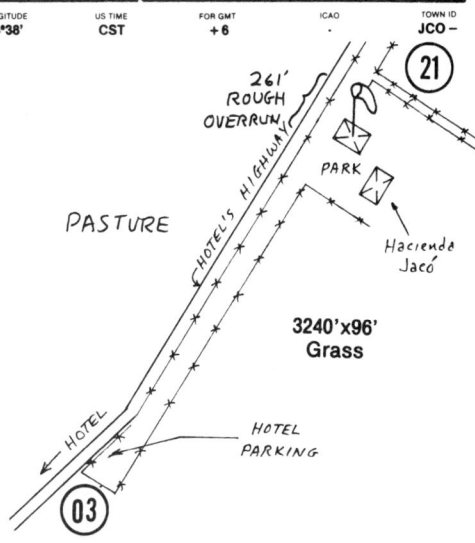

600　Puerto Quepos, Costa Rica　　　　　*PWAIR-toe KAY-poce*

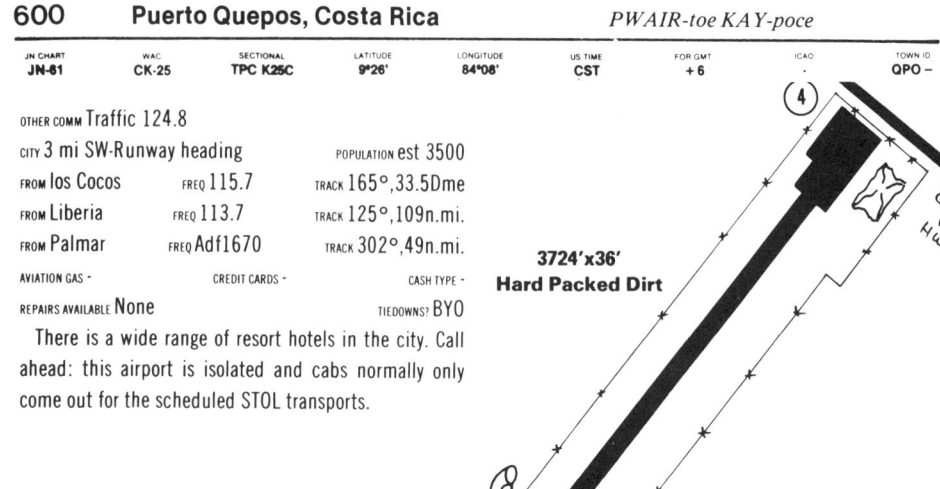

JN CHART	WAC	SECTIONAL	LATITUDE	LONGITUDE	US TIME	FOR GMT	ICAO	TOWN ID
JN-61	CK-25	TPC K25C	9°26'	84°08'	CST	+6	-	QPO-

OTHER COMM Traffic 124.8
CITY 3 mi SW-Runway heading　　POPULATION est 3500
FROM los Cocos　　FREQ 115.7　　TRACK 165°,33.5Dme
FROM Liberia　　FREQ 113.7　　TRACK 125°,109n.mi.
FROM Palmar　　FREQ Adf1670　　TRACK 302°,49n.mi.
AVIATION GAS -　　CREDIT CARDS -　　CASH TYPE -
REPAIRS AVAILABLE None　　　　TIEDOWNS? BYO

There is a wide range of resort hotels in the city. Call ahead: this airport is isolated and cabs normally only come out for the scheduled STOL transports.

**3724'x36'
Hard Packed Dirt**

ELEVATION
est 370'

Palmar Sur – Costa Rica

pall-MARR SIR 601

JET CHART	WAC	SECTIONAL	LATITUDE	LONGITUDE	US TIME	FOR GMT ADD	ICAO IDENT	TOWN IDENT
JNC-61	CK-25 So.	TPC K-25C	08°57'	83°28'	CST	6	MRPM	TIPM

OTHER COMM Traffic 118.1
CITY Adjacent all sides   POPULATION 7,000
LOCAL Ndb FREQ 1670 WHERE 3 miles SW HOURS Request
FROM los Coco   FREQ 115.7   TRACK 138°, 77Dme
FROM David   FREQ 114.3   TRACK 112°, 73Dme
FROM Puntarenas FREQ airport TRACK 124°, 98n.mi.
FUEL -   CARDS -   CASH? -
REPAIRS Minor   TIEDOWN BYO

HOTEL	RATE	WHERE	TEL
Motel Sierpe	-$	Central	-
Tico Aleman	-$	Palmar No.	-

In the lush tropical lowlands of Costa Rica's West Coast near the Panamanian border. There is some thought this may become an internacional airport so as to expedite traffic and open the area.

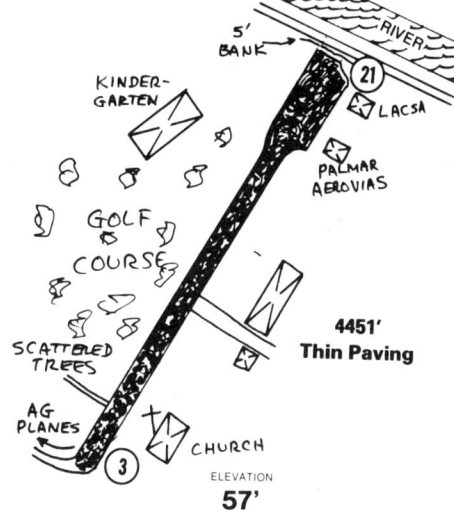

4451'
Thin Paving

ELEVATION
57'

602 Golfito — Costa Rica

goal-FEE-toe

JET CHART	WAC	SECTIONAL	LATITUDE	LONGITUDE	US TIME	FOR GMT ADD	ICAO IDENT	TOWN IDENT
JN-61	CK-25	TPC K-25C	08°39	83°11'	CST	6	MRGF	-

OTHER COMM Radio 126.9
CITY 0.5 mile S   POPULATION 4500
FROM Palmar Sur FREQ 1670 TRACK 132°, 25 n.mi.,
FROM Cocos Vor FREQ 115.7 TRACK 137°, 101 n.mi.
FROM David FREQ 114.3 TRACK 285°, 47Dme,
FUEL -   CARDS -   CASH? -
REPAIRS Minor   TIEDOWN BYO

    New internacional airport here in the SW corner of Costa Rica. Low ceilings and short visibilities are common; have an alternate in mind when filing into here. Delightful fishing and all other water sportings. Several rustic hideaways where you can become well tropicalized at modest rates.

Clearance is by part-time officers. When not clearing the monthly airplane the Inspector runs his shoe store in town. A pleasant twenty minute walk from this airport.

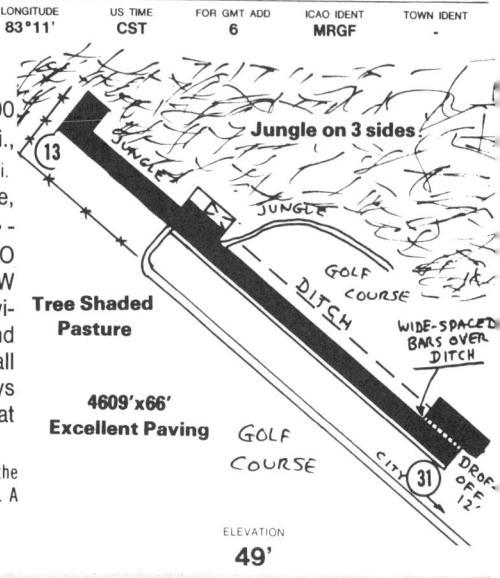

Tree Shaded Pasture

**4609'x66'
Excellent Paving**

ELEVATION
49'

Puerto Armuelles Int'l, Panama

PWAIR-toe arm-WAY-yess

603

JN CHART	WAC	SECTIONAL	LATITUDE	LONGITUDE	US TIME	FOR GMT	ICAO	TOWN ID
JN-61	CK-25	TPC K25C	8°16'	82°52'	CST	+6	-	ARM

OTHER COMM Traffic 124.0
AOE AOE
TOWN Adjacent N thru E
FROM David   FREQ 114.3
FROM Cocos   FREQ 115.7
FROM Palmar   FREQ Adf1670
AVIATION GAS 100   CREDIT CARDS -
REPAIRS AVAILABLE Minor

HOURS 9am-1pm, 3pm-5pm
POPULATION est 12,000
TRACK 251°, 26.7Dme
TRACK 137°, 131n.mi.
TRACK 134°, 54.3n.mi.
CASH TYPE Dollars(many)
TIEDOWNS? BYO

Overall 2990'x80' Grass includes: 416'x36' Paved

These fields and sheds are responsible for the shiploads of Chiquita brand bananas we find in our markets. A bustling small port at the tippy top of Panama a few hundred yards from a busier petroleum pipeline. The latter allows oil to cross the country and be picked up on the Atlantic side without the tankers going through the Canal.

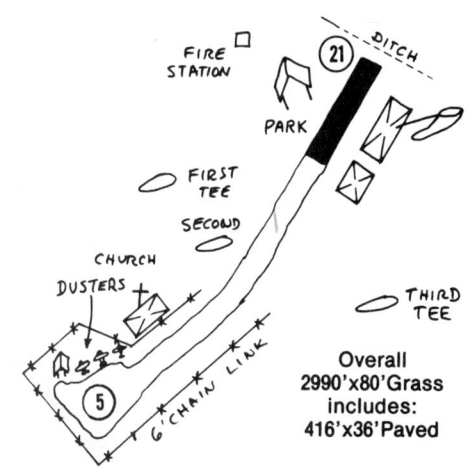

VOR RWY 4

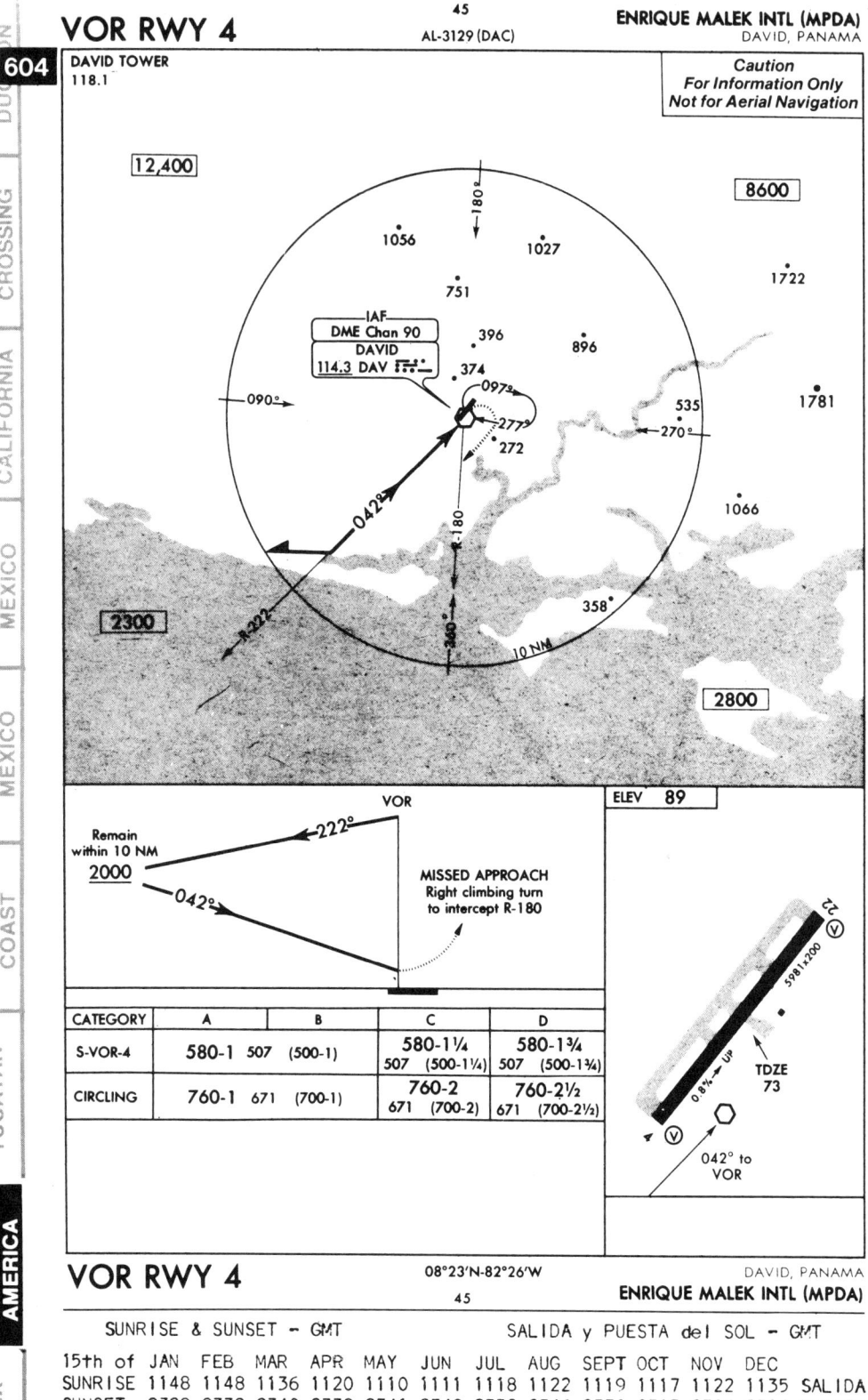

ENRIQUE MALEK INTL (MPDA)
DAVID, PANAMA

AL-3129 (DAC)

DAVID TOWER
118.1

*Caution
For Information Only
Not for Aerial Navigation*

IAF
DME Chan 90
DAVID
114.3 DAV

MISSED APPROACH
Right climbing turn to intercept R-180

Remain within 10 NM
2000
222°
042°
VOR

ELEV 89
TDZE 73

CATEGORY	A	B	C	D
S-VOR-4	580-1 507 (500-1)		580-1¼ 507 (500-1¼)	580-1¾ 507 (500-1¾)
CIRCLING	760-1 671 (700-1)		760-2 671 (700-2)	760-2½ 671 (700-2½)

042° to VOR

VOR RWY 4

08°23'N-82°26'W

DAVID, PANAMA
ENRIQUE MALEK INTL (MPDA)

SUNRISE & SUNSET – GMT   SALIDA y PUESTA del SOL – GMT

15th of   JAN   FEB   MAR   APR   MAY   JUN   JUL   AUG   SEPT OCT   NOV   DEC
SUNRISE   1148 1148 1136 1120 1110 1111 1118 1122 1119 1117 1122 1135   SALIDA
SUNSET   2329 2339 2340 2339 2341 2348 2352 2346 2330 2313 2306 2314   PUESTA
15° de   ENE   FEB   MAR   ABR   MAY   JUN   JUL   AGO   SEP   OCT   NOV   DIC

To get local time just subtract 'GMT ADD'
PARA OBTENER TIEMPO LOCAL SUSTRIAGA 'GMT ADD'

David Internacional, Panama   dah-VEED   605

JET CHART	WAC	SECTIONAL	LATITUDE	LONGITUDE	US TIME	FOR GMT ADD	ICAO IDENT	TOWN IDENT
JNC-61	CK-25 So.	TPC K-25C	08°23'	82°26'	EST	5	MPDA	DAV

tca to 700'msl   CENTER AT Ndb   RADIUS 5n.mi.

APPROACH 125.5   TOWER 118.1   GROUND 118.1

OTHER COMM Enroute 126.9 or 118.1

CITY 2 miles No.   POPULATION 90,000

B'CAST FREQ 660   WHERE -   HOURS Daylight

LOCAL VorDme   FREQ 114.3   WHERE here   HOURS 24

FROM Palmar   FREQ 1670   TRACK 112°, 73n.mi.

FROM Bocas del Toro   FREQ 114.9   TRACK 186°, 58n.mi.

FROM Taboga   FREQ 110.0   TRACK 259°, 173 n.mi.

FUEL 100   CARDS -   CASH? Yes

REPAIRS Yes   TIEDOWN BYO

HOTEL	RATE	WHERE	TEL
Hotel Nacional	$	Central	5-22-21

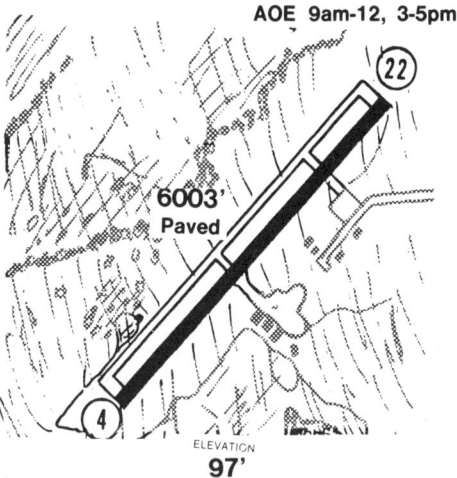

AOE 9am-12, 3-5pm

6003' Paved

ELEVATION 97'

A rich agricultural area, you hardly realize the deep tropical rainforest of Darien is only a couple hundred miles away. Almost a dry tropical city, they do raise lots of rice, coffee, and bananas. Interesting city on the Pan American Highway.

606 Santiago, Panama

sahn-tee-OGG-oh

JET CHART	WAC	SECTIONAL	LATITUDE	LONGITUDE	US TIME	FOR GMT ADD	ICAO IDENT	TOWN IDENT
JNC-61	CK-26 So.	TPC K-26L	08°05'	80°57'	EST	5	MPSA	STG

← to Santiago   to Panama City →

APPROACH · TOWER 124.0   GROUND 124.0: 6am-6pm
CITY 3 mi West   POPULATION est 7000
LOCAL Vor FREQ 114.5 WHERE Here HOURS 24
B'CAST FREQ 690   WHERE -   HOURS Daylight
FROM David   FREQ 114.3   TRACK 098°, 89.9Dme
FROM Taboga FREQ 110.0   TRACK 241°, 92.2Dme
FROM Bocas   FREQ 114.9   TRACK 131°, 107.6Dme

AVIATION GAS ·   CREDIT CARDS? ·   CASH TYPE ·
REPAIRS AVAILABLE ·   TIEDOWNS? BYO

2486'x84' Paved part

Uphill 16'

GAS PUMPS – NO GAS

CONTROL TOWER ON LOW RIDGE

1,000'++ Mowed Grass

We are looking forward to getting back to this part of Panama, this peninsula has a lot of sightseeing appeal that we want to see about. There are any number of intricate beaches with associated tidy bays. There are several plants we saw this time and have on our list for next time. As seen out here, this is a rich, productive country.

Rio Hato Panama

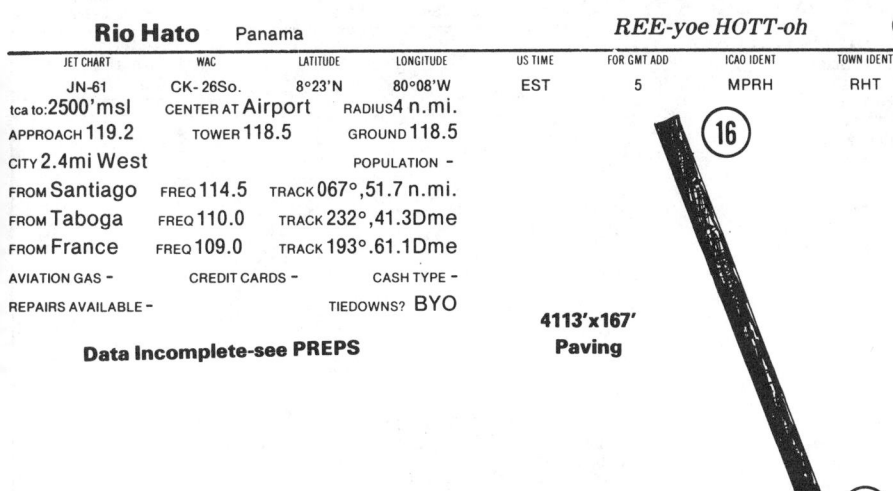

REE-yoe HOTT-oh 607

JET CHART	WAC	LATITUDE	LONGITUDE	US TIME	FOR GMT ADD	ICAO IDENT	TOWN IDENT
JN-61	CK-26So.	8°23'N	80°08'W	EST	5	MPRH	RHT

tca to: 2500'msl CENTER AT Airport RADIUS 4 n.mi.
APPROACH 119.2 TOWER 118.5 GROUND 118.5
CITY 2.4mi West POPULATION -
FROM Santiago FREQ 114.5 TRACK 067°, 51.7 n.mi.
FROM Taboga FREQ 110.0 TRACK 232°, 41.3Dme
FROM France FREQ 109.0 TRACK 193°, 61.1Dme
AVIATION GAS - CREDIT CARDS - CASH TYPE -
REPAIRS AVAILABLE - TIEDOWNS? BYO

Data Incomplete-see PREPS

(16)

4113'x167'
Paving

(34)

ELEVATION
102'msl

VOR OR NDB RWY 36

HOWARD AFB (MBHO)
BALBOA, CANAL ZONE

AL-2262 (USAF)

PANAMA CENTER APP CON
119.7 263.0
HOWARD TOWER
126.2 257.8
GND CON
130.8 275.8
ASR/PAR

**Caution
For Information Only
Not for Aerial Navigation**

IAF
TABOGA ISLAND
110.0 TBG
Chan 37
311

MISSED APPROACH
5.5 NM past "TBG" right to 2100 on heading 110°

339° 1.8 NM
1600 VOR
1700 NDB

Remain within 10 NM

ELEV 51
REIL Rwy 18
HIRL Rwy 18-36

Elev 25
PAD #1
PAD #3
PAD #4
PAD #5

339° 7.3 NM
From NDB and VORTAC

CATEGORY	A	B	C	D
S-VOR-36 †	700-1½	675 (600-1½)		700-2 675 (600-2)
S-NDB-36 †	740-1½	715 (700-1½)	760-1½ 735 (800-1½)	900-2½ 875 (900-2½)
VOR CIRCLING *	740-2	689 (700-2)		800-2¾ 749 (800-2¾)
NDB CIRCLING *	740-2	689 (700-2)	760-2 709 (800-2)	900-3 849 (900-3)

* Not authorized W of runway centerline extended due to high terrain 2½ NM W
† When ALS inop all vis 2 mi

FAF to MAP 5.5 NM

Knots	60	90	120	150	180
Min:Sec	5:30	3:40	2:45	2:12	1:50

VOR OR NDB RWY 36

08°55'N–79°36'W

BALBOA, CANAL ZONE
HOWARD AFB (MBHO)

SUNRISE & SUNSET – GMT   SALIDA y PUESTA del SOL – GMT

15th of	JAN	FEB	MAR	APR	MAY	JUN	JUL	AUG	SEPT	OCT	NOV	DEC
SUNRISE	1138	1137	1125	1108	1058	1059	1106	1110	1108	1106	1111	1125	SALIDA
SUNSET	2317	2327	2329	2328	2330	2338	2342	2335	2318	2302	2254	2301	PUESTA
15° de	ENE	FEB	MAR	ABR	MAY	JUN	JUL	AGO	SEP	OCT	NOV	DIC

To get local time just subtract 'GMT ADD'
PARA OBTENER TIEMPO LOCAL SUSTRIAGA 'GMT ADD'

Howard Air Force Base, Panama 609

JET CHART	WAC	SECTIONAL	LATITUDE	LONGITUDE	US TIME	FOR GMT ADD	ICAO IDENT	TOWN IDENT
JNC-61	CK-26 So.	TPC K-26D	08°55'	79°36'	EST	5	MBHO	HOW

tca to: 2500'msl CENTER AT Airport RADIUS 5n.mi.
APPROACH 119.7 TOWER 126.2 GROUND 130.8
OTHER COMM VFR Radar 119.2, Rescue 123.1, FSS 126.9
CITY Military base POPULATION Adjacent
LOCAL Tacan FREQ Channel 112 WHERE here HOURS 24
FROM Santiago FREQ 114.5 TRACK 057°, 92n.mi.
FROM Taboga Island FREQ 110.0 TRACK 343°, 7Dme
FUEL 115/145, JP-4 CARDS Military CASH? -
REPAIRS - TIEDOWN BYO
HOTEL RATE WHERE TEL
See Paitilla
US Air Force: for offical business only

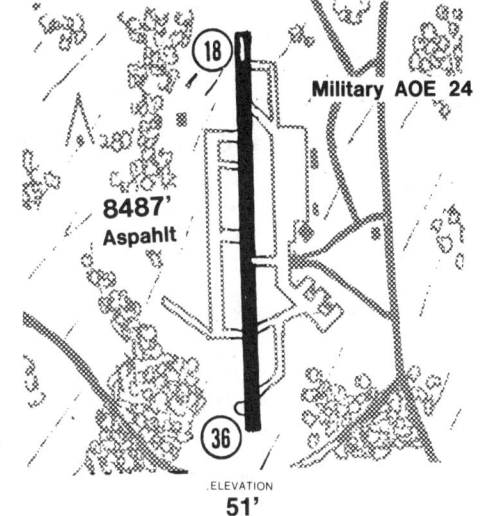

Military AOE 24

8487'
Aspahlt

ELEVATION 51'

610 Paitilla Int'l, Panama

pie-TEE-yah

JET CHART	WAC	SECTIONAL	LATITUDE	LONGITUDE	US TIME	FOR GMT ADD	ICAO IDENT	TOWN IDENT
JNC-61	CK-26 So.	TPC K-26D	08°58'	79°31'	EST	5	MPMG	MAG

tca to: 2500'msl CENTER AT Airport RADIUS 5n.mi.
APPROACH 119.2 TOWER 118.3 GROUND 121.7
OTHER COMM VFR Radar advisories 119.2
CITY Adjacent W POPULATION 550,000
B'CAST FREQ 610 WHERE - HOURS Daylight
LOCAL VorDme FREQ 117.1 WHERE 8 miles NE HOURS 24
FROM Taboga Island FREQ 110.0 TRACK 016°,12Dme
FROM Santiago FREQ 114.5 TRACK 054°,100n.mi.
FROM France FREQ 109.0 TRACK 131°,29Dme
FUEL 100LL CARDS - CASH? Yes
REPAIRS Yes TIEDOWN BYO

HOTEL	RATE	WHERE	TEL
Holiday Inn	$$	Central	69-11-22
Continental	$$	Central	64-66-66
Executive	$	Central	800-223-6764

And dozens of others.

Handy downtown internacional airport for air taxis and general aviation.

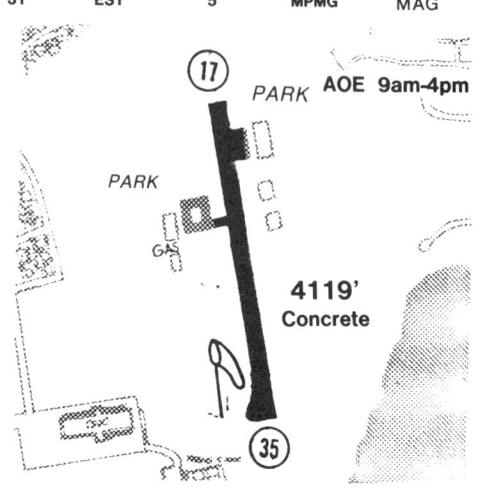

AOE 9am-4pm
4119' Concrete
ELEVATION 8' to 20'

Panama Shopping

Sitting at the world's crossroads for trade, Panama is a unique place to shop. Ladies of the Baja Bush Pilots have long since added Panama City (not Colon at the other end of the Canal) to their list of special shopping spots.

Here we were in the gift shop out at the Old City Park where handicrafts are seen not only from the Cuna Indians molas, but from Guatemala, El Salvador, and the rest of the Caribbean basin.

Several of us were shopping together when I took this picture, among us were Elsie and Bob McCaslin. Part way through the time exposure for this picture, Elsie spotted something she just had to see. She's the blur between her husband Bob at the rear and the lady in a dark dress over to his left. Better luck next time Elsie.

VOR/DME RWY 3L

TOCUMEN INTL (MPTO)
PANAMA CITY, PANAMA

AL-2069 (DAC)
115

612

PANAMA CENTER APP CON
119.7 263.0
TOCUMEN TOWER
118.1
GND CON
121.9
ASR

Caution
For Information Only
Not for Aerial Navigation

ALBROOK AAF
841
1575
320
447
570
700
1095
700
HOWARD AFB
4200
2100
2700
7 DME Arc
7 DME
13 DME
R-028
R-340
R-300
R-209
R-130
028°
208°
270°
340°
10 NM
(IAF)
DME Chan 37
JABOGA ISLAND
110.0 TBG
2100

MISSED APPROACH
Right to 3100 on 130° then direct to "TBG" and hold

ELEV 135
REIL Rwys 21L, 21R
HIRL Rwys 3L, 3R, 21L, 21R
TDZE 81
8800 x 200
10006 x 150
028° 18.3 NM from VOR

	VOR	7 DME	13 DME	18.3 DME
2100	028°	2100 / 028°	1600	1.5
	7 NM	6 NM	5.3 NM	

CATEGORY	A	B	C	D	E
S-VOR 3	660-1¾	579	(600-1¾)	660-2	579 (600-2)
CIRCLING *	660-1¾	525	(600-1¾)	700-2 565 (600-2)	760-2¼ 625 (700-2¼)

* Circling not authorized NW of Rwy 3L-21R centerline extended

FAF to MAP 5.3 NM					
Knots	60	90	120	150	180
Min:Sec	5:18	3:32	2:39	2:07	1:46

VOR/DME RWY 3L
09°04'N-79°23'W
115

PANAMA CITY, PANAMA
TOCUMEN INTL (MPTO)

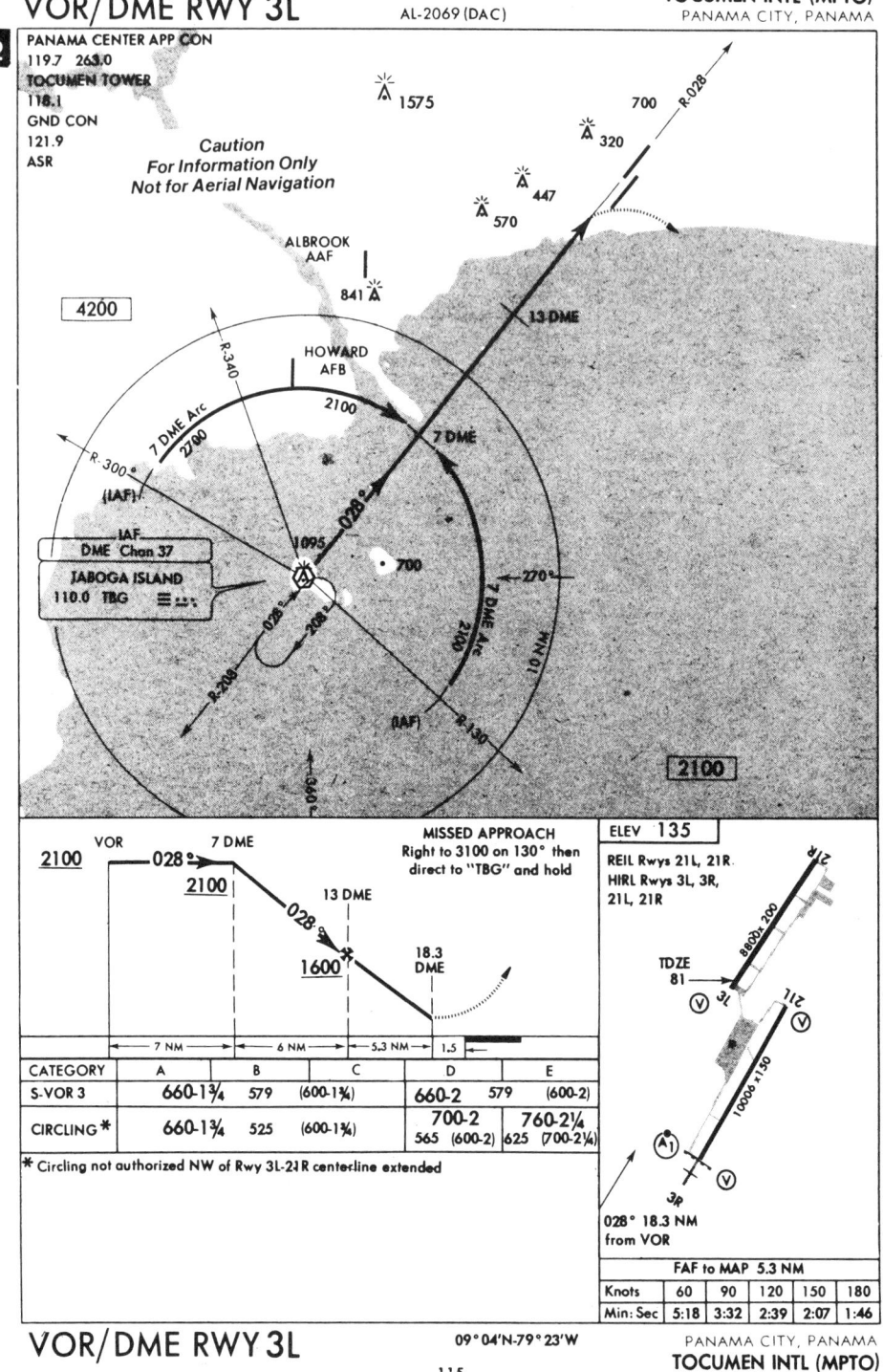

SUNRISE & SUNSET — GMT   SALIDA y PUESTA del SOL — GMT

15th of	JAN	FEB	MAR	APR	MAY	JUN	JUL	AUG	SEPT	OCT	NOV	DEC	
SUNRISE	1137	1136	1124	1107	1057	1058	1105	1109	1107	1105	1110	1124	SALIDA
SUNSET	2316	2326	2328	2327	2329	2337	2341	2334	2318	2301	2253	2300	PUESTA
15" de	ENE	FEB	MAR	ABR	MAY	JUN	JUL	AGO	SEP	OCT	NOV	DIC	

To get local time just subtract 'GMT ADD'
PARA OBTENER TIEMPO LOCAL SUSTRIAGA 'GMT ADD'

Tocumen Int'l, Panama

toe-COO-men **613**

JET CHART	WAC	SECTIONAL	LATITUDE	LONGITUDE	US TIME	FOR GMT ADD	ICAO IDENT	TOWN IDENT
JNC-61	CK-26 So.	TPC K-26D	09°05'	79°23'	EST	5	MPTO	TUM

tca to: 2500'msl CENTER AT Vor RADIUS 5n.mi.
APPROACH 119.7 TOWER 118.1 GROUND 121.9
OTHER COMM Radar advisories 119.2
CITY 13 miles NW POPULATION 550,000
B'CAST FREQ 840 WHERE - HOURS Daylight
LOCAL VorDme FREQ 117.1 WHERE 1 mile SW HOURS 24
FROM Taboga Island FREQ 110.0 TRACK 028°, 20Dme
FROM Santiago FREQ 114.5 TRACK 057°, 109n.mi.
FROM la Palma FREQ 113.1 TRACK 295°, 85n.mi.
FUEL 100LL CARDS - CASH? Yes
REPAIRS Minor TIEDOWN BYO
HOTEL RATE WHERE TEL
see Paitilla

AOE 9am-12, 3-5pm
10007' Concrete
ELEVATION 133'

Panama City's big airport, designed for the 747, DC-10, L1011 trade and frankly general aviation here is a pain. Fees are high, services difficult, and transportation not at all handy. Paitilla, in town, is for us.

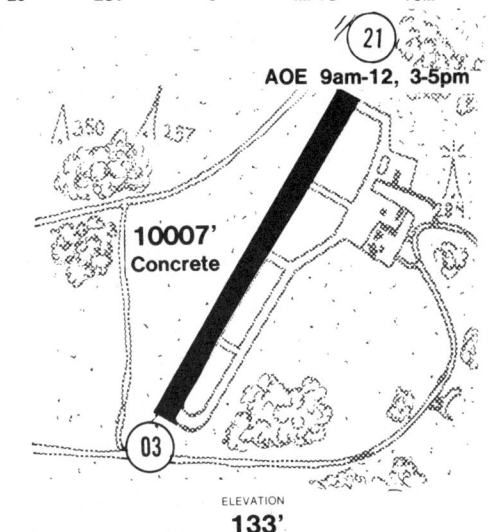

614   Isla Contadora, Panama   *EES-lah cone-tah-DARE-oh*

JN CHART	WAC	SECTIONAL	LATITUDE	LONGITUDE	US TIME	FOR GMT	ICAO	
JN-61	CK-26	TPC K26D	8°38'	79°02'	EST	+5	-	COZ

OTHER COMM Traffic 124.6
FROM Taboga   FREQ 110.0   TRACK 103°, 32.8Dme
FROM Las Palmas   FREQ 113.1   TRACK 285°, 55.5n.mi.
FROM Santiago   FREQ 114.5   TRACK 97°, 114.4n.mi.
AVIATION FUEL -   CREDIT CARDS? -   CASH TYPE?
REPAIRS AVAILABLE No   TIEDOWNS? BYO

Beautiful small resort island set in delicious water you have trouble believing when you are sitting looking at it. Clean white sandy beaches, an architecture which adds to the tropics atmosphere without intruding on it.

A vacation spot you won't want to leave and one you sure won't ever forget.

San Miguel, Panama

SAHN mee-GELL **615**

JN CHART	WAC	SECTIONAL	LATITUDE	LONGITUDE	US TIME	FOR GMT	ICAO	TOWN ID
JN-61	CK-26	TPC K26D	8°27'	78°56'	EST	+5	·	SMI

OTHER COMM Traffic 124.7
SETTLEMENT Adjacent West
POPULATION est 400
FROM Taboga FREQ 110.0 TRACK 115°, 42.6Dme
FROM La Palma FREQ 113.1 TRACK 274°, 47.7n.mi.
FROM Santiago FREQ 114.5 TRACK 079°, 121.8n.mi.
AVIATION GAS · CREDIT CARDS? · CASH TYPE ·
REPAIRS · TIEDOWNS? BYO

Pretty island-dotted point on another of the treasure islands which seem to dot both coasts of Panama. When camping here be sure to move your airplane completely out of the way of the airtaxi planes to be a good neighbor. To do? Fishing, yes, diving yes, superlative sweimming, yes, island explorationing, yes, jungle walking, yes, boredom, never.

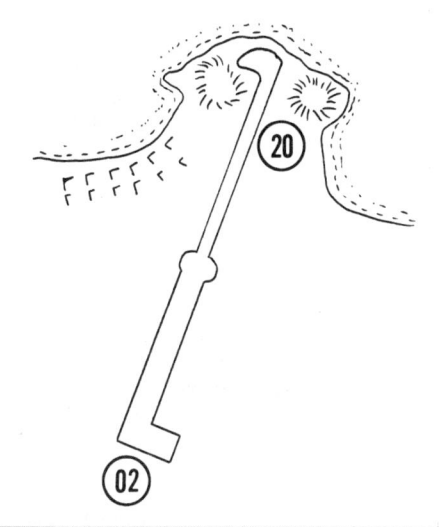

616 Punta Cocos, Panama. *POON-tah COE-coce*

JN CHART	WAC	SECTIONAL	LATITUDE	LONGITUDE	US TIME	FOR GMT	ICAO	TOWN ID
JN-61	CK-26	TPC K26D	8°13'	78°55'	EST	+$	·	PCO

OTHER COMM Traffic 122.8
SETTLEMENT Adjacent South POPULATION est 1
FROM Taboga   FREQ 110.0   TRACK 129°51.4Dme
FROM La Palma   FREQ 113.1   TRACK 257°, 47.6n.mi.
FROM Santiago   FREQ 114.5   TRACK 085°, 121n.mi.
AVIATION GAS -   CREDIT CARDS -   CASH TYPE -
REPAIRS AVAILABLE No   TIEDOWNS? BYO

Except for the watchman, this privately owned south end of Isla del Rey is quietly waiting the owner's chance to get out from Panama City and relax. He picked a winner: in less than two minutes walk there are six of the prettiest views I've ever seen.

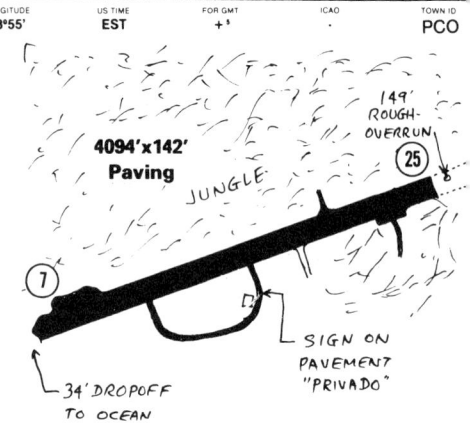

4094'x142' Paving — JUNGLE — 149' ROUGH-OVERRUN — 25 — SIGN ON PAVEMENT "PRIVADO" — 7 — 34' DROPOFF TO OCEAN

ELEVATION
48'msl

Chagres, Panama

CHOGG-ress

617

JN CHART	WAC	SECTIONAL	LATITUDE	LONGITUDE	US TIME	FOR GMT	ICAO	TOWN ID
JN-61	CK-26	TPC K26D	9°07'	79°44'	EST	+5	·	CAG

OTHER COMM Traffic 124.3
CITY 1 mi SW
POPULATION est 3500
FROM France   FREQ 109.0   TRACK 151°, 16.9Dme
FROM Taboga   FREQ 110.0   TRACK 331°, 22.3Dme
FROM Santiago FREQ 114.5   TRACK 098°, 95.1Dme
AVIATION GAS Emergency 100   CREDIT CARDS –   CASH TYPE Dollars
REPAIRS AVAILABLE Minor   TIEDOWNS? BYO

Former US Armed Forces Aeroclub on the banks of The Canal, the club now leases the runway and shelter hangars from the Panamanian government who own the Canal. This is a fine place to sit and watch the seaborne world go by. While I was measuring in the rain at least five ships passed close enough to easily read their names and ports of registry. Overnight camping with permission.

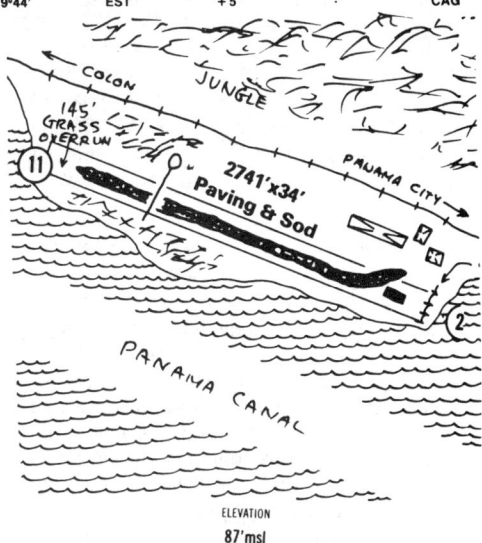

ELEVATION
87' msl

618 France Field, Panama

JET CHART	WAC	SECTIONAL	LATITUDE	LONGITUDE	US TIME	FOR GMT ADD	ICAO IDENT	TOWN IDENT
JNC-61	CK-26 So.	TPC K-26D	09°22'	79°52'	EST	5	MBFF	NFF

OTHER COMM FSS 126.9, Radar 119.2
CITY Colón 3 miles SW   POPULATION 67,000
B'CAST FREQ 1090   WHERE -   HOURS Daylight
LOCAL VorDme   FREQ 109.0   WHERE here   HOURS 24
FROM Paitilla   FREQ airport   TRACK 311°, 31 n.mi.
FROM Cartagena   FREQ 255   TRACK 256°, 266 n.mi.
FROM Bocas del Toro   FREQ 114.9   TRACK 085°, 140 n.mi.
FUEL —   CARDS —   CASH? —
REPAIRS Minor   TIEDOWN BYO

HOTEL	RATE	WHERE	TEL
Washington Hyatt	$$	Central	47-18-70

4579' Paved

ELEVATION 49'

Panamanians who hear you are going to Colon, at this Atlantic end of the Canal, will fear for your safety and with good reason. The policemen working on the street in this city advised members of the Baja Bush Pilots, on our only Colon trip, that they are unable to maintain order more than a few yards from themselves even in daylight.

Santa Isabel   Panama   *SONN-tah ees-ah-BELL*   **618A**

JET CHART	WAC	LATITUDE	LONGITUDE	US TIME	FOR GMT ADD	ICAO IDENT	TOWN IDENT
JN-61	CK-26 No.	09°32'	79°12'	EST	5	-	SIE

OTHER COMM Traffic 122.8
SETTLEMENT Adjacent So.   POPULATION Est 800
FROM France   FREQ 109.0   TRACK 073°,40.7Dme
FROM Taboga Is.   FREQ 110.0   TRACK 023°50.0Dme
FROM La Palma   FREQ 113.1   TRACK 315°,92.8n.mi.
AVIATION GAS-   CREDIT CARDS-   CASH TYPE-
REPAIRS AVAILABLE -   TIEDOWNS? BYO

A definite test for one's ability to handle a short, narrow runway with a spanking good prevailing crosswind, purely for its own sake. There are farms in the interior from here and one could make up an interesting jungle tour safe with the knowledge that you are the onliest ones ever to do so.

Store, very basic supplies.

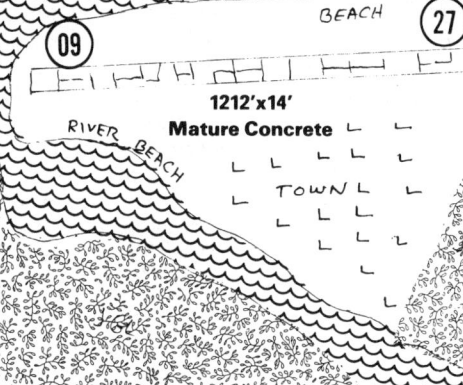

1212'x14' Mature Concrete

ELEVATION
08'msl

| 618B | **Nombre de Dios** | Panama | | | *NOME-bray day DEE-oce* |

JET CHART	WAC	LATITUDE	LONGITUDE	US TIME	FOR GMT ADD	ICAO IDENT	TOWN IDENT
JN-61	CK-26 So.	09°35'	79°29'	EST	5	-	NDI

OTHER COMM Traffic 122.8
FROM France   FREQ 109.0   TRACK 058°, 26.1Dme
FROM Taboga Is.   FREQ 110.0   TRACK 003°, 48.2Dme
FROM La Palma   FREQ 113.1   TRACK 309°, 107n.mi.
AVIATION GAS-   CREDIT CARDS-   CASH TYPE-
REPAIRS AVAILABLE -   TIEDOWNS? -

Assuming you do get stopped safely, try not to park under a coconut palm; you could find it necessary to compose a 'bizarre' letter to your insurance adjusters. A fully ripened falling coco weighs in the ten to fifteen pound range but what your insurer sees in his supermarket lacks all that armor. It will be an uphill struggle.

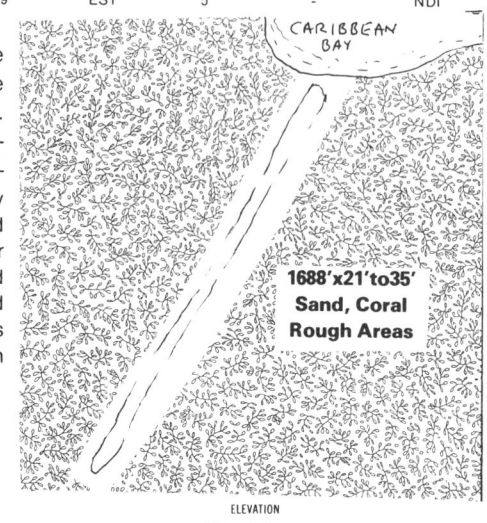

**1688'x21'to35'
Sand, Coral
Rough Areas**

CARIBBEAN BAY

ELEVATION
08'to22'msl

Isla Porvenir, Panama

EES-lah pore-venn-NEER 619

JET CHART	WAC	SECTIONAL	LATITUDE	LONGITUDE	US TIME	FOR GMT ADD	ICAO IDENT	TOWN IDENT
JNC-61	CK-26 So.	TPC K-26D	09°33'	78°57'	EST	5	-	PVR

APPROACH - TOWER 123.4 GROUND 123.4
SETTLEMENT West end POPULATION 31
FROM France FREQ 109.0 TRACK 079°,56Dme
FROM Taboga Island FREQ 110.0 TRACK 035°,59Dme
FROM Tocumen FREQ 117.1 TRACK 038°,40Dme
FUEL By airtaxi only CARDS - CASH? Yes
REPAIRS - TIEDOWN BYO

HOTEL	RATE	WHERE	TEL
Hotel Porvenir	$$	here	Tvl Agt

Delightful rustic island paradise set in the San Blas islands whose scenic vistas are merely unreal. Hundreds of square miles of water whose depth hardly ever gets all the way down to fifteen feet, there are shellfish, fishfish, coral outpoppings, fascinating islands, everything.

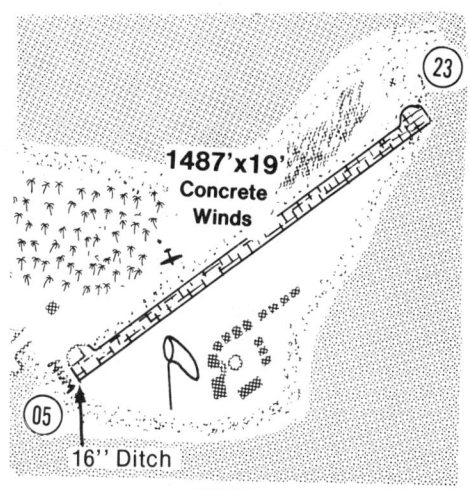

1487'x19' Concrete
Winds
16" Ditch
ELEVATION
5'6"

620 Cartí, Panama

coor-TEE

JET CHART	WAC	SECTIONAL	LATITUDE	LONGITUDE	US TIME	FOR GMT ADD	ICAO IDENT	TOWN IDENT
JN-61	CK-26 So.	TPC K-26D	9°27'	78°48'	EST	5	-	-CUR-

OTHER COMM Traffic 123.4
SETTLEMENT varies   POPULATION varies
FROM France   FREQ 109.0   TRACK 084°, 63.3 Dme
FROM Taboga   FREQ 110.0   TRACK 046°, 60.5 Dme
FUEL -   CARDS -   CASH? -
REPAIRS -   TIEDOWN BYO

Airtaxi Islanders about have this runway to themselves here in the midst of the Cuna Indian reservation. There is an official Indian frown against any foreigner, non-indian, staying the night except at Isla Porvenir. Do expect, therefore, to be received with something less than VIP treatment.

Fantastic watersports in these shallow azure waters. The water is so nice you might not want to get out after that first dip.

Copyright © 1979 Arnold D Senterfitt

1215' x 17' Concrete

ELEVATION
11'

NDB RWY 36

CRESPO (MCCG)
CARTAGENA, COLOMBIA

AL-1055 (AVN)

CARTAGENA TOWER 118.3

Caution
For Information Only
Not for Aerial Navigation

10 NM

Also Missed Approach holding

IAF
CARTAGENA
255 CTG

558°
463
1194

MIN SAFE ALT 25 NM 2800

TA 3000
TLv FL 50

NDB
2500
155°
Remain within 10 NM
1800
005°

MISSED APPROACH
To 2500 in holding pattern

ELEV 7

18
7301 x 148
TWR
36

360° to NDB

CATEGORY	A	B	C	D
S-36		1020-3¼	1013	(1100-3¼) *
CIRCLING		1020-3¼	1013	(1100-3¼) *

* Night vis 6¼

NDB RWY 36

10°27'N-75°31'W

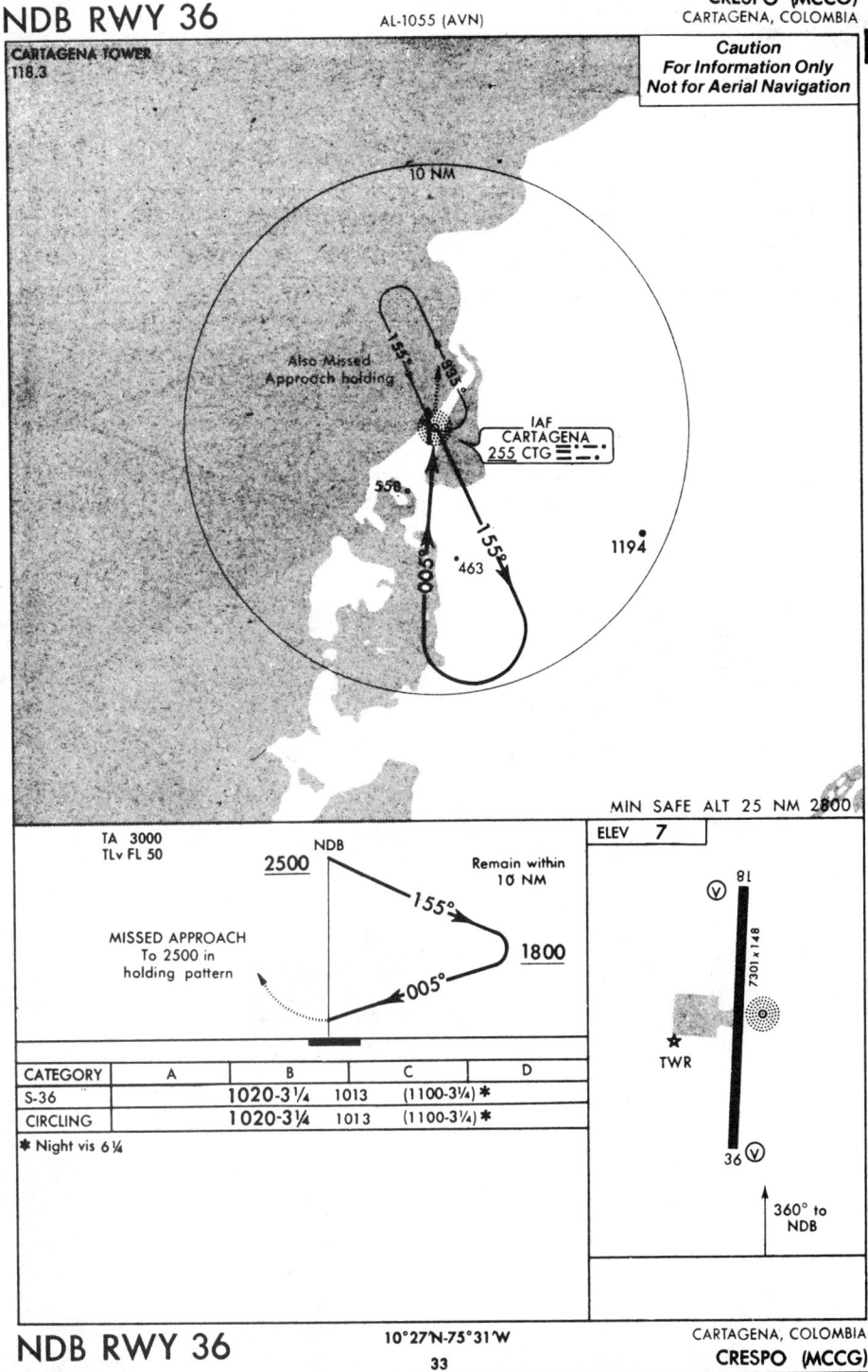

CARTAGENA, COLOMBIA
CRESPO (MCCG)

SUNRISE & SUNSET - GMT   SALIDA y PUESTA del SOL - GMT

15th of JAN FEB MAR APR MAY JUN JUL AUG SEPT OCT NOV DEC
SUNRISE 1124 1122 1109 1051 1040 1040 1047 1052 1051 1050 1057 1111 SALIDA
SUNSET   2258 2310 2312 2312 2316 2324 2328 2320 2302 2244 2236 2242 PUESTA
15° de   ENE FEB MAR ABR MAY JUN JUL AGO SEP OCT NOV DIC

To get local time just subtract 'GMT ADD'
PARA OBTENER TIEMPO LOCAL SUSTRIAGA 'GMT ADD'

622 Cartagena Int'l — Colombia

carr-tah-HAY-nah

JET CHART	WAC	SECTIONAL	LATITUDE	LONGITUDE	US TIME	FOR GMT ADD	ICAO IDENT	TOWN IDENT
JN-61	CK-26 So.	TPC K-26D	10°27'	75°31'	EST	5	MCCG	CTG

APPROACH —	TOWER 118.3	GROUND 118.3	
CITY 1 mile SW		POPULATION 145,000	
B'CAST FREQ 920	WHERE 2 mi SE	HOURS Daylight	
LOCAL Ndb	FREQ 255	WHERE here	HOURS 24
FROM Taboga	FREQ 110.0	TRACK 064°, 262 n.mi.	
FROM Turbo	FREQ 234	TRACK 026°, 156n.mi.	
FROM Barranqilla	FREQ 113.7	TRACK 242°, 44Dme	
FUEL 100	CARDS —	CASH? Dollars only	
REPAIRS Minor		TIEDOWN BYO	

HOTEL	RATE	WHERE	TEL
Don Blas	$$	Beach	4-77-10
el Dorado	$	Central	Tvl Agt
Hotel Bahia	$	Central	Local

All your childhood fantasies about pirates, the Spanish Main, tons and tons of gold, can come to real life here where it all happened.

AOE 9am-12, 2:30-4:30pm

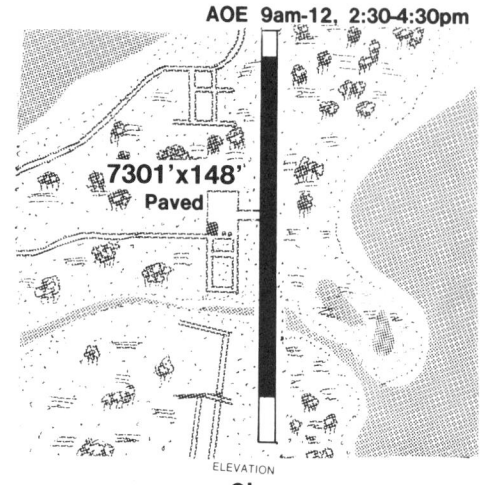

7301'x148' Paved

ELEVATION **9'**

Mexico and Centro America Climates

Climate Chart (including seasonal clothing and sanitary condition of water, milk and food)

Abbreviations:
Mex. = Mexico;
B.C.S. = Baja California
Norte; B.C.S. Baja California Sur;
Camp. = Campeche; Chih. = Chihuahua;
Chis. = Chiapas; Coah. = Coahuila;
Col. = Colima; D.F. = Distrito Federal;
Dgo. = Durango; Gro. = Guerrero;
Gto. = Guanajuato; Hgo. = Hidalgo;
Jal. = Jalisco; Méx. = México;
Mich. = Michoacán; Mor. = Morelos;
N.L. = Nuevo León; Oax. = Oaxaca;
Pue. = Puebla; Qro. = Querétaro;
Q.Roo = Quintana Roo; S.L.P. = San Luis
Potosí; Sin. = Sinaloa; Son. = Sonora;
Tab. = Tabasco; Tamps. = Tamaulipas;
Ver. = Veracruz; Yuc. = Yucatan;
Zac. = Zacatecas.

Altitude:
The altitude is indicated in meters (m) and in feet (ft.) under the name of each city. An asterisk (*) directs you to the IAMAT publication, "How to Adapt to Altitude."

Water, Milk and Food Code:
The lower case letters underneath the altitude represent the sanitary condition of Water (W), Milk (M) and Food (F).

a Drinking water is chlorinated and has no ill effect on local people. However, some strains of E.Coli, a main component of the bacterial population of the bowel, may at times be present in very small concentrations in the water. Some local strains are different than those that we are accustomed to and may cause diarrhea in those people who, like visitors, could not develop immunity because of short exposure—See IAMAT publication "Travellers' Diarrhea."
b A safe course is to drink bottled water for the first few weeks.
c All local water has to be considered contaminated.
d All tap water used for drinking, brushing teeth and making ice cubes should be boiled for ten minutes. Good brands of bottled water are available; assure that the bottle is uncapped in your presence.
e All local water is potable and safe to drink.
f Due to the presence of Giardia lamblia, a protozoan which may cause chronic diarrhea, all local water has to be considered contaminated.
g Milk is not pasteurized and should be boiled for ten minutes. Powdered and evaporated milk are available and safe.
h Milk is pasteurized and safe to drink. Butter, cheese, yoghurt and ice-cream are safe.
i Milk should be boiled for ten minutes because of improper refrigeration during distribution. Powdered and evaporated milk are available and safe.
j Butter should not be used as a table food. Local cheese, yoghurt, whipped cream and ice-cream should not be consumed.
k All meat, poultry and sea-food must be well cooked and served while hot. Pork is best avoided; vegetables should be well cooked and served hot. Salads and mayonnaise are best avoided. Fruits with intact skins should be peeled by you just prior to consumption. Avoid cold buffets, custards and any frozen dessert.
n Local meat, poultry, sea-food, vegetables and fruits are safe to eat.
o First class hotels and restaurants serve purified drinking water and reliable food. However, the hazard is left to your judgement.
p All water used for drinking, brushing teeth and making ice cubes should be boiled for ten minutes. Hot tea is advised as beverage.

Climate.
Under each month the numbers in the first column indicate, in degrees Celsius, the average daily maximum (upper) and average daily minimum (lower) temperatures that can be expected in that month. The second column represents the same readings in degrees Fahrenheit. The upper number in the third column represents the mean relative humidity %, while the lower number represents the average number of days with a measurable amount of precipitation.

Clothing Code:
Capital letters underneath the climate data.
A Lightweight cottons including cotton underwear are a must. They should permit full freedom of ventilation and movement.—See IAMAT publication "Cotton" the essential fiber to help adjust yourself to warm climates.
B Lightweight cottons are a must. Light shoulder wrap or sweater may be needed for cool evenings.
C Lightweight cottons for daytime; lightweight wool suits or dresses, sweaters for evenings are necessary.
D Light wool suits or dresses, sweaters, with lightweight topcoat for evenings.
E Wool suits and dresses, sweaters and warm topcoat are needed.
G Long, woolen underwear; thick woolen socks (two pairs); thick-soled, waterproof boots; thick trousers; heavy sweaters; long, wind-proof, fleecy-lined overcoat; inner gloves and outer mittens; fur hat with ear flaps.
H Rainwear advisable.
I Rainwear is a must.
K Sunglasses are a must.
L Sun hat is advisable.
N Travellers visiting historical sites should wear comfortable, well broken-in leather shoes. The heel should be from 1 cm (⅜ in.) to 4 cm (1½ in.) in height.
O Walking on coral reefs requires shoes with thick rubber soles.
e.g. Panamá, Panamá, 61 meters/200 feet above sea level. The Water "a", drinking water is chlorinated and has no ill effect on local people. However, some strains of E.Coli, a main component of the bacterial population of the bowel, may at times be present in very small concentrations in the water. Some local strains are different than those we are accustomed to and may cause diarrhea in those people who, like visitors, could not develop immunity because of short exposure. "b", a safe course is to drink bottled water for the first few weeks. The Milk "h" is pasteurized and safe to drink. Butter, cheese, yoghurt and ice-cream are safe. The Food "n", local meat, poultry, sea-food, vegetables and fruits are safe to eat. In January the highest average temperature is 32 degrees Celsius/89 Fahrenheit, the lowest average 23 degrees Celsius/73 Fahrenheit. The mean relative humidity is 78% and the average number of days with a measurable amount of precipitation is 3. Clothing "A", lightweight cottons including cotton underwear are a must. They should permit full freedom of ventilation and movement; "K" sunglasses are a must; "L" sun hat is advisable.

Copyright © 1979 Arnold D Senterfitt

Courtesy of IAMAT

624 Mexico and Centro America Climates

		JAN.	FEB.	MAR.	APRIL	MAY	JUNE	JULY	AUG.	SEPT.	OCT.	NOV.	DEC.
Acapulco, Gro., Mex. 28 m; 92 ft W:cdo M:ijo F:ko		31 88 75 22 72 1 AKL	31 88 74 22 72 0 AKL	31 88 74 22 72 0 AKL	31 88 75 23 73 0 AKL	32 90 74 25 77 2 AKL	32 90 76 25 77 13 AHKL	33 91 76 25 77 13 AHKL	33 91 76 25 77 13 AHKL	32 90 78 25 77 16 AKL	32 90 78 25 77 8 AKL	32 90 76 24 75 2 AKL	31 88 76 23 73 1 AKL
Belize City, Belize 5 m; 17 ft W:cdo M:ijo F:ko		27 81 91 19 67 12 B	28 82 89 21 69 6	29 84 89 22 71 4	30 86 89 23 74 5 AKL	31 87 89 24 75 7	31 87 90 24 75 13 AKL	31 87 90 24 75 15 AKL	31 88 91 24 75 14 AKL	31 87 91 24 74 15 AHKL	30 86 91 23 74 16 AHKL	28 83 93 20 68 12 BH	27 81 92 20 68 14 BH
Bluefields, Nicaragua 9 m; 28 ft W:cd M:ij F:k		29 85 78 21 69 : A	29 85 77 21 69 16 AH	31 87 76 22 72 ft	31 88 76 22 72 6 AKL	31 88 79 23 73 : AKL	31 87 80 23 73 : AKL	29 85 83 23 73 : AKL	31 87 82 23 73 : AKL	32 89 79 22 72 19 AHKL	31 88 79 22 72 20 AHKL	30 86 80 21 70 : AHKL	29 85 81 21 69 : A
Campeche, Camp., Mex. 5 m; 16 ft W:cd M:ij F:k		27 81 79 19 66 3 B	28 82 76 20 68 2 B	30 86 73 22 72 1 AKL	32 90 72 23 73 1 AKL	33 91 73 24 75 4 AKL	33 91 75 25 77 10 AKL	32 90 77 24 75 16 AKL	32 90 79 24 75 15 AKL	31 88 80 24 75 15 AHKL	30 86 79 23 73 8 AHKL	28 82 80 21 70 4 A	27 81 80 20 68 3 B
Changuinola, Panama 5 m; 16 ft W:cd M:ij F:k		32 90 : 21 70 14 AHKL	31 88 : 21 70 10 AKL	31 87 : 22 72 : AKL	32 90 : 22 72 7 AKL	32 90 : 23 73 10 AKL	32 88 : 22 72 11 AHKL	32 90 : 22 72 6 AKL	32 90 : 22 72 9 AKL	32 90 : 22 72 12 AKL	32 90 : 22 72 15 AKL	32 90 : 22 72 3 AKL	32 90 : 21 70 12 AHKL
Chihuahua, Chih., Mex. 1423 m; 4669 ft W:cdo M:ijo F:ko		18 64 50 2 36 2 D	20 68 42 4 39 1 D	24 75 35 7 45 1 C	28 82 31 12 54 1 C	31 87 31 15 59 2 CKL	34 93 36 19 66 5 BKL	32 90 51 19 66 10 BKL	31 88 54 18 64 11 BHKL	29 84 57 16 61 7 B	27 81 51 11 52 3 C	22 72 49 6 43 2 D	18 64 51 2 36 2 D
Ciudad Juárez, Chih., Mex. 1167 m; 3830 ft W:ab M:h F:n		14 57 48 0 32 1 E	17 62 41 3 37 1 D	21 69 33 6 42 1 C	25 77 28 10 50 1 C	30 86 27 14 58 1 C	34 94 31 19 67 0 BKL	34 93 45 21 70 4 AKL	33 91 49 20 68 3 BKL	30 86 49 17 63 3 BKL	25 77 46 11 52 3 C	19 66 48 6 40 0 D	14 57 50 1 33 : E
Coatzacoalcos, Ver., Mex. 14 m; 46 ft W:cd M:ij F:k		24 76 79 19 66 15 AKL	27 80 88 19 67 5 B	28 83 85 21 69 5 A	30 86 79 21 70 3 AKL	31 87 82 23 73 9 AKL	31 87 86 23 73 15 AHKL	30 86 88 23 74 19 AHKL	30 86 86 23 73 18 AHKL	29 85 88 23 73 : AKL	28 83 87 22 71 : AKL	26 79 88 20 68 20 BH	24 76 90 19 67 : B
Cobán, Guatemala 1306 m; 4285 ft W:cd M:ij F:k		23 73 84 11 52 14 C	24 75 80 11 52 10 C	25 77 77 12 53 9 C	26 79 79 13 56 10 C	26 79 82 15 59 16 CH	26 78 86 16 61 22 CI	25 77 87 16 60 25 CI	26 78 86 16 59 22 CI	25 77 87 15 60 19 CH	24 75 87 15 59 23 CH	22 72 87 14 57 21 CI	23 73 84 12 53 17 CH
Colón, Panama 4 m; 13 ft W:cd M:ij F:k		24 84 79 24 76 7 AKL	29 84 78 24 76 5 AKL	29 85 77 24 76 4 AKL	30 86 79 25 77 5 AKL	31 87 86 24 76 15 AHKL	30 86 87 24 75 17 AHKL	30 86 88 24 75 19 AHKL	30 86 88 24 75 18 AHKL	31 87 87 24 75 18 AHKL	30 86 88 23 74 19 AHKL	29 84 89 23 74 22 AIKL	29 85 85 24 74 16 AHKL
Cuernavaca, Mor., Mex. 1560 m; 5118 ft W:cdo M:ijo F:ko		25 77 : 13 55 1 C	27 81 67 13 55 1 C	29 84 68 15 59 1 C	30 86 : 17 63 3 B	27 81 : 17 63 18 BH	27 81 : 17 63 18 BH	26 79 : 16 61 19 CI	26 78 : 16 61 20 CI	25 77 : 15 59 19 CH	26 79 : 14 57 10 C	26 79 : 13 55 2 C	26 79 : 13 55 : C
David, Panama 27 m; 89 ft W:cd M:ij F:k		33 91 78 19 67 1 BKL	34 93 67 21 68 2 BKL	34 94 68 21 69 1 B	34 93 77 22 72 4 B	32 90 85 22 71 13 AHKL	31 88 88 22 71 16 AHKL	31 88 88 22 71 13 AHKL	31 88 88 22 71 14 AHKL	31 88 88 21 70 15 AHKL	30 86 90 22 70 17 BHKL	31 87 89 22 70 14 AHKL	31 88 86 21 69 8 AKL
Durango, Dgo. Mex. 1889 m; 6198 ft W:cdo M:ijo F:ko		19 66 49 5 41 2 C	21 70 44 6 43 1 C	24 75 36 8 46 1 C	27 81 36 11 52 1 C	29 84 39 14 57 : C	29 84 49 16 61 8 C	27 81 59 15 59 15 CH	26 79 61 15 59 16 CH	26 79 62 14 57 12 CH	24 75 57 11 52 6 C	22 72 49 8 46 2 C	19 66 52 6 43 5 D
Ensenada, B.C.N., Mex. 13 m; 43 ft W:cdo M:ijo F:ko		18 64 76 7 45 4 D	19 66 78 8 46 4 D	19 66 78 8 48 4 D	20 68 78 11 52 3 C	21 70 79 12 54 1 C	22 72 80 14 57 : C	25 77 82 16 61 0 B	26 78 82 17 63 0 B	25 77 82 16 61 : B	23 73 81 13 55 1 C	22 72 74 9 48 3 C	19 66 75 8 46 5 D
Guadalajara, Jal., Mex. 1589 m; 5213 ft W:cdo M:ijo F:ko		24 75 52 7 45 3 C	25 77 46 8 46 2 C	28 82 41 9 48 1 D	30 86 37 12 54 1 C	31 88 42 14 57 1 C	29 84 61 16 61 14 CH	26 79 71 15 59 23 CI	26 79 73 15 59 20 CH	26 79 73 15 59 20 CH	26 79 66 12 54 8 C	25 77 58 9 48 2 C	24 75 56 8 46 3 C

Mexico and Centro America Climates 625

	JAN.	FEB.	MAR.	APRIL	MAY	JUNE	JULY	AUG.	SEPT.	OCT.	NOV.	DEC.
Guanajuato, Gto., Mex. 2500 m; 8202 ft.* W:cdo M:ijo F:ko	21 70 47 8 46 2 C	23 73 40 16 61 2 C	25 77 34 18 64 2 C	27 81 34 20 68 3 B	28 82 41 21 70 7 B	26 79 56 20 68 13 BH	25 77 60 19 66 13 BH	25 77 60 19 66 14 BH	24 75 62 18 64 12 B	24 75 56 18 64 6 B	23 73 52 16 61 3 C	21 70 50 15 59 2 C
Guatemala, Guatemala 1480 m; 4855 ft. W:cdo M:ijo F:ko	23 73 80 12 53 4 CN	25 77 76 12 54 2 CN	27 81 69 14 57 3 CN	28 82 66 14 58 5 CN	29 84 69 16 60 15 BH	27 81 80 16 61 23 BHKLN	26 78 79 16 60 21 BIKLN	26 79 81 16 60 21 BIKLN	26 79 82 16 60 22 BIKLN	24 76 82 16 60 18 CHN	24 74 80 14 57 7 CN	22 72 80 13 55 4 CN
Guaymas, Son., Mex. 8 m; 26 ft. W:cdo M:ijo F:ko	23 73 66 13 55 2 C	24 75 73 14 57 1 C	26 79 72 16 60 2 C	29 84 79 18 64 1 BKL	31 88 84 21 69 1 BKL	34 93 87 24 76 1 AKL	34 94 90 27 80 7 AKL	35 95 93 27 80 8 AKL	35 95 87 26 78 6 AKL	29 84 82 22 72 2 AKL	28 82 74 18 64 3 B	23 74 73 13 56 5 B
Hermosillo, Son., Mex. 187 m; 615 ft. W:cdo M:ijo F:ko	25 77 50 8 46 1 C	27 81 44 8 47 1 C	29 84 40 10 50 1 C	31 88 36 11 52 1 CKL	36 96 32 15 59 1 BKL	39 102 33 19 67 0 BKL	39 102 51 23 73 6 AKL	39 103 51 23 73 7 AKL	39 102 51 22 73 3 AKL	36 97 45 18 65 2 BKL	29 85 42 13 55 2 CKL	25 77 44 8 47 2 C
La Paz, B.C.S., Mex. 13 m; 43 ft. W:cdo M:ijo F:ko	22 72 64 14 57 1 C	23 74 64 13 56 1 C	27 80 66 13 56 0 C	27 83 72 16 60 0 C	31 88 77 18 64 0 C	33 92 82 21 69 1 BKL	35 95 85 24 75 3 AKL	34 93 86 24 76 4 AKL	33 92 85 24 76 4 AKL	32 89 90 22 71 1 AKL	27 81 73 19 66 0 B	25 77 65 8 C
Limón, Costa Rica m; ft. W:cd M:ij F:k	32 90 86 18 64 BKL	33 91 63 18 64 BIKL	31 88 78 17 63 10 C	32 90 86 19 66 0 C	31 88 85 19 66 BKL	30 86 86 19 66 15 BHKL	31 88 86 19 66 22 BKL	31 88 88 19 66 16 BKL	86 9	33 91 85 20 68 13 BHKL	31 88 86 19 66 18 BHKL	31 87 84 19 66
Managua, Nicaragua 55 m; 180 ft. W:cdo M:ijo F:ko	31 88 69 21 69 0 AKL	32 89 63 21 70 0 AKL	33 91 61 22 72 0 AKL	34 94 54 23 74 1 AKL	34 93 66 23 74 1 AKL	31 88 82 23 73 13 AHKL	31 88 81 23 73 11 AHKL	32 89 84 23 73 10 AHKL	32 89 84 23 73 11 AHKL	31 88 80 22 72 10 AHKL	31 88 75 22 71 3 AKL	31 87 70 21 70 1 AKL
Manzanillo, Col., Mex. 8 m; 26 ft. W:cdo M:ijo F:ko	30 86 76 20 68 1 BKL	29 85 78 19 67 0 BKL	30 86 76 19 66 0 BKL	31 87 77 19 67 0 BKL	32 89 82 22 71 1 AKL	33 91 86 24 76 6 AKL	34 93 87 24 76 10 AKL	34 93 85 24 76 11 AKL	32 90 85 24 76 11 AKL	33 91 84 24 76 5 AKL	32 89 83 22 73 1 AKL	31 87 78 21 70 1 AKL
Matamoros, Tamps., Mex. 7 m; 24 ft. W:ab M:h F:n	21 69 77 11 51 3 C	22 72 77 12 54 2 C	25 77 70 13 56 4 C	28 82 75 19 66 4 B	31 87 76 22 71 6 AKL	33 91 76 23 74 7 AKL	34 93 75 24 75 5 AKL	34 93 77 24 75 9 AHKL	32 90 77 23 73 9 AHKL	29 85 75 19 66 6 B	24 76 73 15 59 4 C	22 71 78 12 53 3 C
Mazatlán, Sin., Mex. 78 m; 256 ft. W:cdo M:ijo F:ko	22 71 65 16 61 1 C	22 71 66 17 62 1 C	23 73 69 17 63 0 C	28 82 75 19 66 0 B	27 80 73 21 70 0 B	29 84 76 24 76 4 AKL	30 86 80 25 77 14 AHKL	30 86 81 25 77 15 AHKL	30 86 79 25 77 14 AHKL	29 85 79 24 76 4 AKL	27 80 75 22 71 2 AKL	24 75 74 18 65 2 B
Mérida, Yuc., Mex. 22 m; 72 ft. W:cdo M:ijo F:ko	28 83 73 17 62 8 BN	29 85 73 17 63 6 BN	32 89 75 19 66 6 BKLN	33 92 82 22 71 2 AKLN	34 94 84 22 72 10 AKLN	33 92 86 23 73 19 AHKLN	33 92 81 23 73 20 AHKLN	33 91 84 23 73 19 AHKLN	32 90 82 23 73 20 AHKLN	31 87 79 22 71 17 AHKLN	29 85 74 22 71 12 BHN	28 82 74 18 64 9 BN
México, D.F., Mex. 2308 m; 7572 ft.* W:cdo M:ijo F:ko	21 70 54 5 41 2 CN	23 73 48 7 45 2 CN	26 79 44 9 48 3 C	27 81 45 10 50 8 B	26 79 53 11 52 13 CHN	25 77 64 12 54 18 CHN	23 73 70 11 52 23 CIN	23 73 72 11 52 22 CIN	22 72 72 11 52 19 CIN	22 72 66 10 50 9 CN	22 72 61 7 45 4 CN	21 70 58 6 43 3 CN
Monterrey, N.L., Mex. 538 m; 1765 ft. W:cdo M:ijo F:ko	20 68 66 9 48 5 D	23 73 65 11 52 5 C	26 79 61 13 55 4 C	30 86 63 18 64 5 B	31 88 66 20 68 4 B	33 91 66 22 72 6 AKL	34 93 63 22 72 4 AKL	34 93 66 22 72 8 AKL	31 88 70 21 70 9 B	27 81 71 17 63 7 B	24 75 70 13 55 5 C	21 70 68 10 50 4 D
Morelia, Mich., Mex. 1941 m; 6368 ft. W:ab M:ijo F:ko	21 70 60 7 45 2 C	23 73 61 8 46 1 C	26 79 59 11 52 1 C	27 81 48 12 54 3 C	27 81 54 14 57 7 C	25 77 67 15 59 17 CH	23 73 72 14 57 21 CI*	23 73 73 14 57 19 CH	23 73 73 14 57 17 CH	23 73 69 12 54 9 C	22 72 66 9 48 3 C	21 70 65 8 46 3 C
Nuevo Laredo, N.L., Mex. 125 m; 410 ft. W:ab M:h F:n	19 66 65 7 44 2 D	23 73 64 10 50 3 C	26 79 57 13 56 0 C	31 88 59 18 64 2 BKL	34 94 60 22 71 2 AKL	37 98 59 24 75 2 CH	38 100 56 24 76 2 AKL	37 100 56 25 77 7 AKL	34 94 64 23 73 4 AKL	31 87 63 18 65 3 BKL	24 75 65 12 54 3 C	21 70 67 8 47 3 C

626 Mexico and Centro America Climates

	CENTRO AMERICA	YUCATAN	COCONUT COAST	NORTHEAST MEXICO	NORTHWEST MEXICO	BAJA CALIFORNIA	BORDER CROSSING	
Oaxaca, Oax., Mex. 1528 m; 5012 ft W:cdo M:ijo F:ko	25 77 59 8 47 2 C	27 81 58 10 50 2 C	29 85 55 12 54 2 C	31 88 56 14 57 4 CKL	31 87 62 15 59 12 C	28 83 72 16 60 12 CKL	27 81 71 15 59 9 CKL	27 80 75 14 58 7 CKL	26 79 70 13 56 4 C	26 79 64 11 52 2 C	25 77 62 9 48 2 C
Pachuca, Hgo., Mex. 2426 m; 7959 ft* W:cdo M:ijo F:ko	19 66 ... 5 41 2 D	21 70 ... 6 43 3 C	23 73 ... 8 46 3 C	24 75 ... 10 50 7 C	23 73 ... 10 50 9 C	21 70 ... 11 52 11 DH	20 68 ... 10 50 12 DH	19 66 ... 10 50 12 DH	19 66 ... 8 46 6 C	19 66 ... 7 45 4 D	19 66 ... 6 43 3 D
Panamá, Panama 61 m; 200 ft W:ab M:h F:n	32 89 78 23 73 3 AKL	32 90 75 23 74 2 C	33 91 73 23 74 1 C	33 92 74 24 74 3 AKL	32 89 84 24 76 12 AHKL	31 88 86 24 75 13 AHKL	31 88 86 24 75 14 AHKL	31 87 86 23 73 11 AHKL	31 87 87 23 74 14 AHKL	31 87 83 23 74 16 AHKL	31 88 82 23 74 10 AKL
Progreso, Yuc., Mex. 8 m; 26 ft W:ab M:h F:n	25 77 77 19 66 2 B	26 79 74 19 66 2 B	29 84 73 21 70 1 B	30 86 74 22 72 1 C	30 86 77 23 73 2 AKL	30 86 80 24 75 5 AKL	30 86 83 24 75 5 AKL	31 87 81 24 75 8 AHKL	32 89 77 24 75 5 AKL	30 86 75 23 73 3 AKL	26 79 75 20 68 3 B
Puebla, Pue., Mex. 2162 m; 7093 ft* W:cdo M:ijo F:ko	21 70 54 7 45 2 C	23 73 49 8 46 1 C	25 77 43 11 52 3 C	27 81 45 12 54 6 C	29 84 54 13 55 11 C	28 83 64 13 55 18 CH	24 75 67 12 54 19 CH	24 75 70 12 54 19 CH	24 75 65 12 54 10 C	23 73 59 8 46 4 C	22 72 57 7 45 1 C
Puerto Cabezas, Nicaragua 15 m; 50 ft W:cd M:ij F:k	29 84 88 21 69 24 AI	30 86 87 22 72 9 AKL	31 88 84 22 73 5 AKL	32 89 84 22 74 6 AKL	32 89 87 23 74 ... AKL	32 89 86 23 73 18 AIKL	32 89 83 23 73 17 AHKL	32 89 89 23 73 18 AHKL	32 89 87 23 73 19 AHKL	30 86 88 22 71 19 AHKL	29 85 89 21 70 ... A
Puerto Vallarta, Jal., Mex. 5 m; 16 ft W:cdo M:ijo F:ko	29 84 ... 17 63 1 B	... 30 86 ... 16 61 1 BKL	... 30 86 ... 17 63 ... BKL	31 88 ... 18 64 1	32 90 ... 20 68 4 BKL	33 91 ... 20 68 1 BKL	35 95 ... 23 73 18 AHKL	34 93 ... 23 73 18 AHKL	34 93 ... 22 72 7	33 91 ... 20 68 1 BKL	30 86 ... 18 64 1 BKL
Puntarenas, Costa Rica 3 m; 10 ft W:cd M:ij F:k	33 91 66 24 75 3 AKL	33 91 67 23 73 ... AKL	33 91 69 25 77 2 AKL	32 90 80 25 77 4 AKL	31 88 81 24 74 7 AKL	31 88 85 24 75 17 AHKL	31 88 83 24 75 19 AHKL	30 86 82 23 73 20 AHKL	30 86 83 23 73 17 AHKL	30 86 82 23 73 11 AHKL	31 88 75 22 72 3 AKL
Querétaro, Qro., Mex. 1842 m; 6043 ft W:cdo M:ijo F:ko	23 73 50 7 45 2 C	25 77 46 8 46 1 C	28 82 41 10 50 2 C	30 86 47 13 55 6 CKL	31 88 41 14 57 3 CKL	29 84 56 15 59 10 CKL	27 81 61 14 57 11 CHKL	26 79 63 13 55 8 C	26 79 59 11 52 5 C	25 77 54 9 48 2 C	24 75 53 7 45 2 C
Rio Hato, Panama 30 m; 100 ft W:cd M:ij F:k	32 90 74 22 72 1 C	33 91 70 23 74 0 C	33 91 71 23 74 0 C	33 91 73 23 74 7 CKL	31 88 81 23 74 7 AKL	31 87 86 23 73 10 AKL	31 87 85 23 73 10 AKL	31 87 86 23 73 8 AKL	31 87 88 23 73 12 AHKL	31 87 86 23 73 11 AHKL	31 88 83 23 74 6 AKL
San Cristobal de las Casas, Chs., Mex. 2276 m; 7467 ft* W: M: F:	20 68 81 4 40 2 D	20 68 79 5 41 2 D	20 68 78 6 43 3 D	22 72 79 9 49 13 CH	22 72 79 9 49 12 CH	22 72 79 10 50 17 CH	22 72 78 10 50 17 CH	21 70 80 10 50 21 CI	21 70 81 9 49 12 CH	20 68 81 7 45 7 D	20 68 81 5 41 1 D
San José, Costa Rica 1146 m; 3760 ft W:ab M:h F:k	24 75 73 14 58 3 C	24 76 70 14 58 1 C	24 76 78 14 58 3 C	27 80 78 15 59 19 CH	27 80 79 16 60 14 CH	25 77 82 17 62 23 BI	26 78 85 16 61 24 BI	25 77 84 16 60 21 CI	25 77 85 16 60 25 CH	25 77 79 16 60 14 CH	24 75 76 14 58 6 C
San Lucas, B.C.S., Mex. 25 m; 82 ft W:cdo M:ijo F:ko	26 79 ... 14 57 2 C	26 79 ... 13 55 0 C	26 79 ... 14 57 2 B	26 79 ... 15 59 0 B	27 81 ... 16 61 0	30 86 ... 18 64 0 BKL	33 91 ... 25 77 1 BI	33 91 ... 25 77 4 AKL	32 90 ... 22 72 2 AKL	29 84 ... 19 66 0 B	27 81 ... 16 61 1 C
San Luis Potosi, S.L.P., Mex. 1859 m; 6100 ft W:cdo M:ijo F:ko	20 68 61 6 42 1 D	23 74 58 8 46 1 C	26 79 56 11 51 2 C	26 79 56 13 55 4 C	28 82 62 15 59 6 C	26 79 66 14 58 6 C	26 79 66 13 56 4 C	24 76 68 13 56 4 C	24 75 67 11 52 3 C	22 71 65 8 47 2 C	21 69 65 7 45 1 C
San Miguel, El Salvador 106 m; 348 ft W:cdo M:ij F:ko	35 95 58 19 66 0 BKL	36 97 53 19 66 0 C	37 99 53 20 68 0 C	38 100 63 23 73 0 AKL	36 97 67 24 75 11 AHKL	34 93 76 23 73 20 AHKL	33 91 77 22 72 16 AHKL	32 90 80 22 72 18 AHKL	33 91 80 22 72 18 AHKL	33 91 73 21 70 9 AKL	35 95 63 20 68 1 BKL

Mexico and Centro America Climates 627

Location	Jan	Feb	Mar	Apr	May	Jun	Jul	Aug	Sep	Oct	Nov	Dec
San Miguel, Cozumel I., Q.Roo, Mex. 3 m; 10 ft. W:cdo M:ijo F:ko	29 84 20 68 BKL	29 84 22 71 AKL	31 87 23 73 AHKL	32 89 24 75 AHKL	33 91 24 75 AHKL	32 89 24 75 AHKL	32 89 24 75 AHKL	32 89 24 75 AHKL	32 89 23 73 AKL	32 89 22 71 AKL	30 86 21 69 AKL	29 84 20 68 BKL
San Miguel de Allende, Gto. Mex. 1852 m; 6076 ft. W:cdo M:ijo F:ko	26 79 9 48 C	27 81 11 52 C	28 82 14 57 C	28 82 16 61 BKL	28 82 16 61 BKL	25 77 17 63 C	25 77 16 61 C	25 77 16 61 C	25 77 15 59 C	25 77 14 57 C	25 77 12 54 C	26 79 9 48 C
San Salvador, El Salvador 682 m; 2238 ft. W:cdo M:ijo F:ko	32 90 16 60 BKL	31 87 17 63 C	31 87 18 65 BHKL	31 87 19 66 BHKL	31 87 19 66 BHKL	29 84 19 66 BIKL	29 84 19 66 BIKL	29 85 19 66 BIKL	29 85 19 66 BHKL	29 85 18 64 BHKL	30 86 18 64 BKL	32 90 15 59 CKL
Santa Ana, El Salvador 647 m; 2123 ft. W:cd M:ij F:k	29 84 12 54 CKL	31 87 11 52 C	31 88 17 63 BKL	31 88 19 66 BIKL	32 89 21 69 BHKL	29 84 21 69 BHKL	29 84 21 69 BHKL	29 84 21 69 BIKL	29 84 21 69 BIKL	29 84 21 69 BHKL	29 84 21 69 BHKL	29 84 18 64 BKL
Tampico, Ver., Mex. 12 m; 39 ft. W:cdo M:ijo F:ko	23 73 14 57 C	27 81 17 63 C	29 84 21 70 AKL	31 88 24 75 AKL	31 88 24 75 AKL	31 88 24 75 AKL	31 88 24 75 AKL	31 88 24 75 AKL	31 88 24 75 AKL	30 86 23 73 AKL	26 79 18 64 B	25 77 14 57 C
Tapachula, Chis., Mex. 109 m; 356 ft. W:cd M:ij F:k	33 91 17 63 BKL	32 90 17 63 BKL	32 90 17 63 BKL	31 88 19 67 BHKL	31 88 21 69 BHKL	29 84 21 69 BHKL	29 84 21 69 BHKL	29 84 21 69 BHKL	29 84 21 69 BHKL	29 84 21 69 BHKL	30 86 18 64 BKL	33 91 17 63 BKL
Taxco, Gro., Mex. 1171 m; 3842 ft. W:cd M:ij F:k	26 79 14 57 C	25 77 16 61 C	26 79 17 63 BH	30 86 19 67 BHKL	25 77 19 67 BH	25 77 19 67 BH	26 79 17 63 BH	25 85 19 67 BHKL	27 81 18 64 BH	30 86 18 64 BHKL	26 79 15 59 C	26 79 14 57 C
Tegucigalpa, Honduras 1004 m; 3294 ft. W:cdo M:ijo F:ko	26 78 6 43 C	27 81 4 40 C	28 82 5 41 B	28 82 5 41 B	30 86 12 53 CKL	31 87 11 51 CI	31 87 11 51 CI	31 87 11 51 CI	29 85 11 52 CI	29 84 12 54 CI	26 78 10 50 B	27 81 8 46 B
Toluca, Mex., Mex. 2680 m; 8793 ft. W:cdo M:ijo F:ko	16 61 3 37 D	18 64 4 39 D	18 64 4 39 D	19 66 10 50 DH	19 66 10 50 DH	18 64 9 48 DH	18 64 9 48 DI	18 64 9 48 DI	18 64 7 45 DH	19 66 8 46 C	17 63 5 41 D	16 61 3 37 D
Torreón, Coah., Mex. 1143 m; 3750 ft. W:cdo M:ijo F:ko	27 80 5 41 C	28 82 7 44 B	31 88 12 53 C	34 94 15 59 BKL	37 99 16 60 BKL	38 100 16 60 BKL	37 99 16 60 BKL	36 97 16 61 BKL	34 94 15 59 CKL	32 90 11 52 CKL	28 83 6 43 B	27 80 5 41 C
Tuxpan, Ver., Mex. 3 m; 9 ft. W:cdo M:ijo F:ko	23 73 14 57 C	26 78 17 62 B	29 84 19 66 C	32 89 22 72 C	33 91 23 74 AHKL	32 89 23 74 AHKL	32 89 23 74 AHKL	32 89 23 74 AHKL	32 89 22 72 AKL	30 86 21 70 AKL	28 83 18 64 BH	24 75 14 57 C
Uruapan, Mich., Mex. 1634 m; 5361 ft. W:cdo M:ijo F:ko	24 75 7 45 C	25 77 10 50 C	25 77 12 54 C	25 77 14 57 CI	25 77 14 57 CI	25 77 15 59 CI	25 77 14 57 CI	25 77 14 57 CI	25 77 14 57 CI	25 77 10 50 C	25 77 10 50 B	24 75 8 46 C
Veracruz, Ver., Mex. 16 m; 52 ft. W:cdo M:ijo F:ko	25 77 19 66 B	26 78 19 67 B	27 80 20 68 B	28 83 22 72 A	30 86 23 74 AHKL	31 87 23 74 AHKL	31 87 23 74 AHKL	31 87 23 74 AHKL	30 86 23 73 AHKL	29 85 23 73 AHKL	27 80 21 69 B	26 78 19 67 B
Villahermosa, Tab., Mex. 17 m; 55 ft. W:cdo M:ijo F:ko	24 76 19 66 B	26 78 19 67 B	28 83 21 69 B	31 87 21 70 B	32 89 23 73 AKL	31 87 23 73 AHKL	31 87 23 73 AHKL	31 87 23 73 AHKL	30 86 23 73 BH	30 86 23 73 AKL	26 79 20 68 B	24 76 19 67 B
Zacatecas, Zac., Mex. 2446 m; 8025 ft. W:cdo M:ijo F:ko	20 68 4 39 D	20 68 5 41 D	23 73 7 45 C	25 77 9 48 C	26 79 12 54 C	26 79 12 54 BH	24 75 11 52 C	24 75 11 52 C	24 75 11 52 C	24 75 11 52 C	21 70 5 41 D	20 68 4 39 D

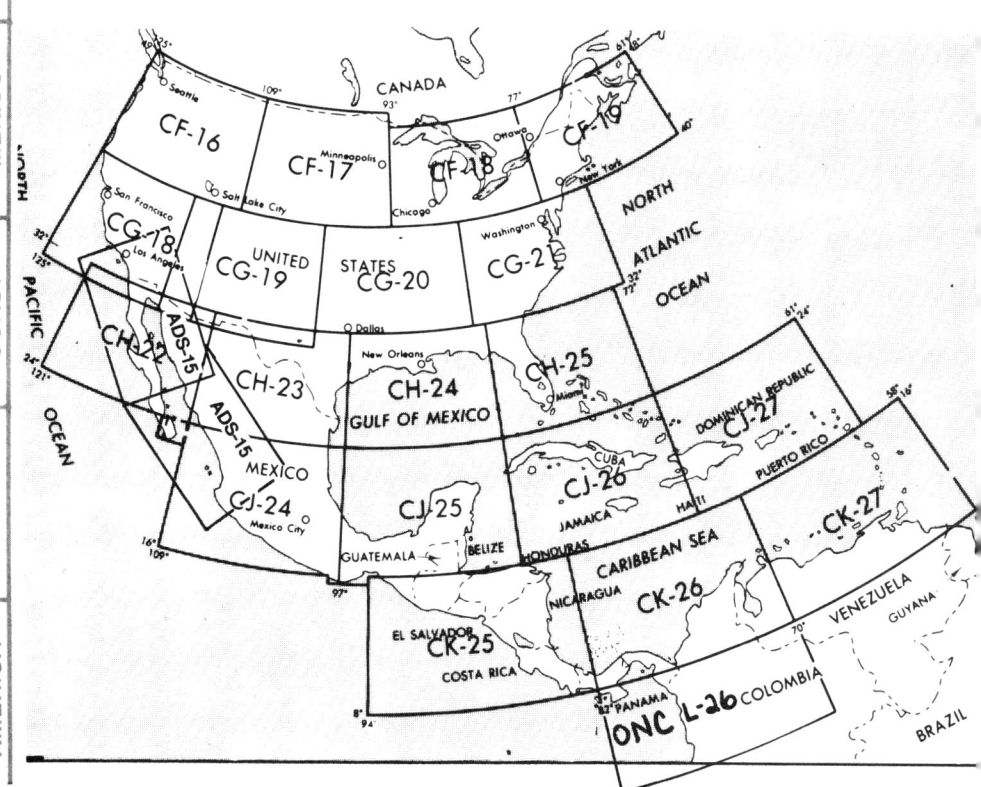

627A World Aeronautical Charts, WACs

WORLD AERONAUTICAL CHARTS
Scale 1:1,000,000

	Current Edition Number and Date		Next Edition
WAC CF-16	11	Feb 18 82	2/17/83
*WAC CF-17	11	Sep 3 81	9/2/82
WAC CF-18	11	Nov 26 81	11/25/82
WAC CF-19	12	May 13 82	5/12/83
WAC CG-18	12	Jun 10 82	6/9/83
WAC CG-19	12	Jul 8 82	7/7/83
WAC CG-20	11	Aug 5 82	8/4/83
WAC CG-21	12	Oct 29 81	10/28/82
WAC CH-22	5	Oct 29 81	10/27/83
WAC CH-23	12	Apr 15 82	4/14/83
WAC CH-24	12	Oct 1 81	9/30/82
WAC CH-25	12	Jan 21 82	1/20/83
WAC CJ-24	5	Dec 24 81	12/22/83
WAC CJ-25	5	Jan 21 82	1/19/84
WAC CJ-26	5	Mar 18 82	3/15/83
WAC CJ-27	5	May 13 82	5/11/84
WAC CK-25	4	Mar 18 82	3/15/84
WAC CK-26	4	Oct 30 80	10/28/82
'WAC CK-27	4	Sep 4 80	9/2/82

The Last Page 627B

I know this is a funny place to have "The Last Page" but there you are. Unless I have miscounted we have 655 pages, the printer must work in 16 page multiples. Here are a couple of things I wanted to say but didn't get done so let's clear them up now.

$50 Telephone Calls

There are two ways to make a Long Distance (Larga Distancia) telephone call in Latin America: the local Larga Distancia agency or via a hotel switchboard. The hotel will recommend you use their service for speed, modern equipment, ease of billing, no language problem. And they are right on those points. But the hotel generally charges a service fee that can be an unwelcome surprise at checkout time.

I have paid more than $45 US dollars service charge for a call home on which the long distance bill portion was just over $5 US dollars.

There are two alternatives: negotiate the service charge first, or go to the Larga Distancia office and place your call without a service charge. There is a LD facility in each city I've looked for one, down to the 4,000 population Palenque.

You will need to be patient about language and waiting. In some places such as remote Chetumal I've waited half an hour to get through on a call to the states.

Helicopter Entries To Mexico

The thrust of this book is to provide information for fixed wing pilots wishing to do the administrative things to visit Mexico and Central America. Because they can land anywhere, helicopters are handled differently both at border crossing and for incountry handling.

Basically the reason for special handling is that the officials want to know why you are going to the huge expense of flying a chopper. Marvin Patchen is known as an explorer type so he gets through easily, one medical group has a rich doctor who likes to fly his Bell. The officials know that now.

I am indebted to Marvin Patchen for the following procedure for getting advance permission to fly a helicopter in Mexico. He has tried it out by doing it several times so I know the method works.

1. Write a letter to the airport commandante at your intended border crossing point at least a month before the planned flight. Identify yourself, the aircraft, passengers, and date plus purpose of the planned flight.
2. Check with the commandante of that airport two weeks before to see if there are any unanswered questions.
3. On the day of crossing the first time, don't be surprised if it takes nearly a full day of telephone calls and pieces of paper. Some pilots have told me that getting through the border at all that first time could be expecting a lot.
4. Get names and telephone numbers. Latin countries are very people oriented so knowing how to directly reach someone who was helpful and effective this time is vital to getting through more easily next time.
5. Write and tell me any usual experiences you have. Use the address on page 4 of this book. In the next edition I plan a helo section up front to cover the complete process.

That's It

This book has gone together a lot differently than all the editions which have gone before. Cancer got in the way, some   I wrote or researched and photographed on data gathering trips between sessions of radiation and chemotherapy.

But in all honesty writing about the fun Grace and I have had and you will have in these places extends our enjoyment. In the months ahead we'll be filling in some of the blanks in this book and working on the next edition. You will get a PREP or two by mail which will tell you what we are doing and how to make updating notes to your book.

With 100/130 now costing 70 cents a gallon at the controlled airports in Mexico you can bet we are going to be going a lot!

Have tailwinds wherever you go,

Arnold

628 Emergency Air Rescue Signals

VISUAL EMERGENCY SIGNALS

NEED MEDICAL ASSISTANCE - URGENT - USED ONLY WHEN LIFE IS AT STAKE	ALL OK - DO NOT WAIT	CAN PROCEED SHORTLY - WAIT IF PRACTICAL	NEED MECHANICAL HELP OR PARTS - LONG DELAY	DO NOT ATTEMPT TO LAND HERE
LIE SUPINE	WAVE ONE ARM OVERHEAD	ONE ARM HORIZONTAL	BOTH ARMS HORIZONTAL	BOTH ARMS WAVED ACROSS FACE
LAND HERE	USE DROP MESSAGE	OUR RECEIVER IS OPERATING	NEGATIVE (NO)	AFFIRMATIVE (YES)
BOTH ARMS FORWARD HORIZONTALLY, SQUATTING AND POINTING IN DIRECTION OF LANDING - REPEAT	MAKE THROWING MOTION	CUP HANDS OVER EARS	CLOTH WAVED HORIZONTALLY	CLOTH WAVED VERTICALLY
PICK US UP - PLANE ABANDONED	AFFIRMATIVE (YES)	NEGATIVE (NO)	HOW TO USE THEM	
BOTH ARMS VERTICAL	DIP NOSE OF PLANE SEVERAL TIMES	FISHTAIL PLANE		

HOW TO USE THEM: IF YOU ARE FORCED DOWN AND ARE ABLE TO ATTRACT THE ATTENTION OF THE PILOT OF A RESCUE AIRPLANE, THE BODY SIGNALS ILLUSTRATED ON THIS PAGE CAN BE USED TO TRANSMIT MESSAGES TO HIM AS HE CIRCLES OVER YOUR LOCATION. STAND IN THE OPEN WHEN YOU MAKE THE SIGNALS. BE SURE THAT THE BACKGROUND, AS SEEN FROM THE AIR, IS NOT CONFUSING. GO THROUGH THE MOTIONS SLOWLY AND REPEAT EACH SIGNAL UNTIL YOU ARE POSITIVE THAT THE PILOT UNDERSTANDS YOU.

GROUND TO AIR EMERGENCY CODE DISTRESS SIGNALS

REQUIRE DOCTOR, SERIOUS INJURIES	I	REQUIRE SIGNAL LAMP WITH BATTERY, AND RADIO	I	REQUIRE FUEL AND OIL	L
REQUIRE MEDICAL SUPPLIES	II	INDICATE DIRECTION TO PROCEED	K	ALL WELL	LL
UNABLE TO PROCEED	X	AM PROCEEDING IN THIS DIRECTION	↑	NO	N
REQUIRE FOOD AND WATER	F	WILL ATTEMPT TAKE-OFF	❘>	YES	Y
REQUIRE FIREARMS AND AMMUNITION	⩔	AIRCRAFT SERIOUSLY DAMAGED	L⏋	NOT UNDERSTOOD	JL
REQUIRE MAP AND COMPASS	▢	PROBABLY SAFE TO LAND HERE	△	REQUIRE MECHANIC	W
		IF IN DOUBT, USE INTERNATIONAL SYMBOL	SOS		

INSTRUCTIONS:

1. Lay out symbols by using strips of fabric or parachutes, pieces of wood, stones, or any available material.
2. Provide as much color contrast as possible between material used for symbols and background against which symbols are exposed.
3. Symbols should be at least 10 feet high or larger, if possible. Care should be taken to lay out symbols exactly as shown to avoid confusion with other symbols.
4. In addition to using symbols, every effort is to be made to attract attention by means of radio, flares, smoke, or other available means.
5. When ground is covered with snow, signals can be made by dragging, shoveling or tramping the snow. The depressed areas forming the symbols will appear to be black from the air.
6. Pilot should acknowledge message by rocking wings from side to side.

Symbol	Meaning
	ON LAND & AT SEA: O.K. TO LAND. ARROW SHOWS LANDING DIRECTION
	LAND & SEA: DO NOT ATTEMPT LANDING
	ON LAND: WALKING IN THIS DIRECTION / AT SEA: DRIFTING
	ON LAND: NEED GAS AND OIL, PLANE IS FLYABLE
	AT SEA: NEED EQUIPMENT AS INDICATED, SIGNALS FOLLOW
	ON LAND & AT SEA: NEED FOOD AND WATER
	ON LAND: NEED WARM CLOTHING / AT SEA: NEED EXPOSURE SUIT OR CLOTHING INDICATED
	ON LAND & AT SEA: PLANE IS FLYABLE, NEED TOOLS
	ON LAND & AT SEA: NEED MEDICAL ATTENTION
	ON LAND & AT SEA: NEED FIRST AID SUPPLIES
	ON LAND: SHOULD WE WAIT FOR RESCUE PLANE / AT SEA: NOTIFY RESCUE AGENCY OF MY POSITION
	ON LAND: INDICATE DIRECTION OF NEAREST CIVILIZATION / AT SEA: INDICATE RESCUE CRAFT, DIRECTION OF

Search and Rescue

The Mexican government's normal communications search for lost or overdue aircraft can be supplemented in one of two ways.

A 1935 US/Mexico treaty provides for each country to search the other's territory for its own planes after notification and acceptance. Our Coast Guard and Air Force could search in Mexico depending, frankly, on how much political pressure is brought to bear.

That notifying and accepting process will be speeded considerably if a U.S. Senator or Representative is interested enough to call our Department of State often and encourage them to work faster.

Volunteer Search Teams

In Southern California and Northwestern Mexico the bi-national Search and Rescue Group of the Californias fills in the open spots. U.S. pilot participants from the San Diego Sheriff's Aerosquadron join mountain rescue teams and four wheel drive units. When an aircraft, boat, or person is missing in northwestern Mexico there is very fast exchange of information and help between the Mexico coordinator and the San Diego Sheriff's office. Aircraft or other units are dispatched as needed.

These searches happen faster than when the two national capitals get involved. This past month a San Felipe fishing boat, one airplane, and a missing hiker were involved, about usual.

The author has participated in a few dozen searches as one of the fifty or so pilots. He was U.S. Coordinator for two years. Once he was a passenger in a searched for airplane. Being the searchee is definitely last place on my list.

Searchee Must Help

However it starts, the search is only as good as the information the searched-for pilot has provided. We all should list a person on our roundrobin flight plan who knows our itinerary and who will be told of any changes to it. Places we'll visit should be listed sequentially. Searchers can trail him by gasoline sales books if nothing else.

The searchers' task would be even easier if each pilot would imagine he was going to fly the search and ask himself what he would need so he could find these people right quick?

Survival Gear: Water

Based on my being a one-time survivor may I suggest the most important survival item to carry is water. Typically aircraft are found in 72 hours or less so starvation isn't the big danger. But anyone will be in bad shape long before he is found if he has not had at least a quart a day to sip.

Stay With The Airplane

Whatever its condition, an airplane is a treasure of things you can use to help searchers find you, to salvage and use for comfort or warmth, or with which to signal.

We used the plastic fresh air pipe for a successful water still. Engine oil added to a fire makes a signal fire seen ten to twenty miles. Seats or sidepanels will keep you warm.

But primarily the airplane gives the searcher something to recognize. If an airplane's usual arrangement of wings, fuselage, and tail becomes disorganized in the process of whatever happened, by all means get them back into a semblance of normal.

No matter how much we tell new searchers they will probably find a bunch of aluminum trash, they are mentally looking for a classic wings on each side, fuselage in the middle, airplane. The more it looks like an airplane in the tiedown area the faster it will be spotted and the people rescued.

Survival Mirror

My candidate for highest honors is the inventor of the Survival Mirror with the aiming screen. You can lay a totaly non-ignorable sunlight beam on an airplane as far as you can see him. At less than five miles the pilot will even be holding up a hand to shield his eyes from you.

Why?

The idea of Search and Rescue is to save your life in the unlikely event that you have a problem. If each of us does a few precautionary things on each flight the likelihood of a timely, successful search is increased.

Helps to keep in mind who benefits most.

Spanish Phrases

AROUND THE PLANE

ENGLISH	SPANISH	PRONUNCIATION
Gasoline	gasolina	gaws-oh-LEE-nah
Do you have ... ?	¿Tiene ... ?	tee-ENN-eh?
80 octane	ochenta octano	oh-CHEN-tah oke-TAHN-oh
100 octane	cien octano	see-ENN oke-TAHN-oh
Jet fuel	turbosina	toor-boh-SEEN-ah
Please fill ...	Por favor llene ...	por fah-VORE YENN-eh
the right tank	el tanque derecho	ell TAHN-kay deh-RAY-cho
the left tank	el tanque izquierdo	ell TAHN-kay ees-CARE-doh
the rear tank	el tanque posterior	ell TAHN-kay pos terr-ee-ORE
the tip tanks	los tanques tips	los TAHN-kase teeps
the wing tanks	los tanques alas	los TAHN-case AH-las
Oil	aceite	ah-say-EE-tay
40 wt.	grado ochenta	GRAH-doh oh-CHEN-tah
50 wt.	grado cien	GRAH-doh see-ENN
Chief	jefe	HEFF-eh
control tower	torre de control	TORR-eh deh con-TROL
course	rumbo	ROOM-bow
dispatcher	despachador	dess-pah-cha-DORR
flight plan	plan de vuelo	PLAHN deh voo-EH-loh
landing	aterrizaje	eh-tairr-ee-SAH-hay
oil change	cambio de aceite	CAHM-bee-yoh deh ah-SAY-teh
route	ruta	ROO-tah
runway	pista	PEE-stah
runway lights	luces de la pista	LOO-ses deh lah PEE-sta
stops (as fuel stops)	escalas	ess-CALL-ahs

Airplane Spanish

taxiway	rodaje	row-DAH-hay
VOR	VOR	BORE
wind	viento	vee-ENN-toh

DIRECTIONS

north	norte	NOR-teh
northeast	nordeste	nord-ESS-teh
east	este	ESS-teh
southeast	sudeste	sood-ESS-teh
south	sur	SOOR
southwest	sudoeste	sood-oh-ESS-teh
west	oeste	oh-ESS-teh
northwest	nordoeste	nord-oh-ESS-teh

BORDER CROSSING

ENGLISH	SPANISH	PRONUNCIATION
age	edad	eh-DOD
color	color	coh-LORE
tourist card	tarjeta (de turista)	tar-HAY-tah day too-REE-stah
signature	firma	FEER-mah
occupation	ocupación	oh-coo-pah-see-OWN
address	dirección	dee-rek-see-OWN
city	ciudad	see-oo-DAD
state	estado	ess-TAH-doh
name	nombre	NOME-bray
marital status	estado civil	ess-TAH-doh see-VEEL
single (m. and f.)	soltero (a)	sole-TAIR-oh (ah)
married	casado (a)	cah-SAH-doh (ah)
widower / widow	viudo (a)	vee-OO-doh (ah)
divorced	divorciado (a)	dee-vor-see-AH-doh (dah)
license	matrícula	mah-TREE-coo-lah
type (as airplane)	tipo	TEE-poh

COLORS

ENGLISH	SPANISH	PRONUNCIATION
amber	ámbar	AHM-barr
black	negro	NAY-grow
blue	azul	ah-SOOL
brown	café	cah-FAY
gray	gris	GREASE
green	verde	VAIR-day

632 Airplane Spanish

orange	naranjo	nar-AHN-hoe
pink	rosa	ROCE-ah
purple	morado	more-AH-doe
red	rojo	ROE-hoe
white	blanco	BLON-coh

1.	uno	OO-noh	18.	diez y ocho	dee-ACE ee OH-cho
2.	dos	DOSE	19.	diez y nueve	dee-ACE ee noo-EVV-ay
3.	tres	trace	20.	veinte	BAIN-tay
4.	cuatro	KWOT-roe	21.	veinte y uno	BAIN-tay ee OO-no
5.	cinco	SINK-oh	30.	treinta	TRAIN-tah
6.	seis	SACE	40.	cuarenta	kwar-ENN-tah
7.	siete	see-ATE-ay	50.	cincuenta	seen-KWEN-tah
8.	ocho	OH-cho	60.	sesenta	say-SENN-tah
9.	nueve	noo-EVV-ay	70.	setenta	say-TENN-tah
10.	diez	dee-ACE	80.	ochenta	oh-CHENN-tah
11.	once	OWN-say	90.	noventa	no-VENN-tah
12.	doce	DOE-say	100.	cien, ciento	see-ENN, see-ENN-to
13.	trece	TRAY-say	200.	doscientos	doe-see-ENN-tose
14.	catorce	kah-TORR-say	500.	quinientos	kee-nee-ENN-tose
15.	quince	KEEN-say	1,000.	mil	MEEL
16.	diez y seis	dee-ACE ee sace	2,000.	dos mil	DOSE MEEL
17.	diez y siete	dee-ACE ee see-ATE-ay	5,000.	cinco mil	SEEN-koh MEEL

USEFUL ADJECTIVES

bad	malo	MAH-low
beautiful	hermosa	air-MOH-sah
cheap	barato	bah-RRAH-toe
clean	limpio	LEEM-pee-oh
difficult	difícil	dee-FEE-seel
dirty	sucio	SOO-see-oh
early	temprano	tem-PRAH-noh
easy	fácil	FAH-seel
expensive	caro	CAH-roh
fast	rápido	RAH-pee-doh
good	bueno	BWAY-noh
high	alto	ALL-toh
kind (as to me)	amable	ah-MAH-bleh
large	grande	GRAHN-deh
late	tarde	TARR-deh
low	bajo	BAH-hoe
polite	cortés	corr-TESS
sharp	agudo	ah-GOO-doh
slow	lento	LEN-toh
small	pequeño	peh-KEHN-yo

Spanish Phrases

POLITE PHRASES

ENGLISH	SPANISH	PRONUNCIATION
Good morning	Buenos días	BWAY-nos DEE-uss
Good afternoon	Buenas tardes	BWAY-nahs TAR-dace
Good evening	Buenas noches	BWAY-nas NO-chess
Goodbye	Hasta la vista	AH-stah lah VEE-stah
Yes, very good	Sí, muy bueno	SEE MOO-ee BWAY-noh
Please	por favor	pore fah-VORR
Pardon me	Perdóneme	pair-DOE-nah-may
Thank you	Gracias	GRAH-see-uss
I am very sorry	Lo siento mucho	low see-ENN-toe MOO-cho

TO EXPLAIN YOUR NEEDS

I need	Necesito	nay-say-SEE-toh
We need	Necesitamos	nay-say-see-TAHM-ose
We are hungry	Tenemos hambre.	tay-NAY-mose OMM-bray
We are thirsty	Tenemos sed.	tay-NAY-mose SED.
We are cold / warm	Tenemos frío / calor..	tay-NAY-mose FREE-oh / kah-LORE
We are tired	Estamos cansados..	ess-TAH-mose con-SOD-ose
He (she) is sick (point)	Está enfermo (a).	ess-TAH enn-FAIR-moh (mah).

TIME

today	hoy	OY
tomorrow	mañana	ma-NYA-nah
yesterday	ayer	ah-YAIR
tonight	esta noche	ESS-tah NO-chay
noon	el mediodía	ell may-dee-oh-DEE-ah
morning	mañana	ma-NYA-nah
afternoon	la tarde	lah TAR-day
night	la noche	lah NO-chay
midnight	la medianoche	lah may-dee-ah-NO-chay

DAYS OF THE WEEK

Sunday	domingo	doe-MEEN-go
Monday	lunes	LOO-nehs
Tuesday	martes	MAR-tess
Wednesday	miércoles	mee-AIR-coh-less
Thursday	jueves	WHEH-vess
Friday	viernes	vee-AIR-ness
Saturday	sábado	SAH-bah-doe

ENGLISH	SPANISH	PRONUNCIATION
string beans	ejotes	eh-HO-tess
sweet potatoes	camotes	cah-MO-tess
tomatoes	tomates	toh-MAH-tess
vegetables	legumbres	leh-GOOM-bress

Bread

toast	pan tostado	pahn toh-STAH-doh
crackers	galleta	gah-YAY-tahs
bread	pan	PAHN
bread and butter	pan con mantequilla	pahn cohn mon-teh-KEE-yah
pastries	pasteles	pahs-TELL-ess
*pastry shop	pastelería	pah-stell-air-REE-yah
*bakery shop	panadería	pahn-ah-dair-REE-yah

*(Pick out one of each near where you're staying --- it is a real treat to have fresh pastry and coffee and maybe a papaya for breakfast.)

Fruit

apple	manzana	mon-SSAHN-ah
avocado	aguacate	ah-way-COT-eh
banana	plátano	PLOT-ah-noh

(Ever tried the red ones? Get them in the Indian markets.)

figs	higos	EE-gose
fruit	fruta	FROO-tah
grapes	uvas	OO-vahs
guava	guayaba	gwy-YAH-bah
lemon	limón	lee-MOAN
lime	lima	LEE-mah
mango	mango	MONN-goh
nut, nuts	nuez, nueces	noo-ESS, noo-ESS-ess
olives	aceitunas	as-sayee-TOO-nahs
oranges	naranjas	nah-RON-hahs
papaya	papaya	pah-PYE-yah

(Delicious for breakfast with lime squeezed over it.)

peach	durazno	doo-ROSS-noh
pineapple	piña	PEEN-yah

(Around the Coconut Coast it isn't tart like Hawaii's.)

strawberries	fresas	FRAY-suss

food and eating

Spanish Phrases

ENGLISH	SPANISH	PRONUNCIATION
breakfast	desayuno	dess-ah-YUNE-oh
lunch	comida	coh-MEE-dah
spoon	cuchara	coo-CHAR-ah
cup	taza	TAH-sah
glass	vaso	VAH-soh
napkin	servilleta	sehr-vee-YAY-tah
bill (check)	cuenta	KWEN-tah
tip	propina	pro-PEEN-ah
knife	cuchillo	coo-CHEE-yo
fork	tenedor	ten-ay-DORR

Meat, Fish, Eggs

ENGLISH	SPANISH	PRONUNCIATION
bacon	tocino	toe-SEE-no
meat	carne	CAR-neh
beef	res	RACE
chicken	pollo	POY-yo
duck	pato	POT-oh
ham	jamón	hah-MOAN
lamb	carnero	car-NAIR-oh
chops	chuletas	choo-LET-ahs
pork	puerco	PWAIR-coh
roast	asado	ah-SOD-oh
turkey	pavo	PAH-vo
veal	ternera	tehr-NAIR-ah
eggs	huevos	WHAY-vose
fried	fritos	FREE-toh
soft boiled	tibios	TEE-bee-ohs
hard boiled	cocidos duros	coh-SEE-dohs DOO-rohs
with hot sauce	rancheros	ron-CHAIR-ose

Vegetables

ENGLISH	SPANISH	PRONUNCIATION
beans	frijoles	free-HOLE-ess
beets	betabeles	beh-tah-BAIL-ess
cabbage	repollo	reh-POY-yoh
corn	elote	eh-LOTE-eh
lettuce	lechuga	leh-CHOO-gah
onion	cebolla	seh-BOY-yah
peas	chícharos	CHEE-chah-rose
potatoes	papas	PAH-pahs
rice	arroz	ah-ROHS

These days the Immigration officers at airports of entry are so ready to provide single entry Tourist Permits it is hardly worth the time to get one before leaving. But if you like to be totally prepared, here are the Tourism offices where you may get single or multiple entry permits. In addition you may get the permits at Mexican consulates or at the Embassy in Washington D.C.

When applying for a Tourist Permit be sure to have proof of your citizenship in the form of a passport, or a notarized voters registration, or a notarized statment giving your citizenship, or your birth certificate.

A married woman whose last name is different from that shown on her birth certificate should consider carrying an affidavit verifying her different name. A notarized statement that the name on the birth certificate is of the same person who has since changed via marriage will do.

Take It With You

Whatever proof of citizenship is used for a tourist permit must be carried on the trip where that tourist permit is used. For more detailed information contact one of these offices of the Mexican Government National Tourism Council.

405 Park Avenue No. 1002
New York, NY 10022

1156 15th Street NW No. 329
Washington, DC 20005

Peachtree Center No. 2201
Cain Tower
Atlanta, GA 30303

Tower Bldg No. 612
100 N. Biscayne Blvd
Miami, Florida 33132

John Hancock Center No. 3615
Chicago, IL 60611

1 Shell Square Bldg. Concourse
New Orleans, LA 70130

2 Turtle Creek Village No. 1230
Dallas, Texas 75219

711 Louisiana St No. 1080
South Tower Pennzoil Pl.
Houston, TX 77002

304 N. St Mary's St.
San Antonio, TX 78205

633 17th Street No. 2010
First Denver Plaza Bldg.
Denver, CO 80202

3443 N. Central Avenue No. 101
Phoeniz, AZ 85012

2744 East Broadway
Tucson, AZ 85716

9701 Wilshire Blvd No. 1110
Beverly Hills, CA 90212

San Diego Federal Bldg No. 1200
600 B Street
San Diego, CA 92101

50 California Street
San Francisco, CA 94111

Canada

1 Place Villa Marie No. 2409
Montreal, Que. H3B 3M9

101 Richmond St West No. 1212
Toronto, Ont. M5H 2E1

700 West Georgia Street
Vancouver, BC. V7Y 1B6

Reprinted from

THE WESTERN Journal of Medicine

From the Department of Medicine, Cedars-Sinai Medical Center and UCLA Center for the Health Sciences (Dr. Kahn); and the Division of Epidemiology, UCLA School of Public Health (Dr. Visscher).
Reprint requests to: F. H. Kahn, MD, 123 North San Vicente Blvd., Beverly Hills, CA 90211.

Refer to: Kahn FH, Visscher BR: Water disinfection in the wilderness—A simple, effective method of iodination (Information). West J Med 122:450-453, May 1975

Water Disinfection in the Wilderness

A Simple, Effective Method of Iodination

FREDRICK H. KAHN, MD
BARBARA R. VISSCHER, MD, DR. P.H.
Los Angeles

BEFORE WORLD WAR II, when backpacking and foreign travel were less common, the traveler gave little or no thought to water contamination. It was assumed that mountain streams were pure. With improved surveillance it is known that most streams of the United States are polluted.[1] Waterborne disease continues to be important in undeveloped areas, here and abroad,[2-4] though in urban areas of the United States it is uncommon. Reliable data on the incidence of waterborne disease among travelers are not available, yet potentially waterborne diseases including Salmonella infections, amebic dysentery, giardiasis and infectious hepatitis are commonly observed among travelers returning from abroad and from remote areas of the United States.

The authors' interest in water disinfection was sharpened when they acquired giardiasis after drinking from a partly frozen stream on the Long Valley trail to Mount San Jacinto, California. At this time in early May 1971, human habitation of the area was sparse, and snow covered the ground. Cold weather is no protection from intestinal parasitism, and may present a problem in water purification, as will be explained later.

A water disinfectant must be able to kill the hardiest of each group of organisms, especially amebic cysts, which are hardier than their active forms, and enteroviruses, the most resistant to disinfection of the pathogenic microorganisms. At the same time, the toxicity of the chemical must be very low compared with its germicidal potency. A water disinfectant for the traveler presents special requirements which are of less importance to the municipal water sanitary engineer. These include simplicity, effectiveness in the presence of nitrogenous pollutants, rapidity of antimicrobial action over a wide pH range and immediate palatability. The backpacker will, of course, demand light weight.

Iodination meets these requirements,[5-7] and offers a number of advantages over the time-honored chlorination[8,9] of small quantities of water with p-dichlorosulfamoyl benzoic acid (Halazone®).

During World War II, Halazone was issued for individual use when other forms of water treatment were not available. Though Halazone produced potable water in the absence of heavy contamination, its efficacy in treating cold, heavily polluted water containing resistant forms such as viruses and amebic cysts was seriously questioned. In 1942, at the request of the armed forces, investigators at Harvard University initiated a search for a more dependable technique of water sterilization. This study recommended the use of iodine for treatment of small quantities of water. A technique for iodination was developed and adapted by the armed forces.[10] Subsequent investigations confirm the superiority of iodination as a personal water germicide, yet Halazone continues to be widely used and is currently the only commercially available agent for this purpose in Southern California.

Chlorination

Chlorination by Halazone in the recommended dose depends on the slow release of 2.8 parts per million (ppm) of free chlorine for its immediate antimicrobial action.[11] Chlorine under ideal conditions, namely a pH of 7 or lower and the absence of nitrogenous compounds, hydrolyzes to hypochlorous acid (HClO). The highly active HClO is an excellent germicide.[12,13] The high reactivity of HClO is its main defect as a personal water disinfectant, since in the presence of amino and ammonia ions HClO is quickly converted to relatively inactive monochloramine.[14] Above pH 7 HClO hydrolyzes to the less active hypochlorite.

Furnished by Arnold D Senterfitt

These two problems are solved in water purification plants by the practice of breakpoint chlorination. Breakpoint chlorination is the application of sufficient chlorine to bind with the organic materials in the water, while leaving a biocidal residual of free chlorine. But this technique requires continual testing and is not practical for rapid treatment of small quantities of water. The individual traveler must resort to simple chlorination, the practice of adding a fixed dose of a chlorine compound to water of uncertain quality. Simple chlorination is unpredictable,[15] and may be useless against bacteria[16] and enteroviruses[9,17] when water is contaminated with organic material.

A number of waterborne disease outbreaks have occurred when simple chlorination was practiced.[18] Neefe's classic study of an infectious hepatitis epidemic demonstrated the failure of combined chlorine to inactivate the hepatitis virus.[19] Enteroviruses were recovered from chlorinated tap water in Paris when breakpoint chlorination was not practiced.[20]

Additional disadvantages of Halazone are slow solubility and a short shelf life of five months when stored at 32°C (89.6°F). Potency is reduced 50 percent when stored at 40° to 50°C (104° to 122°F),[21] the temperature range one might expect in an automobile glove compartment on a summer day. Halazone loses 75 percent of its activity when exposed to air for two days.[22]

Iodination

Iodination, in contrast, with a weak aqueous solution of 3 to 5 ppm of elemental iodine (I_2) will destroy amebae and their cysts, bacteria and their spores, algae and enteroviruses at 25°C (77°F)[4] in 15 minutes or less (see Chart 1).[4,7,8] At near freezing (3°C, 37.4°F) disinfection will require 20 to 30 minutes at the same concentration of iodine, since germicidal potency is roughly proportional to temperature. Elemental iodine does not react readily with ammonia and amino ions, and therefore will remain an effective disinfectant in water polluted with nitrogenous wastes.[7,8] Iodine is effective over a wide pH range, hydrolyzing at pH above 6 to hydroiodous acid, which is a faster virucide than I_2.[8]

Iodination can be accomplished in three ways. One method is the addition of eight drops of 2 percent tincture of iodine to a quart of water, but this results in water of less than acceptable palatability.[22] A second is the addition of a tablet of Globaline® (tetraglycine hydroperiodide) to a quart of water, releasing active iodine in a concentration of 8 ppm. Globaline tablets lose 20 percent of their effectiveness when stored in sealed bottles at 75°C (167°F) for 24 weeks. They lose 33 percent of their initial activity when exposed to air for four days.[22] The third method, described below, using crystals of elemental iodine, has been recommended for treatment of water supplies of villages in underdeveloped countries,[8] but has not been previously described for use as a personal water germicide.

Procedure for Iodination Using Crystalline Iodine

The only equipment needed for iodination with crystalline iodine is a one ounce clear glass bottle, with a leak-proof bakelite cap, containing 4 to 8 grams (or any small quantity) of USP grade resublimed iodine (I_2). The bottle is filled with water and capped, shaken vigorously for 30 to 60 seconds, then held upright for a few moments to permit the heavy iodine crystals (specific gravity 4.6) to fall to the bottom. The iodine crystals are not to be used directly. Disinfection is accomplished at 25°C (77°F) by the addition of 12½ cubic centimeters (cc) of the near saturated supernatant iodine solution to one liter of water, to achieve a final concentration of 4 ppm iodine. Since the concentration of the saturated iodine solution varies with its temperature (see Table 1), only 10 cc of iodine solution would be needed if the bottle were kept at body temperature. At

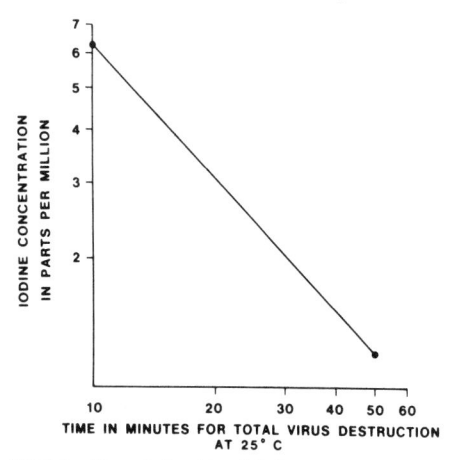

Chart 1.—The relationship of iodine concentration to contact time for the inactivation of enterovirus (Coxsackie B₁), taken from Chang.[5] This enterovirus has a high resistance to disinfection, estimated to be comparable to that of the infectious hepatitis virus.[1]

near freezing, 20 cc of iodine solution would be used per liter. (The cap of the iodine bottle may serve as a measuring device.) After a contact time of 15 minutes, the water is disinfected. When more disinfected water is desired, the above steps are repeated almost 1,000 times without replenishing the iodine crystals. The shelf life of crystalline iodine is unlimited. Under usual circumstances, a 2 ppm iodine solution with a contact time of 40 minutes would offer improved palatability and effective disinfection.

Furnished by Arnold D Senterfitt

If increased germicidal potency is necessary because the water is turbid, cold or known to be heavily contaminated, the concentration of the iodine solutions could be increased to 8 ppm, with contact time of 20 minutes.[5] However, in the interest of palatability, one may prefer not to increase the concentration, but instead increase the contact time (see Chart 1).

A clear glass bottle is recommended for the above procedure to permit observation of the iodine crystals. Plastic bottles of all types take on an opaque brown stain after long exposure to the working solution. Further, plastic bottles tend to leak as one travels to high altitude, and distort and crack on descent to low altitude.

By all measures, the toxicity of iodine is remarkably low in the concentrations used for water disinfection.[9,23-25] Only persons with a specific sensitivity to iodine, and perhaps those who have been treated for hyperthyroidism risk any ill effects. The only danger of the above procedure is the inadvertent ingestion of iodine crystals, although an ounce of iodine solution would be harmless. No fatality from ingestion of less than 15 grams of iodine has been reported.

Conclusion

The use of iodine releasing tablets for emergency water disinfection has been employed by the United States Army since World War II, replacing chlorination with Halazone tablets. Chlorine,

TABLE 1.—The Volume at Various Temperatures of a Near Saturated Solution of Iodine Added to One Liter of Water to Yield an Iodine Concentration of Four Parts per Million

Temperature	Volume	ppm	Capfuls*
3°C (37°F)	20.0 cc	200	8
20°C (68°F)	13.0 cc	300	5+
25°C (77°F)	12.5 cc	320	5
40°C (104°F)	10.0 cc	400	4

*Assuming a capful of standard 1 ounce glass bottle is 2½ cc.

except when breakpoint chlorination is practiced, is not a reliable disinfectant. This is so because the hydrolysis products of chlorine are less active at pH over 7 and in the presence of amino and ammonia ions. Iodination rapidly inactivates the known human pathogens, including the enteroviruses which are the most resistant to disinfection. Iodination is effective over a wide pH range, and in the presence of nitrogenous pollutants. A simple, lightweight iodination method using iodine crystals with unlimited shelf life is described for use by travelers and backpackers.

For a more detailed and technical discussion of water disinfection the reader is referred to papers from the Sanitary Engineering Center, United States Public Health Service, Cincinnati, Ohio,[5,8,9,18] and the most current review of water disinfectants.[26]

Summary

There is a need among travelers and hikers for an effective, palatable water disinfectant with rapid action and long shelf life. A method of iodine disinfection which meets these requirements is described. A one ounce glass bottle containing 4 to 8 grams of iodine crystals is filled with water, then shaken vigorously to produce a near saturated solution of iodine. At 25°C (77°F), 12.5 cubic centimeters of this supernatant solution is added to one liter of water to be disinfected. In less than 15 minutes pathogenic bacteria, amebic cysts and viruses will be inactivated. This procedure can be repeated almost 1,000 times without replenishing the iodine crystals.

This method is compared with Halazone disinfection and other iodination methods, some of which are not currently available.

REFERENCES

1. Third Annual Report of the Council on Environmental Quality. U.S. Government Printing Office, Washington, DC, Stock Number 411-0011. Aug 1972, pp 11-16
2. Craun GK: Microbiology—Waterborne outbreaks (A Review). Water Pollution Control Federation J 44:1175-1182, 1972
3. Water treatment and examination, chap 7, In Holden WS (Ed): Water Supply and Public Health. Baltimore, Williams and Wilkins Co., 1970, pp 89-101
4. Bobb RR, Peck OC, Vescia FG: Giardiasis—A cause of traveler's diarrhea. JAMA 217:1359-1361, 1971
5. Chang SL: The use of active iodine as a water disinfectant. J Am Pharm Assoc 47:417-423, 1958
6. Chambers CW, Kabler PW, Malaney G, et al: Iodine as a bactericide. Soap and Sanitary Chemicals 28:149-165, 1952
7. Berg G, Chang SL, Harris EK: Devitalization of microorganisms by iodine. Virology 22:469-481, 1964
8. Chang SL: Waterborne viral infections and their prevention. Bull WHO 38:401-414, 1968
9. Berg G: Viral transmission by the water vehicle—III. Health Lab Science 3:170-181, 1966
10. Fair GM: Water disinfection and allied subjects, chap 34, Advances in Military Medicine—Vol. 2. Boston, Little, Brown and Co., 1948, pp 520-531
11. Esplin DW: Antiseptic and disinfectants, chap 50, In Goodman LS, Gilman A (Eds): The Pharmacological Basis of Therapeutics. New York, Macmillan Publishing Co., 1965, p 1036
12. Dychdala GR: Chlorine and chlorine compounds, chap 19, In Lawrence CA, Block SS (Eds): Disinfection, Sterilization, and Preservation. Philadelphia, Lea and Febiger, 1968
13. Clarke NA, Kabler PW: Disinfection of drinking water, chap 40, In Lawrence CA, Block SS (Eds): Disinfection, Sterilization, and Preservation. Philadelphia, Lea and Febiger, 1968
14. Marks HC, Strandskov FB: Halogens and their mode of action. Ann NY Academy of Sciences 53:163-171, 1950
15. Bacterial purification of water by chlorine, chap 33, In Holden WS (Ed): Water Treatment and Examination. Baltimore, Williams and Wilkins Co., 1970, p 368
16. Butterfield CT, Wattie E: Influence of pH and temperature on the survival of coliforms and enteric pathogens when exposed to chloramine. Public Health Rep 61:157-192, 1946
17. Kelly SM, Sanderson WW: The effect of chlorine on enteric viruses—II. The effect of combined chlorine on polio and Coxsackie viruses. Am J Public Health 48:1323-1334, 1958, 50:14-20, 1960
18. Kabler PW: Purification and sanitary control of water (potable and waste). Annu Rev Microbiol pp 127-138, 1962
19. Neefe JR, Baty JB, Reinbold JB, et al: Inactivation of the virus of infectious hepatitis in drinking water. Am J Public Health 37:365-372, 1947
20. Coin L, Labonde MJ, Hannoun M: Modern microbiological and virological aspects of water pollution. Advances in Water Pollution Research 1:1-18, 1964
21. Hadfield WA: Chlorine and chlorine compounds, chap 23, In Reddish GF (Ed): Antiseptics, Disinfectants, Fungicides, and Chemical and Physical Sterilization. Philadelphia, Lea and Febiger, 1957
22. Morris VC, Chang SL, Fair GM, et al: Disinfection of drinking water under field conditions. Indust Engineer Chem 45:1013-1015, 1953
23. Black AP, Thomas WC, Kinman WB, et al: Iodine for disinfection of water. J Am Wat Wks Assoc 60:69-83, 1968
24. Freund G, Thomas WC Jr, Bird ED, et al: Effect of iodinated water supplies on thyroid function. J Clin Endocrinol Metab 26:619-624, 1966
25. Gershenfeld L, Witlin B: Iodine as an antiseptic. Ann NY Acad Sci 52:172-181, 1950
26. Poynter SFB, Slade JS, Hones HH: Disinfection of water with special reference to viruses—Water Treatment and Examination 22:194-206, 1973

Furnished by Arnold D Senterfitt

640

Wherever in the world you fly, we can provide the pilot-aids.

global chart coverage • aviation books • guidebooks • airway manuals • plotters • electronic and manual computers • radio headsets and mikes • knee-desks • flight bags • sun glasses • timers • weather recorders • pilot training manuals • exam guides • logbooks • FAA publications • Jeppesen • Telex • Ray Ban • Airguide • Government Printing Office

Pan Am Nav Service, the one-stop center for all the best in pilot-aids and cockpit accessories. Order by mail or toll-free telephone. Master Charge and Visa cards. Free catalog!

CALL TOLL-FREE
USA: 800-423-5932
Calif: 800-382-3328

PAN AMERICAN NAVIGATION SERVICE
16934 SATICOY ST., P.O. BOX 9046, VAN NUYS, CA 91409
(Adjacent to VNY, the world's busiest general-aviation airport)

Index 641

Abreojos,Punta,PAB,167
Acaponeta,ACP,317
Acapulco,ACA,463
Acapulco IFR,ACA,462
Acapulco Map,ACA,461
Agriculture,US,58
Agua Azul,GUA-,509
Agua Prieta,APA,276
Aircraft Spanish,631
Alamos,ALA,302
Aleman,GRO,460
Alfonsina's,ALF-,246
All Border Data,42
Allende,San Miguel,SMA,364
Altamirano,ALT,441
Angostura,ARA,277
Apatzingan,AZG,474
Aquascalientes,AGS,360
Arcelia,ARC,442
Arrival in Mexico,45
Arrive/Departure,550
Asuncion,Bahia,BSU,164
Author's Preface,5
Avgas in Mexico,25

B los Angeles-Munoz,BLX4-,239
BLX-Diaz,BLX2-,240
Bad Picture,261
Bahia Asuncion,BSU,164
Bahia Ballenas,BBS-,168
Bahia Ballenas Map,BBS,169
Bahia Chamela,ELA-,485
Bahia Chileno,HCB-,190
Bahia Concepcion,MLG5-,222
Bahia Escondida,DID-,292B
Bahia Kino,KIO-,292
Bahia Magdalena,MAG-,182
Bahia Tortugas,BTO,163
Bahia Vermillion,292A
Bahia la Ventana,VNT-,204
Bahia los Angeles New,BLX1-,242
Bahia los Angeles-SE,BLX3-,238
Bahia's Hotels,241
Baja Adventures,17
Baja Bush Pilots,18
Baja Calif Index,108
Baja Calif. Area,106
Baja Calif. Briefing,109
Baja Cfa Shipwrecks,179
Baja Mar,BJM-,119
Baptist Mission,BPT-,136
Barra Cazones,CAZ-,380
Barra Navidad,BRR-,480
Belice Int'l,ZDZ,557
Belice Municipal,ZDZ2-,558
Belize IFR,ZDZ,556
Belmopan,BMO-,559
Benjamin Hill,BJN-,283
Bisbee Douglas IFR,IFR,274
Bisbee Douglas Int'l,DUG,275
Black Warrior Map,GNO,155
Blue Form,47
Boarding Pass,548
Boca Paila,PEZ-,534
Briefing,Coconut Coast,421
Briefing-Malarrimo,MMO-,160
Brown Field Int'l,SDM,113
Brown IFR,SDM,112
Brownsville IFR,BRO,406
Brownsville Int'l,BRO,407

Cabo San Lucas,CSL,188
Cabo San Lucas detail,CBO-,187
Cadaje,CJE-,172
Cadena,DNA-,249B
Calentura,HOT-,125
Calexico International,CXL,256
Calmalli,CAI,233
Campeche,CPE,519
Campeche IFR,CPE,518
Camping,34
Campo de la Costa,CST-,487
Cananea,CNA,281
Cancun IFR,CUN,528
Cancun Int'l,CUN,529
Candelaria,CDL-,513
Cartagena IFR,CTG,621
Cartagena Int'l,CTG,622
Carti,CAW,620
Castel Resort Hotel,SFE,251
Catch 22,C22-,293
Cay Ambergris,MBR-,553
Caye Chapel,HPL-,554
Celaya,CYA,362
Central Farm,CFM-,560
Centro America All Borders,542
Centro America Area,538
Centro America Briefing,541
Centro America Flt Plan,551
Centro America Gen.Decl.,546
Centro America Index,540
Centro America Perm. Form,545
Centro America Permission,544
Cerro Azul,CER-,382
Chagres,CAG,617
Chetumal IFR,CTM,536
Chetumal Int'l,CTM,537
Chichen-Itza,CZA,522
Chichen-Itza Briefing,523
Chihuahua,CUU,331
Chihuahua IFR,CUU,330
Chilpancingo,CHG,443
Choix,Chih.,CHX,305A
Cielito Lindo,MTA-,142
Citizenship,51
Ciudad Acuna Int'l,CAC,348
Ciudad Aleman,ALM-,372
Ciudad Guzman,CGZ,476
Ciudad Juarez IFR,CJS,332
Ciudad Juarez Int'l,CJS,333
Ciudad Mante,CDM,391
Ciudad Obregon,CEN,299
Ciudad Obregon IFR,CEN,298
Ciudad Victoria,CVM,395
Ciudad Victoria IFR,CVM,394
Ciudad del Carmen,CME,515
Ciudad del Carmen IFR,CME,514
Club Grulla,GRU-,121
Coconut Coast Area,418
Coconut Coast Briefing,421
Coconut Coast Index,420
Colima,IMA,477
Colnett West,CNT-,133
Colnett-East,CNT-,132
Coloradito,DTO-,249A
Concepcion,Bahia,MLG5-,222
Corozal,552
Covadonga,OVA-,385
Cozumel IFR,CZM,530
Cozumel Int'l,CZM,531
Creel,CRL,329

Culiacan,CUL,311
Culiacan IFR,CUL,310
Customs Guide:Pilots,67

David IFR,DAV,604
David Int'l,DAV,605
Del Rio IFR,DRT,346
Del Rio Int'l,DRT,347
Delicias,DEL,328
Depart Mexico Checklist,56
Desemboque,DES,289
Desengano,DNO-,243
Dexter Products,337
Dictionary,104
Dirt Field,22
Divisadero,DRO-,305B
Durango,DGO,323
Durango IFR,DGO,322

EL Paso IFR,ELP,334
EL Paso Int'l,ELP,335
Eagle Pass Int'l,EPS,350
Ebano,EBN-,384
El Alamo,LAM-,126
El Arco,LRC-,232
El Fuerte,FRT,304
El Huerfanito,HFO-,248
El Llano,PNT,319
El Marmol,MRM-,150
El Rosario East,ERO,146
El Rosario West,ERO,147
El Salvador Internacional,CAT,584
El Tule,HCB-,190
Emergency Rescue Signals,628
Emiliano Zapata,EZT,512
Ensenada,ENS,120
Esmeralda,ESM-,371

Felipe Carrill Pto.,535
Fifth of February,CEN2-,297
Finca Lutz,LUT-,598
Flamingo Beach,NGO-,591
Flight Plan Fee,50
Flores,FLS,568
Flying Samaritans,40
For Women Only,11
Fort Royal,FTK-,578
Francisquito,FQT-,234
Franklin Insurance,20
Fresnillo,FRS,356
Fulano's Restaurant,FOOD,209

Gamboa,CAG,617
Gasoline,Mexico,25
General Declaration,54
Golfito Int'l,MRGF,602
Goloson Int'l,LCE,573
Guadalajara,GDL,429
Guadalajara IFR,GDL,428
Guadalupe New,TCT,118
Guadalupe Old,LIF,117
Guamuchil,GCH,312
Guanaja,GJA,579
Guanajuato,GTO,363
Guasave,GUS-,309
Guatemala City IFR,AUR,570
Guatemala City Int'l,AUR,571
Guaymas IFR,GYM,294
Guaymas Int'l,GYM,295
Guerrero Negro Map,155

642 Index

Guerrero Negro So.,GNO,157
Guerrero Negro-N,GNO,156

Hamilton Ranch,HAM-,134
Health,16
Hermosillo IFR,HMO,284
Hermosillo Int'l,HMO,285
Hermosillo South,HMO2-,286
Hidalgo del Parral,HPC,324
Hidalgo,Presa,DLG-,303
Holbox,BOX-,526
Holiday-los Mochis,LMM,308
Hortaliza,HRT-,131
Hotel Baja Mar,BJM-,189
Hotel Borrego de Oro,PCH,228
Hotel Cabo San Lucas,HCB-,190
Hotel Castel,251
Hotel De Anza,257
Hotel Francisquito,FQT-,235
Hotel Palmilla,PMA-,191
Hotel Punta Pescadero,PES-,203
Hotel Serenidad,SRD-,223
Hotel las Arenas,205
Howard AFB,HOW,609
Howard IFR,HOW,608
Huapa,UAP-,484
Huetamo, M,439

Iguala New,IGA,455
Ilopango IFR,YSX,582
Ilopango Int'l,YSX,583
Imperial IFR,IPL,258
Imperial VFR,IPL,259
Incountry Tourist Offices,549
Index,640
Ingenio de la Joya,JOY-,517
Insurance,21
Irapuato,IPO,361
Isla Carmen,ICM,219
Isla Cedros,ICD,161
Isla Contadora,COZ,614
Isla Maria Madre,IMM,321
Isla Mujeres,IMU,527
Isla Natividad,TVD-,162
Isla Porvenir,PVR,619
Isla San Jose,ISJ,214
Isla del Rey North,SMI,615
Isla del Rey South,PCO,616
Isla,Veracruz,ILA-,370
Ixtepec,IZT,446
Ixtepec Hurricane Damage,448
Ixtepec Military,IZT,447

Jaco Beach,JCO-,599
Jamiltepec,JAM,453
Jimenez,CJM,325
Jiquilpan,JQL,431
Juanito-Creel,CRL,329

Know Before You Go,92

La Aurora IFR,AUR,570
La Aurora Int'l,AUR,569
La Bocana,BCN1-,165
La Bocana,BCN2-,166
La Cruz,CRU-,313
La Mesa Int'l IFR,LMS,575
La Paz IFR,LAP,210
La Paz Internacional,LAP,211
La Paz Military,LAP,212
La Penita,PNT-,319
La Pesca,PSA-,396

La Petaca,PET-,457
La Purisima,PUR,175
La Venta,LAV-,503
La Ventana,ABU-,197
La Viga,FIG-,456
Lago Azucar,AZU-,412
Lago Mocuzari,CUZ-,301
Laguna San Ignacio,LSG-,169
Lands End,CBO-,187
Laredo IFR,LRD,416
Laredo Int'l,LRD,417
Las Coloradas,ADS-,525
Las Cruces,RAC,206
Las Palmas,BHP,201
Legal Notices,4
Leon,LEO,359
Leon IFR,LEO,358
Liberia Int'l,MRLB,590
Lindbergh IFR,LIF,114
Lindbergh Int'l,LIF,115
Llano Colorado,LLN-,124
Loreto IFR,LTO,216
Loreto Int'l,LTO,217
Loreto Map,LTO,218
Los Brasiles,587
Los Cocos IFR,TIO,596
Los Frailes South,FRY-,196
Los Mochis Holiday,LMM,308
Los Mochis IFR,LMM,306
Los Mochis New,LMM,307

MacKenzie Aviation,24
Magdalena Village 1,MVG1-,180
Magdalena Village 2,MVG2-,181
Magdalena,Son,STO-,282
Malarrimo,MAL-,159
Malarrimo Briefing,160
Managua IFR,MGA,588
Managua Int'l,MGA,589
Manzanillo,ZLO,479
Manzanillo IFR,ZLO,478
Map-Black Warrior,GNO,155
Map: Bahia Ballenas,BBS-,169
Map: Loreto Area,LTO,218
Map: Mulege,MLG,225
Map:Laguna San Ignacio,LSG-,169
Marihuata,UAT-,471
Matamoros IFR,MAM,404
Matamoros Int'l,MAM,405
Matancitas,MTB,178
Maya Beach,MAY-,563
Mazatlan,MZT,315
Mazatlan IFR,MZT,314
McAllen IFR,MFE,410
McAllen Int'l,MFE,411
Mechanical Help,28
Melchor de Mencos Int'l,MCH-,566
Melinda,MDA-,562
Meling Ranch,MEL-,130
Merida,MID,521
Merida IFR,MID,520
Mexicali IFR,MXL,254
Mexicali Internacional,MXL,255
Mexican Gasoline,25
Mexican Money,15
Mexican Regulations,32
Mexican TCAs,33
Mexican Tourist Offices in US,636
Mexico Checklist,44
Mexico City,MEX,367

Mexico Flight Plan,48
Mexico IFR,MEX,366
Mexico and C.A. Climate,623
Mike's Skyranch New,MSK-,129
Mina Volcanes,VOL-,141
Minatitlan,MTT,497
Minatitlan IFR,MTT,496
Miraflores,MFL-,194
Mision San Borja,BRJ-,237
Mision Santa Catalina,CAT-,127
Mocuzari,Lago,CUZ-,301
Monclova,MOV,353
Monclova IFR,MOV,352
Monterrey,MTY,401
Monterrey IFR,MTY,400
Monterrey del Norte,ADN,403
Monterrey del Norte IFR,ADN,402
Morelia,MLM,437
Morelia IFR,MLM,436
Mulege Map,225
Mulege Municipal,MLG,227
Mulege View,MLG,224
Mulege West,MLGW-,226
Mustang Aviation,30
Muzquiz,MUZ-,351

Naranjos,NAR-,383
Natividad,Isla,TVD-,162
Navajoa,NVJ,300
New France,FTD,618
Nogales IFR,278
Nogales Int'l,AZ,OLS,279
Nogales Int'l,Sonora,NOG,280
Nombre de Dios,NDI,618B
Norport,NPT-,561
Northeast Area Chart,338
Northeast Area,intro,341
Northeast Index,340
Northwest Area,262
Northwest Briefing,265
Northwest Index,264
Notarized Permission,46
Novillero,NOV-,316
Nueva Italia,NAT-,472
Nuevas Casas Grandes,NCG,336
Nuevo Laredo IFR,NLD,414
Nuevo Laredo Int'l,NLD,415

Oaxaca,OAX,445
Oaxaca IFR,OAX,444
Ocotlan,OCO-,430
Ojinaga,OJA,344
Ojo de Liebre,SCM-,158
Old Mill,MOL-,139
Ometepec,OMT,458
Orange Walk,555
Overall Areas,1

P.San Carlos Briefing,PSC-,148
Paitilla Int'l,MAG,610
Palenque Aerial View,PQE,506
Palenque Airport,PQE,508
Palenque's Airport,PQE,507
Palmar,TIPM,601
Palmas de Cortes,BHP,201
Panama Shopping,611
Papa Fernandez',PPF-,247
Parral,HPC,324
Patzcuaro,PTZ,433
Pavas Int'l,PAV,595
Pedregal,EGA-,140